ADVANCED ACCOUNTING

DENNIS M. BLINE
Bryant College

MARY L. FISCHER
The University of Texas at Tyler

TED D. SKEKEL
The University of Texas at San Antonio

WILEY

JOHN WILEY & SONS, INC.

To Bonnie, my wife, without whom accomplishments are hollow
To Don, husband, mentor and companion
To Mary, my spouse, friend and inspiration

ACQUISITIONS EDITOR	Mark Bonadeo
MARKETING MANAGER	Steve Herdegan
SENIOR PRODUCTION EDITOR	Norine M. Pigliucci
SENIOR DESIGNER	Karen Kincheloe
ASSOCIATE EDITOR	Ed Brislin
EDITORIAL ASSISTANT	Brian Kamins
PRODUCTION MANAGEMENT SERVICES	Hermitage Publishing Services

This book was set in Times Roman by Hermitage Publishing Services and printed and bound by Hamilton Printing. The cover was printed by Lehigh Press.

This book is printed on acid free paper. ∞

Library of Congress Cataloging in Publication Data

ISBN 0-471-32775-1 (pbk.)
WIE ISBN 0-471-65667-4

Printed in the United States of America

10 9 8 7 6 5 4 3 2 1

PREFACE

RELEVANCE, CLARITY, AND TECHNOLOGY

The philosophy and purpose of *Advanced Accounting* is to provide concise, current coverage of material most commonly taught in a one-semester Advanced Accounting course. The text is designed to be both instructor and student friendly. It is structured to make it as easy and efficient as possible for both student and faculty to effectively cover highly technical material. The overall goal is to prepare the student to be an effective accounting practitioner capable of appropriately applying Generally Accepted Accounting Principles as well as addressing current accounting problems by conducting research using various sources of authoritative support (e.g., FARS) that are critical to the modern practice of professional accounting.

In developing a text of this kind, it is important to understand who your audience is—both students and instructors. Students who enroll in an advanced accounting course are committed accounting majors. Many plan to pursue professional accounting careers that include being either external auditors in public accounting (CPAs) or internal auditors. This is a course also taken by students who expect to work in a corporate accounting environment. Additionally, advanced accounting provides initial education for both auditors and preparers of financial information in the government and not-for-profit sectors. Faculty who teach advanced accounting tend to be veteran teachers. This means that they have already had several years of teaching financial accounting courses, typically including principles and both intermediate accounting classes.

Given the general goals and the nature of the students and faculty audience, *Advanced Accounting* has been designed to be efficient in its presentation. The chapters in the text cover the same basic material that is covered in 16–20 chapters included in many advanced accounting texts. While shorter in number of chapters and in total page count than the typical advanced accounting text, *Advanced Accounting* is complete because the reduced length is accomplished via the elimination of many redundancies. In addition, *Advanced Accounting* uses a highly efficient system of undertaking the basics of business consolidation procedures which reduces the time that it takes for the instructor to present the material and for the student to master the material.

One of the basic premises of *Advanced Accounting* is that average accounting majors at this level are generally able to master the complexities of advanced accounting topics as long as the presentation of those topics is logically structured and well organized. *Advanced Accounting* places great emphasis on logical structure and organization.

Research Component

Research skills are critical to the success of a professional accountant. A practicing accountant must be able to search for answers to accounting problems that routinely arise. Beginning in 2004, the CPA exam will include an accounting research component that will require keyword searches of resources such as the FARS.

To meet student's need to be proficient researchers, the authors have integrated materials into the text that will educate students on how to conduct practical accounting research. The authors believe that there is a confluence of events that makes a text having an "easy to use" research component particularly attractive to faculty teaching advanced accounting due to the increased pressure to better prepare students to conduct accounting research, the forthcoming change in the CPA exam structure, and recent corporate accounting and auditing failures in high profile cases such as Enron and Worldcom.

Although there is increased pressure to teach research skills, the primary goals of most accounting instructors include preparing their students to understand and be able to apply the accounting concepts covered in each course. Furthermore, intermediate accounting courses typically contain so much text material that many faculty cannot allocate time for an introduction to research tools in these courses. That makes advanced accounting an attractive and logical point in the curriculum to introduce research skills using databases such as the FARS. Even when faculty require students to conduct advanced research in subsequent classes as a part of the 150-hour education requirement, the resources provided by *Advanced Accounting* can be used as an introduction to research and a first exposure to use of the FARS.

Many faculty do not want to make the CPA exam the main focus of a course. However, the authors believe that better preparation for the CPA exam can be achieved as a byproduct within the existing course structure without diluting existing academic goals. With the restructured CPA exam as well as current knowledge demands within the accounting profession, *Advanced Accounting* provides skill development to address these changes. As a part of these changes, CPA candidates and those entering the accounting profession will be required to conduct on-line searches of the FARS and other research databases to identify the appropriate authoritative support for proposed solutions to accounting problems. *Advanced Accounting's* research component is designed to simultaneously augment the concepts in chapters and provide guidance and practice in using the FARS.

One effect of the recent corporate and accounting scandals is that there will is a renewed emphasis on providing clear and complete documentation of the authoritative support that accounting professionals rely upon to justify their choices of accounting treatments to report business transactions. The public (as well as the SEC and Congress) will demand that of corporate accountants and the auditing profession. Thus, knowing how to use the FARS and other databases, the primary source of Generally Accepted Accounting Principles, to provide such authoritative support is going to become even more important. Increased emphasis on teaching the use of databases and the FARS in the formal education of accounting students will logically follow. If this is the students' first exposure to using the FARS, they can employ the research appendix as a learning tool.

ACKNOWLEDGMENTS

We received invaluable input and support through the years from present and former colleagues and students. In particular, we thank Professor Emeritus Richard Samuelson of San Diego State University, who, with Ted Skekel, first explored ways to improve the pedagogy of teaching consolidations. Development of the pedagogy continued when Dr. Skekel joined the University of North Texas (UNT) faculty. We thank UNT accounting students for the many hours spent working the exercises and problems to address the complexities and structure of consolidation elimination entries. Furthermore, we appreciate the additional and continued comments, suggestions, and support of our students and colleagues at Bryant College, The University of Texas at Tyler, and The University of Texas at San Antonio.

We extend our appreciation to all of the following colleagues who assisted in some way with the development of this effort. Thanks for your support and constructive comments.

Tom Beime
California State University,
Sacramento

Martin Birr
Indiana University – Purdue
University, Indianapolis

Penny Clayton
Drury University

Lynn Clements
Florida Southern College

Charles Cullinan
Bryant College

David Eichelberger
Austin Peay State University

Teresa Gordon
University of Idaho

Janet Greenlee
University of Dayton

Jeff Harkins
University of Idaho

Glen Hanson
Pennsylvania State University

Sarah Hughes
Butler University

Steve Hunt
Western Illinois University

Bikki Jaggi
Rutgers University – New
Brunswick

Elizabeth Keating
Harvard University

Ellen Landgraf
Loyola University – Chicago

Trini Melcher
California State University,
San Marcos

Bonnie Moe
University of Illinois,
Springfield

Beth Murphy
DePaul University

Wilda Meixner
Southwest Texas State
University

Keith Smith
George Washington
University

Dave Smith
Iowa State University

Dave Wallin
Ohio State University

Leonard Wells
Valdosta State University

Nancy Whittaker
Texas Tech University

Sharon Williamson
Texas Tech University

G. Lee Willinger
University of Oklahoma

Finally, we would like to acknowledge the extraordinary efforts of a talented group of individuals at Wiley who made all of this come together. We would especially like to thank our sponsoring editor, Mark Bonadeo; editorial program assistant, Brian Kamins; and Steve Herdegan, marketing coordinator.

Dennis Bline
Mary Fischer
Ted Skekel

ABOUT THE AUTHORS

Dennis M. Bline is professor of accounting at Bryant College where he teaches graduate and undergraduate financial and managerial accounting. Dennis previously taught at The University of Texas at San Antonio. He received his baccalaureate degree in business administration at Indiana University Southeast and his MBA and Ph.D. from the University of Arkansas.

Professor Bline's research interests include behavioral, education, ethics, and financial accounting. He has published in *Behavioral Research in Accounting, The Accounting Educators' Journal, Issues in Accounting Education, Research on Accounting Ethics, Advances in Managerial Accounting,* and other accounting journals. He serves as the Editor of *Global Perspectives on Accounting Education* and the Associate Editor of *Issues in Accounting Education.* He has also served on the editorial boards of *Advances in Accounting Behavioral Research, Behavioral Research in Accounting,* and *Accounting Enquiries.* Dennis is an active leader in various sections of the American Accounting Association.

Mary Fischer is the Pirtle Professor of Free Enterprise and Professor of Accounting at The University of Texas at Tyler where she teaches the advanced and government accounting courses. She previously taught at Fairfield University in Connecticut. She received her B.S., M.A., and Ph.D. from the University of Connecticut. She also holds the CGMA designation.

Mary is a widely published author specializing in not-for-profit and financial accounting. The Southwestern American Accounting Association named her as the 2003 Outstanding Accounting Educator. In 2002, she was selected as the Texas Society of CPA Outstanding Accounting Educator. She has published numerous articles in the *Journal of Accounting and Public Policy, Accounting Horizons, Journal of Public Budgeting, Accounting and Financial Management, Critical Perspective on Accounting,* and other accounting journals. She is on the editorials boards of *Issues in Accounting Education, Journal of Public Budgeting, Accounting and Financial Management,* and *Research in Healthcare Financial Management.*

Ted D. Skekel is associate professor of accounting in the College of Business Administration at The University of Texas at San Antonio. He holds a B.S. with a major in accounting from Florida State University and a Ph.D. with emphasis in accounting and finance from the University of Oregon.

He has also served on the faculties of the University of Houston, San Diego State University, and the University of North Texas. He primarily teaches in the financial reporting area. He has taught at all levels, including principles, intermediate, advanced, masters level theory and case study classes, and doctoral seminars. His current focus is in the intermediate and advanced accounting areas. His research includes a broad range of academic and professional publications including articles in *The Accounting Review, Issues in Accounting Education, Journal of Accountancy,* and *The CPA Journal.* Ted is actively involved in Beta Alpha Psi, the national honors fraternity for financial information professionals. He is currently a faculty advisor at UT–San Antonio and previously served as a faculty advisor at the University of North Texas. Beyond the Beta Alpha Psi local level, he has been the regional director for the Southwest Region, and served for several years on the Beta Alpha Psi National Council and National Board of Directors. He was awarded Beta Alpha Psi's 1992 Arthur Andersen Outstanding Faculty Advisor Award. In addition, he has received several teaching and service awards at The University of Texas at San Antonio.

BRIEF CONTENTS

CONTENTS

CHAPTER 1

INTRODUCTION TO BUSINESS COMBINATIONS

LEARNING OBJECTIVES

After reading this chapter, you should be able to:

- Discuss the differences among horizontal, vertical, and conglomerate combinations.
- Differentiate among different types of defensive measures potential acquirees may pursue.
- Analyze the different ways in which business combinations can be organized.
- Discuss the differences that exist among the three legal forms of business combinations.
- Understand contingencies that may impact the consideration given in a business combination.
- Describe the general features required for a business combination to qualify as a nontaxable exchange.

Internal expansion: when the business is expanded through new product development or geographic expansion without acquiring another company

External expansion: when two or more businesses join together and operate as one entity, or related entities, under the direction and control of one management group

Business combination: when two companies join in an external form of expansion

Business expansion is often viewed as an indicator of a successful business. Expansion may occur internally or externally. **Internal expansion** is often the result of an entity undertaking research and development activities that culminate in the development and marketing of new products. An example is RCA's expansion into direct television. Alternatively, an entity may expand internally by selling new or existing products in new markets. This may be either the sale of existing products to new consumers in current geographic markets or the sale of new or existing products to new consumers in new geographic markets. An example is when Outback Steakhouse expanded from its home base of Florida to become a nationwide restaurant chain.

External expansion occurs when two or more businesses join together and operate as one entity, or related entities, under the direction and control of one management group. Generally such an expansion is known as a **business combination** and may be an offensive or a defensive maneuver. Two entities may combine to grow larger and take advantage of economies of scale or increased influence in the marketplace, or they may combine to survive the threat of increased competition or takeover by other entities. For example, Kemper Corporation combined with Conseco in 1994 to prevent Kemper from being acquired by GE Capital Corporation.

This chapter presents an introduction to business combinations. The first part of the chapter presents the economic reasons for, history of, and legal restrictions on business combinations. In addition, an introduction to the takeover process in both a friendly and hostile environment is provided. The second part of the chapter illustrates the more common ways by which one entity can take control of the net assets of another entity. Discussion of the different legal forms of business combinations is presented in the third part of the chapter. Subsequent parts of the chapter present a discussion of substance versus form, contingent consideration, and some tax implications of business combinations.

BUSINESS COMBINATIONS IN THE UNITED STATES

Economic Motivation for Business Combinations

Given that business expansion may be achieved through the development of new products and the construction of new production facilities, there must be perceived advantages to external expansion (combination) to explain why management often chooses to expand externally. One reason is that internal expansion is often a slow process because the entity may be required to develop a distribution system, generate demand for its new product, and/or build new production facilities to support new products or expanding sales. In addition, internal expansion may be viewed as risky in that the development and marketing of new products are often difficult tasks.

To overcome some of these perceived shortcomings of internal expansion, management may choose to expand through business combinations. The following is a summary list of advantages of business combinations. It is not intended to be all-inclusive, nor should it be inferred that each of these advantages exists in every business combination.

1. Expansion can be achieved more rapidly through combinations. Alternatively, the time necessary to construct a new facility, staff it, and develop a market for the output is comparatively long.

2. Combinations may provide an established, experienced management group immediately.

3. Combinations may lead to economies of scale. For example, the same sales force or accounting staff may be able to service two corporate structures as well as one.

4. The overall cost of capital may be reduced as a result of a combination because of the increased size of the entity.

5. Federal income tax laws provide some advantages to certain combined corporate entities that are not available to one corporation.

6. External expansion does not increase the total supply of goods available from that industry, whereas internal expansion may increase supply beyond existing demand levels.

7. Control over a greater market share may enable the combined entity to become a price leader in the market.

8. For some combinations, the guaranteed raw material sources and product markets provided by combinations provide a significant management advantage. In addition, the profits at each level accrue to the combined entity.

9. Diversification accomplished through combinations may provide a less volatile income stream. This reduces the riskiness of the entity, which, in turn, lowers borrowing rates.

A business combination results in one entity taking control of another entity's net assets. Regardless of the manner in which the business combination occurs or the accounting required to recognize the combination, all business combinations are the result of one entity (the investor or acquirer) investing in the other entity (the investee or acquiree). The decision by the acquirer to undertake such an investment will involve the same type of analysis as is performed when deciding whether to make capital expenditures for other assets. Managers of the acquiring entity may prepare budgets and perform capital budgeting analysis using techniques such as net present value and internal rate of return to determine whether the investment is in the best interest of the acquirer. The difference between the purchase of an individual asset and the acquisition of another entity is that projecting the future cash flows may be more involved for an entity acquisition. When purchasing a piece of machinery, the relevant cash flows will be such items as the change in the operating costs, the tax implications of differences in depreciation, and the future salvage value of the machine. When considering the acquisition of another entity, some of the cash flows that may need to be evaluated result from the disposal of redundant facilities, reduction of fixed costs by eliminating duplicate operations, and internal coordination of operations when one part of the combined entity produces input for another part of the combined entity. In addition to the directly measurable cash flows, the acquisition of another entity also may result in benefits not directly measurable, such as (1) a readily available supply of scarce inputs (raw materials), (2) production and/or marketing expertise, (3) established market share for products, and (4) the potential synergy resulting from sales of complementary products.

History of Business Combinations in the United States

With the age of industrialization, which began in the second half of the nineteenth century, came the growth of large corporations and separation of ownership and management. Three types of business combinations have occurred since the first significant American business combination in the late 1800s. Business combinations may be categorized into three types by examining the nature of the combining companies and their relationship with one another.

The first type of business combination began about 1880. This type of combination may occur when management attempts to dominate or monopolize particular industries. In fact, early combinations in the steel industry, lead by J. P. Morgan's U. S. Steel, and in the oil industry, led by Standard Oil, resulted in almost total domination within each industry by the combined companies. The business combinations that took place during this time period primarily resulted from entities acquiring competitors. This permitted the acquirers to increase sales by entering new product markets, increasing production capacity, and expanding into new geographic regions. This type of combination is generally referred to as a **horizontal combination** (a combination involving two or more entities that are in competition in the same industry).

Horizontal combination: a combination involving two or more entities that are in competition in the same industry

The second type of business combination started in the 1920s. This type of business combination seems to be dominated by companies attempting to improve the efficiency of

Vertical combination: a combination involving two or more entities that have a potential buyer–seller relationship

operations by purchasing suppliers of inputs or purchasers of outputs. For example, General Motors, a manufacturing company, acquired an electrical equipment company, Alambrados Y Circuitos, and a car rental company, National Car Rental Systems. These acquisitions provided General Motors with a source of supply for electrical components for automobile engines and an outlet for selling output to the car rental company. A business combination of this nature is generally referred to as a **vertical combination** (a combination involving two or more entities which have a potential buyer–seller relationship).

Conglomerate combination: a combination that occurs when the acquired company is in an unrelated or tangentially related business

The third type of business combination began in the late 1950s. Overall, the value of business combinations exceeded $3.4 trillion for 1999. Horizontal combinations (e.g., Exxon's 1999 acquisition of Mobil for $79 billion) and vertical combinations (e.g., Eli Lilly's 1994 acquisition of PCS Health Systems for $4 billion) still occur; however, now entities are also attempting to diversify business risk by acquiring companies in unrelated or tangentially related businesses (e.g., America Online's 2000 acquisition of Time Warner for $156 billion). This type of business combination is often referred to as a **conglomerate combination** (a combination involving two or more entities in unrelated industries). One reason for the rise of conglomerates is that management has become more aware of the increased income stability provided by diversifying the asset base of an entity. Another reason for the increase in conglomerate combinations is that it has been considerably more difficult for the government to challenge a conglomerate business combination on the basis of antitrust regulations.

Legal Restrictions on Business Combinations

Business combinations may result in the concentration of economic power in the hands of fewer entities, resulting in an industry having only a small number of dominant entities (**oligopoly**) or, at the extreme, only one entity (**monopoly**). This concentration of economic power may result in business practices by the combined entities that are contrary to the public interest. Recognizing that such actual and potential abuses were not in the public interest, Congress passed legislation restricting the ability of entities to effect business combinations. The first of these legislative actions, the Sherman Act, was passed by Congress in 1890. Its basic purpose is to make illegal any action that would hinder free competition. Specifically, Section I of the Sherman Act in part reads:

> *Every contract, combination in the form of a trust or otherwise, or conspiracy, in restraint of trade or commerce among the Several States, or with foreign nations, is hereby declared to be illegal ...*

The Sherman Act is directed at controlling monopolistic practices, but the act is worded in such a way that the burden of proof is placed on the government to show that trade had been restrained. Thus, combinations could not be prevented, only broken up after the fact. The Sherman Act was the basis for breaking up both Standard Oil and American Tobacco in 1911. However, because the Sherman Act proved to be inadequate, additional legislation was passed.

The Clayton Act, which became law in 1914, provided additional power to control business combination activities. In part, Section 7 of the Clayton Act (amended) reads:

> *... no corporation engaged in commerce shall acquire, directly or indirectly, the whole or any part of the stock or other share of capital and no corporation subject to the jurisdiction of the Federal Trade Commission shall acquire the whole or any part of the assets of another corporation engaged also in commerce, where in any line of commerce in any section of the country, the effect of such acquisition may be substantially to lessen competition, or to tend to create a monopoly.*

This wording prevents "the acquisition" when "the effect of such acquisition may" be contrary to the public policy of ensuring free competition. Thus, through the Clayton Act, the government can anticipate restraint of trade and legally stop proposed mergers based on arguments concerning the potential results.

Today, the Federal Trade Commission works closely with the Antitrust Division of the Department of Justice in enforcing the antitrust laws. As part of the ongoing scrutiny of business combinations, the Hart-Scott Rodino Amendment was passed in 1976. This act requires that the Antitrust Division and the Federal Trade Commission be notified of antic-ipated business combinations. This notification enables the Federal Trade Commission to assess the potential impact of the combination on such issues as industry concentration, barriers to entry, and restriction of trade. In 1999 a merger of Exxon and Mobil Oil was proposed. As part of the negotiations with the Federal Trade Commission to satisfy gov-ernment antitrust concerns, late in the year it was announced that approximately 2,400 retail outlets, a refinery, and interests in several U.S. pipelines would be sold by the merg-ing companies.[1] The enforcement of the law does not imply that the government will chal-lenge every business combination. The vast majority of combinations are not disallowed because they involve relatively minor segments of competitive markets and, therefore, would not reduce or control competition in any significant way.

Takeovers

Business combinations may be accomplished by negotiations between the management of the acquirer and the acquiree. If these negotiations result in mutually agreeable terms, an offer will be made to the stockholders of the acquiree (target company). This offer will be publicly supported by the management of the acquiree and a **friendly takeover** will be initiated. An example of such a cash offer is the offer of $55 per share ($1.9 billion) that was made by Martin Marietta Corporation for all 34 million shares of Grumman Corporation.[2] The rationale for this particular combination may have been the perceived need for the existence of a larger entity to successfully compete in the defense industry given expected U. S. military spending reductions in the 1990s. Grumman's chairman, Renso Capporali, stated that "the bidding environment was sure to become 'increasingly difficult' for a smaller enterprise squared off against ever-larger rivals." Martin Marietta's proposed acquisition was a maneuver that left other mid-sized defense contractors scram-bling to locate potential merger candidates. Among the companies known at that time to be searching for a merger candidate was Northrop Corporation. Northrop had been dis-cussing a possible merger with Grumman after it was unsuccessful in attempts to acquire a division of International Business Machines Corporation, the tactical-fighter business of General Dynamics, and the missile division of McDonnell Douglas Corporation. The potential merger of Martin Marietta and Grumman was viewed by the U. S. government as a huge merger that would be "carefully scrutinized" if the companies were competitors in the defense industry.

Tender Offer If negotiations between the management of any two entities consider-ing a combination do not result in mutually agreeable terms, the acquirer will either withdraw the proposal or make the proposal directly to the stockholders of the acquiree.

Friendly takeover: a tender offer that is publicly supported by acquiree management

---

[1] Liesman, Steve, Alexei Barrionuevo, and John R. Wilke, "Exxon, Mobil Offer to Shed 15% of Gas Stations," *The Wall Street Journal,* November 23, 1999, p. A2.

[2] Cole, Jeff, "Martin Marietta Agrees to Buy Grumman Corp.," *The Wall Street Journal,* March 8, 1994, pp. A3, A8.

Tender offer: an offer by an acquirer to buy the stock of another company

An offer by an acquirer to buy the stock of another company is commonly referred to as a **tender offer**. A tender offer is generally published in major newspapers (such as *The Wall Street Journal*) and the tender amount will be above the current market price. The tender offer generally contains stipulations regarding the length of time the offer is valid and the percentage of outstanding shares that must be offered to the acquirer to finalize the acquisition.

Hostile bid: a tender offer that is opposed by acquiree management

A tender offer is sometimes opposed by the acquiree's management and the offer is viewed as a **hostile bid** for the acquiree. Returning to the defense industry example, soon after Grumman's management had agreed to the friendly acquisition proposed by Martin Marietta Corporation, a hostile bid to acquire Grumman was made by Northrop.[3] Northrop's bid of $2.04 billion ($60 per share) exceeded Martin Marietta's original agreement with Grumman's management by $5 per share. Northrop was viewed by defense experts as being under pressure to buy or be bought. Martin Marietta's chairman criticized the proposed acquisition by Northrop as an attempt to disrupt the friendly merger of Martin Marietta and Grumman. After almost 30 days of dispute and discussion, Northrop finally acquired Grumman for $62 per share, or $2.17 billion.[4] During the negotiations, the market value of Grumman Corporation's stock increased from $39.875 to over $65 per share.

Defensive measures: steps taken by a potential acquiree to avoid an undesired acquisition

Defensive Measures Although Grumman Corporation did not engage in **defensive measures** to prevent the takeover by Northrop, these actions are possible when management of the target company perceives that the tender offer should not be accepted. Defensive maneuvers can take a variety of forms. For example, some companies attempt to avoid an undesired acquisition by offering the acquirer a premium over the market price of the stock to sell any stock already owned by the acquirer back to the acquiree. Such a strategy is termed **greenmail**.[5] The potential acquiree may also seek to be acquired by an entity perceived to be a better match with the acquiree. In this instance the friendly replacement acquirer is termed a **white knight**[6] because it has rescued the acquiree from an undesirable acquirer.

The acquiree may also engage in a variety of maneuvers to make itself less desirable to the acquirer. One maneuver used by a number of entities is a **poison pill**.[7] This term is used to describe the issuance of preferred stock that is convertible into common stock of the unwanted acquirer. This would enable the holders of the preferred stock to convert at a later date and regain control by once again having the majority of voting common stock. The danger of the poison pill is that it can deter friendly as well as hostile acquirers. This problem can be avoided with careful planning when designing preferred stock features. In addition to these individual strategies, a potential acquiree can institute a broader plan, often called a **kamikaze strategy**.[8] Under this strategy the potential acquiree takes action to reduce its value to the acquirer.

[3] Cole, Jeff, "Northrop Seeks Grumman in Hostile $2.04 Billion Bid," *The Wall Street Journal,* March 11, 1994, pp. A3–A4.

[4] Harris, Roy J., Jr., "Northrop Offer of $2.17 Billion Wins Grumman," *The Wall Street Journal,* April 5, 1994, pp. A3, A5.

[5] Michel, Allen, and Israel Shaked, *Takeover Madness* (New York: Wiley, 1986), p. 194.

[6] Ibid., pp. 208–221.

[7] Ibid., pp. 236–242.

[8] Ibid., pp. 195–200.

Three common ways to implement a kamikaze strategy are through the **sale of the crown jewels**,[9] the **scorched earth defense**,[10] and the **fatman defense**.[11] The sale of the crown jewels and the scorched earth defenses both result in the target selling profitable assets and distributing the proceeds of the sale to the stockholders to reduce the value of the acquiree. The sale of the crown jewels involves the sale of key assets, while the scorched earth defense involves a more broad-based sale of assets. Either of these defenses can fail to be successful because the rushed sale of assets will likely result in less than optimum prices for the assets sold. In addition, if the acquirer believes that the acquisition can be accomplished before the cash is distributed to the stockholders, the cash may be used to help the acquirer buy the acquiree. The fatman defense takes a different approach in that it results in the acquisition of assets, not the sale. This defense is one where management of the target purchases poorly performing assets of another entity. The fatman defense may be attractive if it is expected to reduce the short-term profits of the target but increase long-term profits. The result of this defense may be to deter the acquirer but make the potential acquiree stronger in the long run.

Rather than attempting to reduce the value of the potential acquiree, management may choose to make the acquiree more difficult to purchase by instituting administrative measures often called **shark repellent**.[12] These defenses may include staggering the terms of the board of directors, thereby preventing an acquirer from attaining control quickly. This defense will buy time and, thus, better enable the potential acquiree to implement other defensive strategies if necessary. Another approach is to have additional requirements for membership on the board of directors, such as residency. Many entities have implemented a supermajority (greater than 50 percent) for approving business combinations. This percentage may be as high as 75 to 95 percent. As a result, hostile takeover of a company that requires a supermajority is more difficult to attain. Another technique often used to deter an unfriendly takeover is **golden parachutes**.[13] This maneuver results in significant compensation to the acquiree's top executives if a "change in control" of the acquiree occurs and the executive is terminated from the position currently held. As a result, golden parachutes transfer assets from the target to the executives, making the target less attractive.

All of the techniques discussed thus far are defensive and reactive. In a limited number of instances, the acquiree takes an offensive, proactive stand, often termed a **packman defense**.[14] The packman defense occurs when the potential acquiree attempts to purchase the acquirer. This defense can take on two forms. First, the target may make a tender offer for some of the acquirer's shares. Second, the target may purchase the acquirer's shares in the open market. Either approach indicates that the target intends to purchase the acquirer rather than be the acquiree.

All the techniques discussed above are based on the assumption that they are in the best interest of the stockholders. Management has a fiduciary duty to undertake the activities that will maximize the benefits of the stockholders. Potential acquirers have contested all these defenses in court on the basis that management is acting in its own self-interest rather than in the interest of the stockholders.

---

[9] Ibid., p. 198.

[10] Ibid., p. 197.

[11] Ibid., p. 199.

[12] Ibid., pp. 344–358.

[13] Ibid., pp. 356–358.

[14] Ibid., pp. 38–39.

THE CONCEPT OF CONTROL IN BUSINESS COMBINATIONS

Control: the power to use or direct the use of the individual assets of an entity to achieve the objectives of the controlling entity

For a business combination to occur, one entity must gain "control" of the "net assets" of another entity. The manner by which **control** over an entity is determined has evolved from a majority ownership of an entity's voting common stock to the "ability by itself to make the decisions that guide the ongoing activities of another entity (subsidiary)."[15] Control over an entity represents a greater involvement than investing in an entity in that control enables the investor to direct the use of individual assets in a manner that will result in the maximum benefit to the controlling entity. In particular, control enables the acquiring entity to (1) direct the use of the controlled entity's assets by having the power over policy-making that guides how the assets are used; and (2) enforce the budgets and policies by selecting, compensating, and terminating those responsible for implementing decisions.[16]

Control over the net assets of an entity may be accomplished in a variety of ways. The two most common ways to attain control are by the purchase of the acquiree's net assets or by the purchase of the acquiree's voting stock, which represents ownership of the assets. While majority ownership is not absolutely required for control, the examples in this text will assume transactions involving at least 50 percent of the acquired firm. To achieve control (i.e., acquire control of net assets), the acquirer may give some of its own assets, issue debt instruments, and/or give shares of its own stock. Thus, the type of exchange may vary; however, a business combination has occurred when one entity gains control over the net assets of another entity.

The remainder of this section provides examples of different ways one entity can gain control of another entity. If the transaction results in the transfer of "control," the transaction is a business combination by definition. The first two examples—Type 1 exchanges—present the acquisition of the *net assets* of an entity by: (1) an exchange of assets for assets and (2) an exchange of stock for assets. The next two examples—Type 2 exchanges—present the acquisition of the *voting stock* of another entity by (3) an exchange of assets for stock and (4) an exchange of stock for stock. Major differences exist in the required accounting recognition for the different types of exchanges, but in substance the economic values in a given exchange are the same (before taxes) no matter what type of exchange occurs. To simplify the examples in this chapter, all illustrations assume the acquirer purchases 100 percent of the acquiree.

Type 1 Exchange: Acquisition of Assets

In the first type of exchange, acquisition of assets, the acquiring entity desires the use and earning power of a particular set of assets that are owned by another entity. Assume that the RST Corporation (RST), a large entity, wishes to gain control of the assets of the growing but relatively small ABC Corporation (ABC). RST may accomplish its objective by either of two methods. First, it may give cash and/or other assets (possibly including promises of future payments in the form of notes) in exchange for ABC's assets. Second, rather than exchanging assets, RST may issue shares of RST Corporation stock for ABC's assets.

Exchange of RST Assets for ABC Assets The upper section of Figure 1-1 outlines the flow of resources between ABC's balance sheet and RST's balance sheet for an asset for asset exchange. The solid line represents the rights to, and ownership of,

[15] *Exposure Draft Revised Proposed Statement of Financial Accounting Standards,* "Consolidated Financial Statements: Purpose and Policy" (Stamford, CT: Financial Accounting Standards Board, 1999), par. 11.

[16] Ibid.

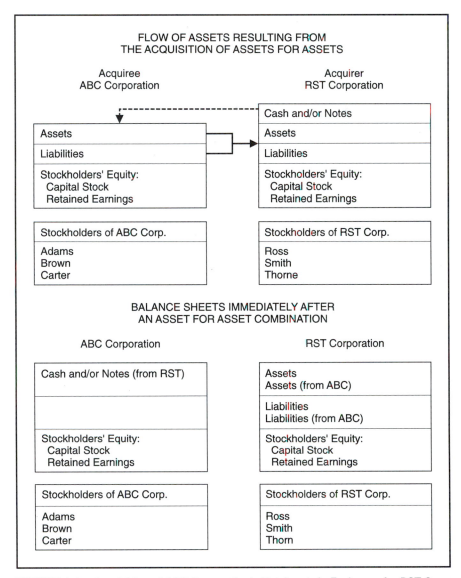

FIGURE 1-1 Acquisition of ABC Corporation's Net Assets in Exchange for RST Corporation's Assets

ABC's net assets transferred to RST. In return, RST exchanges cash and future promises to pay cash, represented by the broken line from RST to ABC. Immediately below each balance sheet is a listing of the stockholders of the respective corporations as the transaction begins.

The lower section of the figure depicts the balance sheets and stockholder lists immediately after the transaction is complete. Immediately after the exchange, the financial records of RST include all the specific asset and liability account balances for the net assets acquired. The stockholders' equity of RST is unchanged, and the individual stockholders of RST are the same. After the exchange, ABC's balance sheet is nothing more than a skeleton. The monetary assets, cash and notes, are all that is left on ABC's books. The stockholders of ABC have not changed. Therefore, Adams, Brown, and Carter may choose to invest the cash in new productive assets and enter into a new line of business. Alternatively, Adams, Brown, and Carter also have the option of declaring a liquidating dividend, distributing all the assets among themselves, and disbanding the corporation. Note that the course of action chosen is controlled by Adams, Brown, and Carter, the original owners. In summary, Figure 1-1 presents an acquisition of assets for assets with no transfer of either ABC or RST common stock.

Exchange of RST Stock for ABC Assets In Figure 1-2, ABC Corporation again relinquishes its net assets to RST Corporation, creating another Type 1 exchange. This is depicted in the upper section of Figure 1-2, again by the solid line from ABC to

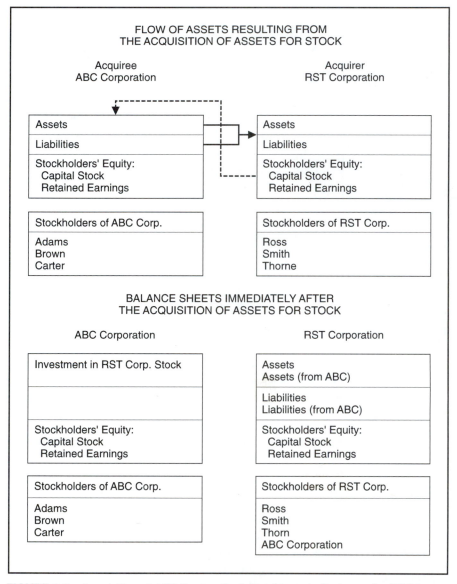

FIGURE 1-2 Acquisition of ABC Corporation's Net Assets in Exchange for RST Corporation's Stock

RST. In this case, however, shares of RST Corporation common stock are issued, with ABC Corporation becoming the registered owner of the shares. No RST assets are surrendered. Instead, the total capitalization of RST increases because the total number of outstanding shares of RST increases, whereas in Figure 1-1, the net assets on RST's balance sheet did not increase. The issuance of the RST shares to ABC is shown by the broken line from the RST stockholders' equity section pointing to the ABC asset section.

In the lower-right-hand section of Figure 1-2, as in Figure 1-1, RST Corporation has recorded the asset and liability accounts for the net assets acquired from ABC. The difference between Figures 1-1 and 1-2 is that the stockholder list for RST now includes not only Ross, Smith, and Thorne, the original owners of RST, but also ABC Corporation, the holder of the shares that were issued as a result of the acquisition. In the lower-left-hand section, the only asset is ABC's investment in RST stock. ABC's stockholder list is unchanged. Again, as in the assets-for-assets exchange, Adams, Brown, and Carter may choose to continue the ABC Corporation, or they may declare a liquidating dividend (this time in RST stock certificates rather than cash) and disband the ABC Corporation.

Because RST Corporation is assumed to be the larger of the two companies involved in the exchange, the percentage of RST owned by ABC Corporation after the exchange is rather small. Therefore, Ross, Smith, and Thorne are not giving up control of RST Corporation, although they no longer collectively own 100 percent of it.

In summary, Figure 1-2 presents an acquisition of assets for shares of stock. ABC's owners still control ABC Corporation's outstanding stock, but ABC Corporation now owns an interest in RST. Again, the assets of ABC may be integrated into the current operations of RST or ABC may become a division of RST. The original RST owners still control RST Corporation stock. Notice that in neither Figure 1-1 nor Figure 1-2 did individual stockholders give up control of their respective corporations. That is, Adams, Brown, and Carter still control ABC while Ross, Smith, and Thorne control RST, although in Figure 1-2 ABC Corporation owns stock of RST Corporation.

Type 2 Exchange: Acquisition of Stock

In an asset acquisition type of combination, control of the net assets of ABC is achieved by acquiring the assets directly. In a stock acquisition type of combination, control of ABC's net assets is accomplished by RST, but control is achieved by acquiring ABC's stock rather than the assets directly. If RST Corporation owns enough of ABC Corporation's stock to set operating policies and enforce the implementation of these policies, then RST controls ABC. This would often be accomplished by RST owning enough of ABC's stock to elect a majority of ABC's board of directors. The type 2 examples assume that RST acquires 100 percent of ABC's stock. This assumption is made to simplify the examples, although control with less than 100 percent ownership is common in practice.

Exchange of RST Assets for Outstanding ABC Stock   In Figure 1-3, RST Corporation transacts with Adams, Brown, and Carter individually, not ABC Corporation, the entity. The upper section shows the flow of the transaction. The solid line from the stockholder list of ABC to the asset section of RST depicts the flow of ABC's stock certificates from the stockholders of ABC to the RST balance sheet. Adams, Brown, and Carter give up their ownership of ABC Corporation. The broken line from RST to the ABC stockholder list represents the assets that the individual stockholders receive in exchange for their shares of ABC stock.

The resulting balance sheet of RST, in the lower-right-hand section of Figure 1-3, includes an *Investment in ABC Corp. Stock.* Also, the stockholder list for RST has not

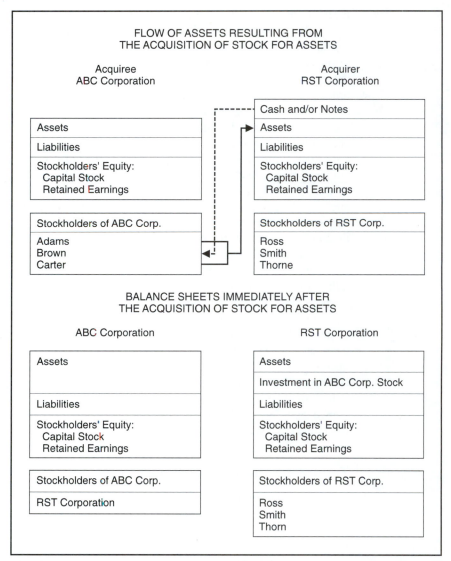

FIGURE 1-3   Acquisition of Outstanding ABC Corporation's Stock in Exchange for RST Corporation's Assets

changed because no shares were issued in this case. Note that the ABC balance sheet, in the lower-left-hand section, is intact. No changes have occurred on the books of ABC. The only change is the configuration of ownership of ABC's shares. The list of ABC stockholders now consists of the RST Corporation only. Adams, Brown, and Carter no longer own any interest in ABC or RST. Instead, they are holding the cash and notes that were distributed to them by RST Corporation.

In summary, Figure 1-3 presents the case where a company, RST, literally buys another, ABC, for cash. RST may do whatever it wishes with ABC Corporation subsequent to the purchase of the stock. ABC may continue to operate as a subsidiary corporation under the guidance of RST management, ABC may be liquidated, or ABC may cease to be a separate corporation and become a division of RST. The decision rests with the management of RST.

Exchange of RST Stock for Outstanding ABC Stock   Figure 1-4 presents the stock-for-stock transaction in which the ABC stockholders give up their shares of ABC Corporation stock in exchange for shares of RST Corporation stock. The solid line from the ABC stockholder list to the RST asset section represents the flow of ABC shares into the RST Corporation balance sheet. The shares issued by RST flow to the individuals who previously owned ABC Corporation, as depicted by the broken line from the RST stockholders' equity section to the ABC stockholders.

After the transaction, all six individuals—Adams, Brown, Carter, Ross, Smith, and Thorne—are stockholders of the RST Corporation, as seen in the lower-right-hand section

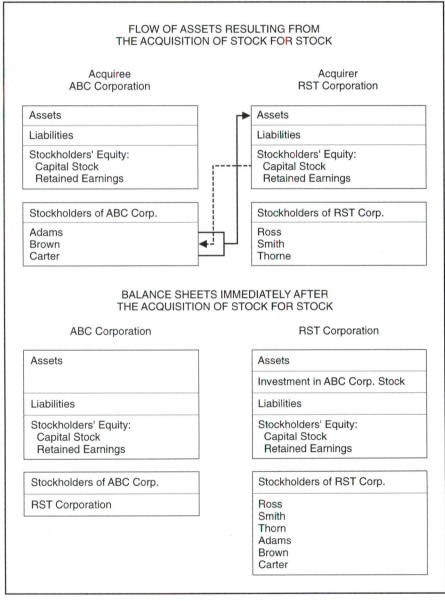

FIGURE 1-4   Acquisition of Outstanding ABC Corporation's Stock in Exchange for RST Corporation's Stock

of Figure 1-4. Also, as with Figure 1-3, RST is now holding an asset: *Investment in ABC Corp. Stock*. Again, the lower-left-hand side of Figure 1-4 displays a balance sheet for ABC Corporation that is unchanged and a stockholder list that consists only of the RST Corporation, as in Figure 1-3. RST's options regarding the future of ABC are identical to those presented in Figure 1-3.

In a stock-for-stock transaction, usually the entity that issues stock gains control of the entity whose existing stockholders give up their shares, although this is not necessarily the case. For example, assume RST is twice as large as ABC, but ABC is the company issuing the shares. Ross, Smith, and Thorne collectively would likely receive twice as many shares of ABC stock as were previously outstanding and owned by Adams, Brown, and Carter. Thus, although ABC is the issuer of additional shares of stock, the stockholders of RST could gain control of ABC. An example of this in practice was the 1993 combination of SoftKey Software Products Incorporated, Spinnaker Software Corporation, and WordStar International Incorporated. SoftKey was the entity making the acquisition, but the three-way stock swap was accomplished using WordStar stock.[17] It is assumed in this text that the larger of the entities is the issuer of shares and that the issuer gains control of the combined entity.

In comparing the assets-for-stock to the stock-for-stock transactions, the only differences are that in Figure 1-3, RST gives up some of its monetary assets but Ross, Smith, and Thorne maintain 100 percent control of RST, whereas in Figure 1-4 all the original RST assets remain intact but some new stockholders are brought into RST.

FORMS OF BUSINESS COMBINATIONS

Business combinations may be structured in ways that result in either one or two entities existing after the combination is completed. These different structures have resulted in three different legal forms of combinations. The relationship between the acquirer and the acquiree in each form of business combination is illustrated in Figure 1-5.

Statutory Mergers

Statutory merger: a business combination that results in one company continuing to operate and the other company liquidating into the survivor

As a part of the business combination plan, one or more participant companies may give up its corporate charter and cease to exist as a separate legal entity. When this occurs and at least one of the participant companies survives and continues to operate using its same legal charter, the combination is formally called a **statutory merger**. The word *statutory* refers to the various state laws (statutes) under which the corporate charters were obtained. These statutes generally provide for certain formal steps that must be followed in executing this type of combination. This form of business combination may result from the acquirer's acquisition of the acquiree's net assets where the acquiree's stockholders decide to liquidate the corporation, or it may result from the acquirer's acquisition of the acquiree's stock. For example, when United HealthCare acquired HMO America in 1993, HMO America ceased to exist as a corporate entity and United HealthCare continued to operate as a single legal entity.

Statutory Merger of RST and ABC

Figure 1-6 demonstrates the results of a statutory merger between ABC and RST, with RST being the surviving corporation. In

---

[17] Wilke, John R., "SoftKey Will Acquire Spinnaker, WordStar in a 3-Way Stock Swap," *The Wall Street Journal*, August 18, 1993, p. B6.

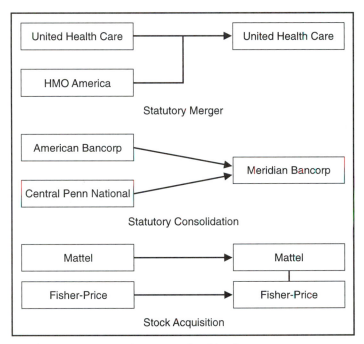

FIGURE 1-5 Forms of Business Combinations

step 1 at the top of Figure 1-6, RST and ABC undertake a stock-for-stock exchange, identical to the one in Figure 1-4. However, in this case, under the terms of the agreement, ABC is to go out of existence. Thus, in step 2, presented in the middle of the figure, the solid line from ABC to RST represents a liquidating dividend that distributes 100 percent of the net assets of ABC to its only stockholder, RST Corporation. This step can occur because RST now owns 100 percent of the ABC stock, so RST is free to declare any dividend that it desires.

The bottom section of Figure 1-6 displays the balance sheet results. RST replaces the *Investment in ABC Corp. Stock* account that appears after the acquisition with the specific asset and liability accounts that underly the investment. ABC Corporation relinquishes its corporate charter and no longer exists.

In summary, the statutory merger is a special case of the acquisition-of-stock (Type 2) business combination. The results in Figure 1-6 differ from Figure 1-4 only in that one set of corporate accounting records and one corporation exist when the combination is completed, rather than two. In this case, Adams, Brown, and Carter received RST stock, though this is not critical to statutory mergers. Adams, Brown, and Carter could have received cash, for example. What is critical to the statutory merger notion is that RST Corporation must gain control of the ABC stock so that the ABC corporate entity may be dissolved.

Statutory Consolidations

Statutory consolidation: a business combination that results in two companies being liquidated into a newly created organization

Another legal form of business combination is called a **statutory consolidation.** As with statutory mergers, the word *statutory* refers to the fact that the combination is subject to certain state laws because a change in the number of existing chartered corporations is again involved. To qualify under the definition of statutory consolidation, however, a new corporation must be formed and a new charter granted by the state of incorporation. The newly created entity acquires the net assets of both combining entities, and the original

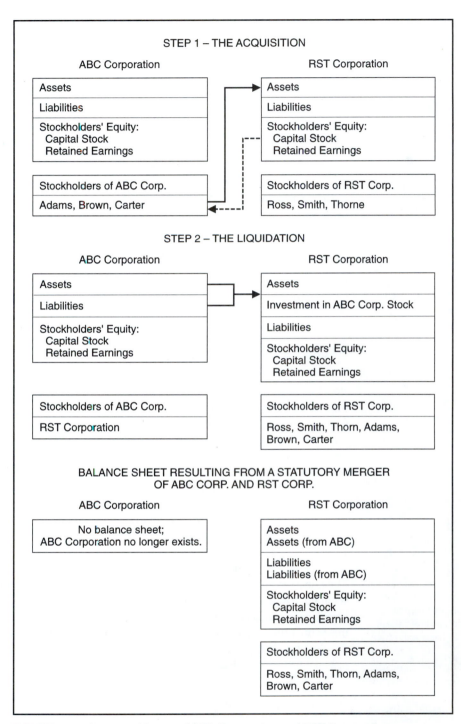

FIGURE 1-6 Statutory Merger of ABC Corporation and RST Corporation

entities cease to exist. The acquisition is typically accomplished by the new entity issuing stock for the stock or assets of the combining entities. For example, American Bancorp and Central Penn National combined in a statutory consolidation in 1983, creating Meridian Bancorp.

Statutory Consolidation of RST and ABC into XYZ If RST and ABC wish to combine as they did in Figure 1-4, but they wish to set up an entirely new corporate structure, a statutory consolidation may be undertaken. Figure 1-7 illustrates the results of a statutory consolidation. In this example, both ABC and RST relinquish their corporate charters and the only remaining entity is XYZ. At the top of Figure 1-7, step 1 displays the issuance of shares by the new XYZ Corporation, as shown by the solid line from XYZ to the stockholders of both ABC and RST. In exchange, outstanding shares of both ABC and RST are transferred by Adams, Brown, Carter, Ross, Smith, and Thorne to XYZ. XYZ records two accounts—*Investment in ABC Corp.* and *Investment in RST Corp.*—for the shares received.

In step 2, XYZ liquidates both ABC and RST by having each corporation declare a dividend of its entire net asset position. The result is that XYZ absorbs ABC's and RST's asset and liability account balances on XYZ's books, with ABC and RST both ceasing to exist. Thus, the resulting balance sheet at the bottom of Figure 1-7 reflects the new structure of XYZ Corporation.

Notice that a *Retained Earnings* balance appears on the new corporate books. This is an example of recording the **substance** versus the **form** of the transaction. Legally, a new corporate shell was created. However, because RST is substantially larger than ABC, Ross, Smith, and Thorne will receive a proportionately larger percentage of the new XYZ shares than will Adams, Brown, and Carter. Essentially, the RST group has achieved control of the newly formed XYZ Corporation and should be treated as the acquirer. Had this been accomplished as it was in Figure 1-6, one set of books (RST's books) including RST's *Retained Earnings* balance would have resulted. The establishment of the XYZ corporate shell was purely a matter of legal form. It is reasonable, then, that the RST *Retained Earnings* be carried forward to the XYZ balance sheet. The substance of the transaction is that the stockholders of RST have gained control of ABC Corporation's net assets and will continue as a going concern. RST's corporate name has changed and it has acquired ABC. There is no substantive reason for RST's retained earnings to disappear.

One common feature of statutory mergers and statutory consolidations is that only one entity exists at the end of the combination. As a result, no special accounting issues exist after the acquisition has been recognized. The single entity continues in existence, and the accounting records are maintained for the single legal entity.

Stock Acquisitions Resulting in Parent–Subsidiary Relationship

The third legal form of business combination is one where both original entities retain their separate legal existence. This form of combination is accomplished through a **stock acquisition**. The acquisition can be accomplished with the acquiree's stockholders receiving part of the acquirer's assets, debt, stock, or some combination of the three. An example of a stock acquisition is Mattel's $1.1 billion acquisition of Fisher-Price through the issuance of Mattel stock to existing Fisher Price stockholders.[18]

Figure 1-4 presents a stock acquisition where RST decided that ABC is not to be liquidated. This form of business combination results in a **parent–subsidiary relationship** between the two entities, with the acquirer being the **parent** and the acquiree being the **subsidiary**. The existence of a parent–subsidiary relationship normally requires the preparation of **consolidated financial statements** for the consolidated entity.

Stock acquisition: a business combination where both original companies retain their separate legal existence

Consolidated financial statements: the financial statements prepared as a result of combining the financial information of a parent company and its subsidiary(ies)

---

[18] Yoshihashi, Pauline, and Joseph Pereira, "Mattel to Buy Fisher-Price in $1.1 Billion Stock Swap," *The Wall Street Journal,* August 20, 1993, pp. A3–A4.

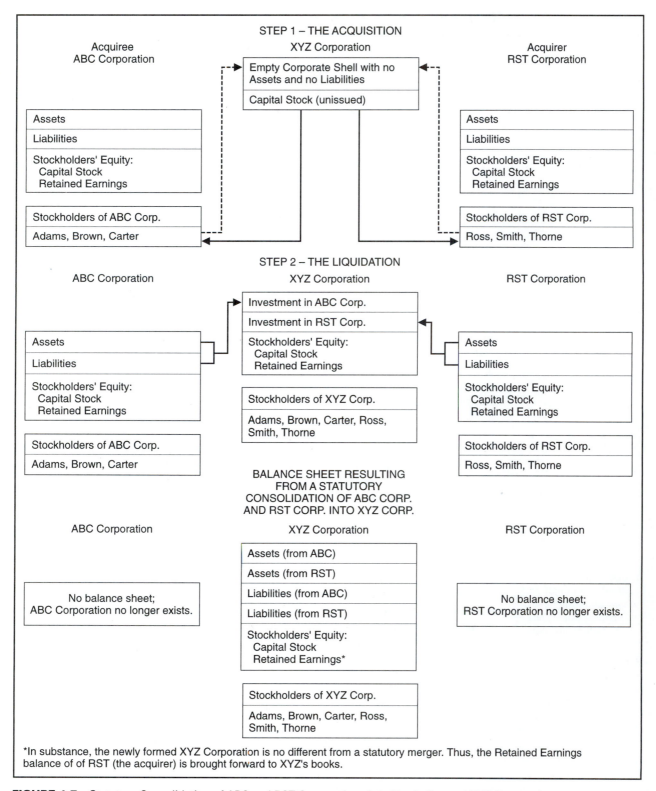

FIGURE 1-7 Statutory Consolidation of ABC and RST Corporations into Newly Formed XYZ Corporation

SUBSTANCE VERSUS FORM IN BUSINESS COMBINATIONS

In the statutory consolidation example, the issue of recording the economic substance versus the form of a business combination arose. Except for differences that result from tax implications, all the different legal forms of business combinations have the same substance. To illustrate this, a hypothetical example of an exchange is examined under the various forms.

Assume that the ABC Corporation and the RST Corporation have the following condensed balance sheets at January 1, 1991:

ABC Corporation Balance Sheet at January 1, 1991		RST Corporation Balance Sheet at January 1, 1991	
Assets	$8,000,000	Assets	$20,000,000
Liabilities	$3,000,000	Liabilities	$ 5,000,000
Capital Stock ($10 par)	4,000,000	Capital Stock ($10 par)	9,000,000
Retained Earnings	$1,000,000	Retained Earnings	6,000,000
Total	$8,000,000	Total	$20,000,000

Further assume that the market value of ABC is equal to its $5,000,000 net assets, while the market value of RST is $45,000,000. RST Corporation approaches ABC about a possible combination. The management of RST and ABC agree that $5,000,000 is the market value of ABC's net assets. The per-share market values of each firm's outstanding stock are computed as follows:

	Market Value of Firm		*Shares Outstanding*		*Market Value per Share*
RST	$45,000,000	÷	900,000 shares	=	$50.00 per share
ABC	$5,000,000	÷	400,000 shares	=	$12.50 per share

The substance of the exchange (ignoring tax aspects) is that ABC's stockholders must receive resources worth $5,000,000 for their sacrifice of ABC's net assets or for their holdings of ABC stock. Table 1-1 summarizes the various forms that result in a $5,000,000 exchange of value and the effects of the transaction on the stockholders of ABC.

In rows 1 and 2 of Table 1-1, the holdings of the ABC stockholders are unchanged. Either ABC Corporation must receive $5,000,000 in cash and notes (row 1) or it must receive 100,000 shares of RST stock (row 2) worth $50 per share. In row 3, the individual ABC stockholders receive assets worth $5,000,000 for their ABC stock. Further, in the cases where RST issues shares of stock directly to the ABC shareholders, rows 4 and 5, the number of shares issued is 100,000 ($5,000,000 / $50 per share).

Finally, with respect to the row 6 case, the $5,000,000 in value is in the form of new shares of XYZ stock. For example, assume the newly formed XYZ Corporation decides to issue 2,000,000 shares of voting common stock. The market value of the new XYZ shares will be $25 per share calculated:

$$\frac{\text{Combined market value in XYZ}}{\text{Number of new shares issued}} = \frac{\$50,000,000}{2,000,000 \text{ shares}} = \$25 \text{ per share}$$

Adams, Brown, and Carter would receive a total of 200,000 shares (10 percent) of XYZ stock if the market value of XYZ's stock is $25 per share because their contribution to the new entity was $5,000,000 of the $50,000,000 total market value contributed.

As is seen in Table 1-1, regardless of the form of the exchange, the substance is identical for all cases. ABC's stockholders have $5,000,000 in resources after the combination. The form of the business combination can vary significantly while, in substance, the value

TABLE 1-1   Summary of Holdings of the Stockholders of ABC before and after the Various Exchanges

Description of form of exchange	Personal holdings of Adams, Brown, and Carter *before* the exchange	Personal holdings of Adams, Brown, and Carter *after* the exchange
Exchange of RST assets for ABC assets (see Figure 1-1)	400,000 shares of ABC stock @ $12.50 = $5,000,000	400,000 shares of ABC stock@ $12.50 = $5,000,000
Exchange of RST stock for ABC assets (see Figure 1-2)		400,000 shares of ABC stock @ $12.50 = $5,000,000
Exchange of RST assets for ABC stock (see Figure 1-3)		Cash and notes = $5,000,000
Exchange of RST stock for ABC stock (see Figure 1-4)		100,000 shares of RST stock @ $50 = $5,000,000
Exchange of RST stock for ABC stock (statutory merger) (see Figure 1-6)		100,000 shares of RST stock @ $50 = $5,000,000
Exchange of XYZ stock for ABC stock and RST stock (statutory consolidation) (see Figure 1-7)		200,000 shares of XYZ stock @ $25 = $5,000,000

exchanged is the same. The resulting relationship between the entities varies from case to case, but a $5,000,000 exchange has to be recorded in each case. In developing accounting principles for business combinations, the profession's goal is to be sure that the accounting treatments capture the economic substance of each exchange.

CONTINGENT CONSIDERATION

Contingent consideration: when the resources to be transferred in an acquisition are subject to change based on future events

In the examples presented thus far, it has been assumed that the two parties involved in the business combination agreed on the value to be transferred by the acquirer for the acquiree's assets or stock. It is also possible that the acquisition agreement may include contingencies making it difficult to determine the total resources to be transferred (i.e., the total price of the exchange) at the date of the acquisition. The typical contingencies relate to the future earnings of the acquiree or the value of noncash securities (debt or stock) given by the acquirer, the potential change in total resources to be transferred is referred to as **contingent consideration**.

A contingency based on the future earnings of the acquiree has a potential impact on the recognized cost of the investment by the acquirer. A common agreement would result in the acquirer giving additional consideration for the investment if the income of the acquiree exceeds a predetermined level during a specified time period. For example, assume that the acquirer is initially exchanging two shares of its common stock for every share of acquiree common stock. If the market value of the acquirer's common stock is $15 and the acquiree has 100,000 shares of common stock outstanding, the dollar amount recognized in the *Investment in Subsidiary* account at the date of acquisition would be $3,000,000 (100,000 shares × 2 × $15). Assume also that the acquiree attains the required level of earnings, resulting in the acquirer exchanging three of its common shares for each acquiree share. The additional number of shares increases the payment by the acquirer, and the cost of the acquisition to the acquirer increases by the amount of the additional payment. This is reflected in an increase in the *Investment in Subsidiary* account from $3,000,000 to $4,500,000.

Conversely, a contingency based on the value of securities given by the acquirer does not impact the acquisition cost to the acquirer. One example may involve an acquirer whose stock price has been volatile (for example, $35–$55 per share). The acquiree may agree to the combination given that the value of the securities provided for the acquiree's stock is at least equal to a predetermined market value at some future specified date (for example, $10,000,000). If the market value of the acquirer's stock is $50 at the date the acquisition is agreed on (200,000 shares) and then declines to $40, the total market value of the stock to be transferred to the acquiree falls below the agreed total market value. The acquirer must issue additional shares of stock (50,000 shares). The issuance of additional shares of stock does not increase the total market value of the acquisition above the original agreed amount; it just returns the acquisition price to the original amount. The only adjustment made for the issuance of the new shares is a reallocation between *Capital Stock* and *Additional Paid-in Capital* on the books of the acquirer.

TAXES AND BUSINESS COMBINATIONS

Like most decisions that occur in business, the structure of a business combination has tax implications for the parties involved in the transaction. A business combination may be structured in a manner that will result in tax obligations for the acquiree and the inability to take advantage of a net operating loss carryforward by the acquirer, or it may result in what is referred to in the tax literature as a nontaxable exchange (in reality, it may result in a tax-deferred exchange to the acquiree stockholders, rather than a nontaxable exchange). A business combination is viewed to be a nontaxable exchange if it qualifies as a reorganization.

Reorganizations can occur regardless of whether the combination is accomplished via the acquisition of assets or the acquisition of stock. Furthermore, reorganizations can also occur regardless of whether the combination is structured as a statutory merger, statutory consolidation, or acquisition of stock.

For a combination to qualify as a reorganization, it must meet three criteria. First, the owners of the acquiree must continue to have an indirect ownership interest in the acquiree (i.e., the acquiree's stockholders cannot sell their ownership interest in the acquired entity). Indirect ownership in the acquiree would be continued through an equity interest in the acquirer, although the equity interest does not have to be in the form of voting common stock. The issuance of preferred stock or a nonvoting class of stock would also qualify as an indirect equity interest in the acquiree.

The continuation of the indirect ownership provision also does not mean that some stockholders of the acquiree cannot accept consideration other than stock and cease to have an indirect ownership in the acquiree. Internal Revenue Service (IRS) regulations indicate that at least 50 percent of the consideration paid to the acquiree's stockholders must be in the form of stock in the acquirer for the transaction to be considered a nontaxable exchange. This first provision essentially states that a reorganization has to result in the restructuring of an entity, which must include the continuation of a significant portion of the original owners.

Second, the acquirer must continue the acquiree's business or employ a significant portion of the acquiree's net assets in an ongoing business. The second provision essentially states that the reorganization must result in the continued use of the assets of the entity. Third, the combination (reorganization) must occur for a valid business purpose. It cannot occur just to avoid the payment of taxes.

Types A and C

A number of different types of reorganizations are defined in the Internal Revenue code, and only the ones relevant to business combinations are discussed here. A statutory merger or a statutory consolidation that meets the three criteria outlined above qualifies as a nontaxable exchange. This type of reorganization is labeled **Type A** because it is addressed in subparagraph A of Section 368(a)(1)(A) of the Internal Revenue code. The benefit of a Type A reorganization is that the acquirer only has to give 50 percent of the consideration in stock; the remainder can be in any form. One disadvantage of the Type A reorganization is that the acquirer becomes liable for all known and contingent liabilities of the acquiree. In addition, another issue managers must consider when accomplishing a Type A reorganization is that statutory mergers and statutory consolidations must be approved by the stockholders of both entities, a potentially timely and costly undertaking for large entities.

Some managers avoid having to attain approval by both groups of stockholders by creating a new company for the purpose of accomplishing the merger or consolidation. Because the acquirer is the sole stockholder of the new company, there is no problem with getting stockholder approval for the statutory merger or statutory consolidation. The new company is then liquidated into the acquirer. To overcome the perceived problems with a Type A reorganization, some entities may choose to accomplish a **Type C** reorganization. This type of reorganization permits the acquirer to gain possession of the acquiree's assets through contract rather than through the provisions of the state of incorporation. As a result, the acquirer does not become liable for contingent liabilities that are not expressly accepted as part of the agreement. The negative aspect of the Type C reorganization is that the acquirer's voting common stock must be issued for 100 percent of the consideration given to the acquiree. In addition, the acquiree must distribute the stock to its shareholders and, in essence, terminate the operations of the target corporation.

Type B

The third type of nontaxable exchange relevant to business combinations, **Type B**, is a stock-for-stock exchange. This type of reorganization is accomplished when the acquirer desires to take possession of the acquiree's voting common stock rather than net assets. The acquirer's voting common stock must be exchanged for the acquiree's outstanding stock. The acquirer must also own at least 80 percent of the acquiree's stock after the reorganization is completed. One provision that the acquirer's management must consider carefully is that *any* acquisition of the acquiree's stock prior to the reorganization for consideration other than stock may result in denial of the nontaxable exchange status.

The acquiree's net operating loss carryforward is not retained by the acquirer if the business combination results in a taxable exchange because it is not possible to purchase the tax aspects of another entity. On the other hand, structuring the reorganization as a nontaxable exchange always results in the acquirer being allowed to retain any net operating loss carryforward of the acquiree. However, the IRS has placed a limit on the amount of the net operating loss carryforward that can be recognized in a tax year for Type A and Type C reorganizations, thus reducing the attractiveness of net operating loss carryforward benefits of potential takeover targets. This reduces the attractiveness of the takeover target.

SUMMARY

This chapter presented an overview of business combinations. First, a background of the environment surrounding business combinations was provided. A wide array of economic motivations for business combinations were listed. Then, some historical and legal perspectives relating to business combinations in the United States were discussed. The Sherman Act and Clayton Act, landmark legislative actions, were briefly covered to provide insights into the government's concerns over the potential for abuses of power that may result when combinations result in potentially oligopolistic or monopolistic concentrations of power. Finally, modern takeover strategies and stockholder defenses were presented to provide an understanding of the dynamics of the business combination negotiating process.

The concept of "control" and the types of exchanges that result in a transfer of control were presented next. First, acquisitions of assets, Type 1 exchanges, were covered. Then,

acquisitions of stock, Type 2 exchanges, were introduced. The forms of the various transactions were illustrated, and the changes in the holdings of the entities and various stockholder groups were diagrammed. Two special cases, statutory mergers and statutory consolidations, which result in a reduction of the total number of legal entities, were also presented, diagrammed, and compared to Type 1 and Type 2 exchanges. A summary example was then provided to illustrate how the same transfer of value (the substance) can be accomplished through various types of exchanges (the form). It was emphasized that accounting should strive to be sure that the substance of the exchange is recorded no matter what form the combination takes.

The last part of the chapter gave a brief introduction of (1) contingent consideration and the complications that result, as well as (2) the tax implications of various forms of business combinations to provide an overview of taxable versus nontaxable exchanges.

QUESTIONS

1-1. Discuss two reasons why external expansion may be preferred over internal expansion.

1-2. Discuss whether expansion from a regional market to a nationwide market is more likely to occur depending on whether the expansion occurs internally or externally.

1-3. Sam and Jim are board members who just left a meeting where external expansion was discussed. An issue presented by one of the consultants was economies of scale. Sam and Jim are confused about this concept. Prepare a brief memo explaining the concept of economies of scale as it is applied to business expansion.

1-4. Discuss the differences between the analysis conducted when acquiring a new piece of machinery and the analysis conducted when acquiring control over the net assets of another company.

1-5. Your company has acquired an interest in another entity that may result in control of that entity. Your CFO has asked you to explain what characteristics in the relationship would lead to the consolidation of this entity.

1-6. Discuss what is meant by horizontal combinations.

1-7. Discuss what is meant by vertical combinations.

1-8. Discuss what is meant by conglomerate combinations.

1-9. Discuss the reasons why the Sherman Act was passed.

1-10. Discuss how the Clayton Act addressed the primary weakness in the Sherman Act.

1-11. Phyllis, a friend, was watching the news when a story on business combinations was presented. One aspect of the story was friendly and hostile takeovers. Phyllis did not hear all of the story and asks for a clarification of the difference between hostile and friendly takeovers. Respond to Phyllis's request.

1-12. The company where you work is being considered as a possible takeover target by a conglomerate entity. Bob Maxell, a board member, has asked your opinion about strategies to avoid being taken over. Your suggestions include a search for a white knight or a packman defense. Bob indicated that he does not understand these terms. Prepare an explanation of these terms for Bob.

1-13. Discuss what is meant by the term *kamikaze strategy*. Be sure to explain what maneuvers are often considered part of this strategy.

1-14. Shark repellent comes in a variety of forms. Discuss some of the more common types of shark repellent and explain what they accomplish.

1-15. Management has proposed that the board of directors institute golden parachutes that would become effective if the company were ever taken over through a business combination. Discuss what is meant by a golden parachute and indicate who, in your opinion, benefits from such a policy.

1-16. Discuss the similarities and differences between attaining control of another entity's net assets through the purchase of the entity's net assets versus through the purchase of the entity's voting common stock.

1-17. Discuss the impact of the purchase of another entity's net assets and the purchase of an entity's voting common stock on the total capitalization of the acquirer.

1-18. When one entity acquires control over the net assets of another entity through the acquisition of net assets, who decides whether the acquired entity remains in existence or ceases to exist as a legal entity? Support your answer.

1-19. The management of your company is deciding whether the acquisition of another entity should be structured as an acquisition of assets or an acquisition of stock. Prepare a memo to provide information regarding any similarities and differences that may exist between the two alternatives.

1-20. Allen Schrader is a friend of yours who is not a business major. Allen has been hearing about mergers and takeovers in the news. One day he said, "If all of these takeovers keep occurring, there will soon be few companies left because every time a takeover occurs, there is one fewer company." How do you respond to Allen?

1-21. Statutory mergers and statutory consolidations are very similar in that each results in only one company existing after the combination is completed. Why would two companies go through all the trouble of setting up another company to accomplish a statutory consolidation when a statutory merger is so similar?

1-22. Explain the meaning of the term *parent company*.

1-23. Explain the meaning of the term *subsidiary company*.

1-24. Jesse Cox is a board member for the Music Company, a company completing an acquisition. The acquiree, Piano Incorporated, is being purchased with stock of Music Company. The agreement states that Music Company will issue additional shares of stock if the market value of Music's stock decreases by more than 5 percent before the stock is exchanged. Jesse has said that the additional shares of stock would not significantly dilute the ownership of the current stockholders and that it would have no impact on the acquisition price because the purchase is being accomplished with a stock-for-stock swap. Do you agree with Jesse? Support your answer.

1-25. Does a business combination have to be a stock-for-stock exchange to qualify as a tax-deferred exchange? Why or why not?

1-26. There are three different types of IRS tax-deferred exchange treatments that may apply to business combinations. Prepare a memo indicating the basic differences that exist among the three.

1-27. What is the primary advantage(s) and disadvantage(s) of a Type A business combination?

1-28. What is the primary advantage(s) and disadvantage(s) of a Type B business combination?

1-29. What is the primary advantage(s) and disadvantage(s) of a Type C business combination?

MULTIPLE CHOICE

1-1. Which of the following would not be a form of external business expansion for Sarah's Dress Shop?
 a. Purchase of a trucking company to deliver dresses to distributors
 b. Purchase of a mill that weaves cloth
 c. Construction of a new store in a neighboring town
 d. Purchase of Millie's Dress Emporium

1-2. When one company acquires a company in the same industry, what type of business combination has occurred?
 a. Horizontal combination
 b. Vertical combination
 c. Conglomerate combination
 d. All of the above

1-3. Which of the following may management be trying to accomplish when a conglomerate form of business combination is undertaken?
 a. Increase efficiency
 b. Guarantee a supply of raw materials
 c. Capitalize on market synergies
 d. Diversify risk across industries

1-4. Which of the following combinations would be considered "horizontal"?
 a. The two entities are unrelated.
 b. The two entities are competitors in the same industry.
 c. The two entities have a potential buyer–seller relationship.
 d. None of the above describe a horizontal combination.

1-5. What type of acquisition occurs when the combination is opposed by the acquiree's management?

    a. Friendly takeover

    b. Tender offer

    c. Defensive measure

    d. Hostile takeover

1-6. What is the term used for the defensive maneuver where management of a potential acquiree sells selected desirable assets to reduce the company's value?

    a. Sale of the crown jewels

    b. Scorched earth defense

    c. Fatman defense

    d. All of the above are kamikaze strategies.

1-7. In an acquisition where there is an exchange of acquirer assets for acquiree equity, how does the reported value of the acquiree's net assets change?

    a. The net assets increase.

    b. The net assets decrease.

    c. There is no change in net assets.

    d. It is not possible to determine whether net assets will increase or decrease.

1-8. In an acquisition where there is an exchange of acquirer equity for acquiree assets, how do the ownership structures of the entities change?

    a. There is no change in the acquirer's ownership structure.

    b. The acquirer's stockholders become the acquiree's stockholders.

    c. The acquirer's and acquiree's stockholders share ownership of the acquiree company stock.

    d. The acquiree company becomes a stockholder of the acquirer.

1-9. Which of the following is not true with regard to a business combination accomplished in the form of a stock acquisition?

    a. Consolidated financial statements are required.

    b. The acquiree stockholders still control the acquiree company.

    c. A parent–subsidiary relationship exists.

    d. Two companies still exist after the acquisition is completed.

1-10. Which of the following is not a feature of a Type A form of reorganization for tax purposes?

    a. Only 50 percent of the consideration given must be in the form of stock.

    b. The acquirer must own at least 80 percent of the acquiree's stock after the reorganization is completed.

    c. The acquirer becomes liable for all known and contingent acquiree liabilities.

    d. Stockholder approval of both entities is required if the reorganization is accomplished via a statutory merger or statutory consolidation.

EXERCISES

EXERCISE 1-1   Bibby, Dyer, and Lozeau are the stockholders of East Coast Yachting Incorporated. These owners have just acquired control over the net assets of East Bay Sailing Company in an asset-for-asset exchange. The stockholders of East Bay Sailing are Clarke and Hartling.

    Required:

    Who are the stockholders of East Coast Yachting and East Bay Sailing immediately after the transaction described above occurs?

EXERCISE 1-2   The owners of Pete's Yard Maintenance, DeSimone and Murphy, just sold all of the company's net assets to Independent Lawn Service, owned by Fortier, Miranda, and Rush. Independent Lawn Service paid for Pete's assets by issuing stock.

    Required:

    Who are the stockholders of Pete's Yard Maintenance and Independent Lawn Service immediately after the transaction described above occurs?

EXERCISE 1-3 The stock of *HealthCare Magazine* was sold by its owners, Armstrong and Hart, to HealthCare Review for $650,000. HealthCare Review is owned by Perreault, Richards, and Sheldon.

Required:
Who are the stockholders of *HealthCare Magazine* and *HealthCare Review* immediately after the transaction described above occurs?

EXERCISE 1-4 The stock of Shawn's Clothing was purchased by Casual Clothing in a stock-for-stock acquisition. The stockholders of Shawn's Clothing before the transaction were Stafford and Vargas, while the stockholders for Casual Clothing were Best, Creeden, and Eikman.

Required:
Who are the stockholders of Shawn's Clothing and Casual Clothing immediately after the transaction described above occurs?

EXERCISE 1-5 Mega Markets is considering combining with Minor Location. The combination would be accomplished with a stock swap. The current agreement is for each share of Minor Location (250,000 shares outstanding) to be exchanged for .6 share of Mega Markets. The current market value of the two stocks are $12 and $20 for Minor Location and Mega Markets, respectively. Minor Location's managers believe the company is going to have an exceptionally high net income this period, so they negotiate an increased exchange ratio from .6 to .75 shares if return on equity is more than one-half percentage point greater than the same period last year.

Required:
Determine two investment amounts that could be recognized by Mega Markets. One amount should be based on Minor Location not meeting the return on equity target and the other based on Minor Location meeting the return on equity target.

EXERCISE 1-6 Philips Industries is in the process of combining with Reynolds Machine Company. The business combination has been negotiated whereby each of Reynolds's 500,000 shares of stock (market value $30) will be exchanged for 1.5 shares of Phillips Industries (market value $20). This exchange ratio will change if the market value of Phillips changes by more than 10 percent before the combination is completed. For example, if the market price of the stock decreases from $20 to $15, then the exchange ratio will increase from 1.5 shares of Phillips per share of Reynolds to 2.0 shares (based on the new market ratio of $30/$15).

Required:
Determine the investment amount that would be recognized by Phillips Industries based on the three following independent situations.

  A. Phillips's stock price increases from $20 to $24, resulting in a change in the exchange rate from 1.5 to 1.25 shares of Phillips stock for each share of Reynolds.
  B. Phillips's stock price decreases from $20 to $12.50, resulting in a change in the exchange rate from 1.5 to 2.4 shares of Phillips stock for each share of Reynolds.
  C. Phillips's stock price decreases from $20 to $19, resulting in no change in the exchange ratio. Reynolds stockholders still receive 1.5 shares of Phillips stock for each share of Reynolds.

PROBLEMS

PROBLEM 1-1 Percentage stock ownership and market value after acquisition
PROBLEM 1-2 Percentage stock ownership based on different types of acquisition
PROBLEM 1-3 Acquisition price with contingent consideration based on income
PROBLEM 1-4 Acquisition price with contingent consideration based on stock price

PROBLEM 1-1 For each of the following independent cases, identify the stockholders of each company immediately after the transaction described, the percentage of the stock owned, and the market value of each group's investment in each company.

A. Conlan, Jackson, and Perron own all 10,000 shares of Han's Import/Export Company's stock, market value $2,500,000. Han's just purchased all of the met assets of Mass Production for $150,000 cash. Mass Production's stock (1,000 shares) is owned by Hartley and Munson and the stock's market value is $140,000.

B. The owners of Universal Plumbing sell all of the entity's net assets to Random Pipefitters for 80,000 unissued shares of Random Pipefitters' stock. Alberto and Amato owned all 25,000 shares of Universal's stock prior to this transaction, and the stock had a market value of $2,750,000. Prior to the purchase of Universal Plumbing's net assets, Random Pipefitters' stock (240,000 shares) was owned by Davis, Hurd, and Ringrose (market value $15,000,000).

C. Heritage Cleaners purchases all of the stock of City Cleaners for $3,600,000. The market values of Heritage and City immediately prior to the transaction were $10,750,000 and $3,400,000, respectively. Prior to the transaction, the owners of Heritage Cleaners are Levin and Levy and the owners of City Cleaners are Bosco and Krone.

D. The owners of Chambers Music Store (Chambers and Garrett) exchange all 16,000 shares of their stock (market value $1,250,000) with Olympia Music Incorporated for 25,000 shares of Olympia's common stock. Prior to this transaction, the market value of Olympia's 100,000 shares of stock was $5,000,000 and the stockholders of Olympia were Forest and Gump.

PROBLEM 1-2

Monti's Tools is owned by Brewer and Herold, and Chester's Machinery is owned by Dorsey, Lawlor, and O'Flaherty. The stockholders of both companies have been discussing a business combination whereby Chester's Machinery would acquire control of the net assets of Monti's Tools. Dorsey, Lawlor, and O'Flaherty have asked for some information regarding how the structuring of the business combination would impact the ownership interest of the two groups of stockholders. Prior to the transaction, Monti's Tools and Chester's Machinery had 337,500 and 600,000 shares of stock outstanding, respectively, and the stock had market value of $6,750,000 and $27,000,000, respectively.

Required:

Complete the following table to indicate the stockholders of each company based on different types of transactions and the ownership interest each group would have in each company. Assume the market values presented above would be used to determine the numbers of shares of stock to be issued.

	TYPES OF EXCHANGES							
	Chester's assets for Monti's assets		Chester's assets for Monti's stock		Chester's stock for Monti's assets		Chester's stock for Monti's stock	
	Monti's	Chester's	Monti's	Chester's	Monti's	Chester's	Monti's	Chester's
Shareholders								
Percentage ownership								

PROBLEM 1-3

Ace Building Products and Home Construction Company have been contemplating a business combination in which Ace Building would take control of Home Construction. The board of directors of Home Construction is concerned that the stockholders of Home Construction will not receive adequate compensation for their stock because the company's net income fluctuates significantly. The current stock-for-stock exchange being considered is that each share of Home Construction stock, par value $1.00 and market value $17.875, would be exchanged for .65 shares of Ace Building Products' stock, par value $.50 and market value $27.50. There are currently 320,000 shares of Home Construction Company stock outstanding. One proposal is that the exchange ratio be increased from .65 to .7 share of Ace Building for each share of Home Construction if the net income of Home Construction increases by more than 15 percent above last year.

Required:

Prepare a report for the board of directors explaining the impact of changing the exchange ratio on the financial records of Ace Building Products. Explain the reason for the impact determined.

PROBLEM 1-4   Management of Microsoft and Intuit discussed a possible merger for some time. While negotiations were eventually stopped, there are some interesting issues that could have come about. Assuming an agreement had been reached whereby Microsoft would have acquired all of the outstanding common stock of Intuit and that this agreement had not been challenged in the courts, a stock-for-stock exchange could have occurred. This type of exchange may have been viewed as risky by the stockholders of Intuit. Microsoft's stock was trading at a 52-week high, approximately $90 per share, when management of the two companies were discussing the merger, while Intuit's stock was trading at approximately $76 per share (approximately $10 below the 52-week high). If the stockholders of Intuit agreed to an exchange of stock—for example .90 shares of Microsoft for each share of Intuit—the exchange value per share of Intuit stock would be $81. However, if the market value of Microsoft stock decreased, the exchange value per share of Intuit stock would also decrease. Suppose management of Intuit agreed to an exchange of stock if the agreement included the stipulation that for any decrease in the value of Microsoft's stock, the ratio of shares exchanged would increase proportionately. For example, if the Microsoft's stock decreased in value from $90 to $72 (a 20 percent decrease), the shareholders of Intuit would receive 1.125 (.9/.8) shares of Microsoft for each share of Intuit. Assume also that there are 5,000,000 shares of Intuit stock outstanding and 35,000,000 shares of Microsoft stock outstanding.

Required:
Prepare a report for Microsoft's board of directors explaining the impact of a decrease in the market price of its stock from $90 per share to $67.50 per share on the financial records of Microsoft. Explain the reason for the impact determined.

CHAPTER 2

CONSOLIDATION AT THE DATE OF ACQUISITION

LEARNING OBJECTIVES

After reading this chapter, you should be able to:

- Discuss why consolidated financial statements are prepared.
- Allocate the difference between the purchase price of a subsidiary and the underlying book value of the subsidiary's assets and liabilities.
- Prepare the worksheet elimination needed to consolidate a parent and subsidiary at the date of acquisition of a subsidiary.
- Prepare a consolidation worksheet at the date a subsidiary is acquired.
- Determine the noncontrolling interest that exists at the date a subsidiary is acquired.

Business combinations are accomplished when one entity acquires control over the net assets of another entity. The legal structure of such a combination may result in either one entity existing after the combination is completed (i.e., statutory merger or statutory consolidation) or two entities continuing to exist after the combination (i.e., stock acquisition). When two legal entities exist after the combination, consolidated financial statements are required.

This chapter presents consolidation objectives and procedures for a parent company and its subsidiary at the date the subsidiary is acquired. Consolidated financial statements may be prepared at the date a subsidiary is acquired, or management may request pro forma consolidated financial statements in anticipation of an acquisition. Pro forma statements may help determine the impact of an acquisition on both the financial position of the combined entity and indicators such as financial statement ratios.

The chapter begins with a brief history of the requirement to prepare consolidated financial statements, including a discussion of the perceived strengths and weaknesses of consolidated financial statements. The subsequent section presents a data set for Pratt Corporation (parent company) and Sterling Products (subsidiary company). Some time should be spent examining the data for the two entities because it provides a basis for consolidation illustrations presented in the remainder of this chapter as well as subsequent consolidation chapters. Following the data set are illustrations of a Pratt and Sterling combination at the date of acquisition. The illustrations developed in this chapter begin with Pratt's acquisition of 100 percent of Sterling's outstanding stock on the balance sheet date at a price equal to Sterling's book value. Subsequent illustrations relax this simplified model by first dropping the assumption that the price equals the book value of the subsidiary. Next, the assumption of balance sheet date acquisition is relaxed. Finally, the concept of noncontrolling interest is introduced by changing the percentage ownership acquired to 90 percent. Also interwoven into the chapter are discussions of new FASB standards that narrow the acceptable methods for combining parent and subsidiary financial statements, alternative concepts of consolidated financial statements, current FASB proposals that change the consolidation concept used to prepare consolidated financial statements, and Securities and Exchange Commission (SEC) push-down accounting requirements.

CONSOLIDATED FINANCIAL STATEMENTS

Consolidated financial statements are the set of financial statements (balance sheet, income statement, and statement of cash flows) prepared for a parent company and all subsidiaries under control of the parent company. The parent company and its subsidiaries are presented as one economic unit for financial reporting purposes. Consolidated financial statements have been required for many entities since 1959.[1] Accounting Research Bulletin (ARB) No. 51 required the preparation of consolidated financial statements but permitted companies to exclude some majority-owned subsidiaries from the consolidated statements if (1) control of the subsidiary is temporary; (2) control of the subsidiary does not rest with the majority owner; (3) the subsidiary has a relatively large minority interest; (4) the subsidiary is a foreign company; or (5) the subsidiary's operations are sufficiently different from those of the parent company, that is, the subsidiary has nonhomogeneous operations. A result of these exceptions was that to some entities chose not to consolidate certain subsidiaries even with ownership in the 80 to 100 percent range. Other entities chose not to consolidate any foreign subsidiaries or to consolidate only foreign subsidiaries that were located in North America. Still other entities, such as some manufacturing companies, did not consolidate finance subsidiaries because of nonhomogeneous operations. The ability of companies to choose not to consolidate many subsidiaries resulted in some companies excluding more specific assets and liabilities from the consolidated financial statements than were included.[2]

The American Institute of Certified Public Accountants (AICPA) asked the Financial Accounting Standards Board (FASB) to reconsider the exclusion of finance subsidiaries from consolidated financial statements. The FASB chose to review all the exclusion provisions as part of its reporting entity project. The result of this deliberation was the issuance of Statement No. 94.[3] As part of its deliberations, the FASB considered the impact of all the different exclusions on the consolidated financial statements. In addition, the

---

[1] **Accounting Research Bulletin**, No. 51, "Consolidated Financial Statements" (New York: American Institute of Certified Public Accountants, 1959).

[2] Ibid., par. 2–3.

[3] **Statement of Financial Accounting Standards**, No. 94, "Consolidation of All Majority-Owned Subsidiaries" (Norwalk, CT: Financial Accounting Standards Board, 1987).

Board also addressed the relative strengths and weaknesses of consolidated statements when compared to other forms of presentation.

One area considered was the impact of including some subsidiaries with highly diverse business operations on the consolidated financial statements. The FASB focused on the difference between using the equity method to account for an investment versus the consolidation of the subsidiary. Some preparers and users of financial statements contended that combining very diverse business operations results in financial statements that are more difficult to interpret. In addition, weak performances by some subsidiaries are more difficult to identify when combined with the entire consolidated entity. The FASB concluded that the diverse nature of business is not a sufficient reason to exclude a subsidiary from the consolidated financial statements.[4] It also decided that the equity method is not a valid substitute for inclusion in the consolidated statements because the equity method omits detailed reporting of significant revenue and expenses from the income statement, significant assets and liabilities from the balance sheet, and significant receipts and payments from the statement of cash flows.[5]

Another area considered was the ability of investors and creditors to compare entities. Some investors and creditors contended that the many mergers that have occurred make it difficult to compare entities to industry standards. In addition, financial ratios calculated from consolidated data are averages and thus, are not representative of any particular part of the consolidated entity. The FASB took the position that investors and creditors are interested in the consolidated entity, not just the parent company, and that if similarities or differences between entities exist because of financial reporting rather than because of the nature of the entities themselves, financial reporting hinders investors and creditors in making decisions.[6] The Board also states in paragraph 36 that

> *if the assets, liabilities, revenues, expenses, and cash flows of "nonhomogeneous" subsidiaries are excluded from consolidation, the consolidated financial statements of the enterprise do not faithfully represent the operating results, financial status, and capital structure of the enterprise ...*

The FASB's final decision was that all majority-owned subsidiaries are to be included in the consolidated financial statements unless control is temporary or the majority owner does not have control. The decision to include all other majority-owned subsidiaries in the consolidated financial statements was based on the importance of relevance, representational faithfulness, and comparability.[7] The FASB concluded that including all majority-owned subsidiaries except those specified above would better meet the objectives of financial reporting than would excluding some subsidiaries.[8]

DATA SET FOR PRATT AND STERLING

Pratt Corporation was organized approximately 40 years ago and is a publicly owned manufacturing concern. Sterling Products is a 10-year-old growing firm that markets a variety of products. Sterling's stockholders have responded favorably to indications that

---

[4] Ibid., par. 29.

[5] Ibid., par. 31.

[6] Ibid., par. 43.

[7] **Statement of Financial Accounting Concepts**, No. 2, "Qualitative Characteristics of Accounting Information" (Stamford, CT: Financial Accounting Standards Board, 1980).

[8] Op. cit., **Statement of Financial Accounting Standards (FAS)**, No. 94, par. 46.

ILLUSTRATION 2-1
Pratt Corporation and Sterling Products
Balance Sheets
October 1, 2005

	Pratt	Sterling
Assets		
Cash	$ 3,400,000	$ 100,000
Accounts Receivable (net)	2,000,000	250,000
Inventory (FIFO)	5,000,000	600,000
Other Current Assets	1,700,000	150,000
Total Current Assets	$12,100,000	$1,100,000
Plant and Equipment (net)	14,100,000	1,400,000
Patents		1,200,000
Other Noncurrent Assets	1,500,000	2,100,000
Total Long-Term Assets	$15,600,000	$4,700,000
Total Assets	$27,700,000	$5,800,000
Liabilities		
Current Liabilities	$ 8,755,000	$1,405,000
Long-Term Notes Payable		1,000,000
7% Bonds Payable (due June 30, 2013)	4,000,000	
Less: Discount on Bonds Payable	(155,000)	
8% Bonds Payable (due December 31, 2010)		1,500,000
Less: Discount on Bonds Payable		(105,000)
Total Liabilities	$12,600,000	$3,800,000
Stockholders' Equity		
Common Stock ($1 par):		
Pratt, 10,000,000 shares authorized, 6,000,000 shares issued and outstanding	$ 6,000,000	
Sterling, 1,000,000 shares authorized, issued, and outstanding		$1,000,000
Additional Paid-In Capital	6,500,000	750,000
Retained Earnings (October 1, 2005)	2,600,000	250,000
Total Stockholders' Equity	$15,100,000	$2,000,000
Total Liabilities and Stockholders' Equity	$27,700,000	$5,800,000

Pratt may wish to acquire control of Sterling. The balance sheets of the two companies at October 1, 2005, are provided in Illustration 2-1.

CONSOLIDATION AT ACQUISITION DATE: 100 PERCENT–OWNED SUBSIDIARY

The acquisition of a subsidiary at book value is an event that would seldom occur in practice because the market value of assets generally exceeds the book value. The following example is based on a book value acquisition of a subsidiary at the balance sheet date (beginning of the fiscal year) to illustrate the basic features of the consolidation process.

Subsequent examples relax the book-value assumption and the beginning-of-year-acquisition assumption.

Acquisition at Beginning of Year: Purchase Price Equals Book Value

Assume that September 30 is the fiscal year-end for both Pratt and Sterling. On October 1, 2005, Pratt acquires all of the outstanding shares of Sterling for cash equal to the net book value of Sterling, $2,000,000. Keep in mind that the market values equal the book values in the accounts of Sterling for this example. This acquisition is recorded on Pratt's books by making the following journal entry:

Journal Entry—Pratt Corporation Books

Oct. 1, 2005	Investment in Sterling Products	2,000,000	
	Cash		2,000,000

To record the acquisition of Sterling Products' stock at book value.

The investment balance represents Pratt's ownership of the 1,000,000 outstanding shares of Sterling common stock, which, in turn, represent the entire $2,000,000 of Sterling's net worth.

Immediately after the business combination has been completed, the combined entity may be viewed as a single economic unit owned by Pratt's stockholders. Reporting the status of Pratt via the Pratt Corporation balance sheet at this time would include reporting a balance in a noncurrent asset account, *Investment in Sterling Products,* at $2,000,000 (see Pratt's balance sheet at October 1, 2005, in Illustration 2-2). The presentation of the *Investment in Sterling Products* account discloses the amount invested; however, a more meaningful presentation is to report the various individual asset and liability account balances of Sterling that constitute the $2,000,000 investment balance. Such a presentation gives a more detailed and useful disclosure of the combined entity's financial position. For example, the breakdown of current assets and long-term assets would be clearer. The current and long-term obligations of the parent and subsidiary together would also be disclosed more completely. Thus, the primary objective of the consolidation procedures that follow is to present to the Pratt Corporation stockholders (1) the detailed asset, liability, and net worth position represented by the Pratt Corporation separate books plus (2) the individual values of the Sterling Products assets and liabilities.

Illustration 2-2 presents the consolidating worksheet to combine Pratt and Sterling at October 1, 2005, immediately after the investment on the first day of the fiscal year. The first two numeric columns show the respective balance sheets at October 1, 2005. Notice that Pratt's asset section shows $2,000,000 less in cash than was shown in Illustration 2-1 before the investment entry was posted. Columns 3 and 4 provide the necessary worksheet elimination (discussed below). Column 5 presents the resulting consolidated balances, which achieve the primary objective stated above.

Sterling's assets and liabilities are assumed in this example to have market values equal to book values; therefore, the balances are added across to arrive at the appropriate consolidated balances. For example, adding across the *Inventory* accounts (reproduced from Illustration 2-2) results in the following:

			Adjustments and Eliminations		
	Pratt	Sterling	Debit	Credit	Consolidated Balance
Inventory	5,000,000	600,000			5,600,000

ILLUSTRATION 2-2
Worksheet for Consolidation of Pratt Corporation and Subsidiary, Sterling Products
100 Percent–Owned Subsidiary
Consolidation at Acquisition Date (Beginning of Year)
Price Equal to Book Value
October 1, 2005

	Separate Financial Statements		Adjustments and Eliminations		Consolidated Financial Statements
	Pratt	Sterling	Debit	Credit	
Balance Sheet					
Cash	1,400,000	100,000			1,500,000
Accounts Receivable (net)	2,000,000	250,000			2,250,000
Inventory (FIFO)	5,000,000	600,000			5,600,000
Other Current Assets	1,700,000	150,000			1,850,000
Total Current Assets	10,100,000	1,100,000			11,200,000
Plant and Equipment (net)	14,100,000	1,400,000			15,500,000
Patent		1,200,000			1,200,000
Investment in Sterling Products	2,000,000			(1) 2,000,000	0
Other Noncurrent Assets	1,500,000	2,100,000			3,600,000
Total Long-Term Assets	17,600,000	4,700,000			20,300,000
Total Assets	27,700,000	5,800,000			31,500,000
Current Liabilities	8,755,000	1,405,000			10,160,000
Long-Term Notes Payable		1,000,000			1,000,000
7% Bonds Payable (due 6/30/2013)	4,000,000				4,000,000
Less: Discount on Bonds Payable	(155,000)				(155,000)
8% Bonds Payable (due 12/31/2010)		1,500,000			1,500,000
Less: Discount on Bonds Payable		(105,000)			(105,000)
Total Liabilities	12,600,000	3,800,000			16,400,000
Common Stock ($1 par):					
Pratt, 10,000,000 shares authorized, 6,000,000 shares issued and outstanding	6,000,000				6,000,000
Sterling, 1,000,000 shares authorized, issued and outstanding		1,000,000	(1) 1,000,000		0
Additional Paid-In Capital	6,500,000	750,000	(1) 750,000		6,500,000
Retained Earnings (10/1/2005)	2,600,000	250,000	(1) 250,000		2,600,000
Total Stockholders' Equity	15,100,000	2,000,000			15,100,000
Total Liabilities and Stockholders' Equity	27,700,000	5,800,000			31,500,000
			2,000,000	2,000,000	

(1) To eliminate the subsidiary's date of acquisition stockholders' equity and the parent's date of acquisition Investment in Sterling Products account.

To include both Sterling's asset and liability account balances and Pratt's *Investment in Sterling Products* account on the consolidated balance sheet would result in a double counting of Sterling's net assets because the investment account is the summary account that represents those same assets and liabilities. For this reason, the *Investment in Sterling Products* account should be eliminated from the consolidated financial statements. The owners' equity accounts of Sterling should also be eliminated because the consolidated statements are prepared for the Pratt Corporation stockholders, and Pratt's net worth is already equal to Pratt's net assets, including the Sterling investment. The worksheet elimination from Illustration 2-2, in journal entry form, is presented in Worksheet Elimination 2-2.

Worksheet Elimination 2-2—Journal Entry Form		
(1) Common Stock	1,000,000	
Additional Paid-In Capital	750,000	
Retained Earnings (October 1, 2005)	250,000	
Investment in Sterling Products		2,000,000

To eliminate the subsidiary's date of acquisition stockholders' equity and the parent's date of acquisition Investment in Sterling Products account.

Worksheet Procedures—General Discussion

Particular attention should be given to the fact that *worksheet eliminations are not posted* to either Pratt's or Sterling's books. Pratt maintains its investment balance on its separate books, and Sterling maintains its owners' equity accounts on its separate books. Worksheet eliminations are displayed in journal entry form for clarity of discussion. Note the heading "Worksheet Elimination" in Worksheet Elimination 2-2. This terminology is used as a reminder that these debits and credits are not posted as one would post normal journal entries. Worksheet eliminations are shaded to distinguish them from journal entries that are posted on the books of the parent or subsidiary.

Worksheet elimination (1) is based on account values that exist on Pratt's and Sterling's separate financial records at the date of acquisition or the beginning of the period (in periods subsequent to acquisition). This particular worksheet elimination removes the beginning subsidiary stockholders' equity and the beginning balance in the investment account from the consolidated financial statements. In the presentation of the various cases that follow, the worksheet elimination that removes the parent's date of acquisition investment account and the subsidiary's date of acquisition stockholders' equity will be expanded as some restrictions are relaxed; however, this worksheet elimination will be labeled (1) in all consolidation examples. Notice that, in this case, the investment balance at the acquisition date exactly offsets the reported net worth of the subsidiary. This occurs only when two conditions exist: (1) 100 percent of the subsidiary's stock is acquired, and (2) the acquisition price is equal to the book value of the subsidiary.

Acquisition at Beginning of Year: Purchase Price Exceeds Book Value (Positive Goodwill)

In practice, acquisitions rarely occur at book value. Accounting principles tend toward conservatism, so the market value of an existing company will generally be greater than its book value. Thus, the price paid in an acquisition will generally exceed the subsidiary's book value. Assume that the relevant market value information for Sterling at October 1, 2005, is provided in Illustration 2-3. These values would be determined by appraisals attained while negotiating the purchase. Note that the identified net assets (assets minus liabilities) of Sterling now have a market value of $2,175,000. This information is the market value data (resulting from a negotiated arm's-length transaction) to use for purchase acquisitions occurring at a price other than book value.

ILLUSTRATION 2-3
Sterling Products' Assets and Liabilities
Book Values and Market Values
at October 1, 2005

Accounts	Debit (Credit) Market Value	Debit (Credit) Book Value	Difference
Cash	100,000	100,000	0
Accounts Receivable (net)	250,000	250,000	0
Inventory (FIFO)	730,000	600,000	130,000
Other Current Assets	150,000	150,000	0
Plant and Equipment (net)	1,750,000	1,400,000	350,000
Patents	1,031,400	1,200,000	(168,600)
Other Noncurrent Assets	2,100,000	2,100,000	0
Current Liabilities	(1,405,000)	(1,405,000)	0
Long-Term Notes Payable	(1,136,400)	(1,000,000)	(136,400)
Bonds Payable	(1,395,000)	(1,500,000)	0
Less: Discount on Bonds Payable		105,000	
Net Assets	2,175,000	2,000,000	175,000

Assume also that Pratt acquires 100 percent of Sterling's stock, but Pratt pays $2,400,000 and records this investment as follows:

Journal Entry—Pratt Corporation Books

Oct. 1, 2005	Investment in Sterling Products	2,400,000
	Cash	

2,400,000

To record the acquisition of Sterling Products' stock at $400,000 in excess of book value.

Note that, from the perspective of Pratt's stockholders, the market value of Sterling determines the historical cost of the investment because it is the amount Pratt paid for the investment in Sterling. Recall that the book values of Pratt's accounts were added to the book values of Sterling's accounts in Illustration 2-2 to determine many of the consolidated financial statement balances. This was possible because Sterling's book values were also Sterling's market values. In essence, Sterling's market values became the book values for consolidated financial statements.

The market value of individual assets and liabilities must be considered when determining consolidated financial statement values in the current example. The purchase price for Sterling in the current example includes a $400,000 premium above book value. The amount by which the book value and the market value differ is called the **purchase differential**. To prepare the consolidated financial statements, the purchase differential must be allocated to all individual asset and liability accounts where the book value and market value differ, including any asset that has no book value. Any positive purchase differential remaining after the allocation to all individual assets and liabilities is assigned to goodwill. That is, goodwill is the amount of positive purchase differential that cannot be allocated to any identifiable assets or liabilities. The allocation in the current example is as follows:

Purchase differential:
the amount by which a
subsidiary's book value
and market value differ
at the acquisition date

Purchase price for a 100 percent interest	$2,400,000
Less: Book value of 100 percent acquired (per Illustration 2-1)	2,000,000
Purchase Differential	400,000

Allocation of purchase differential: difference between the market
value and book value of identifiable net assets (per Illustration 2-3):

Inventory	130,000	
Plant and Equipment (net)	350,000	
Patents	(168,600)	
Long-Term Notes Payable	(136,400)	175,000
Goodwill (price in excess of market value of net assets acquired)		$225,000

To consolidate Pratt and Sterling in this case, the value of certain accounts of Sterling must be adjusted so that the consolidated balance sheet reflects the historical cost to the consolidated entity, that is, the market values of the assets acquired. Using the same account illustrated earlier, *Inventory,* the worksheet now should show a consolidated balance of $5,730,000 as follows:

	Pratt	Sterling	Adjustments and Eliminations		Consolidated Balance
			Debit	**Credit**	
Inventory	5,000,000	600,000	130,000		5,730,000

The Pratt and Sterling columns represent the historical cost of inventory on their respective financial records. The $130,000 debit represents the adjustment needed to reflect the historical cost of Sterling's inventory to the consolidated entity, that is, the amount Pratt paid to acquire the inventory. The consolidated balance discloses the total historical cost of inventory to the consolidated entity.

As in Illustration 2-2, the objective of the consolidation process presented in Illustration 2-4 is to eliminate the *Investment in Sterling Products* account of Pratt and the owners' equity accounts of Sterling. However, in this case the owners' equity balance is $2,000,000 while the investment balance is $2,400,000. The difference is exactly equal to the net adjustments made to carrying values of existing Sterling accounts, $175,000, plus the recognition of purchased goodwill, $225,000. Worksheet Elimination 2-4 presents the worksheet elimination in journal entry form.

Recall that worksheet elimination (1) is based on values that exist as of the beginning of the period or the date of acquisition. As discussed previously, the worksheet elimination to some accounts is based on the amounts disclosed in the financial records of Pratt or Sterling. The worksheet elimination to *Common Stock, Additional Paid-In Capital,* and *Retained Earnings* removes the subsidiary's beginning stockholders' equity accounts, while the worksheet elimination to *Investment in Sterling Products* removes the parent's beginning investment balance from the consolidated balance sheet. The other items in Worksheet Elimination 2-4 present adjustments to accounts on the subsidiary's financial records or the creation of accounts that do not exist on the parent's or the subsidiary's financial records. For example, the credit to *Long-Term Notes Payable* is made to adjust for the increase in the date of acquisition market value of the outstanding notes. This adjustment is a function of changed market interest rates.

The adjustments to *Inventory, Plant and Equipment,* and *Patents* reflect the date of acquisition market value adjustments to existing assets. Note that there are both tangible assets (inventory and plant and equipment) as well as intangible assets (patents) in the worksheet elimination. Individual intangible assets are recognized apart from goodwill if they meet either one of two criteria.[9] The first criterion is that the intangible asset arises

[9] **Statement of Financial Accounting Standards**, No. 141, "Business Combinations" (Norwalk, CT: Financial Accounting Standards Board, 2001), par. 39.

ILLUSTRATION 2-4
Worksheet for Consolidation of Pratt Corporation and Subsidiary, Sterling Products
100 Percent–Owned Subsidiary
Consolidation at Acquisition Date (Beginning of Year)
Price More Than Book Value
October 1, 2005

	Separate Financial Statements		Adjustments and Eliminations		Consolidated Financial Statements
	Pratt	Sterling	Debit	Credit	
Balance Sheet					
Cash	1,000,000	100,000			1,100,000
Accounts Receivable (net)	2,000,000	250,000			2,250,000
Inventory (FIFO)	5,000,000	600,000	(1) 130,000		5,730,000
Other Current Assets	1,700,000	150,000			1,850,000
Total Current Assets	9,700,000	1,100,000			10,930,000
Plant and Equipment (net)	14,100,000	1,400,000	(1) 350,000		15,850,000
Patents		1,200,000		(1) 168,600	1,031,400
Investment in Sterling Products	2,400,000			(1) 2,400,000	0
Other Noncurrent Assets	1,500,000	2,100,000			3,600,000
Goodwill			(1) 225,000		225,000
Total Long-Term Assets	18,000,000	4,700,000			20,706,400
Total Assets	27,700,000	5,800,000			31,636,400
Current Liabilities	8,755,000	1,405,000			10,160,000
Long-Term Notes Payable		1,000,000		(1) 136,400	1,136,400
7% Bonds Payable (due 6/30/2013)	4,000,000				4,000,000
Less: Discount on Bonds Payable	(155,000)				(155,000)
8% Bonds Payable (due 12/31/2010)		1,500,000			1,500,000
Less: Discount on Bonds Payable		(105,000)			(105,000)
Total Liabilities	12,600,000	3,800,000			16,536,400
Common Stock ($1 par):					
Pratt, 10,000,000 shares authorized, 6,000,000 shares issued and outstanding	6,000,000				6,000,000
Sterling, 1,000,000 shares authorized, issued and outstanding		1,000,000	(1) 1,000,000		0
Additional Paid-In Capital	6,500,000	750,000	(1) 750,000		6,500,000
Retained Earnings (10/1/2005)	2,600,000	250,000	(1) 250,000		2,600,000
Total Stockholders' Equity	15,100,000	2,000,000			15,100,000
Total Liabilities and Stockholders' Equity	27,700,000	5,800,000			31,636,400
			2,705,000	2,705,000	

(1) To eliminate the subsidiary's date of acquisition stockholders' equity and the parent's date of acquisition Investment in Sterling Products account, and to establish the date of acquisition purchase differentials.

from contractual or other legal rights. These rights do not have to be transferable to other entities or separable from the acquired entity to qualify for separate recognition. The second criterion is that the intangible asset can be separated from the acquired entity and transferred to another entity. If neither of the criteria is met, the intangible asset is not separately recognized. Instead, it is recognized as part of goodwill. In this particular instance,

Worksheet Elimination 2-4—Journal Entry Form		
(1) Common Stock	1,000,000	
Additional Paid-In Capital	750,000	
Retained Earnings (October 1, 2005)	250,000	
Inventory	130,000	
Plant and Equipment (net)	350,000	
Goodwill	225,000	
Patents		168,600
Long-Term Notes Payable		136,400
Investment in Sterling Products		2,400,000

To eliminate the subsidiary's date of acquisition stockholders' equity and the parent's date of acquisition Investment in Sterling Products account, and to establish the date of acquisition purchase differentials.

Patents is assumed to meet the definition of a recognizable intangible asset. Notice that the adjustment to the *Patent* account, a credit, reflects a current market value that is less than book value.

Finally, the debit to *Goodwill* creates a new account balance in the consolidated assets. *Goodwill* is unique in this example in that it is a part of the *Investment in Sterling Products* balance on Pratt's books but is disclosed as a separate asset only in the consolidated balance sheet. Some of the premium paid is due to market value in excess of book value for existing net assets of Sterling (i.e., those already having a nonzero book value on Sterling's books), while goodwill is an amount paid that is not reflected at all in Sterling's financial records. Additional accounts could also be created on the consolidated balance sheet. For example, Sterling may have a copyright that resulted from work in the company. As a result, the copyright may have a carrying value of $0 on Sterling's books yet have market value. A key aspect to worksheet elimination (1) is that all the values included in the worksheet elimination represent date of acquisition amounts.

Illustration 2-4, like Illustration 2-2, achieves the presentation of consolidated balances that reflect (1) the books of Pratt plus (2) the market value of Sterling's net assets, including goodwill. Thus, the second example does not change the objective of consolidated statements; it only illustrates an expanded application of the same objective.

Acquisition at Beginning of Year: Appraisal Value Exceeds Purchase Price (Negative Goodwill)

Negative goodwill: the amount by which the net appraised value of the subsidiary's identifiable assets and liabilities exceeds the acquisition price

In most acquisitions the amount paid for a subsidiary will exceed the subsidiary's recognized book value. Occasionally the amount paid by the parent will not be as great as the net appraised market values of the individual identifiable assets and liabilities. In this circumstance **negative goodwill** exists. There are two likely reasons for the existence of negative goodwill. First, something relating to the subsidiary may reduce its overall value in the marketplace. Some conditions that may lead to such a valuation are rates of return below market expectations, pending litigation, or a general market perception about the subsidiary's future profitability. Second, appraised values for individual assets may contain estimation errors.

When negative goodwill exists, the acquirer should first review the procedures used to identify and value the subsidiary's assets and liabilities. Once it is determined that all the subsidiary's assets and liabilities have been identified and valued at the appropriate market values, any negative goodwill that exists is assigned to the income statement as an extraordinary gain.

To illustrate this occurrence, assume that Pratt's purchase price for 100 percent of Sterling's outstanding common stock is $2,078,000, rather than $2,400,000 as in the previous example. Assume also that the market values to be considered for individual assets and liabilities are those previously presented in Illustration 2-3. The purchase differential allocation and calculation of the negative goodwill are provided in the following table.

Purchase price for a 100 percent interest		$2,078,000
Less: Book value of 100 percent acquired (per Illustration 2-1)		2,000,000
Purchase Differential		78,000
Allocation of purchase differential: difference between the market value and book value of identifiable net assets (per Illustration 2-3):		
Inventory	130,000	
Plant and Equipment (net)	350,000	
Patents	(168,600)	
Long-Term Notes Payable	(136,400)	175,000
Negative Goodwill (price less than market value of net assets acquired)		$(97,000)

The assignment of the purchase differentials to the individual identifiable assets and liabilities is not affected by the existence of negative goodwill. The purchase differentials, totaling $175,000, are first assigned to the identifiable assets and liabilities just as they were in the previous example when Pratt paid $2,400,000 for all of Sterling's stock. In this case, however, the purchase differentials of $175,000 exceed the actual price in excess of book value of $78,000 ($2,078,000 − $2,000,000). The difference is treated as negative goodwill of $97,000 ($175,000 − $78,000) and is recognized in the income statement as an extraordinary gain. The following journal entry would be recorded by Pratt at the acquisition date.

Journal Entry—Pratt Corporation Books

Oct. 1, 2005	Investment in Sterling Products	2,175,000	
	Extraordinary Gain from Acquisition of Sterling Products		97,000
	Cash		2,078,000

To record the acquisition of Sterling Products' stock at $78,000 in excess of book value.

Notice that the *Investment in Sterling Products* account is established at the market value of the underlying net assets, while the *Cash* decreases by the amount actually paid for the investment. The difference between the recorded investment and the cash paid is the extraordinary gain due to the negative goodwill.[10] Worksheet Elimination 2-4a presents the worksheet elimination in journal entry form that would be needed to consolidate Pratt and Sterling based on this information.

---

[10] The investor may initially record the investment on its books at the amount paid ($2,078,000 in this example) and only identify and segregate the extraordinary gain in the consolidation worksheet. This would be acceptable as long as the investor does not publish separate (unconsolidated) parent company financial statements. If the investment is reported as a line item in unconsolidated financial statements, proper application of the equity method by the parent company would require the recognition of the extraordinary gain on the parent company books. The approached used in this text was taken because it simplifies the worksheet elimination process at acquisition as well as subsequent to acquisition.

Worksheet Elimination 2-4a—Journal Entry Form		
(1) Common Stock	1,000,000	
Additional Paid-In Capital	750,000	
Retained Earnings (October 1, 2005)	250,000	
Inventory	130,000	
Plant and Equipment (net)	350,000	
Patents		168,600
Long-Term Notes Payable		136,400
Investment in Sterling Products		2,175,000

To eliminate the subsidiary's date of acquisition stockholders' equity and the parent's date of acquisition Investment in Sterling Products account, and to establish the date of acquisition purchase differentials.

The resulting worksheet elimination is displayed below in comparison to the positive goodwill case (from Illustration 2-4). Note that the only difference pertains to the recognition of the goodwill. The purchase differential recognition for the identifiable assets and liabilities is the same whether there is positive goodwill, negative goodwill, or no goodwill.

Illustration 2-5 compares the positive and negative goodwill cases. In the positive goodwill case, the goodwill is recognized separately only in the process of preparing the consolidation worksheet elimination. Therefore, the asset *Goodwill* appears only on the consolidated balance sheet. On the other hand, in the negative goodwill case the dollar amount of negative goodwill is recognized immediately as an extraordinary gain in the investment entry posted by Pratt at the acquisition date. Furthermore, in the negative goodwill case, the worksheet elimination credit to the investment account for $2,175,000 exactly matches the stockholders' equity (net book value) plus the appraisal value in excess of book value for the net assets of Sterling. Thus, there is no need to identify a separate line item for the extraordinary gain in the elimination process. Pratt identified and recorded the extraordinary gain at the date of acquisition, thus creating a line item on Pratt's books that will flow through to the consolidated financial statements with the rest of Pratt's account balances.

ILLUSTRATION 2-5
Comparative Worksheet Eliminations—Positive Versus Negative Goodwill

Purchase Price:	Positive Goodwill Case (From Worksheet Elimination 2-4) $2,400,000		Negative Goodwill Case (From Worksheet Elimination 2-4a) $2,078,000	
	Debit	**Credit**	**Debit**	**Credit**
Common Stock	1,000,000		1,000,000	
Additional Paid-In Capital	750,000		750,000	
Retained Earnings	250,000		250,000	
Inventory	130,000		130,000	
Plant and Equipment (net)	350,000		350,000	
Goodwill	225,000		0	
Patents		168,600		168,600
Long-Term Notes Payable		136,400		136,400
Investment in Sterling Products		2,400,000		2,175,000

Consolidating Multiple Financial Statements

While the acquisition of a subsidiary can occur at the beginning of the year, acquisition during the year is more common. An acquisition during the year can result in a consolidation worksheet that looks like the one discussed previously if the subsidiary's financial records are closed. The closing process eliminates the need to address revenue earned and expenses incurred during the period and changes in *Retained Earnings* since the beginning of the year. While it is possible to close the subsidiary's books, it is unlikely. The consolidation worksheet generally needed when a subsidiary is acquired during the year includes an income statement section, a statement of retained earnings section, and a balance sheet section.

Illustration 2-6 emphasizes the mechanics for consolidating multiple financial statements. The amounts in the net income line are carried down to the Statement of Retained

ILLUSTRATION 2-6
Vertical Format for Consolidating Worksheet

	Separate Financial Statements		Adjustments and Eliminations		Consolidated Financial Statements
	Parent	**Subsidiary**	**Debit**	**Credit**	
Income Statement					
Revenues and gains					
Expenses and losses					
Net Income (to Statement of Retained Earnings)					
Retained Earnings Statement					
Retained Earnings (1/1)					
Add: Net Income (from Income Statement)					
Subtotal					
Less: Dividends					
Retained Earnings (12/31 to Balance Sheet)					
Balance Sheet					
Cash					
Accounts Receivable (net)					
Inventory (FIFO)					
Other Current Assets					
Total Current Assets					
Plant and Equipment (net)					
Patent					
Investment in subsidiary					
Other Noncurrent Assets					
Total Long-Term Assets					
Total Assets					
Current Liabilities					
Long-Term Debt					
Total Liabilities					
Retained Earnings (from Stmt. of Retained Earnings)					
Total Stockholders' Equity					
Total Liabilities and Stockholders' Equity					

Earnings. This transfers all net income effects into the Statement of Retained Earnings. The forward sloping lines (/////) in the illustration indicate the transfer of net income to the Statement of Retained Earnings. The amounts in these two lines of the worksheet will be identical. Similarly, all items affecting *Retained Earnings* at year-end are carried down from the bottom line of the Statement of Retained Earnings to the Balance Sheet. The backward sloping lines (\\\\\ ) in the illustration indicate the transfer of the ending retained earnings from the Statement of Retained Earnings to the Balance Sheet. The amounts in these two lines of the worksheet will also be identical.

When consolidating multiple financial statements, worksheet eliminations are never posted directly to the year-end *Retained Earnings* balance. They will be posted to either beginning *Retained Earnings* (the first line of the Statement of Retained Earnings) or to one of the temporary accounts (*Revenue, Expense, Gain, Loss,* or *Dividend*) that ultimately affect the ending *Retained Earnings*. By carrying forward the effects of these component eliminations into the balance sheet section, the ending *Retained Earnings* balance is also eliminated.

Acquisition During the Year: Purchase Price Equals Book Value

To illustrate the consolidation of multiple financial statements, assume that Pratt and Sterling have a December 31 fiscal year-end instead of September 30, as assumed previously. Assume also that Pratt purchases all the outstanding shares of Sterling for cash at October 1, 2005, the acquisition thus taking place after nine months of the fiscal year have passed. Under these circumstances, both Pratt and Sterling have income statement accounts and possibly *Dividends Declared* balances on the books at the date of acquisition.

The assumed facts regarding the activity of Pratt and Sterling for the first nine months of 2005 are provided in the following Statement of Retained Earnings:

Statement of Retained Earnings

	Pratt	Sterling
Retained Earnings January 1, 2005	2,300,000	160,000
Net Income (from January 1, 2005, to September 30, 2005)	600,000	90,000
	2,900,000	250,000
Less: Dividends	300,000	0
Retained Earnings at September 30, 2005	2,600,000	250,000

The income statement section at the top of Illustration 2-7 provides the detailed revenue and expense information supporting the net income of the parent and subsidiary. The (X) in the Adjustments and Eliminations column show where amounts have been carried down the worksheet from above. For example, the $90,000 debit adjustment in the Retained Earnings Statement section was carried down from the Income Statement section.

Two alternatives are available for consolidating the income statements at the date of acquisition. Either eliminate the net effect of the Sterling income statement accounts as a single deduction to a new account titled *Preacquisition Earnings,* or eliminate each of Sterling's revenue and expense balances, line by line. The justification for the *Preacquisition Earnings* approach lies in the comparability of results achieved. For example, if a financial statement user examines the consolidated *Sales* number for Pratt and subsidiary for 2005 and 2006, the two *Sales* numbers are comparable under this approach. If *Sales* prior to acquisition for Sterling were eliminated as a separate line item, the sales results for 2005 would not be comparable to the results for 2006 because only in 2006 would the sales of both the

ILLUSTRATION 2-7
Worksheet for Consolidation of Pratt Corporation and Subsidiary, Sterling Products
100 Percent–Owned Subsidiary
Consolidation at Acquisition Date (During the Year)
Price Equal to Book Value
October 1, 2005

	Separate Financial Statements		Adjustments and Eliminations		Consolidated Financial Statements
	Pratt	Sterling	Debit	Credit	
Income Statement					
Sales	9,000,000	1,830,000			10,830,000
Cost of Goods Sold	5,000,000	890,000			5,890,000
Selling Expenses	1,200,000	170,000			1,370,000
General and Administrative Expenses	2,200,000	650,000			2,850,000
Nonoperating Items (net)		30,000			30,000
Preacquisition Earnings			(1) 90,000		90,000
Net Income (to Statement of Retained Earnings)	600,000	90,000	90,000	0	600,000
Retained Earnings Statement					
Retained Earnings (1/1/2005)	2,300,000	160,000	(1) 160,000		2,300,000
Add: Net Income (from Income Statement)	600,000	90,000	(X) 90,000	(X) 0	600,000
Subtotal	2,900,000	250,000			2,900,000
Less: Dividends	(300,000)				(300,000)
Retained Earnings (10/1/2005 to Balance Sheet)	2,600,000	250,000	250,000	0	2,600,000
Balance Sheet					
Cash	1,400,000	100,000			1,500,000
Accounts Receivable (net)	2,000,000	250,000			2,250,000
Inventory (FIFO)	5,000,000	600,000			5,600,000
Other Current Assets	1,700,000	150,000			1,850,000
Total Current Assets	10,100,000	1,100,000			11,200,000
Plant and Equipment (net)	14,100,000	1,400,000			15,500,000
Patent		1,200,000			1,200,000
Investment in Sterling Products	2,000,000			(1) 2,000,000	0
Other Noncurrent Assets	1,500,000	2,100,000			3,600,000
Total Long-Term Assets	17,600,000	4,700,000			20,300,000
Total Assets	27,700,000	5,800,000			31,500,000
Current Liabilities	8,755,000	1,405,000			10,160,000
Long-Term Notes Payable		1,000,000			1,000,000
7% Bonds Payable (due 6/30/2013)	4,000,000				4,000,000
Less: Discount on Bonds Payable	(155,000)				(155,000)
8% Bonds Payable (due 12/31/2010)		1,500,000			1,500,000
Less: Discount on Bonds Payable		(105,000)			(105,000)
Total Liabilities	12,600,000	3,800,000			16,400,000
Common Stock ($1 par):					
Pratt, 10,000,000 shares authorized, 6,000,000 shares issued and outstanding	6,000,000				6,000,000
Sterling, 1,000,000 shares authorized, issued and outstanding		1,000,000	(1) 1,000,000		0
Additional Paid-In Capital	6,500,000	750,000	(1) 750,000		6,500,000
Retained Earnings (10/1/2005 from Statement of Retained Earnings)	2,600,000	250,000	(X) 250,000	(X) 0	2,600,000
Total Stockholders' Equity	15,100,000	2,000,000			15,100,000
Total Liabilities and Stockholders' Equity	27,700,000	5,800,000			31,500,000
			2,000,000	2,000,000	

(1) To eliminate the subsidiary's date of acquisition stockholders' equity and the parent's date of acquisition Investment in Sterling Products account.

parent and the subsidiary for the entire year be included in the consolidated income statement. The potential drawback to the "preacquisition earnings" approach is that it results in an "overstatement" of income statement accounts in the year of acquisition. However, if their separate statements for the partial period prior to acquisition are required, the contribution to total sales from both the parent and the subsidiary can be determined easily. Note that this disclosure issue is unique to the year of acquisition because only in the first year does the possibility of current period preacquisition earnings arise. The approach used in Illustration 2-7 deducts the net income of Sterling for the first nine months of the fiscal year with a single debit to a worksheet elimination account entitled *Preacquisition Earnings.*

To reexamine the acquisition at book value, assume that $2,000,000 is the price paid by Pratt. Illustration 2-7 presents the consolidating worksheet based on the assumption that the date of acquisition is October 1, the beginning of the fourth quarter. In this illustration, it is assumed that Sterling has $160,000 of Retained Earnings at January 1, 2005. Through the first three-quarters of the fiscal year, income has totaled $90,000. It is also assumed that Sterling has paid no dividends during this nine-month period. The worksheet elimination in journal entry form is presented in Worksheet Elimination 2-7.

Worksheet Elimination 2-7—Journal Entry Form

(1)	Common Stock	1,000,000	
	Additional Paid-In Capital	750,000	
	Retained Earnings (January 1, 2005)	160,000	
	Preacquisition Earnings	90,000	
	Investment in Sterling Products		2,000,000

To eliminate the subsidiary's date of acquisition stockholders' equity and the parent's date of acquisition Investment in Sterling Products account.

Compare Worksheet Elimination 2-7 to Worksheet Elimination 2-2. The eliminations of *Common Stock, Additional Paid-In Capital,* and *Investment in Sterling Products* are identical. The difference lies in how Sterling's *Retained Earnings* balance is eliminated. One objective of the consolidation procedures is still to eliminate all of Sterling's *Retained Earnings,* but the method of accomplishing this objective has changed. Sterling's net income at the date of acquisition is part of Sterling's stockholders' equity, but it has not yet been closed to the *Retained Earnings* account. As a result, the date of acquisition worksheet elimination has expanded to include both Sterling's date of acquisition *Retained Earnings* and changes in the book value of Sterling's equity in the form of net income (loss). At the date of acquisition, consolidated net income and retained earnings should not include Sterling's earnings generated for the first nine months of 2005 because Sterling's earnings prior to the date of acquisition are not earnings of the consolidated entity. Thus, instead of simply eliminating the October 1, 2005, subsidiary *Retained Earnings* as it appears in the balance sheet, the component factors that give rise to the ending balance must be eliminated (i.e., beginning retained earnings, net income, and dividends, if any).

Acquisition During the Year: Purchase Price Exceeds Book Value

The most common acquisition of the subsidiary's stock is one that occurs during the period at a price different (usually greater) than book value. The next example parallels Illustration 2-4 except for the interim nature of the acquisition. Again assume a December 31 fiscal year-end. Pratt purchases Sterling at the beginning of the fourth quarter, October 1, 2005, for $2,400,000. This price includes the same components for market values outlined in Illustration 2-3 plus the same $225,000 in goodwill. Illustration 2-8 shows the consolidating worksheet for Pratt and Sterling for these circumstances. Worksheet Elimination 2-8 presents the worksheet elimination in journal entry form.

Worksheet Elimination 2-8—Journal Entry Form			
(1)	Common Stock	1,000,000	
	Additional Paid-In Capital	750,000	
	Retained Earnings (January 1, 2005)	160,000	
	Preacquisition Earnings	90,000	
	Inventory	130,000	
	Plant and Equipment (net)	350,000	
	Goodwill	225,000	
	Patents		168,600
	Long-Term Notes Payable		136,400
	Investment in Sterling Products		2,400,000

To eliminate the subsidiary's date of acquisition stockholders' equity and the parent's date of acquisition Investment in Sterling Products account, and to establish the date of acquisition purchase differentials.

In addition to the $400,000 premium allocated to the appropriate accounts as in Worksheet Elimination 2-4, the same component elimination of *Retained Earnings* as presented in Worksheet Elimination 2-7 occurs.

Whether the acquisition price is the subsidiary's book value or some other value has no bearing on the elimination of the subsidiary's *Retained Earnings* and recognition of a *Preacquisition Earnings* account because any premium paid relates to values other than recorded book values. The current year subsidiary earnings prior to the acquisition date cause the book value to increase. Thus, the book value at acquisition fully reflects the preacquisition earnings.

Consideration Given—Pratt Corporation Stock Instead of Cash

Thus far, it has been presumed that cash was paid to the Sterling Products stockholders to acquire their outstanding shares. If the consideration given is stock instead of assets, the only changes would be the following:

1. The original journal entry on Pratt's books would credit *Common Stock* and *Additional Paid-In Capital* in lieu of *Cash*.
2. The consolidated balance sheet would include (a) a larger cash balance and (b) the additional invested capital generated on Pratt's books when the stock was issued (i.e., the market value of the acquired company).

For example, if Pratt issued 48,000 shares of stock in the Illustration 2-8 case to acquire all the outstanding stock of Sterling, the following journal entry would be recorded:

ILLUSTRATION 2-8
Worksheet for Consolidation of Pratt Corporation and Subsidiary, Sterling Products
100 Percent–Owned Subsidiary
Consolidation at Acquisition Date (During the Year)
Price More Than Book Value
October 1, 2005

	Separate Financial Statements		Adjustments and Eliminations		Consolidated Financial Statements
	Pratt	Sterling	Debit	Credit	
Income Statement					
Sales	9,000,000	1,830,000			10,830,000
Cost of Goods Sold	5,000,000	890,000			5,890,000
Selling Expenses	1,200,000	170,000			1,370,000
General and Administrative Expenses	2,200,000	650,000			2,850,000
Nonoperating Items (net)		30,000			30,000
Preacquisition Earnings			(1) 90,000		90,000
Net Income (to Statement of Retained Earnings)	600,000	90,000	90,000	0	600,000
Retained Earnings Statement					
Retained Earnings (1/1/2005)	2,300,000	160,000	(1) 160,000		2,300,000
Add: Net Income (from Income Statement)	600,000	90,000	(X) 90,000	(X) 0	600,000
Subtotal	2,900,000	250,000			2,900,000
Less: Dividends	(300,000)				(300,000)
Retained Earnings (10/1/2005 to Balance Sheet)	2,600,000	250,000	250,000	0	2,600,000
Balance Sheet					
Cash	1,000,000	100,000			1,100,000
Accounts Receivable (net)	2,000,000	250,000			2,250,000
Inventory (FIFO)	5,000,000	600,000	(1) 130,000		5,730,000
Other Current Assets	1,700,000	150,000			1,850,000
Total Current Assets	9,700,000	1,100,000			10,930,000
Plant and Equipment (net)	14,100,000	1,400,000	(1) 350,000		15,850,000
Patent		1,200,000		(1) 168,600	1,031,400
Investment in Sterling Products	2,400,000			(1) 2,400,000	0
Other Noncurrent Assets	1,500,000	2,100,000			3,600,000
Goodwill			(1) 225,000		225,000
Total Long-Term Assets	18,000,000	4,700,000			20,706,400
Total Assets	27,700,000	5,800,000			31,636,400
Current Liabilities	8,755,000	1,405,000			10,160,000
Long-Term Notes Payable		1,000,000		(1) 136,400	1,136,400
7% Bonds Payable (due 6/30/2013)	4,000,000				4,000,000
Less: Discount on Bonds Payable	(155,000)				(155,000)
8% Bonds Payable (due 12/31/2010)		1,500,000			1,500,000
Less: Discount on Bonds Payable		(105,000)			(105,000)
Total Liabilities	12,600,000	3,800,000			16,536,400
Common Stock ($1 par):					
Pratt, 10,000,000 shares authorized, 6,000,000 shares issued and outstanding	6,000,000				6,000,000
Sterling, 1,000,000 shares authorized, issued and outstanding		1,000,000	(1) 1,000,000		0
Additional Paid-In Capital	6,500,000	750,000	(1) 750,000		6,500,000
Retained Earnings (10/1/2005 from Statement of Retained Earnings)	2,600,000	250,000	(X) 250,000	(X) 0	2,600,000
Total Stockholders' Equity	15,100,000	2,000,000			15,100,000
Total Liabilities and Stockholders' Equity	27,700,000	5,800,000			31,636,400
			2,705,000	2,705,000	

(1) To eliminate the subsidiary's date of acquisition stockholders' equity and the parent's date of acquisition Investment in Sterling Products account, and to establish the date of acquisition purchase differentials.

Journal Entry—Pratt Corporation Books

Oct. 1, 2005	Investment in Sterling Products	2,400,000	
	Common Stock		48,000
	Additional Paid-In Capital		2,352,000

To record the acquisition of Sterling Products' stock at $400,000 in excess of book value.

When stock is issued by Pratt to accomplish the combination, the worksheet eliminations would be identical in every example. Therefore, the **form** of consideration given by the acquiring firm (Pratt) in exchange for stock of the acquired firm (Sterling) has no impact on the worksheet eliminations necessary.

Costs of Consolidation

Whether the consolidation is completed by paying cash, issuing equity securities or long-term debt, or some combination of consideration, a number of different costs are often incurred to complete the transaction. These costs may include various direct costs such as fees to professionals for engineering, accounting, and/or appraisal services. In addition, a finder's fee or broker's commission may be paid when searching for target companies for a possible takeover. All such direct costs are expensed as incurred.[11]

If equity or debt securities are issued as consideration given to complete the acquisition, the normal issuance costs are accounted for as an adjustment to the recorded fair value of the securities. The *Additional Paid-In Capital* account would be reduced in the case of a stock issuance. The *Premium* or *Discount on Bonds Payable* account would be adjusted for costs associated with the issuance of such debt securities.

CONSOLIDATION AT ACQUISITION DATE: LESS THAN 100 PERCENT–OWNED SUBSIDIARY

Noncontrolling Interest

Noncontrolling interest: the owners of the subsidiary's stock other than the parent company

By definition, to be a business combination, control must be achieved. When control is achieved by the parent company, but less than 100 percent of the subsidiary's stock is acquired, the owners of the remaining shares of outstanding subsidiary stock are referred to as the **noncontrolling interest**. The noncontrolling interest has no voting rights in the parent company as a result of owning stock in the subsidiary, and it cannot exercise control over the management of the subsidiary.

Concepts of Consolidated Financial Statements

Several concepts have evolved regarding recognition of noncontrolling interest in the consolidated financial statements. Application of these concepts varies across political boundaries, necessitating an understanding of the differences in a global business environment. The concepts range from no recognition of the noncontrolling interest in the consolidated

---

[11] As of this printing a 2004, first quarter Exposure Draft is expected to propose the expensing of direct costs of consolidation. Prior to the exposure draft, the direct costs were capitalized. Only indirect (internal) costs were expensed.

financial statements to full market value recognition of all ownership interests in the net assets and income of the subsidiary, regardless of the source. The basis for these differing opinions pertains to the perceived importance of control and ownership in the preparation of consolidated financial statements. The ownership and control views of proponents of the three major consolidation concepts are:

1. **Proportionate consolidation concept:** ownership is essential to recognition in the consolidated financial statements.

2. **Parent company concept:** both control and ownership are essential for recognition in the consolidated financial statements.

3. **Economic unit concept:** control is the sole criteria for recognition in the consolidated financial statements.

Proponents of all consolidation concepts agree that the parent's ownership percentage of the subsidiary's income and net assets should be recognized in the consolidated financial statements. The consolidated balance sheet should include the market value of the parent's ownership percentage of the subsidiary's assets (including goodwill) and liabilities. In addition, the consolidated income statement should include the parent's ownership percentage of the subsidiary's revenues and expenses and, as a consequence, the parent's ownership percentage of the subsidiary's net income. The differences that exist among the consolidation concepts pertain to the recognition of the noncontrolling interest's ownership percentage in the subsidiary.

Proportionate Consolidation Concept Proponents of the proportionate consolidation concept support the view that the consolidated financial statements are prepared only for the parent company's stockholders. As a result, these individuals hold the opinion that there should be no recognition of the noncontrolling interest because the noncontrolling interest portion of the subsidiary is not owned by the parent and as such is not relevant to the parent company's stockholders. The percentage of the subsidiary's assets and liabilities as well as revenue and expenses owned by the noncontrolling interest would be eliminated from the consolidated balance sheet and income statement, respectively. This would also result in the noncontrolling interest's percentage of the subsidiary's net assets and net income being excluded from consolidated financial statements.

Parent Company Concept Supporters of the parent company concept believe that, in addition to the percentage of the subsidiary owned by the parent being recognized at market value (price paid), there should also be recognition of the subsidiary's book values of assets and liabilities for the noncontrolling interest's ownership percentage. This opinion is based on the premise that the parent company purchased less than 100 percent of the subsidiary, so there is a verifiable transaction for only the portion of the subsidiary acquired. No purchase of the noncontrolling interest's ownership percentage occurs, so a revaluation of that portion of the subsidiary's assets and liabilities is not justified. Supporters of this concept also contend that the noncontrolling interest should not be classified as a liability in the consolidated balance sheet because the parent company does not have an obligation to make a payment to the noncontrolling interest nor should it be a component of stockholders' equity because the noncontrolling interest is not an owner of the consolidated entity. These individuals would argue that the noncontrolling interest should be displayed in the consolidated balance sheet in a separate category between liabilities and stockholders' equity.

Proponents of the parent company concept also support the position that the consolidated income statement should include all of the subsidiary's revenues and expenses but only the parent's ownership percentage of the subsidiary's net income. This form of presentation would enable financial statement users to know the revenues generated by the entire consolidated entity and the basic cost structure that exists in the entity, while it would indicate to the parent's stockholders that only a portion of the subsidiary's net income is applicable to the parent company. As a result of this view regarding the consolidated income statement, a separate item for income associated with the noncontrolling interest percentage ownership must be subtracted in the consolidated income statement prior to determining consolidated net income.

Economic Unit Concept Proponents of the economic unit concept contend that management of the parent company controls the entire subsidiary regardless of the ownership percentage. The noncontrolling interest is viewed as another ownership group in the combined entity. As a result of this perception, proponents of the economic unit concept believe that the full market value of the subsidiary's identifiable assets and liabilities should be included in the consolidated balance sheet.

Under the economic unit concept, two views exist regarding the amount of goodwill that should be recognized on the consolidated balance sheet. One view, the **economic unit–full goodwill concept**, is supported by those who believe that the subsidiary's entire goodwill should be recognized. This group would propose that the full goodwill can be estimated. One approach to this estimation would be to determine (impute) the amount of goodwill implied in the purchase price of the parent's ownership percentage. For example, if the goodwill applicable to the parent's ownership percentage is $800,000 and the parent owns 80 percent of the subsidiary's stock, the estimated full goodwill would be $1,000,000 ($800,000/.8). Another view, the **economic unit– purchased goodwill concept**, is supported by those who believe that only the goodwill pertaining to the percentage interest acquired should be recognized. This belief is based on the view that estimation of the goodwill related to the noncontrolling interest's percentage ownership is too unreliable. Proponents of purchased goodwill would state that estimation of the noncontrolling interest's goodwill may be reasonable when the parent's ownership percentage is large, but the estimation error may increase dramatically when the parent's ownership percentage decreases. In particular, the parent company may pay a **control premium** to attain more than 50 percent of the subsidiary's stock and thus have legal control over the subsidiary. For example, the amount the parent may be willing to pay to increase its ownership percentage from 40 to 51 percent may be substantially more than 11 percent of the subsidiary's total market value. The existence of a control premium could inflate recognized goodwill under the full-goodwill approach.

The two forms of the economic unit concept are the same when considering recognition of noncontrolling interest in the consolidated income statement. All of the subsidiary's revenue, expense, and income are included in consolidated net income under the economic unit concept. Consolidated net income is then allocated to the controlling interest and the noncontrolling interest below. The allocation is disclosed below the calculation of consolidated net income.

In the consolidated balance sheet, the stockholders' equity applicable to the parent company is the same regardless of the consolidation concept applied. The difference among the consolidation concepts is the method of valuing net assets and the accompanying value assigned to the noncontrolling interest. In addition, the income allocated to the controlling interest on the consolidated income statement is the same under all of the consolidation concepts. The differences that exist among the concepts pertain to the measurement and display of the income allocated to the noncontrolling interest.

Changes in U.S. GAAP The parent company concept has been the basis for U.S. GAAP since the 1950s. While U.S. GAAP has been based on the parent company concept, many other countries apply the economic unit concept for consolidations. An exposure draft[12] was issued by the FASB that changes U.S. GAAP from the parent company concept to the economic unit concept with full-goodwill recognition. In summary, the primary difference that exists between the parent company and the economic unit consolidation concepts is the impact of purchase differential recognition as it pertains to the noncontrolling interest. The economic unit concept recognizes the total market value of the subsidiary when consolidating and then allocates the appropriate pro rata share of the market value to the noncontrolling interest. This text has adopted the economic unit concept in a manner consistent with the principles proposed in the FASB exposure draft or subsequent official standard.

Purchase Price Equals Book Value: 90 Percent–Owned Subsidiary

Thus far, examination of the Pratt–Sterling parent–subsidiary relationship has assumed a 100 percent ownership. The acquisition assumption is now changed such that Pratt acquires only 90 percent of Sterling's outstanding common stock. Referring back to the basic October 1, 2005, financial information developed for Pratt and Sterling (see Illustration 2-1), Sterling's net book value is $2,000,000 at the date of combination. A Pratt purchase of 90 percent of Sterling's outstanding stock at book value would cost $1,800,000 instead of $2,000,000, and Pratt's journal entry to record the acquisition is as follows:

Journal Entry—Pratt Corporation Books

Oct. 1, 2005	Investment in Sterling Products	1,800,000	
	Cash		1,800,000
	To record the acquisition of 90 percent of Sterling Products' outstanding stock at book value.		

Assuming a December 31 year-end, the combination of Pratt and its 90 percent–owned subsidiary, Sterling, at date of acquisition is shown in Illustration 2-9. The journal entry form of the worksheet elimination is presented in Worksheet Elimination 2-9.

Worksheet Elimination 2-9 contains two items that warrant specific consideration. The first item is *Preacquisition Earnings.* Even though only 90 percent of the preacquisition earnings apply to Pratt, the preacquisition earnings are established in the same manner as they were when 100 percent of Sterling's stock was acquired. Thus, *Preacquisition Earnings* are defined as *all* of Sterling's earnings prior to October 1, 2005. The complete elimination of *Preacquisition Earnings* occurs because it represents part of the subsidiary's equity at the date of acquisition. Net income of the subsidiary is equity that has not been closed to *Retained Earnings.* Another way to view this issue is that the subsidiary could close its books at the date of acquisition. In that instance, *Retained Earnings* would increase by the amount of the preacquisition earnings. The economic position of the subsidiary is not changed as a result of closing the income statement, so the particular form of presentation should not result in a change in the worksheet elimination.

---

[12] Exposure Draft Consolidation Procedures (Norwalk, CT: Financial Accounting Standards Board anticipated, first quarter 2004).

ILLUSTRATION 2-9
Worksheet for Consolidation of Pratt Corporation and Subsidiary, Sterling Products
90 Percent–Owned Subsidiary
Consolidation at Acquisition Date (During the Year)
Price Equal to Book Value
October 1, 2005

	Separate Financial Statements		Adjustments and Eliminations		Consolidated Financial Statements
	Pratt	Sterling	Debit	Credit	
Income Statement					
Sales	9,000,000	1,830,000			10,830,000
Cost of Goods Sold	5,000,000	890,000			5,890,000
Selling Expenses	1,200,000	170,000			1,370,000
General and Administrative Expenses	2,200,000	650,000			2,850,000
Nonoperating Items (net)		30,000			30,000
Preacquisition Earnings			(1) 90,000		90,000
Net Income (to Statement of Retained Earnings)	600,000	90,000	90,000	0	600,000
Retained Earnings Statement					
Retained Earnings (1/1/2005)	2,300,000	160,000	(1) 160,000		2,300,000
Add: Net Income (from Income Statement)	600,000	90,000	(X) 90,000	(X) 0	600,000
Subtotal	2,900,000	250,000			2,900,000
Less: Dividends	(300,000)				(300,000)
Retained Earnings (10/1/2005 to Balance Sheet)	2,600,000	250,000	250,000	0	2,600,000
Balance Sheet					
Cash	1,600,000	100,000			1,700,000
Accounts Receivable (net)	2,000,000	250,000			2,250,000
Inventory (FIFO)	5,000,000	600,000			5,600,000
Other Current Assets	1,700,000	150,000			1,850,000
Total Current Assets	10,300,000	1,100,000			11,400,000
Plant and Equipment (net)	14,100,000	1,400,000			15,500,000
Patent		1,200,000			1,200,000
Investment in Sterling Products	1,800,000			(1) 1,800,000	0
Other Noncurrent Assets	1,500,000	2,100,000			3,600,000
Total Long-Term Assets	17,400,000	4,700,000			20,300,000
Total Assets	27,700,000	5,800,000			31,700,000
Current Liabilities	8,755,000	1,405,000			10,160,000
Long-Term Notes Payable		1,000,000			1,000,000
7% Bonds Payable (due 6/30/2013)	4,000,000				4,000,000
Less: Discount on Bonds Payable	(155,000)				(155,000)
8% Bonds Payable (due 12/31/2010)		1,500,000			1,500,000
Less: Discount on Bonds Payable		(105,000)			(105,000)
Total Liabilities	12,600,000	3,800,000			16,400,000
Common Stock ($1 par):					
Pratt, 10,000,000 shares authorized, 6,000,000 shares issued and outstanding	6,000,000				6,000,000
Sterling, 1,000,000 shares authorized, issued and outstanding		1,000,000	(1) 1,000,000	0	
Additional Paid-In Capital	6,500,000	750,000	(1) 750,000	6,500,000	
Retained Earnings (10/1/2005 from Statement of Retained Earnings)	2,600,000	250,000	(X) 250,000	(X) 0	2,600,000
Noncontrolling Interest in Sterling				(1) 200,000	200,000
Total Stockholders' Equity	15,100,000	2,000,000			15,300,000
Total Liabilities and Stockholders' Equity	27,700,000	5,800,000			31,700,000
			2,000,000	2,000,000	

(1) To eliminate the subsidiary's date of acquisition stockholders' equity and the parent's date of acquisition Investment in Sterling Products account, and to create the date of acquisition Noncontrolling Interest in Sterling account.

Worksheet Elimination 2-9—Journal Entry Form		
(1) Common Stock	1,000,000	
Additional Paid-In Capital	750,000	
Retained Earnings (January 1, 2005)	160,000	
Preacquisition Earnings	90,000	
Investment in Sterling Products		1,800,000
Noncontrolling Interest In Sterling		200,000
To eliminate the subsidiary's date of acquisition stockholders' equity and the parent's date of acquisition Investment in Sterling Products account, and to create the date of acquisition Noncontrolling Interest in Sterling account.		

The second item that warrants consideration is the *Noncontrolling Interest* account. The $200,000 noncontrolling interest represents 10 percent of the market value of Sterling's net assets. The book value of the net assets also happens to be the market value in this example.

Purchase Price Greater Than Book Value (Positive Goodwill): 90 Percent–Owned Subsidiary

Imputed market value: the implied total market value of an entity derived by dividing the observed price paid for less than 100 percent of the entity by the actual percentage acquired

The more common acquisition of a subsidiary's stock is one that occurs during the period at a price different from (usually greater than) book value. Assume that Pratt acquires a 90 percent ownership interest in Sterling for $2,160,000. If a $2,160,000 price is observed for a 90 percent acquisition, then that price may be assumed to represent 90 percent of the acquired entity's total market value. Because the Pratt and Sterling example is a continuation from the cases earlier in the chapter, Sterling's total market value is already known to be $2,400,000, the amount Pratt paid for 100 percent of Sterling's stock in a previous example. Generally, however, in acquisitions of less than 100 percent, the total market value will not be known in advance. If the subsidiary's total market value is not known, it can be imputed. For the Pratt and Sterling case, Illustration 2-10 demonstrates the calculation necessary to determine Sterling's **imputed market value**.

Remember that under the economic unit — full goodwill concept, full fair market value is allocated to both the parent company and the noncontrolling interest. It follows, then, that for acquisitions of less than 100 percent, imputing the acquired entity's total market value is required in applying the economic unit — full goodwill concept. The process of imputing the total (100 percent) market value can always be accomplished by dividing the price paid by the percentage acquired. Once the total market value has been imputed, the total (100 percent) purchase differentials can be allocated to identifiable assets and liabilities and full goodwill can be determined. These purchase differential amounts can then be allocated to the parent company and noncontrolling interest accord-

ILLUSTRATION 2-10
Calculation of Imputed Total Value Based on
Acquisition of a 90 Percent Interest in Sterling

Using facts from the observed transaction:	(Total Market Value)(.90) = $2,160,000
Then, dividing by (.90):	(Total Market Value) = $2,160,000/(.90)
Therefore:	(Total Market Value) = $2,400,000

ing to their percentage ownership in the subsidiary. Illustration 2-11 presents the calculation of Sterling's imputed total value and the assignment of the total purchase differential (including goodwill) in the Analysis of Market Value column. These amounts are allocated to Pratt (90 percent) and the noncontrolling interest (10 percent) in the last two columns of the illustration. In summary, the calculated imputed values can be used to determine the total market value and full goodwill implied for any transaction of less than 100 percent.

The consolidation of Pratt and Sterling on October 1, 2005, immediately after the purchase, is shown in Illustration 2-12. Illustration 2-12 is similar to Illustration 2-8 in that it depicts the consolidation of Pratt and Sterling (1) at the date of acquisition, (2) after a purchase for market value, and (3) at the beginning of the fourth quarter of the year. The only difference is that in Illustration 2-12 the purchase is for 90 percent of Sterling rather than 100 percent, as is the case in Illustration 2-8. Worksheet Elimination 2-12 presents the worksheet elimination that is made for a 90 percent acquisition.

The difference between Worksheet Elimination 2-8 (100 percent acquisition) and Worksheet Elimination 2-12 (90 percent acquisition) is the recognition of the noncontrolling interest. The elimination of Sterling's stockholders' equity and recognition of purchase differentials do not change. The full amount of the stockholders' equity is eliminated and the full purchase differential is recognized regardless of the percentage ownership by Pratt. The only difference that exists between the two worksheets is that Worksheet Elimination 2-12 recognizes the imputed market value of the noncontrolling interest.

ILLUSTRATION 2-11
Purchase Differential Allocation for 90 Percent–Owned Subsidiary
October 1, 2005

	100% of Value	Pratt (90%)	Noncontrolling Interest (10%)
Sterling's **imputed** total market value ($2,160,000/.90)	$2,400,000	$2,160,000	$240,000
Less: Book value	2,000,000		
Pratt ($2,000,000 × .90)		1,800,000	
Noncontrolling interest ($2,000,000 × .10)			200,000
Purchase differential to be allocated	$ 400,000	$ 360,000	$ 40,000
Allocation of purchase differential to identifiable accounts and goodwill:			
Account Title			
Inventory (FIFO)	$ 130,000*	$ 117,000	$ 13,000
Plant and Equipment (net)	350,000*	315,000	35,000
Patents	(168,600)*	(151,740)	(16,860)
Long-term Notes Payable	(136,400)*	(122,760)	(13,640)
Total market versus book value for identifiable net assets	$ 175,000	$ 157,500	$ 17,500
Positive Goodwill (to balance)	225,000		
Pratt ($225,000 × .90)		202,500	
Noncontrolling interest ($225,000 × .10)			22,500
Allocated purchase differential	$ 400,000	$ 360,000	$ 40,000

*From Illustration 2-3.

ILLUSTRATION 2-12
Worksheet for Consolidation of Pratt Corporation and Subsidiary, Sterling Products
90 Percent–Owned Subsidiary
Consolidation at Acquisition Date (During the Year)
Price More Than Book Value
October 1, 2005

	Separate Financial Statements		Adjustments and Eliminations		Consolidated Financial Statements
	Pratt	Sterling	Debit	Credit	
Income Statement					
Sales	9,000,000	1,830,000			10,830,000
Cost of Goods Sold	5,000,000	890,000			5,890,000
Selling Expenses	1,200,000	170,000			1,370,000
General and Administrative Expenses	2,200,000	650,000			2,850,000
Nonoperating Items (net)		30,000			30,000
Preacquisition Earnings			(1) 90,000		90,000
Net Income (to Statement of Retained Earnings)	600,000	90,000	90,000	0	600,000
Retained Earnings Statement					
Retained Earnings (1/1/2005)	2,300,000	160,000	(1) 160,000		2,300,000
Add: Net Income (from Income Statement)	600,000	90,000	(X) 90,000	(X) 0	600,000
Subtotal	2,900,000	250,000			2,900,000
Less: Dividends	(300,000)				(300,000)
Retained Earnings (10/1/2005 to Balance Sheet)	2,600,000	250,000	250,000	0	2,600,000
Balance Sheet					
Cash	1,240,000	100,000			1,340,000
Accounts Receivable (net)	2,000,000	250,000			2,250,000
Inventory (FIFO)	5,000,000	600,000	(1) 130,000		5,730,000
Other Current Assets	1,700,000	150,000			1,850,000
Total Current Assets	9,940,000	1,100,000			11,170,000
Plant and Equipment (net)	14,100,000	1,400,000	(1) 350,000		15,850,000
Patent		1,200,000		(1) 168,600	1,031,400
Investment in Sterling Products	2,160,000			(1) 2,160,000	0
Other Noncurrent Assets	1,500,000	2,100,000			3,600,000
Goodwill			(1) 225,000		225,000
Total Long-Term Assets	17,760,000	4,700,000			20,706,400
Total Assets	27,700,000	5,800,000			31,876,400
Current Liabilities	8,755,000	1,405,000			10,160,000
Long-Term Notes Payable		1,000,000		(1) 136,400	1,136,400
7% Bonds Payable (due 6/30/2013)	4,000,000				4,000,000
Less: Discount on Bonds Payable	(155,000)				(155,000)
8% Bonds Payable (due 12/31/2010)		1,500,000			1,500,000
Less: Discount on Bonds Payable		(105,000)			(105,000)
Total Liabilities	12,600,000	3,800,000			16,536,400
Common Stock ($1 par):					
Pratt, 10,000,000 shares authorized, 6,000,000 shares issued and outstanding	6,000,000				6,000,000
Sterling, 1,000,000 shares authorized, issued and outstanding		1,000,000	(1) 1,000,000		0
Additional Paid-In Capital	6,500,000	750,000	(1) 750,000		6,500,000
Retained Earnings (10/1/2005 from Statement of Retained Earnings)	2,600,000	250,000	(X) 250,000	(X) 0	2,600,000
Noncontrolling Interest in Sterling				(1) 240,000	240,000
Total Stockholders' Equity	15,100,000	2,000,000			15,340,000
Total Liabilities and Stockholders' Equity	27,700,000	5,800,000			31,876,400
			2,705,000	2,705,000	

(1) To eliminate the subsidiary's date of acquisition stockholders' equity and the parent's date of acquisition Investment in Sterling Products account, to create the date of acquisition Noncontrolling Interest in Sterling account, and to create the date of acquisition purchase differentials.

Worksheet Elimination 2-12—Journal Entry Form		
(1) Common Stock	1,000,000	
Additional Paid-In Capital	750,000	
Retained Earnings (January 1, 2005)	160,000	
Preacquisition Earnings	90,000	
Inventory	130,000	
Plant and Equipment (net)	350,000	
Goodwill	225,000	
Patents		168,600
Long-Term Notes Payable		136,400
Investment in Sterling Products		2,160,000
Noncontrolling Interest in Sterling		240,000

To eliminate the subsidiary's date of acquisition stockholders' equity and the parent's date of acquisition Investment in Sterling Products account, to create the date of acquisition Noncontrolling Interest in Sterling account (for 10 percent of Sterling's imputed market value), and to create the date of acquisition purchase differentials.

Appraised Value Greater Than Purchase Price (Negative Goodwill): 90 Percent–Owned Subsidiary

While acquisitions for an amount that results in negative goodwill are not common, they do occur. The 100 percent acquisition section of the chapter included a discussion of the reasons that negative goodwill might occur. The current section focuses on the unique procedures that occur when negative goodwill exists in an acquisition of less than 100 percent. Assume that Pratt acquires a 90 percent ownership interest in Sterling for $1,870,200. Illustration 2-13 presents the calculation of Sterling's total imputed market value. It also shows how the purchase differentials are determined and the negative goodwill is calculated.

Notice that the full amount of the purchase differential and the full amount of the negative goodwill are presented in Illustration 2-13. The $97,000 total negative goodwill is the amount that was calculated in the previous example when Pratt acquired 100 percent of Sterling. In the current example, Pratt recognizes 90 percent of the total negative goodwill ($87,300) as an extraordinary gain. The journal entry to record the 90 percent acquisition in Sterling for $1,870,200 is as follows:

Journal Entry—Pratt Corporation Books

Oct. 1, 2005	Investment in Sterling Products	1,957,500	
	Extraordinary Gain from Acquisition of Sterling Products		87,300
	Cash		1,870,200

To record the acquisition of 90 percent of Sterling Products' stock at a price equal to $70,200 in excess of $1,800,000, 90 percent of Sterling's book value.

The consolidation of Pratt and Sterling on October 1, 2005, immediately after the 90 percent acquisition with negative goodwill purchase, is shown in Illustration 2-14.

ILLUSTRATION 2-13
Purchase Differential Allocation for 90 Percent–Owned Subsidiary
Negative Goodwill Case
at October 1, 2005

	100% of Value	Pratt (90%)	Noncontrolling Interest (10%)
Sterling's **imputed** total market value ($1,870,000/.90)	$2,078,000	$1,870,200	$207,800
Less: Book value	2,000,000		
Pratt ($2,000,000 × .90)		1,800,000	
Noncontrolling interest ($2,000,000 × .10)			200,000
Purchase differential to be allocated	$78,000	$70,200	$7,800
Allocation of purchase differential to identifiable accounts and goodwill:			
Inventory (FIFO)	$130,000*	$117,000	$13,000
Plant and Equipment (net)	350,000*	315,000	35,000
Patents	(168,600)*	(151,740)	(16,860)
Long-Term Notes Payable	(136,400)*	(122,760)	(13,640)
Total market versus book value for identifiable net assets	$175,000	$157,500	$17,500
Negative Goodwill (to balance)	(97,000)		
Pratt ($97,000 × .90)		(87,300)	
Noncontrolling interest ($97,000 × .10)			(9,700)
Allocated purchase differential	$78,000	$70,200	$7,800

* From Illustration 2-3.

Illustration 2-14 is similar to Illustration 2-12 in that it depicts the consolidation of Pratt and Sterling (1) at the date of acquisition, (2) after a purchase for market value, and (3) at the beginning of the fourth quarter of the year. The only difference is that in Illustration 2-14 the purchase results in negative goodwill rather than positive goodwill, as is the case in Illustration 2-12. Worksheet Elimination 2-14 presents the worksheet eliminations that are made for a 90 percent acquisition when there is negative goodwill.

Worksheet Elimination 2-14 differs from Worksheet Elimination 2-12 in that Worksheet Elimination 2-14 requires recognition of the extraordinary gain attributable to the noncontrolling interest. Recall that the extraordinary gain with respect to Pratt's ownership percentage was recognized when Pratt acquired 90 percent of Sterling's stock. Under the economic unit concept, the full amount of the extraordinary gain must be recognized. The noncontrolling interest portion of the extraordinary gain can only be created on the consolidation worksheet. The $9,700 extraordinary gain from acquisition of Sterling Products serves to increase the noncontrolling interest reported in the consolidated balance sheet at the acquisition date. A new worksheet elimination (la) is created to allocate the noncontrolling interest's share of the extraordinary gain to the noncontrolling interest.

Two differences exist between Worksheet Elimination 2-12 and Worksheet Elimination 2-14. One difference is the total dollar amount credited to the *Investment in Sterling Products* account and the *Noncontrolling Interest in Sterling* account. While the dollar amount of the eliminations in Worksheet Elimination 2-14 differs from the dollar

ILLUSTRATION 2-14
Worksheet for Consolidation of Pratt Corporation and Subsidiary, Sterling Products
90 Percent–Owned Subsidiary
Consolidation at Acquisition Date (During the Year)
Price More Than Book Value (Negative Goodwill)
October 1, 2005

	Separate Financial Statements		Adjustments and Eliminations		Consolidated Financial Statements
	Pratt	Sterling	Debit	Credit	
Income Statement					
Sales	9,000,000	1,830,000			10,830,000
Extraordinary Gain from Acquisition of Sterling Products	87,300			(1) 9,700	97,000
Cost of Goods Sold	5,000,000	890,000			5,890,000
Selling Expenses	1,200,000	170,000			1,370,000
General and Administrative Expenses	2,200,000	650,000			2,850,000
Nonoperating Items (net)		30,000			30,000
Preacquisition Earnings			(1) 90,000		90,000
Consolidated Net Income					697,000
Income to Noncontrolling Interest			(1a) 9,700		9,700
Net Income (to Statement of Retained Earnings)	687,300	90,000	99,700	9,700	687,300
Retained Earnings Statement					
Retained Earnings (1/1/2005)	2,300,000	160,000	(1) 160,000		2,300,000
Add: Net Income (from Income Statement)	687,300	90,000	(X) 99,700	(X) 9,700	687,300
Subtotal	2,987,300	250,000			2,987,300
Less: Dividends	(300,000)				(300,000)
Retained Earnings (10/1/2005 to Balance Sheet)	2,687,300	250,000	259,700	9,700	2,687,300
Balance Sheet					
Cash	1,529,800	100,000			1,629,800
Accounts Receivable (net)	2,000,000	250,000			2,250,000
Inventory (FIFO)	5,000,000	600,000	(1) 130,000		5,730,000
Other Current Assets	1,700,000	150,000			1,850,000
Total Current Assets	10,229,800	1,100,000			11,459,800
Plant and Equipment (net)	14,100,000	1,400,000	(1) 350,000		15,850,000
Patent		1,200,000		(1) 168,600	1,031,400
Investment in Sterling Products	1,957,500			(1) 1,957,500	0
Other Noncurrent Assets	1,500,000	2,100,000			3,600,000
Total Long-Term Assets	17,557,500	4,700,000			20,481,400
Total Assets	27,787,300	5,800,000			31,941,200
Current Liabilities	8,755,000	1,405,500			10,160,000
Long-Term Notes Payable		1,000,000		(1) 136,400	1,136,400
7% Bonds Payable (due 6/30/2013)	4,000,000				4,000,000
Less: Discount on Bonds Payable	(155,000)				(155,000)
8% Bonds Payable (due 12/31/2010)		1,500,000			1,500,000
Less: Discount on Bonds Payable		(105,000)			(105,000)
Total Liabilities	12,600,000	3,800,000			16,536,400
Common Stock ($1 par):					
Pratt, 10,000,000 shares authorized, 6,000,000 shares issued and outstanding	6,000,000				6,000,000
Sterling, 1,000,000 shares authorized, issued and outstanding		1,000,000	(1) 1,000,000		0
Additional Paid-In Capital	6,500,000	750,000	(1) 750,000		6,500,000
Retained Earnings (10/1/2005 from Statement of Retained Earnings)	2,687,300	250,000	(X) 259,700	(X) 9,700	2,687,300
Noncontrolling Interest in Sterling				(1) 207,800	217,500
				(1a) 9,700	
Total Stockholders' Equity	15,187,300	2,000,000			15,404,800
Total Liabilities and Stockholders' Equity	27,787,300	5,800,000			31,941,200
			2,489,700	2,489,700	

(1) To eliminate the subsidiary's date of acquisition stockholders' equity and the parent's date of acquisition Investment in Sterling Products account, to create the date of acquisition Noncontrolling Interest in Sterling account and the date of acquisition purchase differentials, and the noncontrolling interest's pro rata portion of the extraordinary gain from the acquisition of Sterling.

(1a) To assign the noncontrolling interests' pro rata portion of the extraordinary gain from acquisition of Sterling to the noncontrolling interest account.

Worksheet Elimination 2-14—Journal Entry Form

(1)	Common Stock	1,000,000	
	Additional Paid-In Capital	750,000	
	Retained Earnings (January 1, 2005)	160,000	
	Preacquisition Earnings	90,000	
	Inventory	130,000	
	Plant and Equipment (net)	350,000	
	Patents		168,600
	Long-Term Notes Payable		136,400
	Investment in Sterling Products		1,957,500
	Noncontrolling Interest in Sterling		207,800
	Extraordinary Gain from Acquisition of		9,700
	Sterling Products—NCI		

To eliminate the subsidiary's date of acquisition stockholders' equity and the parent's date of acquisition Investment in Sterling Products account, and to create the date of acquisition Noncontrolling Interest in Sterling account (for 10 percent of Sterling's imputed market value), the date of acquisition purchase differentials, and the noncontrolling interest's pro rata portion of the extraordinary gain from the acquisition of Sterling.

(1a)	Income to Noncontrolling Interest	9,700	
	Noncontrolling Interest in Sterling		9,700

To assign the noncontrolling interest's pro rata portion of the extraordinary gain from acquisition of Sterling to the noncontrolling interest account.

amount of the eliminations in Worksheet Elimination 2-12, the amounts for both accounts represent their respective share of underlying market value of the identifiable net assets. Note, however, that the creation of the $217,500 balance in the noncontrolling interest account is accomplished in two steps—the credit of $207,800 in worksheet elimination (1) and the credit of $9,700 in worksheet elimination (1a). The sum of these two amounts represents 10 percent of the market value of Sterling's net assets. As a result, there will be two worksheet eliminations when consolidating at the acquisition date with less than 100 percent ownership and negative goodwill.

PURCHASE AND POOLING OF INTERESTS

Beginning in the early 1900s, two methods of preparing consolidated financial statements emerged: **purchase** and **pooling of interests**. The fundamental difference between the purchase and pooling of interests methods is the assumption made regarding whether there is a change in ownership as a result of the business combination. The Accounting Principles Board (APB), in Opinion No. 16, states that "the purchase method accounts for a business combination as the acquisition of one company by another."[13] As a result of the

---

[13] **Accounting Principles Board Opinion**, No. 16, "Business Combinations" (New York: American Institute of Certified Public Accountants, 1970), par. 11.

purchase, there is a change in the owners of the subsidiary. Many of the subsidiary's prior owners do not continue to have an ownership interest in the subsidiary, direct or indirect, after the combination. In addition, the arm's-length nature of the business combination results in the ability to determine an acquisition price. The change in ownership and the existence of a purchase price usually result in the revaluation of assets and liabilities at the acquisition date.

The pooling of interests method, on the other hand, was initially viewed as a means by which two entities of approximately equal size could combine their resources and share the risks and rewards of co-ownership. APB Opinion No. 16 stated:

> *The pooling of interest method accounts for a business combination as the uniting of the ownership interests of two or more companies by exchange of equity securities. No acquisition is recognized because the combination is accomplished without disbursing resources of the constituents.*[14]

Pooling was used extensively in recent years to account for large mergers that were consummated as stock-for-stock transactions. In 2001, the FASB discontinued the acceptability of the pooling of interests method.[15] All new combinations now must be accounted for using the purchase method. Combinations completed prior to the effective date of the standard and accounted for by the pooling of interests method do not have to be restated to reflect the purchase method. While this chapter focuses on use of the purchase method, a brief discussion of the accounting treatments applied to combinations accounted for using the pooling of interests method is necessary because of the pooling of interests combinations that occurred prior to the prohibition of the method in 2001.

Pooling produces results that are sometimes vastly different from the results obtained using the purchase method because the theory of pooling assumes that the parties to the combination maintain a continuity of ownership and management. That assumption provides the logical basis to account for the combination by simply combining the book values of the previously independent entities. The application of the pooling concept provided that, subsequent to the combination, the entities should be accounted for as if they had always been together, rather than as if one entity had purchased the other in an arm's-length transaction.

By combining the companies at book value, no adjustments to reflect market value differences from book value (purchase differentials) were created, and no goodwill was recorded. With one exception, the accounting was the same as when a purchase occurred at a price equal to book value. The exception was that under pooling the retained earnings of the acquired company were combined with the acquirer's retained earnings. The reported consolidated *Retained Earnings* was then the sum of the two companies' individual *Retained Earnings* balances.

Once a pooling is recorded, consolidation elimination procedures are the same as in the "purchase at a price equal to book value" case illustrated earlier in the chapter. The same procedure is followed because it is common practice in pooling for the parent company to record the subsidiary's *Retained Earnings* on the parent's books as a part of the entry to record the transaction. Assume that Sterling Products is acquired by Pratt and the pooling of interests method of accounting is applied. The following journal entry illustrates the pooling acquisition:

---

[14] Ibid., par. 12.

[15] Op. cit., **Statement of Financial Accounting Standards (FAS)**, No. 141.

Journal Entry—Pratt Corporation Books

Oct. 1, 2005	Investment in Sterling Products (at book value)	2,000,000	
	Common Stock (assume 880,000 shares of $1 par issued)		880,000
	Retained Earnings (balance on Sterling's books)		250,000
	Additional Paid-In Capital (to balance)		870,000

To record the acquisition of 100 percent of Sterling Products common stock in exchange for 880,000 shares of Pratt common in a pooling of interests.

The transaction above assumes that Pratt exchanges 880,000 shares of its $1 par value common stock for 100 percent of the outstanding stock of Sterling Products, and the combination is accounted for as a pooling of interests. Because Pratt records the *Retained Earnings* balance of Sterling Products in the entry above, the elimination of the Sterling Products stockholders' equity accounts in the worksheet elimination to consolidate the entities can be prepared in exactly the same manner as it is prepared when purchase accounting is employed.

The following worksheet elimination would be prepared when consolidating Pratt and Sterling at the date of acquisition when the transaction was structured as a pooling of interests.

Worksheet Elimination Pooling—Journal Entry Form

(1)	Common Stock	1,000,000	
	Additional Paid-In Capital	750,000	
	Retained Earnings (October 1, 2005)	250,000	
	Investment in Sterling Products		2,000,000

To eliminate the subsidiary's date of acquisition stockholders' equity and the parent's date of acquisition Investment in Sterling Products account.

Thus, the pooling worksheet elimination illustrated above is identical to Worksheet Elimination 2-8, prepared earlier in the chapter for the case of a 100 percent purchase at a price equal to book value.

No additional coverage of pooling of interests is necessary in later chapters for two reasons. First, the accounting and consolidation procedures subsequent to acquisition are identical to those illustrated for subsidiaries purchased at a price equal to the book value of the acquired company. Second, because pooling has been banned, no new combinations are being accounted for using this method.

USING A SEPARATE ACCUMULATED DEPRECIATION ACCOUNT WHEN CONSOLIDATING AT THE DATE OF ACQUISITION

All examples thus far in this chapter have presented depreciable fixed assets *net* of the related accumulated depreciation. As a result, the fixed asset purchase differential adjustment in worksheet elimination (1) has been to the account (net). For example, in both Illustrations 2-8 (100 percent ownership) and 2-12 (90 percent ownership) plant and equipment was increased using one debit adjustment to the account *Plant and Equipment (net)* for the market value in excess of *net* book value.

The net presentation approach simplifies the mechanics of the adjustment to *Plant and Equipment* while correctly reporting the substance of the adjustment to reflect market value in excess of book value for assets acquired. If management of the consolidated entity chooses the net form of presentation, the balance sheet footnotes must still disclose the separate historical cost and accumulated depreciation balances. On the other hand, if the consolidated financial statements include a separate accumulated depreciation account in the consolidation worksheet, both the *Plant and Equipment* and the *Accumulated Depreciation* accounts must be adjusted individually. The rationale and the procedures required to consolidate at the date of acquisition when *Plant and Equipment* and *Accumulated Depreciation* accounts are included as separate items in a consolidation worksheet are provided below.

In the section Acquisition at Beginning of Year: Purchase Price Exceeds Book Value (Positive Goodwill) earlier in the chapter, the *Plant and Equipment* account was presented net of accumulated depreciation. In a detailed consolidation worksheet where separate *Plant and Equipment* and *Accumulated Depreciation* exist, adjustments to both account balances is necessary. The *Accumulated Depreciation* balance on the subsidiary's books is eliminated (debited for its existing credit balance). The *Plant and Equipment* account is adjusted to reflect the difference between current market value and historical cost as recorded on the subsidiary's books.

An analogy can be used to explain the logic behind these adjustments. Assume Company A purchases used equipment from Company B. Company A would record current market value in its equipment account (its cost) rather than recording the historical cost and accumulated depreciation balances that previously existed on the books of Company B (the seller) and then adjusting the historical cost to reflect the market value change. Similarly, in the Pratt and Sterling example, Pratt's acquisition of Sterling includes depreciable fixed assets. As a result, the market value that Pratt paid for those fixed assets with no accumulated depreciation should be added to the Pratt's fixed assets in preparing the consolidated financial statements at the date of acquisition.

The following example demonstrates how the separate accounts would alter the worksheet elimination. Assume that the $1,400,000 net book value of *Plant and Equipment (net)* for Sterling in Illustration 2-3, a 100 percent ownership case, actually consisted of the following components:

Plant and Equipment (historical cost)	$2,600,000
Accumulated Depreciation	(1,200,000)
Net Book Value	$1,400,000

Recall also from Illustration 2-3 that Sterling's plant and equipment has a market value of $1,750,000 at the acquisition date. If the worksheet to consolidate Pratt and Sterling uses separate historical cost and accumulated depreciation accounts, the presentation of the worksheet elimination previously presented in Worksheet Elimination 2-8 would be amended.

In the alternate presentation of the worksheet elimination (2-8a), Sterling's existing $1,200,000 accumulated depreciation balance is completely eliminated, and the historical cost of the plant and equipment is reduced from $2,600,000 to the appropriate current market value paid by Pratt ($1,750,000). Note that the net increase to plant and equipment is still $350,000, as it was in Worksheet Elimination 2-8. In the amended elimination, however, the contribution from Sterling to consolidated assets is now reported at historical cost of $1,750,000 with no accumulated depreciation. Although this illustration is for 100 percent ownership, the dollar amount of adjustment to the *Accumulated Depreciation* and *Plant and Equipment* accounts would be the same for any percentage ownership

Worksheet Elimination 2-8a—Journal Entry Form		
(1) Common Stock	1,000,000	
Additional Paid-In Capital	750,000	
Retained Earnings (January 1, 2005)	160,000	
Preacquisition Earnings	90,000	
Inventory	130,000	
Accumulated Depreciation—P & E *(existing balance)*	*1,200,000*	
Goodwill	225,000	
Plant and Equipment (2,600,000 – 1,750,000)		*850,000*
Patents		168,600
Long-Term Notes Payable		136,400
Investment in Sterling Products		2,400,000

To eliminate the subsidiary's date of acquisition stockholders' equity and the parent's date of acquisition Investment in Sterling Products account, and to establish the date of acquisition purchase differentials.

because the full purchase differential is always recognized when applying the economic unit concept.

In the next chapter, the net approach is again used for the initial examples. Toward the end of the chapter, the alternate (separate *Accumulated Depreciation* account) procedures are presented. The problem sets in both chapters provide opportunities to use the net presentation as well as the separate *Accumulated Depreciation* account approach.

PUSH-DOWN ACCOUNTING

New-basis accounting is a concept that focuses on the identification of events that give rise to a change in the valuation of an entity's assets from existing book value to fair market value. This chapter has illustrated that a business combination is one type of transaction that logically results in a change in valuation.

When a combination occurs, the consolidation process includes a revaluation of the subsidiary's net assets to market values. However, the individual account balances in the subsidiary's books are typically not revalued. In 1983 the SEC issued *Staff Accounting Bulletin No. 54* requiring subsidiaries that are wholly or almost wholly owned (with some exceptions) to report their net assets at the fair value paid for them. That is, the price paid for control of the net assets is considered to be an event that justifies the reporting of those net assets at a new basis—namely, the value of the acquisition transaction. This requirement only creates a need to revalue when the subsidiary issues separate subsidiary financial statements. The procedure for revaluing the subsidiary's net assets to market values is referred to as push-down accounting. The term *push-down* **accounting** comes from the process of pushing the market value (i.e., the parent company's *Investment in Subsidiary* balance when purchase accounting is applied) down into the accounts of the subsidiary. Procedurally, the write-up of the asset accounts is not difficult. When the asset values are written up, however, an adjustment to the owners' equity of the subsidiary must be posted.

The write-up of the assets creates an element of unrealized profit in the balance sheet that is posted to a *Revaluation Capital* account. In addition, the *Retained Earnings* account must be eliminated against the *Additional Paid-In Capital* and/or the *Revaluation Capital* account. The justification of the removal of the *Retained Earnings* is that the purchase transaction has resulted in the subsidiary having a new basis, as if a new entity had been created. The push-down adjustments may be made as worksheet adjustment only, or they may be posted to the subsidiary's books.

If the Pratt and Sterling acquisition at a price greater than book value (Illustration 2-4) resulted in Sterling's use of push-down accounting, the following entries could be made by Sterling to adjust its accounts to meet the SEC separate-reporting requirements:

Inventory	130,000	
Plant and Equipment (net)	350,000	
Goodwill	225,000	
Patents		168,600
Long-Term Notes Payable		136,400
Revaluation Capital		400,000
Retained Earnings	250,000	
Additional Paid-In Capital		250,000

The above entries revalue the net assets of Sterling to market value and create a *Revaluation Capital* account to reflect the $400,000 of market value in excess of book value included in Pratt's price to acquire 100 percent of the Sterling common stock. The *Retained Earnings* is eliminated to reflect the new-basis concept.

Not all subsidiaries must follow the SEC requirements. The details of the exceptions are beyond the scope of this text. Generally, the exceptions are for subsidiaries that have substantial minority common stock holdings, publicly traded debt, or publicly held preferred stock. In these cases the parent does not have the ability to control the form of ownership of the subsidiary and, therefore, could not liquidate the subsidiary at will. The SEC believes that in these cases it would be inappropriate to apply the new-basis concept.

For all subsequent coverage of consolidations in this text, it is assumed that the subsidiary has not formally applied push-down accounting. Therefore, the consolidation eliminations will be presumed to include all appropriate adjustments from historical cost to market for the net assets of an acquired subsidiary.

SUMMARY

This chapter presented the basic concepts and procedures relevant to the consolidation of a parent and a subsidiary at the date of acquisition. Some of the primary features of the consolidation process are that the objective of the consolidation process does not change regardless of whether the acquisition occurs at the beginning of the year or during the year, at the book value of the subsidiary or at some other amount. The consolidation process always results in the complete elimination of the date of acquisition subsidiary stockholders' equity and the elimination of the date of investment in subsidiary account. In addition, certain cases result in the creation of date of acquisition purchase differentials and noncontrolling interest. An understanding of the consolidation procedures at the date of acquisition is essential to understanding the consolidation procedures that occur in periods subsequent to acquisition.

First, the consolidation of a 100 percent–owned subsidiary, purchased at a price equal to book value, was presented. The various complicating factors were then introduced. These included acquisition during the year, acquisition at a price greater than book value, acquisition at a "bargain" price, and acquisition of less than 100 percent of the stock of the acquired entity (noncontrolling interest). Brief coverage was also provided of pooling of interests accounting, which was recently prohibited by the FASB, and push-down accounting, which is sometimes required by the SEC.

QUESTIONS

2-1. Prepare a short report that identifies the current authoritative support for the provisions that permit some subsidiaries to be excluded from the consolidated financial statements under current GAAP. Include references that show how current GAAP requirements differ from the provisions for exclusions that existed under ARB No. 51. (*Hint:* Search ARB No. 51 and FAS No. 94.)

2-2. What are some arguments that support using the equity method to disclose investments and some arguments that support using consolidated financial statements to disclose investments?

2-3. What is the basic criticism of consolidated financial statements with regard to the calculation of ratios?

2-4. Six divisions report to the new U.S. operations manager of a large international company. This manager has never had responsibility for multiple divisions at one time. You just received a phone call from this manager, who is concerned that she cannot use the consolidated financial statements to assess the performance of her six divisions. What do you tell her?

2-5. Jim, a coworker, has come to you with a question regarding when a company in which your company has a large stock ownership does not have to be consolidated. Locate authoritative support and prepare a memo indicating when current GAAP allows a company to exclude a controlled subsidiary from the consolidated financial statements? (*Hint:* Search FAS No. 94.)

2-6. What is the rationale in GAAP to justify the presentation of consolidated financial statements in general rather than the investment account included in the long-term asset section of the parent's balance sheet? (*Hint:* Search ARB No. 51.)

2-7. What is the primary objective of consolidation procedures?

2-8. Why is the investment account on the parent's financial records eliminated as part of the consolidation process?

2-9. A new member of the controller's department is confused about the worksheet eliminations necessary to prepare the consolidated financial statements. He understands why the investment account is eliminated from the consolidated balance sheet but does not understand why the subsidiary's stockholders' equity is eliminated. Prepare a memo to this person to clear up his misunderstanding.

2-10. While it is possible for the worksheet elimination to the investment account to exactly equal the sum of the subsidiary's stockholders' equity accounts, it is not likely. What must occur for the investment account and the subsidiary's stockholders' equity accounts to exactly offset one another?

2-11. A member of the board of directors has questions regarding the preparation of the consolidated financial statements. His main concern pertains to a presentation made by the controller last month. At that presentation, the controller indicated that the parent's book values are included in the consolidated statements at the date a subsidiary is acquired, but the subsidiary's market value must be considered when consolidating at the acquisition date. This seems inconsistent to the board member. Prepare a memo to the board member to clarify this issue.

2-12. Why is it important to assign purchase differentials to individual asset and liability accounts; that is, why can the net purchase differential not be assigned to a generic deferred debit or credit on the balance sheet?

2-13. A medium-sized local company is negotiating the acquisition of a small company. The bank loan officer where the medium-sized company attains financing said the company must prepare pro forma consolidated financial statements to get the necessary funds for the acquisition. The owner of the acquiring company is concerned with the recognition of goodwill. She can understand the other purchase differentials because she can see the appraised values and the book values. Prepare a memo to the owner explaining the meaning of goodwill and how its value is approximated.

2-14. Does the worksheet elimination to the subsidiary's stockholders' equity accounts change at the date of acquisition as the purchase price changes? Why or why not?

2-15. Jim Reynolds is a local bank's loan officer. He has been looking at the pro forma consolidated financial statements of two local companies. Jim's familiarity with the two companies has created some concern regarding the pro forma statements. Jim is aware that neither company has a patent on the books; however, there is a patent listed on the pro forma consolidated balance sheet. Prepare a memo to Jim explaining how this event could occur.

2-16. What are two possible reasons for an acquisition to occur at a price less than the appraised values of the net assets?

2-17. Sarah Hughes has been preparing the consolidated financial statements for Ace Enterprises and its newly acquired subsidiary, Baker Company. She noticed that negative goodwill was calculated in the process of analyzing the acquisition. Sarah knows that positive goodwill appears on the balance sheet, but there is no negative goodwill on the consolidated balance sheet. Prepare a memo to Sarah explaining the required GAAP treatment of negative goodwill at the time of consolidation (*Hint:* Search FASB Exposure Draft on consolidation procedures, released first quarter of 2004, or subsequent official standard.)

2-18. Why might negative goodwill exist?

2-19. The assistant controller of Pacific Company has been asked to prepare pro forma consolidated financial statements based on two possible acquisition prices for a potential subsidiary. One acquisition price results in positive goodwill while the other results in negative goodwill. The assistant controller has reviewed the relevant standards and is confused about the purchase differentials. You receive an e-mail with the following question: "Why are the purchase differentials for assets and liabilities the same whether you have positive or negative goodwill?" Prepare a memo to the assistant controller explaining this issue. In your memo, reference the new GAAP requirements for the application of the economic unit concept, including guidance on how to account for negative goodwill situations. (*Hint:* Search FASB Exposure Draft on consolidation procedures, released first quarter of 2004, or subsequent official standard.)

2-20. The CFO is presenting the pro forma consolidated financial statements to the board of directors to answer final questions prior to an acquisition. One board member asks the CFO about the *Preacquisition Earnings* item on the consolidated income statement. The board member is confused because he has never seen this type of income statement item before. How would you respond to this board member if the CFO turned to you and asked you to address this question?

2-21. What is the impact on the parent's investment account of a stock issuance rather than a cash payment for an acquisition of another company?

2-22. What is the basic underlying reason for the differences that exist among the three consolidation concepts?

2-23. Explain how the three consolidation concepts differ with regard to the importance of control and ownership as they pertain to consolidated financial statements.

2-24. One important similarity among the consolidation concepts pertains to the recognition of the parent company's ownership interest in the subsidiary. What dollar amount is always included in the consolidated financial statements to represent the parent's ownership interest in the subsidiary?

2-25. What is the view of the proportionate consolidation concept with regard to recognition of the noncontrolling interest's portion of the subsidiary's net assets and income statement? Why is this view taken?

2-26. What is the view of the parent company consolidation concept with regard to recognition of the noncontrolling interest's portion of the subsidiary's net assets and income statement? Why is this view taken?

2-27. What is the view of the economic unit consolidation concept with regard to recognition of the noncontrolling interest's portion of the subsidiary's net assets and income statement? Why is this view taken?

2-28. Why do the two views regarding how much goodwill should be recognized under the economic unit concept differ?

2-29. Why is the complete *Preacquisition Earnings* account eliminated even if the parent acquires less than 100 percent of a subsidiary's stock?

2-30. Describe the difference in the valuation of an *Investment in Subsidiary* account under pooling versus purchase accounting.

2-31. Prepare a memo for your CFO explaining the implications of FASB Statement No. 141 on business combinations with regard to pooling of interests. (*Hint:* Search FAS No. 141.)

2-32. Prepare a short memo that discusses the GAAP requirements promulgated in FASB Statement No. 141 (business combinations) for acquisitions that were accounted for using pooling of interests accounting and were completed prior to the issuance of the standard. (*Hint:* Search FAS No. 141.)

2-33. What organization initiated the push-down accounting requirements, and under what conditions is push-down accounting required?

2-34. If push-down accounting is applied, a *Revaluation Capital* account is normally created. Describe what the balance in the *Revaluation Capital* account represents.

2-35. List the exceptions to the push-down accounting requirements.

2-36. Describe a typical consolidation elimination when a subsidiary has been purchased at a price greater than book value and when push-down accounting adjustments have been formally recorded in the subsidiary's books.

MULTIPLE CHOICE

2-1. Richardson, Inc. purchased 80 percent of Frankfort Enterprises at market value. At the acquisition date, Richardson's equipment had a market value of $380,000 and a book value of $250,000, while Frankfort's equipment had a market value of $82,000 and a book value of $60,000. What is the equipment account purchase differential included on the acquisition date consolidated balance sheet?

a. $22,000
b. $17,600
c. $130,000
d. $78,000

2-2. QuietKey acquired 100 percent of Lansing Corporation. At the acquisition date, QuietKey's machinery had a book and market value of $240,000 and $350,000, respectively, while Lansing's machinery had a book and market value of $100,000 and $125,000, respectively. What amount is presented on the consolidated balance sheet for the machinery account at the acquisition date?

a. $475,000

b. $340,000

c. $240,000

d. $365,000

2-3. Able Manufacturing purchased 70 percent of Clark Enterprises. At the acquisition date, Able had common stock and retained earnings of $45,000 and $780,000, respectively. Clark had stock of $30,000 and retained earnings of $300,000. What amount of stockholders' equity is eliminated when preparing the consolidated financial statements at the acquisition date?

a. $330,000

b. $75,000

c. $1,080,000

d. $825,000

2-4. High Flying Airplanes purchased 60 percent of Best Quality Airframes for $420,000. At that date the book and market values of Best Quality were $600,000 and $740,000, respectively. Best Quality had the following assets at the acquisition date.

	Book Value	Market Value
Inventory	$40,000	$50,000
Buildings	$250,000	$300,000
Equipment	$100,000	$180,000

How much extraordinary gain resulting from negative goodwill would appear in the parent company's separate income statement?

a. $0

b. $320,000

c. $24,000

d. $40,000

2-5. HD Corporation owns 75 percent of Digital, Inc. At the acquisition date, Digital had the following trial balance:

Cash	$ 10,000
Receivables	40,000
Inventory	125,000
Plant Assets (net)	950,000
Cost of Goods Sold	530,000
Depreciation Expense	87,000
Other Expenses	62,000
Total Debits	$1,804,000
Current Liabilities	$ 80,000
Long-Term Debt	295,000
Common Stock	25,000
Retained Earnings	304,000
Sales	1,100,000
Total Credits	$1,804,000

What is the amount of preacquisition earnings eliminated at the acquisition date?

a. $725,000

b. $315,750

c. $543,750

d. $421,000

2-6. Soft Tech purchased 80 percent of High Tech's stock by issuing new stock having a market value of $2,500,000. Additional costs incurred to accomplish the acquisition include a finder's fee paid to a consultant ($350,000), stock issuance costs ($165,000), and appraisal fees ($100,000). What is the amount recorded in the investment account at the acquisition date?

a. $3,115,000

b. $2,950,000

c. $2,850,000

d. $2,500,000

2-7. Quickest Products purchased 70 percent of Slowdown Software for $133,000. At the acquisition date Slowdown had common stock and retained earnings of $10,000 and $130,000, respectively. Included in Slowdown's assets was machinery that had a market value and a book value of $200,000 and $150,000, respectively. What is the amount of noncontrolling interest recognized on the consolidated balance sheet at the acquisition date?

a. $42,000

b. $57,000

c. $132,000

d. $87,000

2-8. CHS Corporation acquired 90 percent of EEX Enterprises. At the acquisition date the inventory book and market values for CHS were $250,000 and $370,000, respectively. EEX's book and market values of inventory at that date were $180,000 and $230,000, respectively. What amount of inventory would appear on the consolidated balance sheet at the acquisition date?

a. $480,000

b. $457,000

c. $577,000

d. $600,000

The following data are for Questions 2-9 and 2-10. Wilson Corporation purchased 70 percent of Hoyte Industries for $315,000. At the acquisition date, Hoyte had the following trial balance:

	Book Value	Market Value
Cash	$ 13,000	$ 13,000
Receivables	25,000	25,000
Inventory	80,000	130,000
Buildings (net)	350,000	520,000
Cost of Goods Sold	260,000	

Depreciation Expense	38,000	
Total Debits	$766,000	
Current Liabilities	68,000	68,000
Long-Term Debt	250,000	250,000
Common Stock	20,000	
Retained Earnings	78,000	
Sales	350,000	
Total Credits	$766,000	

2-9. What is the amount of goodwill recognized on the consolidated balance sheet at the acquisition date?

a. $55,000

b. $24,000

c. $80,000

d. $56,000

2-10. What is the amount of revaluation capital that would be recognized on Hoyte's books if push-down accounting is applied using the economic unit concept?

a. $261,000

b. $195,000 *300,000*

c. $107,000

d. $41,000

EXERCISES

Consolidation worksheets for exercises that require a worksheet can be found at the book companion website.

EXERCISE 2-1	Record 100 percent acquisition at beginning of year for book value, debt issued, worksheet elimination, consolidation worksheet
EXERCISE 2-2	Purchase differential allocation, 100 percent acquisition, positive goodwill
EXERCISE 2-3	Purchase differential allocation, 80 percent acquisition, negative goodwill
EXERCISE 2-4	Record 100 percent acquisition at beginning of year for more than book value, no goodwill, stock issued, worksheet elimination, consolidation worksheet, issuance costs
EXERCISE 2-5	100 percent acquisition at beginning of year for more than book value, negative goodwill, worksheet elimination, consolidation worksheet
EXERCISE 2-6	Record 100 percent acquisition during year at book value, preferred stock issued, worksheet elimination, consolidation worksheet
EXERCISE 2-7	100 percent acquisition during year for more than book value, goodwill, worksheet elimination, consolidation worksheet, separate accumulated depreciation account
EXERCISE 2-8	Record 100 percent acquisition during year for more than book value, negative goodwill, worksheet elimination, consolidation worksheet, direct and indirect acquisition costs, separate accumulated depreciation account
EXERCISE 2-9	80 percent acquisition at beginning of year for book value, worksheet elimination, consolidation worksheet
EXERCISE 2-10	Record 75 percent acquisition at beginning of year for more than book value, goodwill, preferred stock issued, worksheet elimination, consolidation worksheet, issuance costs, direct and indirect acquisition costs, separate accumulated depreciation account
EXERCISE 2-11	60 percent acquisition at beginning of year for more than book value, negative goodwill, worksheet elimination, consolidation worksheet, separate accumulated depreciation account
EXERCISE 2-12	Record 90 percent acquisition during year at book value, long-term debt issued, worksheet elimination, consolidation worksheet
EXERCISE 2-13	80 percent acquisition during year for more than book value, goodwill, worksheet elimination, consolidation worksheet, separate accumulated depreciation account
EXERCISE 2-14	Record 60 percent acquisition during year for more than book value, negative goodwill, worksheet elimination, consolidation worksheet, direct and indirect acquisition costs, separate accumulated depreciation account

EXERCISE 2-1	Richard Corporation acquired all of the outstanding common stock of Jacobi Incorporated on January 1, 2005, for $450,000. Richard and Jacobi had the following trial balances immediately prior to the acquisition:

	Richard		Jacobi	
Account	*Book Value*	*Market Value*	*Book Value*	*Market Value*
Cash and Receivables	125,000	125,000	50,000	50,000
Inventory	300,000	500,000	120,000	120,000

Plant Assets (net)	1,500,000	2,600,000	750,000	750,000
Total Debits	1,925,000		920,000	
Current Liabilities	200,000	200,000	100,000	100,000
Long-Term Debt	600,000	580,000	370,000	370,000
Common Stock ($1 par)	40,000		50,000	
Retained Earnings	1,085,000		400,000	
Total Credits	1,925,000		920,000	

Required:

A. Record the acquisition of Jacobi by Richard assuming the acquisition was completely financed by issuing long-term debt.

B. Prepare the worksheet elimination in journal entry form to consolidate Richard and Jacobi on January 1, 2005.

C. Prepare the consolidation worksheet to combine Richard and Jacobi on January 1, 2005.

EXERCISE 2-2

Clark Enterprises purchased 100 percent of Jensen's outstanding common stock for $7,750,000. At the date of acquisition, Jensen had common stock, additional paid-in capital, and retained earnings of $500,000, $2,000,000, and $1,800,000, respectively. The carrying values and market values of Jensen's assets and liabilities at the date of acquisition were the following:

Account	Book Value	Market Value
Cash and Receivables	950,000	950,000
Inventory	1,200,000	1,400,000
Plant Assets (net)	6,050,000	7,500,000
Patents		1,650,000
Current Liabilities	(700,000)	(700,000)
Long-Term Debt	(3,200,000)	(3,350,000)

Required:

Prepare a schedule allocating the purchase differential to the appropriate categories.

EXERCISE 2-3

Macro, Incorporated purchased 80 percent of Micro's stock on October 1, 2005. During the appraisal of assets and liabilities, it was determined that negative goodwill in the amount of $150,000 exists with regard to Macro's ownership interest. The following table presents the book values and market values that exist at the date of acquisition.

Account	Book Value	Market Value
Cash and Receivables	320,000	320,000
Inventory	1,000,000	1,350,000
Land	140,000	300,000
Plant Assets (net)	1,260,000	1,650,000
Patents		450,000
Current Liabilities	(320,000)	(320,000)
Long-Term Debt	(500,000)	(500,000)

Required:

Prepare a schedule allocating the purchase differential to the appropriate accounts.

EXERCISE 2-4

David's Pottery Corporation was acquired (100 percent) by Mitchell's Ceramics, Incorporated on January 1, 2005, for $200,000. The following trial balances existed for Mitchell's Ceramics and David's Pottery immediately prior to the acquisition:

Account	Mitchell's Ceramics		David's Pottery	
	Book Value	Market Value	Book Value	Market Value
Cash and Receivables	75,000	100,000	30,000	30,000
Inventory	130,000	250,000	50,000	60,000
Plant Assets (net)	600,000	950,000	125,000	132,000
Patents				13,000
Total Debits	805,000		205,000	

Current Liabilities	110,000	110,000	35,000	35,000
Long-Term Debt	150,000	150,000		
Common Stock ($5 par)	60,000		40,000	
Retained Earnings	485,000		130,000	
Total Credits	805,000		205,000	

Required:

A. Record the acquisition of David's Pottery by Mitchell's Ceramics assuming the acquisition was accomplished by Mitchell's Ceramics issuing 8,000 new shares of common stock. Registration and issuance costs for the stock are $12,000.

B. Prepare the worksheet elimination in journal entry form to consolidate Mitchell's Ceramics and David's Pottery on January 1, 2005.

C. Prepare the consolidation worksheet to combine Mitchell's Ceramics and David's Pottery on January 1, 2005.

EXERCISE 2-5   APT Corporation purchased 100 percent of Baker's outstanding common stock on January 1, 2005, for $2,000,000. At the date of acquisition, APT and Baker had the following trial balances:

	APT		Baker	
Account	Book Value	Market Value	Book Value	Market Value
Cash and Receivables	750,000	750,000	300,000	300,000
Inventory	1,400,000	1,850,000	480,000	670,000
Land	500,000	650,000	120,000	270,000
Plant Assets (net)	5,400,000	5,950,000	1,300,000	1,530,000
Investment in Baker	2,250,000*			
Total Debits	10,300,000		2,200,000	
Current Liabilities	1,140,000	1,140,000	200,000	200,000
Long-Term Debt	1,500,000	1,550,000	300,000	320,000
Common Stock ($5 par)	260,000		350,000	
Retained Earnings	7,400,000*		1,350,000	
Total Credits	10,300,000		2,200,000	

* Includes Extraordinary Gain from acquisition of Baker.

Required:

A. Record the acquisition of Baker by APT assuming cash was paid to acquire Baker's stock.

B. Prepare the worksheet elimination in journal entry form to consolidate APT and Baker on January 1, 2005.

C. Prepare the consolidation worksheet (balance sheet only) to combine APT and Baker on January 1, 2005.

EXERCISE 2-6   Leslie's Limo Service was acquired (100 percent) by Expert Travel, Incorporated on May 1, 2005, for $250,000. Both companies maintain their records on a calendar-year basis. The following trial balances existed for Expert Travel and Leslie's Limo immediately prior to the acquisition:

	Expert Travel		Leslie's Limo	
Account	Book Value	Market Value	Book Value	Market Value
Cash and Receivables	15,000	15,000	18,000	18,000
Plant Assets (net)	600,000	750,000	450,000	450,000
Expenses	120,000		125,000	
Total Debits	735,000		593,000	
Current Liabilities	10,000	11,000	8,000	8,000
Long-Term Debt	350,000	350,000	210,000	210,000
Common Stock ($2 par)	20,000		40,000	
Retained Earnings (1/1/2005)	85,000		165,000	
Revenues	270,000		170,000	
Total Credits	735,000		593,000	

Required:

A. Record the acquisition of Leslie's Limo by Expert Travel assuming the acquisition was accomplished by Expert Travel issuing 10,000 shares of preferred stock ($10 par).

B. Prepare the worksheet elimination in journal entry form to consolidate Expert Travel and Leslie's Limo on May 1, 2005.

C. Prepare the consolidation worksheet to combine Expert Travel and Leslie's Limo on May 1, 2005.

EXERCISE 2-7

A-1 Electronics Corporation acquired 100 percent of Jeff's Computer Store on November 1, 2005, for $1,300,000. Both companies have a December 31 year-end. At the date of acquisition, A-1 and Jeff's had the following trial balances:

	A-1		Jeff's	
Account	Book Value	Market Value	Book Value	Market Value
Cash and Receivables	600,000	600,000	100,000	110,000
Inventory	650,000	1,250,000	520,000	590,000
Plant Assets (net)	3,800,000	4,200,000	1,700,000	1,880,000
Investment in Jeff's	1,300,000			
Cost of Goods Sold	1,555,000		980,000	
Depreciation Expense	425,000		220,000	
Total Debits	8,330,000		3,520,000	
Current Liabilities	480,000	480,000	350,000	350,000
Long-Term Debt	1,950,000	1,950,000	980,000	980,000
Common Stock	300,000		75,000	
Retained Earnings (1/1/2005)	3,000,000		715,000	
Sales	2,600,000		1,400,000	
Total Credits	8,330,000		3,520,000	

Required:

A. Prepare the worksheet elimination in journal entry form to consolidate A-1 and Jeff's on November 1, 2005.

B. Prepare the consolidation worksheet to combine A-1 and Jeff's on November 1, 2005.

C. Prepare the worksheet elimination in journal entry form to consolidate A-1 and Jeff's on November 1, 2005, assuming Jeff's plant assets had a historical cost of $2,200,000 and accumulated depreciation of $500,000.

EXERCISE 2-8

Mega Computer Corporation purchased 100 percent of Software Development, Incorporated on May 31, 2005, for $1,850,000. Both companies have a December 31 year-end. The following trial balances existed for Mega and Software immediately prior to the acquisition:

	Mega Computer		Software Development	
Account	Book Value	Market Value	Book Value	Market Value
Cash and Receivables	6,300,000	6,300,000	420,000	420,000
Inventory	8,450,000	9,750,000	650,000	700,000
Land	300,000	500,000	100,000	120,000
Plant Assets (net)	20,000,000	21,000,000	3,000,000	3,200,000
Other Noncurrent	5,000,000	6,900,000	600,000	680,000
Cost of Goods Sold	19,650,000		1,300,000	
Depreciation Expense	3,200,000		625,000	
Total Debits	62,900,000		6,695,000	
Current Liabilities	6,000,000	6,000,000	750,000	750,000
Long-Term Debt	10,000,000	10,150,000	2,155,000	2,155,000
Common Stock	1,000,000		90,000	
Retained Earnings (1/1/2005)	7,900,000		800,000	
Sales	38,000,000		2,900,000	
Total Credits	62,900,000		6,695,000	

Required:

A. Record the acquisition of Software Development by Mega Computer assuming Mega pays cash for Software Development's stock. Mega incurred $150,000 of direct acquisition costs and $80,000 of indirect acquisition costs to acquire Software Development.

B. Prepare the worksheet elimination in journal entry form to consolidate Mega Computer and Software Development on May 31, 2005.

C. Prepare the consolidation worksheet to combine Mega and Software on May 31, 2005.

D. Prepare the worksheet elimination in journal entry form to consolidate Mega Computer and Software Development on May 31, 2005, assuming that Software Development's plant assets have a historical cost of $4,600,000 and accumulated depreciation of $1,600,000.

EXERCISE 2-9

Davidson Foods acquired 80 percent of Wholesale Foods on January 1, 2005, for $1,280,000. The following trial balances existed for Davidson and Wholesale Foods at the date of acquisition:

	Davidson		Wholesale	
Account	*Book Value*	*Market Value*	*Book Value*	*Market Value*
Cash and Receivables	600,000	600,000	380,000	380,000
Inventory	1,150,000	1,350,000	690,000	690,000
Plant Assets (net)	4,705,000	5,100,000	2,800,000	2,800,000
Investment in				
Wholesale Foods	1,280,000			
Total Debits	7,735,000		3,870,000	
Current Liabilities	900,000	900,000	450,000	450,000
Long-Term Debt	2,000,000	2,000,000	1,820,000	1,820,000
Common Stock ($5 par)	170,000		130,000	
Retained Earnings	4,665,000		1,470,000	
Total Credits	7,735,000		3,870,000	

Required:

A. Prepare the worksheet elimination in journal entry form to consolidate Davidson and Wholesale Foods on January 1, 2005.

B. Prepare the consolidation worksheet to combine Davidson and Wholesale Foods on January 1, 2005.

EXERCISE 2-10

Small Motor Manufacturing Corporation was acquired (75 percent) by Major Appliance, Incorporated on January 1, 2005, for $600,000. The following trial balances existed for Major Appliance and Small Motor immediately prior to the acquisition:

	Major Appliance		Small Motor	
Account	*Book Value*	*Market Value*	*Book Value*	*Market Value*
Cash and Receivables	295,000	295,000	80,000	88,000
Inventory	680,000	850,000	230,000	250,000
Plant Assets (net)	2,600,000	3,150,000	685,000	725,000
Total Debits	3,575,000		995,000	
Current Liabilities	550,000	550,000	145,000	145,000
Long-Term Debt	350,000	350,000	150,000	150,000
Common Stock ($1 Par)	20,000		95,000	
Retained Earnings	2,655,000		605,000	
Total Credits	3,575,000		995,000	

Required:

A. Record the acquisition of Small Motor by Major Appliance assuming Major Appliance issues 10,000 shares of $20 par value preferred stock for Small Motor's common stock. Registration and issuance costs for the stock are $38,000. Major Appliance also incurs indirect acquisition costs of $25,000 to acquire Small Motor.

B. Prepare the worksheet elimination in journal entry form to consolidate Major Appliance and Small Motors on January 1, 2005.

C. Prepare the consolidation worksheet (balance sheet only) to combine Major Appliance and Small Motors on January 1, 2005. For purposes of part c, any acquisition costs recorded as expenses in part a are a reduction to Retained Earnings.

D. Prepare the worksheet elimination in journal entry form to consolidate Major Appliance and Small Motors on January 1, 2005, assuming that Small Motor's plant assets have a historical cost of $1,000,000 and an accumulated depreciation of $315,000.

EXERCISE 2-11   Amex Corporation purchased 60 percent of Caldwell Corporation's outstanding common stock on January 1, 2005, for $7,500,000. At the date of acquisition, Amex and Caldwell had the following trial balances:

	Amex		Caldwell	
Account	*Book Value*	*Market Value*	*Book Value*	*Market Value*
Cash and Receivables	10,500,000	10,500,000	3,200,000	3,200,000
Inventory	25,500,000	31,200,000	8,700,000	10,300,000
Land	3,600,000	5,000,000	2,000,000	2,860,000
Plant Assets (net)	54,210,000	60,000,000	17,600,000	19,140,000
Investment in Caldwell	8,100,000*			
Total Debits	101,910,000		31,500,000	
Current Liabilities	14,810,000	14,810,000	6,000,000	6,000,000
Long-Term Debt	20,000,000	20,000,000	16,000,000	16,000,000
Common Stock ($5 par)	3,000,000		1,000,000	
Retained Earnings	64,100,000*		8,500,000	
Total Credits	101,910,000		31,500,000	

* Includes Extraordinary Gain from acquisition of Caldwell.

Required:

A. Record the acquisition of Caldwell by Amex assuming cash was paid to acquire Caldwell's stock.

B. Prepare the worksheet elimination in journal entry form to consolidate Amex and Caldwell on January 1, 2005.

C. Prepare the consolidation worksheet (balance sheet only) to combine Amex and Caldwell on January 1, 2005.

D. Prepare the worksheet elimination in journal entry form to consolidate Amex and Caldwell on January 1, 2005, assuming that Caldwell had plant assets and accumulated depreciation in the amounts of $21,600,000 and $4,000,000, respectively.

EXERCISE 2-12   Bill's Machine Tools Corporation was acquired (90 percent) by Keeley Machine, Incorporated on September 30, 2005, for $1,845,000. Both companies maintain their records on a calendar-year basis. The following trial balances existed for Bill's Machine Tools and Keeley Machine immediately prior to the acquisition:

	Keeley Machine		Bill's Machine Tools	
Account	*Book Value*	*Market Value*	*Book Value*	*Market Value*
Cash and Receivables	2,500,000	2,500,000	950,000	950,000
Inventory	4,000,000	3,200,000	1,400,000	1,400,000
Plant Assets (net)	8,800,000	9,600,000	3,900,000	3,900,000
Expenses	5,620,000		2,650,000	
Total Debits	20,920,000		8,900,000	
Current Liabilities	2,700,000	2,700,000	1,000,000	1,000,000
Long-Term Debt	8,000,000	8,000,000	3,200,000	3,200,000
Common Stock	75,000		85,000	
Retained Earnings (1/1/2005)	1,405,000		415,000	
Revenues	8,740,000		4,200,000	
Total Credits	20,920,000		8,900,000	

Required:

A. Record the acquisition of Bill's Machine Tools by Keeley Machine assuming Keeley issued long-term debt for Bill's Machine Tools' stock.

B. Prepare the worksheet elimination in journal entry form to consolidate Keeley's Machine and Bill's Machine Tools on September 30, 2005.

C. Prepare the consolidation worksheet to combine Keeley Machine and Bill's Machine Tools on September 30, 2005.

EXERCISE 2-13

Discount Office Supply Corporation acquired 80 percent of Amy's Computer Supply Company on March 1, 2005, for $2,760,000. Both companies have a December 31 year-end. At the date of acquisition, Discount Office Supply and Amy's Computer Supply had the following trial balances:

Account	Discount Office Supply		Amy's Computer Supply	
	Book Value	Market Value	Book Value	Market Value
Cash and Receivables	950,000	950,000	375,000	375,000
Inventory	1,750,000	2,150,000	870,000	1,010,000
Plant Assets (net)	2,800,000	2,950,000	1,480,000	1,660,000
Patents				100,000
Investment in Amy's	2,760,000			
Cost of Goods Sold	650,000		420,000	
Depreciation Expense	180,000		125,000	
Total Debits	9,090,000		3,270,000	
Current Liabilities	1,030,000	1,030,000	450,000	450,000
Long-Term Debt	870,000	870,000	580,000	580,000
Common Stock ($5 par)	300,000		250,000	
Retained Earnings (1/1/2005)	5,590,000		905,000	
Sales	1,300,000		1,085,000	
Total Credits	9,090,000		3,270,000	

Required:

A. Prepare the worksheet elimination in journal entry form to consolidate Discount Office Supply and Amy's Computer Supply on March 1, 2005.

B. Prepare the consolidation worksheet to combine Discount Office Supply and Amy's Computer Supply on March 1, 2005.

C. Prepare the worksheet elimination in journal entry form to consolidate Discount Office Supply and Amy's Computer Supply on March 1, 2005, assuming that Amy's plant assets have a historical cost and accumulated depreciation of $1,900,000 and $420,000, respectively.

EXERCISE 2-14

Big Surf Ski Jet Corporation purchased 60 percent of Little Surfboard, Incorporated on August 31, 2005, for $780,000. Both companies have a December 31 year-end. The following trial balances existed for Big Surf and Little Surfboard immediately prior to the acquisition:

Account	Big Surf		Little Surfboard	
	Book Value	Market Value	Book Value	Market Value
Cash and Receivables	2,800,000	3,200,000	120,000	120,000
Inventory	6,150,000	7,850,000	380,000	480,000
Land	220,000	500,000	125,000	180,000
Plant Assets (net)	9,750,000	11,175,000	1,450,000	1,530,000
Other Noncurrent	1,600,000	1,850,000	50,000	90,000
Cost of Goods Sold	10,425,000		510,000	
Depreciation Expense	1,325,000		175,000	
Total Debits	32,270,000		2,810,000	
Current Liabilities	3,800,000	3,800,000	250,000	250,000
Long-Term Debt	6,450,000	6,450,000	720,000	720,000
Common Stock	500,000		90,000	
Retained Earnings (1/1/2005)	5,320,000		750,000	
Sales	16,200,000		1,000,000	
Total Credits	32,270,000		2,810,000	

Required:

A. Record the acquisition of Little Surfboard by Big Surf assuming Big Surf pays cash for Little Surfboard's stock. Big Surf incurred $25,000 of direct acquisition costs and $10,000 of indirect acquisition costs to acquire Little Surfboard.

B. Prepare the worksheet elimination in journal entry form to consolidate Big Surf and Little Surfboard on August 31, 2005.

C. Prepare the consolidation worksheet to combine Big Surf and Little Surfboard on August 31, 2005.

D. Prepare the worksheet elimination in journal entry form to consolidate Big Surf and Little Surfboard on August 31, 2005, assuming that Little Surfboard's plant assets have a historical cost of $2,300,000 and accumulated depreciation of $850,000.

PROBLEMS

Consolidation worksheets for problems that require a worksheet can be found at the book companion website.

PROBLEM 2-1   Record 100 percent acquisition at beginning of year, goodwill, worksheet elimination, consolidation worksheet, long-term debt issued; balance sheet assuming 80 percent acquisition, goodwill, long-term debt issued

PROBLEM 2-2   Record 60 percent acquisition at beginning of year, goodwill, worksheet elimination, consolidation worksheet, common stock issued; worksheet elimination assuming 100 percent acquisition, goodwill

PROBLEM 2-3   Record 100 percent acquisition at beginning of year, book value acquisition with individual purchase differentials, worksheet elimination, consolidation worksheet, preferred stock issued; worksheet elimination assuming 85 percent acquisition

PROBLEM 2-4   Record 75 percent acquisition at beginning of year, negative goodwill, worksheet elimination, consolidation worksheet, preferred stock issued; worksheet elimination and consolidation worksheet with separate accumulated depreciation account, balance sheet assuming 100 percent acquisition, negative goodwill, long-term debt issued

PROBLEM 2-5   Record 100 percent acquisition at beginning of year, negative goodwill, worksheet elimination with separate accumulated depreciation account, consolidation worksheet, long-term debt issued; worksheet elimination assuming 70 percent acquisition, negative goodwill

PROBLEM 2-6   Record 60 percent acquisition at beginning of year, goodwill, worksheet elimination with separate accumulated depreciation account, consolidation worksheet, long-term debt issued; balance sheet assuming 100 percent acquisition, goodwill, common stock issued

PROBLEM 2-7   Record 100 percent acquisition during the year, goodwill, worksheet elimination, consolidation worksheet, long-term debt issued; worksheet elimination and consolidation worksheet with separate accumulated depreciation account, balance sheet assuming 80 percent acquisition, goodwill, long-term debt issued

PROBLEM 2-8   Record 100 percent acquisition during the year, book value acquisition with individual purchase differentials, worksheet elimination, consolidation worksheet, preferred stock issued; worksheet elimination assuming 75 percent acquisition

PROBLEM 2-9   Record 60 percent acquisition during the year, goodwill, worksheet elimination, consolidation worksheet, common stock issued; worksheet elimination assuming 100 percent ownership, goodwill

PROBLEM 2-10   Record 80 percent acquisition during the year, negative goodwill, worksheet elimination, consolidation worksheet, common stock issued; balance sheet assuming 100 percent acquisition, negative goodwill

PROBLEM 2-11   Record 100 percent acquisition during the year, negative goodwill, worksheet elimination with separate accumulated depreciation account, consolidation worksheet, long-term debt issued; worksheet elimination assuming 70 percent acquisition, negative goodwill

PROBLEM 2-12   Record 60 percent acquisition during the year, goodwill, worksheet elimination with separate accumulated depreciation account, consolidation worksheet, common stock issued; balance sheet assuming 100 percent acquisition, goodwill, long-term debt issued.

PROBLEM 2-1   Highland Industries acquired Jensen Manufacturing Corporation on January 1, 2005. The following balances exist for Highland and Jensen immediately prior to the acquisition.

Account	Highland Book Value	Highland Market Value	Jensen Book Value	Jensen Market Value
Cash and Receivables	859,000	875,000	287,000	270,000
Inventory	2,074,000	2,180,000	847,000	1,020,000
Land	96,000	230,000	141,000	175,000
Plant Assets (net)	3,267,000	3,600,000	599,000	750,000
Other Non-Current	973,000	875,000	72,000	65,000
Totals	7,269,000		1,946,000	
Current Liabilities	1,500,000	1,500,000	600,000	600,000
Long-Term Debt	2,850,000	2,850,000	570,000	570,000
Common Stock ($10 Par)	252,000		100,000	
Additional Paid-in Capital	350,000		215,000	
Retained Earnings	2,317,000		461,000	
Totals	7,269,000		1,946,000	

Required:

A. Record the acquisition of Jensen by Highland assuming Highland issued long-term debt to purchase 100 percent of Jensen for $1,200,000.

B. Prepare the worksheet elimination in journal entry form to consolidate Highland and Jensen on January 1, 2005.

C. Prepare the consolidation worksheet to combine Highland and Jensen on January 1, 2005 based on the information in part a.

D. Prepare the worksheet elimination in journal entry form to consolidate Highland and Jensen on January 1, 2005 assuming Highland issued long-term debt to purchase 80 percent of Jensen for $960,000.

PROBLEM 2-2   Michigan Automotive Corporation was acquired by Hoosier National Engine Corporation on January 1, 2005. The following balances exist for Hoosier Engine and Michigan Automotive immediately prior to the acquisition.

Account	Hoosier Engine Book Value	Hoosier Engine Market Value	Michigan Automotive Book Value	Michigan Automotive Market Value
Cash and Receivables	920,000	935,000	75,700	85,000
Inventory	2,918,000	3,082,000	213,000	245,000
Land	742,000	826,000	165,600	195,000
Plant Assets (net)	2,826,000	3,389,000	793,000	975,000
Other Non-Current	760,000	870,000	46,400	55,000
Totals	8,166,000		1,293,700	
Current Liabilities	1,850,000	1,850,000	175,000	175,000
Long-Term Debt	3,270,000	3,270,000	300,000	280,000
Common Stock ($5 Par)	91,000		59,800	
Additional Paid-in Capital	800,000		200,000	
Retained Earnings	2,155,000		558,900	
Totals	8,166,000		1,293,700	

Required:

A. Record the acquisition of Michigan Automotive by Hoosier Engine assuming Hoosier Engine issued 11,000 shares of common stock to purchase 60 percent of Michigan Automotive for $750,000.

B. Prepare the worksheet elimination in journal entry form to consolidate Hoosier Engine and Michigan Automotive on January 1, 2005.

C. Prepare the consolidation worksheet to combine Hoosier Engine and Michigan Automotive on January 1, 2005 based on the information in part a.

D. Prepare the worksheet elimination in journal entry form to consolidate Hoosier Engine and Michigan Automotive on January 1, 2005 assuming Hoosier Engine issued 19,200 shares of common stock to purchase 100 percent of Michigan Automotive for $1,250,000.

PROBLEM 2-3

Northern Enterprises acquired Eastern Corporation on January 1, 2005. The following balances exist for Northern and Eastern immediately prior to the acquisition.

Account	Northern		Eastern	
	Book Value	Market Value	Book Value	Market Value
Cash and Receivables	314,000	314,000	119,000	119,000
Inventory	830,000	1,050,000	285,000	245,000
Land	1,850,000	2,130,000	66,000	85,000
Plant Assets (net)	1,931,000	2,389,000	319,000	326,500
Other Non-Current	59,000	870,000	14,500	18,000
Totals	4,984,000		803,500	
Current Liabilities	600,000	1,850,000	200,000	200,000
Long-Term Debt	580,000	3,270,000	190,000	180,000
Common Stock ($2 Par)	61,000		15,000	
Additional Paid-in Capital	189,000		37,000	
Retained Earnings	3,554,000		361,500	
Totals	4,984,000		803,500	

Required:

A. Record the acquisition of Eastern by Northern assuming Northern financed the purchase of 100 percent of Eastern by issuing 5,000 shares of $10 par value preferred stock with a market value of $413,500.

B. Prepare the worksheet elimination in journal entry form to consolidate Northern and Eastern on January 1, 2005.

C. Prepare the consolidation worksheet to combine Northern and Eastern on January 1, 2005 based on the information in part a.

D. Prepare the worksheet elimination in journal entry form to consolidate Northern and Eastern on January 1, 2005 assuming Northern financed the purchase of 85 percent of Eastern by issuing 4,000 shares of $10 par value preferred stock with a market value of $351,475.

PROBLEM 2-4

Creative Electronics Corporation was acquired by General Corporation in a conglomerate type of business combination on January 1, 2005. The following balances exist for General and Creative Electronics immediately prior to the acquisition.

Account	General		Creative Electronics	
	Book Value	Market Value	Book Value	Market Value
Cash and Receivables	854,000	860,000	191,000	191,000
Inventory	2,529,000	2,890,000	353,000	375,000
Land	427,000	520,000	50,000	50,000
Plant Assets (net)	5,761,000	6,000,000	527,000	550,000
Other Non-Current	395,000	425,000	18,500	25,000
Totals	9,966,000		1,139,500	
Current Liabilities	1,500,000	1,500,000	250,000	250,000
Long-Term Debt	2,135,000	2,180,000	330,000	330,000
Common Stock ($10 Par)	413,000		30,000	
Additional Paid-in Capital	950,000		80,000	
Retained Earnings	4,968,000		449,500	
Totals	9,966,000		1,139,500	

Required:

A. Record the acquisition of Creative Electronics by General assuming General purchased 75 percent of Creative Electronics for $443,250 by issuing 10,000 shares of $10 par preferred stock.

B. Prepare the worksheet elimination in journal entry form to consolidate General and Creative Electronics on January 1, 2005.

C. Prepare the consolidation worksheet (balance sheet only) to combine General and Creative Electronics on January 1, 2005 based on the information in part a.

D. Prepare the worksheet elimination in journal entry form to consolidate General and Creative Electronics on January 1, 2005 assuming that Creative's plant assets have a historical cost of $700,000 and accumulated depreciation of $173,000.

E. Prepare the plant assets and accumulated depreciation rows of the consolidation worksheet to combine General and Creative Electronics on January 1, 2005 assuming the information in part d. and assuming that General's plant assets have a historical cost of $7,500,000 and accumulated depreciation of $1,739,000.

F. Prepare the consolidated balance sheet for General and Creative Electronics on January 1, 2005 assuming General purchased 100 percent of Creative Electronics for $591,000 by issuing long-term debt.

PROBLEM 2-5

Coach's Corner is a local sporting goods company that was acquired by Major Shoes, Incorporated (a large shoe manufacturer looking to expand into retail sales) on January 1, 2005. The following balances exist for Coach's Corner and Major Shoes immediately prior to the acquisition.

| | Major Shoes | | Coach's Corner | |
Account	Book Value	Market Value	Book Value	Market Value
Cash and Receivables	2,731,000	731,000	276,000	280,000
Inventory	3,514,000	1,834,000	963,000	1,125,000
Land	189,000	275,000	66,000	75,000
Plant Assets	5,207,000	2,750,000	1,410,000	660,000
Accumulated Depreciation	(2,399,000)		(667,000)	
Other Non-Current	41,000	45,000	18,000	15,000
Totals	9,283,000		2,066,000	
Current Liabilities	3,200,000	1,200,000	480,000	480,000
Long-Term Debt	2,675,000	1,618,000	750,000	750,000
Common Stock ($5 Par)	64,000		54,000	
Additional Paid-in Capital	621,000		149,000	
Retained Earnings	2,723,000		633,000	
Totals	9,283,000		2,066,000	

Required:

A. Record the acquisition of Coach's Corner by Major Shoes assuming Major Shoes purchased 100 percent of Coaches Corner's for $865,000 by issuing long-term debt at face value.

B. Prepare the worksheet elimination in journal entry form to consolidate Major Shoes and Coach's Corner on January 1, 2005.

C. Prepare the consolidation worksheet (balance sheet only) to combine Major Shoes and Coach's Corner on January 1, 2005 based on the information in part a.

D. Prepare the worksheet elimination in journal entry form to consolidate Major Shoes and Coach's Corner on January 1, 2005 assuming Major Shoes purchased 70 percent of Coach's Corner for $605,500.

PROBLEM 2-6

Premium Publishing Corporation acquired a competitor in the magazine industry (Home Journal Corporation) in a horizontal type of business combination on January 1, 2005. The following balances exist for Premium and Home Journal immediately prior to the acquisition.

| | Premium | | Home Journal | |
Account	Book Value	Market Value	Book Value	Market Value
Cash and Receivables	2,407,000	2,407,000	1,123,000	1,123,000
Inventory	5,555,000	5,850,000	1,834,000	1,750,000
Land	3,301,000	3,100,000	427,000	490,000
Plant Assets	8,489,000	7,200,000	4,270,000	3,400,000
Accumulated Depreciation	(1,700,000)		(1,067,000)	
Other Non-Current	486,000	495,000	276,000	255,000
Totals	18,538,000		6,863,000	
Current Liabilities	3,600,000	3,600,000	1,250,000	1,250,000
Long-Term Debt	4,275,000	4,085,000	2,600,000	2,480,000

Common Stock ($2 Par)	500,000	572,000
Additional Paid-in Capital	2,738,000	989,000
Retained Earnings	7,425,000	1,452,000
Totals	18,538,000	6,863,000

Required:
A. Record the acquisition of Home Journal by Premium assuming Premium purchased 60 percent of Home Journal for $2,100,000 by issuing long-term debt with a $2,000,000 face value.
B. Prepare the worksheet elimination in journal entry form to consolidate Premium and Home Journal on January 1, 2005.
C. Prepare the consolidation worksheet to combine Premium and Home Journal on January 1, 2005 based on the information in part a.
D. Prepare the consolidated balance sheet for Premium and Home Journal on January 1, 2005 assuming Premium purchased 100 percent of Home Journal for $3,500,000 by issuing 50,000 shares of common stock.

PROBLEM 2-7   Newton Corporation acquired the common stock of Langsam Corporation on May 1, 2005. Both companies have a December 31 year-end. The following balances exist for Newton and Langsam immediately prior to the acquisition.

Account	Newton Book Value	Newton Market Value	Langsam Book Value	Langsam Market Value
Cash and Receivables	501,000	510,000	228,000	228,000
Inventory	1,546,000	2,320,000	612,000	720,000
Land	607,000	1,760,000	208,000	180,000
Plant Assets (net)	8,342,000	9,200,000	744,000	780,000
Other Non-Current	953,000	1,150,000	50,700	45,000
Cost of Goods Sold	1,600,000		798,000	
Depreciation Expense	96,000		50,000	
Other Expenses	1,850,000		299,600	
Totals	15,495,000		2,990,300	
Current Liabilities	956,000	956,000	325,000	325,000
Long-Term Debt	2,482,000	2,482,000	500,000	500,000
Common Stock ($5 Par)	154,000		51,000	
Additional Paid-in Capital	2,416,000		56,900	
Retained Earnings (1/1/2005)	5,810,000		382,000	
Sales	3,677,000		1,675,400	
Totals	15,495,000		2,990,300	

Required:
A. Record the acquisition of Langsam by Newton assuming Newton issued long-term debt to purchase 100 percent of Langsam's common stock for $1,350,000.
B. Prepare the worksheet elimination in journal entry form to consolidate Newton and Langsam on May 1, 2005.
C. Prepare the consolidation worksheet to combine Newton and Langsam on May 1, 2005 based on the information in part a.
D. Prepare the worksheet elimination in journal entry form to consolidate Newton and Langsam on January 1, 2005 assuming that Langsam's plant assets have a historical cost of $900,000 and accumulated depreciation of $156,000.
E. Prepare the plant assets and accumulated depreciation rows of the consolidation worksheet to combine Newton and Langsam on January 1, 2005 assuming the information in part d. and assuming that Newton's plant assets have a historical cost of $9,750,000 and accumulated depreciation of $1,408,000.
F. Prepare the consolidated balance sheet for Newton and Langsam on May 1, 2005 assuming Newton issued long-term debt to purchase 80 percent of Langsam for $1,080,000.

PROBLEM 2-8   School Supply Corporation acquired Midwestern Book Corporation on February 1, 2005. Both companies have a December 31 year-end. The following balances exist for School Supply and Midwestern immediately prior to the acquisition.

	School Supply		Midwestern	
Account	Book Value	Market Value	Book Value	Market Value
Cash and Receivables	633,000	635,000	192,000	185,000
Inventory	2,501,000	2,750,000	414,000	410,000
Land	854,000	2,085,000	71,000	80,000
Plant Assets (net)	3,985,000	4,254,000	936,000	950,000
Other Non-Current	213,000	258,000	58,000	45,000
Cost of Goods Sold	402,000		75,000	
Depreciation Expense	56,000		10,000	
Other Expenses	257,000		46,000	
Totals	8,901,000		1,802,000	
Current Liabilities	1,600,000	1,600,000	223,000	223,000
Long-Term Debt	1,250,000	1,270,000	340,000	339,000
Common Stock ($1 Par)	22,900		87,000	
Additional Paid-in Capital	647,000		331,000	
Retained Earnings (1/1/2005)	4,231,100		595,000	
Sales	1,150,000		226,000	
Totals	8,901,000		1,802,000	

Required:

A. Record the acquisition of Midwestern by School Supply assuming School Supply purchased 100 percent of Midwestern by issuing 22,000 shares of $20 par value preferred stock with a market value of $1,108,000.

B. Prepare the worksheet elimination in journal entry form to consolidate School Supply and Midwestern on February 1, 2005.

C. Prepare the consolidation worksheet to combine School Supply and Midwestern on February 1, 2005 based on the information in part a.

D. Prepare the worksheet elimination in journal entry form to consolidate School Supply and Midwestern on February 1, 2005 assuming School Supply purchased 75 percent of Midwestern by issuing 16,500 shares of $20 par value preferred stock with a market value of $831,000.

PROBLEM 2-9 Larry's Luxury Tours, Incorporated was acquired by Ted's Tremendous Tours, Incorporated on September 1, 2005. Both companies have a December 31 year-end. The following balances exist for Ted's and Larry's immediately prior to the acquisition.

	Ted's		Larry's	
Account	Book Value	Market Value	Book Value	Market Value
Cash and Receivables	3,130,000	3,250,000	1,590,700	1,550,000
Inventory	8,791,000	9,225,000	5,761,000	6,215,000
Land	636,000	730,000	90,800	295,000
Plant Assets (net)	14,692,000	14,300,000	6,184,200	6,380,000
Other Non-Current	1,244,000	1,350,000	61,900	50,000
Cost of Goods Sold	12,320,000		8,641,000	
Depreciation Expense	623,000		520,000	
Other Expenses	789,000		1,654,000	
Totals	42,225,000		24,503,600	
Current Liabilities	5,160,000	5,160,000	3,225,000	3,225,000
Long-Term Debt	7,760,000	7,760,000	4,300,000	4,100,000
Common Stock ($2 Par)	908,000		422,000	
Additional Paid-in Capital	2,742,000		816,000	
Retained Earnings (1/1/2005)	9,636,000		3,660,900	
Sales	16,019,000		12,079,700	
Totals	42,225,000		24,503,600	

Required:

A. Record the acquisition of Larry's by Ted's assuming Ted's issued 60,000 shares of common stock to purchase 60 percent of Larry's stock for $4,500,000.

B. Prepare the worksheet elimination in journal entry form to consolidate Ted's and Larry's on September 1, 2005.

C. Prepare the consolidation worksheet to combine Ted's and Larry's on September 1, 2005 based on the information in part a.

D. Prepare the worksheet elimination in journal entry form to consolidate Ted's and Larry's on September 1, 2005 assuming Ted's issued 100,200 shares of common stock to purchase 100 percent of Larry's stock for $7,500,000.

PROBLEM 2-10

Premier Cabinet Corporation was acquired by General Construction Corporation in a vertical type of business combination on August 1, 2005. Both companies have a December 31 year-end. The following balances exist for General Construction and Premium Cabinet immediately prior to the acquisition.

Account	General Construction		Premium Cabinet	
	Book Value	Market Value	Book Value	Market Value
Cash and Receivables	67,800	65,000	82,300	80,000
Inventory	367,400	350,000	447,000	475,000
Land	117,300	220,000	105,000	105,000
Plant Assets (net)	509,500	635,500	492,000	562,500
Other Non-Current	9,400	12,000	76,800	82,500
Depreciation Expenses	51,600		46,000	
Other Expenses	348,000		525,000	
Totals	1,471,000		1,774,100	
Current Liabilities	161,900	161,900	260,000	260,000
Long-Term Debt	344,000	344,000	510,000	500,000
Common Stock ($1 Par)	61,000		20,000	
Additional Paid-in Capital	52,900		35,000	
Retained Earnings (1/1/2005)	265,500		172,300	
Revenue	585,700		776,800	
Totals	1,471,000		1,774,100	

Required:

A. Record the acquisition of Premium Cabinet by General Construction assuming General Construction purchased 80 percent of Premium Cabinet for $400,000 by issuing 25,000 shares of common stock.

B. Prepare the worksheet elimination in journal entry form to consolidate General Construction and Premium Cabinet on August 1, 2005.

C. Prepare the consolidation worksheet to combine General Construction and Premium Cabinets on August 1, 2005 based on the information in part a.

D. Prepare the consolidated balance sheet for General Construction and Premium Cabinets on January 1, 2005 assuming General Construction purchased 100 percent of Premium Cabinets for $500,000 by issuing long-term debt.

PROBLEM 2-11

Ultimate Advertising, Incorporated is a national company that specializes in advertising food products. Ultimate Advertising was acquired by Bigger Than Life Advertising, Incorporated (an international advertiser specializing in sporting goods) on May 1, 2005. Both companies have a December 31 year-end. The following balances exist for Bigger Than Life and Ultimate immediately prior to the acquisition.

Account	Bigger Than Life		Ultimate	
	Book Value	Market Value	Book Value	Market Value
Cash and Receivables	9,589,000	9,450,000	3,600,000	3,400,000
Inventory	815,000	1,020,000	764,000	970,000
Plant Assets	1,360,000	1,650,000	1,423,000	1,250,000
Accumulated Depreciation	(247,000)		(93,000)	
Copyrights	61,565,000	98,248,000	19,574,000	21,750,000
Other Non-Current	455,000	430,500	1,880,000	2,000,000

Depreciation Expense	35,000		24,000	
Other Expenses	25,555,000		8,275,000	
Totals	99,127,000		35,447,000	
Current Liabilities	6,200,000	6,200,000	2,650,000	2,650,000
Long-Term Debt	5,240,000	5,240,000	3,000,000	2,750,000
Common Stock ($5 Par)	250,000		100,000	
Additional Paid-in Capital	16,547,000		2,275,000	
Retained Earnings (1/1/2005)	24,563,000		11,044,000	
Revenue	46,327,000		16,378,000	
Totals	99,127,000		35,447,000	

Required:

A. Record the acquisition of Ultimate by Bigger Than Life assuming Bigger Than Life purchased 100 percent of Ultimate's common stock for $22,000,000 by issuing long-term debt at face value.

B. Prepare the worksheet elimination in journal entry form to consolidate Bigger Than Life and Ultimate on May 1, 2005.

C. Prepare the consolidation worksheet to combine Bigger Than Life and Ultimate on May 1, 2005 based on the information in part a.

D. Prepare the worksheet elimination in journal entry form to consolidate Bigger Than Life and Ultimate on May 1, 2005 assuming Bigger Than Life purchased 70 percent of Ultimate for $15,400,000.

PROBLEM 2-12   Julia's Designs Corporation acquired a competitor in the computer graphics industry. (Development Software Corporation) in a horizontal type of business combination on November 1, 2005. Both companies have a December 31 year-end. The following balances exist for Julia's Designs and Development Software immediately prior to the acquisition.

	Julia's Designs		Development Software	
Account	*Book Value*	*Market Value*	*Book Value*	*Market Value*
Cash and Receivables	145,000	145,000	73,000	73,000
Inventory	116,000	143,000	51,500	75,000
Land	61,400	72,000	189,000	175,000
Plant Assets	985,000	825,000	1,207,400	860,000
Accumulated Depreciation	(212,000)		(399,000)	
Other Non-Current	16,000	15,000	41,400	54,000
Depreciation Expense	42,000		64,100	
Other Expenses	350,000		262,000	
Totals	1,503,400		1,489,400	
Current Liabilities	120,000	120,000	80,000	80,000
Long-Term Debt	168,000	170,000	100,000	112,000
Common Stock ($1 Par)	150,000		225,000	
Additional Paid-in Capital	190,000		264,000	
Retained Earnings (1/1/2005)	286,000		371,000	
Revenue	589,400		449,400	
Totals	1,503,400		1,489,400	

Required:

A. Record the acquisition of Development Software by Julia's assuming Julia's Designs purchased 60 percent of Development Software for $805,200 by issuing 26,000 shares of common stock.

B. Prepare the worksheet elimination in journal entry form to consolidate Julia's Designs and Development Software on November 1, 2005.

C. Prepare the consolidation worksheet to combine Julia's Designs and Development Software on November 1, 2005 based on the information in part a.

D. Prepare the consolidated balance sheet for Julia's Designs and Development Software on November 1, 2005 assuming Julia's Designs purchased 100 percent of Development Software for $1,342,000 by issuing long-term debt at a 10 percent premium.

CHAPTER 3

CONSOLIDATION SUBSEQUENT TO THE DATE OF ACQUISITION

LEARNING OBJECTIVES

After reading this chapter, you should be able to:

- Determine the amounts to be recognized on the parent's financial records subsequent to a subsidiary's acquisition.
- Construct the worksheet eliminations necessary to prepare a consolidation worksheet for a parent and subsidiary in periods subsequent to acquisition.
- Construct the consolidation worksheet in periods subsequent to acquisition.
- Determine the noncontrolling interest balance subsequent to the date of acquisition of a subsidiary.

Subsequent to the date of acquisition, consolidation of the same parent and subsidiary normally occurs every time financial statements are prepared. Regardless of whether the consolidation occurs one month subsequent to the parent's acquisition of the subsidiary or 20 years after acquisition, the general procedures and the rationale for the procedures are the same. This chapter focuses on procedures for consolidating a parent and a subsidiary subsequent to the date of acquisition. The first section addresses book value acquisitions while the second addresses acquisitions at a price greater than book value. Both the cost method and the equity method are available for accounting for certain investments. While some companies choose to use the cost method for internal accounting purposes, the issuance of separate parent company (unconsolidated) financial statements requires that the equity method be used to report the investment accounts for unconsolidated subsidiaries.[1] For the purpose of illustrating consolidation procedures subsequent to date of acquisition, this text assumes that the parent uses the equity method for internal accounting purposes.[2] The illustrations in this chapter assume that the parent (Pratt) acquired the subsidiary's (Sterling) stock during the year (October 1, 2005) when the fiscal year ends on December 31.

[1] A review of the cost and equity methods of accounting for investments is presented in Appendix 3-1.

[2] If the parent uses the cost method internally, the consolidation elimination procedures differ slightly. The cost method is presented in Appendix 3-2.

PRATT AND STERLING DATA SUBSEQUENT TO ACQUISITION DATE

Subsequent to the date of acquisition, the parent and subsidiary continue conducting normal business operations. As a result, both the parent and the subsidiary may separately earn income and pay dividends. The parent company, in its separate financial records, recognizes its ownership percentage of the subsidiary's income and dividends through equity method journal entries. The income and dividend information presented in Illustration 3-1 is used to prepare worksheet eliminations and consolidation worksheets in 2005 and 2006 under various purchase assumptions.

ILLUSTRATION 3-1
Income and Dividend Data for Pratt and Sterling for 2005 and 2006

Period of Measurement	Separate Net Income Reported by		Dividend Declared by	
	Pratt	Sterling	Pratt	Sterling
January 1–September 30, 2005	600,000	90,000	300,000	0
October 1–December 31, 2005	70,000	50,000	80,000	0
January 1–December 31, 2006	885,000	205,000	400,000	110,000

CONSOLIDATION SUBSEQUENT TO ACQUISITION DATE: PURCHASE PRICE EQUALS BOOK VALUE

First Year of Ownership

To illustrate the accounting and consolidation procedures necessary subsequent to acquisition, the first illustration in this chapter extends the case in which Pratt purchases all of the outstanding stock of Sterling at a price equal to Sterling's book value. In this example, Pratt had originally invested $2,000,000 cash in Sterling on October 1, 2005. As a result, Pratt will recognize 100 percent of Sterling's net income and any dividends subsequent to acquisition as adjustments to the *Investment in Sterling Products* account when applying the equity method to account for its investments. The appropriate December 31, 2005, journal entry on Pratt's books to record investment income is:

Journal Entry—Pratt Corporation Books

Dec. 31, 2005	Investment in Sterling Products	50,000	
	Investment Income		50,000
	To record investment income based on Sterling's reported fourth quarter, 2005, net income.		

As many as three equity method journal entries may be needed by the parent each year. These entries recognize: (1) the parent's ownership percentage of the subsidiary's net income; (2) purchase differential amortizations to adjust the parent's share of subsidiary income; and (3) the parent's ownership percentage of dividends paid by the subsidiary. The acquisition in the current example was at book value, so there were no purchase differentials and, therefore, no second journal entry was required. The third journal entry is not recorded by Pratt in 2005 for the current example because Sterling did not pay dividends.

Illustration 3-2 presents the consolidating worksheet to combine Pratt and Sterling at December 31, 2005, three months after acquisition. Note the following assumptions made in this illustration:

(1) Pratt Corporation's trial balance provided in the worksheet assumes that the end-of-year entry (as illustrated above) to record investment income has already been posted to Pratt's books. Thus, the *Investment in Sterling Products* account

ILLUSTRATION 3-2
Worksheet for Consolidation of Pratt Corporation and Subsidiary, Sterling Products
100 Percent–Owned Subsidiary
Consolidation Subsequent to Acquisition Date
Price Equal to Book Value
December 31, 2005

	Separate Financial Statements		Adjustments and Eliminations		Consolidated Financial Statements
	Pratt	Sterling	Debit	Credit	
Income Statement					
Sales	10,000,000	2,120,000			12,120,000
Investment Income, Sterling Products	50,000		(2) 50,000		0
Cost of Goods Sold	5,600,000	1,010,000			6,610,000
Selling Expenses	1,400,000	190,000			1,590,000
General and Administrative Expenses	2,330,000	750,000			3,080,000
Nonoperating Items (net)		30,000			30,000
Preacquisition Earnings			(1) 90,000		90,000
Net Income (to Statement of Retained Earnings)	720,000	140,000	140,000	0	720,000
Retained Earnings Statement					
Retained Earnings (1/1/2005)	2,300,000	160,000	(1) 160,000		2,300,000
Add: Net Income (from Income Statement)	720,000	140,000	(X) 140,000	(X) 0	720,000
Subtotal	3,020,000	300,000			3,020,000
Less: Dividends	(380,000)				(380,000)
Retained Earnings (12/31/2005 to Balance Sheet)	2,640,000	300,000	300,000	0	2,640,000
Balance Sheet					
Cash	1,300,000	240,000			1,540,000
Accounts Receivable (net)	1,800,000	270,000			2,070,000
Inventory (FIFO)	5,500,000	650,000			6,150,000
Other Current Assets	1,600,000				1,600,000
Total Current Assets	10,200,000	1,160,000			11,360,000
Plant and Equipment (net)	14,290,000	1,330,000			15,620,000
Patent		1,140,000			1,140,000
Investment in Sterling Products	2,050,000			(1) 2,000,000	0
				(2) 50,000	
Other Noncurrent Assets	1,400,000	2,290,000			3,690,000
Total Long-Term Assets	17,740,000	4,760,000			20,450,000
Total Assets	27,940,000	5,920,000			31,810,000

(Continued)

ILLUSTRATION 3-2 *Continued*

	Separate Financial Statements		Adjustments and Eliminations		Consolidated Financial Statements
	Pratt	**Sterling**	**Debit**	**Credit**	
Current Liabilities	8,950,000	1,470,000			10,420,000
Long-Term Notes Payable		1,000,000			1,000,000
7% Bonds Payable (due 6/30/2013)	4,000,000				4,000,000
Less: Discount on Bonds Payable	(150,000)				(150,000)
8% Bonds Payable (due 12/31/2010)		1,500,000			1,500,000
Less: Discount on Bonds Payable		(100,000)			(100,000)
Total Liabilities	12,800,000	3,870,000			16,670,000
Common Stock ($1 par):					
Pratt, 10,000,000 shares authorized, 6,000,000 shares issued and outstanding	6,000,000				6,000,000
Sterling, 1,000,000 shares authorized, issued and outstanding		1,000,000	(1) 1,000,000		0
Additional Paid-In Capital	6,500,000	750,000	(1) 750,000		6,500,000
Retained Earnings (12/31/2005 from					
Statement of Retained Earnings)	2,640,000	300,000	(X) 300,000	(X) 0	2,640,000
Total Stockholders' Equity	15,140,000	2,050,000			15,140,000
Total Liabilities and Stockholders' Equity	27,940,000	5,920,000			31,810,000
			2,050,000	2,050,000	

(1) To eliminate the subsidiary's date of acquisition stockholders' equity and the parent's beginning Investment in Sterling Products account.
(2) To eliminate the change in the Investment in Sterling Products account and the parent's Investment Income account.

balance is $2,050,000, and Pratt's reported net income includes $50,000 of investment income in addition to Pratt's total separate net income of $670,000 for all of 2005.

(2) Because there are no purchase differentials to amortize, the reported net income of Sterling is the basis for Pratt's reported *Investment Income* balance.

The worksheet eliminations, in journal entry form, are presented in Worksheet Eliminations 3-2.

Worksheet Eliminations 3-2—Journal Entry Form

(1) Common Stock   1,000,000
     Additional Paid-In Capital   750,000
     Retained Earnings (January 1, 2005)   160,000
     Preacquisition Earnings   90,000
          Investment in Sterling Products   2,000,000

To eliminate the subsidiary's date of acquisition stockholders' equity and the parent's beginning Investment in Sterling Products account.

(2) Investment Income   50,000
          Investment in Sterling Products   50,000

To eliminate the change in the Investment in Sterling Products account and the parent's Investment Income account.

The Consolidated Financial Statements column in Illustration 3-2 presents $0 in the *Investment in Sterling Products* account and $0 for the *Investment Income* account. The investment account must be completely eliminated because it represents the parent's ownership interest in the subsidiary's stockholders' equity (net assets). This ownership is disclosed in the consolidated balance sheet through the inclusion of the subsidiary's individual assets and liabilities. Recall, however, that worksheet elimination (1) is based on dollar amounts that exist at the beginning of the period, or the date of acquisition. As a result, only the original investment balance of $2,000,000 is eliminated in worksheet elimination (1). The change that has been posted to the investment account during the period is eliminated in a second worksheet elimination. The change in the *Investment in Sterling Products* account is eliminated via worksheet elimination (2), which reverses the journal entries recorded by the parent during the year. Simultaneously, this worksheet elimination removes the parent's *Investment Income* account. The *Investment Income* balance is eliminated because the same $50,000 is reflected in the net effect of Sterling's various revenue and expense accounts that are consolidated line by line.

The consolidated net income for the year ending December 31, 2005, is Pratt's separate net income for 2005 ($670,000) plus Sterling's fourth-quarter net income ($50,000). Consolidated net income does not include the $90,000 of income earned by Sterling prior to Pratt's investment. This income was eliminated as preacquisition earnings in worksheet elimination (1). Consolidated *Retained Earnings* at December 31 is Pratt's entire balance of $2,640,000, including the $50,000 income generated since Sterling was acquired. Finally, the consolidated net assets include the book values from both Pratt and Sterling with no adjustments to market value because, in this case, this purchase price (market value) was equal to book value.

Second Year of Ownership

During 2006, Pratt records the following two journal entries under the equity method to recognize its ownership interest in Sterling. The first entry recognizes Pratt's interest in Sterling's net income and the second entry recognizes the payment of a dividend by Sterling to Pratt. This is the first dividend payment Sterling made to Pratt because Sterling did not declare a dividend in 2005.

Journal Entry—Pratt Corporation Books

Dec. 31, 2006	Investment in Sterling Products	205,000	
	Investment Income		205,000
	To record investment income based on Sterling's reported 2006 net income.		
	Cash	110,000	
	Investment in Sterling Products		110,000
	To record dividends declared by Sterling in 2006.		

The next worksheet, Illustration 3-3, consolidates Pratt and Sterling at December 31, 2006, one year later. Again, the worksheet assumes that Pratt's equity method entries have already been posted. The worksheet eliminations for Illustration 3-3, in journal entry form, are provided in Worksheet Eliminations 3-3.

Worksheet Eliminations 3-3 is again composed of two worksheet eliminations. Worksheet elimination (1) removes the investment balance, as it appeared *at the beginning of the current fiscal period (January 1, 2006)* as well as Sterling's stockholders' equity account balances *as of January 1, 2006*. The investment exactly offsets the stockholders'

ILLUSTRATION 3-3
Worksheet for Consolidation of Pratt Corporation and Subsidiary, Sterling Products
100 Percent–Owned Subsidiary
Consolidation Subsequent to Acquisition Date
Price Equal to Book Value
December 31, 2006

	Separate Financial Statements		Adjustments and Eliminations		Consolidated Financial Statements
	Pratt	Sterling	Debit	Credit	
Income Statement					
Sales	10,158,000	1,400,000			11,558,000
Nonoperating Items (net)	127,000				127,000
Investment Income, Sterling Products	205,000		(2) 205,000		0
Cost of Goods Sold	5,800,000	855,000			6,655,000
Selling Expenses	1,200,000	180,000			1,380,000
General and Administrative Expenses	2,400,000	160,000			2,560,000
Net Income (to Statement of Retained Earnings)	1,090,000	205,000	205,000	0	1,090,000
Retained Earnings Statement					
Retained Earnings (1/1/2006)	2,640,000	300,000	(1) 300,000		2,640,000
Add: Net Income (from Income Statement)	1,090,000	205,000	(X) 205,000	(X) 0	1,090,000
Subtotal	3,730,000	505,000			3,730,000
Less: Dividends	(400,000)	(110,000)		(2) 110,000	(400,000)
Retained Earnings (12/31/2006 to Balance Sheet)	3,330,000	395,000	505,000	110,000	3,330,000
Balance Sheet					
Cash	490,000	150,000			640,000
Accounts Receivable (net)	2,000,000	300,000			2,300,000
Inventory (FIFO)	5,500,000	600,000			6,100,000
Other Current Assets	1,500,000				1,500,000
Total Current Assets	9,490,000	1,050,000			10,540,000
Plant and Equipment (net)	15,000,000	1,500,000			16,500,000
Patent		900,000			900,000
Investment in Sterling Products	2,145,000			(1) 2,050,000	0
				(2) 95,000	
Other Noncurrent Assets	1,935,000	1,950,000			3,885,000
Total Long-Term Assets	19,080,000	4,350,000			21,285,000
Total Assets	28,570,000	5,400,000			31,825,000
Current Liabilities	8,870,000	835,000			9,705,000
Long-Term Notes Payable		1,000,000			1,000,000
7% Bonds Payable (due 6/30/2014)	4,000,000				4,000,000
Less: Discount on Bonds Payable	(130,000)				(130,000)
8% Bonds Payable (due 12/31/2011)		1,500,000			1,500,000
Less: Discount on Bonds Payable		(80,000)			(80,000)
Total Liabilities	12,740,000	3,255,000			15,995,000

(Continued)

ILLUSTRATION 3-3 *Continued*

	Separate Financial Statements		Adjustments and Eliminations		Consolidated Financial Statements
	Pratt	Sterling	Debit	Credit	
Common Stock ($1 par):					
Pratt, 10,000,000 shares authorized, 6,000,000 shares issued and outstanding	6,000,000				6,000,000
Sterling, 1,000,000 shares authorized, issued and outstanding		1,000,000	(1) 1,000,000		
Additional Paid-In Capital	6,500,000	750,000	(1) 750,000		6,500,000
Retained Earnings (12/31/2006 from Statement of Retained Earnings)	3,330,000	395,000	(X) 505,000	(X) 110,000	3,330,000
Noncontrolling Interest in Sterling					0
Total Stockholders' Equity	15,830,000	2,145,000			15,830,000
Total Liabilities and Stockholders' Equity	28,570,000	5,400,000			31,825,000
			2,255,000	2,255,000	

(1) To eliminate the subsidiary's beginning of current period stockholders' equity and the parent's beginning of period Investment in Sterling Products account.

(2) To eliminate the change in the Investment in Sterling Products account, the parent's Investment Income account, and the subsidiary's dividends declared.

Worksheet Eliminations 3-3—Journal Entry Form

(1)   Common Stock   1,000,000
        Additional Paid-In Capital   750,000
        Retained Earnings (January 1, 2006)   300,000
                Investment in Sterling Products   2,050,000

To eliminate the subsidiary's beginning of current period stockholders' equity and the parent's beginning of period Investment in Sterling Products account.

(2)   Investment Income   205,000
                Investment in Sterling Products   95,000
                Dividends   110,000

To eliminate the change in the Investment in Sterling Products account, the parent's Investment Income account, and the subsidiary's dividends declared.

---

equity because the investment was for 100 percent of Sterling at a price equal to the book value. Under these conditions, the investment balance will always equal the subsidiary's total stockholders' equity. The elimination to the investment account in worksheet elimination (1) is equal to the sum of the worksheet eliminations of the prior year. Worksheet elimination (1) in 2005 removed $2,000,000, the original investment account balance. Worksheet elimination (2) in 2005 removed $50,000, the net change in the investment account that had been posted during 2005. Therefore, worksheet elimination (1) in 2006 must remove $2,050,000, the investment balance carried forward from 2005.

Worksheet elimination (2) reverses the effect of the 2006 changes that have been entered into the *Investment in Sterling Products* balance. In worksheet elimination (2), the debit is to eliminate the investment income that was recognized by Pratt while the offsetting credits are to Sterling's *Dividends* account and Pratt's *Investment in Sterling Products* account. As with the previous illustration, the individual revenue and expense accounts on Sterling's books, included in the consolidated income statement, present the same information that is summarized in the *Investment Income* account on Pratt's books. The dividend declared by Sterling is an intercompany transfer of cash because Pratt owns the stock of Sterling. The consolidated Statement of Retained Earnings should not report the $110,000 as a distribution of consolidated *Retained Earnings* because these assets have not been distributed by the consolidated entity to Pratt's stockholders. Only Pratt's dividends of $400,000 represent a distribution of consolidated assets.

Keep in mind that *the worksheet eliminations are not posted* to either Pratt's or Sterling's accounting records. Pratt, for instance, will continue to account for its investment in Sterling using the equity method. Pratt's balance in *Investment in Sterling Products* at January 1, 2007, will be $2,145,000, calculated as follows:

Original purchase price	$2,000,000
Add: 2005 investment income	50,000
Balance at January 1, 2006	2,050,000
Add: 2006 investment income	205,000
Less: 2006 dividends	(110,000)
Balance at January 1, 2007	$2,145,000

Moreover, Pratt's *Retained Earnings* at January 1, 2007, will reflect both the 2005 and 2006 investment income from Sterling even though the line item *Investment Income* is eliminated for the consolidated income statement presentation in 2005 and 2006. Understanding the consolidation process depends on having a thorough understanding of what is, and what is not, posted to the books of both the parent and the subsidiary.

CONSOLIDATION SUBSEQUENT TO ACQUISITION DATE: PURCHASE PRICE MORE THAN BOOK VALUE

The previous example was based on the assumption that the book values of Sterling's assets and liabilities equaled the market values. This assumption is relaxed for the remainder of the chapter. Subsequent examples in this chapter are based on the following differences between the book values and market values of Sterling's assets and liabilities:

	Debit (Credit) Market Value	Debit (Credit) Book Value	Purchase Differentials
Inventory	$730,000	$600,000	$130,000
Plant and Equipment (net)	1,750,000	1,400,000	350,000
Patent	1,031,400	1,200,000	(168,600)
Long-Term Notes Payable	(1,136,400)	(1,000,000)	(136,400)
Total			$175,000

In addition, $225,000 of goodwill is established.

100 Percent–Owned Subsidiary

This example presents the consolidation of Pratt and Sterling subsequent to acquisition assuming that Pratt paid $2,400,000 for 100 percent of Sterling's outstanding common stock on October 1, 2005. For consolidation purposes, the purchase differentials (differences between book values and market values) result in adjustments to revalue the amounts carried on Sterling's books. The values created on the consolidated balance sheet are the market values of the assets and liabilities acquired at the acquisition date.

ILLUSTRATION 3-4
Schedule of Estimated Lives and Amortization Adjustments for Purchase Differentials in Pratt's Investment in Sterling Products

Account	Maturity Date or Estimated Life	Purchase Differentials Subject to Straight-Line Amortization	Increase (Decrease) to Investment Income (4th quarter) 2005	2006	Remaining Unamortized Balance at 1/1/2007
Inventory	FIFO flow assumed: turnover rate is once every 8 months	$130,000	($48,750)	($81,250)	$0
Plant and Equipment (net)	Ten years remaining useful life assumed at October 1, 2005	$350,000	($8,750)	($35,000)	$306,250
Patent	Five years remaining useful life assumed at October 1, 2005	($168,600)	$8,430 (Note: Reduction of patent value reduces subsequent patent amortization, thereby increasing income)	$33,720	($126,450)
Long-Term Notes Payable	Maturity date is June 30, 2013 (31 quarters after October 1, 2005)	($136,400)	$4,400 (Note: Increasing the notes payable reduces subsequent interest expense, thereby increasing income)	$17,600	($114,400)
Net purchase differential to be amortized		$175,000			
Net purchase differential amortization			($44,670)	($64,930)	

As a result of the change in the assigned values to the assets and liabilities, there will also be a change in the cost allocations of those assets and liabilities to the income statement over their remaining lives. Remember that subsequent to acquisition, the subsidiary continues to measure and report net income using its historical cost as a basis for allocation to various expense accounts. Recorded depreciation expense by Sterling, for example, is based on $1,400,000, the recorded plant and equipment net book value, rather that the market value. For consolidated depreciation expense to reflect the historical cost to the consolidated entity, the purchase differential for identifiable assets must be amortized during the asset's remaining life.

The purchase differential amortizations for Sterling's identifiable assets and liabilities are presented in Illustration 3-4. Note that the second column of Illustration 3-4 presents information regarding the economic lives and maturity date assumptions. These assumptions provide the basis for Pratt's systematic allocation of the various purchase differentials to income.

As a result of guidelines set forth in FASB Statement No. 142 for all intangibles having an indefinite life, the $225,000 value assigned to goodwill is not amortized in a systematic manner,[3] and therefore it does not appear in Illustration 3-4. Rather, it is reduced in subsequent periods only when it is determined that the goodwill has been impaired. Detailed discussion of the assessment process for intangible asset impairment is beyond the scope of this chapter. For illustration purposes, the dollar amount of impairment, if any, will be given. The purchase differential amortization and/or goodwill impairment adjustment is recognized as a change in the investor's recognized percentage of the investee's reported net

---

[3] FAS No. 142 also requires that certain other intangible assets with an indefinite life be capitalized but not amortized systematically. Rather, such assets shall be tested for impairment and written down if an impairment is found to exist. In addition, if an intangible asset with an indefinite life is subsequently determined to have a finite remaining life, it is tested for impairment and then amortized over its estimated remaining life.

income. This amortization must also occur in the consolidated statements to adjust the individual line item in the consolidated income statement and balance sheet.

First Year of Ownership Pratt's journal entries at December 31, 2005, are based on the assumption that goodwill impairment did not occur in 2005. The following journal entries are prepared to record Pratt's equity in net income of Sterling and amortization of identifiable asset and liability purchase differentials (no dividend entry for 2005), resulting in a net *Investment Income* of $5,330:

Journal Entry—Pratt Corporation Books

Dec. 31, 2005	Investment in Sterling Products	50,000	
	Investment Income		50,000

To record investment income of $50,000 based on Sterling's reported fourth-quarter 2005 net income.

	Investment Income	44,670	
	Investment in Sterling Products		44,670

To recognize the net amortization of purchase differentials against Sterling's reported 2005 net income (see Illustration 3-4).

The $50,000 *Investment Income* recognized in the first journal entry is based on Sterling's reported net income, which has been calculated by Sterling using *its* book values as the basis for cost allocations. However, the market values rather than the book values of Sterling's assets and liabilities are relevant to Pratt. The purchase differential amortizations recognize the amount of change ($44,670) to Pratt's share of Sterling's net income. This adjustment to net income is relevant to Pratt's financial records because it reflects the amortization of the historical cost values *to Pratt*, that is, the market value of Sterling's assets and liabilities at the date of acquisition.

In this example the net adjustment to reported income is a reduction of $44,670 for the fourth quarter of 2005 and a reduction of $64,930 in 2006. These amortizations continue until the purchase differentials have been fully amortized. For example, the $350,000 purchase differential associated with plant and equipment is amortized over the 10-year remaining useful life on a straight-line basis. The quarterly amortization rate is $8,750 = $350,000/40 quarters.

Notice that the inventory write-off is assumed to be completed over the eight months beginning in October, 2005. The monthly amortization is $16,250 = $130,000/8 months. Market value in excess of book value for inventory is normally amortized over the period associated with the actual inventory turnover rate as a matter of practicality. Thus, the write-off period implicitly follows a FIFO flow even though many companies actually use a LIFO cost flow to account for inventory.

Illustration 3-5 presents the consolidation worksheet for Pratt and Sterling at December 31, 2005, under the $2,400,000 purchase price assumption.

Notice that three worksheet eliminations are prepared in the process of consolidating Pratt and Sterling in this example. The three worksheet eliminations are reproduced, in journal entry form, in Worksheet Eliminations 3-5. The beginning investment account is offset in worksheet elimination (1) against the net worth of Sterling. At the same time, the unamortized purchase differentials *as of October 1, 2005*, are recognized.

Worksheet elimination (2) adjusts the consolidated income statement to remove Pratt's recognition of Sterling's income net of purchase differential amortizations. The balances created as a result of Pratt's equity method journal entries are eliminated because

ILLUSTRATION 3-5
Worksheet for Consolidation of Pratt Corporation and Subsidiary, Sterling Products
100 Percent–Owned Subsidiary
Consolidation Subsequent to Acquisition Date
Price More Than Book Value
December 31, 2005

	Separate Financial Statements		Adjustments and Eliminations		Consolidated Financial Statements
	Pratt	Sterling	Debit	Credit	
Income Statement					
Sales	10,000,000	2,120,000			12,120,000
Investment Income, Sterling Products	5,330		(2) 5,330		0
Cost of Goods Sold	5,600,000	1,010,000	(3) 48,750		6,658,750
Selling Expenses	1,400,000	190,000			1,590,000
General and Administrative Expenses	2,330,000	750,000		(3) 4,080	3,075,920
Nonoperating Items (net)		30,000			30,000
Preacquisition Earnings			(1) 90,000		90,000
Net Income (to Statement of Retained Earnings)	675,330	140,000	144,080	4,080	675,330
Retained Earnings Statement					
Retained Earnings (1/1/2005)	2,300,000	160,000	(1) 160,000		2,300,000
Add: Net Income (from Income Statement)	675,330	140,000	(X) 144,080	(X) 4,080	675,330
Subtotal	2,975,330	300,000			2,975,330
Less: Dividends	(380,000)				(380,000)
Retained Earnings (12/31/2005 to Balance Sheet)	2,595,330	300,000	304,080	4,080	2,595,330
Balance Sheet					
Cash	900,000	240,000			1,140,000
Accounts Receivable (net)	1,800,000	270,000			2,070,000
Inventory (FIFO)	5,500,000	650,000	(1) 130,000	(3) 48,750	6,231,250
Other Current Assets	1,600,000				1,600,000
Total Current Assets	9,800,000	1,160,000			11,041,250
Plant and Equipment (net)	14,290,000	1,330,000	(1) 350,000	(3) 8,750	15,961,250
Patent		1,140,000	(3) 8,430	(1) 168,600	979,830
Investment in Sterling Products	2,405,330			(1) 2,400,000	0
				(2) 5,330	
Other Noncurrent Assets	1,400,000	2,290,000			3,690,000
Goodwill			(1) 225,000		225,000
Total Long-Term Assets	18,095,330	4,760,000			20,856,080
Total Assets	27,895,330	5,920,000			31,897,330
Current Liabilities	8,950,000	1,470,000			10,420,000
Long-Term Notes Payable		1,000,000	(3) 4,400	(1) 136,400	1,132,000
7% Bonds Payable (due 6/30/2013)	4,000,000				4,000,000
Less: Discount on Bonds Payable	(150,000)				(150,000)
8% Bonds Payable (due 12/31/2010)		1,500,000			1,500,000
Less: Discount on Bonds Payable		(100,000)			(100,000)
Total Liabilities	12,800,000	3,870,000			16,802,000

(Continued)

ILLUSTRATION 3-5 *Continued*

	Separate Financial Statements		Adjustments and Eliminations		Consolidated Financial Statements
	Pratt	Sterling	Debit	Credit	
Common Stock ($1 par):					
Pratt, 10,000,000 shares authorized, 6,000,000 shares issued and outstanding	6,000,000				6,000,000
Sterling, 1,000,000 shares authorized, issued and outstanding		1,000,000	(1) 1,000,000		0
Additional Paid-In Capital	6,500,000	750,000	(1) 750,000		6,500,000
Retained Earnings (12/31/2005 from Statement of Retained Earnings)	2,595,330	300,000	(X) 304,080	(X) 4,080	2,595,330
Total Stockholder's Equity	15,095,330	2,050,000			15,095,330
Total Liabilities and Stockholders' Equity	27,895,330	5,920,000			31,897,330
			2,771,910	2,771,910	

(1) To eliminate the subsidiary's date of acquisition stockholders' equity as well as parent's beginning of period Investment in Sterling Products account, and to establish the beginning of period purchase differentials.

(2) To eliminate the change in the Investment in Sterling Products account and the parent's Investment Income account.

(3) To amortize identifiable asset and liability purchase differentials for the current period.

Worksheet Eliminations 3-5—Journal Entry Form

(1)	Common Stock	1,000,000	
	Additional Paid-In Capital	750,000	
	Retained Earnings (January 1, 2005)	160,000	
	Preacquisition Earnings	90,000	
	Inventory	130,000	
	Plant and Equipment (net)	350,000	
	Goodwill	225,000	
	Patent		168,600
	Long-Term Notes Payable		136,400
	Investment in Sterling Products		2,400,000

To eliminate the subsidiary's date of acquisition stockholder's equity as well as the parent's beginning of period Investment in Sterling Products account, and to establish the beginning of period purchase differentials.

| (2) | Investment Income ($50,000 – $44,670) | 5,330 | |
| | Investment in Sterling Products | | 5,330 |

To eliminate the change in the Investment in Sterling Products account and the parent's Investment Income account.

(3)	Cost of Goods Sold	48,750	
	Long-Term Notes Payable	4,400	
	Patent	8,430	
	Inventory		48,750
	General and Administrative Expenses		4,080
	Plant and Equipment (net)		8,750

To amortize identifiable asset and liability purchase differentials for the current period.

Sterling's individual revenue and expense accounts are included on the consolidated income statement.

Worksheet elimination (3) amortizes the identifiable asset and liability purchase differentials for the quarter ending December 31, 2005, and adjusts specific income statement and balance sheet accounts for the amortizations. This worksheet elimination reflects the fact that the market values of the subsidiary's assets and liabilities are the appropriate values for the consolidated entity to use as a basis when making cost allocations for the consolidated financial statements. As a result of the combined effect of worksheet eliminations (1) and (3), the consolidated assets and liabilities reflect the December 31, 2005, unamortized purchase differentials. An analysis of the worksheet postings of purchase differential amortizations in worksheet elimination (3) of Illustration 3-5 is provided below:

Reduction of Investment Income for Inventory allocation to Cost of		($48,750)
Goods Sold		
Adjustments due to all other systematic amortizations:		
Plant and Equipment (net)	($8,750)	
Patent	8,430	
Long-Term Notes Payable	4,400	
Net decrease to General and Administrative Expenses		$4,080
Net adjustment to Investment Income		($44,670)

Second Year of Ownership Continuing with this example, and using data from Illustration 3-1, in 2006 Sterling reports $205,000 net income and declares $110,000 in dividends. Assume that one of Sterling's major customers recently signed a long-term contract with a competitor. As a result, forecasts of future sales and profitability have been revised downward. This is an event that prompts a goodwill impairment appraisal. The assessment suggests that goodwill has been impaired in the amount of $34,000. At the end of 2006, Pratt prepares the following three entries:

Journal Entry—Pratt Corporation Books

Dec. 31, 2006	Investment in Sterling Products	205,000	
	Investment Income		205,000
	To record equity in Sterling's 2006 net income.		
	Investment Income	98,930	
	Investment in Sterling Products ($64,930 + $34,000)		98,930
	To recognize the net amortization of purchase differentials (see Illustration 3-4) and goodwill impairment against Sterling's reported 2006 net income.		
	Cash	110,000	
	Investment in Sterling Products		110,000
	To reduce the investment by the equity distributed in the form of dividends during 2006.		

These entries have been posted to Pratt's books prior to preparation of the consolidating worksheet displayed in Illustration 3-6.

The consolidation of Pratt and Sterling at the end of 2006 requires three worksheet eliminations to be prepared in a manner similar to those in the 2005 worksheet. The Illustration 3-6 worksheet eliminations in journal entry form are presented in Worksheet Eliminations 3-6.

ILLUSTRATION 3-6
Worksheet for Consolidation of Pratt Corporation and Subsidiary, Sterling Products
100 Percent–Owned Subsidiary
Consolidation Subsequent to Acquisition Date
Price More Than Book Value
December 31, 2006

	Separate Financial Statements		Adjustments and Eliminations		Consolidated Financial Statements
	Pratt	Sterling	Debit	Credit	
Income Statement					
Sales	10,158,000	1,400,000			11,558,000
Nonoperating Items (net)	127,000				127,000
Investment Income, Sterling Products	106,070		(2) 106,070		0
Cost of Goods Sold	5,800,000	855,000	(3) 81,250		6,736,250
Selling Expenses	1,200,000	180,000			1,380,000
General and Administrative Expenses	2,400,000	160,000		(3) 16,320	2,543,680
Goodwill Impairment Loss			(3) 34,000		34,000
Net Income (to Statement of Retained Earnings)	991,070	205,000	221,320	16,320	991,070
Retained Earnings Statement					
Retained Earnings (1/1/2006)	2,595,330	300,000	(1) 300,000		2,595,330
Add: Net Income (from Income Statement)	991,070	205,000	(X) 221,320	(X) 16,320	991,070
Subtotal	3,586,400	505,000			3,586,400
Less: Dividends	(400,000)	(110,000)		(2) 110,000	(400,000)
Retained Earnings (12/31/2006 to Balance Sheet)	3,186,400	395,000	521,320	126,320	3,186,400
Balance Sheet					
Cash	90,000	150,000			240,000
Accounts Receivable (net)	2,000,000	300,000			2,300,000
Inventory (FIFO)	5,500,000	600,000	(1) 81,250	(3) 81,250	6,100,000
Other Current Assets	1,500,000				1,500,000
Total Current Assets	9,090,000	1,050,000			10,140,000
Plant and Equipment (net)	15,000,000	1,500,000	(1) 341,250	(3) 35,000	16,806,250
Patent		900,000	(3) 33,720	(1) 160,170	773,550
Investment in Sterling Products	2,401,400		(2) 3,930	(1) 2,405,330	0
Other Noncurrent Assets	1,935,000	1,950,000			3,885,000
Goodwill			(1) 225,000	(3) 34,000	191,000
Total Long-Term Assets	19,336,400	4,350,000			21,655,800
Total Assets	28,426,400	5,400,000			31,795,800
Current Liabilities	8,870,000	835,000			9,705,000
Long-Term Notes Payable		1,000,000	(3) 17,600	(1) 132,000	1,114,400
7% Bonds Payable (due 6/30/2013)	4,000,000				4,000,000
Less: Discount on Bonds Payable	(130,000)				(130,000)
8% Bonds Payable (due 12/31/2010)		1,500,000			1,500,000
Less: Discount on Bonds Payable		(80,000)			(80,000)
Total Liabilities	12,740,000	3,255,000			16,109,400

(Continued)

ILLUSTRATION 3-6 *Continued*

	Separate Financial Statements		Adjustments and Eliminations		Consolidated Financial Statements
	Pratt	Sterling	Debit	Credit	
Common Stock ($1 par):					
Pratt, 10,000,000 shares authorized, 6,000,000 shares issued and outstanding	6,000,000				6,000,000
Sterling, 1,000,000 shares authorized, issued and outstanding		1,000,000	(1) 1,000,000		0
Additional Paid-In Capital	6,500,000	750,000	(1) 750,000		6,500,000
Retained Earnings (12/31/2006 from Statement of Retained Earnings)	3,186,400	395,000	(X) 521,320	(X) 126,320	3,186,400
Total Stockholders' Equity	15,686,400	2,145,000			15,686,400
Total Liabilities and Stockholders' Equity	28,426,400	5,400,000	2,974,070	2,974,070	31,795,800

(1) To eliminate the subsidiary's beginning of current period stockholders' equity as well as the parent's beginning of period Investment in Sterling Products account, and to establish the beginning of period purchase differentials.

(2) To eliminate the change in the Investment in Sterling Products account, the parent's Investment Income account, and the subsidiary's dividends declared.

(3) To amortize identifiable asset and liability purchase differentials for the current period and recognize goodwill impairment.

The amounts included in the 2006 worksheet elimination (1) for the investment account and the unamortized purchase differential can be determined from the 2005 worksheet eliminations. The *Investment in Sterling Products* account can be determined from the beginning 2005 *Investment in Sterling Products* balance [worksheet elimination (1)] and the change in the investment account [worksheet elimination (2)] in Worksheet Eliminations 3-5. The purchase differential balances presented in worksheet elimination (1) for 2006 can be determined from worksheet eliminations (1) and (3) in 2005. The purchase differentials established in 2005 [worksheet elimination (1)] were partially amortized in worksheet elimination (3), resulting in the January 1, 2006, unamortized amounts presented in Worksheet Eliminations 3-6 [worksheet elimination (1)].

Worksheet elimination (2) offsets the change that occurred in the *Investment in Sterling Products* account during 2006. Note that the dividend declared ($110,000) in 2006 was greater than the net revenue recognized by Pratt ($106,070). As a result, worksheet elimination (2) contains a debit adjustment to the *Investment in Sterling Products* account to complete the elimination of the investment from the consolidated balance sheet.

Worksheet elimination (3) provides the 2006 amortization of the purchase differentials and the recognition of goodwill impairment. The eliminations appear in the appropriate lines of the consolidated income statement and balance sheet in lieu of the net recognition that had been included in Pratt's *Investment Income.*

Less Than 100 Percent–Owned Subsidiary

The final case presented in this chapter changes the example to an acquisition where Pratt pays 90 percent of Sterling's market value ($2,400,000 × .9 = $2,160,000) for 90 percent of Sterling's outstanding stock. As a result, the worksheet eliminations in this example will differ from the worksheet eliminations presented in Illustrations 3-5 and 3-6 in two ways. One difference is that the purchase differential recognition and the amortization of those

Worksheet Eliminations 3-6 — Journal Entry Form

(1)	Common Stock	1,000,000	
	Additional Paid-In Capital	750,000	
	Retained Earnings (January 1, 2006)	300,000	
	Inventory ($130,000 − $48,750)	81,250	
	Plant and Equipment (net) ($350,000 − $8,750)	341,250	
	Goodwill	225,000	
	Patent ($168,600 − $8,430)		160,170
	Long-Term Notes Payable ($136,400 − $4,400)		132,000
	Investment in Sterling Products		2,405,330
	($2,400,000 + $5,330)		

To eliminate the subsidiary's beginning of current period stockholders' equity as well as the parent's beginning of period Investment in Sterling Products account, and to establish the beginning of period purchase differentials.

(2)	Investment Income ($205,000 − $98,930)	106,070	
	Investment in Sterling Products	3,930	
	Dividends		110,000

To eliminate the change in the Investment in Sterling Products account, the parent's Investment Income account, and the subsidiary's dividends declared.

(3)	Cost of Goods Sold	81,250	
	Long-Term Notes Payable	17,600	
	Patent	33,720	
	Goodwill Impairment Loss	34,000	
	Inventory		81,250
	General and Administrative Expenses		16,320
	Plant and Equipment (net)		35,000
	Goodwill		34,000

To amortize identifiable asset and liability purchase differentials for the current period and recognize goodwill impairment.

differentials must be allocated between Pratt and the noncontrolling interest. The recognition of the entire purchase differential is required under the economic unit–full goodwill concept of consolidation. As a result, the purchase differentials initially established and the amortizations of identifiable asset and liability purchase differentials in subsequent periods are the same as those presented in Illustration 3-4.

The second difference is that the 10 percent noncontrolling interest in Sterling must be recognized in the current example. Recall from Chapter 2 that the value to be assigned to the noncontrolling interest is 10 percent of the imputed total market value of Sterling based on the price paid by Pratt for its 90 percent interest in Sterling, ($2,160,000/.90) (.10) = $240,000.

First Year of Ownership In this example, Pratt recognizes revenue equal to 90 percent of Sterling's net income. However, the income recognized by Sterling is based on the allocation of Sterling's book values for such items as *Inventory (Cost of Goods Sold)* and *Plant and Equipment (Depreciation Expense)*. As in the previous example, these amounts must be adjusted to reflect amortization of market value via purchase differential amortizations. Assuming a goodwill impairment adjustment is not necessary in 2005, Pratt makes the following entries on December 31, 2005:

Journal Entry—Pratt Corporation Books

Dec. 31, 2005	Investment in Sterling Products	45,000	
	Investment Income		45,000

To record 90 percent of Sterling's reported net income [($50,000 × .9) = $45,000].

	Investment Income	40,203	
	Investment in Sterling Products		40,203

To recognize the net amortization of purchase differentials against Sterling's reported net income. Purchase differential amortizations (see Illustration 3-4):

Inventory ($48,750 × .9)	$43,875
Plant and Equipment (net) ($8,750 × .9)	7,875
Patent ($8,430 × .9)	(7,587)
Long-Term Notes Payable ($4,400 × .9)	(3,960)
	$40,203

Illustration 3-7 presents the consolidating worksheet that combines Pratt and Sterling at December 31, 2005. The eliminations in journal entry form are presented in Worksheet Eliminations 3-7.

ILLUSTRATION 3-7
Worksheet for Consolidation of Pratt Corporation and Subsidiary, Sterling Products
90 Percent–Owned Subsidiary
Consolidation Subsequent to Acquisition Date
Price More Than Book Value
December 31, 2005

	Separate Financial Statements		Adjustments and Eliminations		Consolidated Financial Statements
	Pratt	Sterling	Debit	Credit	
Income Statement					
Sales	10,000,000	2,120,000			12,120,000
Investment Income, Sterling Products	4,797		(2) 4,797		0
Cost of Goods Sold	5,600,000	1,010,000	(3) 48,750		6,658,750
Selling Expenses	1,400,000	190,000			1,590,000
General and Administrative Expenses	2,330,000	750,000		(3) 4,080	3,075,920
Nonoperating Items (net)		30,000			30,000
Preacquisition Earnings			(1) 90,000		90,000
Consolidated Net Income					675,330
Noncontrolling Interest in Net Income of Sterling			(4) 533		533
Net Income (to Statement of Retained Earnings)	674,797	140,000	144,080	4,080	674,797
Retained Earnings Statement					
Retained Earnings (1/1/2005)	2,300,000	160,000	(1) 160,000		2,300,000
Add: Net Income (from Income Statement)	674,797	140,000	(X) 144,080	(X) 4,080	674,797
Subtotal	2,974,797	300,000			2,974,797
Less: Dividends	(380,000)				(380,000)
Retained Earnings (12/31/2005 to Balance Sheet)	2,594,797	300,000	304,080	4,080	2,594,797

(Continued)

ILLUSTRATION 3-7 *Continued*

	Separate Financial Statements		Adjustments and Eliminations				Consolidated Financial Statements
	Pratt	Sterling	Debit		Credit		
Balance Sheet							
Cash	1,140,000	240,000					1,380,000
Accounts Receivable (net)	1,800,000	270,000					2,070,000
Inventory (FIFO)	5,500,000	650,000	(1)	130,000	(3)	48,750	6,231,250
Other Current Assets	1,600,000						1,600,000
Total Current Assets	10,040,000	1,160,000					11,281,250
Plant and Equipment (net)	14,290,000	1,330,000	(1)	350,000	(3)	8,750	15,961,250
Patent		1,140,000	(3)	8,430	(1)	168,600	979,830
Investment in Sterling Products	2,164,797				(1)	2,160,000	0
					(2)	4,797	
Other Noncurrent Assets	1,400,000	2,290,000					3,690,000
Goodwill			(1)	225,000			225,000
Total Long-Term Assets	17,854,797	4,760,000					20,856,080
Total Assets	27,894,797	5,920,000					32,137,330
Current Liabilities	8,950,000	1,470,000					10,420,000
Long-Term Notes Payable		1,000,000	(3)	4,400	(1)	136,400	1,132,000
7% Bonds Payable (due 6/30/2013)	4,000,000						4,000,000
Less: Discount on Bonds Payable	(150,000)						(150,000)
8% Bonds Payable, (due 12/31/2010)		1,500,000					1,500,000
Less: Discount on Bonds Payable		(100,000)					(100,000)
Total Liabilities	12,800,000	3,870,000					16,802,000
Common Stock ($1 par):							
Pratt, 10,000,000 shares authorized, 6,000,000 *shares issued and outstanding*	6,000,000						6,000,000
Sterling, 1,000,000 shares authorized, *issued and outstanding*		1,000,000	(1)	1,000,000			0
Additional Paid-In Capital	6,500,000	750,000	(1)	750,000			6,500,000
Retained Earnings (12/31/2005 from Statement of Retained Earnings)	2,594,797	300,000	(X)	304,080	(X)	4,080	2,594,797
Noncontrolling Interest in Sterling					(1)	240,000	240,533
					(4)	533	
Total Stockholders' Equity	15,094,797	2,050,000					15,335,330
Total Liabilities and Stockholders' Equity	27,894,797	5,920,000					32,137,330
				2,771,910		2,771,910	

(1) To eliminate the subsidiary's date of acquisition stockholders' equity as well as the parent's beginning of period Investment in Sterling Products account, to establish the beginning of period purchase differentials, and to create the beginning of period Noncontrolling Interest in Sterling account.
(2) To eliminate the change in the Investment in Sterling Products account and the parent's Investment Income account.
(3) To amortize identifiable asset and liability purchase differentials for the current period.
(4) To recognize the change in the Noncontrolling Interest in Sterling account during the period.

The Illustration 3-7 worksheet eliminations may be compared to those in Illustration 3-5, which depicted the December 31, 2005, consolidation under the 100 percent–ownership assumption. Elimination (1) in Worksheet Eliminations 3-5 and 3-7 are identical with one exception. That is, elimination (1) in Worksheet Eliminations 3-7 eliminates the *Investment in Sterling Products* account for Pratt's 90 percent ownership interest and establishes

Worksheet Eliminations 3-7—Journal Entry Form

(1)	Common Stock	1,000,000	
	Additional Paid-In Capital	750,000	
	Retained Earnings (January 1, 2005)	160,000	
	Preacquisition Earnings	90,000	
	Inventory	130,000	
	Plant and Equipment (net)	350,000	
	Goodwill	225,000	
	Patent		168,600
	Long-Term Notes Payable		136,400
	Investment in Sterling Products		2,160,000
	Noncontrolling Interest in Sterling ($2,160,000/.90)(.10)		240,000

To eliminate the subsidiary's date of acquisition stockholders' equity as well as the parent's beginning of period Investment in Sterling Products account, to establish the beginning of period purchase differentials, and to create the beginning of period Noncontrolling Interest in Sterling account.

(2)	Investment Income ($45,000 – $40,203)	4,797	
	Investment in Sterling Products		4,797

To eliminate the change in the Investment in Sterling Products account and the parent's Investment Income account.

(3)	Cost of Goods Sold	48,750	
	Long-Term Notes Payable	4,400	
	Patent	8,430	
	Inventory		48,750
	General and Administrative Expenses		4,080
	Plant and Equipment (net)		8,750

To amortize identifiable asset and liability purchase differentials for the current period.

(4)	Noncontrolling Interest in Net Income of Sterling	533	
	($50,000 – $48,750 + $4,080)(.1)		
	Noncontrolling Interest in Sterling Products		533

To recognize the change in the Noncontrolling Interest in Sterling account during the period. Note that the $48,750 and $4,080 used in the calculation are the two income statement amortization adjustments in elimination (3) above. Alternatively, the net amount ($44,670) also appears in Illustration 3-4 as the net purchase differential amortization for the fourth quarter of the year.

The **Noncontrolling Interest in Net Income (Loss) of Subsidiary** is the prorated share of consolidated net income that increases (decreases) the equity interest of the noncontrolling stockholders.

Noncontrolling Interest in Sterling for the remaining 10 percent. The sum of these amounts ($2,160,000 + $240,000 = $2,400,000) is the same as the elimination of the *Investment in Sterling Products* in Worksheet Eliminations 3-5. The worksheet elimination (2) *Investment Income* amount in Illustration 3-7 is smaller than in Illustration 3-5 because only 90 percent of Sterling's net income and purchase differentials are recognized by Pratt. The Worksheet Eliminations 3-7 amortizations of the identifiable asset and liability purchase differentials in elimination (3) are the same as in Illustration 3-5. The *Noncontrolling Interest in Net Income of Sterling* is recognized in a new elimination, worksheet elimination (4). The **Noncontrolling Interest in Net Income (Loss) of Subsidiary** is the prorated share of consolidated net income that increases (decreases) the equity interest of the noncontrolling stockholders. It consists of 10 percent of Sterling's reported net income adjusted for purchase differential amortizations because the noncontrolling interest is created at the market value when applying the economic unit–full goodwill concept. Thus, the *Noncontrolling Interest in Net Income of Sterling* is the noncontrolling interest's percentage of Sterling's adjusted net income.

Second Year of Ownership

As with previous examples, Sterling reports $205,000 net income and declares $110,000 in dividends in 2006. Assume again that Sterling is required to recognize a $34,000 goodwill impairment loss. At December 31, 2006, Pratt's journal entries to reflect its share of Sterling's 2006 income and dividends are the following:

Journal Entry—Pratt Corporation Books

Dec. 31, 2006	Investment in Sterling Products	184,500	
	Investment Income		184,500

To record a 90 percent share of Sterling's reported net income [($205,000 × .9) = $184,500].

	Investment Income	89,037	
	Investment in Sterling Products		89,037

To recognize the amortization of purchase differentials and goodwill impairment against Starling's reported net income. Purchase differential amortizations (see Illustration 3-8):

Inventory ($81,250 × .9)	$73,125	
Plant and Equipment (net) ($35,000 × .9)	31,500	
Patent ($33,720 × .9)	(30,348)	
Long-Term Notes Payable ($17,600 × .9)	(15,840)	$58,437
Goodwill Impairment ($34,000 × .9)		30,600
		$89,037

	Cash	99,000	
	Investment in Sterling Products		99,000

To record 90 percent Sterling's 2006 dividends declared [($110,000 × .9) = $99,000].

Illustration 3-8 consolidates Pratt and Sterling after the above entries have been made by Pratt at December 31, 2006. The worksheet eliminations in journal entry form are presented in Worksheet Eliminations 3-8.

Worksheet elimination (1) removes Sterling's equity account balances and Pratt's investment account balance as of January 1, 2006, and establishes the purchase differentials and noncontrolling interest at their January 1, 2006, unamortized levels. These amounts can be determined by adjusting the purchase differential balance in worksheet elimination (1) in Worksheet Eliminations 3-7 for the change that occurred during 2005. For example, the purchase differential assigned to *Inventory* in Worksheet Eliminations 3-7 was $130,000. The *Cost of Goods Sold* amortization in elimination (3) in Worksheet Eliminations 3-7 was $48,750. As a result, the debit to the *Inventory* purchase differential in elimination (1) in Worksheet Eliminations 3-8 is ($130,000 − $48,750 = $81,250). Worksheet elimination (2) offsets the effects of Pratt's current year entries for its investment income (net of purchase differential amortizations and goodwill impairment recognition) and dividends. Worksheet elimination (3) provides the amortization of the purchase differential balances for the appropriate 2006 amortizations and the recognition of goodwill impairment. Worksheet elimination (4) establishes the change in noncontrolling interest

ILLUSTRATION 3-8
Worksheet for Consolidation of Pratt Corporation and Subsidiary, Sterling Products
90 Percent–Owned Subsidiary
Consolidation Subsequent to Acquisition Date
Price More Than Book Value
December 31, 2006

	Separate Financial Statements		Adjustments and Eliminations		Consolidated Financial Statements
	Pratt	Sterling	Debit	Credit	
Income Statement					
Sales	10,158,000	1,400,000			11,558,000
Nonoperating Items (net)	127,000				127,000
Investment Income, Sterling Products	95,463		(2) 95,463		0
Cost of Goods Sold	5,800,000	855,000	(3) 81,250		6,736,250
Selling Expenses	1,200,000	180,000			1,380,000
General and Administrative Expenses	2,400,000	160,000		(3) 16,320	2,543,680
Goodwill Impairment Loss			(3) 34,000		34,000
Consolidated Net Income					991,070
Noncontrolling Interest in Net Income of Sterling			(4) 10,607		10,607
Net Income (to Statement of Retained Earnings)	980,463	205,000	221,320	16,320	980,463
Retained Earnings Statement					
Retained Earnings (1/1/2006)	2,594,797	300,000	(1) 300,000		2,594,797
Add: Net Income (from Income Statement)	980,463	205,000	(X) 221,320	(X) 16,320	980,463
Subtotal	3,575,260	505,000			3,575,260
Less: Dividends	(400,000)	(110,000)		(2) 99,000	(400,000)
				(4) 11,000	
Retained Earnings (12/31/2006 to Balance Sheet)	3,175,260	395,000	521,320	126,320	3,175,260
Balance Sheet					
Cash	330,000	150,000			480,000
Accounts Receivable (net)	2,000,000	300,000			2,300,000
Inventory (FIFO)	5,500,000	600,000	(1) 81,250	(3) 81,250	6,100,000
Other Current Assets	1,489,000				1,489,000
Total Current Assets	9,319,000	1,050,000			10,369,000
Plant and Equipment (net)	15,000,000	1,500,000	(1) 341,250	(3) 35,000	16,806,250
Patent		900,000	(3) 33,720	(1) 160,170	773,550
Investment in Sterling Products	2,161,260		(2) 3,537	(1) 2,164,797	0
Other Noncurrent Assets	1,935,000	1,950,000			3,885,000
Goodwill			(1) 225,000	(3) 34,000	191,000
Total Long-Term Assets	19,096,260	4,350,000			21,655,800
Total Assets	28,415,260	5,400,000			32,024,800
Current Liabilities	8,870,000	835,000			9,705,000
Long-Term Notes Payable		1,000,000	(3) 17,600	(1) 132,000	1,114,400
7% Bonds Payable (due 6/30/2013)	4,000,000				4,000,000
Less: Discount on Bonds Payable	(130,000)				(130,000)
8% Bonds Payable (due 12/31/2010)		1,500,000			1,500,000
Less: Discount on Bonds Payable		(80,000)			(80,000)
Total Liabilities	12,740,000	3,255,000			16,109,400

(Continued)

ILLUSTRATION 3-8 *Continued*

	Separate Financial Statements		Adjustments and Eliminations		Consolidated Financial Statements
	Pratt	Sterling	Debit	Credit	
Common Stock ($1 par):					
Pratt, 10,000,000 shares authorized, 600,000,000 shares issued and outstanding	6,000,000				6,000,000
Sterling, 1,000,000 shares authorized, issued and outstanding		1,000,000	(1) 1,000,000		0
Additional Paid-In Capital	6,500,000	750,000	(1) 750,000		6,500,000
Retained Earnings (12/31/2006 from Statement of Retained Earnings)	3,175,260	395,000	(X) 521,320	(X) 126,320	3,175,260
Noncontrolling Interest in Sterling			(4) 393	(1) 240,533	240,140
Total Stockholders' Equity	15,675,260	2,145,000			15,915,400
Total Liabilities and Stockholders' Equity	28,415,260	5,400,000			32,024,800
			2,974,070	2,974,070	

(1) To eliminate the subsidiary's beginning of current period stockholders' equity as well as the parent's beginning of period Investment in Sterling Products account, to establish the beginning of period purchase differentials, and to create the beginning of period Noncontrolling Interest in Sterling account.

(2) To eliminate the change in the Investment in Sterling Products account and the parent's Investment Income account.

(3) To amortize identifiable asset and liability purchase differentials for the current period and recognize goodwill impairment.

(4) To recognize the change in the Noncontrolling Interest in Sterling account during the period.

during 2006. The change in noncontrolling interest results from the noncontrolling interest's share of the adjusted net income of Sterling and the dividends distributed to the noncontrolling interest. The net change in the noncontrolling interest balance on the consolidated financial statements at December 31, 2006, is calculated as follows:

Beginning Noncontrolling Interest balance			$240,533
Noncontrolling Interest percentage of Sterling's reported net income ($205,000 × .1)		20,500	
Purchase differential amortization			
Inventory ($81,250 × .1)	(8,125)		
Plant and Equipment (net) ($35,000 × .1)	(3,500)		
Patent ($33,720 × .1)	3,372		
Long-Term Notes Payable ($17,600 × .1)	1,760	(6,493)	
Goodwill impairment ($34,000 × .1)		(3,400)	10,607
Dividends to Noncontrolling Interest ($110,000 × .1)			(11,000)
Ending Noncontrolling Interest balance			$240,140

Remember that the noncontrolling interest balance never appears in either company's separate accounting records. The noncontrolling interest must be reconstructed each year in the consolidating worksheet via the worksheet eliminations. Similarly, both the appropriate subsidiary account balance market adjustments and goodwill must be reestablished each year to reflect unamortized purchase differentials because none of the purchase differentials are recorded or amortized on the subsidiary's or the parent's books as separate line items.

Worksheet Eliminations 3-8—Journal Entry Form		
(1) Common Stock	1,000,000	
Additional Paid-In Capital	750,000	
Retained Earnings (January 1, 2006)	300,000	
Inventory ($130,000 – $48,750)	81,250	
Plant and Equipment (net) ($350,000 – $8,750)	341,250	
Goodwill	225,000	
Patent ($168,600 – $8,430)		160,170
Long-Term Notes Payable ($136,400 – $4,400)		132,000
Investment in Sterling Products		2,164,797
($2,160,000 + $4,797)		
Noncontrolling Interest in Sterling		240,533
($240,000 + $533)		

To eliminate the subsidiary's beginning of current period stockholders' equity as well as the parent's beginning of period Investment in Sterling Products account, to establish the beginning of period purchase differentials, and to create the beginning of period Noncontrolling Interest in Sterling account.

(2) Investment Income ($184,500 – $89,037)	95,463	
Investment in Sterling Products	3,537	
Dividends ($110,000 × .9)		99,000

To eliminate the change in the Investment in Sterling Products account and the parent's Investment Income account.

(3) Cost of Goods Sold	81,250	
Long-Term Notes Payable	17,600	
Patent	33,720	
Goodwill Impairment Loss	34,000	
Inventory		81,250
General and Administrative Expenses		16,320
Plant and Equipment (net)		35,000
Goodwill		34,000

To amortize identifiable asset and liability purchase differentials for the current period and recognize goodwill impairment.

(4) Noncontrolling Interest in Net Income of Sterling	10,607	
[($205,000 – $81,250 – $34,000 + $16,320)(.1)]		
Noncontrolling Interest in Sterling	393	
Dividends ($110,000 × .1)		11,000

To recognize the change in the Noncontrolling Interest in Sterling account during the period.

USE OF A SEPARATE ACCUMULATED DEPRECIATION ACCOUNT

Continuing the alternate approach introduced in Chapter 2, if accumulated depreciation is reported as a separate line item in the consolidation worksheet, then elimination (1) in Worksheet Eliminations 3-8 is prepared with a credit to *Plant and Equipment* for $850,000 ($2,600,000 – $1,750,000) to adjust the account to market value at the acquisition date of Sterling. This amount of adjustment will be the same every period because the value at the acquisition date does not change. Also in elimination (1), a debit to *Accumulated Depreciation* for $1,191,250 is posted, reflecting the elimination of the original accumulated depreciation of $1,200,000 less the $8,750 amortization of purchase differential taken in the prior period. Posting the two separate line items results in the same net adjustment of $341,250 ($1,191,250 – $850,000) that appears using the net approach above in elimination (1) of Worksheet Eliminations 3-8. Elimination (3) is for the same amount, $35,000, but is posted to *Accumulated Depreciation.* Eliminations (2) and (4) are not affected. The alternate, separate accumulated depreciation account format presentations of eliminations (1) and (3) are presented below:

Worksheet Eliminations 3-8—Journal Entry Form
Separate Accumulated Depreciation Account Format

(1)	Common Stock	1,000,000	
	Additional Paid-In Capital	750,000	
	Retained Earnings (January 1, 2006)	300,000	
	Inventory ($130,000 – $48,750)	81,250	
	Accumulated Depreciation (1,200,000 – 8,750)	*1,191,250*	
	Goodwill	225,000	
	Plant and Equipment (2,600,000 – 1,750,000)		*850,000*
	Patent ($168,600 – $8,430)		160,170
	Long-Term Notes Payable ($136,400 – $4,400)		132,000
	Investment in Sterling Products		2,164,797
	($2,160,000 + $4,797)		
	Noncontrolling Interest in Sterling		240,533
	($240,000 + $533)		

To eliminate the subsidiary's beginning of current period stockholders' equity as well as the parent's beginning of period Investment in Sterling Products account, to establish the beginning of period purchase differentials, and to create the beginning of period Noncontrolling Interest in Sterling account.

(3)	Cost of Goods Sold	81,250	
	Long-Term Notes Payable	17,600	
	Patent	33,720	
	Goodwill Impairment Loss	34,000	
	Inventory		81,250
	General and Administrative Expenses		16,320
	Accumulated Depreciation		*35,000*
	Goodwill		34,000

To amortize identifiable asset and liability purchase differentials for the current period and recognize goodwill impairment.

SIMPLE VERSUS MODIFIED EQUITY METHOD

When applying the equity method to account for investments, investing companies may adopt one of three different forms. For internal recordkeeping some investors do not adjust their share of reported investee income by amortizing purchase differentials when calculating *Investment Income.* If the purchase differentials are not amortized on the separate parent company records, the method is referred to as the "simple equity method." Other companies follow the procedures illustrated in this chapter, where the equity method entries include the amortization of purchase differentials. The procedures followed in this chapter are known as the "modified equity method" (or partial equity method).

For consolidation purposes, whether or not the *Investment Income* is adjusted for amortization of purchase differentials has no impact on the calculation of consolidated net income. The *Investment Income* account balance, whether calculated by the parent using the simple or the modified equity method, must be eliminated when preparing consolidation worksheet elimination (2). Furthermore, appropriate amortizations of purchase differentials *must* occur in worksheet elimination (3). Thus, the form of the equity method used by the investing company for its separate accounting affects only the dollar amount of worksheet elimination (2)—not the accounts eliminated or the resulting consolidated net income reported.

A third form, the "complete equity method," is occasionally used internally by *investing* companies and is required when separate parent company (unconsolidated) financial statements are prepared and issued under GAAP.[4] Application of the complete equity method extends the modified equity method by also adjusting *Investment Income* for unrealized profits included in reported subsidiary net income resulting from intercompany transactions (discussed in Chapter 4). Throughout this text it is assumed that the parent company applies the modified equity method for internal accounting purposes.

SUMMARY

This chapter presented the consolidation worksheet and worksheet eliminations needed to consolidate a parent and its subsidiary subsequent to the date of acquisition. The chapter began with a 100 percent ownership acquired at book value. The restrictive assumptions were eliminated by first illustrating 100 percent acquisitions at a price greater than book value followed by acquisitions of less than 100 percent ownership acquired at an amount greater than book value. The final example resulted in four worksheet eliminations. This four-step elimination forms the "basic eliminations" for all consolidations. The summary format for these eliminations is:

(1) Eliminate the beginning of period investment account balance against the underlying beginning of period subsidiary stockholders' equity values that it represents as of that date; establish beginning of

period unamortized purchase differentials, including goodwill; establish the beginning of period noncontrolling interest balance.

(2) Eliminate the change that occurred in the investment account balance during the period.

(3) Charge current year write-off of amortizable purchase differentials established in (1) to the appropriate accounts on the consolidated income statement and record any necessary goodwill impairment.

(4) Recognize the change that occurs in the noncontrolling interest account during the period.

These worksheet eliminations are referred to as the "basic eliminations" because they are an integral part of all worksheet procedures subsequent to acquisition.

APPENDIX 3-1
ACCOUNTING FOR LONG-TERM INVESTMENTS

When a parent–subsidiary relationship arises, an investment account is carried on the books of the parent company. Accounting Principles Board Opinion Number 18 discusses

---

[4] **Accounting Principles Board Opinion**, No. 18, "The Equity Method of Accounting for Investments in Common Stock" (New York: American Institute of Certified Public Accountants, 1971), par. 19.

the appropriate method for accounting for such investments. Basically, two methods are appropriate, depending on the percentage of the investee owned by the investor. Normally, *the cost method is appropriate for investments in less than 20 percent* of the investee's common stock and *the equity method is applied to investments of 20 percent or more.* The overriding criteria for the method to be used is the investor's ability to exert "significant influence" over the investee regarding management policies and practices.[5] The 20 percent cutoff is arbitrary, so the choice of method is sometimes a matter of professional judgment. For example, if an investor can show that it cannot or does not exert "significant influence" over the investee even though the investor owns more than 20 percent of the investee's stock, it may use the cost method.

The Cost Method of Accounting for Investments

Under the cost method, the investment is normally reported at historical cost with fair value adjustments as required by FAS No. 115.[6] An entry is made to the investor's investment account only when the investment is sold, market adjustments are required, or a liquidating dividend is declared. Income from the investment is recognized as *Dividend Revenue* on the investor's books only when dividends are declared by the investee.

Assume that Brannon Corporation purchases 20 percent of Smith Corporation's common stock on January 1, 2005, for $25,000. The journal entry to record this transaction on Brannon's books is:

Journal Entry—Brannon Corporation Books

Jan. 1, 2005	Investment in Smith Corporation	25,000	
	Cash		25,000
	To record a 20 percent investment in Smith's common stock.		

Information for the next three years for Smith is provided in Illustration 3A-1.

ILLUSTRATION 3A-1
Financial Information for Smith Corporation
For the Three-Year Period Ending December 31, 2007

Date	Net Income Reported	Dividend Declared
December 31, 2005	$10,000	$4,000
December 31, 2006	14,000	5,000
December 31, 2007	12,000	8,500
Total	$36,000	$17,500
× 20% share	× .2	× .2
Brannon's share	**$7,200**	**$3,500**

Assuming that Brannon cannot exert "significant influence" over Smith, the cost method is appropriate. Under the cost method, Brannon records the dividends from Smith as they are declared. Assuming that dividends are declared and paid at December 31 of each year, Brannon's journal entries are:

[5] Ibid.

[6] **Statement of Financial Accounting Standards**, No. 115, "Accounting for Certain Investments in Debt and Equity Securities" (Norwalk, CT: Financial Accounting Standards Board, 1993).

Dec. 31, 2005   Cash   800
        Dividend Revenue   800
    To record the 2005 dividends from Smith: [(.2) ($4,000) = $800].

Dec. 31, 2006   Cash   1,000
        Dividend Revenue   1,000
    To record the 2006 dividends from Smith: [(.2) ($5,000) = $1,000].

Dec. 31, 2007   Cash   1,700
        Dividend Revenue   1,700
    To record the 2007 dividends from Smith: [(.2) ($8,500) = $1,700].

Using the cost method, the ledger balances for Brannon, at January 1, 2008, appear below:

Ledger of Brannon Corporation—Cost Method

Investment in Smith Corporation

January 2, 2005	25,000	
Balance	25,000	

Retained Earnings

	800	2005 Income
	1,000	2006 Income
	1,700	2007 Income
	3,500	Balance

The credit to *Retained Earnings* is made when the *Dividend Revenue* is closed each year. At the beginning of 2008, the balance of $3,500 in *Retained Earnings* is equal to Brannon's percentage of total earnings distributed since the acquisition.

THE EQUITY METHOD OF ACCOUNTING FOR INVESTMENTS

In that assets are generally accounted for using a method based on historical cost, the rationale for deciding when investors should use the equity method is important. The rationale lies in the notion of "control." While a standard of absolute control is not used, a subjectively determined degree of control called "significant influence" is the basis for application of the equity method. In theory, the larger the percentage of an investee that an investor owns, the greater the influence the investor is able to exercise over investee management policies.

A small percentage ownership in the investee's voting stock indicates that the investor is primarily interested in dividend revenue. This may imply that the investor is willing to take a somewhat passive role in the organization's operations and accept the dividends declared by the investee's board of directors. A large percentage ownership of the investee's voting stock is generally purchased for reasons other than dividend revenue. The investor may be attempting to accomplish such goals as ensuring input sources through vertical integration. The result would be the active participation by the investor in the investee's decision-making process.

The primary rationale for using the equity method comes from the argument that any investor who owns enough stock to exert "significant influence" over the investee should value the investment at the appropriate share of the net assets of the investee that underlie the investment. In theory, at some point along the continuum of increasing degree of control, the investor becomes able to influence the investee's management decisions. Therefore, the growth or decline in the net assets should be recorded immediately by the investor. Thus, when net assets grow, evidenced by reported net income of the investee, the investment balance should be increased. Similarly, when the investee's net assets shrink, evidenced by dividend distributions or net losses, the investment balance should be reduced.

A secondary and more practical rationale for the equity method is that an investor who can exert "significant influence" can potentially manipulate its own net income under the cost method. The investor would achieve this by influencing the timing of the dividend declaration by the investee, thereby controlling the timing of recognition of dividend revenue. Use of the equity method alleviates this problem.

Unlike the cost method, the equity method investment account balance is adjusted periodically for the investor's share of the subsidiary's (1) income reported (debit adjustment) and (2) dividends declared (credit adjustment). Furthermore, the market valuation procedures that are required for marketable securities do not have to be applied when using the equity method unless a permanent impairment of the investment value has occurred.[7]

The equity method assumes that the investor can exert "significant influence" over the investee. Thus, both the underlying value in the investment and the income from the investment are presumed to be partially a result of investor management decisions because of the "influence" exerted by the investor. APB Opinion No. 18 emphasizes this notion in the requirement that the investor recognize its share of the income generated by the investee in the same period that the investee records that income. That is, the investor recognizes its increase in investment value when the investee *earns* the income, not when it distributes the income (declares dividends). Under the equity method all dividends are viewed as a return *of* investment rather than return *on* investment to the investor (liquidating dividends).

Assume again that Brannon Corporation buys 20 percent of Smith Corporation's outstanding stock for $25,000. The acquisition entry is the same as it was under the cost method:

Journal Entry—Brannon Corporation Books

Jan. 1, 2005	Investment in Smith Corporation	25,000	
	Cash		25,000
	To record the purchase of 20 percent of Smith's common stock.		

This time it is assumed that Brannon has "significant influence" over Smith, and therefore, the equity method of accounting for the investment is appropriate.

In applying the equity method, one important factor is the price paid relative to the book value acquired. First, assume that the net book value of Smith Corporation is $125,000. A 20 percent acquisition for $25,000, therefore, represents a purchase price equal to 20 percent of book value. Using Illustration 3A-1 data again, Brannon's entries for 2005–2007 are:

---

[7] Ibid.

Journal Entries—Brannon Corporation Books

Dec. 31, 2005	Investment in Smith Corporation	2,000	
	Investment Income		2,000

To record Brannon's share of Smith's reported 2005 net income [(.2)($10,000) = $2,000].

	Cash	800	
	Investment in Smith Corporation		800

To record Brannon's share of dividends declared by Smith in 2005 [(.2)($4,000) = $800].

Dec. 31, 2006	Investment in Smith Corporation	2,800	
	Investment Income		2,800

To record Brannon's share of Smith's reported 2006 net income [(.2)($14,000) = $2,800].

	Cash	1,000	
	Investment in Smith Corporation		1,000

To record Brannon's share of dividends declared by Smith in 2006 [(.2)($5,000) = $1,000].

Dec. 31, 2007	Investment in Smith Corporation	2,400	
	Investment Income		2,400

To record Brannon's share of Smith's reported 2007 net income [(.2)($12,000) = $2,400].

	Cash	1,700	
	Investment in Smith Corporation		1,700

To record Brannon's share of dividends declared by Smith in 2007 [(.2)($8,500) = $1,700].

Using the equity method for the investment made at book value, the January 1, 2008, Brannon Corporation ledger balances are:

Ledger of Brannon Corporation—Equity Method

Investment in Smith Corporation

January 2, 2005	25,000		
Share of Smith's Reported 2005 Income	2,000	800	2005 Dividend
Share of Smith's Reported 2006 Income	2,800	1,000	2006 Dividend
Share of Smith's Reported 2007 Income	2,400	1,700	2007 Dividend
Balance	28,700		

Retained Earnings

	2,000	2005 Income
	2,800	2006 Income
	2,400	2007 Income
	7,200	Balance

The credit entry made to *Retained Earnings* each year is for the closing of the *Investment Income* account. The January 1, 2008, balance in *Retained Earnings* equals Brannon's share of total earnings *reported* by Smith since Brannon's acquisition. Furthermore, the investment account represents the initial investment plus the undistributed earnings (earnings less dividends) subsequent to the investment.

The equity method requires that any amount paid that differs from the book value of the net assets acquired should be (1) associated with differences between market values and book values of identifiable accounts and/or (2) associated with purchased goodwill. Purchase differentials (except goodwill and other intangible assets with indefinite lives) are amortized over the estimated remaining lives of the accounts involved. In the case of Smith and Brannon, the amortization of Smith's underlying premiums would cause *Investment Income* to be reduced. This reduction of *Investment Income* is justified because the amortization of assets (which is matched against reported revenue) as reported in Smith's income statement is calculated based on book values. Thus, Smith's reported net income is based entirely on Smith's **book values**. Brannon's investment in Smith, however, is 20 percent of the **market values** of Smith. This market value is the appropriate value to be amortized from Brannon's perspective. As a result, Brannon's appropriate share of income should reflect amortization of market values rather than book values matched against Smith's revenues. If the assets had been purchased directly by Brannon, the market values of individual net assets acquired would appear on Brannon's balance sheet in lieu of the *Investment in Smith Corporation* and, therefore, the annual amortization would have been based on the purchase price (market value at time of acquisition). The same amortization should be recognized even if the asset purchase is accomplished through the acquisition of another firm's stock because the economic substance of an acquisition of assets and an acquisition of stock is identical.

To illustrate, assume that the underlying book value of Smith at January 1, 2005, is $100,000 instead of $125,000. Also, assume the following book and market values for Smith:

Smith Corporation
Net Assets—Book Values and Market Values January 1, 2005

Assets	Book Value	Market Value
Current Assets	50,000	50,000
Fixed Assets	175,000	190,000
Total Assets	225,000	240,000
Liabilities		
Current Liabilities	30,000	30,000
Long-Term Liabilities	95,000	95,000
Total Liabilities	125,000	125,000
Net Assets	100,000	115,000

Brannon's investment of $25,000 for a 20 percent interest in Smith may be analyzed as follows:

Price paid for a 20 percent interest	$25,000
Less: 20 percent of book value acquired: (.2) ($100,000)	20,000
Purchase Differential	5,000
Less: 20 percent of market value in excess of book value for fixed assets: (.2) ($190,000 – $175,000)	3,000
Goodwill (price in excess of market value of net assets acquired)	$2,000

The analysis shows that the $5,000 premium paid over book value is identified as $3,000 excess paid for fixed assets and $2,000 for goodwill. Assuming that the fixed assets are being depreciated straight-line over 10 years, an adjustment is made by Brannon to its *Investment Income* each year until the fixed asset purchase differential is fully amortized. The adjustment converts the 20 percent share of reported net income based on Smith's book values to a 20 percent share of Smith's income based on market values. The actual entries on Brannon's books using the equity method are:

Journal Entries—Brannon Corporation Books

Dec. 31, 2005	Investment in Smith Corporation	2,000	
	Investment Income		2,000
	To record Brannon's share of Smith's reported 2005 net income [(.2)($10,000) = $2,000].		
	Investment Income	300	
	Investment in Smith Corporation		300
	To amortize the fixed asset purchase differential for 2005 [$3,000/10 years = $300].		
	Cash	800	
	Investment in Smith Corporation		800
	To record Brannon's share of dividends declared by Smith in 2005 [(.2)($4,000) = $800].		
Dec. 31, 2006	Investment in Smith Corporation	2,800	
	Investment Income		2,800
	To record Brannon's share of Smith's reported 2006 net income [(.2)($14,000) = $2,800].		
	Investment Income	300	
	Investment in Smith Corporation		300
	To amortize the fixed asset purchase differential for 2006.		
	Cash	1,000	
	Investment in Smith Corporation		1,000
	To record Brannon's share of dividends declared by Smith in 2006 [(2)($5,000) = $1,000].		
Dec. 31, 2007	Investment in Smith Corporation	2,400	
	Investment Income		2,400
	To record Brannon's share of Smith's reported 2007 net income: (.2)($12,000) = $2,400.		
	Investment Income	300	
	Investment in Smith Corporation		300
	To amortize the fixed asset purchase differential for 2007.		
	Cash	1,700	
	Investment in Smith Corporation		1,700
	To record Brannon's share of dividends declared by Smith in 2007 [(.2)($8,500) = $1,700].		

In this case, the ledgers of Brannon appear as follows at January 1, 2008:

Ledger of Brannon Corporation—Equity Method

Investment in Smith Corporation

January 2, 2005	25,000		
Share of Smith's Reported 2005 Income	2,000	300	2005 Amortization of Fixed Asset Purchase Differential
		800	2005 Dividend
Share of Smith's Reported 2006 Income	2,800	300	2006 Amortization of Fixd Asset Purchase Differentials
		1,000	2006 Dividend
Share of Smith's Reported 2007 Income	2,400	300	2007 Amortization of Fixed Asset Purchase Differential
		1,700	2007 Dividend
Balance	27,800		

Retained Earnings

1,700	2005 Income
2,500	2006 Income
2,100	2007 Income
6,300	Balance

COMPARISON OF RESULTS UNDER COST AND EQUITY METHODS

The results for the three years of accounting for the investment using the cost and equity methods are summarized in Illustration 3A-2 assuming $300 per year of amortized purchase differential.

ILLUSTRATION 3A-2
Investment and Retained Earnings
Using the Cost Versus the Equity Method on Investor's Books
for Brannon's Investment in Smith for the Years 2005–2007

	Investment Balance		
At End of Year	Cost Method	Equity Method	Cumulative Difference
2005	25,000	25,900	900
2006	25,000	27,400	2,400
2007	25,000	27,800	2,800

	Annual Retained Earnings Effect		
At End of Year	Cost Method	Equity Method	Cumulative Difference
2005	800	1,700	900
2006	1,000	2,500	2,400
2007	1,700	2,100	2,800

The cumulative difference between using the cost and equity methods is the same for the *Investment* and the *Retained Earnings* accounts. The similarity is due to the way in which each account balance evolves over time. Using the cost method, the *Investment* account does not change, while the *Retained Earnings* account increases by the **distributed** portion of the income from Smith (i.e., the dividends). Under the equity method, Brannon's *Investment* account increases by the net of Brannon's share of Smith's reported income less both purchase differential amortization and dividends. Meanwhile, under the equity method the *Retained Earnings* increases by the net investment income. The effects are summarized below:

	Investment	Retained Earnings
Cost	No Change	Increased by Dividends
Equity	Increased by Net Investment Income – Dividends	Increased by Net Investment Income
Equity Method Account Change in Excess of Cost Method Change	Net Investment Income – Dividends	Net Investment Income – Dividends

Therefore, the cumulative difference in both the *Investment* account and the *Retained Earnings* account resulting from the difference in methods is the investor's share of **undistributed** net income generated since acquisition (Net Investment Income – Dividends).

An example of a common application of this relationship is when an investor must convert from the cost to the equity method. APB No. 18 states that when a firm acquires enough stock in an investee that the investor must convert from the cost to the equity method, the equity method must be applied retroactively to the actual percentage of investment previously held.

Assume that on January 3, 2008, Brannon acquires an additional 60 percent of Smith's stock and that Brannon previously had been using the cost method to account for its 20 percent holdings. Retroactive application requires that an adjustment be made to convert to the equity method as of the beginning of the year when the equity method is adopted. The adjusting entry and supporting calculation are given below for the Brannon and Smith case, where the original purchase was at a price greater than book value:

Jan. 3, 2008   Investment in Smith Co.   2,800
                   Retained Earnings   2,800
               To record retroactive conversion to the equity method as of the beginning of 2008 as follows:

$$\text{Net Adjustment} = \left[\begin{array}{c} \text{Share of Cumulative} \\ \text{Net Income} \\ \text{Reported by} \\ \text{Subsidiary} \end{array} - \begin{array}{c} \text{Parent Share of} \\ \text{Cumulative Purchase} \\ \text{Differential} \\ \text{Amortization} \end{array} \right] - \begin{array}{c} \text{Parent's Share} \\ \text{of Cumulative} \\ \text{Dividends} \end{array}$$

$$= [.2(\$10{,}000 + \$14{,}000 + \$12{,}000) - 3(\$300)] - \$3{,}500$$

$$= \$2{,}800$$

After the entry is made, the equity method can be applied for 2008. An additional entry may have to be made to reverse out any fair value adjustments that had been recorded previously. This conversion approach also will be a convenient tool in Appendix 3-2 when consolidation procedures are examined for cases in which the parent accounts for its investment in the subsidiary using the cost method.

APPENDIX 3-2
COST METHOD CONSOLIDATION PROCEDURES

As a matter of internal corporate bookkeeping convenience, a number of parent companies use the cost method of accounting for investments internally, even though external reporting requires use of the equity method. When the cost method is used, the *Investment in Subsidiary* account balance is not revised over time, and the only income reported is dividend income.

To consolidate when the parent is using the cost method, some modifications of the four basic worksheet eliminations developed in this chapter are required. Recall from the body of the chapter that worksheet elimination (1) removes the *Investment in Subsidiary* balance that existed at the beginning of the year. Conversion of the cost method balance to an equity method balance on the worksheet adjusts the investment balance so that the normal format of worksheet elimination (1) can be used.

Appendix 3-1 discussed the rationale for converting from the cost to equity methods in accounting for investments. To convert from cost to equity, the parent company's *Investment in Subsidiary* and *Retained Earnings* accounts must be adjusted to reflect the parent's share of net undistributed income of the subsidiary from the date of acquisition *to the first day of the current year.* The calculation is:

$$\text{Net Adjustment} = \begin{bmatrix} \text{Share of Cumulative} \\ \text{Net Income} \\ \text{Reported by} \\ \text{Subsidiary} \end{bmatrix} - \begin{bmatrix} \text{Parent Share of} \\ \text{Cumulative Purchase} \\ \text{Differential} \\ \text{Amortization} \end{bmatrix} - \begin{bmatrix} \text{Parent's Share} \\ \text{of Cumulative} \\ \text{Dividends} \end{bmatrix}$$

Acquisition of Less Than 100 Percent With Positive Goodwill

Assume that Pratt uses the cost method to account for its investment in Sterling. Using the current chapter example where Pratt purchases 90 percent of Sterling's stock for more than book value ($2,160,000) to illustrate the cost to equity method adjustment, the following calculations are made to determine the size of the adjustment that must be made to consolidate Pratt and Sterling at the end of 2006:

	2005
Pratt's Share of Reported Sterling Net Income in 2005	$45,000
Purchase Differential Amortization	(40,203)
Pratt's Share of Dividend Declared by Sterling in 2005	(0)
Net adjustment to Investment in Sterling and Retained Earnings as of Jan. 1, 2006	$ 4,797

The special elimination to be posted to the worksheet to consolidate Pratt and Sterling at the end of 2006 is labeled (1X) and appears as follows:

(1X)	Investment in Sterling Products	4,797	
	Retained Earnings (January 1, 2006)		4,797
	To adjust the January 1, 2006, balances by ($45,000 − $40,203) − $0 to reflect the equity method.		

Notice that this elimination converts the *Investment in Sterling Products* balance from $2,160,000 to $2,164,797, the amount that appears in worksheet elimination (1) in Worksheet Eliminations 3-8, the final case presented in the body of the chapter. Thus, by first preparing (1X), as of January 1, 2006, Pratt's balances are effectively converted to the equity method, and worksheet elimination (1) does not need to be amended. If consolidated financial statements are prepared at the end of 2006, for example, then the adjustment would be prepared to reflect the cumulative net income, amortizations, and dividends from the date of acquisition up to January 1, 2006.

The form of worksheet elimination (2) in Worksheet Eliminations 3-8 now appears as follows:

(2)	Dividend Revenue	99,000	
	Dividends ($110,000 × .9)		99,000
	To eliminate Dividend Revenue recorded by Pratt during 2006 against the dividends account of Sterling.		

This eliminates the only existing account in Pratt's income statement (under the cost method) relating to current year Sterling Products activity.

In summary, if the parent company uses the cost method for internal bookkeeping for a subsidiary, the consolidation procedures [worksheet eliminations (1)–(4)] can be followed as presented in Chapter 3 with modifications. For consolidation at the end of the first year, the only modification is that worksheet elimination (2) must eliminate the *Dividend Revenue* reported by the parent against the related subsidiary dividend account. In years subsequent to the year of acquisition, two modifications must be made. First, the (1X) cumulative adjustment must be made to convert the parent company's *Investment in Subsidiary* and *Retained Earnings* balances from cost to equity method as of the first day of the current reporting period. Then worksheet elimination (2), in its revised form, is prepared to eliminate the current year *Dividend Revenue* effects of the cost method being applied.

Acqusition of Less Than 100 Percent With Negative Goodwill

Acquisition at a price less than appraisal value creates special problems when the cost method is employed by the parent company in accounting for its investment in a subsidiary. Recall the negative goodwill case developed in Chapter 2, wherein Pratt paid $1,870,200 for a 90 percent share of Sterling's common stock. Using the cost method, Pratt likely would record only the actual cost of its investment as follows:

Journal Entry—Pratt Corporation Books

Oct. 1, 2005	Investment in Sterling Products	1,870,200	
	Cash		1,870,200
	To record the acquisition of 90 percent Sterling's stock at $87,300 below appraised value of the underlying identifiable net assets: ($2,175,000 – $2,078, 000)(.9) = $87,300.		

The $1,870,200 price results in negative goodwill of $87,300 as analyzed in Illustration 2-13. The extraordinary gain of $87,300 is not booked by Pratt unless there is a need to issue separate financial statements of the parent company. Further, the normal carrying value of the investment will remain at $1,870,200 indefinitely.

Year of Acquisition When the cost method is used and negative goodwill arises, the effect on the form of the consolidation eliminations is unique in the year of acquisition. Note that Pratt has not recorded the extraordinary gain separately on its books and the investment carrying value is less than Sterling's appraisal value. In this case, the special elimination either at the date of acquisition or at any time that consolidation occurs during the year of acquisition must now take the following form:

(IX)	Investment in Sterling [($2,175,000 − $2,078,000)(.9)]	87,300	
	Extraordinary Gain on Acquisition of Sterling Products		87,300

To recognize the extraordinary gain associated with the negative goodwill in the price paid for Sterling, and to adjust the carrying value of the investment account to its equivalent value under the equity method.

Once the account balances are converted to their equity method equivalents in worksheet elimination (IX) above, eliminations at the date of acquisition (October 1,2005) can be prepared as they were in Illustration 2-14. To consolidate at the end of 2005, the same eliminations as were prepared at the date of acquisition plus appropriate eliminations (2) (for dividend revenue if any), (3), and (4) would be necessary.

Years Subsequent to the Year of Acquisition The special elimination (IX) is prepared each year subsequent to the year of acquisition in the same format whether there is positive or negative goodwill at the acquisition date. The dollar amount of the adjustment to the investment account and to retained earnings, however, is larger in the negative goodwill case because using the cost method Pratt would not have booked the extraordinary gain resulting from the negative goodwill. In the 90 percent acquisition for $1,870,200 case, the cumulative effect of using the cost method at the end of 2005 is the $4,797 calculated above in the positive goodwill case plus the $87,300 of negative goodwill. When Pratt and Sterling are consolidated at the end of 2006, the special worksheet elimination (IX) to adjust the January 1, 2006, investment and retained earnings balances is now calculated as follows:

Extraordinary Gain not recognized by Pratt	$87,300
Cumulative adjustment to convert to equity method as of January 1, 2006	4,797
Total adjustment to *Investment in Sterling* and *Retained Earnings*	$92,097

and the (IX) consolidation elimination at December 31, 2006, would include

(IX)	Investment in Sterling ($87,300 + $4,797)	92,097	
	Retained Earnings (January 1, 2006)		92,097

To adjust the investment account to the equivalent values under the equity method.

Worksheet eliminations (1), (3), and (4) would be the same as they would be under the equity method, and in the Pratt and Sterling case, worksheet elimination (2) for 2006 would now be

| (2) Dividend Revenue | 99,000 | |
| Dividends ($110,000 × .9) | | 99,000 |

To eliminate Dividend Revenue recorded by Pratt during 2006 against the dividends account of Sterling.

QUESTIONS

3-1. Shawn Robinson and Mary McDonald are owners of a closely held corporation. They recently acquired 80 percent of another corporation, and they are discussing how the new company will be reported as part of their corporation's financial statements. Shawn would like to apply the cost method, but Mary says that the equity method is required. Prepare a memo clarifying this issue for Shawn and Mary.

3-2. (Refer to the information in Question 3-1.) Shawn and Mary have approached their banker about obtaining a $10 million line of credit for their corporation. Their banker informs them that bank policy requires that all loan applications for more than $5 million must be accompanied by audited financial statements with full application of GAAP. The bank wants both separate parent company financial statements and consolidated financial statements to be prepared. Provide authoritative support to justify the required method of accounting for the investment in subsidiary account in the separate parent company financial statements. (*Hint:* Search APB No. 18.)

3-3. What are the three equity method journal entries typically recorded by a parent?

3-4. Why is the investment in subsidiary account completely eliminated when preparing the consolidation worksheet in periods subsequent to acquisition?

3-5. Why is the investment income account completely eliminated when preparing the consolidation worksheet in periods subsequent to acquisition?

3-6. The board of directors has asked you to make a brief presentation explaining the reason consolidated financial statements are prepared as the company's primary financial statements. During the presentation a new board member asks whether the income figure calculated is different for consolidated financial statements when compared to the income figure calculated when using the equity method. The board member then goes on to ask why consolidated statements must be prepared, since they are more expensive both in time and money. How do you respond to this board member? (*Hint:* Search SFAS No. 94 to support your response.)

3-7. It takes more than one worksheet elimination to completely remove the investment in subsidiary account when preparing the consolidation worksheet in periods subsequent to acquisition. Which worksheet eliminations accomplish that task? What part of the investment balance is eliminated in each of the worksheet eliminations?

3-8. Jason Perry is helping prepare his first set of consolidated financial statements. He notices that consolidated net income is the same as the parent's net income. During lunch he asks, "Why is the consolidation process necessary if we end up in the same place we started?" How do you respond?

3-9. Albert Hall and Jessica Morse are new members of the board of directors. As such, they are attending a one-day workshop to become familiar with the corporation's financial reporting. Part of the afternoon discussion includes the consolidated financial statements. Albert and Jessica comment that they do not understand why the dividends received from the subsidiary are not included in the consolidated financial statements. Prepare a response to this comment.

3-10. Why are purchase differentials amortized subsequent to the acquisition of a subsidiary?

3-11. A substantial amount of goodwill has been calculated as part of the analysis of the price paid by Walters Company to acquire controlling interest in Givens Corporation. Your supervisor, the controller of Walters, explains to you that he has recently read of new FASB standards regarding accounting for goodwill. He has requested that you write a memo to him outlining the required accounting treatment for the goodwill subsequent to the acquisition providing appropriate authoritative support. (*Hint:* Search FASB No. 142 for support.)

3-12. High Plains Airlines has recently been established, with headquarters in North Platte, Nebraska. Other than airplanes, its major asset is landing rights (rights to use of specific gates) that it acquires from various airports. A few of these contracts give permanent rights to High Plains for one fee paid in advance. Other airports grant rights for 10-year periods (fee paid each 10 years) on a renewable basis. Both types of contracts create intangible assets. FASB No. 142, however, requires different treatment of the two types of contracts. Write a memo that explains the different treatment for the different types of intangibles belonging to High Plains. (*Hint:* Search FASB No. 142 for "indefinite life intangibles.")

3-13. Marsha Carroll is a new corporate accountant attending a training session. This particular session is addressing the consolidated financial statements. Marsha states that she does not understand what occurs with purchase differential amortizations. She states, "I understand that they are part of the journal entries on the parent's books and that they are removed in one of the worksheet eliminations. What I do not understand is why they are put back on the consolidated financial statements in another worksheet elimination. Why can't they just be left alone?" Prepare a response to Marsha's question.

3-14. Jim Philips is attending a training session for the controller's staff. The topic of discussion is purchase differential amortizations. Jim asks, "Why are purchase differentials created on the consolidated balance sheet for the same dollar amounts for different parent ownership interest levels in the subsidiary?" Find the authoritative support in FARS to answer Jim's question. (*Hint:* Search the FASB Exposure Draft and/or Standard on, "Consolidation Procedures.")

MULTIPLE CHOICE

3-1. Atkins Enterprises purchases 100 percent of Baker Company at January 1, 2005. One purchase differential was created as a result of the acquisition. Plant assets were appraised at $600,000 more than book value. What is the purchase differential amortization in 2005 if plant assets have an estimated remaining life of 10 years?

  a. $45,000

  b. $0

  c. $60,000

  d. $100,000

3-2. Richardson acquired 100 percent of Smith Corporation at January 1, 2005. At that date the patent controlled by each company had the following book value, appraised value, and estimated remaining economic life.

	Richardson			Smith	
Book	Market	Life	Book	Market	Life
$56,000	$84,000	7 years	$25,000	$35,000	5 years

What is the balance in the patent account on the consolidated balance sheet at December 31, 2005?

  a. $100,000

  b. $76,000

  c. $92,000

  d. $68,000

3-3. PH Corporation purchased 80 percent of Classic Pool Supply's stock at January 1, 2005. At that time, equipment of Classic Pool had book and market values of $69,000 and $93,000, respectively. Equipment has a remaining life of three years. What is the amount of purchase differential amortization recognized in 2005?

  a. $6,400

  b. $23,000

  c. $8,000

  d. $24,800

3-4. Denver, Inc. acquired 80 percent of Colorado Corporation at January 1, 2005. At that date the equipment owned by each company had the following book value, appraised value, and estimated remaining economic life.

	Denver			Colorado	
Book	Market	Life	Book	Market	Life
$88,000	$96,000	8 years	$48,000	$72,000	6 years

What is the balance in the equipment account on the consolidated balance sheet at December 31, 2005?

  a. $144,000

  b. $117,000

  c. $133,000

  d. $137,000

3-5. Drill Corporation acquired 100 percent of Bit Tools at January 1, 2005, for $350,000. At that date, Bit Tools had a net book value of $300,000. Purchase differentials of $25,000, $35,000, and $45,000 were assigned to inventory, land, and equipment, respectively. The following book and market values exist for all of Bit Tools' noncurrent assets at the acquisition date.

	Book Value	Market Value
Land	$65,000	$100,000
Equipment	$155,000	$200,000
Buildings	$700,000	$700,000

Assuming the equipment has an estimated remaining life of 10 years, what is the amount of purchase differential allocated to equipment at January 1, 2005, and December 31, 2005?

	January 1	December 31
a.	$45,000	$40,500
b.	$45,000	$41,600
c.	$34,000	$30,600
d.	$34,000	$29,500

3-6. Peasant purchased 80 percent of Slave at the beginning of 2005 for book value and used the equity method to account for its investment. Peasant's investment account balance at the beginning of 2006 was $581,000. During 2006 Slave reports a net loss of $60,000 yet pays dividends totaling $25,000. Calculate the balance in the Investment in Peasant account at the end of 2006.

a. $496,000

b. $513,000

c. $553,000

d. $561,000

Items 7–10 are based on the following information for Perch and Salmon: Perch acquired 70 percent of Salmon for $875,000 at the beginning of 2005. The book value of Salmon at that date was $1,000,000, and the entire purchase differential was identified as goodwill. The reported net income for Perch during 2005 and 2006 was $46,000 and $54,000, respectively, while the dividends declared during the two years were $30,000 per year.

3-7. How much noncontrolling interest would be reported in the 2006 end-of-year consolidated balance sheet?

a. $300,000

b. $312,000

c. $387,000

d. $903,000

3-8. How much Investment Income would Perch record during 2006 presuming there is no goodwill impairment?

a. $37,800

b. $28,000

c. $70,000

d. $12,000

3-9. At the end of 2005, what balance would appear in Perch's Investment in Salmon account presuming there is no goodwill impairment?

a. $799,000

b. $886,200

c. $877,200

d. $951,000

3-10. At the end of 2006, it is determined that 40 percent of the goodwill is impaired and is written off. What is the Investment in Salmon balance at the end of 2006?

a. $971,000

b. $917,000

c. $833,000

d. $789,000

EXERCISES

Consolidation worksheets for exercises that require a worksheet can be found at the book companion website.

EXERCISE 3-1	Purchase differential amortization on parent's books and consolidated income statement, 100 percent acquisition
EXERCISE 3-2	Extension of Exercise 3-1, purchase differential amortization on parent's books and consolidated income statement, 80 percent acquisition
EXERCISE 3-3	Purchase differential amortization on parent's books and consolidated income statement, 60 percent acquisition, negative goodwill
EXERCISE 3-4	Extension of Exercise 3-3, purchase differential amortization on parent's books and consolidated income statement, 100 percent acquisition, negative goodwill
EXERCISE 3-5	Investment account balance for 100 percent and 75 percent acquisition, three years
EXERCISE 3-6	Investment income, investment account balance, purchase differential amortization for 80 percent and 100 percent acquisition, three years, goodwill impairment
EXERCISE 3-7	Investment income, investment account balance for 60 percent ownership, three years, goodwill, goodwill impairment
EXERCISE 3-8	Extension of Exercise 3-7, investment income, investment account balance for 100 percent ownership, three years, negative goodwill
EXERCISE 3-9	Equity method journal entries, no purchase differentials, worksheet eliminations for change in investment and change in noncontrolling interest
EXERCISE 3-10	Equity method journal entries, 70 percent ownership, purchase differentials, worksheet eliminations, consolidation worksheet
EXERCISE 3-11	Equity method journal entries, 75 percent ownership, purchase differentials, negative goodwill, worksheet eliminations, consolidation worksheet
EXERCISE 3-12	Equity method journal entries, 60 percent ownership, purchase differentials, negative goodwill, worksheet eliminations for change in investment and change in noncontrolling interest, consolidation worksheet

NOTE: Exercises 3-13 and 3-14 repeat Exercises 3-10 and 3-11 using a separate accumulated depreciation account.

EXERCISE 3-13   Equity method journal entries, 70 percent ownership, purchase differentials, worksheet eliminations with separate accumulated depreciation account, consolidation worksheet

EXERCISE 3-14   Equity method journal entries, 75 percent ownership, purchase differentials, negative goodwill, worksheet eliminations with separate accumulated depreciation account, consolidation worksheet

NOTE: Exercises 3-15, 3-16, and 3-17 repeat Exercises 3-10, 3-11, and 3-12 with the parent company using the cost method to account for the investment.

EXERCISE 3-15   Cost method journal entries, 70 percent ownership, purchase differentials, worksheet eliminations, consolidation worksheet

EXERCISE 3-16   Cost method journal entries, 75 percent ownership, purchase differentials, negative goodwill, worksheet eliminations

EXERCISE 3-17   Cost method journal entries, 60 percent ownership, purchase differentials, negative goodwill, worksheet eliminations for change in investment and change in noncontrolling interest

EXERCISE 3-1   Schneider Corporation purchased 100 percent of the outstanding stock of Kane, Incorporated on January 1, 2005, for $2,590,000. The following information existed for Kane at the acquisition date.

	Book Value	Market Value
Cash and Receivables	$90,000	$90,000
Inventory	390,000	390,000
Plant Assets (net)	2,220,000	2,880,000
Current Liabilities	(150,000)	(150,000)
Long-Term Debt	(620,000)	(620,000)
Stockholders' Equity	(1,750,000)	

At the acquisition date, Schneider assigns a six-month amortization period to the inventory and a five-year amortization period to the plant assets.

Required:
A. What is the amount of purchase differential amortization included in the calculation of Investment Income on Schneider's books in 2005 and 2006?
B. What amounts appear on the income statement portion of the 2005 consolidation worksheet with regard to the purchase differential amortizations?

EXERCISE 3-2   Use the information from Exercise 3-1 but assume that Schneider Corporation purchased 80 percent of Kane for $2,072,000.

Required:
A. What is the amount of purchase differential amortization included in the calculation of Investment Income on Schneider's books in 2005 and 2006?
B. What amounts appear on the income statement portion of the 2005 consolidation worksheet with regard to the purchase differential amortizations?

EXERCISE 3-3   SlipStream Airplane Corporation purchased 60 percent of the outstanding stock of Krash and Burn Aviation, Incorporated on January 1, 2005, for $630,000. The following information existed for Krash and Burn at the date of acquisition.

	Book Value	Market Value
Cash and Receivables	$50,000	$50,000
Inventory	150,000	150,000
Plant Assets (net)	850,000	1,080,000
Other Noncurrent Assets	120,000	120,000
Current Liabilities	(40,000)	(40,000)
Long-Term Debt	(220,000)	(220,000)
Stockholders' Equity	(870,000)	

SlipStream

At the acquisition date, ~~Schneider~~ assigns a remaining estimated life of 10 months to the inventory, 10 years to the plant assets, and 3 years to the other noncurrent assets.

Required:
A. What is the amount of purchase differential amortization included in the calculation of Investment Income on SlipStream's books in 2005?
B. What amounts appear on the income statement portion of the 2005 consolidation worksheet with regard to the purchase differential amortizations?

EXERCISE 3-4   Use the information from Exercise 3-3 but assume that SlipStream purchases 100 percent of Krash and Burn for $1,050,000.

Required:
A. What is the amount of purchase differential amortization included in the calculation of Investment Income on SlipStream's books in 2005?
B. What amounts appear on the income statement portion of the 2005 consolidation worksheet with regard to the purchase differential amortizations?

EXERCISE 3-5   Griffin Corporation purchased 100 percent of Harper, Incorporated on June 1, 2005, for $2,276,000, the underlying book value of Harper. The following table presents the income earned by Harper and the dividends paid by Harper since the date of acquisition.

	Income	Dividends
June 1–December 31, 2005	$175,000	$60,000
2006	230,000	75,000
2007	190,000	90,000

Required:
A. Determine the Investment in Harper account balance at December 31, 2005, 2006, and 2007.
B. Determine the Investment in Harper account balance at December 31, 2005, 2006, and 2007 assuming Griffin paid $1,707,000 for a 75 percent–ownership interest in Harper.

EXERCISE 3-6   Dreamworld, Incorporated purchased 80 percent of Pocahontas Enterprises on February 1, 2005, for $6,875,000. At that time, Pocahontas had inventory appraised at $300,000 more than book value and plant assets appraised at $562,500 more than book value. Dreamworld estimated that it paid $384,000 goodwill for the 80 percent ownership acquired. The estimated remaining lives were eight months and five years for inventory and plant assets, respectively. The following table presents the income earned by Pocahontas from the date of acquisition until the end of 2007.

	Income	Dividends
February 1–December 31, 2005	$1,150,000	$450,000
2006	1,375,000	525,000
2007	1,600,000	650,000

Required:
A. Determine the annual purchase differential amortizations for 2005, 2006, and 2007.
B. Determine the Investment in Pocahontas account balances at December 31, 2005, 2006, and 2007 assuming that it is determined that goodwill impairment requires writing off 40 percent of the goodwill in 2006.
C. Determine the annual purchase differential amortizations for 2005, 2006, and 2007 assuming Dreamworld paid $8,593,750 for 100 percent of Pocahontas's stock on February 1, 2005, resulting in $480,000 of goodwill.
D. Determine the the Investment in Pocahontas account balances at December 31, 2005, 2006, and 2007 assuming the information presented in part C is applicable and that it is determined that goodwill impairment requires writing off 40 percent of the goodwill in 2006.

EXERCISE 3-7

Southern Publishing Corporation purchased 60 percent of the outstanding common stock of Western Publishing Corporation on May 1, 2005, for $10,656,000. The following table indicates the book and market values of Western Publishing's assets and liabilities at the date of acquisition.

	Book Value	Market Value
Cash and Receivables	$3,900,000	$3,900,000
Inventory	7,700,000	8,600,000
Land	2,500,000	4,000,000
Plant Assets (net)	14,000,800	16,000,000
Current Liabilities	(5,600,000)	(5,600,000)
Long-Term Debt	(10,000,000)	(10,000,000)

The inventory is estimated to have a remaining life of four months, and the plant assets have an estimated remaining life of 17 years. Western has had income of $1,400,000, $2,750,000, and $2,400,000 subsequent to the date of acquisition in 2005, during 2006, and during 2007, respectively. In addition, Western, paid dividends of $1,100,000, $1,500,000, and $1,700,000 in the three respective periods.

Required:
A. Determine Investment Income for 2005, 2006, and 2007, assuming that at the end of 2006 it was determined that the entire goodwill balance was impaired and needed to be written off.
B. Determine the Investment in Western Publishing account balance at December 31, 2005, 2006, and 2007.

EXERCISE 3-8

Use the information from Exercise 3-7 but assume that Southern Publishing had acquired 100 percent of Western Publishing's stock for the bargain price of $15,000,250.

Required:
A. Determine Investment Income for 2005, 2006, and 2007.
B. Determine the Investment in Western Publishing account balance at December 31, 2005, 2006, and 2007.

EXERCISE 3-9

TPC Enterprises acquired 80 percent of Jones, Incorporated on May 1, 2005, for $2,940,000, the book value of Jones at the date of acquisition. During the remainder of 2005, Jones had income of $610,000 and paid dividends of $400,000.

Required:
A. Record the journal entries necessary on TPC's books for 2005 assuming that TPC uses the equity method to account for its investment in Jones.
B. Prepare the worksheet elimination to remove the change in the Investment in Jones during 2005 from the consolidated financial statements.
C. Prepare the worksheet elimination to recognize the income to noncontrolling interest on the 2005 consolidated financial statements.

EXERCISE 3-10

OfficePro, a local office supply company, was acquired (70 percent) by Mega Office Corporation, a national office supply wholesaler, on August 31, 2005, for $6,440,000. OfficePro's book value at the date of acquisition was $8,000,000. Mega assigned purchase differentials of $210,000 to Inventory and $378,000 to net Plant and Equipment. The purchase differential for Inventory is to be amortized over three months and Plant and Equipment over five years. OfficePro has $894,000 of income and pays $500,000 in dividends for the remainder of 2005 (no dividends were paid in 2005 prior to the acquisition). A review of goodwill revealed that no impairment adjustments were necessary. The following balances exist for Mega Office and OfficePro at December 31, 2005.

	Mega	OfficePro
Cash	$2,552,000	$1,750,000
Inventory	5,900,000	3,300,000
Plant and Equipment (net)	14,258,000	7,894,000

Investment in OfficePro	6,480,600	
Cost of Goods Sold	30,600,000	7,560,000
Depreciation Expense	1,200,000	984,000
Other Expenses	3,950,000	2,746,000
Dividends	2,000,000	500,000
Total Debits	$66,940,600	$24,734,000
Current Liabilities	$2,300,000	$1,900,000
Long-Term Debt	3,800,000	2,650,000
Common Stock	2,100,000	700,000
Additional Paid-In Capital	5,800,000	2,870,000
Retained Earnings	12,550,000	4,014,000
Sales	40,000,000	12,600,000
Investment Income	390,600	
Total Credits	$66,940,600	$24,734,000

Required:

A. Record the journal entries necessary on Mega's books for 2005 assuming that Mega uses the equity method to account for its investment in OfficePro.

B. Prepare all worksheet eliminations in journal entry form necessary to consolidate Mega and OfficePro at December 31, 2005.

Test → **C.** Prepare the consolidation worksheet for Mega and OfficePro at December 31, 2005.

EXERCISE 3-11   Crane Mechanics acquired 75 percent of Downey Enterprises on March 31, 2005, for $3,645,000. Downey's book value at that date totaled $4,000,000. Appraisal values differed from book values for identifiable assets in the following amounts: Inventory ($300,000) and Plant and Equipment ($700,000). The purchase differential for Inventory is to be amortized over five months and Plant and Equipment over 10 years. For the remainder of 2005 Downey reports $635,000 of income and pays $100,000 in dividends. The following balances exist for Crane at December 31, 2005, and Downey at March 31 and December 31, 2005.

	Crain	Downey	
	12/31	*3/31*	*12/31*
Cash	$730,000	$175,000	$180,000
Inventory	1,950,000	260,000	340,000
Plant and Equipment (net)	12,995,000	4,215,000	4,515,000
Investment in Downey	3,886,875		
Expenses	6,400,000	1,000,000	4,265,000
Dividends	1,275,000	150,000	250,000
Total Debits	$27,236,875	$5,800,000	$9,550,000
Liabilities	$3,550,000	$650,000	$500,000
Common Stock	350,000	100,000	100,000
Additional Paid-In Capital	2,650,000	850,000	850,000
Retained Earnings	9,720,000	2,800,000	2,800,000
Sales	10,650,000	1,400,000	5,300,000
Extraordinary Gain From Acquisition of Downey	105,000		
Investment Income	211,875		
Total Credits	$27,236,875	$5,800,000	$9,550,000

Required:

A. Record the journal entries necessary on Crain's books for 2005 assuming that Crain uses the equity method to account for its investment in Downey.

B. Prepare all worksheet eliminations in journal entry form necessary to consolidate Crain and Downey at December 31, 2005.

C. Prepare the consolidation worksheet for Crain and Downey at December 31, 2005.

EXERCISE 3-12   Miniature Trains, Incorporated purchased 60 percent of the outstanding voting common stock of Little Steam Engine Corporation on March 1, 2005, for $750,000. The book values, market values, and estimated remaining life of Little Steam Engine's assets and liabilities at the date of acquisition are the following:

	Book Value	Market Value	Remaining Life
Cash and Receivables	$200,000	$200,000	
Inventory	425,000	665,000	12 months
Land	300,000	900,000	Not applicable
Plant Assets (net)	1,400,000	1,600,000	100 months
Current Liabilities	(560,000)	(560,000)	
Long-Term Debt	(1,500,000)	(1,500,000)	

During the remainder of 2005, Little Steam Engine had net income and paid dividends of $300,000 and $190,000, respectively.

Required:

A. Record the journal entries necessary on Miniature Trains' books for 2005 assuming that Miniature Trains uses the equity method to account for its investment in Little Steam Engine.

B. Prepare the worksheet elimination to remove the change in the Investment in Little Steam Engine that had been recorded during 2005.

C. Prepare the worksheet elimination to recognize the income to noncontrolling interest on the 2005 consolidated financial statements.

NOTE: **Exercises 3-13 and 3-14 repeat Exercises 3-10 and 3-11 using a separate accumulated depreciation account.**

EXERCISE 3-13   OfficePro, a local office supply company, was acquired (70 percent) by Mega Office Corporation, a national office supply wholesaler, on August 31, 2005, for $6,440,000. OfficePro's book value at the date of acquisition was $8,000,000. Mega assigned purchase differentials of $210,000 to Inventory and $378,000 to Plant and Equipment. The purchase differential for Inventory is to be amortized over three months and Plant and Equipment over five years. OfficePro has $894,000 of income and pays $500,000 in dividends for the remainder of 2005 (no dividends were paid in 2005 prior to the acquisition). A review of goodwill revealed that no impairment adjustments were necessary. The following balances exist for Mega Office and OfficePro at December 31, 2005.

	Mega	OfficePro
Cash	$2,552,000	$1,750,000
Inventory	5,900,000	3,300,000
Plant and Equipment	21,000,000	11,740,000
Accumulated Depreciation	(6,742,000)	(3,846,000)
Investment in OfficePro	6,480,600	
Cost of Goods Sold	30,600,000	7,560,000
Depreciation Expense	1,200,000	984,000
Other Expenses	3,950,000	2,746,000
Dividends	2,000,000	500,000
Total Debits	$66,940,600	$24,734,000
Current Liabilities	$2,300,000	$1,900,000
Long-Term Debt	3,800,000	2,650,000
Common Stock	2,100,000	700,000
Additional Paid-In Capital	5,800,000	2,870,000
Retained Earnings	12,550,000	4,014,000
Sales	40,000,000	12,600,000
Investment Income	390,600	
Total Credits	$66,940,600	$24,734,000

Required:

A. Record the journal entries necessary on Mega's books for 2005 assuming that Mega uses the equity method to account for its investment in OfficePro.

B. Prepare all worksheet eliminations in journal entry form necessary to consolidate Mega and OfficePro at December 31, 2005. Assume that OfficePro has an August 31 accumulated depreciation balance of $3,518,000.

C. Prepare the consolidation worksheet for Mega and OfficePro at December 31, 2005.

EXERCISE 3-14 Crane Mechanics acquired 75 percent of Downey Enterprises on March 31, 2005, for $3,645,000. Downey's book value at that date totaled $4,000,000. Appraisal values were greater than book values for identifiable assets in the following amounts: Inventory ($300,000) and Plant and Equipment ($700,000). The purchase differential for Inventory is to be amortized over five months and Plant and Equipment over ten years. For the remainder of 2005 Downey reports $635,000 of income and pays $100,000 in dividends. The following balances exist for Crane at December 31, 2005, and Downey at March 31 and December 31, 2005.

	Crain	*Downey*	
	12/31	*3/31*	*12/31*
Cash	$730,000	$175,000	$180,000
Inventory	1,950,000	260,000	340,000
Plant and Equipment	17,650,000	5,150,000	5,765,000
Accumulated Depreciation	(4,655,000)	(935,000)	(1,250,000)
Investment in Downey	3,886,875		
Expenses	6,400,000	1,000,000	4,265,000
Dividends	1,275,000	150,000	250,000
Total Debits	$27,236,875	$5,800,000	$9,550,000
Liabilities	$3,550,000	$650,000	$500,000
Common Stock	350,000	100,000	100,000
Additional Paid-In Capital	2,650,000	850,000	850,000
Retained Earnings	9,720,000	2,800,000	2,800,000
Sales	10,650,000	1,400,000	5,300,000
Extraordinary Gain From Acquisition of Downey	105,000		
Investment Income	211,875		
Total Credits	$27,236,875	$5,800,000	$9,550,000

Required:

A. Record the journal entries necessary on Crain's books for 2005 assuming that Crain uses the equity method to account for its investment in Downey.

B. Prepare all worksheet eliminations in journal entry form necessary to consolidate Crain and Downey at December 31, 2005.

C. Prepare the consolidation worksheet for Crain and Downey at December 31, 2005.

NOTE: **Exercises 3-15, 3-16, and 3-17 repeat Exercises 3-10, 3-11, and 3-12 with the parent company using the cost method to account for the investment.**

EXERCISE 3-15 OfficePro, a local office supply company, was acquired (70 percent) by Mega Office Corporation, a national office supply wholesaler, on August 31, 2005, for $6,440,000. OfficePro's book value at the date of acquisition was $8,000,000. Mega assigned a purchase differential of $210,000 to Inventory and $378,000 to net Plant and Equipment. The purchase differential for Inventory is to be amortized over three months and Plant and Equipment over five years. OfficePro has $894,000 of income and pays $500,000 in dividends for the remainder of 2005 (no dividends were paid in 2005 prior to the acquisition). The following balances exist for Mega Office and OfficePro at December 31, 2005.

	Mega	*OfficePro*
Cash	$2,552,000	$1,750,000
Inventory	5,900,000	3,300,000
Plant and Equipment (net)	14,258,000	7,894,000
Investment in OfficePro	6,440,000	
Cost of Goods Sold	30,600,000	7,560,000

Depreciation Expense	1,200,000	984,000
Other Expenses	3,950,000	2,746,000
Dividends	2,000,000	500,000
Total Debits	$66,900,000	$24,734,000
Current Liabilities	$2,300,000	$1,900,000
Long-Term Debt	3,800,000	2,650,000
Common Stock	2,100,000	700,000
Additional Paid-In Capital	5,800,000	2,870,000
Retained Earnings	12,550,000	4,014,000
Sales	40,000,000	12,600,000
Dividend Revenue	350,000	
Total Credits	$66,900,000	$24,734,000

Required:

A. Record the journal entries necessary on Mega's books for 2005 assuming that Mega uses the cost method to account for its investment in OfficePro.

B. Prepare all worksheet eliminations in journal entry form necessary to consolidate Mega and OfficePro at December 31, 2005.

C. Prepare the consolidation worksheet for Mega and OfficePro at December 31, 2005.

EXERCISE 3-16   Crane Mechanics acquired 75 percent of Downey Enterprises on March 31, 2005, for $3,645,000. Downey's book value at that date totaled $4,000,000. Appraisal values were greater than book values for identifiable assets in the following amounts: Inventory ($300,000) and Plant and Equipment ($700,000). The purchase differential for Inventory is to be amortized over five months and Plant and Equipment over ten years. For the remainder of 2005 Downey reports $635,000 of income and pays $100,000 in dividends. The following balances exist for Crane at December 31, 2005, and Downey at March 31 and December 31, 2005.

	Crain	Downey	
	12/31	3/31	12/31
Cash	$730,000	$175,000	$180,000
Inventory	1,950,000	260,000	340,000
Plant and Equipment (net)	12,995,000	4,215,000	4,515,000
Investment in Downey	3,645,000		
Expenses	6,400,000	1,000,000	4,265,000
Dividends	1,275,000	150,000	250,000
Total Debits	$26,995,000	$5,800,000	$9,550,000
Liabilities	$3,550,000	$650,000	$500,000
Common Stock	350,000	100,000	100,000
Additional Paid-In Capital	2,650,000	850,000	850,000
Retained Earnings	9,720,000	2,800,000	2,800,000
Sales	10,650,000	1,400,000	5,300,000
Dividend Revenue	75,000		
Total Credits	$26,995,000	$5,800,000	$9,500,000

Required:

A. Record the journal entries necessary on Crain's books for 2005 assuming that Crain uses the cost method to account for its investment in Downey.

B. Prepare all worksheet eliminations in journal entry form necessary to consolidate Crain and Downey at December 31, 2005.

C. Prepare the consolidation worksheet for Crain and Downey at December 31, 2005.

EXERCISE 3-17   Miniature Trains, Incorporated purchased 60 percent of the outstanding voting common stock of Little Steam Engine Corporation on March 1, 2005, for $750,000. The book values, market values, and estimated remaining life of Little Steam Engine's assets and liabilities at the date of acquisition are the following:

	Book Value	Market Value	Remaining Life
Cash and Receivables	$200,000	$200,000	
Inventory	425,000	665,000	12 months
Land	300,000	900,000	Not applicable
Plant Assets (net)	1,400,000	1,600,000	100 months
Current Liabilities	(560,000)	(560,000)	
Long-Term Debt	(1,500,000)	(1,500,000)	

During the remainder of 2005 Little Steam Engine had net income and paid dividends of $300,000 and $190,000, respectively.

Required:

A. Record the journal entries necessary on Miniature Trains's books for 2005 assuming that Miniature Trains uses the cost method to account for its investment in Little Steam Engine.

B. Prepare the worksheet elimination to remove the Dividend Revenue recognized in 2005 by Miniature Train.

C. Prepare the worksheet elimination to recognize the income to noncontrolling interest on the 2005 consolidated financial statements.

PROBLEMS

Consolidation worksheets for problems that require a worksheet can be found at the book companion website.

PROBLEM 3-1 Equity method journal entries, 100 percent acquisition; basic worksheet eliminations for year of acquisition; consolidation worksheet

PROBLEM 3-2 Continuation of Problem 3-1, second year of ownership, journal entries, 100 percent ownership, basic worksheet eliminations; consolidation worksheet

PROBLEM 3-3 Equity method journal entries, 80 percent acquisition; basic worksheet eliminations for year of acquisition; consolidation worksheet; basic worksheet eliminations [(1) and (3)] for year of acquisition with separate accumulated depreciation account

PROBLEM 3-4 Continuation of Problem 3-3, second year of ownership, goodwill impairment, journal entries, 80 percent ownership, basic worksheet eliminations; consolidation worksheet; basic worksheet eliminations [(1) and (3)] for year of acquisition with separate accumulated depreciation account

PROBLEM 3-5 Equity method journal entries, 90 percent acquisition; basic worksheet eliminations for year of acquisition; consolidation worksheet; negative goodwill

PROBLEM 3-6 Continuation of Problem 3-5, second year of ownership, journal entries, 90 percent ownership, basic worksheet eliminations; consolidation worksheet; negative goodwill

PROBLEM 3-7 Equity method journal entries, 100 percent mid-year acquisition; basic worksheet eliminations for year of acquisition; consolidation worksheet

PROBLEM 3-8 Continuation of Problem 3-7, second year of ownership, journal entries, 100 percent ownership, basic worksheet eliminations

PROBLEM 3-9 Extension of Problem 3-7, equity method journal entries, 75 percent mid-year acquisition; basic worksheet elimination for year of acquisition, consolidation worksheet

PROBLEM 3-10 Continuation of Problem 3-9, second year of ownership, journal entries, 75 percent ownership, basic worksheet eliminations

PROBLEM 3-11 Equity method journal entries, 60 percent mid-year acquisition, separate accumulated depreciation account; basic worksheet eliminations, two years

PROBLEM 3-12 Worksheet elimination at date of acquisition (January 1); date of acquisition consolidation worksheet, separate accumulated depreciation account; negative goodwill; equity method journal entries and basic worksheet eliminations for first and second years of ownership assuming 100 percent and 80 percent ownership; contrast 100 percent and 80 percent solutions

PROBLEM 3-13 Consolidation worksheet and financial ratios at date of acquisition and end of first year of ownership under two methods to finance 80 percent acquisition; worksheet eliminations at end of first year of ownership; report to board of directors on method of financing to be pursued

PROBLEM 3-1

Jennifer Enterprises acquired 100 percent of David's Materials on January 1, 2005, for $1,850,000. Appraisals reveal that David's plant assets have a market value $60,000 greater than book value and an estimated remaining economic life of six years. David's financial records disclose net income and dividends declared and paid during 2005 of $700,000 and $140,000, respectively. The following balances exist for Jennifer and David's on December 31, 2005.

	Jennifer	David's
Cash and Receivables	$1,950,000	$250,000
Inventory	2,500,000	600,000
Plant Assets (net)	11,500,000	3,700,000
Investment in David's	2,400,000	
Cost of Goods Sold	4,350,000	1,957,000
Depreciation Expense	1,720,000	275,000
Other Expenses	1,060,000	848,000
Dividends	325,000	140,000
Totals	$25,805,000	$7,770,000
Liabilities	$3,685,000	$2,200,000
Common Stock	250,000	50,000
Additional Paid-In Capital	3,500,000	240,000
Retained Earnings	8,000,000	1,500,000
Sales	9,680,000	3,780,000
Investment Income	690,000	
Totals	$25,805,000	$7,770,000

Required:
A. Prepare the equity method journal entries on Jennifer Enterprises's financial records during 2005.
B. Prepare the basic worksheet eliminations in journal entry form to consolidate Jennifer Enterprises and David's Materials at December 31, 2005.
C. Prepare the consolidation worksheet for Jennifer Enterprises and David's Materials at December 31, 2005.

PROBLEM 3-2

(Refer to the information in Problem 3-1.) David's financial records disclose net income and dividends declared and paid during 2006 of $850,000 and $250,000, respectively. The following balances exist for Jennifer and David's on December 31, 2006.

	Jennifer	David's
Cash and Receivables	$2,030,000	$390,000
Inventory	3,400,000	700,000
Plant Assets (net)	13,600,000	4,660,000
Investment in David's	2,990,000	
Cost of Goods Sold	5,165,000	2,700,000
Depreciation Expense	2,390,000	380,000
Other Expenses	1,490,000	1,260,000
Dividends	600,000	250,000
Totals	$31,665,000	$10,340,000
Liabilities	$4,685,000	$2,800,000
Common Stock	250,000	50,000
Additional Paid-In Capital	3,500,000	240,000
Retained Earnings	10,915,000	2,060,000
Sales	11,475,000	5,190,000
Investment Income	840,000	
Totals	$31,665,000	$10,340,000

Required:
A. Prepare the equity method journal entries on Jennifer Enterprises's financial records during 2006.
B. Prepare the basic worksheet eliminations in journal entry form to consolidate Jennifer Enterprises and David's Materials at December 31, 2006.

C. Prepare the consolidation worksheet for Jennifer Enterprises and David's Materials at December 31, 2006.

PROBLEM 3-3

Gatron Electronics purchased 80 percent of Circuit Village on January 1, 2005, for $6,750,000. At the acquisition date, inventory had an appraised value $350,000 greater than book value (five-month estimated remaining life) and plant assets had an appraised value $780,000 greater than net book value (eight year estimated remaining life). Circuit Village reports $1,525,000 net income and declares dividends of $600,000 on December 31, 2005. The following balances exist for Gatron and Circuit Village on December 31, 2005, immediately prior to the recognition of all equity method journal entries for the year.

	Gatron	Circuit Village
Cash and Receivables	$980,000	$205,000
Inventory	1,860,000	650,000
Plant Assets (net)	17,747,000	7,220,000
Investment in Circuit Village	6,750,000	
Cost of Goods Sold	7,960,000	2,700,000
Depreciation Expense	2,040,000	370,000
Other Expenses	12,900,000	1,050,000
Dividends	1,000,000	600,000
Totals	$51,237,000	$12,795,000
Liabilities	$9,600,000	$2,150,000
Common Stock	268,000	73,000
Additional Paid-In Capital	3,619,000	658,000
Retained Earnings	10,850,000	4,269,000
Sales	26,900,000	5,645,000
Totals	$51,237,000	$12,795,000

Required:

A. Prepare the equity method journal entries on Gatron's financial records during 2005.
B. Prepare the basic worksheet eliminations in journal entry form to consolidate Gatron and Circuit Village at December 31, 2005.
C. Prepare the consolidation worksheet for Gatron and Circuit Village at December 31, 2005.
D. Prepare worksheet elimination (1) and (3), in journal entry form, to consolidate Gatron and Circuit Village at December 31, 2005, assuming that Circuit Village's plant assets have a historical cost and accumulated depreciation of $9,300,000 and $2,080,000, respectively.

PROBLEM 3-4

(Refer to the information in Problem 3-3.) Circuit Village earned net income of $2,200,000 and declared dividends of $700,000 in 2006. The following balances exist for Gatron and Circuit Village at December 31, 2006.

	Gatron	Circuit Village
Cash and Receivables	$1,050,000	$270,000
Inventory	2,600,000	820,000
Plant Assets (net)	19,942,000	8,210,000
Investment in Circuit Village	7,146,400	
Cost of Goods Sold	9,100,000	3,500,000
Depreciation Expense	2,200,000	400,000
Other Expenses	13,050,000	1,100,000
Dividends	1,785,000	700,000
Totals	$56,873,400	$15,000,000
Liabilities	$9,250,000	$1,875,000
Common Stock	268,000	73,000
Additional Paid-In Capital	3,619,000	658,000
Retained Earnings	14,712,000	5,194,000
Sales	28,450,000	7,200,000
Investment Income	574,400	
Totals	$56,873,400	$15,000,000

Required:

A. Prepare the equity method journal entries on Gatron's financial records during 2006 assuming that a competitor's introduction of a new product reduces projected sales and results in the write-off of 60 percent of the goodwill associated with Circuit Village.

B. Prepare the basic worksheet eliminations in journal entry form to consolidate Gatron and Circuit Village at December 31, 2006.

C. Prepare the consolidation worksheet for Gatron and Circuit Village at December 31, 2006.

D. Prepare Worksheet elimination (1) and (3) in journal entry form to consolidate Gatron and Circuit Village at December 31, 2006, assuming that Circuit Village's plant assets have date of acquisition historical cost and accumulated depreciation as presented in Problem 3-3.

PROBLEM 3-5   Total Interiors purchased 90 percent of Tropical Design on January 1, 2005, for $4,500,000. Book values equaled market values at the acquisition date with two exceptions. Inventory had an appraised value of $670,000 and a book value of $300,000 (six-month estimated remaining life). Land had an appraised value of $1,450,000 and a net book value of $100,000. Tropical Design had net income and dividends in 2005 of $820,000 and $270,000, respectively. The following balances exist for Total Interiors and Tropical Design at December 31, 2005.

	Total Interiors	*Tropical Design*
Cash and Receivables	$4,168,000	$145,000
Inventory	950,000	320,000
Land	2,800,000	100,000
Plant Assets (net)	14,750,000	4,985,000
Investment in Tropical Design	4,860,000	
Cost of Goods Sold	3,140,000	984,000
Depreciation Expense	1,100,000	480,000
Other Expenses	1,652,000	996,000
Dividends	1,450,000	270,000
Totals	$34,870,000	$8,280,000
Liabilities	$7,295,000	$1,500,000
Common Stock	550,000	150,000
Additional Paid-In Capital	3,890,000	750,000
Retained Earnings	14,682,000	2,600,000
Sales	7,850,000	3,280,000
Extraordinary Gain from Acquisition of Tropical Design	198,000	
Investment Income	405,000	
Totals	$34,870,000	$8,280,000

Required:

A. Prepare the equity method journal entries on Total Interiors's financial records during 2005.

B. Prepare the basic worksheet eliminations, in journal entry form, to consolidate Total Interiors and Tropical Design at December 31, 2005.

C. Prepare the consolidation worksheet for Total Interiors and Tropical Design at December 31, 2005.

PROBLEM 3-6   (Refer to the information in Problem 3-5.) Tropical Design's financial records disclose net income and dividends declared and paid during 2006 of $1,650,000 and $460,000, respectively. The following balances exist for Total Interiors and Tropical Design at December 31, 2006.

	Total Interiors	*Tropical Design*
Cash and Receivables	$3,567,000	$575,000
Inventory	1,150,000	380,000
Land	2,800,000	100,000
Plant Assets (net)	15,600,000	5,385,000
Investment in Tropical Design	5,931,000	
Cost of Goods Sold	3,600,000	1,050,000

Depreciation Expense	1,250,000	230,000
Other Expenses	1,900,000	1,370,000
Dividends	1,750,000	460,000
Totals	$37,548,000	$9,550,000
Liabilities	$6,800,000	$1,200,000
Common Stock	550,000	150,000
Additional Paid-In Capital	3,890,000	750,000
Retained Earnings	15,793,000	3,150,000
Sales	9,030,000	4,300,000
Investment Income	1,485,000	
Totals	$37,548,000	$9,550,000

Required:
A. Prepare the equity method journal entries on Total Interior's financial records during 2006.
B. Prepare the basic worksheet eliminations in journal entry form to consolidate Total Interiors and Tropical Design at December 31, 2006.
C. Prepare the consolidation worksheet for Total Interiors and Tropical Design at December 31, 2006.

PROBLEM 3-7   WorldWide Enterprises acquired an ownership interest in Import/Export Corporation on October 1, 2005. The following amounts were determined from an examination of Import/Export's financial records and appraisals at the date of acquisition.

	Book Value	Market Value	Remaining Life
Cash	$125,000	$125,000	
Receivables	350,000	350,000	
Inventory	1,750,000	1,850,000	8 months
Land	1,520,000	1,520,000	
Plant and Equipment (net)	4,799,000	4,739,000	10 years
Other Noncurrent Assets	160,000	120,000	40 months
Cost of Goods Sold	850,000		
Depreciation Expense	300,000		
Other Expenses	275,000		
Dividends	50,000		
Totals	$10,179,000		
Current Liabilities	$1,100,000	$1,100,000	
Long-Term Debt	2,000,000	2,000,000	
Common Stock	230,000		
Additional Paid-In Capital	1,624,000		
Retained Earnings	3,425,000		
Sales	1,800,000		
Totals	$10,179,000		

At December 31, 2005, the following balances were compiled by each company.

	WorldWide	Import/Export
Cash	$3,750,000	$162,000
Receivables	5,240,000	410,000
Inventory	13,759,000	1,990,000
Land	3,200,000	1,520,000
Plant and Equipment (net)	28,368,000	4,777,000
Investment in Import/Export	5,706,000	
Other Noncurrent Assets	159,000	130,000
Cost of Goods Sold	18,450,000	1,350,000
Depreciation Expense	750,000	450,000
Other Expenses	2,049,000	460,000
Dividends	350,000	80,000
Totals	$81,781,000	$11,329,000

Current Liabilities	$13,000,000	$1,250,000
Long-Term Debt	18,500,000	2,000,000
Common Stock	600,000	230,000
Additional Paid-In Capital	2,243,000	1,624,000
Retained Earnings	15,600,000	3,425,000
Sales	31,706,000	2,800,000
Investment Income	132,000	
Totals	$81,781,000	$11,329,000

Required:

A. Determine the amount WorldWide paid for Import/Export's stock assuming there is no goodwill and assuming that WorldWide purchased 100 percent of Import/Export.

B. Prepare all the equity method journal entries that would have been made on WorldWide's financial records during 2005, including the original investment in Import/Export.

C. Prepare the worksheet eliminations in journal entry form to consolidate WorldWide and Import/Export at December 31, 2005.

D. Prepare the consolidation worksheet for WorldWide and Import/Export at December 31, 2005.

PROBLEM 3-8 (Refer to the information in Problem 3-7.) Assume that in 2006 Import/Export continues to operate as a separate legal entity. At the end of 2006, the controller of Import/Export forwards the following balances to WorldWide Enterprises.

	Import/Export
Cash	$285,000
Receivables	460,000
Inventory	2,330,000
Land	1,680,000
Plant and Equipment (net)	4,494,000
Other Noncurrent Assets	155,000
Cost of Goods Sold	1,635,000
Depreciation Expense	475,000
Other Expenses	490,000
Dividends	170,000
Totals	$12,174,000
Current Liabilities	$1,600,000
Long-Term Debt	2,000,000
Common Stock	230,000
Additional Paid-In Capital	1,624,000
Retained Earnings	3,885,000
Sales	2,835,000
Totals	$12,174,000

Required:

A. Prepare all the journal entries that would be made on WorldWide's financial records during 2006 with regard to the investment in Import/Export.

B. Prepare the worksheet eliminations in journal entry form to consolidate WorldWide and Import/Export at December 31, 2006.

PROBLEM 3-9 Assume that the information in Problem 3-7 is applicable in this problem except that WorldWide acquires only 75 percent of Import/Export's stock. This change in ownership percentage results in the following December 31 WorldWide changes in account balances.

Account	*Problem 3-7 Amount*	*Problem 3-9 Amount*
Cash	$3,750,000	$5,143,500
Investment in Import/Export	5,706,000	4,279,500
Investment Income	132,000	99,000

Required:

A. Determine the amount WorldWide paid for Import/Export's stock assuming there is no goodwill.

B. Prepare all the equity method journal entries that would have been made on WorldWide's financial records during 2005, including the original investment in Import/Export.

C. Prepare the worksheet eliminations in journal entry form to consolidate WorldWide and Import/Export at December 31, 2005.

D. Prepare the consolidation worksheet for WorldWide and Import/Export at December 31, 2005.

PROBLEM 3-10   (Refer to the information in Problem 3-9.) Assume that in 2006 Import/Export continues to operate as a separate legal entity. At the end of 2006, the controller of Import/Export forwards the following balances to WorldWide Enterprises.

	Import/Export
Cash	$285,000
Receivables	460,000
Inventory	2,330,000
Land	1,680,000
Plant and Equipment (net)	4,494,000
Other Noncurrent Assets	155,000
Cost of Goods Sold	1,635,000
Depreciation Expense	475,000
Other Expenses	490,000
Dividends	170,000
Totals	$12,174,000
Current Liabilities	$1,600,000
Long-Term Debt	2,000,000
Common Stock	230,000
Additional Paid-In Capital	1,624,000
Retained Earnings	3,885,000
Sales	2,835,000
Totals	$12,174,000

Required:

A. Prepare all the journal entries that would be made on WorldWide's financial records during 2006 with regard to the investment in Import/Export.

B. Prepare the worksheet eliminations in journal entry form to consolidate WorldWide and Import/Export at December 31, 2006.

PROBLEM 3-11   Marine Supply Corporation is a subsidiary of Navy, Incorporated. At the date of acquisition (May 1, 2005), Marine Supply had the following book and market values of its assets and liabilities (revenue and expense accounts have been closed to Retained Earnings).

	Book Value	Market Value
Cash	$624,000	$624,000
Receivables	490,000	490,000
Inventory	$1,386,000	1,620,000
Land	940,000	1,570,000
Plant and Equipment	5,680,000	4,600,000
Accumulated Depreciation	(1,146,000)	
Other Noncurrent Assets	207,000	207,000
Totals	$8,181,000	
Current Liabilities	$985,000	$985,000
Long-Term Debt	1,200,000	1,236,000
Common Stock	300,000	
Additional Paid-In Capital	1,394,000	
Retained Earnings	4,302,000	
Totals	$8,181,000	

The inventory is expected to be sold over nine months, plant and equipment is estimated to have a remaining life of ten years, and the long-term debt matures in three years.

Required:

A. Prepare the 2005 equity method journal entries on Navy's books assuming that 60 percent of Marine Supply's outstanding common stock was acquired for $4,499,400 and that Marine Supply had net income and dividends from May 1 to December 31, 2005, of $900,000 and $250,000, respectively. A goodwill impairment adjustment is not required in 2005.

B. Prepare the worksheet eliminations in journal entry form to consolidate Navy and Marine Supply on December 31, 2005.

C. Prepare the 2006 equity method journal entries on Navy's books assuming that Marine Supply had net income and dividends of $1,354,000 and $330,000, respectively. Assume also that the 2006 goodwill assessment results in a write-off of 30 percent of the goodwill associated with Marine Supply.

D. Prepare the worksheet eliminations in journal entry form for to consolidate Navy and Marine Supply on December 31, 2006.

PROBLEM 3-12 Control over Creative Electronics, Incorporated was acquired by Traditional Publishing Corporation on January 1, 2005. The following table presents the account balances for each company immediately prior to Traditional attaining control as well as the estimated market value of Creative Electronics assets and liabilities at the same date.

	Traditional	*Creative—Book*	*Creative—Market*
Cash	$15,708,000	$2,350,000	$2,350,000
Receivables	35,810,000	4,842,000	4,842,000
Inventory	160,584,000	12,271,000	25,000,000
Land	8,651,000	1,500,00	4,342,000
Plant and Equipment	650,486,000	80,498,000	75,000,000
Accumulated Depreciation	(180,584,000)	(20,876,000)	
Patents	350,600,000	850,000	17,000,000
Other Noncurrent Assets	4,058,000	3,658,000	3,658,000
Totals	$1,045,313,000	$85,093,000	
Current Liabilities	$126,870,000	$10,694,000	$10,694,000
Long-Term Debt	480,650,000	30,506,000	30,200,000
Common Stock ($5 par)	10,571,000	2,648,000	
Additional Paid-In Capital	60,875,000	15,688,000	
Retained Earnings	366,347,000	25,557,000	
Totals	$1,045,313,000	$85,093,000	

The inventory is expected to be sold over eight months, plant and equipment has an estimated remaining life of 5 years, patents have an average economic and legal life of 100 months, and long-term debt has a maturity of 6 years.

Creative's controller provides the following balances to Traditional at the end of 2005 and 2006.

	2005	*2006*
Cash	$3,548,000	$4,524,000
Receivables	$6,748,000	8,542,000
Inventory	17,274,000	22,345,000
Land	1,500,000	1,500,000
Plant and Equipment	87,413,000	93,989,000
Accumulated Depreciation	(30,246,000)	(39,428,000)
Patents	800,000	750,000
Other Noncurrent Assets	5,028,000	6,120,000
Cost of Goods Sold	42,524,000	62,034,000
Depreciation Expense	9,370,000	10,842,000

Other Expenses	7,086,000	9,847,000
Dividends	3,500,000	5,000,000
Totals	$154,545,000	$186,065,000
Current Liabilities	$11,656,000	$13,404,000
Long-Term Debt	30,650,000	30,584,000
Common Stock ($5 par)	2,648,000	2,648,000
Additional Paid-In Capital	15,688,000	15,688,000
Retained Earnings	25,557,000	31,423,000
Sales	68,346,000	92,318,000
Totals	$154,545,000	$186,065,000

Required:

A. Prepare the worksheet elimination at the date of acquisition assuming that Traditional paid $80,298,000 for 100 percent of Creative's outstanding common stock.

B. Prepare the date of acquisition consolidation worksheet assuming that Traditional issued 4,000,000 shares of common stock to acquire Creative's stock.

C. Prepare the equity method journal entries for 2005 using the information provided by Creative's controller.

D. Prepare the worksheet eliminations for 2005 in journal entry format.

E. Prepare the equity method journal entries for 2006 using the information provided by Creative's controller.

F. Prepare the worksheet eliminations for 2006 in journal entry format.

G. Rework parts A–F assuming that Traditional paid $64,238,400 for 80 percent of Creative's outstanding common stock by issuing 3,200,000 shares of Traditional stock in exchange for Creative's stock.

H. What are some of the similarities and differences that exist between the 100 percent and the less than 100 percent solutions prepared for the information in this problem?

PROBLEM 3-13   Advanced Computer Systems, Incorporated is in the process of acquiring 80 percent of Statistical Software Corporation. The board of directors of Advanced Computer want to know how the acquisition of Statistical Software will impact the financial ratios of the consolidated entity based on the following assumed methods of financing the combination: (1) the issuance of 300,000 shares of Advanced common stock with a market value of $50 per share or (2) the issuance of $15,000,000 of long-term debt at face value. The following balances are expected to exist for Advanced Computer and Statistical Software immediately prior to the expected combination (January 1, 2005). The table also presents the estimated market value of Statistical Software's assets and liabilities at the expected combination date.

	Advanced	Statistical–Book	Statistical–Market
Cash	$3,518,000	$2,548,000	$2,548,000
Receivables	5,243,000	6,826,000	6,826,000
Inventory	16,045,000	10,050,000	11,030,000
Land	2,248,000	1,200,000	2,750,000
Plant and Equipment (net)	37,469,000	19,006,000	22,551,000
Patents	19,270,000	3,870,000	3,100,000
Other Noncurrent Assets	1,450,000	1,005,000	860,000
Totals	$85,243,000	$44,505,000	
Current Liabilities	$17,474,000	$7,194,000	$7,194,000
Long-Term Debt	18,650,000	28,950,000	28,950,000
Common Stock ($2 par)	1,000,000	500,000	
Additional Paid-In Capital	8,465,000	5,154,000	
Retained Earnings	39,654,000	2,707,000	
Totals	$85,243,000	$44,505,000	

Inventory will be sold over six months. The estimated remaining lives of plant and equipment, patents, and other noncurrent assets are ten years, seven years, and four years, respectively.

The board has also asked the controller to determine a projected balances for Advanced Computer and Statistical Software at the end of the first year of ownership (December 31, 2005). The pro forma balances for Advanced and Statistical are presented in the following table. These balances do not reflect any recognition of the proposed investment, that is, the investment account stock or debt issued, investment income, receipt of dividends from the subsidiary, or payment of interest or dividends. The payment of interest and dividends by Advanced would be affected by the financing used to acquire Statistical. Assume that the debt has a 10 percent interest rate and that a $5 per share dividend is paid on the stock (ignore income taxes).

	Advanced	Statistical
Cash	$3,925,000	$3,200,000
Receivables	6,480,000	7,518,000
Inventory	18,408,000	12,540,000
Land	2,248,000	1,200,000
Plant and Equipment (net)	37,368,000	21,620,000
Patents	17,950,000	3,050,000
Other Noncurrent Assets	1,380,000	1,250,000
Cost of Goods Sold	50,624,000	40,520,000
Depreciation Expense	4,420,000	2,370,000
Other Expenses	5,654,000	3,950,000
Dividends	2,500,000	1,000,000
Totals	$150,957,000	$98,218,000
Current Liabilities	$20,100,000	$9,303,000
Long-Term Debt	18,100,000	29,175,000
Common Stock ($2 par)	1,000,000	500,000
Additional Paid-In Capital	8,465,000	5,154,000
Retained Earnings	39,654,000	2,707,000
Sales	63,638,000	51,379,000
Totals	$150,957,000	$98,218,000

Required:

A. Prepare the consolidation worksheet that would be needed to combine Advanced Computer and Statistical Software at the acquisition date based on each financing assumption.

B. Compare financial statement ratios that may be of value to the board in determining the impact of the financing assumptions on the consolidated entity's financial position at the proposed acquisition date.

C. Prepare the worksheet eliminations that would be needed to combine Advanced Computer and Statistical Software at the end of the first year of ownership based on the pro forma balances prepared by the controller.

D. Prepare the consolidation worksheet that would be needed to combine Advanced Computer and Statistical Software at the end of the first year of ownership based on each financing assumption.

E. Compare financial statement ratios that may be of value to the board in determining the impact of the financing assumptions on the consolidated entity's financial position at the end of the first year of ownership if the proposed acquisition occurs.

F. Prepare a report to the board of directors of Advanced Computer Systems outlining the differences that exist under the financing methods proposed.

CHAPTER 4

INTERCOMPANY TRANSACTIONS

LEARNING OBJECTIVES

After reading this chapter, you should be able to:

- Understand the different types of intercompany transactions that can occur.
- Understand why intercompany transactions are addressed when preparing consolidated financial statements.
- Prepare the worksheet eliminations necessary for intercompany transactions in the period of the transaction.
- Prepare the worksheet eliminations necessary for intercompany transactions in periods subsequent to the transaction.
- Differentiate between upstream and downstream intercompany transactions.

Most economic transactions involve two unrelated entities, although transactions may occur between units of one entity (intercompany transactions). Intercompany transactions may involve such items as the declaration and payment of dividends, the purchase and sale of assets such as inventory or plant assets, and borrowing and lending. Regardless of the type of transaction, the occurrence of an intercompany transaction, if not removed (eliminated) from the consolidated financial statements, will often result in a misrepresentation of the consolidated entity's financial position.

This chapter presents a framework for evaluating intercompany transactions. The next section presents a theoretical discussion of intercompany transactions. The subsequent section presents a framework for interpreting such transactions, including two-year examples of downstream (parent-to-subsidiary) transactions to assist in applying the framework to specific situations. The examples in this section are simplified in that each intercompany transaction occurs at, or near, year-end. This is followed by examples where the simplifying assumption is relaxed. The chapter then presents how upstream (subsidiary-to-parent) intercompany transactions differ from downstream transactions.

BASIC CONCEPTS

Intercompany transaction: a transaction that occurs between two units of the same entity

An **intercompany transaction** occurs when one unit of an entity is involved in a transaction with another unit of the same entity. While these transactions can occur for a variety of reasons, they often occur as a result of the normal business relationships that exist between the units of the entity. These units may be the parent and a subsidiary, two

Downstream transaction: an intercompany transaction flowing from the parent to the subsidiary

Upstream transaction: an intercompany transaction flowing from the subsidiary to theparent

Lateral transaction: an intercompany transaction flowing from one subsidiary to another subsidiary

subsidiaries, two divisions, or two departments of one entity. It is common for vertically integrated organizations to transfer inventory among the units of the consolidated entity. On the other hand, a plant asset may be transferred between organizational units to take advantage of changes in demand across product lines.

An intercompany transaction is recognized in the financial records of both units of the entity as if it were an arm's-length transaction with an unrelated party. From the consolidated entity's perspective, the transaction is initially unrealized because unrelated parties are not involved; therefore, the intercompany transaction needs to be interpreted differently than it was by either of the participating units. The difference in interpretation generally results in the elimination of certain account balances from the consolidated financial statements.

Transactions between units of an entity can take several forms and can occur between any units of the entity. Figure 4-1 illustrates possible directions of intercompany transactions. Transactions flowing from the parent to the subsidiary are commonly called **downstream transactions**, transactions from the subsidiary to the parent are commonly called **upstream transactions**, and transactions between subsidiaries are commonly called **lateral transactions**.

The volume of intercompany transactions eliminated from the financial records of many large conglomerate organizations is significant. For example, Exxon Mobil Corporation reported the elimination of intercompany revenue of $98.1 billion, $113.4 billion, and $136.6 billion for 2000, 2001, and 2002, respectively.[1] These amounts represented 29.7 percent, 34.8 percent, and 40.0 percent of the entity's total sales and other revenue before eliminating intercompany transactions for the three years, respectively.

The views developed in ARB No. 51 have long served as the basic philosophy of the accounting profession toward consolidations and intercompany transactions. In stating the purpose of consolidated financial statements, ARB No. 51 provides a justification for the elimination of intercompany transactions. Regardless of the direction, the intercompany transaction must be removed when preparing the consolidated entity's financial statements because, as discussed in ARB No. 51:

> *The purpose of consolidated statements is to present, primarily for the benefit of the shareholders and creditors of the parent company, the results of operations and the financial position of a parent company and its subsidiaries essentially as if the group were a single company with one or more branches or divisions.*[2]

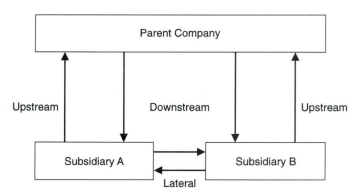

FIGURE 4-1 Directions of Intercompany Transaction

[1] Exxon Mobil Corporation, 2002 10-K.

[2] **Accounting Research Bulletin**, No. 51, "Consolidated Financial Statements" (New York: American Institute of Certified Public Accountants, 1959), par. 1.

In addition, ARB No. 51 also states that "…any intercompany profit or loss on assets remaining within the group should be eliminated; the concept usually applied for this purpose is gross profit or loss" (par. 6). Addressing profit or loss on assets transferred as a result of intercompany transactions is important because many organizations, such as Exxon Mobil, record intercompany inventory transactions (typically the largest dollar amount of intercompany transactions) on a market value basis. For example, failure to eliminate intercompany inventory transactions recorded at market value would result in an overstatement of *Sales, Cost of Goods Sold,* and *Inventory.* Even if the intercompany inventory transaction is recorded at cost, the *Sales* and *Cost of Goods Sold* accounts would be overstated if they are not eliminated when preparing the consolidated financial statements.

The percentage ownership interest by the parent in the subsidiary does not alter the requirement to eliminate intercompany transactions. ARB No. 51 states:

> *The amount of intercompany profit or loss to be eliminated in accordance with paragraph 6 is not affected by the existence of a minority interest. The complete elimination of the intercompany profit or loss is consistent with the underlying assumption that consolidated statements represent the financial position and operating results of a single business enterprise. The elimination of the intercompany profit or loss may be allocated proportionately between the majority and minority interests.*[3]

Paragraph 14 states that intercompany profit or loss *may* be allocated between majority (controlling interest) and minority (noncontrolling) interest. In a downstream transaction, all profit or loss accrues to the parent company because the parent company records the sale. None of the gain or loss is recognized on the subsidiary's books. As a result, the profit or loss is not shared between the parent company stockholders and the noncontrolling interest; that is, all the profit or loss accrues to the parent company stockholders.

This chapter takes the position that the allocation of profit or loss to parent company stockholders and the noncontrolling interest is theoretically preferable in upstream and lateral transactions. The gain or loss is divided between the parent stockholders and the noncontrolling interest in an upstream or a lateral transaction because the subsidiary records the sale and, therefore, records the gain or loss on the sale. Because the parent and noncontrolling stockholders share ownership interest in the subsidiary, the gain or loss is allocated proportionately to the two groups.

IMPACT OF INTERCOMPANY TRANSACTIONS ON FINANCIAL STATEMENTS

Interpreting the impact of intercompany transactions on the financial records of the units involved begins with understanding how the transactions are initially recognized on each unit's financial records. It is also important to understand how each intercompany transaction impacts the income statement and balance sheet of the units involved in the period of the intercompany transaction as well as in subsequent periods. From this understanding it is possible to determine how to adjust the consolidated financial statements for intercompany transactions using worksheet eliminations.

This section presents the journal entries that would be recorded by each entity when selected intercompany transactions occur. Accompanying the journal entries are the worksheet

---

[3] Ibid., par. 14.

eliminations that are necessary to prepare the consolidated financial statements. The remainder of the chapter examines intercompany transactions in the order outlined below:

- Downstream
  - o Intercompany transactions initiated at year-end
    - . Elimination in year of transaction
    - . Second-year elimination
  - o Intercompany transactions initiated during the year
    - . Elimination in year of transaction
    - . Second-year elimination
- Upstream intercompany transactions initiated during the year
  - o Intercompany transactions initiated during the year
    - . Elimination in year of transaction
    - . Second-year elimination

Period of Intercompany Transaction—Downstream (at or near Year-End)

To adjust for the effects of intercompany transactions, additional worksheet eliminations, labeled (5), are required. The purpose of such worksheet eliminations is to adjust the financial information so that it is presented from the perspective of the consolidated entity rather than from the perspective of either the parent or the subsidiary. These adjustments restate the consolidated financial statements to recognize that the effect of intercompany transactions on the consolidated entity is different from the effect recognized on the financial records of either the parent or the subsidiary. The following examples (machine, inventory, and debt) analyze three downstream intercompany transactions. The presentation includes the journal entries recorded by both Pratt and Sterling as well as the worksheet eliminations necessary to prepare the consolidated financial statements.

Fixed Asset Transaction at the End of the Period The following data pertain to the sale of a machine from Pratt to Sterling.

EXAMPLE 4-1A
Downstream sale of a machine on December 31, 2006

Assume a machine was purchased by Pratt on January 1, 2001, for $9,000. The machine is being depreciated using the straight-line method assuming a 10-year life with no salvage value. The machine is sold to Sterling for $6,000 on December 31, 2006. Pratt records its 2006 depreciation expense prior to the sale. At the date of the sale, six years have passed since the purchase of the machine. Thus, the accumulated depreciation is $5,400 ($900 × 6). The remaining useful life of the asset to Sterling is four years.

At the date of the intercompany sale of the machine, Pratt and Sterling record the following entries:

Journal Entry—Pratt Corporation Books

Cash	6,000	
Accumulated Depreciation ($900 × 6)	5,400	
Gain on Sale of Machine		2,400
[$6,000 – ($9,000 – $5,400)]		
Machine		9,000
To record sale of machine to Sterling.		

Journal Entry—Sterling Products Books

Machine	6,000	
Cash		6,000

To record purchase of machine from Pratt.

After completing this transaction, the recognized historical cost of the machine is $6,000 and the accumulated depreciation is $0. In addition, a gain of $2,400 has been recognized on Pratt's income statement. From the consolidated entity's perspective, this transaction never occurred because it did not involve an unrelated party. The December 31, 2006, worksheet elimination must return the *Machine* account to its original historical cost, $9,000, because this amount is the historical cost to the consolidated entity. The worksheet elimination must also reestablish the $5,400 balance in the *Accumulated Depreciation* account. In addition, the $2,400 gain on Pratt's financial records must be eliminated because the transaction is viewed as having not occurred.

The T-account format presented below is used throughout the remainder of the chapter to calculate the dollar amounts necessary for the worksheet eliminations. The T-account format does not specifically represent a ledger account on either company's accounting records. Rather, it is a tool used to calculate the adjustment necessary for the appropriate presentation of the consolidated financial statements. The first entry of each balance sheet T-account is the beginning of year balance (or date of original purchase) on the books where the account was recorded prior to the intercompany transaction. Income statement accounts are presumed to have a zero beginning balance; therefore, the beginning balance is not shown in the T-account. Entries made during the year, on both unit's books, are then displayed below the beginning balance. The consolidated balance for the account is shown as the required ending balance. The amount shaded is the dollar amount of the worksheet elimination needed to convert the existing balance to the correct consolidated balance.

Pratt's machine had a $9,000 historical cost on its financial records at January 1, 2001. The historical cost of the machine was removed from Pratt's financial records on December 31, 2006, and is presented as a $9,000 credit in the T-account. Sterling's recording of the machine purchase appears as a $6,000 debit in the T-account. Because the consolidated financial statements must disclose the original historical cost ($9,000), a debit worksheet elimination of $3,000 is required.

Machine

Pratt purchases machine	1/1/2001	9,000		
Sterling buys machine from Pratt	12/31/2006	6,000	9,000	12/31/2006 Pratt sells machine to Sterling
Worksheet elimination	12/31/2006	3,000		
Consolidated balance	12/31/2006	9,000		

The January 1, 2006, balance in *Accumulated Depreciation* was reported as $4,500 on Pratt's books. A $900 increase in *Accumulated Depreciation* was posted in 2006 to reflect the current year depreciation expense recorded by Pratt. The December 31 balance of $5,400 ($4,500 + $900) was debited by Pratt at the date of sale. Because the consolidated balance at December 31, 2006, should be $5,400, the worksheet elimination must include a $5,400 credit to restore the balance.

Accumulated Depreciation

			4,500	1/1/2006	Pratt's beginning balance
Pratt sells machine to Sterling	12/31/2006	5,400	900	12/31/2006	Pratt's 2006 depreciation expense
			5,400	12/31/2006	Worksheet elimination
			5,400	12/31/2006	Consolidated balance

Because there was no sale by the consolidated entity, the *Gain on Sale of Machine* must be eliminated.

Gain on Sale of Machine

Worksheet elimination	12/31/2006	2,400	2,400	12/31/2006	Pratt sells machine to Sterling
			-0-	12/31/2006	Consolidated balance

The T-account analysis indicates the amounts needed in the Example 4-1a worksheet elimination presented to remove the impact of the intercompany machine sale. Preparing this worksheet elimination will return the balances in the *Machine, Accumulated Depreciation,* and *Gain on Sale of Machine* accounts to the amounts that would have existed had the intercompany transaction never occurred (i.e., the amounts relevant for the consolidated financial statements).

Worksheet Elimination 4-1A—Journal Entry Form		
December 31, 2006		
Machine	3,000	
Gain on Sale of Machine	2,400	
Accumulated Depreciation		5,400

Remember that in the previous two chapters, for efficiency purposes, the fixed asset account was presented net of accumulated depreciation in many of the examples. In this chapter, however, the fixed asset account and accumulated depreciation account are presented separately because tracking the historical cost and accumulated depreciation accounts individually makes it easier to follow the logic of the eliminations necessary in each period.

In Pratt's sale of machinery to Sterling, at the date of the intercompany sale, the accumulated depreciation is removed from the books of Pratt, the seller, and a revised historical cost is recorded on the books of Sterling, the buyer. At the date of sale, therefore, for consolidated reporting purposes the historical cost and accumulated depreciation balances must be restored because there has been no transaction with an unrelated party. In the subsection, Fixed Asset Transaction One Period Subsequent, later in the chapter, it will be shown that additional adjustments must be made to depreciation expense and accumulated depreciation in subsequent periods because Sterling's depreciation expense is based on the price paid rather than the historical cost of the asset to the consolidated entity. Reconstructing the specific effects of the intercompany machinery sale on the machinery account separate from the accumulated depreciation account simplifies the analysis because the restatement of the historical cost is removed from the adjustment due to depreciation expense recognition.

Inventory Transaction at the End of the Period   The following data pertain to the sale of inventory from Pratt to Sterling.

EXAMPLE 4-1B
Downstream sale of inventory on December 30, 2006

Assume Pratt purchases 8,000 units of inventory on November 10, 2006, at a cost of $6 per unit. Pratt sells this inventory to Sterling on December 30, 2006, for $8 per unit. Assume that none of this inventory is sold by Sterling to an unrelated party prior to December 31.

At the date of the intercompany sale of inventory, Pratt and Sterling record the following entries:

Journal Entry—Pratt Corporation Books

Cash	64,000	
Sales (8,000 × $8)		64,000
To record sale of inventory to Sterling.		
Cost of Goods Sold (8,000 × $6)	48,000	
Inventory		48,000
To record cost of inventory sold to Sterling.		

Journal Entry—Sterling Products Books

Inventory	64,000	
Cash		64,000
To record purchase of inventory from Pratt.		

After completing this transaction, the recognized historical cost in Sterling's *Inventory* account is $64,000. In addition, *Sales* of $64,000 and *Cost of Goods Sold* of $48,000 have been recognized on Pratt's income statement. As in the machine example, from the consolidated entity's perspective, this transaction never occurred because it does not involve an unrelated party. The December 31, 2006, worksheet elimination must return the inventory to its original historical cost of $48,000. In addition, the $16,000 gross profit ($64,000 − $48,000) on Pratt's financial records must be eliminated by adjusting *Sales* and *Cost of Goods Sold*. The following T-accounts depict the worksheet eliminations necessary to accomplish this objective.

Sales

Worksheet elimination 12/31/2006	64,000	64,000	12/30/2006	Pratt sells inventory to Sterling
		-0-	12/31/2006	Consolidated balance

Cost of Goods Sold

Pratt sells inventory to Sterling	12/30/2006	48,000	48,000	12/31/2006	Worksheet elimination
Consolidated balance	12/31/2006	-0-			

The *Inventory* T-account shows that Pratt purchases inventory on November 10 for $48,000. This inventory is sold to Sterling on December 30, resulting in a credit of $48,000 by Pratt and a debit of $64,000 by Sterling. The $64,000 also represents Sterling's

Inventory account balance at December 31 because none of the inventory is sold before year-end. The consolidated balance sheet must include inventory at its original historical cost ($48,000). Therefore, a credit worksheet elimination of $16,000 is required.

		Inventory			
Pratt buys inventory	11/10/2006	48,000			
Sterling purchases inventory from Pratt	12/30/2006	64,000	48,000	12/30/2006	Pratt sells inventory to Sterling
			16,000	12/31/2006	Worksheet elimination
Consolidated balance	12/31/2006	48,000			

The T-accounts indicate the amounts needed in the worksheet elimination presented in Example 4-1b to eliminate the intercompany inventory sale. Preparing this worksheet elimination will return the balances in the *Sales, Cost of Goods Sold,* and *Inventory* accounts to the amounts that would have existed had the intercompany transaction never occurred (i.e., the amounts relevant for the consolidated financial statements).

Worksheet Elimination 4-1B—Journal Entry Form

December 31, 2006

Sales	64,000	
Cost of Goods Sold		48,000
Inventory		16,000

Direct intercompany debt transaction: when one unit of an entity makes a loan directly to another unit of the same entity

Indirect intercompany debt transaction: when one unit of an entity acquires, from an unrelated party, debt previously issued by another unit of the same entity

Debt Transaction at the End of the Period Two types of intercompany debt transactions can exist: direct or indirect. **Direct intercompany debt transactions** exist when the two units of the consolidated entity enter into a transaction where one unit makes a loan directly to the other unit. This type of transaction results in an additional worksheet elimination that removes the notes payable and notes receivable, any accrued interest receivable or payable, and any accompanying interest expense or interest revenue. In all periods in which the note is outstanding, the amounts in the worksheet elimination for the notes payable and notes receivable will exactly offset, as will the interest expense and interest revenue, because the two units are recording the loan using the same dollar amount and interest rate at the date of the transaction. **Indirect intercompany debt transactions** occur when one unit of a consolidated entity borrows from an unrelated party and the other unit of the consolidated entity acquires the debt instrument from the unrelated party. If the two transactions occur at different points in time, they are viewed as a borrowing transaction by the debtor and as an investment by the creditor, but the two transactions create an early retirement of debt from the consolidated entity's perspective.

The following data pertain to Sterling's indirect purchase of bonds issued by Pratt.

EXAMPLE 4-1C
Downstream debt transaction on December 31, 2006

Assume Pratt had issued 4,000 20-year bonds payable, each in the amount of $1,000, on June 30, 1994, to finance the construction of a new manufacturing facility. The bonds had a stated interest rate of 7 percent, with interest paid quarterly (80 periods) on a calendar-year basis. Pratt received $3,600,000 on June 30, 1994 (present value of the cash flows discounted at approximately 8.25

percent). The discount is being amortized using the straight-line method.[4] Sterling (the subsidiary) acquires $300,000 of the bonds (7.5 percent) as an investment on December 31, 2006—30 quarters prior to maturity—for $327,000 (the present value of the cash flow discounted at approximately 5.6 percent). Sterling elects to amortize the premium using the straight-line method.

The intercompany debt transaction outlined in Example 4-1c is a downstream indirect purchase of bonds wherein the date Sterling purchases the bonds is not the date on which they are issued by Pratt. On the date the bonds are acquired, the following entry is recorded on Sterling's financial records:

Journal Entry—Sterling Products Books

Investment in Bonds	327,000	
Cash		327,000

To record purchase of Pratt Corporation bonds.

No entry is recorded on Pratt's books at the date of Sterling's investment. From Pratt's perspective, the bonds payable is still outstanding, so no journal entry is required. On the other hand, the consolidated entity would view Sterling's investment in Pratt's bonds as an early retirement of debt, because the debt instrument is acquired by a member of the consolidated entity. As a result, the *Bonds Payable* acquired by Sterling must be eliminated from the consolidated balance sheet. The T-accounts below depict the consolidated entity's view of this transaction. Note that the T-accounts provide information on the intercompany bonds only. The accounting entries for the remainder of the bonds outstanding ($3,700,000) are not affected by the intercompany transaction.

Bonds Payable

			300,000	6/30/1994	Pratt issues bonds
Worksheet elimination	12/31/2006	300,000			
			-0-	12/31/2006	Consolidated balance

Discount on Bonds Payable

Pratt issues bonds: $400,000 × .075	6/30/1994	30,000			
			750	1994	July–Dec. amortization: ($30,000/80)(2)
			18,000	1995–2006	12 years amortization: ($30,000/80)(48)
			11,250	12/31/2006	Worksheet elimination (unamortized balance)
Consolidated balance	12/31/2006	-0-			

The beginning *Discount on Bonds Payable* balance ($30,000) is the discount on the 7.5 percent of the total bond issue acquired by Sterling. The original discount on the total bond issue was $400,000. The quarterly discount amortization ($375) is the straight-line amortization of the $30,000 discount relevant to the bonds acquired by Sterling. Because the bonds pay interest quarterly, the bond discount is amortized over 80 three-month periods.

---

[4] While the effective interest method is generally required, the straight-line method is permissible when the resulting difference in calculated interest expense or revenue is not material. The straight-line method is used in this chapter to simplify calculations.

Investment in Bonds (net)

Sterling's Investment in Pratt's bonds	12/31/2006	327,000			
			327,000	12/31/2006	Worksheet elimination
Consolidated balance	12/31/2006	-0-			

Loss on Early Debt Retirement

Worksheet elimination	12/31/2006	38,250	
Consolidated balance	12/31/2006	38,250*	

* Purchase Price		$327,000
Face Value of Bond	$300,000	
Unamortized Discount	11,250	
Carrying Value		288,750
Loss on Early Debt Retirement		$38,250

The worksheet elimination presented in Example 4-1c removes $300,000 of *Bonds Payable* (the amount acquired by Sterling) and the entire *Investment in Bonds* account from the consolidated balance sheet. The elimination of the *Bonds Payable* is accompanied by the elimination of a proportionate share of the *Discount on Bonds Payable*. The difference between the carrying value of the bonds payable eliminated and the amount paid for the bonds by the investor is recognized as a *Loss on Early Debt Retirement* on the consolidated income statement.

Worksheet Elimination 4-1C—Journal Entry Form		
December 31, 2006		
Bonds Payable	300,000	
Loss on Early Debt Retirement	38,250	
Discount on Bonds Payable		11,250
Investment in Bonds		327,000

Comparison of Intercompany Asset Versus Indirect Intercompany Debt Transactions A major difference between Example 4-1c and Examples 4-1a (machine) and 4-1b (inventory) discussed previously is the creation of the loss on the consolidated income statement. Gains and losses were eliminated in Examples 4-1a and 4-1b, while a loss is created in Example 4-1c. This difference occurs because the consolidated entity views the Example 4-1c transaction differently from the previous examples. An intercompany sale of assets is viewed by the consolidated entity as being a transaction that has not occurred, although it has been recorded on the books of the buyer and seller. The gain or loss reported on the seller's books, therefore, must be removed when preparing the consolidated financial statements. An indirect intercompany effective retirement of debt is viewed by the consolidated entity as a transaction that has occurred because cash is paid to a party other than the parent or subsidiary. The worksheet elimination is prepared to record the loss because neither party recognized that an early debt retirement has occurred from the consolidated point of view.

Basic Worksheet Eliminations The Examples 4-1a, 4-1b, and 4-1c worksheet eliminations are prepared in addition to the required basic worksheet eliminations. With regard to the current examples (downstream), the basic worksheet eliminations are not altered by the occurrence of intercompany transactions in the current period.

First, consider worksheet elimination (1), which eliminates the parent's beginning investment account and the subsidiary's beginning stockholders' equity accounts while it establishes the beginning purchase differentials and the beginning noncontrolling interest. An intercompany transaction that occurs *during* the current period cannot impact any of these amounts because this worksheet elimination eliminates/establishes *beginning* of period balances.

Also, consider worksheet elimination (2), which removes the parent's *Investment Income* and subsidiary *Dividends* allocated to the parent from the consolidated financial statements. Recall that Pratt's adjusting entry to recognize *Investment Income* is based on Sterling's reported net income and Pratt's ownership percentage. The downstream intercompany transactions have no impact on Sterling's income statement and do not impact this worksheet elimination.

Next, recall that the amortization of purchase differentials, worksheet elimination (3), is based on the amounts established when the subsidiary is acquired. These amounts are not impacted by intercompany transactions even if subsidiary assets that are assigned purchase differentials are sold to the parent or to another subsidiary. In such a case the asset is adjusted to its original value on the subsidiary's financial records, and the cost allocation (e.g., *Depreciation Expense* or *Cost of Goods Sold*) and purchase differential amortization is recognized as if the asset had not been sold.

Finally, worksheet elimination (4) establishes the *Noncontrolling Interest in Net Income of Subsidiary* and adjusts the *Noncontrolling Interest* account. This basic worksheet elimination allocates the noncontrolling interest proportion of subsidiary net income to the noncontrolling stockholders. Again, because downstream intercompany transactions have no impact on the subsidiary's income statement, worksheet elimination (4) is not adjusted for the intercompany transactions presented thus far.

Period Subsequent to Intercompany Transaction—Downstream

Worksheet eliminations are required in periods subsequent to an intercompany transaction until the asset is sold or abandoned (or the liability matures) because the worksheet eliminations prepared in the year of the intercompany transaction are not posted to the books of either the parent or the subsidiary. The worksheet elimination in subsequent periods differs from the worksheet elimination prepared in the period of the intercompany transaction in that an adjustment to the beginning of year *Retained Earnings* is generally included in each subsequent-period worksheet elimination. Subsequent period worksheet eliminations are discussed next as a continuation of the examples developed earlier in the chapter.

Fixed Asset Transaction One Period Subsequent

EXAMPLE 4-2A
Downstream sale of a machine (4-1A continued)

Assume that in 2007 Sterling uses the machine acquired from Pratt on December 31, 2006, and records depreciation as appropriate.

The machine is recorded on Sterling's books at an amount different from the original value on Pratt's books. The worksheet elimination is used to return the machine to its original historical cost because, from the consolidated perspective, the intercompany transaction has not occurred. That is, the fixed asset still belongs to the consolidated entity. The adjustment to any long-term asset account, except intangible assets, will be the same in all periods until the asset is sold or abandoned. Intangible assets differ because periodic amortizations are posted directly to the asset account rather than to a contra account such as *Accumulated Depreciation.*

The adjustment to the *Machine* account will remain at $3,000 every period until the machine is sold or abandoned. Recall that this is the amount by which the cost basis changed when it was sold by Pratt to Sterling. From the consolidated entity's perspective, this change in cost basis has not occurred because the asset has not left the consolidated entity.

Recall that the sale of the machine by Pratt to Sterling occurred on December 31, 2006. During 2007, Sterling recognizes $1,500 ($6,000/4 years) depreciation expense on its income statement. The T-accounts below indicate the amounts recognized on the books of Pratt and Sterling with regard to the machine and the worksheet elimination necessary to prepare the consolidated financial statements at December 31, 2007.

Machine

Pratt purchases machine	1/1/2001	9,000			
Sterling buys machine from Pratt	12/31/2006	6,000	9,000	12/31/2006	Pratt sells machine to Sterling
Worksheet elimination	12/31/2007	3,000			
Consolidated balance	12/31/2007	9,000			

Depreciation Expense

Sterling's 2007 depreciation expense	12/31/2007	1,500	600	12/31/2007	Worksheet elimination
Consolidated balance ($9,000/10)	12/31/2007	900			

The cost allocation recognized by the purchaser will often differ from the amount that would have been recognized by the consolidated entity had the intercompany transaction not occurred. This is because any gain or loss on the sale causes a change in the cost basis. Keep in mind that the seller's historical cost is the basis for the consolidated entity's cost allocations because the change in the historical cost resulting from the intercompany transaction is not recognized. In Example 4-2a, Pratt's 2007 *Depreciation Expense* would have been $900 had the asset not been sold to Sterling. Sterling's *Depreciation Expense* is booked at $1,500 ($6,000/4 years). Therefore, an adjustment must be made to reduce *Depreciation Expense* by $600. The *Depreciation Expense* adjustment in subsequent periods will be the same dollar amount if straight-line depreciation is used. The amount will change from period to period if other depreciation methods are used.

Accumulated Depreciation

			4,500	1/1/2006	Pratt's beginning balance
Pratt sells machine to Sterling	12/31/2006	5,400	900	12/31/2006	Pratt's 2006 depreciation expense
			1,500	12/31/2007	Sterling's 2007 depreciation expense
			4,800	12/31/2007	Worksheet elimination
			6,300	12/31/2007	Consolidated balance: ($9,000/10)(7)

In conjunction with the adjustment to the *Depreciation Expense* account, the adjustment to *Accumulated Depreciation* also changes. Recall that the *Accumulated Depreciation* account ($5,400) was removed from Pratt's financial records at the date of the intercompany transaction. A worksheet elimination was necessary to restate the *Accumulated Depreciation* as of that date. Subsequent to the acquisition, the purchaser (Sterling) recognizes *Depreciation Expense* at a faster rate ($1,500 per year) than the consolidated entity recognizes *Depreciation Expense* ($900 per year). As a result, Sterling increases its *Accumulated Depreciation* balance faster than the consolidated entity, and the periodic adjustment to *Accumulated Depreciation* becomes smaller by $600 each year.

Retained Earnings

			-0-	1/1/2006	Beginning balance
Worksheet elimination	1/1/2007	2,400	2,400	12/31/2006	Pratt sells machine to Sterling
			-0-	1/1/2007	Consolidated balance

The amount disclosed as *Retained Earnings* on the consolidated balance sheet will also be adjusted in subsequent periods until the historical cost of the asset *to the purchaser* is allocated to the income statement. This adjustment occurs because of the impact of the original transaction and subsequent cost allocations on the buyer's and seller's income statements. At the intercompany transaction date, Pratt recognizes a $2,400 gain while Sterling's recognizes a book value ($6,000) that is $2,400 greater than the machine's book value on Pratt's accounting records ($9,000 – $5,400). The higher book value on Sterling's accounting records will result in $2,400 additional depreciation expense over the machine's remaining life being recorded by Sterling. Thus, over the machine's remaining life, Pratt's recognized gain is completely offset by the difference between Sterling's recognized *Depreciation Expense* and the *Depreciation Expense* reported on the consolidated income statement. The worksheet elimination to *Retained Earnings* in the current example is a $2,400 debit. This amount will be reduced in subsequent years by $600 per year and the adjustment to *Retained Earnings* will no longer be necessary the year after the machine's cost is fully allocated to Sterling's income statement.

Example 4-2a presents the 2007 worksheet elimination for the machine example.

Worksheet Elimination 4-2A—Journal Entry Form		
December 31, 2007		
Machine	3,000	
Retained Earnings (January 1, 2007)	2,400	
Depreciation Expense		600
Accumulated Depreciation		4,800

To understand how the *Accumulated Depreciation* and *Retained Earnings* adjustments change in worksheet elimination (5) from year to year, it is important to examine the dollar amount of adjustments to worksheet elimination accounts over time. The following table presents a summary of selected information that impacts the worksheet elimination each year over the remaining life of the machine sold downstream to Sterling.

	Gain on Sale of Machine	Depreciation Expense to Adjust Sterling to Consolidated ($1,500 – $900)	Accumulated Depreciation	Retained Earnings
2006	$2,400		$5,400	
2007		$600	4,800	$2,400
2008		600	4,200	1,800
2009		600	3,600	1,200
2010		600	3,000	600
2011			3,000	0

Note that in the period of the intercompany sale (2006) there is an income statement adjustment *(Gain on Sale of Machine)* but no adjustment to *Retained Earnings*. The $2,400 adjustment to *Retained Earnings* resulting from the gain on sale is not part of the worksheet elimination until 2007 because the gain is not closed to *Retained Earnings* until the end of the accounting period during which the sale occurred. In subsequent years, 2008–2011, the worksheet elimination to *Retained Earnings* decreases by $600 ($1,500 – $900) per year due to the excess *Depreciation Expense* recorded on Sterling's financial records relative to the consolidated income statement. The *Accumulated Depreciation* worksheet elimination amount in 2006 returns Pratt's recognized *Accumulated Depreciation* to the consolidated balance sheet. In each subsequent period, Sterling recognizes *Depreciation Expense* ($1,500) greater than the consolidated *Depreciation Expense* ($900). As a result, the worksheet elimination to *Accumulated Depreciation* will decrease by $600 each year. Note that the worksheet elimination to *Accumulated Depreciation* does not cease to exist when the machine is fully depreciated. Rather, the dollar amount of the *Accumulated Depreciation* worksheet elimination will equal the worksheet elimination to the *Machine* account and both will be eliminated in equal dollar amounts until the machine is sold or abandoned.

Inventory Transaction One Period Subsequent

EXAMPLE 4-2B
Downstream sale of inventory (4-1B Continued)

Assume that during 2007 Sterling sold, to unrelated parties, all 8,000 units of inventory that had been acquired from Pratt on December 30, 2006. The selling price was $96,000. As a result of these sales, Sterling recognized $64,000 cost of goods sold (8,000 units × $8 cost per unit). In addition, assume that during 2007 Sterling purchased an additional 18,000 units from Pratt for $9 per unit. These goods also had cost Pratt $6 per unit. Note that the markup per unit on goods sold by Pratt to Sterling increased from $2 per unit in 2006 to $3 per unit in 2007. Of the 18,000 units of inventory purchased by Sterling in 2007, 14,000 units were sold to unrelated parties in the same year for a total of $168,000.

The T-accounts below indicate the amounts recognized on Pratt's and Sterling's books plus the worksheet elimination necessary (the shaded values) to prepare the consolidated financial statements at December 31, 2007.

		Sales			
			264,000	2007	Sterling sells to unrelated entity: $96,000 + $168,000
Worksheet elimination	12/31/2007	162,000	162,000	2007	Pratt sells 18,000 units to Sterling
			264,000	12/31/2007	Consolidated balance

The current period intercompany sale by Pratt must be removed from the consolidated income statement as in the previous inventory example. In this case, the *Sales* amount must be adjusted to eliminate the current period intercompany sale of $162,000. Note that Sterling's $264,000 of sales to unrelated parties are not eliminated because such sales are transactions with parties outside the consolidated entity.

Cost of Goods Sold

Sterling sells inventory to unrelated entity: (8,000 × $8) + (14,000 × $9)	2007	190,000			
Pratt sells inventory to Sterling: (18,000) ($6)	2007	108,000	166,000	12/31/2007	Worksheet elimination: (18,000) ($6) + 8,000 × ($2) + (14,000) × ($3)
Consolidated balance: (22,000) ($6)	12/31/2007	132,000			

The *Cost of Goods Sold* worksheet elimination ($166,000) is comprised of three parts in the current example:

1. *The Cost of Goods Sold reported by Pratt relating to its 2007 sales to Sterling.* The 2007 intercompany sales resulted in $108,000 (18,000 × $6) of *Cost of Goods Sold* to be eliminated.

2. *Sterling's markup in the beginning inventory sold to unrelated parties during 2007.* In conjunction with the higher historical cost basis of the inventory on Sterling's books from the 2006 intercompany inventory transaction, the *Cost of Goods Sold* recognized by Sterling will be higher than the amount that would have been recognized by Pratt had the intercompany inventory transaction not taken place. The per-unit beginning inventory cost on Sterling's books is $8 while the per-unit cost that had been on Pratt's books is $6. Therefore, *Cost of Goods Sold* must be reduced by the $2 per unit cost difference for each of the 8,000 beginning inventory units sold by Sterling to unrelated parties. The result is a $16,000 adjustment to *Cost of Goods Sold.*

3. *Sterling's markup in Cost of Goods Sold relating to current period purchases sold to unrelated parties. Cost of Goods Sold* must be reduced by $3 per unit for each of the 14,000 units purchased from Pratt in 2007 for $9 and resold to unrelated parties in the same year.

The three component parts ($108,000 + $16,000 + $42,000) total to the $166,000 *Cost of Goods Sold* elimination.

Inventory

Sterling's beginning inventory: 8,000 × $8	1/1/2007	64,000			
Pratt purchase of inventory: 18,000 × $6	2007	108,000	108,000 2007		Pratt sells 18,000 units to Sterling
Sterling purchases from Pratt: 18,000 × $9	2007	162,000	190,000 2007		Sterling sells inventory to unrelated entities: (8,000×$8) + (14,000×$9)
			12,000 12/31/2007		Worksheet elimination: 4,000 × $3
Consolidated balance: 4,000 × $6	12/31/2007	24,000			

The *Inventory* T-account reveals that Sterling's beginning 2007 inventory is valued at $64,000. During 2007 Pratt purchased 18,000 units of inventory for $108,000 and sold that inventory to Sterling, resulting in a debit and a credit entry to the T-account. Sterling recognized the 2007 intercompany purchase of inventory for $162,000. Sterling also sold inventory to unrelated entities during 2007. The *Cost of Goods Sold* recognized from all Sterling's sales to unrelated parties is $190,000 (8,000 × $8 + 14,000 × $9). As a result, the ending inventory on Sterling's books is $36,000 [(18,000 units purchased − 14,000 units sold) × $9 cost per unit]. The amount that would be recognized if the ending inventory was still on Pratt's books is $24,000 (4,000 units × $6 cost per unit). Therefore, the worksheet elimination must reduce the inventory's carrying value by $12,000.

Retained Earnings

			-0-	1/1/2006	Beginning balance
Worksheet elimination	1/1/2007	16,000	16,000	12/31/2006	Pratt's 2006 Net Income due to inventory sold to Sterling
			-0-	1/1/2007	Consolidated balance

During 2006 Pratt recognized $16,000 gross profit (*Sales − Cost of Goods Sold*) when inventory was sold to Sterling. At the end of 2006, this gross profit was transferred to Pratt's *Retained Earnings* when the financial records were closed. As a result, the gross profit from 2006 downstream intercompany sales is included in the beginning 2007 *Retained Earnings* account balance. The 2007 adjustment to beginning *Retained Earnings* removes this gross profit because the inventory was not sold to unrelated parties before the end of 2006, and therefore Pratt's January 1, 2007, *Retained Earnings* balance is overstated by the unrealized profit. The unrealized profit remains in *Retained Earnings* until the period after the intercompany inventory is sold to a party outside the consolidated entity.

Worksheet Elimination 4-2B—Journal Entry Form		
December 31, 2007		
Sales	162,000	
Retained Earnings (January 1, 2007)	16,000	
Cost of Goods Sold		166,000
Inventory		12,000

The worksheet elimination related to the 2007 inventory transactions is presented in Example 4-2b. Notice that there is no structural difference between the worksheet elimination for the downstream sale of a machine (Example 4-2a) and the worksheet elimination for the downstream sale of inventory (Example 4-2b). Specifically, the adjustments to the asset account, the cost allocation, and the equity are accomplished similarly for both transactions. The asset account (*Machine* or *Inventory*) is returned to the value that would be disclosed on the original owner's financial records had the intercompany transaction not taken place. In accord with the change in the recognized historical cost, the cost allocation (*Depreciation Expense* or *Cost of Goods Sold*) is adjusted to reflect the allocation of the historical cost to the original owner. Finally, the *Retained Earnings* adjustment reflects the net consolidation worksheet eliminations made to the income statement accounts in previous periods due to the intercompany transaction.

The primary issue to consider when preparing the worksheet elimination for intercompany inventory transactions is the removal of the intercompany markup from the consolidated financial statements. The volume of inventory activity can sometimes require a very detailed analysis when using T-accounts to determine the dollar amount of markup in beginning inventory, current period activity, and ending inventory. A matrix of inter-company inventory activity can be a useful tool when analyzing the inventory markup and constructing the required worksheet elimination. Generally the worksheet elimination in Example 4-2b can be developed using the system illustrated below.

	Number of Units	*Cost to Seller*	*Markup*	*Price to Buyer*
Beginning Inventory (Buyer's Books)			①	
Current Period Intercompany Transfers (Seller's Books)		④		⑤
Less Ending Inventory (Buyer's Books)			③	
Sold (by Buyer to unrelated parties)			②	

	Debit	*Credit*
Sales	⑤	
Retained Earnings	①	
Cost of Good Sold		② + ④
Inventory		③

Notice that all of the dollar values in the markup column are eliminated in steps. First, the markup in the buyer's beginning inventory ① results in an adjustment to the seller's beginning *Retained Earnings* balance because this markup represents the, as yet, unrealized profit. Second, the markup in those goods sold by the buyer to unrelated parties in the current year results in an adjustment to the *Cost of Goods Sold* ② reported by the buyer. This adjustment is needed because the recognized *Cost of Goods Sold* includes the markup, so it is overstated from the consolidated entity's perspective. Third, markup on those intercompany goods still in the buyer's year-end *Inventory* ③ is the amount eliminated from the ending *Inventory* balance.

Finally, the markup on goods sold intercompany during the current period is eliminated. This part of the elimination is slightly more involved because the entire intercompany balances on the seller's books in *Sales* ⑤ and *Cost of Goods Sold* ④ must be eliminated because the sales are to a related party. By eliminating both balances, the equivalent of the amount in the markup column is removed. That is, the net of these two amounts, ⑤ minus ④, equals the markup on current period intercompany sales. Thus, the components of the inventory matrix markup column explain the entire flow of markup on intercompany goods and provide the basis for the line items of the inventory worksheet elimination.

To demonstrate the use of the matrix approach, the following information is taken from Example 4-2b.

	Number of Units	Cost to Pratt	Markup	Pratt's Selling Price
Beginning Inventory	8,000	$48,000	$16,000	$ 64,000
2007 Sales to Sterling	18,000	108,000	54,000	162,000
Less Ending Inventory*	(4,000)	(24,000)	(12,000)	(36,000)
Sold	22,000	$132,000	$58,000	$190,000

* Assumes a first-in, first-out cost flow.

The five values shaded in the table combine to make up the worksheet elimination presented in Example 4-2b. Two of the values ($108,000 and $58,000) combine to make up the *Cost of Goods Sold* adjustment, while the other three amounts are adjustments to individual accounts (*Sales,* $162,000; *Retained Earnings*, $16,000; *Inventory* $12,000).

Debt Transaction One Period Subsequent

EXAMPLE 4-2C
Downstream debt transaction (4-1C Continued)

Assume that Sterling holds the investment in Pratt's bonds made in 2006 for the entire year and that Pratt and Sterling record the appropriate interest amounts in 2007.

During 2007, Pratt and Sterling record the following journal entries to recognize the payment and receipt of interest for each quarter.

Journal Entry—Pratt Corporation Books

Quarterly Entry	Interest Expense ($300,000 .07) × (3/12) + ($30,000/80)	5,625	
	Discount on Bonds Payable ($30,000/80)		375
	Cash ($300,000 .07) × (3/12)		5,250
	To record 2007 interest payment for three months.		

Journal Entry—Sterling Products Books

Quarterly Entry	Cash ($300,000 .07) × (3/12)	5,250	
	Investment in Bonds ($27,000/30)		900
	Interest revenue		4,350
	To record 2007 interest receipt for three months.		

The T-accounts below illustrate the worksheet elimination necessary to remove the relevant part of the *Bonds Payable* and all related accounts and the entire *Investment in Bonds* as well as adjust *Retained Earnings* due to income statement effects from the prior period.

Bonds Payable

			300,000	6/30/1994 Pratt issues bonds
Worksheet elimination 12/31/2007	300,000			
			-0-	12/31/2007 Consolidated balance

Discount on Bonds Payable

Pratt issues bonds: $400,000 × .075	6/30/1994	30,000		
			750	1994 July–Dec. amortization: ($30,000/80)(2)
			19,500	1995–2007 13 years amortization: ($30,000/80)(52)
			9,750	12/31/2007 Worksheet elimination (unamortized balance)
Consolidated balance	12/31/2007	-0-		

Investment in Bonds

Sterling's investment in Pratt's bonds	12/31/2006	327,000			
			3,600	2007	Premium amortization: ($27,000/30)(4)
			323,400	12/31/2007	Worksheet elimination
Consolidated balance	12/31/2007	-0-			

As was the case at the end of 2006, the 7.5 percent of the *Bonds Payable* acquired by Sterling ($300,000) is eliminated in 2007 when preparing the consolidated financial statements because worksheet eliminations were not posted to any entity's financial records in 2006. The discount eliminated is reduced from $11,250 on December 31, 2006 (Example 4-1c) to $9,750 on December 31, 2007 (Example 4-2c). The decrease in the worksheet elimination to the *Discount on Bonds Payable* ($11,250 vs. $9,750) is equal to the discount amortized by Pratt during 2007 on the $300,000 of bonds purchased by Sterling. The worksheet elimination to the *Discount on Bonds Payable* will continue to decrease each period as the discount is amortized. Similarly, the change in the worksheet elimination to the *Investment in Bonds* account reflects the premium amortization recorded by Sterling. This amount will also continue to change throughout the remaining life of the bonds until the bonds mature, at which time the *Investment in Bonds* account will equal the face value of the bonds acquired ($300,000 in the current example).

Interest Revenue

Worksheet elimination	12/31/2007	17,400	17,400	2007	Sterling interest revenue: ($300,000 × .07) − ($27,000/30)(4)
			-0-	12/31/2007	Consolidated balance

Interest Expense

Pratt interest expense: $300,000 × .07 + ($30,000/80)(4)	2007	22,500	22,500	12/31/2007	Worksheet elimination
Consolidated balance	12/31/2007	-0-			

The entire amount of *Interest Revenue* recorded by Sterling is viewed by the consolidated entity as intercompany revenue because it was received from Pratt. Similarly, the portion of the *Interest Expense* recorded by Pratt and relating to the bonds purchased by Sterling is viewed by the consolidated entity as an intercompany expense. The *Interest Expense* recorded by Pratt and paid to unrelated parties (not shown here) is not an intercompany transaction. In summary, the entire *Interest Revenue* and *Interest Expense* balances relating to the $300,000 of bonds retired are intercompany, so they are fully eliminated.

Retained Earnings

Beginning balance	1/1/2006	-0-	
Worksheet elimination	1/1/2007	38,250	
Consolidated balance	1/1/2007	38,250	

The worksheet elimination prepared at December 31, 2007, to adjust the January 1, 2007, *Retained Earnings* balance reflects the *Loss on Early Debt Retirement* included in the 2006 worksheet elimination. Remember that the $38,250 *Loss on Early Debt Retirement* was not recognized on the books of either Pratt or Sterling in 2006; therefore, the *Retained Earnings* accounts were unaffected at that time. This amount was subtracted in calculating consolidated net income in 2006 and therefore reduced the consolidated *Retained Earnings* at December 31, 2006. It now must be subtracted from beginning *Retained Earnings* on the 2007 consolidated financial statements. The worksheet elimination to *Retained Earnings* will decrease in future periods as the intercompany *Interest Revenue* and *Interest Expense* are eliminated in subsequent worksheet eliminations. The difference between *Interest Revenue* and *Interest Expense* eliminated in a given year is the amount by which the next year's *Retained Earnings* worksheet elimination will decrease. For example, the 2008 *Retained Earnings* worksheet elimination will be $33,150 = $38,250 – ($22,500 – $17,400). Also, notice that the *Interest Expense* worksheet elimination (credit) is greater than the *Interest Revenue* worksheet elimination (debit). This will always occur when the worksheet elimination at the date of the intercompany debt transaction results in a *Loss on Early Debt Retirement*. The opposite will occur if an intercompany bond transaction results in a *Gain on Early Debt Retirement* (illustrated later in the chapter).

Worksheet Elimination 4-2C—Journal Entry Form

December 31, 2007

Bonds Payable	300,000	
Interest Revenue	17,400	
Retained Earnings (January 1, 2007)	38,250	
Discount on Bonds Payable		9,750
Interest Expense		22,500
Investment in Bonds		323,400

Example 4-2c presents the worksheet elimination in journal entry form. The 2007 worksheet elimination differs from the 2006 worksheet presented in Example 4-1c in that the *Interest Revenue, Interest Expense,* and *Retained Earnings* must be adjusted, but the *Loss on Early Debt Retirement* is not recreated.

Periods Subsequent to Intercompany Transaction—Summary

Worksheet eliminations in subsequent periods are prepared to remove the impact of intercompany transactions initiated in a previous period from the consolidated income statement and balance sheet as long as balance sheet accounts are valued incorrectly and/or income, as measured by the buyer and seller, does not match the income that should be reported for the consolidated entity. The worksheet eliminations in the periods subsequent to intercompany transactions result in: (1) the removal of current period of income statement amounts related to intercompany transactions (e.g., *Depreciation Expense, Sales* and *Cost of Goods Sold,* and *Interest Expense* and *Interest Revenue* for the three examples presented above, respectively); (2) the restatement of balance sheet accounts to the historical values that would have existed on the financial records where initially recorded if the intercompany transaction had not occurred (e.g., *Machine* and *Accumulated Depreciation; Inventory;* and *Bonds Payable, Premium (Discount) on Bonds Payable,* and *Investment in Bonds,* respectively); and (3) the adjustment made to *Retained Earnings* (January 1) relating to all unrealized intercompany income statement effects existing at the end of the prior year. *Retained Earnings* (January 1) must be adjusted in subsequent years for all intercompany transactions because prior period income statement worksheet eliminations affect the beginning *Retained Earnings* in subsequent years.

The adjustments to cost allocations for intercompany asset transactions are necessary because the historical cost to the seller is the relevant basis for allocations on the consolidated income statement, not the historical cost to the buyer (buyer's cost includes seller's profit margin). The restatement of the asset to the seller's historical cost occurs because, from the consolidated perspective, an arm's-length transaction with an unrelated party has not occurred. Therefore, there is no justification for revaluing the asset.

The balances in the accounts relating to intercompany debt transactions are eliminated because the debt is viewed as retired from a consolidated entity perspective, so no liability or investment exists, and there is no interest to recognize. Once the maturity date is reached, no further adjustments are necessary because the debt and the investment are removed from the issuer's and investor's accounting records, respectively.

Period of Intercompany Transaction— Downstream (During the Year)

Few intercompany transactions actually occur at the end of a year. As a result, additional accounts are affected due to the passage of time between the date of the intercompany transaction and year-end. Complexities in the consolidation procedures arise because in the year of the intercompany transaction, for example, the plant asset will be depreciated by the new owner, inventory may be sold by the purchaser, or the investor purchasing the intercompany bonds will record interest revenue and amortization of a discount or premium. The following examples (machine, inventory, and debt) present three downstream intercompany transactions that occur during the year. The journal entries recorded by Pratt and Sterling as well as the worksheet eliminations necessary to prepare the consolidated financial statements are presented.

Fixed Asset Transaction During the Period with Change in Estimated Life   The following example is based on the facts presented in Example 4-1a, with two exceptions. First, the date that Pratt sells the machine to Sterling is changed. Second, the estimated remaining life assigned to the asset by Sterling is different from the remaining life to Pratt.

EXAMPLE 4-3A
Downstream sale of a machine on May 1, 2006

Assume a machine was purchased by Pratt on January 1, 2001, for $9,000. The machine is being depreciated using the straight-line method assuming a 10-year life with no salvage value. The machine is sold to Sterling for $6,000 on May 1, 2006. Pratt recorded depreciation expense for the period from January 1 to April 30, 2006. At the date of the sale, 64 months have passed since Pratt purchased the machine. Thus, the accumulated depreciation is $4,800 [$9,000 (64/120)]. Sterling increases the machine's estimated remaining life to eight years.

The following journal entries are recorded on Pratt's and Sterling's accounting records at the date of the intercompany transaction:

Journal Entry—Pratt Corporation Books

Cash	6,000	
Accumulated Depreciation ($9,000) (64/120)	4,800	
Gain on sale of machine [$6,000 – ($9,000 – $4,800)]		1,800
Machine		9,000
To record sale of machine to Sterling.		

Journal Entry—Sterling Products Books

Machine	6,000	
Cash		6,000

To record purchase of machine from Pratt.

The T-accounts that follow display the determination of the dollar amounts for the worksheet elimination in Example 4-3a. The *Machine* account has the same $3,000 worksheet elimination amount as in Example 4-1a. The purchase price by Sterling is $3,000 less than the original purchase price by Pratt. Therefore, the *Machine* account worksheet elimination will be a debit of $3,000 each year.

Machine

Pratt purchases machine	1/1/2001	9,000			
Sterling buys machine from Pratt	5/1/2006	6,000	9,000	5/1/2006	Pratt sells machine to Sterling
Worksheet elimination	12/31/2006	3,000			
Consolidated balance	12/31/2006	9,000			

When an intercompany sale of a plant asset occurs at any time other than the end of an accounting period, there are two income statement accounts that must be considered when preparing worksheet elimination (5) in the period of the intercompany transaction. First, gain or loss on sale of the plant asset must be eliminated as in Example 4-1a. The amount of gain to be eliminated in the current example differs from the amount eliminated in Example 4-1a because the date of sale was changed, so the book value at the date of sale differed. The elimination of the entire gain is still required as discussed previously.

Gain on Sale of Machine

Worksheet elimination	12/31/2006	1,800	1,800	5/1/2006	Pratt sells machine to Sterling
			-0-	12/31/2006	Consolidated balance

Second, the difference between the purchaser's depreciation expense and the required consolidated depreciation expense subsequent to the date of the intercompany transaction must be eliminated. The *Depreciation Expense* recognized by the original owner (Pratt in a downstream transaction) prior to the intercompany transaction date is always the relevant amount for the consolidated income statement with regard to the period prior to the intercompany transaction. Thus, it does not result in a worksheet elimination adjustment. The *Depreciation Expense* adjustment that must be made as part of worksheet elimination (5) pertains only to the difference between the *Depreciation Expense* recognized by the purchaser (Sterling in a downstream transaction) and the *Depreciation Expense* that should be on the consolidated income statement for the period from the date of the intercompany transaction until year-end.

The worksheet elimination (5) adjustment to depreciation expense is more involved when the estimated remaining life changes at the intercompany transaction date. Sterling's recognized *Depreciation Expense* is based on Sterling's historical cost ($6,000) and the eight-year estimated remaining life assigned to the machine. In Example 4-2a, Sterling's recognized *Depreciation Expense* was compared to the *Depreciation Expense* that would have been recorded by Pratt to determine the worksheet elimination (5) adjustment. When Sterling changes the machine's estimated remaining life, the revised estimated life must be used to calculate consolidated *Depreciation Expense.* Pratt's book value remains the basis for calculating consolidated *Depreciation Expense* because Pratt was the original owner and Pratt's book value is the unamortized amount of the expenditure. However, Sterling's assigned estimated life must be used to calculate consolidated *Depreciation Expense* because it now represents the revised remaining time over which the machine will be used by the consolidated entity. Thus, subsequent to the date Sterling acquires the machine, consolidated *Depreciation Expense* is calculated using Pratt's book value and Sterling's estimated remaining life. This is basically the same approach to recording depreciation expense on any asset when there is a change in estimated life. Pratt had already depreciated the asset for 5 years, 4 months out of an original estimated 10-year life at the date Sterling acquired the machine. The estimated remaining useful life became 8 years as compared to the 4 years, 8 months remaining to Pratt had the machine not been sold. The new estimated remaining life assigned by Sterling is a change in accounting estimate from the consolidated perspective.

The adjustment to depreciation expense impacts the worksheet elimination from the date of the intercompany transaction until the end of the asset's estimated remaining life. The amount of the *Depreciation Expense* adjustment for 2006 in Example 4-3a is based on the following information:

			Depreciation Expense	
	Pratt	Sterling	Recognized	Consolidated
Jan. 1–April 30, 2006 [($9,000/10)4/12]	$300	N/A	$300	$300
May 1–Dec. 31, 2006 [($9,000 − $4,800)/8](8/12)				$350
[($6,000/8)8/12]	N/A	$500	$500	
Totals			$800	$650

Depreciation Expense

Pratt's 2006 depreciation expense	5/1/2006	300			
Sterling's 2006 depreciation expense	12/31/2006	500	150	12/31/2006	Worksheet elimination
Consolidated balance	12/31/2006	650			

In the year Pratt sells the machine to Sterling, *Depreciation Expense* is recognized on Pratt's accounting records for four months and on Sterling's accounting records for eight months. Pratt's recognized *Depreciation Expense* prior to the intercompany transaction ($300) is reflected on the consolidated income statement, and it does not impact the worksheet elimination because it is based on the seller's (Pratt's) historical cost and estimated remaining life. This amount is correct from the consolidated entity's point of view. The $150 ($500 − $350) of *Depreciation Expense* recognized by Sterling above what would have been recognized on the consolidated income statement from May 1 to December 31 results in an adjustment to worksheet elimination (5). This amount is subtracted from depreciation expense when removing the impact of the intercompany transaction from the consolidated financial statements. The *Depreciation Expense* T-account shows the amounts recorded by Pratt and Sterling as well as the worksheet elimination necessary to present the correct consolidated *Depreciation Expense.*

Accumulated Depreciation

		4,500	1/1/2006	Pratt's beginning balance
Pratt sells machine to Sterling 5/1/2006	4,800	300	5/1/2006	Pratt's 2006 depreciation expense
		500	12/31/2006	Sterling's 2006 depreciation expense
		4,650	12/31/2006	Worksheet elimination
		5,150*	12/31/2006	Consolidated balance

* Consolidated accumulated depreciation

from 1/1/2001 to 4/30/2006 ($9,000/10) × 5 years 4 months	$4,800
from 5/1/2006 to 12/31/2006 [($9,000 − $4,800)/8]8/12 year	350
Consolidated balance in accumulated depreciation 12/31/2006	$5,150

The worksheet adjustment to *Accumulated Deprecation* is a direct extension of the *Depreciation Expense* T-account. *Accumulated Depreciation* on Pratt's accounting records ($4,800) is completely removed at the date of the intercompany transaction. Sterling then starts to recognize *Depreciation Expense* ($500) based on its cost basis and remaining economic life. At the end of the accounting period, consolidated *Accumulated Depreciation* is the amount removed from Pratt's accounting records at the intercompany transaction date plus the consolidated *Depreciation Expense* ($350) for the period from the intercompany transaction date to the end of the year. Thus, the $500 recognized balance in the *Accumulated Depreciation* account must be increased by $4,650 to create the required consolidated balance ($5,150).

Worksheet Elimination 4-3A—Journal Entry Form

December 31, 2006

Machine	3,000	
Gain on Sale of Machine	1,800	
Depreciation Expense		150
Accumulated Depreciation		4,650

The worksheet elimination presented in Example 4-3a presents the adjustments discussed above in journal entry form. As in previous examples, the values included in this worksheet elimination can be found by referring to the shaded amounts in the T-accounts.

Inventory Transaction During the Period An intercompany sale of inventory that occurs early enough in the year that some of the inventory is sold to unrelated parties before year-end results in a worksheet elimination that has the same accounts as an intercompany sale that occurs at the end of the year, but the dollar amounts change. The intercompany sale must always be completely eliminated from the consolidated financial statements (this was demonstrated in the 2006 worksheet elimination in Example 4-1b). In addition, the sale to the unrelated party has to be adjusted in a manner similar to the adjustment demonstrated in the 2007 worksheet elimination in Example 4-2b. The interpretation of the information results in a worksheet elimination that is basically a combination of the two years.

The following example is an extension of Example 4-1b where some of the inventory acquired by Sterling is sold to an unrelated party before the end of the period during which the intercompany transaction occurred.

EXAMPLE 4-3B
Downstream sale of inventory on December 30, 2006

Assume Pratt purchases 8,000 units of inventory on November 10, 2006, at a cost of $6 per unit. Pratt sells this inventory to Sterling on December 30, 2006, for $8 per unit. Assume that Sterling sells 1,500 units of inventory acquired from Pratt to unrelated parties for $18,000 on December 31, 2006. As a result of these sales, Sterling recognizes $12,000 cost of goods sold (1,500 units × $8 cost per unit).

The T-accounts below indicate the amounts recorded on Pratt's and Sterling's books plus the worksheet elimination necessary to prepare the consolidated financial statements at December 31, 2006.

Sales

	64,000	2006	Pratt sells 8,000 units to Sterling
Worksheet elimination 12/31/2006 64,000	18,000	2006	Sterling sells 1,500 units to an unrelated entity
	18,000		12/31/2006 Consolidated balance

The entire amount of the intercompany sale ($64,000) must be eliminated, while the entire amount of Sterling's sale to unrelated parties ($18,000) is included on the consolidated income statement.

Cost of Goods Sold

Pratt sells inventory to Sterling:	8,000 × $6	2006	48,000	
Sterling sells to unrelated entity:	1,500 × $8	2006	12,000	51,000 12/31/2006 Worksheet elimination: 8,000 × $6 + 1,500 × $2
Consolidated balance: 1,500 × $6		12/31/2006	9,000	

The *Cost of Goods Sold* worksheet elimination ($51,000) consists of two parts in the current example: (1) current period intercompany sale by Pratt and (2) Sterling sales of current period inventory purchases to unrelated parties. The current period intercompany sale by Pratt must always be removed from the consolidated income statement. The 2006 intercompany sales resulted in the elimination of $48,000 of *Cost of Goods Sold*. In conjunction with the higher historical cost basis of the inventory on Sterling's books from the intercompany inventory transaction, the *Cost of Goods Sold* recognized by Sterling will be higher than the amount that would have been recognized by Pratt had the intercompany inventory transaction not taken place. The per-unit inventory cost on Sterling's books is $8, while the per-unit cost that had been on Pratt's books is $6. As a result, *Cost of Goods Sold* must be reduced by the $2 per unit cost difference for each of the 1,500 units sold by Sterling to unrelated parties, resulting in an additional $3,000 adjustment to *Cost of Goods Sold*.

Inventory

Pratt purchases 8,000 units of inventory	2006	48,000	48,000	2006	Pratt sells 8,000 units to Sterling
Sterling purchases from Pratt 8,000 × $8	2006	64,000	12,000	2006	Sterling sells inventory inventory to unrelated entity 1,500 × $8
			13,000	12/31/2006	Worksheet elimination: 6,500 × $2
Consolidated balance: 12/31/2006 6,500 × $6		39,000			

The remaining intercompany inventory is carried on Sterling's books at $52,000 at the end of 2006. This amount is based on the $8 per unit purchase price by Sterling and the 6,500 units remaining in ending inventory. The consolidated balance sheet must disclose the inventory at its cost when acquired by the consolidated entity (when purchased by Pratt). As a result, the consolidated balance sheet will include *Inventory* at $39,000 (6,500 units × $6 per unit). The worksheet elimination ($13,000) restates the *Inventory* from its current carrying value ($52,000) to its required consolidated balance ($39,000).

The worksheet elimination related to the 2006 inventory transactions is presented in Example 4-3b.

Worksheet Elimination 4-3B—Journal Entry Form		
December 31, 2006		
Sales	64,000	
Cost of Goods Sold		51,000
Inventory		13,000

Debt Transaction During the Period The intercompany debt transaction presented previously (Example 4-1c) resulted in a loss recognition in the period during which Sterling acquired some of Pratt's outstanding bonds. In the subsequent period, the intercompany *Interest Revenue* and *Interest Expense* were eliminated from the consolidated income statement. The loss recognition and the interest were included in worksheet eliminations in different years because the intercompany debt transaction occurred at the end of 2006. Therefore, there was no interest recognized subsequent to the intercompany transaction in 2006. In Example 4-3c presented here, the intercompany debt transaction occurs during the year, so the period of the intercompany transaction will include both loss or gain recognition and subsequent interest revenue and expense in 2006.

EXAMPLE 4-3C
Downstream debt transaction on March 31, 2006

Assume Pratt had issued 4,000 20-year bonds payable, each in the amount of $1,000, on June 30, 1994, to finance the construction of a new manufacturing facility. The bonds had a stated interest rate of 7 percent, with interest paid quarterly (80 periods) on a calendar-year basis. Pratt received $3,600,000 on June 30, 1994 (present value of the cash flows discounted at approximately 8.25 percent). The discount is being amortized using the straight-line method. Sterling (the subsidiary) acquires $300,000 of the bonds (7.5 percent) as an investment on March 31, 2006—33 quarters prior to maturity—for $328,215 (the present value of the cash flows discounted at approximately 5.7 percent). Sterling elects to amortize the premium using the straight-line method.

The following T-accounts illustrate the entries recognized on Pratt's and Sterling's books with respect to the bonds acquired by Sterling and the accompanying consolidated financial statement amounts and worksheet eliminations.

Bonds Payable

			300,000	1/1/1994	Pratt issues bonds
Worksheet elimination	12/31/2006	300,000			
			-0-	12/31/2006	Consolidated balance

The face value of the outstanding bond must always be removed from the consolidated balance sheet. From the consolidated entity's perspective, the bond has been retired.

Discount on Bonds Payable

Pratt issues bonds: $400,000 × .075	6/30/1994	30,000			
			750	1994	July–Dec. amortization: ($30,000/80)(2)
			16,500	1995–2005	11 years amortization: ($30,000/80)(44)
			375	3/31/2006	Jan. 1–Mar. 31 amortization (to date of retirement): ($30,000/80)
			1,125	2006	Apr. 1–Dec. 31 amortization: ($30,000/80)(3)
			11,250	12/31/2006	Worksheet elimination (unamortized balance)
Consolidated balance	12/31/2006	-0-			

The *Discount on Bonds Payable* worksheet elimination amount is exactly the same as in Example 4-1c when Sterling acquired Pratt's bond at December 31. The date of the investment by Sterling has no impact on Pratt's accounting records. The balance ($30,000) is the discount on the 7.5 percent of the total bond issue acquired by Sterling. The original issue discount was $400,000. The quarterly amortization ($375) is the straight-line amortization of the $30,000 discount relevant to the bonds acquired by Sterling. At December 31, 2006, these bonds have a remaining unamortized discount of $11,250 that must be eliminated. Thus, at December 31, 2006, the worksheet elimination to the *Discount on Bonds Payable* is the same regardless of the date when acquired by a related party.

Investment in Bonds

Sterling's investment in Pratt's bonds	3/31/2006	328,215			
			2,565	2006	Apr.–Dec. Sterling premium amortization: ($28,215/33)(3)
			325,650	12/31/2006	Worksheet elimination
Consolidated balance	12/31/2006	-0-			

Sterling's *Investment in Bonds* account is created at the amount paid and reduced by the premium amortization on the investment. The total premium in this example ($28,215) is amortized straight-line over the remaining life (33 quarters) at a rate of $855 per quarter. Three quarters are amortized from March 31 to December 31, 2006, resulting in a remaining account balance of $325,650. The *Investment in Bonds* account must be completely eliminated because the investment is in a related party (Pratt).

Loss on Early Debt Retirement

Worksheet elimination	12/31/2006	40,590	
Consolidated balance	12/31/2006	40,590*	

*Purchase Price		$328,215
Face Value of Bond	$300,000	
Unamortized Discount [$30,000 − ($750 + $16,500 + $375)]	12,375	
Carrying Value		287,625
Loss on Early Debt Retirement		$40,590

The consolidated entity will disclose a *Loss on Early Debt Retirement* because the amount paid by Sterling is more than the book value of the bond liability on Pratt's accounting records. Pratt's book value takes into consideration that the discount has been amortized from June 30, 1994, to March 31, 2006, a total of 47 quarters.

Interest Revenue

Worksheet elimination	12/31/2006	13,185	13,185	2006	Apr.–Dec. Sterling interest revenue: ($300,000 × .07 × 9/12) − ($855 × 3)
			-0-	12/31/2006	Consolidated balance

Interest Expense

July–Dec. Pratt interest expense: ($300,000 × .07 × 9/12) + ($375 × 3)	2006	16,875	16,875	12/31/2006	Worksheet elimination
Consolidated balance	12/31/2006	-0-			

Interest Revenue and *Interest Expense* are both based on the cash flow from Pratt to Sterling adjusted for the relevant amortization. The amounts shown in the T-accounts represent only April 1 to December 31, 2006. The period from January 1 to March 31 is not relevant to the intercompany transaction.

Worksheet Elimination 4-3C—Journal Entry Form		
December 31, 2006		
Bonds Payable	300,000	
Loss on Early Debt Retirement	40,590	
Interest Revenue	13,185	
Discount on Bonds Payable		11,250
Interest Expense		16,875
Investment in Bonds		325,650

Example 4-3c illustrates the worksheet elimination in journal entry form. Note that only two values are exactly the same as they were in Example 4-1c: *Bonds Payable* and *Discount on Bonds Payable*. These amounts are the same because they represent the balance sheet values on the debt issuer's (Pratt's) financial records, and these amounts are not altered by the timing of the intercompany transaction or the amount paid by the purchaser (Sterling). The *Investment in Bonds* and the intercompany *Interest Revenue* and *Interest Expense* are always fully eliminated, but the dollar amount of intercompany interest is a function of the date Sterling made the investment. Finally, the loss or gain recognized on the consolidated income statement is always determined by comparing the amount paid for the debt instrument (market value) with the book value on the bond issuer's records.

Period Subsequent to Intercompany Transaction— Downstream (During the Year)

Worksheet eliminations are required in periods subsequent to an intercompany transaction until the asset is sold or abandoned (or the liability matures) because the worksheet eliminations prepared in the year of the intercompany transaction are not posted to the books of either the parent or the subsidiary. The worksheet eliminations prepared in the period subsequent to an intercompany transaction are conceptually the same regardless of whether the intercompany transaction occurs at the end of the year or during the year. Subsequent-period worksheet eliminations following an intercompany transaction that occurs during a period are discussed next as a continuation of the examples developed in Example 4-3.

EXAMPLE 4-4A
Downstream sale of a machine (4-3A Continued)

Assume that in 2007 Sterling uses the machine acquired from Pratt on May 1, 2006, and records depreciation as appropriate in 2007.

EXAMPLE 4-4B
Downstream sale of inventory (4-3B Continued)

Assume that during 2007 Sterling sold to unrelated parties all the remaining 6,500 units of inventory that had been acquired from Pratt on December 30, 2006. The selling price was $78,000. As a result of these sales, Sterling recognized $52,000 cost of goods sold (6,500 units × $8 cost per unit). In addition, assume that during 2007 Sterling purchased an additional 18,000 units from Pratt for $9 per unit. These goods also had cost Pratt $6 per unit. Note that the markup per unit on goods sold by Pratt to Sterling increased from $2 per unit in 2006 to $3 per unit in 2007. Of the 18,000 units of inventory purchased by Sterling in 2007, 14,000 units were sold to unrelated parties in the same year for a total selling price of $168,000.

EXAMPLE 4-4C
Downstream debt transaction (4-3C Continued)

Assume that Sterling holds the investment in Pratt's bonds made in 2006 for the entire year and that Pratt and Sterling record the appropriate interest amounts in 2007.

Below are three sets of comparative worksheet eliminations, one for each type of intercompany transaction discussed above (machinery, inventory, and debt). The three examples present the period subsequent to intercompany transaction worksheet eliminations (in 2007). Subsequent year eliminations for the transactions that occur during the period (Examples 4-4a, 4-4b, and 4-4c) are compared to the previously presented subsequent year eliminations for transactions that occur at the end of the period (Examples 4-2a, 4-2b, and 4-2c).

EXAMPLE 4-4A
(Machine)

Worksheet Elimination 4-4A—Journal Entry Form

December 31, 2007

	From Example 4-2a		Example 4-4a	
Machine	3,000		3,000	
Retained Earnings (January 1, 2007)	2,400		1,650	
Depreciation Expense		600		225
Accumulated Depreciation		4,800		4,425

The *Machine* account adjustment is the same in both examples because the selling price ($6,000) and the historical cost to Pratt ($9,000) are the same in both cases. The *Retained Earnings* adjustment in the machine Example 4-4a column differs from the adjustment in the Example 4-2a column for two reasons. First, the gain recognized in the year of the machine sale was $1,800 in Example 4-3a while it was $2,400 in Example 4-1a. Second, the intercompany sale of the machine during the year (Example 4-3a) results in a $150 credit *Depreciation Expense* adjustment in the period of the transaction. As a result, the 2007 *Retained Earnings* adjustment in Example 4-4a is $1,650 ($1,800 – $150), whereas it was $2,400 ($2,400 – $0) in Example 4-2.

The differences pertaining to *Depreciation Expense* and *Accumulated Depreciation* are related. The difference in *Depreciation Expense* between Examples 4-2a and 4-4a pertains to the change in the cost basis being depreciated by Sterling and the length of time over which depreciation is being recognized. In Example 4-2a, the $2,400 gain on sale affects *Depreciation Expense* over a period of four years. On the other hand, in Example 4-4a, the $1,800 gain affects *Depreciation Expense* over eight years. The *Accumulated Depreciation* worksheet elimination decreases each year by the amount of the previous year's *Depreciation Expense* worksheet elimination. The *Accumulated Depreciation* will stop changing in value when the machine is fully depreciated.

EXAMPLE 4-4B
(Inventory)

Worksheet Elimination 4-4B—Journal Entry Form

December 31, 2007

	From Example 4-2b		Example 4-4b	
Sales	162,000		162,000	
Retained Earnings (January 1, 2007)	16,000		13,000	
Cost of Goods Sold		166,000		163,000
Inventory		12,000		12,000

Example 4-4b presents a comparison of the inventory worksheet elimination when there is no intercompany inventory sold to unrelated parties before year-end (Example 4-2b) and when there is partial sale of the intercompany inventory to unrelated parties before year-end (Example 4-4b). The worksheet elimination to *Sales* represents the inventory sold by Pratt to Sterling in 2007. Because this amount pertains only to 2007, the intercompany sale of inventory in 2006 is not relevant. Similarly, the *Inventory* worksheet elimination removes the gross profit from the inventory still in Sterling's possession at the end of 2007. The amount of the ending inventory in 2007 is not impacted by the sale of some inventory in 2006.

The *Retained Earnings* and *Cost of Goods Sold* worksheet elimination values differ between columns due to the sale of 1,500 units of inventory that Sterling purchased from

Pratt in Example 4-3b. The adjustment to *Retained Earnings* is smaller because the sale of 1,500 units of inventory to an unrelated party in 2006 makes part of the gross profit on the intercompany sale (1,500 units × $2 per unit) realized; therefore, *Retained Earnings* is reduced by a smaller amount. Because the inventory examples have the same amount of ending inventory at the end of 2007, the same amount of inventory must be sold in both examples over the two-year period. Example 4-4b has fewer units sold during 2007 than Example 4-2b (8,000 vs 6,500), resulting in a $3,000 smaller adjustment to *Cost of Goods Sold*.

To help organize the inventory intercompany transaction in 2007, the following table is prepared to summarize the intercompany transaction as well as Sterling's sales to unrelated parties.

	Number of Units	*Cost to Pratt*	*Markup*	*Pratt's Selling Price*
Beginning Inventory	6,500	$39,000	$13,000	$ 52,000
2007 Sales to Sterling	18,000	108,000	54,000	162,000
Less Ending Inventory*	(4,000)	(24,000)	(12,000)	(36,000)
Sold	20,500	$123,000	$55,000	$178,000

* Assumes a first-in, first-out cost flow.

The shaded values in the table represent the amounts that are considered when preparing the worksheet elimination. As discussed previously in this chapter, the markup on the intercompany inventory, both in the current year and from the previous year, is the basis for the inventory worksheet elimination.

EXAMPLE 4-4C
(Debt)

Worksheet Elimination 4-4C—Journal Entry Form				
December 31, 2007				
	From Example 4-2c		**Example 4-4c**	
Bonds Payable	300,000		300,000	
Interest Revenue	17,400		17,580	
Retained Earnings (January 1, 2007)	38,250		36,900	
Discount on Bonds Payable		9,750		9,750
Interest Expense		22,500		22,500
Investment in Bonds		323,400		322,230

The dollar amounts eliminated for *Bonds Payable, Discount on Bonds Payable,* and *Interest Expense* are the same in Examples 4-2c and 4-4c because the amounts represent ending balance sheet amounts (*Bonds Payable* and *Discount on Bonds Payable*) and the bonds were held by a related party for the entire year (*Interest Expense*). Three values in the worksheet elimination differ because of the change in the assumed investment price and Sterling's investment date in Pratt's bonds. Even though the dollar amounts of the adjustments to *Investment Revenue, Retained Earnings,* and *Investment in Bonds* differ, the procedures for determining the amounts are the same in both examples. *Interest Revenue* represents the cash paid by Pratt to Sterling, adjusted for the premium amortization on the amount invested. The *Retained Earnings* adjustment reflects the income statement account adjustments in 2006 [$40,590 – ($16,875 – $13,185)] (see Example 4-3c worksheet elimination). The *Investment in Bonds* adjustment eliminates the remaining book value of the investment on Pratt's accounting records.

Period of Intercompany Transaction— Upstream (During the Year)

The discussion thus far in the chapter has been based on downstream transactions. This section illustrates the differences between downstream and upstream intercompany transactions. The examples used are modified versions of the previous examples wherein the intercompany transactions were initiated during the period. The modification changes the direction of the intercompany transaction from downstream to upstream.

It is shown through these examples that the general difference between downstream and upstream transactions pertains to the recognition necessary with regard to the noncontrolling interest. The noncontrolling interest is allocated a share of the subsidiary's contribution to consolidated net income. The existence of unrealized profit in upstream intercompany transactions creates a need to adjust the subsidiary's reported net income because the profit cannot be included in consolidated net income until it is realized. The resulting adjustments to Sterling's recognized net income in the upstream examples impact the calculation of the noncontrolling interest's share of net income and the value allocated to the noncontrolling interest on the consolidated balance sheet. Below are the three examples to be used in this section. The facts in the examples are identical to those in Examples 4-3a, 4-3b, and 4-3c, with two exceptions. First, all three intercompany transactions are upstream, whereas they were downstream in previous examples. Second, the facts of the intercompany bond transaction are changed because Sterling's bonds have a different interest rate and maturity date than Pratt's bonds.

EXAMPLE 4-5A
Upstream sale of a machine on May 1, 2006

Assume a machine was purchased by Sterling on January 1, 2001, for $9,000. The machine is being depreciated using the straight-line method assuming a 10-year life with no salvage value. The machine is sold to Pratt for $6,000 on May 1, 2006. Sterling recorded depreciation expense for the period January 1–April 30, 2006. At the date of the sale, 64 months have passed since Sterling purchased the machine. Thus, the accumulated depreciation is $4,800 [$9,000 (64/120)]. Pratt increases the machine's estimated remaining life to 8 years.

EXAMPLE 4-5B
Upstream sale of inventory on December 30, 2006

Assume Sterling purchases 8,000 units of inventory on November 10, 2006 at a cost of $6 per unit. Sterling sells this inventory to Pratt on December 30, 2006, for $8 per unit. Assume that Pratt sells 1,500 units of inventory acquired from Sterling to unrelated parties for $18,000 on December 31, 2006. As a result of these sales, Pratt recognizes $12,000 cost of goods sold (1,500 units × $8 cost per unit).

EXAMPLE 4-5C
Upstream debt transaction on March 31, 2006

Assume Sterling had issued 1,500, 10-year bonds payable, each in the amount of $1,000, on January 1, 2002, to finance the construction of a new manufacturing facility. The bonds had a stated interest rate of 8 percent, with interest paid quarterly (40 periods) on a calendar-year basis. Sterling received $1,300,000 on January 1, 2002 (present value of the cash flows discounted at approximately 10.5 percent). The discount is being amortized using the straight-line method. Pratt (the parent) acquires $300,000 of the bonds (20 percent) as an investment on March 31, 2006—23 quarters prior to maturity—for $275,850 (the present value of the cash flows discounted at approximately 10.2 percent). Pratt elects to amortize the discount using the straight-line method.

The following T-accounts illustrate the entries recognized on Pratt's and Sterling's books with respect to the bonds acquired by Pratt and the accompanying consolidated financial statement amounts and worksheet eliminations.

Bonds Payable

			300,000	1/1/2002 Sterling issues bonds
Worksheet elimination	12/31/2006	300,000		
			-0-	12/31/2006 Consolidated balance

Discount on Bonds Payable

Sterling issues bonds: 1/1/2002 $200,000 × .2	40,000				
		16,000	2002–2005	4 years amortization: ($40,000/40)(16)	
		1,000	3/31/2006	Jan. 1–Mar. 31 amortization (to date of retirement): ($40,000/40)	
		3,000	2006	Apr. 1–Dec. 31 amortization: ($40,000/40)(3)	
		20,000	12/31/2006	Worksheet elimination (unamortized balance)	
Consolidated balance 12/31/2006	-0-				

The *Discount on Bonds Payable* worksheet elimination amount removes the unamortized discount from the consolidated balance sheet with regard to the bonds acquired by Pratt. The balance ($40,000) is the discount on the portion of the bonds acquired by Pratt. The discount amortization ($1,000 quarterly) is the straight-line amortization of the $40,000 discount relevant to the bonds acquired by Pratt. At December 31, 2006, these bonds have a remaining unamortized discount of $20,000 that must be eliminated.

Investment in Bonds

Pratt's investment in 3/31/2006 Sterling's bonds	275,850			
Apr.–Dec. Pratt discount 2006 amortization: ($24,150/23)(3)	3,150	279,000	12/31/2006	Worksheet elimination
Consolidated balance 12/31/2006	-0-			

Pratt's *Investment in Bonds* account is created at the amount paid and increased by the discount amortization on the investment. The total discount in this example ($24,150) is amortized straight-line over the remaining life (23 quarters) at a rate of $1,050 per quarter. Three quarters are amortized from March 31 to December 31, 2006, resulting in a remaining account balance of $279,000.

Gain on Early Debt Retirement

1,150	12/31/2006	Worksheet elimination
1,150*	12/31/2006	Consolidated balance

*Purchase Price		$275,850
Face Value of Bond	$300,000	
Unamortized Discount [$40,000 – ($16,000 + $1,000)]	23,000	
Carrying Value		277,000
Gain on Early Debt Retirement		$1,150

The consolidated entity will disclose a *Gain on Early Debt Retirement* because the amount paid by Pratt is less than the book value of the bond liability on Sterling's accounting records.

Interest Revenue

Worksheet elimination 12/31/2006	21,150	21,150 2006		Apr.–Dec. Sterling interest revenue: ($300,000 × .08 × 9/12) + $3,150
		-0-	12/31/2006	Consolidated balance

Interest Expense

Apr.–Dec. Sterling interest expense: [($300,000 × .08) (9/12)] + $3,000	2006 21,000	21,000 12/31/2006	Worksheet elimination
Consolidated balance 12/31/2006	-0-		

Interest Revenue and *Interest Expense* are both based on the cash flow from Sterling to Pratt adjusted for the relevant amortization. The amounts shown in the T-accounts represent only April 1 to December 31. The period from January 1 to March 31 is not relevant to the intercompany transaction. The following worksheet elimination presents the journal entry form of the worksheet elimination needed to prepare the consolidated financial statements.

Worksheet Elimination—Journal Entry Form

Example 4-5a

December 31, 2006

Machine	3,000	
Gain on Sale of Machine	1,800	
Depreciation Expense		150
Accumulated Depreciation		4,650

Example 4-5b

Sales	64,000	
Cost of Goods Sold		51,000
Inventory		13,000

Example 4-5c

Bonds Payable	300,000	
Interest Revenue	21,150	
Discount on Bonds Payable		20,000
Gain on Early Debt Retirement		1,150
Interest Expense		21,000
Investment in Bonds		279,000

A comparison of the worksheet eliminations presented in Examples 4-5a and 4-5b with Examples 4-3a and 4-3b reveals that the downstream and upstream worksheet eliminations (5) are identical both in the accounts affected in the period of the intercompany transaction and in the dollar amounts. The worksheet elimination for Example 4-5c would be identical to the worksheet elimination for Example 4-3c had it been possible for the upstream transaction to be the same as the downstream transaction. The downstream and upstream intercompany bond transactions differ because the interest rates on Pratt's and Sterlilng's bonds payable differ.

Although the accounts and balances in the upstream machine and inventory examples are identical to the downstream examples, the company's account balances that are affected by each line of the worksheet eliminations are reversed. Now, for example, the elimination of *Gain on Sale of Machine* and the adjustment to *Depreciation Expense* in Example 4-5a are revising balances that affect Sterling's net income. These amounts, as well as the income statement accounts presented in Examples 4-5b (inventory) and 4-5c (debt), represent adjustments that must be made to Sterling's income statement, while in previous examples all the income statement impact was on Pratt's income statement. The importance of this distinction is revealed when considering basic worksheet elimination (4), where *Noncontrolling Interest in Net Income of Subsidiary* is recognized.

Below is a set of basic facts about Pratt and Sterling that will be used to demonstrate how the upstream intercompany transactions impact basic worksheet elimination (4).

BASIC INFORMATION 2006

Pratt Corporation owns 90 percent of Sterling Products' outstanding voting common stock. Assume that, including intercompany transactions, Sterling reported net income of $205,000 and paid dividends of $110,000 in 2006. Assume further that Pratt pays book value for Sterling.

Worksheet elimination (4) is used to establish the *Noncontrolling Interest in Net Income of Subsidiary*. To the extent that worksheet elimination (5) modifies the recognized contribution to consolidated net income provided by the subsidiary, the *Noncontrolling Interest in Net Income of Subsidiary* must also be adjusted. The following table summarizes the impact of the three intercompany transaction on Sterling's income statement in the period of the intercompany transaction.

Reported Sterling Net Income		$205,000
Upstream machine adjustments:		
Gain on sale	($1,800)	
Depreciation expense	150	(1,650)
Upstream inventory adjustments:		
Intercompany Gross profit ($64,000 Sales –	($16,000)	
$48,000 Cost of Goods Sold)		
Cost of Goods Sold (realized gross profit)	3,000	(13,000)
Upstream debt adjustments:		
Gain on Early Debt Retirement	$1,150	
Interest Revenue – Interest Expense ($21,150 – $21,000)	(150)	1,000
Adjusted Sterling income		$191,350

The *Gain on Sale of Machine* now reported by Sterling is subtracted from Sterling's reported net income because the gain must be removed from the consolidated income statement. The gain will gradually be allocated to Sterling (and therefore to the noncontrolling interest) via the reduced depreciation expense recognized annually on the consolidated income statement. The *Depreciation Expense* reduction is viewed as an adjustment to Sterling's income even though it is recorded on Pratt's income statement. Therefore, it is added back into the calculation of adjusted Sterling income. Thus, Sterling is allowed to recognize the additional income not at the point of the sale, but rather over the remaining life of the asset. That is, over the life of the machine, the reduction to *Depreciation*

Expense will exactly equal the amount of the *Gain on Sale of Machine* eliminated in the period of the intercompany sale of machine.

In a similar manner, the *Sales* and *Cost of Goods Sold* adjustments net to a $13,000 decrease in Sterling's reported net income. This amount represents both the gross profit of $16,000 in intercompany sale of inventory (*Sales* of $64,000 and *Cost of Goods Sold* of $48,000) in the current year and the $3,000 *Cost of Goods Sold* overstatement recorded by Pratt when it sells 1,500 units of inventory to an unrelated party. Over time, the overstatement in the inventory's cost basis on Pratt's books is added back to Sterling's reported income when the inventory is sold to unrelated parties; that is, Sterling will recapture the gross profit eliminated at the time of the intercompany sale of inventory when the inventory is sold to an unrelated party.

Finally, the *Gain on Early Debt Retirement* is added to Sterling's reported net income because Sterling is the bond issuer in the upstream debt transaction. This gain is credited because the *Gain on Early Debt Retirement* is being created (rather than eliminated) on the consolidated income statement. As a result, it increases Sterling's recognized contribution to consolidated net income. Subsequent to the indirect intercompany debt transaction, the recognized *Interest Revenue* and *Interest Expense* are adjusted, resulting in a gradual offset to the *Gain on Early Debt Retirement*. Thus, the *Gain on Early Debt Retirement* increases Sterling's reported net income by $1,150, while the difference between *Interest Revenue* ($21,150) and *Interest Expense* ($21,000) offsets the gain by $150. The net effect on Sterling's recognized net income is an increase of $1,000.

The net of the three intercompany transaction adjustments results in a contribution from Sterling to consolidated net income of $191,350. Thus, Sterling's $205,000 of reported net income is adjusted downward by $13,650. The basic information and the adjustments discussed above lead to worksheet elimination (4) as displayed in journal entry form below.

Worksheet Elimination 4-5—Journal Entry Form		
(4) Noncontrolling Interest in Net Income of Sterling ($205,000 − $1,650 − $13,000 + $1,000)(.10)	19,135	
Noncontrolling Interest in Sterling Products		8,135
Dividends ($110,000 × .10)		11,000
To recognize the change in the Noncontrolling Interest in Sterling account during the period.		

Period Subsequent to Intercompany Transaction— Upstream (During the Year)

The previous examples (machine and inventory) demonstrated that worksheet elimination (5) in the year of an intercompany transaction is the same regardless of the transaction's direction (upstream, downstream, lateral). While the equality of worksheet elimination (5) in the period subsequent to the intercompany transaction is not absolute, there is only one difference between downstream transactions and upstream (lateral) transactions. This difference pertains to the allocation of the equity impact to only *Retained Earnings* in downstream transactions but to *Retained Earnings* and *Noncontrolling Interest* for upstream (lateral) transactions.

In addition to the equity adjustments from the 2006 upstream intercompany transactions, the impact of current period adjustments must be considered. The following brief summaries outline the information relevant to the intercompany machine, inventory, and debt transactions for 2007.

EXAMPLE 4-6A
Upstream sale of a machine (4-5A Continued)

Assume that in 2007 Pratt uses the machine acquired from Sterling at May 1, 2006, and records depreciation as appropriate in 2007.

EXAMPLE 4-6B
Upstream sale of inventory (4-5B Continued)

Assume that during 2007 Pratt sold to unrelated parties all the remaining 6,500 units of inventory that had been acquired from Sterling on December 30, 2006. The selling price was $78,000. As a result of these sales, Pratt recognized $52,000 cost of goods sold (6,500 units × $8 cost per unit). In addition, assume that during 2007 Pratt purchased an additional 18,000 units for $9 per unit from Sterling. These goods also had cost Sterling $6 per unit. Note that the markup per unit on goods sold by Sterling to Pratt increased from $2 per unit in 2006 to $3 per unit in 2007. Of the inventory (18,000 units) purchased by Pratt in 2007, 14,000 units were sold to unrelated parties in the same year for a total of $168,000.

EXAMPLE 4-6C
Upstream sale of bond (4-5C Continued)

Assume that Pratt holds the investment in Sterling's bonds made in 2006 for the entire year and that Pratt and Sterling record the appropriate interest amounts in 2007.

Below is the 2007 worksheet elimination (5) for each of the upstream transactions. Comparison of these 2007 worksheet eliminations to the downstream worksheet elimination (5) amounts illustrates that, for the machine and inventory transactions, the only difference is that the *Retained Earnings* adjustment in Examples 4-4a and 4-4b is divided proportionately between *Retained Earnings* and *Noncontrolling Interest* in Examples 4-6a and 4-6b. The allocation of the income statement amounts (e.g., *Gain on Sale of Machine* and *Cost of Goods Sold*) in periods subsequent to the upstream intercompany transaction to *Retained Earnings* and *Noncontrolling Interest* is necessary because the source of intercompany income is Sterling and the noncontrolling stockholders must be allocated a 10-percent interest in Sterling's income.

Worksheet Elimination—Journal Entry Form		
Example 4-6a		
December 31, 2007		
Machine	3,000	
Retained Earnings (January 1, 2007) ($1,650)(.90)	1,485	
Noncontrolling Interest ($1,650)(.10)	165	
Depreciation Expense		225
Accumulated Depreciation		4,425
Example 4-6b		
Sales	162,000	
Retained Earnings (January 1, 2007) ($13,000)(.90)	11,700	
Noncontrolling Interest ($13,000)(.10)	1,300	
Cost of Goods Sold		163,000
Inventory		12,000
Example 4-6c		
Bonds Payable	300,000	
Interest Revenue ($14,100)(2)	28,200	
Discount on Bonds Payable [$20,000 – ($40,000/20)(2)]		16,000
Interest Expense ($14,000)(2)		28,000
Retained Earnings (January 1, 2007) ($1,000)(.90)		900
Noncontrolling Interest ($1,000)(.10)		100
Investment in Bonds [$279,000 + ($2,100)(2)]		283,200

When the intercompany transactions are upstream, the profit that is unrealized from the consolidated point of view (a net of $13,650 in 2006) is reported on Sterling's income statement. Ninety percent of the $13,650 ($12,285) is reported on Pratt's income statement via the *Investment Income* account. The *Investment Income* account is eliminated in 2006 worksheet elimination (2). However, the $12,285 is actually closed to Pratt's *Retained Earnings* account because worksheet eliminations are not posted. Therefore, Pratt's January 1, 2007, *Retained Earnings* balance includes 90 percent of the unrealized profit. The *Retained Earnings* adjustments in the worksheet eliminations illustrated in Examples 4-6a, 4-6b, and 4-6c ($1,485, $11,700, and $900, respectively) remove Sterling's income statement effect from Pratt's January 1, 2007, *Retained Earnings* balance.

The 2007 adjustments to *Noncontrolling Interest* in the worksheet eliminations illustrated in Examples 4-6a, 4-6b, and 4-6c are adjustments to worksheet elimination (1). Recall that worksheet elimination (1) in 2007 removes Sterling's reported stockholders' equity as of January 1, 2007 (*including the 2006 reported income now closed to Retained Earnings*) and establishes the beginning *Noncontrolling Interest*. To the extent that Sterling has unrealized intercompany profit included in its January 1, 2007, *Retained Earnings, Noncontrolling Interest* is misstated, when established in worksheet elimination (1), by its pro rata share in the unrealized profit. The amount of this misstatement is corrected by the adjustment to *Noncontrolling Interest* in Examples 4-6a, 4-6b, and 4-6c ($165, $1,300, and $100, respectively).

BASIC INFORMATION 2007

Assume Pratt continues its 90-percent ownership interest in Sterling during 2007. For 2007, Sterling reported net income of $222,775 and paid dividends of $140,000.

Beyond the worksheet elimination (5) amounts that must be included on the consolidation worksheet, an adjustment is required to worksheet elimination (4) as in the 2006 example. The following table shows the calculation of the adjusted Sterling net income.

Reported Sterling Net Income		$222,775
Upstream machine adjustments:		
Depreciation expense		225
Upstream inventory adjustments:		
Intercompany Gross Profit ($162,000 – $108,000)		
Cost of Goods Sold (realized gross profit)	($54,000)	
($13,000 + 14,000 × $3)	55,000	1,000
Upstream debt adjustments:		
Interest Revenue – Interest Expense ($28,200 – $28,000)		(200)
Adjusted Sterling income		$223,800

As in the 2006 example, the reduction in *Depreciation Expense* resulting from the intercompany machine sale is allocated to Sterling and adjusts reported income by $225. The $1,000 net inventory adjustment is again due to the gross profit on the intercompany sale (*Sales* of $162,000 and *Cost of Goods Sold* of $108,000) and the overstatement of *Cost of Goods Sold* when Pratt sells inventory to unrelated parties (6,500 units × $2 per unit + 14,000 units × $3 per unit). Finally, the difference between *Interest Revenue* ($28,200) and *Interest Expense* ($28,000) results in a $200 adjustment to Sterling's reported net income. The *Depreciation Expense* and the net of *Sales* and *Cost of Goods Sold* adjustments in the current example increase Sterling's contribution to consolidated net income, while the net of *Interest Revenue* and *Interest Expense* adjustment decreases Sterling's contribution to consolidated net income. The basic information and the adjustments discussed above lead to worksheet elimination (4) as displayed in journal entry form below.

Noncontrolling Interest in Subsidiary Net Income and Consolidated Net Income

Generally, the *Noncontrolling Interest in Net Income of Subsidiary* amount in worksheet elimination (4) is calculated by multiplying the noncontrolling interest percentage owned by the reported subsidiary net income modified by the worksheet elimination (5) adjustments to consolidated net income that result from upstream transactions. Recall that only the income effects from upstream transactions impact the calculation of *Noncontrolling Interest in Net Income of Subsidiary*. When both upstream and downstream intercompany transactions occur, the income effects of the downstream transactions do not cause adjustments to *Noncontrolling Interest in Net Income of Subsidiary*. The basic information and the adjustments discussed above lead to worksheet elimination (4) as displayed in journal entry form below.

Worksheet Elimination 4-6—Journal Entry Form

(4)	Noncontrolling Interest in Net Income of Sterling	22,380	
	($222,775 + $225 + $1,000 − $200)(.10)		
	Noncontrolling Interest in Sterling Products		8,380
	Dividends ($140,000 × .10)		14,000

To recognize the change in the Noncontrolling Interest in Sterling account during the period.

Consolidated net income is the income of the combined economic unit. In the simplest of circumstances (i.e., when there are no intercompany transactions), the income statements can be added together after eliminating the *Investment Income* account. When intercompany transactions exist, consolidated net income is affected by downstream and upstream intercompany transactions. All unrealized profits are eliminated regardless of whether it is the parent's (downstream) or the subsidiary's (upstream) reported income that is impacted by the intercompany transaction. Finally, if the parent has paid more than book value, the calculation of consolidated net income must also include purchase differential amortizations. When preparing a consolidating worksheet, the consolidated net income that results may verified by the following calculation:

Reported Net Incomes:	
Parent Company	$xxx
Subsidiary	xxx
	xxx
Adjustments: Investment Income	− xxx
All current period income effects relating to intercompany transactions	± xxx
All current period purchase differential amortizations	± xxx
Consolidated Net Income	xxx
Less: Noncontrolling Interest in Net Income of Subsidiary	− xxx
Net Income (to Consolidated Retained Earnings)	$xxx

Notice that *Consolidated Net Income* is not the amount that is transferred to *Consolidated Retained Earnings*. Applying the economic unit concept, the combined income of the entire entity is titled *Consolidated Net Income*. That amount is allocated, in part, to the noncontrolling interest, leaving the parent company's share, *Net Income,* to be transferred to *Retained Earnings* and reported to the parent company stockholders in the consolidated Statement of Retained Earnings and consolidated Balance Sheet.

SUMMARY OF IMPACT OF UPSTREAM INTERCOMPANY TRANSACTIONS

In summary, the upstream direction of the intercompany transaction impacts the worksheet eliminations only because of the requirement to distribute a percentage of subsidiary net income to the noncontrolling interest and the corresponding measurement of the *Noncontrolling Interest* disclosed on the consolidated balance sheet. The worksheet eliminations in Illustration 4-1 present the overall impact in the year of the upstream intercompany transactions and the related impact on the eliminations in the year subsequent to intercompany transactions using the three upstream examples presented. The unaffected accounts in basic worksheet eliminations (1–4) are shown with —.

Notice that the debit to *Retained Earnings* and the credit to *Noncontrolling Interest* in worksheet elimination (1) are not adjusted by the existence of the upstream transactions. Remember that elimination (1) removes the subsidiary's *Retained Earnings* balance that exists at the beginning of the year while it establishes the beginning balance in the *Noncontrolling Interest* account. Because the upstream transactions have created unrealized profit on the subsidiary's books, worksheet elimination (1) establishes an overstatement in the *Noncontrolling Interest* account.

The overstatement of the January 1 *Retained Earnings* (parent company) and *Noncontrolling Interest* [created in worksheet elimination (1)] are corrected in worksheet elimination (5). Any year-end net unrealized profit on upstream transactions carried forward to the next year will give rise to a pro rata adjustment to *Retained Earnings* and *Noncontrolling Interest* in elimination (5) in the subsequent year. The amount is divided between *Retained Earnings* and *Noncontrolling Interest* because the parent's portion has flowed through *Investment Income* to *Retained Earnings* while the *Noncontrolling Interest* portion was created in worksheet elimination (1) as discussed above. The arrows in the side- by-side eliminations illustrate how the unrealized profit (loss) at the end of the first year equals the total adjustment to the January 1 *Retained Earnings* and *Noncontrolling Interest* in the subsequent year for each of the three upstream intercompany transactions presented. In each subsequent year, *Retained Earnings* and *Noncontrolling Interest* worksheet elimination (5) amounts are reduced by the amount of adjustments recognized in the preceding year's income statement. For example, the 2008 worksheet elimination (5) *Retained Earnings* and *Noncontrolling Interest* adjustments will be based on the 2007 *Retained Earnings* and *Noncontrolling Interest* adjustment minus the 2007 income statement account adjustments.

Finally, in any given year the amount of adjustment to reported subsidiary net income in elimination (4) equals the net income statement effect in elimination (5) for the same year. In the 2006 and 2007 examples, the net effect of the three upstream intercompany transactions was ($13,650) and $1,025, respectively.

TEST YOUR KNOWLEDGE

Use the information from Examples 4-5 and 4-6 (a, b, and c) and assume Sterling continues to be Pratt's 90 percent–owned subsidiary. The following information is relevant to preparing the consolidation eliminations at December 31, 2008:

1. The machine purchased by Pratt from Sterling continues to be used throughout the year.

2. All of the intercompany inventory held by Pratt at the end of 2007 is sold to unrelated parties during 2008. Pratt makes no additional purchases of Sterling's inventory during 2008.

ILLUSTRATION 4-1
Overall Impact of Upstream Intercompany Transactions

		Year of Upstream Transaction		Year Subsequent to Upstream Transaction	
		Debit	Credit	Debit	Credit
(1)	Common Stock	—		—	
	Paid-In Capital	—		—	
	Retained Earnings (Jan. 1)	—		—	
	Purchase Differentials (adjust to market)	—		—	
	Investment in Subsidiary (balance Jan. 1)		—		—
	Noncontrolling Interest (value Jan. 1)		—		—
(2)	Investment Income	—		—	
	Investment in Subsidiary		—		—
	Dividends		—		—
(3)	Depreciation and Amortization Expenses	—		—	
	Purchase Differentials		—		—
(4)	Noncontrolling Interest in Net Income of Subsidiary				
	Year of upstream transaction ($205,000 − $13,650)(.10)	19,135			
	Year subsequent ($222,775 + $1,025)(.10)			22,380	
	Noncontrolling Interest		8,135		8,380
	Dividends		—		—
(5a)	Machine	3,000		3,000	
	Retained Earnings (balance Jan. 1)	0		1,485	
	Noncontrolling Interest (value Jan. 1)	0		165	
	Gain on Sale of Machine	1,800		0	
	Depreciation Expense		150		225
	Accumulated Depreciation		4,650		4,425
(5b)	Retained Earnings (balance Jan. 1)	0		11,700	
	Noncontrolling Interest (value Jan. 1)	0		1,300	
	Sales	64,000		162,000	
	Cost of Goods Sold		51,000		163,000
	Inventory		13,000		12,000
(5c)	Bonds Payable	300,000		300,000	
	Interest Revenue	21,150		28,200	
	Interest Expense		21,000		28,000
	Gain on Early Debt Retirement		1,150		0
	Discount on Bonds Payable		20,000		16,000
	Retained Earnings (balance Jan. 1)		0		900
	Noncontrolling Interest (value Jan. 1)		0		100
	Investment in Bonds		279,000		283,200

3. The intercompany bond investment continues to be held by Pratt throughout 2008.

4. Sterling's 2008 reported net income and dividends paid are $290,000 and $180,000, respectively.

5. Purchase differential amortization continues on schedule and no further goodwill impairment is identified or recorded. The 2008 amortization of purchase differentials and unamortized balances remaining at the beginning of 2008 are provided below and are based on extension of the amortization schedule in Illustration 3-4.

Account	Remaining Unamortized Purchase Differential Balance at January 1, 2008	Increase (Decrease) to Investment Income Resulting from Annual Amortization for 2008
Plant and Equipment	(850,000)	0
Accumulated Depreciation	1,121,250	(35,000)
Patent	(92,730)	33,720
Long-Term Notes Payable	(96,800)	17,600
Goodwill	191,000	0
Net Change in Investment Income		16,320

Using the information above, prepare the worksheet eliminations that would be necessary to consolidate Pratt and Sterling at December 31, 2008. (*Hint:* The investment account balance as of January 1, 2008, can be reconstructed by analyzing the changes that occur in the account during 2008.) Post the worksheet eliminations to the worksheet provided—Pratt and Sterling's financial statements provided in the worksheet can be used as the basis for worksheet eliminations (1)–(4). The solution follows the chapter summary.

Worksheet for Consolidation of Pratt Corporation and Subsidiary, Sterling Products
90 Percent Owned Subsidiary
Consolidation with Intercompany Transactions
December 31, 2008

	Separate Financial Statements		Adjustments and Eliminations		Consolidated Financial Statements
	Pratt	Sterling	Debit	Credit	
Income Statement					
Sales	10,100,000	1,450,000			
Non-operating Items (net)	120,000				
Investment Income, Sterling Products	275,688				
Cost of Goods Sold	6,000,000	880,000			
Selling Expenses	1,300,000	130,000			
General and Administrative Expenses	2,200,000	150,000			
Consolidated Net Income					
Noncontrolling Interest in Net Income of Sterling					
Net Income (to Statement of Retained Earnings)	995,688	290,000			

(Continued)

Worksheet *(Continued)*

	Separate Financial Statements		Adjustments and Eliminations		Consolidated Financial Statements
	Pratt	**Sterling**	**Debit**	**Credit**	
Retained Earnings Statement					
Retained Earnings (1/1/2008)	3,357,448	515,000			
Add: Net Income (from Income Statement)	995,688	290,000			
Subtotal	4,353,136	805,000			
Less: Dividends	(400,000)	(180,000)			
Retained Earnings (12/31/2008 to Balance sheet)	3,953,136	625,000			
Balance Sheet					
Cash	615,000	280,000			
Accounts Receivable (net)	1,800,000	380,000			
Inventory (FIFO)	5,700,000	550,000			
Other Current Assets	1,480,000				
Total Current Assets	9,595,000	1,210,000			
Plant and Equipment	31,000,000	3,135,000			
Accumulated Depreciation	(16,500,000)	(1,600,000)			
Patent		700,000			
Investment in Sterling Products	2,397,636				
Investment in Bonds	287,400				
Other Noncurrent Assets	1,803,100	2,025,000			
Goodwill					
Total Long-Term Assets	18,988,136	4,260,000			
Total Assets	28,583,136	5,470,000			
Current Liabilities	8,240,000	635,000			
Long-Term Notes Payable		1,000,000			
7% Bonds Payable (due 6/30/2013)	4,000,000				
Less: Discount on Bonds Payable	(110,000)				
8% Bonds Payable (due 12/31/2010)		1,500,000			
Less: Discount on Bonds Payable		(40,000)			
Total Liabilities	12,130,000	3,095,000			
Common Stock ($1 par):					
Pratt, 10,000,000 shares authorized, 6,000,000 shares issued and outstanding	6,000,000				
Sterling, 1,000,000 shares authorized, issued and outstanding		1,000,000			
Additional Paid-In Capital	6,500,000	750,000			
Retained Earnings (12/31/2008 from Statement of Retained Earnings)	3,953,136	625,000			
Noncontrolling Interest in Sterling					
Total Stockholders' Equity	16,453,136	2,375,000			
Total Liabilities and Stockholders' Equity	28,583,136	5,470,000			

SUMMARY

This chapter presented a format for evaluating intercompany transactions. These transactions may take many forms, and some of the more common were presented as examples. A number of assumptions were made in the examples. Some of these assumptions will generally be true while others may often not exist in practice. One assumption that may or may not exist is the parent and subsidiary preparing financial statements using the same fiscal period. Differences in fiscal periods increase the detail of the adjusting entries and worksheet eliminations, but they do not change the underlying theory applied to prepare consolidated financial statements. Other assumptions made relate to such items as straight-line depreciation and straight-line bond discount or premium amortization.

Practice would often differ from the simplified approach taken in the examples, resulting in alternative numerical values, but the procedures and logic would not change.

The intercompany transactions presented do not represent all possible transactions. For example, another type of intercompany transaction that may exist is intercompany leases. This type of transaction would involve the transfer of an asset as well as a direct debt obligation between the two units of the consolidated entity. An intercompany lease would result in a large number of accounts in the worksheet elimination. The asset and liability could be separated for analysis, resulting in an intercompany sale of an asset and a direct intercompany loan transaction.

TEST YOUR KNOWLEDGE SOLUTION

Worksheet Elimination—Journal Entry Form		
December 31, 2008		
(1) Common Stock	1,000,000	
Additional Paid-In Capital	750,000	
Retained Earnings (January 1, 2008)	515,000	
Accumulated Depreciation	1,121,250	
Goodwill	191,000	
Plant Assets		850,000
Patent		92,730
Long-Term Notes Payable		96,800
Investment in Sterling Products ($2,397,636 + $162,000 − $275,688)		2,283,948
Noncontrolling Interest in Sterling [($2,283,948/.90) (.10)]		253,772
(2) Investment Income [($290,000 + $16,320) (.90)]	275,688	
Investment in Sterling Products		113,688
Dividends ($180,000 × .9)		162,000
(3) Depreciation Expense	35,000	
Patent	33,720	
Long-Term Notes Payable	17,600	
Accumulated Depreciation		35,000
Amortization Expense—Patent		33,720
Interest Expense		17,600
(4) Noncontrolling Interest in Net Income of Sterling [($290,000 + $16,320 + $225 + $12,000 + $28,000 − $28,200)(.10)]	31,835	
Noncontrolling Interest in Sterling Products		13,835
Dividends ($180,000 × .10)		18,000

(5a)	Machine		3,000	
	Retained Earnings (January 1, 2008) [($1,650 − $225)(.90)]		1,283	
	Noncontrolling Interest [($1,650 − $225)(.10)]		142	
	Depreciation Expense			225
	Accumulated Depreciation			4,200
(5b)	Retained Earnings (January 1, 2008) ($12,000 × .90)		10,800	
	Noncontrolling Interest ($12,000 × .10)		1,200	
	Cost of Goods Sold			12,000
(5c)	Bonds Payable		300,000	
	Interest Revenue ($14,100 × 2)		28,200	
	Discount on Bonds Payable [$16,000 − ($40,000/20)(2)]			12,000
	Interest Expense ($14,000 × 2)			28,000
	Retained Earnings (January 1, 2008)			720
	[$1,000 − ($28,200 − $28,000)](.90)			
	Noncontrolling Interest [$1,000 − ($28,200 − $28,000)](.10)			80
	Investment in Bonds [$283,200 + ($2,100 × 2)]			287,400

QUESTIONS

4-1. You are the controller for a moderate-sized company. Several new board members have requested that you make a presentation on how consolidated financial statements are prepared. One board member asked why worksheet eliminations are needed for all intercompany transactions. How will you respond to this question?

4-2. A new division manager of your company is confused about the worksheet eliminations prepared for her division. She is particularly concerned with the letter sent explaining the worksheet eliminations. After a telephone conversation with the manager, it becomes apparent that her confusion centers around a lack of understanding of some terms used in the letter, such as *upstream, downstream,* and *lateral.* Prepare a brief memo to the manager explaining each term, with particular emphasis on differentiating among the terms.

4-3. Write a summary of the theoretical basis for the elimination of 100 percent of the profit or loss from an intercompany transaction even when the parent owns less than 100 percent of the subsidiary's outstanding voting common stock? (*Hint:* Research APB No. 51.)

4-4. Why are intercompany transaction worksheet eliminations required in periods subsequent to the intercompany transaction?

4-5. Why is the worksheet elimination to the historical cost of an equipment account resulting from an intercompany transaction the same each period?

4-6. When does the organization stop making worksheet eliminations to income statement accounts resulting from the intercompany sale of inventory?

4-7. When does the organization stop making worksheet eliminations to balance sheet accounts resulting from the intercompany sale of a tangible fixed asset?

4-8. Why does part of the worksheet elimination in periods subsequent to a downstream intercompany transaction affect retained earnings?

4-9. What is the difference between a direct intercompany debt transaction and an indirect intercompany debt transaction?

4-10. Jim, a new manager in the controller department, is not familiar with indirect intercompany bond transactions. He has asked for an explanation of why the consolidated entity is recognizing a loss on early debt retirement when the bond is still on the books of the issuer. Prepare a response to Jim's question.

4-11. Why is 100 percent of the interest revenue pertaining to an intercompany bond always eliminated while part of the interest expense may still be on the consolidated income statement?

4-12. Why are worksheet eliminations for an indirect intercompany debt transaction prepared in subsequent periods when the transaction occurs only once?

4-13. Why does the worksheet elimination for intercompany transactions differ if the transaction occurs during the year rather than at the end of the accounting period?

4-14. Why does the worksheet elimination in periods subsequent to a downstream intercompany transaction not affect noncontrolling interest?

Worksheet for Consolidation of Pratt Corporation and Subsidiary, Sterling Products
90 Percent Owned Subsidiary
Consolidation with Intercompany Transactions
December 31, 2008

	Separate Financial Statements		Adjustments and Eliminations				Consolidated Financial Statements
	Pratt	Sterling		Debit		Credit	
Income Statement							
Sales	10,100,000	1,450,000					11,550,000
Non-operating Items (net)	120,000						120,000
Investment Income, Sterling Products	275,688		(2)	275,688			0
Cost of Goods Sold	6,000,000	880,000			(5b)	12,000	6,868,000
Selling Expenses	1,300,000	130,000					1,430,000
General and Administrative Expenses	2,200,000	150,000	(3)	35,000	(3)	33,720	2,333,655
			(5c)	28,200	(3)	17,600	
					(5a)	225	
					(5c)	28,000	
Consolidated Net Income							1,038,345
Noncontrolling Interest in Net Income of Sterling			(4)	31,835			31,835
Net Income (to Statement of Retained Earnings)	995,688	290,000		370,723		91,545	1,006,510
Retained Earnings Statement							
Retained Earnings (1/1/2008)	3,357,448	515,000	(1)	515,000	(5c)	720	3,335,285
			(5a)	1,283			
			(5b)	10,800			
Add: Net Income (from Income Statement)	995,688	290,000	(X)	370,723	(X)	91,545	1,006,510
Subtotal	4,353,136	805,000					4,341,795
Less: Dividends	(400,000)	(180,000)			(2)	162,000	(400,000)
					(4)	18,000	
Retained Earnings (12/31/2008 to Balance sheet)	3,953,136	625,000		897,806		272,265	3,952,595
Balance Sheet							
Cash	615,000	280,000					895,000
Accounts Receivable (net)	1,800,000	380,000					2,180,000
Inventory (FIFO)	5,700,000	550,000					6,250,000
Other Current Assets	1,480,000						1,480,000
Total Current Assets	9,595,000	1,210,000					10,805,000
Plant and Equipment	31,000,000	3,135,000	(5a)	3,000	(1)	850,000	33,288,000
Accumulated Depreciation	(16,500,000)	(1,600,000)	(1)	1,121,250	(3)	35,000	(17,017,950)
					(5a)	4,200	

(Continued)

Account	Pratt	Sterling	Elim. Dr	Elim. Cr	Consolidated
Patent		700,000	(3) 33,720	(1) 92,730	640,990
Investment in Sterling Products	2,397,636			(1) 2,283,948	0
				(2) 113,688	
Investment in Bonds	287,400			(5c) 287,400	0
Other Non-current Assets	1,803,100	2,025,000			3,828,100
Goodwill			(1) 191,000		191,000
Total Long-Term Assets	18,988,136	4,260,000			20,930,140
Total Assets	28,583,136	5,470,000			31,735,140
Current Liabilities	8,240,000	635,000			8,875,000
Long-Term Notes Payable		1,000,000	(3) 17,600	(1) 96,800	1,079,200
7% Bonds Payable (due 6/30/2013)	4,000,000				4,000,000
Less: Discount on Bonds Payable	(110,000)				(110,000)
8% Bonds Payable (due 12/31/2010)		1,500,000	(5c) 300,000		1,200,000
Less: Discount on Bonds Payable		(40,000)		(5c) 12,000	(28,000)
Total Liabilities	12,130,000	3,095,000			15,016,200
Common Stock ($1 par):					
Pratt, 10,000,000 shares authorized, 6,000,000 shares issued and outstanding	6,000,000				6,000,000
Sterling, 1,000,000 shares authorized, issued and outstanding		1,000,000	(1) 1,000,000		0
Additional Paid-In Capital	6,500,000	750,000	(1) 750,000		6,500,000
Retained Earnings (12/31/2008 from Statement of Retained Earnings)	3,953,136	625,000	(X) 897,806	(X) 272,265	3,952,595
Noncontrolling Interest in Sterling			(5a) 142	(1) 253,772	266,345
			(5b) 1,200	(4) 13,835	
				(5c) 80	
Total Stockholders' Equity	16,453,136	2,375,000			16,718,940
Total Liabilities and Stockholders' Equity	28,583,136	5,470,000	4,315,718	4,315,718	31,735,140

(1) To eliminate the subsidiary's beginning of current period stockholders' equity and the parent's beginning of period Investment in Sterling Products account, to establish the beginning of period purchase differentials, and to create the beginning of period Noncontrolling Interest in Sterling account.

(2) To eliminate the change in the Investment in Sterling Products account and the parent's Investment Income account.

(3) To amortize identifiable asset and liability purchase differentials for the current period and recognize goodwill impairment.

(4) To recognize the change in the Noncontrolling Interest in Sterling account during the period.

(5a) To eliminate impact of previous period upstream intercompany machine transaction and adjust beginning Retained Earnings and Noncontrolling Interest.

(5b) To eliminate impact of previous period upstream intercompany inventory transaction and adjust beginning Retained Earnings and Noncontrolling Interest.

(5c) To eliminate impact of previous period upstream intercompany bond transaction and adjust beginning Retained Earnings and Noncontrolling Interest.

4-15. Why does an upstream intercompany transaction not require an adjustment with regard to the worksheet elimination of Investment Income?

4-16. Why does part of the worksheet elimination in periods subsequent to an upstream intercompany transaction affect retained earnings?

4-17. Under what circumstances does part of the worksheet elimination in periods subsequent to an upstream intercompany transaction affect noncontrolling interest?

4-18. Why does an upstream or lateral intercompany transaction in the current period impact the basic worksheet eliminations while a downstream intercompany transaction does not?

4-19. Why is the additional worksheet elimination needed to remove the impact of an intercompany transaction (a) *not altered* by the direction of the transaction in the period of the intercompany transaction and (b) *altered* by the direction of the transaction in the period(s) subsequent to the intercompany transaction?

4-20. A member of management has just been promoted to a level where part of his compensation is based on the company's overall performance. As a result of this change in compensation, this manager has become more interested in how the consolidated financial statements are prepared. He recently asked why upstream intercompany transactions in prior periods do not have to be considered when eliminating the stockholders' equity of the subsidiary, even though the transaction impacts the subsidiary's prior period net income such that it would impact this period's retained earnings. Prepare a response to this manager.

MULTIPLE CHOICE

4-1. Southern Materials owns 75 percent of Western Furniture's common stock. On December 31, 2005, Southern sells a machine costing $65,000 with $15,000 accumulated depreciation at the date of sale to Western for $36,000. What amount will be debited in the December 31, 2005, worksheet elimination for the machine account as a result of this transaction?

   a. $15,000

   b. $29,000

   c. $14,000

   d. $44,000

4-2. Pete's Farm Equipment owns 60 percent of Donovan's Agricultural Supply. Pete's has $1,000,000 of bonds payable outstanding with an unamortized discount of $38,000. Donovan's buys $400,000 of the bonds from an unrelated party for $360,000. What is the amount of worksheet elimination at the end of the year of the investment with regard to the Loss or Gain on Early Retirement of Debt?

   a. $24,800 loss

   b. $2,000 gain

   c. $24,800 gain

   d. $2,000 loss

4-3. Reading Retailers owns 80 percent of Miller Manufacturing. Reading sells a machine to Miller for $50,000 on December 31, 2005. The machine had a cost and accumulated depreciation of $80,000 and $32,000, respectively, at the date of sale. In the preparation of the 2006 consolidated financial statements, what is the adjustment to Retained Earnings with regard to this transaction?

   a. $2,000 debit

   b. $2,000 credit

   c. $1,600 debit

   d. $1,600 credit

4-4. Division Corporation owns 85 percent of Regional Operations Company. During 2005, Division sells inventory costing $30,000 to Regional for $40,000. Regional does not sell any of this inventory to unrelated parties before the end of 2005. During 2006, Division sells inventory costing $50,000 to Regional for $65,000. Also during 2006, Regional sells all the inventory purchased in 2005 and 70 percent of the inventory purchased in 2006 to unrelated entities. What is the adjustment to Cost of Goods Sold in the 2006 worksheet elimination?

   a. $70,500 credit

   b. $70,500 debit

   c. $20,500 credit

   d. $20,500 debit

4-5. Becker Corporation owns 60 percent of Conviser Company. During 2006, Becker sells inventory costing $10,000 to Conviser for $14,000. Conviser sells 75 percent of this inventory to unrelated parties before the end of 2006. What is the adjustment to Sales in the 2006 worksheet elimination?

   a. $4,000 debit

   b. $4,000 credit

   c. $14,000 debit

   d. $14,000 credit

4-6. Ace owns 75 percent of Baker. On June 1, 2006, Baker purchases $100,000 of Ace's 9 percent outstanding bonds payable for $106,000. The bonds have a maturity date of June 1, 2011. With regard to this bond, how much interest revenue is reported on the consolidated income statement in 2006?

a. $9,000

b. $0

c. $5,250

d. $4,550

4-7. Ma Tel owns 80 percent of Baby Tel. On March 1, 2006, Baby Tel sells a building to Ma Tel for $350,000. The building's cost and accumulated depreciation at the date of the sale are $450,000 and $260,000, respectively. What is the dollar amount of the worksheet elimination to the loss or gain on sale of building in 2006?

a. $100,000 debit

b. $90,000 debit

c. $160,000 debit

d. $540,000 credit

4-8. Cummings owns 90 percent of Richardson. On October 1, 2005, Cummings purchases $400,000 of Richardson's 8-percent outstanding bonds payable for $379,840. The bonds have an unamortized premium of $3,240 on October 1, 2005, and they mature on September 30, 2011. What is the dollar amount of the worksheet elimination to interest expense at December 31, 2005?

a. $0

b. $31,352

c. $7,460

d. $7,865

4-9. Little Company, a 70 percent–owned subsidiary of Giant Corporation, sold a building to Giant on May 1, 2005, for $480,000. The building had a cost of $850,000 and accumulated depreciation of $430,000 at the date of sale. The building is depreciated using the straight-line method and an estimated remaining life of 10 years. In the preparation of the 2006 consolidated financial statements, what is the dollar amount of the worksheet elimination to 2006 Retained Earnings with respect to this transaction?

a. $39,200

b. $4,000

c. $56,000

d. $60,000

4-10. Nashville Enterprises owns 90 percent of Frankfurt Corporation's stock. During 2005, Frankfurt sold inventory costing $140,000 to Nashville for $190,000. Before year-end, Nashville sold 70 percent of this inventory to unrelated parties for $127,000. In the preparation of the 2006 consolidated financial statements, what is the dollar amount of the adjustment to noncontrolling interest as it relates to this transaction?

a. $15,000

b. $50,000

c. $1,500

d. $3,500

EXERCISES

Number	Intercompany Transaction Direction	Percent Owned	Intercompany Transaction Type	Years of Worksheet Eliminations	Calculation of Consolidated Net Income	Description of Other Factors
4-1	Downstream	80	Inventory	2 years	2 years	0%/60% sold, compare with 20% sold in year 1
4-2	Downstream	90	Inventory	2 years	1 year	30%/45% sold
4-3	Downstream	70	Inventory	2 years		Intercompany sales in both years
4-4	Upstream	60	Inventory	2 years	2 years	15%/80% sold, noncontrolling interest adjustment in year 2
4-5	Upstream	90	Inventory	1 year		60% sold, consolidated sales and cost of goods sold
4-6	Upstream	75	Inventory	2 years		Intercompany sales in both years, intercompany inventory at beginning of first year
4-7	Lateral	80/60	Inventory	2 years	1 year	0%/70% sold, compare with sale of 40% in year 1
4-8	Lateral	70/90	Inventory	2 years		65%/35%, consolidated sales and cost of goods sold Income to noncontrolling interest in year 1

(Continued)

Number	Intercompany Transaction Direction	Percent Owned	Intercompany Transaction Type	Years of Worksheet Eliminations	Calculation of Consolidated Net Income	Description of Other Factors
4-9	Downstream	100	Plant Assets	1 year	1 year	End-of-year and beginning-of-year comparison, consolidated depreciation expense year
4-10	Downstream	80	Plant Assets	3 years	2 years	Consolidated depreciation expense 2 years
4-11	Upstream	80	Plant Assets	2 years	1 year	Prepare discussion of worksheet elimination
4-12	Upstream	90	Plant Assets	1 year		Income to noncontrolling interest year 1, noncontrolling interest adjustment year 2
4-13	Lateral	80/75	Plant Assets	1 year		Income to noncontrolling interest 1 year, compare to solution if direction of transaction changed
4-14	Lateral	60/90	Plant Assets	2 years	2 years	Consolidated depreciation expense 2 years, worksheet elimination if asset sold to unrelated party in year 2
4-15	Downstream	75	Debt	2 years		Income to noncontrolling interest and consolidated interest expense 1 year
4-16	Downstream	80	Debt	2 years		Determine original bond issue date, consolidated interest revenue and expense 2 years
4-17	Upstream	75	Debt	2 years		Income to noncontrolling interest and consolidated interest expense 1 year
4-18	Upstream	80	Debt	2 years	1 year	Adjustment to noncontrolling interest in year 3, consolidated interest revenue and expense 2 years
4-19	Lateral	75/90	Debt	2 years	1 year	Adjustment to noncontrolling interest in year 3
4-20	Lateral	70/80	Debt	2 years		Income to noncontrolling interest and consolidated interest expense 1 year

EXERCISE 4-1

Montana Enterprises sold $25,000 of inventory to Idaho Industries for $40,000 during 2005. Idaho was still in possession of all the inventory at year-end. Montana owns 80 percent of Idaho's stock.

Required:

A. Prepare the intercompany inventory worksheet elimination needed to present consolidated financial statements on December 31, 2005.

B. Assuming Idaho sold 60 percent of the inventory purchased from Montana during 2006, prepare the intercompany inventory worksheet elimination needed to present consolidated financial statements on December 31, 2006.

C. Montana had operating income of $80,000 in 2005 and $105,000 in 2006, while Idaho had operating income of $36,000 in 2005 and $40,000 in 2006. Determine consolidated net income in 2005 and 2006.

D. How would the solution to part A change if Idaho had sold 20 percent of the inventory purchased from Montana in 2005?

EXERCISE 4-2

Sunfish Company purchased inventory from Carp Corporation, its parent, for $64,000 in 2005. The inventory was carried on the books of Carp at $48,000 at the time of the sale. Before the end of 2005, Sunfish sold 30 percent of the inventory purchased from Carp to unrelated parties for $24,500. Carp owns 90 percent of Sunfish's stock.

Required:

A. Prepare the intercompany inventory worksheet elimination needed to present consolidated financial statements on December 31, 2005.

B. Carp and Sunfish had operating income of $250,000 and $90,000, respectively, in 2005. Determine consolidated net income for 2005.

C. Prepare the intercompany inventory worksheet elimination needed to present consolidated financial statements on December 31, 2006, assuming that Sunfish sold an additional 45 percent of the inventory purchased from Carp to unrelated parties for $32,000.

D. How would the solution to part C change if the sales price to the unrelated parties is $35,000.

EXERCISE 4-3

Bear Manufacturing sells 4,000 units of inventory to Cub Enterprises, its subsidiary, for $7 each in 2005. The inventory had a cost basis to Bear of $5 each at the time of the sale. Cub sells 1,500 units of the inventory purchased from Bear to unrelated parties for $11 each before year-end. Bear owns 70 percent of Cub's stock.

Required:

A. Prepare the intercompany inventory worksheet elimination needed to present consolidated financial statements on December 31, 2005.

B. Prepare the intercompany inventory worksheet elimination needed to present consolidated financial statements on December 31, 2006, assuming that Bear sold an additional 5,000 units of inventory (cost $6 each) to Cub for $9 each during 2006. Also assume that Cub sells 5,500 units to unrelated parties for $14 each before year-end and that a FIFO flow is used for inventory transactions.

EXERCISE 4-4

Pokers Unlimited, a 60 percent–owned subsidiary, sold inventory costing $150,000 to its parent, Fireplace Fixtures, for $200,000 in 2005. Fireplace sold 15 percent of this inventory to unrelated parties in 2005 for $35,000. Fireplace sold an additional 80 percent of the inventory to unrelated parties in 2006 for $180,000.

Required:

A. Prepare the intercompany inventory worksheet elimination needed to present consolidated financial statements on December 31, 2005, and December 31, 2006.

B. Fireplace had operating income of $480,000 and $525,000 in 2005 and 2006, respectively. Pokers had operating income of $90,000 and $110,000 in 2005 and 2006, respectively. Determine consolidated net income for 2005 and 2006.

C. Assuming there are no other intercompany transactions, what is the amount of adjustment to noncontrolling interest in the 2007 worksheet elimination for intercompany inventory transactions?

EXERCISE 4-5

Broadcasting Enterprises purchased $100,000 of inventory from its subsidiary, Cable Company, when the inventory was carried on the financial records of Cable for $75,000. Broadcasting sold 60 percent of this inventory to unrelated parties during the same period for $70,000. During the period, Broadcasting recorded sales and cost of goods sold of $2,500,000 and $1,500,000, respectively. Also, Cable recorded sales and cost of goods sold of $850,000 and $400,000, respectively. Broadcasting owns 90 percent of Cable's stock.

Required:

A. Prepare the intercompany inventory worksheet elimination needed to present consolidated financial statements.

B. Determine the amounts that would be presented on the consolidated income statement as Sales and Cost of Goods Sold.

C. What are the worksheet elimination adjustments to Retained Earnings and Noncontrolling Interest (if applicable) in the next period regarding the above intercompany inventory transaction?

EXERCISE 4-6

Sanderson Company is a 75 percent–owned subsidiary of Flip, Incorporated. Sanderson regularly supplies Flip with one of the main raw materials for Flip's manufacturing process. The information below summarizes recent intercompany sales activity between the two companies.

	Units Sold to Flip	Intercompany Units on Hand at Flip	Cost per Unit	Intercompany Markup per Unit
January 1, 2005	—	0	—	—
2005 activity	70,000	—	$11.00	$6.00
December 31, 2005	—	22,000	$11.00	$6.00
2006 activity	80,000	—	$12.00	$6.50
December 31, 2006	—	15,000	$12.00	$6.50

Required:

A. Prepare the intercompany inventory worksheet elimination needed to present consolidated financial statements at December 31, 2005.

B. Prepare the intercompany inventory worksheet elimination needed to present consolidated financial statements at December 31, 2006.

C. Assume that Flip holds some inventory acquired from Sanderson at January 1, 2005. Rework parts A and B to reflect the information set above with the change in information outlined below.

	Units Sold to Flip	Intercompany Units on Hand at Flip	Cost per Unit	Intercompany Markup per Unit
January 1, 2005	—	10,000	$10.00	$4.00

D. Explain your answers for 2005 and 2006 in part C regarding where and why the answers change and do not change.

EXERCISE 4-7

Furniture Enterprises owns 80 percent of Cushion Company's stock and 60 percent of Pillow Corporation's stock. Cushion sold inventory costing $60,000 to Pillow for $75,000 in 2005. Pillow did not sell any of this inventory to unrelated parties during 2005.

Required:

A. Prepare the intercompany inventory worksheet elimination needed to present consolidated financial statements in 2005.

B. Prepare the intercompany inventory worksheet elimination needed to present consolidated financial statements in 2006 assuming that Pillow sold 70 percent of the inventory purchased from Cushion to unrelated parties for $58,000.

C. Assume that Furniture had operating income of $380,000 in 2005 and $415,000 in 2006; Cushion had operating income of $67,000 in 2005 and $80,000 in 2006; and Pillow had operating income of $93,000 in 2005 and $85,000 in 2006. Determine consolidated net income in 2005 and 2006.

D. How would part A change if Pillow had sold 40 percent of the inventory purchased from Cushion in 2005?

EXERCISE 4-8

Apex Monitors purchased inventory from Delta Keyboards for $179,200 in 2005. The inventory had a carrying value on Delta's books of $140,000 at the time of the sale. Apex sold 65 percent of this inventory to unrelated parties in 2005 for $135,000. The remainder of this inventory was sold to unrelated parties in 2006 for $67,000. Computer Unlimited owns 70 percent of Apex's stock and 90 percent of Delta's stock. Apex, Delta, and Computer had sales and cost of goods sold in 2005 and 2006 as follows.

	Sales		Cost of Goods Sold	
	2005	2006	2005	2006
Apex	$1,000,000	$1,130,000	$470,000	$510,000
Delta	3,365,000	2,840,000	1,346,000	1,280,000
Computer	4,200,000	6,300,000	2,700,000	3,100,000

Required:

A. Prepare the intercompany inventory worksheet elimination needed to present consolidated financial statements in 2005 and 2006.

B. Determine the amounts that would be presented on the consolidated income statement as Sales and Cost of Goods Sold for 2005 and 2006.

C. Assuming Apex and Delta had operating income in 2005 of $95,000 and $210,000, respectively, and there are no other intercompany transactions, what is the income to noncontrolling interest for each company in 2005?

EXERCISE 4-9   National Corporation sold equipment to Local Company on December 31, 2005, for $24,000. The equipment was carried on the financial records of National at a cost of $66,000, and accumulated depreciation was $44,000 at the time of the sale. The equipment had an estimated remaining life of two years on the records of National and was assigned an estimated remaining life of four years when purchased by Local. Straight-line depreciation is used by National and Local. National owns 100 percent of Local's stock.

Required:

A. Prepared the intercompany asset transaction worksheet elimination needed to present the consolidated financial statements in 2005.

B. What would be presented on National's income statement, Local's income statement, and the consolidated income statement for depreciation expense for 2005?

C. Prepare the intercompany asset transaction worksheet elimination needed to present the consolidated financial statements in 2005, assuming all the values in the problem exist at January 1, 2005.

D. How would the use of a different depreciation method impact the worksheet elimination prepared in parts A and C above?

EXERCISE 4-10   Small Change Corporation, an 80 percent–owned subsidiary, purchased a building from its parent, Big Bucks Enterprises, for $264,000 on January 1, 2005. The building had a historical cost and accumulated depreciation on Big Bucks' books at the time of the sale of $500,000 and $300,320, respectively. The building had an estimated remaining life of 8 years on the financial records of Big Bucks and was assigned a new estimated life of 20 years when purchased by Small Change. Big Bucks and Small Change both calculate depreciation using the straight-line method.

Required:

A. Prepare the intercompany asset transaction worksheet elimination needed to present the consolidated financial statements in 2005, 2006, and 2007.

B. Assume that Big Bucks has operating income of $675,000 in 2005 and $729,000 in 2006, while Small Change has operating income of $290,000 in 2005 and $326,000 in 2006. Determine consolidated net income assuming that there are no other intercompany transactions in 2005 and 2006.

C. What would be recognized as consolidated depreciation expense in 2005 and 2006 if the sale had occurred on May 1, 2005, assuming all the values in the problem exist at May 1, 2005?

EXERCISE 4-11   Engine Manufacturing Corporation acquired a machine from Piston-Ring Company, its 80 percent–owned subsidiary, for $120,000 on January 1, 2005. The machine had a historical cost of $675,000 and accumulated depreciation of $525,000 in Piston-Ring's financial records at the date of the sale. Piston-Ring was depreciating the machine at a rate of $75,000 per year. Engine assigns the machine a three-year estimated life at the date of purchase.

Required:

A. Prepare the intercompany asset transaction worksheet elimination needed to present the consolidated financial statements in 2005 and 2006.

B. Write a brief explanation of the 2006 worksheet elimination prepared in part a.

C. Assume that Engine has operating income of $1,740,000 and Piston-Ring has operating income of $580,000 in 2005. Determine consolidated net income for 2005.

EXERCISE 4-12   Little Exposure Insurance sells a building with a historical cost of $1,180,000 and accumulated depreciation of $388,000 to Mega Insurance Company on January 1, 2005 for $1,008,000. Little Exposure had assigned the building a 15-year estimated life at the date it was originally purchased. Mega assigns the building an estimated remaining life of 12 years when it is acquired from Little Exposure. Mega owns 90 percent of Little Exposure's stock.

Required:
A. Prepare the intercompany asset transaction worksheet elimination needed to present the consolidated financial statements in 2005.
B. What amount of income would be allocated to noncontrolling interest if Little Exposure has operating income of $750,000 and there are no other intercompany transactions?
C. Assuming there are no other intercompany transactions, what would be the adjustment to noncontrolling interest in the 2006 intercompany asset transaction worksheet elimination?

EXERCISE 4-13   Baseball Company sells a machine to Bowling Shoe Enterprises on March 31, 2006, for $120,000. The machine has a historical cost and accumulated depreciation of $160,000 and $46,000, respectively, on Baseball's books at the date of the sale. The machine had a remaining life of 40 months on Baseball's books at the date of sale and was assigned an estimated remaining life of 60 months when purchased by Bowling Shoe. Ultimate owns 80 percent of Baseball's stock and 75 percent of Bowling Shoe's stock.

Required:
A. Prepare the intercompany asset transaction worksheet elimination needed to present the consolidated financial statements in 2006.
B. How would the solution to part A be different if the buyer had been Ultimate rather than Bowling Shoe?
C. How would the solution to part A be different if the seller had been Ultimate rather than Baseball?
D. Assume that Baseball has operating income of $360,000 and Bowling Shoe has operating income of $285,000. What is the amount of income allocated to the noncontrolling interest of Baseball and Bowling Shoe on the consolidated income statement if there are no other intercompany transactions?

EXERCISE 4-14   Oil Rig Enterprise (a 60 percent–owned subsidiary of Huge Oil Company) buys a building from Pipeline Pumps Company (a 90 percent–owned subsidiary of Huge Oil Company) for $6,300,000 on June 1, 2006. The building is assigned an estimated life of 21 years when purchased. The building has a historical cost and accumulated depreciation of $8,400,000 and $1,596,000, respectively, on Pipeline Pumps' books when the building is sold. Annual depreciation on the books of Pipeline Pumps for years before the sale was $285,000.

Required:
A. Prepare the intercompany asset transaction worksheet elimination needed to present the consolidated financial statements in 2006 and 2007.
B. Assume that Huge Oil had operating income of $8,150,000 in 2006 and $9,200,000 in 2007, Oil Rig had operating income of $1,550,000 in 2006 and $1,700,000 in 2007, and Pipeline Pumps had operating income of $955,000 in 2006 and $875,000 in 2007. Determine consolidated net income in 2006 and 2007.
C. Determine consolidated depreciation expense in 2006 and 2007.
D. Assume that Oil Rig sells the building to an unrelated party on October 1, 2007, for $6,000,000. Prepare the worksheet elimination needed to present the consolidated financial statements in 2007.

EXERCISE 4-15   Eagle Corporation issues a 20-year, $500,000, 12-percent bond payable on January 1, 2001, for $423,200. The discount on bonds is amortized using the straight-line method. Sparrow Enterprises, a 75 percent–owned subsidiary of Eagle, purchased $50,000 of the bond as an investment from an unrelated party on June 1, 2006, for $43,000.

Required:

A. Prepare the indirect intercompany debt transaction worksheet elimination needed to present the consolidated financial statements in 2006 and 2007.

B. Assuming that Sparrow has operating income of $145,000 for 2006 and no other intercompany transactions have occurred, what is the amount of income allocated to noncontrolling interest?

C. Determine consolidated interest expense for 2006.

EXERCISE 4-16   Commuter Airways purchases Big Plane Airline's bond from an unrelated party as an investment for $66,000 on December 1, 2006. The bond has a face value of $60,000, a stated interest rate of 12 percent, and a remaining life of five years. The bond was originally issued for $87,000 and has a carrying value on the issuer's books of $64,500 at the date purchased by Computer. Big Plane owns 80 percent of Commuter's stock. The straight-line method is used to amortize premiums.

Required:

A. Prepare the indirect intercompany debt transaction worksheet elimination needed to present the consolidated financial statements in 2006 and 2007.

B. Determine the date of the original bond issuance.

C. Determine the amount of interest revenue and interest expense to be recognized on the consolidated income statements in 2006 and 2007.

EXERCISE 4-17   Porpoise Products issued, for $281,800, a 10-year, $250,000, 12 percent bond payable on May 1, 2003. On September 1, 2005, Orka Enterprises acquired $150,000 of this bond from an unrelated party for $181,280. The premium is amortized using the straight-line method. Orka owns 75 percent of Porpoise's stock.

Required:

A. Prepare the indirect intercompany debt transaction worksheet elimination needed to present the consolidated financial statements in 2005 and 2006.

B. Determine the amount of interest expense to be recognized on the 2005 consolidated income statement.

C. Assume that Orka has operating income of $650,000 and pays dividends of $150,000 in 2005 while Porpoise has operating income of $400,000 and pays dividends of $90,000. Determine the income allocated to noncontrolling interest.

D. How would the income to noncontrolling interest change if the dividends paid by Porpoise were $120,000 rather than $90,000?

EXERCISE 4-18   Little Magazine Enterprises is an 80 percent owned subsidiary of Big Book Company. Big Book Company purchased $1,000,000 of Little Magazine's outstanding bonds payable from an unrelated party for $1,070,215 on March 31, 2006. The bonds were initially issued by Little Magazine on November 1, 1998, for $1,044,400. At the date of issuance the bonds had a 10 percent stated interest rate. The premium is being amortized straight-line on Little Magazine's books at a rate of $185 per month.

Required:

A. Prepare the indirect intercompany debt transaction worksheet elimination needed to present the consolidated financial statements in 2006 and 2007.

B. What is the amount of the adjustment to noncontrolling interest that would appear in the 2008 worksheet elimination for the indirect intercompany debt transaction?

C. Determine the amount of interest revenue and interest expense recognized on the 2006 and 2007 consolidated income statements.

D. Determine 2006 consolidated net income based on the assumption that Big Book has operating income of $2,650,000, Little Magazine has operating income of $1,100,000, and there are no other intercompany transactions.

E. How would the existence of a $10,000 increase in depreciation expense resulting from a purchase differential on equipment impact the worksheet elimination for this indirect intercompany debt transaction?

EXERCISE 4-19   Syracuse Company, a 75 percent–owned subsidiary of Phoenix Enterprises, issued $500,000, 10-year, 9 percent bonds payable to unrelated parties on January 1, 2006, for $516,800. Toledo

Corporation, a 90 percent–owned subsidiary of Phoenix, acquires $200,000 of these bonds from an unrelated party on August 31, 2006, for $213,104. Syracuse and Toledo both amortize premiums using the straight-line method.

Required:

A. Prepare the indirect intercompany debt transaction worksheet elimination needed to present the consolidated financial statements in 2006 and 2007.

B. Determine the 2007 consolidated net income if Phoenix has operating income of $750,000, Syracuse has operating income of $300,000, and Toledo has operating income of $220,000.

C. Determine the adjustment to noncontrolling interest in the 2008 worksheet elimination for the indirect intercompany debt transaction.

EXERCISE 4-20   Basket Company purchased $300,000 of the bonds payable of Nylon Rope Enterprises from an unrelated party on October 1, 2005, for $263,600. These bonds had originally been issued by Nylon Rope for $246,000 on February 1, 2000. The bonds have a stated interest rate of 12 percent and an original life of 15 years. The discount on the bonds is amortized using the straight-line method. Basket is a 70 percent–owned subsidiary of Hot Air Balloon Corporation, while Nylon Rope is an 80 percent–owned subsidiary of Hot Air Balloon.

Required:

A. Prepare the indirect intercompany debt transaction worksheet elimination needed to present the consolidated financial statements in 2010 and 2011.

B. Determine the interest expense recognized on the 2010 consolidated income statement related to these bonds.

C. Determine the 2010 income allocated to noncontrolling interest assuming that there are no other intercompany transaction and that Basket has operating income of $170,000 and Nylon Rope has operating income of $225,000.

PROBLEMS

Number	Intercompany Transaction Direction	Percent Owned	Transaction Type	Year of Consolidation	Description of Other Factors
4-1	Both	75	Inventory	First	
4-2	Both	75	Inventory	Second	Continuation of Problem 4-1
4-3	Both	75	Inventory	Third	Continuation of Problem 4-2
4-4	Both	60	Inventory	First	Mid-year acquisition
4-5	Both	60	Inventory	Second	Continuation of Problem 4-4
4-6	Both	60	Inventory	Third	Continuation of Problem 4-5
4-7	Down	80	Plant Assets	First	Mid-year sale of asset, negative goodwill, separate accumulated depreciation accounts
4-8	Both	80	Plant Assets	Second	Continuation of Problem 4-7, end-of-year upstream sale of plant asset
4-9	Both	80	Plant Assets	Third	Continuation of Problem 4-8, sale to unrelated party of downstream asset in Problem 4-7
4-10	Down	100	Plant Assets	First	Mid-year acquisition, separate accumulated depreciation accounts, mid-year sale of asset
4-11	Both	100	Plant Assets	Second	Continuation of Problem 4-10, sale to unrelated party of downstream asset in Problem 4-10, mid-year upstream and end-of-year downstream downstream sale of plant asset

Number	Intercompany Transaction Direction	Percent Owned	Transaction Type	Year of Consolidation	Description of Other Factors
4-12	Both	100	Plant Assets	Third	Continuation of Problem 4-11, mid-year upstream sale of plant asset, sale to unrelated party of upstream asset in Problem 4-11
4-13	Down	100	Debt	First	Mid-year acquisition
4-14	Down	100	Debt	Second	Continuation of Problem 4-13
4-15	Down	100	Debt	Third	Continuation of Problem 4-14, additional downstream intercompany debt purchased
4-16	Both	80	Debt	First	Beginning-of-year acquisition
4-17	Both	80	Debt	Second	Continuation of Problem 4-16, additional downstream and upstream intercompany debt purchased
4-18	Both	80	Debt	Third	Continuation of Problem 4-17, retirement of upstream intercompany debt purchased in Problem 4-16
4-19	Both	80	Inventory, Plant Asset, and Debt	First and Second	Beginning-of-year acquisition, separate accumulated depreciation account, upstream inventory, downstream plant assets, downstream debt in year 1, additional upstream inventory in year 2
4-20	Both	100	Inventory	First, second, and third	Beginning-of-year acquisition, upstream and downstream inventory in each year
4-21	Both	60	Plant Asset	First, second, and third	Mid-year acquisition, separate accumulated depreciation accounts, upstream and downstream plant asset in each year, downstream sale in year 1 is sold to unrelated party in year 3 and upstream sale in year 2 is sold to unrelated party in year 3
4-22	Up	60	Debt	First, second, and third	Beginning-of-year acquisition, upstream debt in each year, debt acquired in year 1 is retired by subsidiary in year 2

PROBLEM 4-1 Penman Corporation acquired 75 percent of Shedd Industries' stock on January 1, 2005, for $1,647,750. The balance sheets for Penman and Shedd and market value information at the date of acquisition are presented below.

	Penman Corporation		Shedd Industries	
	Book Value	Market Value	Book Value	Market Value
Cash	$ 250,000	$ 250,000	$ 82,000	$ 82,000
Receivables	350,000	350,000	140,000	140,000
Inventory	800,000	875,000	260,000	300,000
Investment in Shedd	1,650,000	1,650,000		
Land	1,100,000	1,600,000	431,000	481,000
Buildings (net)	3,750,000	3,850,000	900,000	872,000
Equipment (net)	1,660,000	2,400,000	387,000	450,000
Patents	165,000	320,000		
Total Assets	$9,725,000		$2,200,000	

Current Liabilities	$ 650,000	600,000	$ 200,000	200,000
Bonds Payable	2,000,000	2,100,000		
Premium on Bonds Payable	50,000			
Common Stock	1,450,000		600,000	
Additional Paid-In Capital	3,050,000		850,000	
Retained Earnings	2,525,000		550,000	
Total Liabilities and Equity	$9,725,000		$2,200,000	

The estimated remaining life (in years) of each item with a purchase differential is listed below.

	Penman	Shedd
Inventory	1	1
Land	Indefinite	Indefinite
Buildings	15	7
Equipment	5	9
Patents	8	
Current Liabilities	1	
Bonds Payable	10	

Throughout the year Shedd sold inventory to Penman for a total of $96,000. The inventory sold to Penman was carried on Shedd's books at $80,000 at the time of the sale. Seventy percent of this inventory was sold by Penman to unrelated parties during 2005 for $76,000. Near the end of 2005, Penman sold inventory costing $40,000 to Shedd for $46,000. Shedd did not sell any of this inventory to unrelated parties during 2005.

Abbreviated income statements for Penman and Shedd for 2005 are provided below.

	Penman Corporation	Shedd Industries
Sales	$3,500,000	$700,000
Cost of Goods Sold	2,275,000	285,000
Gross Profit	1,225,000	415,000
Depreciation Expense	425,000	86,000
Other Expenses	200,000	109,000
Income Before Taxes	600,000	220,000
Income Taxes	180,000	60,000
Net Income	$420,000	$160,000

Dividends in 2005 for Penman and Shedd were $230,000 and $90,000, respectively.

Required:
Prepare, in journal entry form, the worksheet eliminations needed to present the consolidated financial statements at December 31, 2005.

PROBLEM 4-2

(Refer to the information in Problem 4-1.) During 2006, Shedd sold additional inventory to Penman for $130,000. Shedd originally paid $105,000 for this inventory. Penman sold all the remaining inventory purchased from Shedd during 2005 to unrelated parties and 80 percent of the inventory purchased during 2006 for $150,000.

Penman sold $82,000 of additional inventory to Shedd during 2006. This inventory was carried on Penman's books for $68,000 at the time of sale. Shedd sold 90 percent of the inventory purchased from Penman during 2005 and 30 percent of the inventory purchased during 2006 for $73,000.

Penman's net income and dividends paid during 2006 are $550,000 and $260,000, respectively, while Shedd's net income and dividends paid are $210,000 and $100,000, respectively.

Required:

Prepare, in journal entry form, the worksheet eliminations needed to present the consolidated financial statements at December 31, 2006.

PROBLEM 4-3

(Refer to the information in Problems 4-1 and 4-2.) Penman recorded net income of $675,000 and paid $300,000 of dividends during 2007, while Shedd recorded net income of $250,000 and paid $110,000 of dividends. Shedd sold $160,000 (cost) of inventory to Penman for $225,000 during 2007, while Penman sold $92,000 (cost) of inventory to Shedd for $115,000. During 2007, Penman sold an additional 10 percent of the inventory purchased from Shedd in 2006 to unrelated parties for $16,000. In addition, Penman sold 60 percent of the inventory purchased from Shedd in 2007 to unrelated parties for $147,000. Shedd sold all the remaining inventory purchased from Penman in 2005 to unrelated parties during 2007. Shedd also sold, to unrelated parties, an additional 40 percent of the inventory purchased from Penman during 2006 and 70 percent of the inventory purchased during 2007. Total sales by Shedd to unrelated parties are $131,000.

Required:

Prepare, in journal entry form, the worksheet eliminations needed to present the consolidated financial statements at December 31, 2007.

PROBLEM 4-4

Cardinal Corporation purchased 60 percent of Bishop Company March 31, 2005, for $15,078,000. The balance sheet of Bishop Company on that date follows.

Cash	$2,600,000	Accounts Payable	$1,500,000
Marketable Securities	1,200,000	Notes Payable (short-term)	3,300,000
Accounts Receivable	5,750,000	Notes Payable (long-term)	1,400,000
Inventory	8,260,000	Bonds Payable	10,000,000
Land	750,000	Discount on Bonds Payable	(65,000)
Buildings (net)	6,300,000	Common Stock	350,000
Equipment (net)	850,000	Additional Paid-In Capital	4,150,000
Copyrights	200,000	Retained Earnings	5,275,000
Total Assets	$25,910,000	Total Liabilities and Equity	$25,910,000

Purchase differentials exist for three identifiable assets: land, buildings, and copyrights. The amounts of the purchase differentials applicable to Cardinal's ownership percentage are $648,000, $1,800,000, and $2,565,000, respectively. The remaining estimated life of the buildings is 10 years and the copyrights have an estimated remaining life of 25 years.

Bishop Company records net income of $3,000,000 for the last nine months of 2005 and pays $600,000 in dividends quarterly (three dividend payments were made after the acquisition). In addition, Cardinal records $4,500,000 net income and pays $1,000,000 of dividends in 2005.

Cardinal sold $2,400,000 of inventory to Bishop in 2005 for $2,850,000. Bishop sold 75 percent of this inventory to unrelated parties during 2005. Also in 2005, Bishop sold inventory costing $780,000 to Cardinal for $875,000. Cardinal resells 40 percent of this inventory to unrelated parties before the end of 2005.

Required:

Prepare, in journal entry form, the worksheet eliminations needed to present the consolidated financial statements at December 31, 2005.

PROBLEM 4-5

(Refer to the information in Problem 4-4.) Bishop Company had net income of $4,200,000 and paid dividends of $2,700,000 in 2006.

During 2006, Cardinal sold inventory to Bishop for $2,900,000. The inventory cost Cardinal $2,100,000. Bishop sold all the remaining inventory purchased from Cardinal in 2005 to unrelated parties and 30 percent of the inventory purchased in 2006. Bishop sold inventory costing $950,000 to Cardinal for $1,350,000. Cardinal sold an additional 45 percent of the inventory purchased in 2005 and 20 percent of the inventory purchased in 2006.

Required:

Prepare, in journal entry form, the worksheet eliminations needed to present the consolidated financial statements at December 31, 2006.

PROBLEM 4-6

(Refer to the information in Problems 4-4 and 4-5.) Net income and dividends paid by Bishop Company are $5,200,000 and $3,450,000, respectively.

Cardinal sold inventory costing $3,100,000 to Bishop in 2007 for $3,900,000, while Bishop sold inventory costing $1,300,000 to Cardinal for $1,550,000. Bishop sold an additional 60 percent of the inventory purchased from Cardinal in 2006 to unrelated parties in 2007. In addition, Bishop also sold 90 percent of the inventory purchased from Cardinal in 2007 to unrelated parties. In 2007 Cardinal sold the remaining inventory that had been purchased from Bishop in 2005 and 2006 to unrelated parties. Cardinal also sold 70 percent of the inventory purchased from Bishop in 2007.

Required:

Prepare, in journal entry form, the worksheet eliminations needed to present the consolidated financial statements at December 31, 2007.

PROBLEM 4-7

Micro Techniques Corporation purchased 80 percent of Spreadsheet Development Company for $830,000 on January 1, 2005. The balance sheets for Micro Techniques and Spreadsheet Development and market value information at the date of acquisition are presented below.

	Micro Techniques		*Spreadsheet*	
	Book Value	*Market Value*	*Book Value*	*Market Value*
Cash	$ 210,000	$ 210,000	$ 110,000	$110,000
Receivables	550,000	550,000	165,000	165,000
Inventory	600,000	725,000	340,000	370,000
Investment in Spreadsheet	850,000	850,000		
Land	675,000	780,000	300,000	350,000
Buildings	2,050,000	2,150,000	800,000	680,000
Accumulated Depreciation—Buildings	(450,000)		(175,000)	
Equipment	1,400,000	1,250,000	300,000	220,000
Accumulated Depreciation—Equipment	(300,000)		(90,000)	
Patents	110,000	140,000		
Total Assets	$5,695,000		$1,750,000	
Current Liabilities	$ 625,000	$ 625,000	$ 275,000	$275,000
Bonds Payable	1,000,000	980,000	500,000	500,000
Discount on Bonds Payable	(35,000)			
Common Stock	750,000		225,000	
Additional Paid-In Capital	1,660,000		325,000	
Retained Earnings	1,695,000		425,000	
Total Liabilities and Equity	$5,695,000		$1,750,000	

The estimated remaining life (in years) of each of the items with a purchase differential is listed below.

	Micro	*Spreadsheet*
Inventory	1	1
Land	Indefinite	Indefinite
Buildings	12	8
Equipment	10	4
Patents	5	
Bonds Payable	5	

On April 1, 2005, Micro sells equipment to Spreadsheet for $15,000. The equipment has a historical cost of $24,000 and accumulated depreciation of $9,500 after recording the April 1 adjusting entry.

The equipment has an estimated remaining life of $7\frac{1}{4}$ years when sold by Micro and an estimated remaining life of 5 years by Spreadsheet. Straight-line depreciation is recorded on a monthly basis. Abbreviated income statements for Micro Techniques and Spreadsheet for 2005 are provided below.

	Micro	*Spreadsheet*
Sales	$4,125,000	$950,000
Cost of Goods Sold	2,475,000	370,000
Gross Profit	1,650,000	580,000
Depreciation Expenses	300,000	105,000
Other Expenses	250,000	175,000
Income Before Taxes	1,100,000	300,000
Income Taxes	180,000	90,000
Net Income	$920,000	$210,000

Dividends in 2005 were $190,000 and $60,000 for Micro Techniques and Spreadsheet Development, respectively.

Required:
Prepare, in journal entry form, the worksheet eliminations needed to present the consolidated financial statements at December 31, 2005.

PROBLEM 4-8   (Refer to the information in Problem 4-7.) On December 31, 2006, Spreadsheet sells equipment to Micro Techniques for $20,000. This piece of equipment had an original cost of $32,000 and accumulated depreciation of $9,600 at the date of sale (the adjusting entry has been made). The equipment has an eight-year remaining life on December 31, 2006.

Micro Techniques' net income and dividends paid during 2006 are $975,000 and $225,000, respectively, while Spreadsheet's net income and dividends paid are $300,000 and $100,000, respectively.

Required:
Prepare, in journal entry form, the worksheet eliminations needed to present the consolidated financial statements at December 31, 2006.

PROBLEM 4-9   (Refer to the information in Problems 4-7 and 4-8.) On September 30, 2007, Spreadsheet sells the equipment acquired from Micro Techniques in 2005 to an unrelated party for $13,000. Net income and dividends for Spreadsheet in 2007 are $375,000 and $115,000, respectively.

Required:
Prepare, in journal entry form, the worksheet eliminations needed to present the consolidated financial statements at December 31, 2007.

PROBLEM 4-10   Big Boat Manufacturing Corporation purchased 100 percent of LifeLine Incorporated on September 30, 2005, for $2,870,000. The balance sheet of LifeLine Inc. on that date follows.

Cash	$ 195,000	Accounts Payable	$ 300,000
Accounts Receivable	430,000	Notes Payable (short-term)	450,000
Inventory	720,000	Notes Payable (long-term)	2,100,000
Land	275,000	Common Stock	100,000
Buildings	3,000,000	Additional Paid-In Capital	1,000,000
Accumulated Depreciation—Buildings	(600,000)	Retained Earnings	970,000
Equipment	1,300,000	Total Liabilities and Equity	$4,920,000
Accumulated Depreciation—Equipment	(400,000)		
Total Assets	$4,920,000		

Purchase differentials exist for two identifiable assets: inventory and buildings. The amounts of the purchase differentials are $180,000 and $316,800, respectively. The remaining estimated life of the inventory is four months and the buildings have an estimated remaining life of eight years.

LifeLine Inc. records net income of $125,000 for the last three months of 2005, and LifeLine pays $25,000 of dividends quarterly (one dividend payment is declared and paid in 2005 after the acquisition).

Big Boat sold precision machining equipment to LifeLine on December 1, 2005, for $12,240. This equipment had a historical cost and accumulated depreciation, on the financial records of Big Boat, of $15,000 and $4,200, respectively, after the adjusting entry at the time of sale. The machine had a remaining estimated life of 10 years on Big Boat's records at the time of the sale. The machine was assigned an estimated life of 15 years when place on LifeLine's financial records.

Required:
Prepare, in journal entry form, the worksheet eliminations needed to present the consolidated financial statements at December 31, 2005.

PROBLEM 4-11

(Refer to the information in Problem 4-10.) LifeLine Inc. reports net income of $550,000 and pay dividends of $120,000 in 2006.

On December 31, 2006, Big Boat sold additional equipment to LifeLine for $62,400. This equipment had a historical cost of $90,000 and accumulated depreciation of $25,200 on Big Boat's books at the date of the sale. In addition, Big Boat recorded depreciation expense of $13,000 in the year of the sale. The machine had a remaining life of five years on Big Boat's books and was assigned a life of eight years by LifeLine.

LifeLine sold a storage building to Big Boat on March 1, 2006, for $408,000. The building had a historical cost, accumulated depreciation, and estimated remaining life on LifeLine's books of $750,000, $301,200, and 17 years, respectively, at the time of the sale. Big Boat assigned the building a life of 20 years.

LifeLine sold the equipment purchased from Big Boat on December 1, 2005, to an unrelated party for $14,000 on October 31, 2006.

Required:
Prepare, in journal entry form, the worksheet eliminations needed to present the consolidated financial statements at December 31, 2006.

PROBLEM 4-12

(Refer to the information in Problems 4-10 and 4-11.) Net income and dividends paid by LifeLine Inc. are $430,000 and $150,000, respectively.

LifeLine sold a machine to Big Boat on February 1, 2007. The machine had a remaining life, historical cost, and accumulated depreciation on LifeLine's financial records of six years, $45,000, and $19,800, respectively, at the time of the sale. Big Boat placed the machine on its financial records for $22,320 and assigned a five-year life to the machine.

On June 1, 2007, Big Boat sold the storage building purchased from LifeLine in 2006 for $500,000.

Required:
Prepare, in journal entry form, the worksheet eliminations needed to present the consolidated financial statements at December 31, 2007.

PROBLEM 4-13

Eastbrook Products acquired 100 percent of Westcott Enterprises' stock on June 1, 2005, for $59,384,000. Relevant balance sheet and market value information for Eastbrook and Westcott at the date of acquisition are presented below.

	Eastbook Products		*Westcott Enterprises*	
	Book Value	*Market Value*	*Book Value*	*Market Value*
Cash	$22,750,000	$22,750,000	$ 8,285,000	$ 8,285,000
Receivables	73,500,000	73,500,000	5,450,000	5,450,000
Inventory	151,600,000	180,250,000	9,260,000	11,600,000
Investment in Westcott	50,000,000	50,000,000		
Land	46,300,000	49,600,000	6,275,000	6,350,000

Buildings (net)	123,600,000	124,800,000	16,900,000	19,300,000
Equipment (net)	42,900,000	50,640,000	8,125,000	10,375,000
Patents				3,264,000
Total Assets	$510,650,000		$54,295,000	
Current Liabilities	$140,000,000	140,000,000	$11,000,000	$11,000,000
Bonds Payable	200,000,000	201,200,000		
Premium on Bonds Payable	3,600,000			
Common Stock	11,500,000		6,000,000	
Additional Paid-In Capital	46,150,000		30,850,000	
Retained Earnings	109,400,000		6,445,000	
Total Liabilities and Equity	$510,650,000		$54,295,000	

The estimated remaining life (in months) at the date of acquisition for each of the items with a purchase differential is listed below.

	Eastbook	Westcott
Inventory	2	5
Land	Indefinite	Indefinite
Buildings	144	120
Equipment	180	150
Patents		204
Bonds Payable	240	

On September 30, 2005 (four months after the acquisition date), Westcott purchased $5,000,000 of Eastbrook's outstanding Bonds Payable for $5,031,860. The carrying value (adjusted to September 30, 2005) of these bonds on Eastbrook's financial records is $5,088,500. The premium on bonds is amortized straight-line on the books of both companies. The stated interest rate on the bonds is 8 percent. Interest Revenue and Interest Expense recognized for October1–December 31 on the bonds acquired by were $99,595 and $98,875, respectively.

Abbreviated income statements for Eastbook and Westcott for June1–December 31, 2005 are provided below.

	Eastbook	Westcott
Sales	$280,000,000	$38,000,000
Cost of Goods Sold	161,950,000	26,700,000
Gross Profit	118,050,000	11,300,000
Depreciation Expenses	12,530,000	2,400,000
Interest Expense	15,820,000	650,000
Interest Revenue		99,595
Other Expenses	37,200,000	3,250,000
Income Before Taxes	52,500,000	5,099,595
Income Taxes	21,000,000	2,099,595
Net Income	$31,500,000	$3,000,000

Eastbrook and Westcott distributed $8,250,000 and $600,000, respectively, for dividends during 2005. Dividends are paid in equal amounts at the end of each quarter.

Required:
Prepare, in journal entry form, the worksheet eliminations needed to present the consolidated financial statements at December 31, 2005.

PROBLEM 4-14   (Refer to the information in Problem 4-13.) No additional intercompany bond transactions occurred during 2006.
Eastbrook's net income and dividends paid during 2006 are $35,075,000 and $9,100,000, respectively, while Westcott's net income and dividends paid are $5,6000,000 and $3,360,000, respectively.

Eastbrook had interest expense of $395,500 and Westcott had interest revenue of $398,380 related to the bonds purchased by Westcott on its 2006 income statements.

Required:
Prepare, in journal entry form, the worksheet eliminations needed to present the consolidated financial statements at December 31, 2006.

PROBLEM 4-15   (Refer to the information in Problems 4-13 and 4-14.) Westcott purchased another $12,000,000 of Eastbrook's outstanding bonds payable on April 30, 2007 for $12,299,460. The carrying value of the bonds on that date would have been $12,195,300 if an adjusting entry had been recorded.
Eastbrook recognized net income (including interest expense of $395,500 for bonds purchased by Westcott in 2005 and $632,800 for bonds purchased by Westcott in 2007) and paid dividends of $28,000,000 and $9,750,000, respectively, for 2007. Westcott recognized $5,800,000 of net income (including interest revenue of $398,380 for 2005 bonds and $628,960 for 2007 bonds). Westcott paid dividends of $4,100,000 in 2007.

Required:
Prepare, in journal entry form, the worksheet eliminations needed to present the consolidated financial statements at December 31, 2007.

PROBLEM 4-16   Office Equipment Company purchased 80 percent of Home Copying Equipment, Incorporated on January 1, 2005, for $25,997,160. The balance sheet of Home Copying Equipment on that date follows.

Cash	$ 3,390,000	Accounts Payable	$ 1,674,000
Marketable Securities	1,050,000	Notes Payable (short-term)	2,100,000
Accounts Receivable	1,375,000	Notes Payable (long-term)	3,800,000
Inventory	2,650,000	Bonds Payable (12 percent)	15,000,000
Land	3,150,000	Premium on Bonds Payable	205,800
Buildings (net)	15,600,000	Common Stock	3,000,000
Equipment (net)	8,750,000	Additional Paid-in Capital	10,340,200
Patents	6,880,000	Retained Earnings	6,725,000
Total Assets	$42,845,000	Total Liabilities and Equity	$42,845,000

Purchase differentials exist for three identifiable assets: land, buildings, and patents. The amounts of the purchase differentials applicable to Office Equipment's ownership percentage are $675,000, $2,150,000, and $4,540,000, respectively. The remaining estimated life of the buildings is 20 years and the patents have an estimated remaining life of 8 years.

Home Copying Equipment records net income of $5,000,000 for 2005 and pays $400,000 of dividends quarterly. Discounts and premiums are amortized using the straight-line method by both organizations.

The treasurer of each company is responsible for keeping the cash resources of that organization invested. Beginning in 2005, each organization began investing in the debt securities of the other organization. On March 1, 2005, Office Equipment Company purchased $1,500,000 of the outstanding Home Copying Equipment bonds payable for $1,548,000. The bonds have a remaining life of eight years and a $1,520,160 carrying value on the books of Home Copying Equipment at the time of the investment by Office Equipment. Home Copying recorded $147,900 interest expense on the bonds purchased by Office Equipment for the remainder of the year and Office Equipment recorded $145,000 interest revenue.

On September 30, 2005, Home Copying Equipment purchased $600,000 of the outstanding 10-percent bonds payable of Office Equipment for $639,000. The bonds had a remaining life of five years and a carrying value of $645,000 at the time of the investment. Home Copying Equipment recognized $13,050 of interest revenue for these bonds in 2005 while Office Equipment recognized $12,750 interest expense for the remainder of the year.

Required:

Prepare, in journal entry form, the worksheet eliminations needed to present the consolidated financial statements at December 31, 2005.

PROBLEM 4-17

(Refer to the information in Problem 4-16.) Home Copying Equipment reports net income of $4,000,000 and pay dividends of $1,600,000 in 2006.

On June 1, 2006, Office Equipment purchased an additional $3,000,000 of Home Copying's bonds payable for $3,060,750. The bonds had a carrying value of $3,034,020 at the acquisition date. Home Copying recorded $177,480 of interest expense related to the bonds purchased by Office Equipment in 2005 and $207,060 (for June 1–December 31) related to the 2006 purchase. Office Equipment recorded interest revenue of $174,000 and $204,750 for the 2005 and 2006 bond purchases, respectively.

On October 31, 2006, Home Copying purchased an additional $960,000 of Office Equipment's outstanding bonds payable for $1,008,504. The bonds had a carrying value of $1,016,400 at the date of the acquisition. Home Copying recognized interest revenue of $52,200 and $13,936 on the bonds purchased in 2005 and 2006 (partial year), respectively. Office Equipment recognized interest expense on these same bonds in the amounts of $51,000 and $13,600 for 2005 and 2006, respectively.

Required:

Prepare, in journal entry form, the worksheet eliminations needed to present the consolidated financial statements at December 31, 2006.

PROBLEM 4-18

(Refer to the information in Problems 4-16 and 4-17.) Net income and dividends paid by Home Copying are $5,750,000 and $1,800,000, respectively.

On March 1, 2007, Office Equipment sold (to Home Copying) the $1,500,000 face value bonds purchased in 2005 to provide cash for expanding plant facilities. The sales price on the bonds was $1,490,000. Home Copying recognized interest expense for the 2005 and 2006 bond purchased during the period held by Office Equipment in the following amounts: 2005, $29,580; 2006, $354,960. Office Equipment's financial records disclosed interest revenue in the amounts of $29,000 and $351,000 for the 2005 and 2006 bond investments, respectively.

Home Copying did not have any additional bond investments during 2007. Interest expense recognized by Office Equipment on the bonds held by Home Copying during 2007 were $51,000 for the 2005 investment and $81,600 for the 2006 investment. Home Copying recognized interest revenue for $52,200 and $83,616 for the 2005 and 2006 investments, respectively.

Required:

Prepare, in journal entry form, the worksheet eliminations needed to present the consolidated financial statements at December 31, 2007.

PROBLEM 4-19

Pleasure Company acquired 80 percent of the outstanding no par stock of Sorrow Company on January 1, 2005, by issuing new shares of its common stock having a par value of $24,000 and market value of $260,000. The premium over book value paid for the interest in Sorrow was due to certain fixed assets that were undervalued plus unrecognized goodwill in Sorrow. Sorrow's balance sheet information at the date of the acquisition is provided below.

	Book Value	*Market Value*
Cash and Receivables	$ 40,000	$40,000
Inventory (FIFO)	90,000	90,000
Plant and Equipment (net)	270,000	175,000
Accumulated Depreciation	(145,000)	
Patents	75,000	75,000
Total Assets	$330,000	
Current Liabilities	$ 30,000	30,000
Bonds Payable	50,000	50,000
Common Stock (no par)	130,000	
Retained Earnings	120,000	
Total Liabilities and Equities	$330,000	

Additional information:

1. The remaining useful life of the equipment having the market value in excess of book value is five years.
2. During 2005 Sorrow reports $75,000 of net income and declares $45,000 of dividends.
3. Pleasure uses the equity method to account for the investment in Sorrow's stock.
4. Intercompany transactions began immediately after the combination. The 2005 activities are described here:

- On January 2, 2005, Pleasure sold equipment having a cost of $32,000 and accumulated depreciation of $21,000 to Sorrow for $15,000 cash. The remaining useful life of that equipment was four years at the date of sale. Schedules of depreciation over the remaining life of the equipment are provided.

- Sorrow began selling inventory to Pleasure during 2005. Goods costing $28,000 were sold to Pleasure for $42,000 in 2005. Pleasure resold 45 percent of those units to outside parties for a total of $31,000 before December 31, 2005. A schedule of the intercompany inventory activity is provided.

- Pleasure has 10 percent, 10-year bonds payable outstanding. Those bonds pay interest semiannually on June 30 and December 31. The bonds were sold to yield 8 percent on January 1, 1998. On July 1, 2005, Sorrow buys 20 percent of the bond issue in the open market for $37,767. Sorrow was able to buy the bonds at a discount because market interest rates had risen to 12 percent. The amortization schedules that result from the original price and the buyback price are provided.

Required:

A. Prepare, in journal entry form, all worksheet eliminations necessary to consolidate Pleasure and Sorrow at December 31, 2005. Then post them to the worksheet provided at the end of this problem (additional accounts will need to be added to complete the worksheet).
B. In 2006 Sorrow sold additional inventory to Pleasure. The cost of these items was $60,000 and they were sold to Pleasure for $85,000. By the end of 2006, all the beginning intercompany inventory and 75 percent of the new items acquired in 2006 from Sorrow had been sold to unrelated entities. Prepare the worksheet eliminations that relate to the intercompany transactions for Property, Plant, and Equipment; Inventory; and Bonds that would be necessary as part of the December 31, 2006, consolidation of Pleasure and Sorrow.

Pleasure Company Bonds Payable amortization schedule:

Date	Cash Interest	Interest Expense	Premium Amortized	Carrying Value
Issue date 1/1/1998				$227,181
6/30/1998	$10,000	$9,087	$913	$226,268
12/31/1998	$10,000	$9,051	$949	$225,319
6/30/1999	$10,000	$9,013	$987	$224,332
12/31/1999	$10,000	$8,973	$1,027	$223,305
6/30/2000	$10,000	$8,932	$1,068	$222,237
12/31/2000	$10,000	$8,889	$1,111	$221,127
6/30/2001	$10,000	$8,845	$1,155	$219,972
12/31/2001	$10,000	$8,799	$1,201	$218,771
6/30/2002	$10,000	$8,751	$1,249	$217,521
12/31/2002	$10,000	$8,701	$1,299	$216,222
6/30/2003	$10,000	$8,649	$1,351	$214,871
12/31/2003	$10,000	$8,595	$1,405	$213,466
6/30/2004	$10,000	$8,539	$1,461	$212,005
12/31/2004	$10,000	$8,480	$1,520	$210,485
6/30/2005	$10,000	$8,419	$1,581	$208,904
12/31/2005	$10,000	$8,356	$1,644	$207,260
6/30/2006	$10,000	$8,290	$1,710	$205,551
12/31/2006	$10,000	$8,222	$1,778	$203,773

(Continued)

Date	Cash Interest	Interest Expense	Premium Amortized	Carrying Value
6/30/2007	$10,000	$8,151	$1,849	$201,924
12/31/2007	$10,000	$8,077	$1,923	$200,001

Sorrow Company Investment in Bonds amortization schedule:

Date	Cash Interest	Interest Revenue	Discount Amortized	Carrying Value
Investment date				$37,767
12/31/2005	$2,000	$2,266	$266	$38,033
6/30/2006	$2,000	$2,282	$282	$38,315
12/31/2006	$2,000	$2,299	$299	$38,614
6/30/2007	$2,000	$2,317	$317	$38,931
12/31/2007	$2,000	$2,336	$336	$39,267
6/30/2008	$2,000	$2,356	$356	$39,623
12/31/2008	$2,000	$2,377	$377	$40,000

Schedule of inventory transferred from Sorrow to Pleasure:

2005 Transactions	Cost Basis	Marlup on Transfers	Retail Price to Pleasure
Beginning Inventory—at Pleasure	$0	$0	$0
2005—Sold to Pleasure	$30,000	$14,000	$44,000
Ending Inventory—at Pleasure	$16,500	$7,700	$24,200
Sold by Pleasure to third parties	$13,500	$6,300	$19,800

Schedule of depreciation and book values for intercompany fixed assets transferred:

	Pleasure's Expected Depreciation Schedule Prior to Sale		Sorrow's Depreciation Schedule Subsequent to Sale	
	Depreciation Expense	Accumulated Depreciation	Depreciation Expense	Accumulated Depreciation
1/2/2005		$21,000		$0
12/31/2005	$2,750	$23,750	$3,750	$3,750
12/31/2006	$2,750	$26,500	$3,750	$7,500
12/31/2007	$2,750	$29,250	$3,750	$11,250
12/31/2008	$2,750	$32,000	$3,750	$15,000

	Separate Financial Statements		Adjustments and Eliminations		Consolidated Financial Statements
	Pleasure	Sorrow	Debit	Credit	
Income Statement					
Sales	601,000	322,000			
Interest Revenue		2,266			
Gain on Sale of Equipment	4,000				
Investment Income	52,000				
Cost of Goods Sold	300,000	167,000			
Depreciation Expense	88,000	41,000			
Operating Expenses	102,981	38,266			
Patent Amortization Expense		3,000			
Bond Interest Expense	17,019				
Net Income (to Statement of Retained Earnings)	149,000	75,000			

(Continued)

Retained Earnings Statement

Retained Earnings	280,000	120,000
Add: Net Income (from Income Statement)	149,000	75,000
Subtotal	429,000	195,000
Less: Dividends	(100,000)	(45,000)
Retained Earnings (to Balance Sheet)	329,000	150,000

Balance Sheet

Cash and Receivables	127,000	24,967
Inventory	210,000	133,000
Total Current Assets	337,000	157,967
Plant and Equipment	600,000	280,000
Accumulated Depreciation	(347,000)	(180,000)
Patents		72,000
Investment in Sorrow Stock	276,000	
Investment in Pleasure Bonds		38,033
Total Long-Term Assets	529,000	210,033
Total Assets	866,000	368,000
Current Liabilities	76,516	38,000
Bonds Payable	200,000	50,000
Premium on Bonds Payable	10,484	
Total Liabilities	287,000	88,000
Common Stock	100,000	130,000
Additional Paid-In Capital	150,000	
Retained Earnings	329,000	150,000
Total Stockholders' Equity	579,000	280,000
Total Liabilities and Stockholders' Equity	866,000	368,000

PROBLEM 4-20 Richmond Enterprises purchased 100 percent of the stock of Atlanta Products on January 1, 2005. The acquisition price was $1,250,000. Book values, market values, and estimated remaining lives for Atlanta on that date follow.

	Book Value	Market Value	Estimated Life (in Years)
Cash and Receivables	$275,000	$275,000	
Inventory	490,000	550,000	1
Land	300,000	325,000	n/a
Buildings (net)	650,000	800,000	15
Equipment (net)	200,000	248,000	8
Total Assets	$1,915,000		
Current Liabilities	$370,000	$370,000	
Mortgage Payable	850,000	920,000	14
Common Stock	100,000		
Additional Paid-In Capital	265,000		
Retained Earnings	330,000		
Total Liabilities and Equity	$1,915,000		

Richmond and Atlanta are involved in intercompany inventory transactions. The tables below presents the volume of intercompany transactions and the periods in which this inventory is sold to an unrelated party for 2005, 2006, and 2007.

Intercompany Sales of Inventory

	2005		2006		2007	
Sales by:	Market Value	Book Value	Market Value	Book Value	Market Value	Book Value
Richmond	$95,000	$90,000	125,000	$100,000	$175,000	$160,000
Atlanta	$60,000	$56,000	$50,000	$45,000	$75,000	$68,000

Sales of Intercompany Inventory to Unrelated Parties

		Percent Sold/Sales Price				
Unrelated Party Sales:		2005	2006		2007	
Sold by: Intercompany Transfer:		2005	2005	2006	2006	2007
Richmond		100%	N/A	60%	40%	80%
		$69,000		$33,000	$24,000	$66,000
Atlanta		70%	30%	100%	N/A	75%
		$73,000	$31,000	$137,000		$142,000

Atlanta had net income of $150,000, $180,000, and $140,000 for 2005, 2006, and 2007, respectively. In addition, Atlanta paid dividends of $40,000, $45,000, and $48,000 in 2005, 2006, and 2007, respectively.

Required:
Prepare, in journal entry form, the worksheet eliminations necessary to prepare the consolidated financial statements in each of the three years.

PROBLEM 4-21   Argon Industries purchased 60 percent of the stock of Oxygen Gas Products, Incorporated on March 1, 2005, for $1,446,780. Book values, market values, and estimated remaining lives for Oxygen Gas Product's on that date follow.

	Book Value	Market Value	Estimated Life (in Months)
Cash and Receivables	$ 50,000	$ 50,000	
Inventory	250,000	250,000	
Land	175,000	225,000	n/a
Buildings	800,000	550,000	180
Accumulated Depreciation—Buildings	(475,000)		
Equipment	400,000	180,000	96
Accumulated Depreciation—Equipment	(280,000)		
Total Assets	$920,000		
Current Liabilities	$ 35,000	$ 35,000	
Mortgage Payable	315,000	308,700	140
Common Stock	20,000		
Additional Paid-In Capital	160,000		
Retained Earnings	390,000		
Total Liabilities and Equity	$920,000		

Argon Industries and Oxygen Gas Products are involved in many transactions with each other. Below is a table indicating sales of equipment between the two companies during 2005, 2006, and 2007. Assume straight-line depreciation is recorded on a monthly basis with no salvage values for all plant assets.

	2005		2006		2007	
Buyer Seller	Oxygen Argon	Argon Oxygen	Oxygen Argon	Argon Oxygen	Oxygen Argon	Argon Oxygen
Date of Sale	April 1	Dec. 31	Dec. 31	Oct. 1	May 1	Oct. 1
Sales Price	$27,000	$16,800	$4,900	$16,000	$32,760	$10,080
Year of sale depreciation by seller	$500	$2,000	$420	$1,500	$1,120	$540
Cost and Accumulated Depreciation (seller)	$30,000 $8,220	$15,500 $3,500	$5,000 $1,220	$24,000 $4,000	$40,000 $5,056	$10,000 $1,360
Estimated Life (seller)	11	6	9	10	13	12
Estimated Life (buyer)	15	4	7	8	14	20
Date sold to unrelated party and sales price	April 1, 2007 $23,900		Oct. 1, 2007 $13,000			

Oxygen Gas Products had net income of $105,000, $130,000, and $152,000 for 2005 (March 1–December 31), 2006, and 2007, respectively. In addition, Oxygen paid dividends of $25,000, $25,000, and $35,000 in 2005, 2006, and 2007, respectively.

Required:

A. Prepare, in journal entry form, the worksheet eliminations necessary to prepare the consolidated financial statements in each of the three years.

B. Why are the equipment transactions that took place prior to the acquisition of Oxygen by Argon not viewed as intercompany transactions?

PROBLEM 4-22   Baker Company purchased 60 percent of Muffin Mania, Incorporated on January 1, 2005, for $948,000. Book values, market values, and estimated remaining lives for Muffin Mania on that date follow.

	Book Value	Market Value	Estimated Life (in years)
Cash and Receivables	$103,720	$103,720	
Inventory	210,000	230,000	1
Land	250,000	300,000	n/a
Buildings (net)	550,000	680,000	13
Equipment (net)	315,000	355,000	8
	$1,428,720		
Current Liabilities	$147,440	147,440	
Bonds Payable	300,000	281,280	10
Discount on Bonds Payable	(18,720)		
Common Stock	150,000		
Additional Paid-In Capital	275,000		
Retained Earnings	575,000		
	$1,428,720		

Muffin Mania had net income of $175,000, $215,000, and $250,000 for 2005, 2006, and 2007, respectively. In addition, Muffin Mania paid dividends of $60,000, $70,000, and $80,000 in 2005, 2006, and 2007, respectively.

Baker Company began purchasing the bonds of Muffin Mania as an investment soon after the acquisition. The stated interest rate on Muffin Mania's bonds is 9 percent and the discount on bonds payable is amortized using the straight-line method. The table below presents the indirect intercompany debt purchases by Baker Company in 2005, 2006, and 2007 and the sale of debt instruments to Muffin Mania in 2006.

	2005	2006	2007
Date of purchase	May 1, 2005	Oct. 1, 2006	Mar. 1, 2007
Purchase price	$44,780	$96,337	$69,924
Face value of bonds purchased	$50,000	$100,000	$75,000
Book value of bonds purchased	$46,984	$94,852	$71,334
Intercompany interest expense*	$3,208^A	$4,411^B	$15,639^C
Intercompany interest revenue*	$3,360^D	$4,461^E	$15,609^F
Date sold to Muffin Mania	June 1, 2006		
Sales price	$48,500		

* Supplemental supporting interest expense and interest revenue calculations.

Interest Expense = [(face value of debt × stated interest rate) + (discount amortization)] (fraction of year intercompany) (fraction of total bond intercompany).

2005:		[($300,000 × .09) + ($18,720/10)] (8/12) (1/6)		$3,208^A
2006:	On bonds purchased by Baker in 2005	[($300,000 × .09) + ($18,720/10)] (5/12) (1/6)	2,005	
	On bonds purchased by Baker in 2006	[($300,000 × .09) + ($18,720/10)] (3/12) (1/3)	2,406	$4,411^B
2007:	On bonds purchased by Baker in 2006	[($300,000 × .09) + ($18,720/10)] (12/12) (1/3)	9,624	
	On bonds purchased by Baker in 2007	[($300,000 × .09) + ($18,720/10)] (10/12) (1/4)	6,015	$15,639^C

Interest Revenue = [(face value of debt x stated interest rate)/12 + (monthly discount amortization)] (number of months held)

2005:		[($50,000 × .09)/12 + ($5,220/116)] (8)		$3,360^D
2006:	On bonds purchased by Baker in 2005	[($50,000 × .09)/12 + ($5,220/116)] (5)	2,100	
	On bonds purchased by Baker in 2006	[($100,000 × .09)/12 + ($3,663/99)] (3)	2,361	$4,461^E

(Continued)

| 2007: | On bonds purchased by Baker in 2006 | [($100,000 × .09)/12 + ($3,663/99)] (12) | 9,444 | |
| | On bonds purchased by Baker in 2007 | [($75,000 × .09)/12 + ($5,076/94)] (10) | 6,165 | $15,609[F] |

Required:

Prepare, in journal entry form, the worksheet eliminations necessary to prepare the consolidated financial statements in each of the three years.

FOREIGN CURRENCY TRANSACTIONS

LEARNING OBJECTIVES

After reading this chapter, you should be able to:

- Distinguish between foreign transactions and foreign currency transactions.
- Understand some basic causes and impacts of changes in exchange rates.
- Understand some basic features of forward contracts and option contracts.
- Distinguish among different types of foreign currency transactions.
- Distinguish among different types of foreign currency hedges.
- Prepare the necessary journal entries related to foreign currency transactions and hedges.

United States based entities are involved regularly in transactions around the globe. For example, Pepsi is sold in Russia and John Deere tractors are sold in France, while Fuji film from Japan and Kia cars from Korea are sold in the United States. The number and value of transactions with entities located in foreign countries has increased in recent years. In addition, the volume of these foreign transactions is likely to continue to increase if governments are successful in lowering tariffs and trade barriers. The amounts presented in Table 5-1 are the dollar volumes of recent import and export activities in the United States (in billions of dollars). These values are significantly greater than the 1980 import and export activity levels of $291.2 and $271.8 billion, respectively.

U.S. business entities of any size may be involved in transactions with other entities located in a foreign country.[1] The business risks relevant when engaging in transactions with another U.S. entity also apply when conducting business with an entity located in a foreign country, although the level of risk may be greater. For example, the risk of not collecting on an account receivable resulting from making a credit sale may be greater when the customer is located in Italy because the seller may be less familiar with the financial condition of the Italian purchaser. In addition, transactions with entities located outside the United States may be conducted in U.S. dollars or they may be conducted in a foreign currency. Determining the currency to be exchanged is

---

[1] The examples presented in this chapter assume that the financial statements are being prepared for an entity based in the United States.

TABLE 5-1   U.S. Imports and Exports, 1991–1999 (in billions of dollars)

	1991	1992	1993	1994	1995	1996	1997	1998	1999
Imports	609.4	652.9	711.7	800.5	891.0	954.1	1,043.3	1,098.2	1,227.6
Exports	580.0	615.9	641.8	702.1	793.5	849.8	938.5	933.9	960.1

Source: Department of Commerce, *Statistical Abstracts of the United States,* July 2000.

Denominated: the expressed currency in which a transaction is to be completed

generally a negotiated term of the transaction. If the currency to be exchanged is the U.S. dollar, there is no additional risk to the U.S. entity; however, if the currency to be exchanged is a currency other than the U.S. dollar, the U.S. entity is at risk if the value of the foreign currency changes relative to the U.S. dollar. The currency that is ultimately received or paid as a result of the transaction is the currency in which the transaction is **denominated**.

Foreign currency transaction: a transaction in a currency other than the one in which the financial records are maintained

The most noticeable **foreign currency transactions** involve large international entities purchasing and selling products all over the world. One example of such an entity is Coca-Cola. Coke recognized 62 percent of its 1999 net operating revenue (almost $20 billion) as a result of sales outside the United States.[2] While not all these sales involved foreign currency transactions, the volume of foreign currency transactions related to Coke's sales may be in the billions of dollars. Firms such as Coke exchange a large volume of foreign currency and may have a section of the corporate treasurer's office monitor and coordinate these transactions. On a different scale, a relatively small company located near the U.S. border with Mexico or Canada may be involved in foreign currency transactions with neighboring companies across the border. These small companies face the same foreign exchange risk as do the large entities. In fact, the exposure may be more important to small companies because they often do not have the expertise, or the ability, to manage foreign exchange risk in a way that takes advantage of economies of scale.

The purpose of this chapter is to introduce the accounting procedures for transactions denominated in a currency different from the local currency of an entity (assumed to be the U.S. dollar). The chapter begins with an overview of exchange rate terminology. This is followed by specific discussions of four types of foreign currency transactions. Examples are presented for purchase and sale transactions denominated in a foreign currency, commitments to engage in future foreign currency transactions, forecasted foreign currency transactions, and speculative contracts in foreign currencies.

THE NATURE OF EXCHANGE RATES

Exchange rate: the ratio at which one currency can be converted into another currency

Exchange rates are measures of the relative value of two currencies. These rates may be mandated by the governmental body of the country issuing that currency or established by market conditions.

[2] Compact Disclosure, 2000.

Fixed Exchange Rates

Fixed exchange rate:
official exchange rate
between currencies
established and
maintained by public
officials

Fixed exchange rates may be established by the government to accomplish specific objectives, such as encouraging export trade or discouraging foreign investors from taking capital out of the country. To accomplish these objectives, the official exchange rates may differ for different types of transactions. For example, the exchange rate established for capital investment expenditures may be favorable when compared to the exchange rate established for dividend distributions to nonresident stockholders. If the official exchange rates are permitted to deviate too greatly from what would be the market exchange rates, pressure will exist for the government to change the official exchange rates for the currency. Fixed exchange rates may also be established to accomplish a variety of political objectives. One example is Europe's exchange rate mechanism (ERM). The ERM was established by members of the European Economic Community to move the members toward adopting a common European currency. As a result of the ERM, a number of countries increased interest rates to maintain the agreed-upon relationships among the values of the currencies. In September 1992, the ERM started to break up when the Bank of England raised interest rates by 2 percentage points in an unsuccessful effort to increase the value of the British pound. England's central bank then suspended the pound sterling from the ERM.[3] The dissolution of the ERM led to the realignment of European currencies based on market conditions. In the late 1990s many European countries formed the European Monetary System and established a common currency (euro). Until 2002, European Monetary System countries supported their local currency (e.g., French franc) and the euro. On January 1, 2002, the local currencies were discontinued and the euro became the sole currency for transactions in European Monetary System countries.

Floating Exchange Rates

Floating exchange rate:
exchange rate between
currencies determined
by market conditions

In contrast to fixed exchange rates, **floating exchange rates** (market condition rates) permit the value of currencies to fluctuate against each other based on supply and demand. Supply and demand for currencies depend partially on interest rate differences that exist between the respective economies, differences in balance of trade, political stability, and anticipated inflation. Changes in any of these factors may result in the values of the currencies fluctuating against one another.

If, for example, market conditions result in the U.S. dollar becoming more desirable than other currencies, the value of the U.S. dollar increases relative to other currencies and thus the dollar is said to strengthen against other currencies. This occurred in the early 1980s when interest rates in the United States were higher than interest rates in many other countries. Foreign currency was invested in the United States to take advantage of greater rates of return; however, the foreign currency had to be converted into U.S. dollars by investors before they could acquire the U.S. financial instruments. The increased demand for the U.S. dollar resulted in the value of the dollar reaching record highs. One result of changes in the relative value of currencies is that the balance of trade changes. In the early 1980s, the increase in the value of the U.S. dollar caused exports to become more expensive to foreign purchasers because it took more units of foreign currency to acquire the dollars needed to buy U.S. products. As a result of the higher U.S. dollar value, the demand for U.S. products declined; therefore, the balance of trade for the United States weakened.

---

[3] Sease, Douglas R., "Pound Crisis Shakes World Currency Markets," *The Wall Street Journal*, September 17, 1992, pp. C1, C13.

The weakening in U.S. exports caused demand for the U.S. dollar to decrease, and the value of the dollar retreated from its record highs. The increase in the value of the currency has an impact on the rest of the economy. This ultimately creates pressure on the exchange rate to move back toward historical levels.

It should be noted that a floating exchange rate does not mean that a currency will fluctuate without bounds. Decreases in the value of the U.S. dollar against most major currencies in 1994 prompted action by many central banks (the monetary authorities in many foreign countries). In March 1994, the Bank of Japan intervened in an unsuccessful effort to halt the decline in the value of the U.S. dollar in relation to the Japanese yen.[4] In May 1994, 16 countries joined together to halt the decrease in the value of the U.S. dollar. In that second effort, the central banks purchased U.S. dollars and sold Japanese yen and German marks to stabilize the dollar against the yen and the mark.[5] It is possible that trade negotiations between the United States and Japan caused by attempts to reduce Japan's trade surplus failed, making the banks' attempt to drive up the value of the dollar unsuccessful.

Countries with a relatively small volume of foreign trade have a different type of problem in that the exchange rates for their currencies may fluctuate a great deal if based on market conditions. The demand for the currency of these countries may increase substantially because of a few transactions. Such fluctuations could create economic problems, such as highly volatile interest rates. One alternative available in these countries is to peg the value of their currencies to one of the world's major currencies (e.g., the British pound, Canadian dollar, Japanese yen, Swiss franc, U.S. dollar, and euro) and allow the value of their currencies to fluctuate as the value of the major currency fluctuates. For example, Argentina, Ethiopia, and Panama are among the countries that peg their currency to the U.S. dollar. Another alternative is to adopt one of the major currencies as the country's official currency. For example, Kiribati and Nauru Island use the Australian dollar, while Guam and Puerto Rico use the U.S. dollar. The currency selected is often determined by past political and/or economic ties between the two countries.

Direct and Indirect Exchange Rates

Indirect exchange rate: number of units of a foreign currency equivalent to one unit of the domestic currency

The relationship between two currencies (whether floating or fixed exchange rates exist) can be stated in terms of either currency (domestic or foreign). The **indirect exchange rate** is stated in terms of the number of foreign currency units required to acquire one unit of the domestic currency. An example of an indirect exchange rate is:

$$\$1.00 = 1.55 \text{ Swiss francs}$$

Direct exchange rate: number of units of the domestic currency equivalent to one unit of a foreign currency

A **direct exchange rate** is stated in terms of the number of domestic currency units required to acquire one unit of the foreign currency. An example of a direct exchange rate is:

$$1 \text{ Swiss franc} = \$.645$$

The reciprocal of one exchange rate is the other exchange rate. This text is written from the perspective of U.S. domestic entities. Thus, the direct exchange rate is the exchange rate of particular interest because the primary objective of this chapter is to measure the

---

[4] Rosenberger, Gary, "Dollar Drops Against Despite Bid By Bank of Japan to Prop U.S. Currency," *The Wall Street Journal*, March 31, 1994, p. C15.

[5] Wessel, David, Kenneth H. Bacon, and Michael R. Sesit, "Biggest Show of Force in a Decade Halts Slide of the Dollar — for Now," *The Wall Street Journal*, May 5, 1994, pp. A1, A7.

economic substance of transactions denominated in units of foreign currency in their U.S. dollar equivalents.

Spot Rate

The economic substance of many transactions is based on an immediate exchange of currency. The exchange rate applicable to an immediate exchange of currency is called the **spot rate**. An example of an exchange occurring at the spot rate is a college student who stops at an airport currency exchange broker's window prior to boarding a plane to spend spring break in Mexico. The U.S. dollars will be converted into Mexican pesos using the exchange rate that exists at the time of the exchange, that is, the spot rate. Businesses, like individuals, use exchange brokers to convert one currency into another.

Spot rate: exchange rate that exists for an immediate exchange of currency

The exchange rate applicable when converting currencies differs depending on whether a foreign currency purchase or sale occurs because different exchange rates exist when buying or selling foreign currency units. For example, a person who converts U.S. dollars into Mexican pesos at one window of a bank that exchanges currencies and then converts the Mexican pesos just received back into U.S. dollars at the next window will have fewer dollars at the end than at the beginning. The reason for the decrease in the number of dollars is that the exchange rate for buying pesos is higher than the exchange rate for selling pesos. The difference between the buy and sell rates enables the exchange broker to make a profit on the difference between the rates (spread). The size of the spread is a function of the supply and demand for the currency. For example, turmoil in currency markets in 1992 greatly increased the spread for the British pound.[6]

To maximize long-term profits, many exchange brokers do not actively trade in anticipation of changes in the currency exchange rates. Chase Manhattan, for example, attempts to enter into equal buy and sell contracts for a currency to ensure that fluctuations offset, leaving the spread between the buy and sell prices as a profit. For convenience, this chapter will only give one currency exchange rate for a given situation. This chapter focuses on one exchange rate because an entity is not interested in the exchange rate applicable for selling foreign currency units if it is going into the market to acquire foreign currency units. That is, only one exchange rate will be relevant to an entity that is a party to a foreign currency transaction in a given situation.

PURCHASE OR SALE TRANSACTION

An entity's financial accounting system is designed to measure and record the economic substance of transactions with independent parties. Statement of Financial Accounting Concepts No. 1 states that the values in the financial records "are usually exchange prices or amounts derived from exchange prices."[7] Therefore, when an entity enters into an exchange transaction with an unrelated party, the transaction should be measured (recorded) at the economic value (exchange price) of the transaction. This value may be reflected in the exchange of currency or it may be presented in the form of a payable or receivable in the entity's financial records.

[6] Smith, Randall, "European Exchange-Rate Chaos Is Bedlam for Currency Traders at Chase Manhattan," *The Wall Street Journal*, September 17, 1992, p. C1.

[7] **Statement of Financial Accounting Concepts**, No. 1, "Objectives of Financial Reporting by Business Enterprises" (Stamford, CT: Financial Accounting Standards Board, 1978), par. 18.

The two parties in a transaction may be located in the same country or in different countries. The location of the parties does not alter the underlying economic reality of the initial transaction. When the currency of the buyer's country is to be exchanged (domestic currency—U.S. dollar), the transaction is recorded on the buyer's financial records at the number of currency units exchanged or to be exchanged at a future date. On the other hand, when the currency to be exchanged is the currency of the seller's country (foreign currency), the buyer measures and records the transaction at the current *estimated* U.S. dollar equivalent value of the foreign currency units exchanged or to be exchanged at a future date. That is, the spot rate of the currency units exchanged or to be exchanged is the economic substance of the transaction because the U.S. dollar equivalent value at this date represents the best estimate of the economic sacrifice (in a purchase transaction for the acquisition of goods or services) or the economic benefit (in a transaction involving the sale of goods or services). Potential future changes in the value of the foreign currency are not recognized at the date of the initial transaction because the direction and magnitude of any changes in exchange rates are unpredictable and recognition of such changes would be unreliable. Furthermore, as will be discussed later in the chapter, such changes are viewed as financing events and are recorded as separate transactions.

Immediate Payment

The most common type of foreign currency transaction involves a purchase or sale of goods or services. This transaction could be the purchase or sale of any asset, but the purchase or sale of inventory is the most common. The following example illustrates this type of purchase transaction.

Driskell Enterprises (a U.S.-based entity) enters into a transaction with Frankfurt Manufacturing (a German-based supplier) on November 8, 2005, to purchase 12,500 units of an inventory item costing 20 euros each. Driskell takes possession of the inventory and makes immediate payment in euros on November 8. The exchange rate on November 8 is 1 euro = $.8555.

The journal entry used to initially record a transaction denominated in a foreign currency is identical to the journal entry to record a transaction denominated in U.S. dollars. The critical factor is the value assigned. The transaction is recorded at the spot rate of the currency exchanged at the transaction date. As a result of this transaction, Driskell records a cash purchase on November 8 for $213,875 (12,500 × 20 euros × $.8555). No other entries are necessary because no time passes between the initial purchase and the payment date; therefore, the exchange rate has no time to fluctuate. The following journal entry would be recorded on Driskell's books.

Journal Entry—Driskell Enterprise Books

Nov. 8	Inventory	213,875	
	Cash (12,500 × 20 euros × $.8555)		213,875
	To record the acquisition of inventory.		

The *Cash* account is used for all currency transactions in this chapter regardless of the currency in which the transaction is denominated. In reality, an entity will seldom be in possession of foreign currency units (unless the U.S. entity has a division located in the foreign country). Many foreign currency transactions are accomplished via wire transfer between U.S. and foreign financial institutions. To accomplish these transactions, the U.S.-based entity will likely instruct the U.S. financial institution to adjust its account balance in U.S. dollars by the amount necessary to recognize the receipt or payment of the foreign currency. The currency conversion will take place between the U.S. and the foreign financial institutions. As a result, the U.S. entity can always view the transaction in its U.S. dollar equivalents.

Delayed Payment—No Balance Sheet Date

The currency exchanged (domestic or foreign) does not make a difference when payment occurs immediately. On the other hand, the currency exchanged does make a difference when there is a time lag between the date of the initial transaction and the date of the currency exchange. When the initial transaction and the currency exchange do not occur simultaneously and the transaction is denominated in the domestic currency, the entity records the payment or receipt of the number of currency units regardless of the date of the cash flow. The economic value of the payable/receivable removed from the financial records is equal to the economic value of the currency paid/received. However, when the initial transaction and the currency exchange do not occur simultaneously and the transaction is denominated in a foreign currency, the economic value of a receivable/payable may change subsequent to the initial transaction date. The part of the initial recognition that is denominated in a foreign currency is only estimated when payment does not occur immediately. The estimation is required because the entity does not currently know what the value of the currency will be on the date it will be exchanged. The Financial Accounting Standards Board (FASB) has taken the position that an entity enters into two separate transactions when involved in a foreign currency transaction.[8] The first transaction is the initial purchase or sale, while the second transaction is the settlement of the currency obligation. Any change that occurs in the value of the foreign currency between the date of the initial transaction and the date the currency is received/paid results in a change in estimate and is generally recognized as a gain or loss in the period in which the change occurs.

The following example illustrates the case where Frankfurt ships inventory and bills Driskell for payment at a later date.

Driskell Enterprises (a U.S.-based entity) enters into a transaction with Frankfurt Manufacturing (a German-based supplier) on November 8, 2005, to purchase 12,500 units of an inventory item costing 20 euros each. Driskell takes possession of the inventory on November 8, with payment in euros due on February 8, 2006. The exchange rates on November 8 and February 8 are 1 euro = $.8555 and 1 euro = $.9187, respectively. Driskell prepares financial statements on September 30 and March 31.

Transaction Date The initial transaction date is when the economic substance of the transaction is recorded at the spot rate, that is, the best estimate of the obligation or receivable based on objective information. The first entry, on November 8, would be as follows.

Journal Entry—Driskell Enterprise Books

Nov. 8	Inventory	213,875	
	Accounts Payable (12,500 × 20 euros × $.8555)		213,875
	To record the acquisition of inventory.		

---

[8] **Statement of Financial Accounting Standards (FAS)**, No. 52, "Foreign Currency Translation" (Stamford, CT: Financial Accounting Standards Board, 1981).

This entry is the same as the entry in the previous example except the credit is to *Accounts Payable* instead of *Cash*. The exchange rate that exists on November 8 provides Driskell's best estimate of the number of dollars it will be required to give up to acquire the 250,000 euros to be paid to Frankfurt on February 8. Driskell must now decide whether to accept the risk that the exchange rate may fluctuate between November 8 and February 8 or enter into a contract to buy euros for future delivery at a known price. It is assumed in this example that Driskell opts to accept the risk of currency exchange rate fluctuation.

Settlement date: the date on which the foreign currency transaction is satisfied through the transfer of currency.

Settlement Date The **Settlement date** is the date on which the foreign currency transaction is satisfied through the transfer of currency. If the spot rate has changed since the transaction date, the monetary account denominated in the foreign currency is updated to the spot rate at the settlement date. Such adjustments would result in the recognition of *Exchange Losses or Gains*. The U.S. dollar equivalent of the foreign currency actually paid is recorded, and the *Accounts Payable* is removed at its carrying value at the date the currency is exchanged. Therefore, at the date the *Accounts Payable* is settled (February 8), Driskell must record the economic substance of the settlement transaction and recognize any applicable *Exchange Losses and Gains*. The following journal entries would be recorded on Driskell's books at the settlement date.

Journal Entry—Driskell Enterprise Books

Feb. 8	Exchange Losses and Gains [12,500 × 20 euros × ($.9187 – $.8555)]	15,800	
	Accounts Payable		15,800

To increase *Accounts Payable* and recognize the exchange loss due to the increase in the value of the euro from $.8555 to $.9187.

	Accounts Payable	229,675	
	Cash (12,500 × 20 euros × $.9187)		229,675

To record the payment of 250,000 euros to Frankfurt.

The first entry restates the *Accounts Payable* to the amount Driskell expends to settle its obligation (250,000 euros × $.9187). Keep in mind that Driskell is required to pay 250,000 euros to Frankfurt on February 8 when the exchange rate happened to be 1 euro = $.9187. The $.9187 exchange rate requires Driskell to pay $229,675 to deliver the agreed number of euros ($229,675/$.9187 = 250,000 euros). As a result of this transaction, Driskell settled an *Accounts Payable* of $213,875 by expending $229,675 in *Cash*, resulting in an exchange loss of $15,800. Such exchange losses can be recorded in a generic *Exchange Losses and Gains* account to permit Driskell to efficiently group all such losses and gains that occur during the year for financial statement presentation. The second entry recognizes the payment to Frankfurt. The credit portion of this entry is recorded to *Cash* rather than to *Foreign Currency* because Driskell's bank will reduce Driskell's account by the number of U.S. dollars equivalent to 250,000 euros at the date of payment and wire transfer to a German bank, where euros will be deposited into Frankfurt's account.

Delayed Payment—Balance Sheet Date

The third example assumes that Driskell again decides to accept the risk of exchange rate fluctuation existing as a result of the purchase transaction between Driskell and Frankfurt.

This example includes an intervening balance sheet date between the initial transaction date and the settlement date as described below.

Driskell Enterprises (a U.S.-based entity) enters into a transaction with Frankfurt Manufacturing (a German-based supplier) on November 8, 2005, to purchase 12,500 units of an inventory item costing 20 euros each. Driskell takes possession of the inventory on November 8, with payment in euros due on February 8. Driskell prepares quarterly financial statements, and the balance sheet date is December 31. The exchange rates on November 8, December 31, and February 8 are 1 euro = $.8555, 1 euro = $.9389, and 1 euro = $.9187, respectively.

Transaction Date   Driskell is now required to prepare three journal entries. The first entry is on November 8.

Journal Entry—Driskell Enterprise Books

Nov. 8	Inventory	213,875	
	Accounts Payable (12,500 × 20 euros × $.8555)		213,875
	To record the acquisition of inventory.		

This entry is identical to the first entry made in the previous example. Recognition of the inventory acquisition is independent of when the foreign currency obligation is to be settled or the presence of balance sheet dates.

Balance Sheet Date   A required recognition date occurs when an intervening balance sheet date(s) occur(s) between the initial transaction date and the date of the currency exchange. The reason for this entry is that some accounts on the financial records are **monetary accounts**. The monetary accounts are fixed in units of currency (e.g., *Accounts Receivable, Accounts Payable, Notes Payable*). The U.S. dollar amount(s) recorded on the original transaction date is (are) based on an estimate of the economic value to be given up or received in the future because the future value of the foreign currency is not known. An entry is required on the balance sheet date to adjust the balance in the monetary account(s) denominated in foreign currency units to reflect any change in the estimated value of the currency to be exchanged in the future.

> **Monetary account:** account fixed in units of currency

Driskell must now recognize, on the balance sheet date, the change in the estimated value of the foreign currency (to be exchanged in the future) using the difference between the spot rate at the date of the initial transaction and the spot rate that exists on the balance sheet date. This adjustment is required because the monetary accounts are fixed in terms of units of foreign currency; they are not fixed in terms of U.S. dollar equivalents. Monetary accounts denominated in a fixed number of U.S. dollars do not require revaluation because their carrying values are stated in terms of the equivalent units of the measuring unit, the dollar.

The FASB has taken the position that the changes in value due to exchange rate changes must be recognized at interim reporting dates because the change in the value of the monetary account denominated in a foreign currency will have cash flow effects. Thus, these changes in value are recognized when the event causing the effect takes place rather than when the currency exchange occurs.[9] The adjusting entry will change the balance in the payable or receivable denominated in the foreign currency with the corresponding recognition of an *Exchange Losses and Gains*.

---

[9] Ibid., par. 124.

The recognition of the change in the value of the foreign currency is accomplished in the current example by revaluing the *Accounts Payable* from its current carrying value to the amount that Driskell would have to expend to pay the obligation at the balance sheet date (i.e., the December 31 spot rate). Thus, *Accounts Payable* is adjusted so that the ending balance is $234,725 (250,000 euros × $.9389). The theory applied to revalue the *Accounts Payable* in this example is identical to the revaluation procedures applied for several other financial accounting issues that require a particular value on the balance sheet. For example, a similar procedure is applied to mark marketable securities to market value. The journal entry to recognize the change in *Accounts Payable* and the accompanying exchange loss in the current period is as follows.

Journal Entry—Driskell Enterprise Books

Dec. 31	Exchange Losses and Gains	20,850	
	Accounts Payable [12,500 × 20		20,850
	euros × ($.9389 – $.8555)]		

To increase *Accounts Payable* and recognize the exchange loss due to the increase in the value of the euro from $.8555 to $.9389.

Settlement Date   The final entries are recorded on the date the foreign currency obligation is settled. Driskell must give up $229,675 to acquire the 250,000 euros needed to settle the obligation ($229,675/$.9187 = 250,000 euros). This results in the recognition of an exchange gain as presented in the following entry.

Journal Entry—Driskell Enterprise Books

Feb. 8	Accounts Payable [12,500 × 20 euros ($.9187 – $.9389)]	5,050	
	Exchange Losses and Gains		5,050

To decrease *Accounts Payable* and recognize the exchange gain due to the decrease in the value of the euro from $.9389 to $.9187.

	Accounts Payable	229,675	
	Cash (12,500 × 20 euros × $.9187)		229,675

To record the payment of 250,000 euros to Frankfurt.

The first February 8 entry restates the *Accounts Payable* from its December 31 balance to the amount Driskell expends on February 8 to settle its obligation. Notice that the last two examples both resulted in the same $15,800 net exchange loss being recognized during the November 8 to February 8 time period. In the previous example, the $15,800 exchange loss was recorded on February 8, while in the current example, a $20,850 exchange loss was recorded on December 31 followed by a $5,050 exchange gain on February 8. The net loss or gain recognized from the initial transaction date to the settlement date is not altered by the presence or absence of balance sheet dates. The allocation of the loss or gain to applicable accounting periods is the only difference. The second entry recognizes the payment of $229,675 (250,000 euros × $.9187).

HEDGING

The transactions discussed thus far have assumed that management is willing to accept the risk of exchange rate fluctuation. In reality, management is often not willing to accept such risk. As illustrated in Table 5-2, currency values can fluctuate significantly over a relatively short time period. During a one-month period in early 2001, the U.S. dollar strengthened over 3 percent relative to the value of the British pound, euro, New Zealand dollar, and Swiss franc. The pound was 11.6 percent lower in value on February 8, 2001, than it had been one year previously; however, it strengthened during the subsequent nine months (the change in relative values moved from 11.67% to −1.4% over the nine-month period). The pound then weakened against the U.S. dollar in the next two months (from −1.4% to 3.5%). On the other hand, the Japanese yen was weaker (6.6%) one year prior to February 8, 2001, continued to weaken for the next nine months (8.7%), but gained strength over the subsequent two months (.5%). The large percentage movements illustrate the importance of shifting exchange rate fluctuation risk to the exchange broker for the entire period of the contract, that is, from the day the contract is initiated through the date the contract is settled.

To avoid the unfavorable impact of exchange rate fluctuation, management often enters into a financial instrument (derivative) contract with a currency broker. Such a contract is designed to manage exchange rate fluctuation risk. The contract establishes a fixed exchange rate between the currencies. It is executory in nature because neither party fulfills its part of the contract until a later date. Knowing the amount that will be collected or paid, even though some cost is involved, may be preferred to not knowing the amount that will be collected or paid if the exchange rate fluctuates before the settlement date. The process of using financial instruments to manage foreign currency exchange rate fluctuation risk is known as **hedging**. SFAS No. 133 outlines how financial derivatives are to be valued and how changes in value are to be included in the entity's financial records.

Hedging: the use of a financial instrument contract to eliminate exchange rate fluctuation risk

The risk associated with exchange rate fluctuations can occur over several different time periods. Figure 5-1 illustrates the three different time periods during which management may desire to address potential exchange rate fluctuation.

Time period ① occurs when there is a purchase or sale but settlement does not occur immediately. As a result, there is an *Accounts Payable* or *Accounts Receivable* denominated in a foreign currency. This type of transaction was discussed previously in the chapter under the assumption that management chose to not hedge the risk of exchange rate fluctuation. The risk of currency rate fluctuation exists from the time of the transaction until the settlement date.

Time period ② occurs when a firm commitment to either purchase or sell exists but the transaction does not occur until a later date. The currency rate risk relevant to the commitment begins when the commitment is made and continues until the transaction date.

TABLE 5-2   Percentage Change in Value of the U.S. Dollar Relative to Other Currencies

Country	Currency	1 Month	3 Months	1 Year
Britain	Pound	0.035	−0.014	0.116
Canada	Dollar	0.011	−0.020	0.045
Chile	Peso	−0.027	−0.027	0.087
Europe	Euro	0.032	−0.069	0.074
Japan	Yen	0.005	0.087	0.066
New Zealand	Dollar	0.039	−0.086	0.129
South Korea	Won	0.002	0.115	0.121
Switzerland	Franc	0.039	−0.059	0.025

Source: The Wall Street Journal, February 9, 2001; January 9, 2001; November 9, 2000; and February 9, 2000.

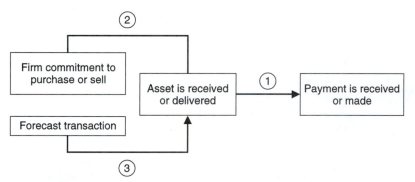

FIGURE 5-1 Time Line of Foreign Currency Transactions

Settlement can occur on the purchase/sales transaction date, or the seller may extend credit to the purchaser. If credit is extended, time period ① follows time period ②.

Time period ③ exists because of a forecast of future transactions. This occurs when management is projecting future transactions based on transactions that occurred in previous periods, and there is the expectation that relationships with foreign customers/suppliers will continue. In this instance, a firm commitment often does not occur so a commitment period, ②, does not exist. The currency rate risk relevant to the forecast exists from the date of the forecast until the transaction date. Again, if credit is extended, time period ① follows time period ③.

The general intent of a hedging transaction is to have the loss or gain on a hedged item (such as an accounts receivable) offset by a corresponding gain or loss on the hedging financial instrument. Management can hedge using a variety of financial instruments, but this text focuses on the two most commonly used—forward contracts and currency options.

Forward Contracts

Forward contract: agreement between individual buyer and seller to exchange currency units at a later date and at an agreed-upon exchange rate

Forward rate: exchange rate that currently exists for an exchange of currency at a future date

A common way to avoid fluctuating currency values (both favorable and unfavorable) is to enter into a **forward contract**, which is an agreement to exchange currency units at a later date and at an agreed-upon exchange rate. In such contracts the **forward rate** (currency exchange rate at a future date) is guaranteed by a currency exchange broker (often a bank) at the date the contract is established. The forward rate is an estimate of the currency's future value based on the market's expectations of factors determining currency value, as discussed earlier in the chapter. Regardless of the exchange rate that exists on the settlement date, the entity and the exchange broker will give/receive the agreed number of dollars for the agreed number of foreign currency units. As a result, the entity knows, with certainty, the number of dollars that will be paid or received depending on whether the forward contract is for the purchase or sale of the foreign currency.

The cost of entering into a forward contract is often negligible because the exchange broker's fee is incorporated into the difference between the buy and sell rates for the currencies. A result of this type of contract is that the contracting entity has a known cash flow and the exchange broker has a guaranteed revenue equal to the difference between buy and sell exchange rates. The exchange broker has an exposure to exchange rate fluctuation to the extent that the investment buy and sell contracts for the currency are not equal.

A forward contract generally results from negotiations between an individual buyer and seller of foreign currency units. This type of contract may be for any number of currency units and the currency exchange may take place at any time. The forward exchange

TABLE 5-3 Foreign Currency Spot and Forward Exchange Rates (as of February 8, 2001)

	U.S. Dollar Equivalent
Australia (dollar)—spot	.5375
1 month forward	.5376
3 months forward	.5377
1 year forward	.5379
Canada (dollar)—spot	.6614
1 month forward	.6616
3 months forward	.6617
1 year forward	.6626
Euro—spot	.9187
1 month forward	.9193
3 months forward	.9201
1 year forward	.9242
Japan (yen)—spot	.008610
1 month forward	.008645
3 months forward	.008717
1 year forward	.009032
Mexico (new peso)—spot	.1036
1 month forward	.1026
3 months forward	.1004
1 year forward	.0922
Switzerland (franc)—spot	.5991
1 month forward	.6001
3 months forward	.6019
1 year forward	.6101

Source: Financial Times, February 9, 2001, p. 27.

rates presented in Table 5-3 include only selected time intervals for the settlement of the forward contract; they are not meant to represent the full range of such contracts.

To illustrate how a forward contract is used, assume a student enters into an agreement in February to accept delivery (purchase) of Mexican pesos in March (immediately prior to departing for Mexico during spring break). The U.S. dollars will be converted into pesos using the predetermined exchange rate (forward rate) that exists at the time of the agreement to exchange currency (February). Table 5-3 provides example spot and forward exchange rates as of February 8, 2001. The table indicates that the student will pay $.1026 per peso and the currencies will be exchanged one month after the contract date. Notice that the one-month forward rate ($.1026) is lower than the spot rate ($.1036) that exists on February 8. As a result, the student will pay $.001 less per peso by taking delivery in one month as compared to the amount that would be exchanged for taking possession of the pesos immediately.

The exchange rate that will exist at a later date can be higher or lower than the exchange rate that currently exists. Table 5-3 illustrates that, as of February 8, 2001, the Australian dollar, Canadian dollar, euro, Japanese yen, and Swiss franc were expected to strengthen relative to the U.S. dollar in the future (it would take more dollars in the future than it did currently to buy one unit of these currencies) while the Mexican peso was expected to weaken relative to the U.S. dollar in the future (it would take fewer U.S. dollars to buy one unit of this currency).

Option Contracts

Option contract: an agreement wherein the writer will exchange currencies with the holder at a predetermined rate if the holder chooses to exercise the option

Strike price: the agreed-upon rate at which the option writer will exchange currencies with the option holder

Another common way to avoid the risk associated with unfavorable fluctuations in currency values is to enter into a foreign currency option contract (**option contract**). Option contracts involve two parties—the writer of the option and the holder of the option. The writer of the option guarantees that the holder, at the holder's option, can exchange currencies at a predetermined rate called the **strike price**. It is important to recognize that the option contract gives the holder the *right, but not the obligation*, to exchange currencies. If the exchange rate is favorable to the holder, the option will be exercised; conversely, the option will be allowed to expire if the exchange rate is not favorable to the holder.

Table 5-4 presents information for selected February 8, 2001, euro option contracts for 62,500 euros. Each currency option has several pieces of relevant information: the option size, the strike price, the type of option (call or put), the option expiration month, and the end-of-day option price (per unit of currency) for each maturity month and strike price.

The option size (62,500 euros in Table 5-4) indicates the number of foreign currency units that will be exchanged if the holder exercises the option. Option contracts are offered only in fixed numbers of currency units. Some of the more common option sizes are 31,250 (British pounds), 50,000 (Australian dollars and Canadian dollars), 62,500 (euro and Swiss francs), and 6,250,000 (Japanese yen).

The strike price, listed in column 1, is the price at which the option writer agrees to exchange currency with the holder. Notice that the *Financial Times* listed three different strike prices for the euro ($.920, $.940, and $.960). Referring back to Table 5-3, the spot rate on February 8, 2001, was $.9187. Note that the strike prices listed in Table 5-4 are all higher than the current spot rate, but strike prices can also be lower than the spot rate.

The remainder of the table is divided into two sections: calls and puts. Calls are option contracts that give the holder the right to purchase the currency; puts are option contracts that give the holder the right to sell the currency. The calls and puts sections of the table are divided into three columns based on the option's expiration month. The value in each cell indicates the price, in cents per euro, that holders were willing to pay to have the right to exchange U.S. dollars for euros at the strike price.

For example, in Table 5-4 holders were willing to pay .63 cents ($.0063) per euro for the right to buy euros (call option) for $.920 each. As a result, the holder would pay the option writer $393.75 (62,500 × $.0063) for the right to purchase 62,500 euros during February 2001 for $57,500 (62,500 × $.920). Purchasing such a call option when the spot rate for the euro is $.9187 may not seem like a wise choice because the holder could acquire the currency for a lower price than that offered by the option writer. On the other hand, the holder may not need the euros until the end of the month, and the euro's value will likely change before it is needed. The holder will save money by exercising the option if the spot rate rises above $.920 before the end of February 2001. The actual exchange rate on February 28, 2001, is $.9196. As a result, the holder of the call option would allow

TABLE 5-4 Euro Options (62,500 Euros) (Philadelphia Exchange)

	Calls (cents per euro)				Puts (cents per euro)		
Strike price	February	March	April		February	March	April
.920	.63	1.42	1.90		.76	1.45	1.94
.940	.12	.67	1.12		2.18	2.78	—
.960	.01	.31	.61		—	4.28	—

Source: Financial Times, February 9, 2001, p. 27.

the option to purchase euros at $.920 to expire unexercised and would purchase euros for $.9196. Had the spot rate on February 28 exceeded $.920 (e.g., spot rate $.925), the holder would have exercised the option and purchased euros from the writer for $.920.

The option price is determined by numerous factors including the spot exchange rate and the forward exchange rate as well as the variability of the currency's exchange rate. The last item, the variability of the currency's exchange rate, is the likely reason the option holder would pay the option writer for the contract discussed previously. Holders will acquire such an option as protection against fluctuations in the currency value greater than the strike price.

In the case of call options, the premium that an option writer requires to guarantee an exchange rate for euros in February goes down ($.0063, $.0012, $.0001) as the strike price increases ($.920, $.940, $.960). The decrease in the premium exists because the writers have less risk of loss for a higher strike price. On the other hand, the premium that writers require increases ($.0063, $.0142, $.0190) as the length of the option contract increases (February, March, April). The increased price exists because there is a longer time during which the euro's value could fluctuate.

In the money: when the currency spot rate for a call (put) option is less (more) than the option strike price

When the spot rate for a currency is less than the put strike price or more than the call strike price, the contract is said to be **in the money**. For example, the put option premium for a $.940 March strike price is $.0278. The option premium guarantees the holder that the euro can be sold in March for $.940 when the February 8, 2001, spot rate for the euro is $.9187, a difference of $.0213. The euro is in the money for this put option and is said to have an intrinsic value of $.0213. The remainder of the option premium—$.0065 ($.0278 – $.0213)—is due to the other factors discussed previously, such as the currency's exchange rate variability. In Table 5-4, all the put options are in the money. If the strike price on a put option is less than the spot rate or the strike price on a call option is more than the spot rate, the contract is said to be **out of the money**. In Table 5-4, all the call options are out of the money. It is also possible to also have put options out of the money and call options in the money.

Out of the money: when the currency spot rate for a call (put) option is more (less) than the option strike price

Several important similarities and differences are identifiable when comparing forward contracts and options. One similarity is that the balance sheet presentation of both is based on the fair value of the contract at the balance sheet date. For purposes of this chapter, the fair value of the forward contract or the option contract will be provided. One difference is that the forward contract may result in both gains and losses to the holder, while the option contract can only result in gains to the holder. Another difference is that the forward contract does not require an initial cash outlay to acquire the contract, while the option contract requires the payment of a premium (as shown in the body of Table 5-4) to the option writer.

Purchase or Sale—Hedge (Forward Contract)

The next example pertains to a purchase or sale denominated in a foreign currency wherein Driskell decides to shift the risk of exchange rate fluctuation to the exchange broker by entering into a forward contract. This example is based on Driskell Enterprises' purchase of inventory.

Driskell Enterprises (a U.S.-based entity) enters into a transaction with Frankfurt Manufacturing (a German-based supplier) on November 8, 2005, to purchase 12,500 units of an inventory item costing 20 euros each. Driskell takes possession of the inventory on November 8, with payment in euros due on February 8, 2006. Driskell immediately negotiates a forward contract to buy euros for delivery on February 8 to shift the risk of exchange rate fluctuation to the exchange broker. Driskell prepares quarterly financial statements, and the balance sheet date is December 31. The relevant exchange rates and account balances for the period from November 8, 2005, to February 8, 2006, are as follows.

Date	Spot Rate	Accounts Payable Balance	February 8 Forward Rate	Forward Contract Fair Value
November 8	$.8555	$213,875	$.8475	$ 0
December 31	$.9389	$234,725	$.9450	$24,375
February 8	$.9187	$229,675	$.9187	$17,800

Transaction Date   Driskell must now prepare two series of entries. The first series of entries relates to the inventory purchase and the ultimate settlement of that obligation. The second series of entries relates to the forward contract and the currency exchange that will take place with the exchange broker. The following entry recognizes the inventory purchase.

Journal Entry—Driskell Enterprise Books

Nov. 8	Inventory	213,875	
	Accounts Payable (12,500 × 20 euros × $.8555)		213,875
	To record the acquisition of inventory.		

The above entry records the acquisition of inventory in the same manner as displayed in previous examples. The *Inventory* and *Accounts Payable* are recorded in Driskell's financial records using the spot rate that exists at the transaction date.

While the inventory purchase results in a journal entry, there is no journal entry for the creation of the forward contract. Forward contracts meet the definition of executory commitments; that is, each party has agreed to perform (exchange currency) based on known terms but neither party has yet performed. Driskell does not have to pay anything to the currency broker at the creation of the forward contract. The agreed-upon exchange price equals the forward exchange rate, so the forward contract has a $0 initial fair value.

Balance Sheet Date   The next relevant event is Driskell's recognition of the change in the value of the monetary account balances denominated in foreign currency units at the balance sheet date. The monetary accounts adjusted in this example are *Accounts Payable* and the *Foreign Currency Forward Contract*. The following entries would result.

Journal Entry—Driskell Enterprise Books

Dec. 31	Exchange Losses and Gains	20,850	
	Accounts Payable [12,500 × 20 euros × ($.9389 – $.8555)]		20,850
	To increase *Accounts Payable* and recognize the exchange loss due to the increase in the value of the euro from $.8555 to $.9389.		
	Foreign Currency Forward Contract	24,375	
	Forward Contract Losses and Gains		24,375
	To recognize the change in the *Foreign Currency Forward Contract*'s fair value from $0 to $24,375.		

The first journal entry results from the restatement of the *Accounts Payable*. This account is fixed in units of currency and denominated in euros. The U.S. dollar equivalent value of the 250,000 euros was estimated on November 8 and, therefore, must be reestimated using the spot rate that exists at the balance sheet date.

The second journal entry recognizes the fair value of the *Foreign Currency Forward Contract*. The contract's change in fair value from $0 to $24,375 is based on the change in the forward exchange rate having a February 8 maturity date. The forward rate indicates the amount that investors would currently pay to own the contract. The contract initially had a $0 fair value because the contract price equaled the existing forward exchange rate. At the December 31 balance sheet date, Driskell has a contract to exchange U.S. dollars into euros at $.8475 per euro. The current forward exchange rate for 1 euro is $.9450. Therefore, Driskell has a contract to purchase euros at less than their projected market rate, resulting in a $24,375 [($.9450 − $.8475) × 250,000] positive fair value for the contract.

Settlement Date   Finally, Driskell prepares entries on the settlement date of both transactions initiated on November 8. The required entries for Driskell are the following.

Journal Entry—Driskell Enterprise Books

Feb. 8	Accounts Payable [12,500 × 20 euros × ($.9187 − $.9389)]	5,050	
	Exchange Losses and Gains		5,050

To decrease *Accounts Payable* and recognize the exchange gain due to the decrease in the value of the euro from $.9389 to $.9187.

	Foreign Currency Losses and Gains	6,575	
	Foreign Currency Forward Contract		6,575

To recognize the change in the *Foreign Currency Forward Contract*'s fair value from $24,375 to $17,800.

	Accounts Payable ($213,875 + $20,850 − $5,050)	229,675	
	Foreign Currency Forward Contract ($24,375 − $6,575)		17,800
	Cash (250,000 euros × $.8475)		211,875

To record the wire transfer of currencies to/from the foreign currency broker and closing of the *Forward Currency Forward Contract*.

The first two entries revalue the *Accounts Payable* and the *Foreign Currency Forward Contract* accounts in the same manner as they were revalued on the December 31 balance sheet date. The *Accounts Payable* is revalued to the spot rate that exists on February 8 and represents the amount Driskell is obligated to expend to pay for the inventory. The *Foreign Currency Forward Contract* is also revalued to its fair value on February 8. The *Foreign Currency Forward Contract*'s fair value at the settlement date is based on the difference between the settlement date spot rate ($.9187) and the forward rate when the forward contract was created ($.8475). The reason the spot rate can be used on February 8 is that it is the contract maturity date. When a forward contract matures, the forward rate and the spot rate become the same.

The last entry shows the payment of the obligation to the supplier and the closure of the forward contract. While Driskell owes Frankfurt 250,000 euros, Driskell is going to wire transfer dollars to the foreign currency exchange broker who will transfer euros into Frankfurt's account. The difference between the dollars that Driskell transfers to the exchange broker ($211,875) and the recognized value in the *Accounts Payable* account ($229,675) is the ending value of the *Foreign Currency Forward Contract* ($17,800).

Purchase or Sale—Hedge (Option Contract)

The next example presents a purchase or sale denominated in a foreign currency hedged with an option contract. This example is based on the same purchase transaction used in the previous section.

Driskell Enterprises (a U.S.-based entity) enters into a transaction with Frankfurt Manufacturing (a German-based supplier) on November 8, 2005, to purchase 12,500 units of an inventory item costing 20 euros each. Driskell takes possession of the inventory on November 8, with payment in euros due on February 8. Driskell immediately purchases a February call option in euros with a strike price of $.86. The option premium paid by Driskell is $5,250. Driskell prepares quarterly financial statements, and the balance sheet date is December 31. The relevant exchange rates for the period from November 8 to February 8 are as follows.

Date	Spot Rate	Accounts Payable Balance	Option Contract Fair Value
November 8	$.8555	$213,875	$5,250
December 31	$.9389	$234,725	$22,200
February 8	$.9187	$229,675	$14,675

Transaction Date As with the forward contract, Driskell must now prepare two series of entries. The first series of entries relates to the inventory purchase and the ultimate settlement of that obligation. The second series of entries relates to the foreign currency option. The following entry recognizes the inventory purchase.

Journal Entry—Driskell Enterprise Books

Nov. 8	Inventory	213,875	
	Accounts Payable (12,500 × 20 euros × $.8555)		213,875
	To record the acquisition of inventory.		

This entry records the inventory acquisition and the creation of the accounts payable. Notice that the inventory purchase is the same regardless of whether or not management hedges or whether management hedges with a forward contract or an option.

Unlike hedging with a forward contract, a journal entry is required when Driskell purchases the option. The reason for the journal entry is that Driskell has to pay a premium to acquire the option. The option writer agrees to provide Driskell with the opportunity to purchase euros at an agreed-upon price ($.86) at a future date (February, 2006). Even though the option is out of the money (strike price is above the current spot rate), the possibility exists that the euro will increase in value and the length of the option period (three months) results in a $5,250 premium. The limit of Driskell's loss is the premium paid. This loss will occur if the spot rate remains below the strike price and the option is not exercised. Driskell has a gain if the spot rate exceeds the strike price. The greater the spot rate, the greater the gain. Theoretically, there is no limit to Driskell's possible gain. On the other hand, the limit to the writer's gain is the premium received, and there is no limit to the amount of loss the writer can incur. The following entry recognizes the payment of the premium for the option.

Journal Entry—Driskell Enterprise Books

Nov. 8	Foreign Currency Option Contract	5,250	
	Cash		5,250
	To record the payment of the option premium.		

Balance Sheet Date   The next relevant date is December 31. Driskell's balance sheet must reflect the change in the monetary account *(Accounts Payable)* and the change in the fair value of the option. The following two entries occur.

Journal Entry—Driskell Enterprise Books

Dec. 31	Exchange Losses and Gains	20,850	
	Accounts Payable [12,500 × 20 euros × ($.8555 – $.9389)]		20,850

To increase *Accounts Payable* and recognize the exchange loss due to the increase in the value of the euro from $.8555 to $.9389.

	Foreign Currency Option Contract	16,950	
	Losses and Gains on Foreign Currency Option		16,950

To recognize the change in the *Foreign Currency Option Contract*'s fair value from $5,250 to $22,200.

The first journal entry results from the restatement of the *Accounts Payable* to the December 31 spot rate. The accounting for the purchase and liability does not change regardless of whether Driskell hedges or the manner in which Driskell hedges.

The second journal entry reflects the change in the fair value of the foreign currency option. As the spot rate increases, the value of the option increases. Driskell has the option to buy euros at $.86 per euro. When the value of the euro increases, as it did from November 8 through December 31, the ability to buy euros at a fixed price becomes more attractive, and the fair value of the option increases.

Settlement Date   Finally, Driskell prepares three entries on the settlement date.

Journal Entry—Driskell Enterprise Books

Feb. 8	Accounts Payable [12,500 × 20 euros × ($.9187 – $.9389)]	5,050	
	Exchange Losses and Gains		5,050

To decrease *Accounts Payable* and recognize the exchange gain due to the decrease in the value of the euro from $.9389 to $.9187.

	Losses and Gains on Foreign Currency Option	7,525	
	Foreign Currency Option Contract		7,525

To recognize the change in *Foreign Currency Option Contract*'s fair value from $22,200 to $14,675.

	Accounts Payable	229,675	
	Foreign Currency Option Contract		14,675
	Cash (250,000 euros × $.86)		215,000

To record the wire transfer of currency to/from the option writer and the closing of the *Foreign Currency Option Contract*.

The first two entries revalue the *Accounts Payable* and the *Foreign Currency Option Contract* to their fair value on February 8. These recognized balances represent the amount that Driskell must pay Frankfurt and the value of the option contract. Driskell has to pay Frankfurt 250,000 euros on February 8, and the spot rate represents the dollars that will be expended to acquire the euros. The option contract's fair value is the amount that the spot rate for the euro exceeds the strike price. If the strike price is above the spot rate to purchase the euro at the date the option expires, the fair value of the option becomes $0. On the other hand, the option may have a positive fair value even if the spot rate is less than the strike price prior to the expiration date, as illustrated in the November 8 entry.

The last entry shows the payment of the obligation to Frankfurt and the exercising of the option contract. Driskell wire transfers $215,000 to the option writer and has the option writer wire transfer 250,000 euros to Frankfurt's account. The difference between the dollars paid to the option writer and the reduction of the liability when the option writer wires euros to Frankfurt closes the *Foreign Currency Option Contract.*

FOREIGN CURRENCY COMMITMENT

Foreign currency commitment: when an entity enters into an agreement to buy or sell goods denominated in a fixed number of foreign currency units at some time in the future

Executory contract: a contract where neither party has yet fulfilled its part of the agreement

The previous examples all involved transactions where the domestic entity, Driskell Enterprises, purchased and took immediate delivery of a product from a foreign entity, Frankfurt Manufacturing. It is also possible that the domestic entity will make a **Foreign currency commitment**; that is, to purchase or sell something at a future date denominated in a fixed number of foreign currency units. The delay between the agreement to purchase or sell and the physical transfer may result from a variety of reasons, such as a backlog in orders making immediate delivery impossible, the item requiring substantial time to manufacture, the item being too valuable to hold in inventory, or the item having a limited shelf life requiring production to meet demand. Any of these circumstances may require the entity to make a commitment to buy or sell in the future at an established price. An entity may also enter into a purchase or sales commitment to assure the price of a future transaction. A company creates an **executory contract** (a contract where neither party has yet fulfilled its part of the agreement) when it enters into a purchase or sales commitment. Executory contracts are not recorded in the financial records when initiated.

Failure to create a commitment for a future transaction results in management accepting the risk of changes in the transaction price until the date of the transaction. Thus, purchase or sales commitments are ways in which management reduces risk. When the future transaction is to be settled in a currency different from the entity's currency, another type of risk exists, that is, the risk of foreign currency exchange rate fluctuation. A result of entering into a purchase or sales commitment with a foreign entity is that management must decide whether to accept the risk of exchange rate fluctuation from the date of the initial purchase or sale agreement until the underlying transaction date. The alternative to accepting such risk is to enter into a hedging contract.

If a hedge is not established, no journal entries are made with respect to changes in the value of the foreign currency until the item is purchased or sold at the future date. At that time, the entity will record a purchase or sale in the manner discussed in the previous section. If management hedges the exposure, it must account for the change in the value of the hedge instrument and the change in the value of the purchase or sales commitment from the date of the commitment to the transaction date. At the time of the purchase or sale, the transaction is recorded and the hedge becomes a hedge of the exposed asset or liability position resulting from the underlying purchase or sale transaction (discussed previously).

The recognition requirements for a foreign currency commitment hedge differ from the hedge of an asset or liability because the theoretical reasons for the hedging contracts differ. When a transaction has already occurred, the hedge eliminates the risk of a change in the currency value resulting from an existing asset or liability. In the case of a foreign currency commitment, there is no underlying transaction at the date the hedge is initiated.

The entity has hedged to eliminate the risk from a change in the value of a currency resulting from a transaction that has not occurred.

Regardless of the reason for entering into a hedge, the change in the financial (hedge) instrument's value must be recognized. Given that an underlying transaction has not occurred for the hedge of a foreign currency commitment, recognizing the change in the value of the hedge instrument should not impact net income. The amount by which the hedge instrument changes in value is recognized as a gain or loss. The process that keeps this recognition from impacting net income is that it is offset by a corresponding loss or gain on the purchase or sales commitment.

Keep in mind that the recognition of the foreign currency commitment is only applicable from the date the hedge is established until the date the underlying transaction occurs (e.g., the inventory is received). The hedge of a foreign currency commitment also has three potential dates for recognition requirements: (1) the date the hedge is established, (2) any intervening balance sheet dates until the underlying transaction is recognized, and (3) the date the underlying transaction is recognized.

Foreign currency commitments can be hedged with a variety of financial instruments. As with previous examples, this text focuses of two of the most commonly used instruments: forward contracts and option contracts.

Forward Contract Hedge

The following is an example of a foreign currency commitment for a sales transaction when hedged with a forward contract.

Driskell Enterprises (a U.S.-based entity) entered into an agreement on November 8, 2005, to sell inventory to Fabre Manufacturing (a French-based manufacturing entity) for 750,000 euros. Driskell is to deliver the inventory by February 8, 2006, and bill Fabre. Payment in euros is required on April 24, 2006. Driskell prepares financial statements quarterly, with a December 31 year-end. Driskell decided to hedge the foreign exchange risk on November 8 and enters into a forward contract with an exchange broker to sell 750,000 euros for delivery on April 24, 2001. The applicable exchange rates and account balances are the following.

Date	Spot Rate	Accounts Receivable Balance	April 24 Forward Rate	Forward Contract Fair Value
November 8	$.8555		$.9200	$ 0
December 31	$.9389		$.9350	($11,250)
February 8	$.9187	$689,025	$.9195	$375
March 31	$.9070	$680,250	$.9053	$11,025
April 24	$.9036	$677,700	$.9036	$12,300

Commitment Initiation Date   As a result of Driskell choosing to hedge the foreign currency sales commitment, the company has two executory contracts: the sales commitment and the forward contract. There are no journal entries recorded on the date the sales commitment and the hedge of a foreign currency commitment with a forward contract are initiated because neither party in either transaction has performed under the terms of the agreement. It should also be noted that there would be no journal entries on Driskell's books prior to February 8, 2006, if Driskell had not hedged the foreign currency commitment.

Driskell would record the sale at the spot rate on February 8 and would then determine whether to hedge the exposed asset position *(Accounts Receivable).* Whether the hedge exists or not, the sales transactions will still be recorded because hedging the foreign currency commitment does not alter the need to record the underlying transaction when it occurs.

Balance Sheet Date The first relevant recognition date is the December 31 balance sheet date. The forward contract must be revalued to its fair value at the balance sheet date (December 31): The sales commitment is also revalued because it is fixed in euros and its value changes as the exchange rate changes. The following two journal entries are prepared on December 31.

Journal Entry—Driskell Enterprise Books

Dec. 31	Forward Contract Losses and Gains	11,250	
	Foreign Currency Forward Contract		11,250

To recognize the change in the *Foreign Currency Forward Contract*'s fair value from a value of $0 to a liability of $11,250.

	Sales Commitment	11,250	
	Losses and Gains on Sales		11,250
	Commitment		

To recognize the change in the value of the *Sales Commitment.*

Transaction Date The next required date for recognition is the date of the underlying transaction. The objective of these entries is to recognize sales in the amount of cash that Driskell would obtain if the transactions were settled at this date. This objective is accomplished in a three-step process. The following journal entries present the transaction-date recognition.

Journal Entry—Driskell Enterprise Books

Feb. 8	Foreign Currency Forward Contract	11,625	
	Forward Contract Losses and Gains		11,625

To recognize the change in the *Foreign Currency Forward Contract*'s fair value from a liability of $11,250 to an asset of $375.

	Losses and Gains on Sales Commitment	11,625	
	Sales Commitment		11,625

To recognize the change in the value of the *Sales Commitment.*

	Accounts Receivable	689,025	
	Sales (750,000 euros × $.9187)		689,025

To recognize the sale of inventory.

	Sales Commitment ($11,625 − $11,250)	375	
	Sales		375

To close the *Sales Commitment* to the *Sales* account.

The first two journal entries recognize the revaluation of the forward contract and the sales commitment to the fair value of the forward contract as of February 8. These entries accrue the change in the *Sales Commitment* from the initial commitment date to the transaction date. The third entry recognizes the sale at the transaction date spot rate. This is the same entry that would be recorded had the commitment not occurred. The last entry closes the *Sales Commitment* to *Sales*.

Balance Sheet Date   As soon as the underlying transaction occurs, the forward contract becomes the hedge of the exposed asset position *(Accounts Receivable)*. The procedures then applied for the remainder of this example are the same as those discussed earlier in the chapter for the forward contract hedge of an exposed asset or liability. The change in the forward contract's fair value is recognized on the balance sheet date using the forward exchange rate with the April 24 settlement date, while *Accounts Receivable* is revalued using the spot rate at the balance sheet date. The following are Driskell's March 31 adjusting entries.

Journal Entry—Driskell Enterprise Books

Mar. 31	Exchange Losses and Gains	8,775	
	Accounts Receivable [750,000 euros × ($.9070 – $.9187)]		8,775

To decrease *Accounts Receivable* and recognize the exchange loss due to the decrease in the value of the euro from $.9187 to $.9070.

	Foreign Currency Forward Contract ($11,025 – $375)	10,650	
	Foreign Currency Losses and Gains		10,650

To recognize the change in the *Foreign Currency Forward Contract*'s fair value from $375 to $11,025.

Settlement Date   The final set of entries occur at the date of the cash flows. The first entry recognizes the revaluation of the *Accounts Receivable* to the April 24 spot rate. The second entry recognizes the revaluation of the forward contract to the forward rate at the date of the cash flow (spot rate). The third entry discloses the receipt of 750,000 euros from Fabre Manufacturing, resulting in a decrease in *Accounts Receivable*. Driskell directs Fabre to make payment to the exchange broker, and the exchange broker then transfers $690,000 (750,000 euros × $.9200) to Driskell. The difference between the value of the euros transferred to the exchange broker and the cash received from the exchange broker is equal to the fair value of the *Foreign Currency Forward Contract*.

Journal Entry—Driskell Enterprise Books

Apr. 24	Exchange Losses and Gains	2,550	
	Accounts Receivable [750,000 euros × ($.9036 – $.9070)]		2,550

To decrease *Accounts Receivable* and recognize the exchange loss due to the decrease in the value of the euro from $.9070 to $.9036.

	Foreign Currency Forward Contract	1,275	
	Foreign Currency Losses and Gains		1,275

To recognize the change in the *Foreign Currency Forward Contract*'s fair value from $11,025 to $12,300.

	Cash (750,000 euros × $.920)	690,000	
	Foreign Currency Forward Contract		12,300
	Accounts Receivable (750,000 euros × $.9036)		677,700

To record the wire transfer of currencies to/from the foreign currency broker and closing of the *Foreign Currency Forward Contract*.

Option Contract Hedge

The following example presents a foreign currency commitment for a sales transaction when hedged with an option contract.

Driskell Enterprises (a U.S.-based entity) entered into an agreement on November 8, 2005, to sell inventory to Fabre Manufacturing (a French-based manufacturing entity) for 750,000 euros. Driskell is to deliver the inventory by February 8, 2006, and bill Fabre. Payment in euros is required on April 24, 2006. Driskell prepares financial statements quarterly, with a December 31 year-end. Driskell decided to hedge the foreign exchange risk on November 8 and purchases a put option in euros with a strike price of $.9100. The option premium paid by Driskell is $45,000. The relevant exchange rates and account balances for the period from November 8 till April 24 are as follows.

Date	Spot Rate	Accounts Receivable Balance	Option Contract Fair Value
November 8	$.8555		$45,000
December 31	$.9389		$0
February 8	$.9187	$689,025	$900
March 31	$.9070	$680,250	$2,625
April 24	$.9036	$677,700	$4,800

Commitment Initiation Date Consistent with the previous example, there is no journal entry recorded at the date the sales commitment is initiated. Consistent with hedging purchases or sales with option contracts, there is a journal entry recorded on the date the hedge of a foreign currency commitment option contract is initiated because Driskell has to pay the option premium ($45,000) to buy the right to sell 750,000 euros at $.9100 each on April 24. Also consistent with the previous example, there would be no journal entries on Driskell's books prior to February 8, 2006, if Driskell had not hedged the foreign currency commitment.

Journal Entry—Driskell Enterprise Books

Nov. 8	Foreign Currency Option Contract	45,000	
	Cash		45,000
	To record the payment of the option premium.		

Balance Sheet Date The next relevant recognition date is the December 31 balance sheet date. Driskell's balance sheet must reflect the fair value of the put option and the sales commitment must be revalued, resulting in offsetting losses and gains on the income statement. The reason for the offsetting losses and gains for the foreign currency commitment hedged with an option contract is the same as with a forward contract hedge of a foreign currency commitment. As long as there is not an underlying transaction, there should be no income statement effect due to changes in values of hedging instruments. As a result, the following entries would be made.

Journal Entry—Driskell Enterprise Books

Dec. 31	Losses and Gains on Foreign Currency Option	45,000	
	Foreign Currency Option Contract		45,000
	To recognize the change in the *Foreign Currency Option Contract*'s fair value from $45,000 to $0.		

| Sales Commitment | 45,000 | |
| Losses and Gains on Sales Commitment | | 45,000 |

To recognize the change in the value of the *Sales Commitment*.

The option contract's fair value decreased because of a large increase in the euro's spot rate. Driskell has a put option to sell euros for $.9100 each on April 24. This was purchased when the spot rate was $.8555. As the spot rate for the euro increases, the value of an ability to sell euros at a fixed price decreases. At some point, the spot rate becomes great enough that the option contract's fair value becomes $0. The spot rate is not the only item that impacts the option's fair value. As discussed earlier in the chapter, the length of the option contract and the variability of the currency exchange rate are other major factors in determining the option's fair value. The fair value of the option can be a positive value or $0, it cannot become negative because Driskell can always let the option expire unexercised. The sales commitment is revalued to have an offsetting gain. The sales commitment increases in value because Driskell has a contract to make a sale for a fixed 750,000 euros when the euros have increased in value.

Transaction Date   Driskell's next recognition date is the date of sale. As with the previous example, the objective of these entries is to recognize sales in the amount of cash that Driskell would obtain if the transactions were settled at this date. This objective is accomplished in a three-step process. The following journal entries present the transaction-date recognition.

Journal Entry—Driskell Enterprise Books

| Feb. 8 | Foreign Currency Option Contract | 900 | |
| | Losses and Gains on Foreign Currency Option | | 900 |

To recognize the change in the *Foreign Currency Option Contract*'s fair value from $0 to $900.

| | Losses and Gains on Sales Commitment | 900 | |
| | Sales Commitment | | 900 |

To recognize the change in the value of the *Sales Commitment*.

| | Accounts Receivable | 689,025 | |
| | Sales (750,000 euros × $.9187) | | 689,025 |

To recognize the sale of inventory.

| | Sales | 44,100 | |
| | Sales Commitment ($45,000 − $900) | | 44,100 |

To close the *Sales Commitment* to the *Sales* account.

The first two journal entries recognize the revaluation of the option contract and the sales commitment to the fair value of the option contract as of February 8. These entries accrue the change in the *Sales Commitment* from the initial commitment date to the transaction date. The third entry recognizes the sale at the transaction-date spot rate. This is the same entry that would be recorded had the commitment not occurred. The last entry closes the *Sales Commitment* to *Sales*.

Balance Sheet Date   As with the foreign currency commitment hedged with a forward contract, as soon as the underlying transaction occurs, the option contract becomes the hedge of the exposed asset position *(Accounts Receivable)*. The procedures then applied for the remainder of this example are the same as those discussed earlier in the chapter for the option hedge of an exposed asset or liability. The change in the option contract fair value is recognized on the balance sheet date and the *Accounts Receivable* is revalued, using the spot rate at the balance sheet date. The following are Driskell's March 31 adjusting entries.

Journal Entry—Driskell Enterprise Books

Mar. 31	Exchange Losses and Gains	8,775	
	Accounts Receivable [750,000 euros × ($.9070 – $.9187)]		8,775

To decrease *Accounts Receivable* and recognize the exchange loss due to the decrease in the value of the euro from $.9187 to $.9070.

	Foreign Currency Option Contract	1,725	
	Losses and Gains on Foreign Currency Option		1,725

To recognize the change in the *Foreign Currency Option Contract*'s fair value from $900 to $2,625.

Settlement Date   The final set of entries occur at the settlement date. The first entry recognizes the revaluation of the *Accounts Receivable* to the spot rate. The second entry recognizes the change in the option contract's fair value. The option contract's settlement date fair value ($4,800) equals the difference between the strike price and the spot rate on April 24 [($.9100 – $.9036) × 750,000 euros]. If the spot rate at the settlement date had exceeded the strike price, the option would have a $0 fair value and Driskell would have allowed it to expire unexercised. The third entry discloses the receipt of 750,000 euros from Fabre Manufacturing, resulting in a decrease in *Accounts Receivable*. Driskell directs Fabre to make payment to the option writer, who then transfers $682,500 ($.9100 × 750,000 euros) to Driskell. The difference between the value of the euros transferred to the option writer and the cash received from the option writer is equal to the fair value of the *Foreign Currency Option Contract*.

Journal Entry—Driskell Enterprise Books

Apr. 24	Exchange Losses and Gains	2,550	
	Accounts Receivable [750,000 euros × ($.9036 – $.9070)]		2,550

To decrease *Accounts Receivable* and recognize the exchange loss due to the decrease in the value of the euro from $.9070 to $.9036.

	Foreign Currency Option Contract	2,175	
	Losses and Gains on Foreign Currency Option		2,175

To recognize the change in the *Foreign Currency Option Contract*'s fair value from $2,625 to $4,800.

	Cash (750,000 euros × $.9100)	682,500	
	Foreign Currency Option Contract		4,800
	Accounts Receivable (750,000 euros × $.9036)		677,700

To record the wire transfer of currencies to/from the option writer and closing of the *Foreign Currency Option Contract*.

The key issues in recognizing the substance of foreign currency commitments is the recognition of offsetting gains and losses when the forward (option) contract and purchase or sales commitment are revalued. The net gain or loss on the purchase or sales commitment is then offset against the recognized transaction (revenue or asset). The transactions pertaining to *Accounts Receivable* is the same whether the hedge is undertaken with a forward contract or an option. *Accounts Receivable* is always revalued to the spot rate, and the losses or gains are recognized to the income statement.

FORECASTED TRANSACTION

The previous examples involved transactions between a domestic entity and a foreign entity that had either occurred or where there is a contractual agreement for a future transaction to occur. Whether there is a contractual agreement or not, continuing relationships with foreign customers/suppliers are likely to exist. In fact, it is common for management to prepare budgets based on forecasts that assume continuing relationships with other entities. When the expected continuing relationship is with a foreign entity, management expects to have foreign exchange rate fluctuation risk if previous transactions were denominated in a foreign currency. If management takes no action to protect the company from the risk of exchange rate fluctuations, there are no accounting issues until an actual transaction occurs. At that time, the transaction will be accounted for in the manner discussed previously in this chapter. On the other hand, management may initiate a hedge of the forecasted transaction to protect the company from exchange rate fluctuation risk.

Forecasted transaction: a transaction that is expected to occur rather than one that has occurred or is contracted to occur

The recognition rules for the hedge of a **forecasted transaction** differ from recognition rules discussed previously in that the hedge is based on a transaction that is expected to occur rather than a transaction that has either occurred or is contractually committed to occur. Changes in the value of the hedge instrument (forward contract or option) in previous examples were recognized on the income statement along with the change in the hedged item (i.e., either a payable or receivable or a purchase or sales commitment). The hedge of a forecasted transaction differs from previously discussed hedges because there is no account to revalue that would offset the hedge instrument's income statement effect (either fully or partially). As a result, recognition of the change in the hedge instrument's value on the income statement would add volatility to the entity's financial statements. This volatility is what management is trying to avoid by entering into a hedge contract.

As with other types of hedges, a forecasted transaction can be hedged with either a forward contract or an option contract. The basic premise displayed in the forward contract and option examples in this section is that the change in the hedge instrument's fair value will be held in *Other Comprehensive Income* until the item forecasted to be purchased or sold impacts the income statement via *Sales* or *Cost of Goods Sold*. At that time, *Other Comprehensive Income* is reclassified and becomes part of earnings.

Forward Contract Hedge

The following is an example of a forecasted foreign currency sales transaction when hedged with a forward contract.

Driskell Enterprises (a U.S.-based entity) has sold inventory for several years to a German appliance assembler (Fritz Consumer Electronics, Inc.). Management believes the relationship with Fritz will continue, and on November 8, 2005, additional inventory sales priced at 750,000 euros are forecasted for February 8, 2006. Based on previous experience with Fritz, payment will be received 75 days later (on April 24). Driskell chooses to hedge this forecasted transaction by entering into a forward contract on November 8, 2005, to deliver 750,000 euros to the exchange broker on April 24, 2006. Driskell prepares financial statements quarterly, with a December 31 year-end. Relevant exchange rates and account balances are presented below.

Date	Spot Rate	Accounts Receivable Balance	April 24 Forward Rate	Forward Contract Fair Value
November 8	$.8555		$.9200	$0
December 31	$.9389		$.9350	($11,250)
February 8	$.9187	$689,025	$.9195	$375
March 31	$.9070	$680,250	$.9053	$11,025
April 24	$.9036	$677,700	$.9036	$12,300

Forecast Hedge Initiation Date   As with other forward contract hedges, a journal entry is not required on the date the forward contract hedge is initiated. Although Driskell has contracted to deliver 750,000 euros and receive $690,000 (750,000 euros × $.9200) from the exchange broker, the forward contract's fair value at the date the hedge is initiated is $0.

Balance Sheet Date   Consistent with the recognition requirements for other types of hedges, the purpose of the balance sheet date requirement is to revalue the forward contract to its balance sheet date fair value. The forward rate has increased from its November 8 rate of $.9200 to $.9350 on December 31. As a result, Driskell has entered into a contract whereby it will receive a lesser value for the euros than could be attained currently. This results in a negative fair value for the forward contract. When the forward contract is deceased in value, *Other Comprehensive Income* is charged for the amount of the adjustment, as shown in the following journal entry.

Journal Entry—Driskell Enterprise Books

Dec. 31	Other Comprehensive Income	11,250	
	Foreign Currency Forward Contract		11,250

To recognize the change in the *Foreign Currency Forward Contract*'s fair value from a value of $0 to a liability of $11,250.

Transaction Date   The following entries present the journal entries on Driskell's financial records at the date the inventory is sold to Fritz.

Journal Entry—Driskell Enterprise Books

Feb. 8	Foreign Currency Forward Contract	11,625	
	Other Comprehensive Income		11,625

To recognize the change in the *Foreign Currency Forward Contract*'s fair value from a liability of $11,250 to an asset of $375.

	Accounts Receivable	689,025	
	Sales (750,000 euros × $.9187)		689,025

To recognize the sale of inventory to Fritz.

	Other Comprehensive Income ($11,625 − $11,250)	375	
	Sales	375	

To close the *Other Comprehensive Income* account to the *Sales* account.

The forward contract must be revalued to its fair value at the transaction date so the full amount of the change in fair value, from the date of the original forecast hedge to the transaction date, can be assigned to *Other Comprehensive Income*. In this instance, the forward rate for the euro has decreased from $.9350 to $.9195, resulting in an increase in the forward contract's fair value from ($11,250) to $375, a change of $11,625.

Sales are always recorded at the spot rate on the transaction date. As a result, Driskell records *Sales* for $689,025. *Other Comprehensive Income* is reclassified to earnings at the transaction date because that is when the previously forecasted transaction impacts net income. If the forecast had been for the purchase of inventory, *Other Comprehensive Income* would have been reclassified to *Cost of Goods Sold* in the period in which the inventory was sold.

Balance Sheet Date   The balance sheet date results in recognition of the change in the forward contract's fair value as well as the change in the *Accounts Receivable* value. The following entries present the revaluation of these two amounts.

Journal Entry—Driskell Enterprise Books

Mar. 31	Exchange Losses and Gains	8,775	
	Accounts Receivable [750,000 euros × ($.9070 – $.9187)]		8,775

To decrease *Accounts Receivable* and recognize the exchange loss due to the decrease in the value of the euro from $.9187 to $.9070.

	Foreign Currency Forward Contract ($11,025 – $375)	10,650	
	Foreign Currency Losses and Gains		10,650

To recognize the change in the *Foreign Currency Forward Contract*'s fair value from $375 to $11,025.

Note that the above entries are exactly the same as the March 31 entries on the forward contract hedge of a foreign currency commitment. They are the same because the forecasted transaction hedge becomes the hedge of an *Accounts Receivable* as of the transaction date. This is true whether there was a foreign currency commitment or a forecasted transaction. The *Accounts Receivable* is revalued to its spot rate at the balance sheet date, and *Exchange Losses and Gains* are recognized on the income statement. The forward contract is also revalued to its March 31 fair value ($11,025) from its previous fair value of $375. The resulting $10,650 is recognized on the income statement as *Foreign Currency Losses and Gains*.

Settlement Date   The final set of entries occur at the date of the cash flows. The first entry recognizes the revaluation of the *Accounts Receivable* to the spot rate. The second entry recognizes the revaluation of the forward contract to the forward rate at the date of the cash flow (spot rate). The third entry discloses the receipt of 750,000 euros from Fritz Consumer Electronics, resulting in a decrease in *Accounts Receivable*. Driskell directs Fritz to make payment to the exchange broker, and the exchange broker then transfers $690,000 to Driskell. The difference between the value of the euros transferred to the exchange broker and the cash received from the exchange broker is equal to the fair value of the *Foreign Currency Forward Contract*.

Journal Entry—Driskell Enterprise Books

Apr. 24	Exchange Losses and Gains	2,550	
	Accounts Receivable [750,000 euros × ($.9036 – $.9070)]		2,550

To decrease *Accounts Receivable* and recognize the exchange loss due to the decrease in the value of the euro from $.9070 to $.9036.

Foreign Currency Forward Contract	1,275	
Foreign Currency Losses and Gains		1,275

To recognize the change in the *Foreign Currency Forward Contract*'s fair value from $11,025 to $12,300.

Cash (750,000 euros × $.9200)	690,000	
Foreign Currency Forward Contract		12,300
Accounts Receivable (750,000 euros × $.9036)		677,700

To record the wire transfer of currencies to/from the foreign currency broker and closing of the *Foreign Currency Forward Contract.*

Option Contract Hedge

The following example presents a forecasted foreign currency sales transaction when hedged with an option contract.

Driskell Enterprises (a U.S.-based entity) has sold inventory for several years to a German appliance assembler (Fritz Consumer Electronics, Inc.). Management believes the relationship with Fritz will continue, and on November 8, 2005, additional inventory sales priced at 750,000 euros are forecasted for February 8, 2006. Based on previous experience with Fritz, payment will be received 75 days later (on April 24). Driskell prepares financial statements quarterly, with a December 31 year-end. Driskell decided to hedge the foreign exchange risk on November 8 and purchases a put option in euros with a strike price of $.9100. The option premium paid by Driskell is $45,000. Relevant exchange rates and account balances are presented below.

Date	Spot Rate	Accounts Receivable Balance	Option Contract Fair Value
November 8	$.8555		$45,000
December 31	$.9389		$0
February 8	$.9187	$689,025	$900
March 31	$.9070	$680,250	$2,625
April 24	$.9036	$677,700	$4,800

Forecast Hedge Initiation Date As with other option contract hedges, a journal entry is required on the hedge initiation date to recognize the premium paid by Driskell to acquire the put option. Driskell has the option to deliver 750,000 euros and receive $682,500 (750,000 euros × $.9100) from the option writer. If the exchange rate on April 24 is below $.9100, Driskell will exercise this option. If the exchange rate on April 24 is above $.9100, Driskell will let the option expire and will sell the euros for the higher amount. The journal entry below presents the recognition of the option premium paid on November 8.

Journal Entry—Driskell Enterprise Books

Nov. 8	Foreign Currency Option Contract	45,000	
	Cash		45,000

To record the payment of the option premium.

Balance Sheet Date Consistent with the recognition requirements for other types of hedges, the balance sheet date requirement is to revalue the option contract to its balance sheet date fair value. The spot rate has increased from its November 8 rate of $.8555 to $.9389 on December 31. Diskell has purchased a put option whereby it will receive a lesser value for the euros ($.9100) than could be attained currently. This results in a $0 fair value for the option contract. When the option contract decreases in value, *Other Comprehensive Income* is charged for the amount of the adjustment, as shown in the following journal entry.

Journal Entry—Driskell Enterprise Books

Dec. 31	Other Comprehensive Income	45,000	
	Foreign Currency Option Contract		45,000

To recognize the change in the *Foreign Currency Option Contract*'s fair value from a value of $45,000 to a value of $0.

Transaction Date The following are the journal entries on Driskell's financial records at the date the inventory is sold to Fritz.

Journal Entry—Driskell Enterprise Books

Feb. 8	Foreign Currency Option Contract	900	
	Other Comprehensive Income		900

To recognize the change in the *Foreign Currency Option Contract*'s fair value from $0 to $900.

	Accounts Receivable	689,025	
	Sales (750,000 euros × $.9187)		689,025

To recognize the sale of inventory.

	Sales	44,100	
	Other Comprehensive Income ($45,000 – $900)		44,100

To close the *Other Comprehensive Income* account to the *Sales* account.

The option contract must be revalued to its fair value at the transaction date so the full amount of the change in fair value, from the date of the original forecast hedge to the transaction date, can be assigned to *Other Comprehensive Income*. In this instance, the euro has decreased from $.9389 to $.9187, resulting in an increase in the option contract's fair value from $0 to $900.

Sales are always recorded at the spot rate on the transaction date. As a result, Driskell records *Sales* for $689,025. As with the forward contract hedge, *Other Comprehensive Income* is reclassified to earnings at the transaction date because that is when the previously forecasted transaction impacts net income.

Balance Sheet Date The balance sheet date results in recognition of the change in the option contract's fair value as well as the change in the *Accounts Receivable* value. The following entries present the revaluation of these two amounts.

Journal Entry—Driskell Enterprise Books

Mar. 31	Exchange Losses and Gains	8,775	
	Accounts Receivable [750,000 euros × ($.9070 – $.9187)]		8,775

To decrease *Accounts Receivable* and recognize the exchange loss due to the decrease in the value of the euro from $.9187 to $.9070.

Foreign Currency Option Contract	1,725	
Losses and Gains on Foreign Currency Option		1,725

To recognize the change in the *Foreign Currency Option Contract*'s fair value from $900 to $2,625.

Note that the above entries are exactly the same as the March 31 entries on the option hedge of a foreign currency commitment. They are the same because the hedge becomes the hedge of an *Accounts Receivable* as of the transaction date. This is true whether there was a foreign currency commitment or a forecasted transaction. The *Accounts Receivable* is revalued to its spot rate at the balance sheet date, and *Exchange Losses and Gains* are recognized on the income statement. The option contract is also revalued to its March 31 fair value ($2,625) from its previous fair value of $900. The resulting $1,725 is recognized on the income statement as *Losses and Gains on Foreign Currency Options*.

Settlement Date   The final set of entries occur at the date of the cash flows. The first entry recognizes the revaluation of the *Accounts Receivable* to the spot rate. The second entry recognizes the revaluation of the option contract's fair value. The option contract's settlement-date fair value ($4,800) equals the difference between the strike price and the spot rate on April 24 [($.9100 − $.9036) × 750,000 euros]. If the spot rate at the settlement date had exceeded the strike price, the option would have a $0 fair value and Driskell would have allowed it to expire unexercised. The third entry discloses the receipt of 750,000 euros from Fritz Consumer Electronics, resulting in a decrease in *Accounts Receivable*. Driskell directs Fritz to make payment to the option writer, who then transfers $682,500 (750,000 euros × $.9100) to Driskell. The difference between the value of the euros transferred to the option writer and the cash received from the option writer is equal to the fair value of the *Foreign Currency Option Contract*.

Journal Entry—Driskell Enterprise Books

Apr. 24	Exchange Losses and Gains	2,550	
	Accounts Receivable [750,000 euros × ($.9036 − $.9070)]		2,550

To decrease *Accounts Receivable* and recognize the exchange loss due to the decrease in the value of the euro from $.9070 to $.9036.

Foreign Currency Option Contract	2,175	
Losses and Gains on Foreign Currency Option		2,175

To recognize the change in the *Foreign Currency Option Contract*'s fair value from $2,625 to $4,800.

Cash (750,000 euros × $.9100)	682,500	
Foreign Currency Option Contract		4,800
Accounts Receivable (750,000 euros × $.9036)		677,700

To record the wire transfer of currencies to/from the option writer and closing of the *Foreign Currency Option Contract*.

The key issue in recognizing the substance of forecasted foreign currency transactions is that the change in fair value (forward contract or option) is recognized in *Other Comprehensive Income* until the item purchased or sold impacts the income statement. At that time, *Other Comprehensive Income* is reclassified into earnings. After the transaction date, the forward contract or option contract is a hedge of an accounts receivable or accounts payable.

SPECULATIVE FOREIGN CURRENCY CONTRACTS

Speculative foreign currency contract: agreement to buy or sell foreign currency in the future at a known price when there is no underlying transaction, commitment to a future transaction, or forecasted future transaction

Speculation in the foreign currency market results in a special type of investment that is adjusted when changes in the underlying value of the contract occur. A **speculative foreign currency contract** exists when an entity enters into an agreement to buy or sell foreign currency in the future at a known price when there is no underlying transaction, commitment to a future transaction, or forecasted future transaction. As with hedging, speculative contracts can take many forms, but the most common are forward contracts and option contracts. Some of the unique features of accounting for speculative contracts are presented in the discussion of the following forward contract example.

Driskell Enterprises (a U.S.-based entity) has been involved in a number of foreign currency transactions recently. Some of the financial managers, as a result of their expertise in the foreign currency markets, have determined that the entity should speculate in exchange rate movement of foreign currency as one form of investment. The managers have obtained approval from their supervisors and have investigated the currency markets. As a result of this investigation, the managers determine that the forward exchange rate for the Japanese yen is low. The managers are cautious in their first endeavor into this market and propose on September 1 that Driskell purchase 12,500,000 yen for delivery on February 28 of the following year. Driskell's financial statements are prepared on December 31. The applicable exchange rates are presented below.

Date	February 28 Forward Rate	Forward Contract Fair Value
September 1	$.0102	$0
December 31	$.0095	($8,750)
February 28	$.0103	$1,250

Speculation Initiation Date   Consistent with the accounting treatment for the initiation of other forward contracts, a journal entry is not needed at the initiation of the speculative forward contract because the contract's fair value is $0.

Balance Sheet Date   At the balance sheet date, the *Foreign Currency Forward Contract* is revalued to its December 31 fair value. The entry required at the balance sheet date is the following.

Journal Entry—Driskell Enterprise Books

Dec. 31	Foreign Currency Losses and Gains	8,750	
	Foreign Currency Forward Contract		8,750

To recognize the change in the *Foreign Currency Forward Contract*'s fair value from $0 to a liability of $8,750.

This recognition is consistent with the accounting for other forms of foreign currency derivatives discussed previously. The financial statements should represent the value of the investment, that is, the value of the contract as of the balance sheet date. The fair value of the contract is based on the change in the forward rate with a February 28 maturity date [($.0095 − $.0102) × 12,500,000 yen)].

Settlement Date   On the date the contract matures, the forward and the spot exchange rates become the same, resulting in the following entries.

Journal Entry—Driskell Enterprise Books

Feb. 28	Foreign Currency Forward Contract	10,000	
	Foreign Currency Exchange Losses and Gains		10,000

To recognize the change in the *Foreign Currency Forward Contract*'s fair value from a liability of $8,750 to an asset of $1,250.

	Cash	1,250	
	Foreign Currency Forward Contract ($8,750 − $7,500)		1,250

To record the exchange of currency with the exchange broker and the closing of the *Foreign Currency Forward Contract.*

The first entry recognizes the change in the forward contract's fair value. The increase in the exchange rate from $.0095 to $.0103 makes Driskell's contract to purchase Japanese yen for $.0102 worth $1,250. The second entry records the exchange of currencies between Driskell and the exchange broker and the closing of the forward contract.

The above set of transactions were based on two simplifying assumptions: (1) that Driskell held the speculative contract until the maturity date and (2) that Driskell did not take possession of the 12,500,000 yen. With regard to the first assumption, it is possible that the exchange loss suffered by Driskell between September 1 and December 31 would convince management that Driskell should not be speculating in these currencies. To protect the entity from further losses, Driskell could enter into a 60-day forward contract to sell 12,500,000 yen. The second contract would permit any future gains and losses on one contract to be offset by losses and gains on the other contract. With regard to the second assumption, speculative contracts are often settled by a net flow of cash. The entity with the gain collects the amount of the gain from the entity with the loss. In reality, entities entering into a speculative contract often do not want to take possession of the currency because it would incur costs involved in converting the foreign currency into the domestic currency.

There are times when a currency speculation is a direct result of hedging. When a company hedges with an option contract, a portion of that contract may be speculative if the fixed option contract size is not the same as the receivable or payable being hedged. The number of foreign currency units needed to settle a purchase or sale transaction may be in any amount; however, option contracts in foreign currencies exist only in certain sizes. This often requires the manager to decide whether to buy an option contract that is smaller than the amount of the exposed asset or liability or larger than the exposed asset or liability. If the option contract is smaller than the foreign currency exposure, the firm retains some of the exchange rate fluctuation risk. On the other hand, if the option contract is larger than the foreign currency exposure, the firm enters into a speculative contract for the amount greater than the exposure, again subjecting the entity to the exchange rate fluctuation risk.[10]

STATEMENT OF CASH FLOWS

Foreign currency transactions have a direct impact on an entity's cash flow and income statement. This impact may not be noticed when the direct method is used to prepare the

---

[10] In practice a gain or loss on the amount of a forward contract in excess of the related commitment may be deferred if the excess amount of the contract adjusts the hedge to an after-tax basis. Otherwise no deferral related to an excess contract amount is permitted.

Statement of Cash Flows because the cash flows for such transactions as sales and inventory purchases are based on the spot rate at the date of the sale or purchase, not the ultimate cash flow. To the extent the exchange rate fluctuates, the operating section of the Statement of Cash Flows would be misstated. This would be noticed if the indirect method is used to prepare the Statement of Cash Flows because the exchange gain or loss is a non-cash item that would be included in the Income Statement; however, separating the exchange losses and gains among operating, investing, and financing activities may not be cost-effective. The FASB requires a separate reconciling item for "the effect of exchange rate changes"[11] to be included in the net increase (decrease) in cash on the Statement of Cash Flows.

INTERPERIOD INCOME TAXES

The Income Statement reflects accrual-based recognition of foreign currency exchange losses and gains, while the IRS requires the loss or gain to be determined in the period the currencies are exchanged. To the extent an entity has foreign currency receivables and payables at the balance sheet date, it will have to determine the deferred income tax impact of the difference between accrual accounting and IRS regulations.

SUMMARY

This chapter examined the accounting for various types of transactions between U.S.-based companies and companies whose transactions are conducted in foreign currencies. Specifically, purchase and sale transactions denominated in a foreign currency were the focus of the discussion because of the risk inherent in holding receivables and payables that will be settled in a foreign currency. The source of the risk is in the potential for an unfavorable shift in the exchange rate between any foreign currency and the U.S. dollar.

First, the accounting for basic economic transactions that give rise to foreign currency receivables and payables were presented. The resulting receivable or payable balance will change if the exchange rate changes over time. Accounting for the purchase and sale transactions as well as the recording of gains and losses resulting from exchange rate fluctuations that occur over time were illustrated.

Next, the concept of hedging was introduced. Hedging occurs when a company enters into a contract to buy or sell units of a foreign currency to alleviate the risk of holding foreign receivables and payables. Hedging can be accomplished by entering into either forward or option contracts. Accounting methodologies were presented for forward and option contracts in general, the gains and losses associated with forward and option contracts, and the settling of receivables and payables when forward and option contracts exist.

Some companies enter into hedging contracts prior to the actual purchase or sale transaction that places the company at risk. When a company has a purchase or sale commitment or has a forecasted transaction, the company may choose to protect itself immediately by entering into a forward or option contract. Thus, the forward or option contract may come into existence prior to the consummation of the underlying purchase or sale. In these cases the accounting differs from the previously discussed situations (when the transaction and the hedge occurred at the same date). Accounting for these circumstance was discussed and illustrated.

Finally, the purchase of currency contracts for purely speculative purposes was discussed. Again, such contracts may be in the form of forward contracts or option contracts. For the contract to be classified as speculative, there is no underlying purchase or sale that has exchange risk. Therefore, a new risk position is created rather than hedging an existing or anticipated risk position. Accounting requirements for speculative foreign currency contracts and the recognition of related gains and losses completed the chapter coverage.

---

[11] **Statement of Financial Accounting Standards (FAS)**, No. 95, "Statement of Cash Flows" (Stamford, CT: Financial Accounting Standards Board, 1987), par. 101.

QUESTIONS

5-1. What types of risk are encountered by a U.S. company when it conducts business with a foreign company?

5-2. Sally, Richard, and Beth are division managers in a medium-sized consumer goods company. While the three were discussing senior management's decision to expand sales into Canada, Sally expressed concern that the expansion would make the division's income more volatile because of foreign currency transactions. The division's income is an issue because two-thirds of each manager's salary is based on divisional profits. Richard said that he was not concerned because the company could require all the sales to be made in U.S. dollars. Beth is not certain whether this is possible. Prepare a memo explaining how the currency to be exchanged is often determined.

5-3. Exchange rates between currencies may be fixed or may be established by market conditions. Why might the government of a country have more than one official exchange rate?

5-4. What are some factors that determine the market exchange rates among currencies?

5-5. Jennifer Black recently starting working in the treasurer's department of a large multinational corporation. One day she attended a meeting where changing interest rates were discussed. The treasurer said that if British interest rates continued to increase, she would have to make some significant changes in the company's investment position before the value of the pound increased too much. Jennifer has asked you for an explanation of why changes in British interest rates are related to changes in the value of the pound. Prepare a memo explaining this relationship to Jennifer.

5-6. George Stringfeld, the newly hired controller of your company, had never been involved with foreign sales before accepting this position. Shortly after arriving, he approached you with the following: "I understand that exchange gains and losses have to be recorded over time when we experience exchange rate fluctuations that affect our receivables from foreign customers. What I'm not sure about is the justification for the value assigned to the receivable initially—when the sale is booked. That value assignment is important because it not only affects the subsequent gains or losses due to exchange rate fluctuations but also impacts the recorded value of our Sales account. Would you research the basic issue and provide me with some authoritative support for booking these transactions using the spot rate at the date we record the transaction?" Write a brief memo to Mr. Stringfeld explaining the issue. (*Hint:* Search FASB Concepts Statement No. 1 for guidance on initial valuation of transactions using exchange prices.)

5-7. How are exchange rates related to a country's balance of payments?

5-8. Why is the initial recording of a purchase denominated in a foreign currency the same no matter when the foreign currency transaction will be settled?

5-9. The spot rate is used to recognize a transaction in the financial records of a company when a foreign currency is going to be exchanged at a future date. This is in part because conceptually the two-transaction approach has been adopted as the basis for accounting for foreign exchange transactions. What authoritative support is provided by the FASB to support the use of this approach? (*Hint:* Search FASB Statement No. 52.)

5-10. Why are receivables/payables denominated in a foreign currency revalued at the balance sheet date while receivables/payables denominated in U.S. dollars are not revalued?

5-11. Jerry St. Angelo is a new manager in the treasurer's department. He had not worked with foreign currency transactions prior to his recent promotion. One item that has confused Jerry is exchange gains and losses that result from the revaluation of foreign currency receivables/payables. He has asked why the company recognizes a gain/loss on the payment of a debt. Prepare a memo clarifying Jerry's misunderstanding.

5-12. Why would someone choose not to hedge a foreign currency transaction?

5-13. Springboard Enterprises recently starting making sales to wholesalers in Asia. As a result, the company is exposed to foreign currency exchange fluctuations. Richard, a new assistant to the CFO, has never been involved in managing foreign currency exchange risk. He has heard the term *hedging* but is not certain what it means. Prepare a brief memo explaining the term.

5-14. What is the difference between a spot rate and a forward rate with regard to foreign currencies?

5-15. Why would someone want to enter into a forward contract to exchange currencies at a future date?

5-16. What is the difference between the hedge of a foreign currency purchase or sale and the hedge of a foreign currency purchase or sale commitment?

5-17. Why is there often no cash payment made to an exchange broker when a forward contract is initiated?

5-18. Debbie Anderson is a new member of the controller's staff. She attended a meeting where forward contracts and option contracts were discussed. One manager commented that he prefers to hedge with option contracts because the option holder controls whether the currencies are exchanged. Debbie has asked you to clarify what the manager meant. How do you respond?

5-19. Regarding foreign currency option contracts, what is meant by the phrase *in the money?*

5-20. The change in the fair value of a financial instrument used to hedge a foreign currency commitment does not have a net effect on the income statement. Why?

5-21. Why can a forward contract's fair value be an asset or liability but an option contract's fair value can only be an asset?

5-22. You are conducting a training seminar for new managers. The most recent session was about how hedging is used to control foreign currency exchange rate risk. The following question has been posed: "Why is the recognition of gains and losses on hedges of forecasted transactions different from hedges of foreign currency commitments? Both types of hedges exist because of transactions that have not yet occurred." How do you respond?

5-23. How are changes in exchange rates eventually recognized on the income statement when there is a hedge of a forecasted transaction? Provide authoritative support. (*Hint:* Search FASB Statement No. 52.)

5-24. When does a forward or option contract qualify as a speculative contract?

MULTIPLE CHOICE

5-1. Richie Corporation sold merchandise to Sanchez Company for 300,000 Mexican pesos when the exchange rate was 1 peso = $.102. Mexican pesos were received when the exchange rate was 1 peso = $.105. What is the dollar amount of debit to cash at the date of collection?

  a. $31,500
  b. $2,857,143
  c. $30,600
  d. $2,941,176

5-2. Quest Industries purchased inventory for 130,000 Canadian dollars when the exchange rate was 1 Canadian dollar = $.62. The exchange rates on the balance sheet date and the payment date were 1 Canadian dollar = $.64 and $.65, respectively. What is the amount of the gain or loss recognized on the balance sheet date?

  a. $3,900 gain
  b. $3,900 loss
  c. $2,600 gain
  d. $2,600 loss

5-3. KRL sells product to Frankfort Company for 150,000 euros. KRL entered into a forward contract hedge at the date of the sale. The spot rate and the forward contract fair value at the date of the transaction, balance sheet date, and settlement date are presented in the following table:

	Spot Rate	Forward Contract Fair Value
Transaction date	$.86	$0
Balance sheet date	$.89	($6,000)
Settlement date	$.85	$1,500

What is the amount of gain or loss recognized on the balance sheet date with regard to the Accounts Receivable and the Forward Contract, respectively?

  a. $4,500 loss; $6,000 loss
  b. $4,500 gain; $6,000 gain
  c. $4,500 gain; $6,000 loss
  d. $4,500 loss; $6,000 gain

5-4. Southern Company acquired inventory for 125,000 Swiss francs when the exchange rate was 1 Swiss franc = $.60. Southern paid a $3,100 premium to purchase a call option for 100,000 Swiss francs with a strike price of $.58. At the balance sheet date, the spot rate was $.63 and the option contract fair value was $7,000. At the settlement date, the spot rate was $.61 and the option contract fair value was $1,250. What is the amount recorded for the option contract at the date the contract is initiated?

  a. $0
  b. $3,900
  c. $3,100
  d. $5,750

5-5. Wilson Incorporated entered into an agreement on January 15 to purchase 50,000 British pounds of material to be used in its manufacturing operations. The material is to be delivered on March 31. Payment is scheduled for April 30. At the date the order is placed, Wilson enters into a forward contract hedge. The spot rate and forward contract fair value on the transaction date, balance sheet date, and settlement date are provided below:

	Spot Rate	Forward Contract Fair Value
Commitment initiated	$1.35	$0
Transaction date	$1.38	$1,000
Balance Sheet date	$1.41	$1,300
Settlement date	$1.43	$2,500

What is the carrying value of the inventory account at the transaction date?

a. $70,000

b. $68,000

c. $69,000

d. $68,500

5-6. Trailblazer Company enters into a 4,800,000 yen sales agreement whereby it will deliver 50 motorcycles to a Japanese company in 90 days. At the commitment date (when the spot rate is 1 Japanese yen = $.0080), Trailblazer pays an option writer $7,200 for a put option with a strike price of $.0085 per yen. At the balance sheet date, the spot rate is $.0083 and the option contract fair value is $3,400. At the transaction date, the spot rate is $.0087 and the option contract fair value is $0. What is the amount of gain or loss recognized on the sales commitment at the balance sheet date?

a. $3,800 gain

b. $3,800 loss

c. $3,400 gain

d. $3,400 loss

5-7. Miller Company has made sales to Jeannie Corporation of France for many years. Miller forecasts that sales valued at 100,000 euros will be made in the upcoming period and enters into a forward contract hedge of the forecasted sales. The spot rate at the hedge initiation date is 1 euro = $.90. The sales occur when the spot rate is 1 euro = $.93 and the forward contract has a value of ($3,000). What is the amount of sales recognized after accounting for the transaction and the hedge?

a. $93,000

b. $96,000

c. $87,000

d. $90,000

5-8. Becker Incorporated has purchased inventory from Jensen Manufacturing for many years. Forecasted purchases for the next period will total 250,000 Australian dollars. Becker pays an option writer $6,500 to enter into a call option to purchase 250,000 Australian dollars. At the balance sheet date and the transaction date, the option contract is valued at $3,600 and $4,200, respectively. What is the balance in the Other Comprehensive Income account at the transaction date?

a. $600

b. $4,200

c. $6,500

d. $2,300

5-9. Northward Enterprises has entered into a speculative foreign currency forward contract to purchase 100,000 Canadian dollars. The Canadian dollar spot rate and forward contract fair value on the date the contract is created is $.60 and $0, respectively. At the balance sheet date, the spot rate and forward contract fair value are $.63 and $2,000, respectively. At the date the contract matures, the spot rate is $.61 and the forward contract fair value is $500. What is the amount of gain or loss recognized on the forward contract at the balance sheet date?

a. $3,000 gain

b. $3,000 loss

c. $2,000 gain

d. $2,000 loss

5-10. CEN Corporation pays $8,000 to purchase a speculative call option contract to purchase 93,750 British pounds at a strike price of $1.46 when the spot rate is $1.50. At the balance sheet date, the spot rate and option contract fair values are $1.52 and $8,500, respectively. At the transaction date, the spot rate and option contract fair values are $1.54 and $7,500, respectively. What is the amount of Cash that CEN pays if it takes delivery of the British pounds?

a. $144,375

b. $136,875

c. $142,500

d. $140,625

EXERCISES

EXERCISE 5-1	Inventory purchase, paid when inventory is received
EXERCISE 5-2	Sale, collection when product is delivered
EXERCISE 5-3	Inventory purchase with delayed payment, no hedge, no balance sheet date
EXERCISE 5-4	Sale with delayed collection, no hedge, no balance sheet date
EXERCISE 5-5	Equipment purchase with delayed payment, no hedge, balance sheet date
EXERCISE 5-6	Sale with delayed collection, no hedge, balance sheet date
EXERCISE 5-7	Purchase with delayed payment, forward contract hedge, no balance sheet date
EXERCISE 5-8	Sale with delayed collection, option hedge, no balance sheet date
EXERCISE 5-9	Sale with delayed collection, forward contract hedge, balance sheet date
EXERCISE 5-10	Purchase with delayed payment, option hedge, balance sheet date
EXERCISE 5-11	Foreign currency purchase commitment, forward contract hedge, no balance sheet date, payment on delivery

EXERCISE 5-1
Graphics Enterprises is a processor of negatives and pictures. The firm maintains inventory records using the perpetual method. One inventory item, a chemical used for its development process, is purchased from a Mexican supplier. The agreement with the supplier is that chemicals will be shipped via overnight delivery and Graphics Enterprises will wire payment in pesos the same day the inventory arrives. Chemicals costing 100,000 pesos are received on September 18, and payment is wired the same day. The exchange rate for the Mexican peso on September 18, 2005 is 1 peso = $.1032.

Required:
Record the purchase of the inventory.

EXERCISE 5-2
Computers Made Basic is an assembler of components into personal computers. The firm has an agreement to sell 50 computers to Canada Rail and Freight for a special price of 1,500 Canadian dollars each. This special price was to be granted only if Canada Rail and Freight picked up the computers and paid for the them at the time of delivery. A representative for Canada Rail and Freight paid for the computers and took possession of them on March 3, 2005. The exchange rate on March 3 is 1 Canadian dollar = $.88.

Required:
Record the sales transaction.

EXERCISE 5-3
Miami Import purchases South American sculptures for resale. The firm has recently acquired a new line of items from a Brazilian firm in Rio de Janeiro. The inventory arrived on June 15 with an invoice requiring payment by August 15. Miami Import decided to not hedge the 5,000,000 cruzeiro obligation, and financial statements are prepared annually on December 31. The exchange rates on June 15 and August 15 are 1 cruzeiro = $.00134 and $.00137, respectively.

Required:
Make all journal entries applicable to these circumstances.

EXERCISE 5-4
Dallas Instruments sells electronics components around the world. Inventory was shipped to a French computer manufacturer FOB shipping point on May 1, 2005. The inventory arrived at the French company on May 15, 2005, along with the invoice for 1,500,000 euros. Payment is due on or before June 30, 2005. Payment is received on June 28. The exchange rates on May 1, May 15, and June 28 are 1 euro = $.883, $.881, and $.88, respectively. Dallas Instruments prepares quarterly financial statements on March 31, June 30, September 30, and December 31.

Required:
Prepare all journal entries relating to this sale.

EXERCISE 5-5
Timepiece, Incorporated, a domestic watch manufacturer, purchases much of its equipment from various Swiss machine companies. Timepiece purchased a new precision machine from one of these machine companies at a cost of 250,000 Swiss francs on November 1. Payment is due on February

28. Timepiece prepares financial statements on December 31. The spot rates on November 1, December 31, and February 28 are 1 Swiss franc = $.7035, $.7018, and $.7024, respectively.

Required:
Prepare the journal entries on the books of Timepiece for these events.

EXERCISE 5-6

Pioneer Products sells computer disks in most parts of the western hemisphere. Pioneer recently entered a new market in Chile. As a result of entering this new market, Pioneer shipped a complete line of products to the retailer on October 1, 2005, along with a bill for 10,000,000 pesos. Payment for the inventory is due by December 31. Payment is received on December 20, 2005. Financial statements are prepared on October 31. The spot exchange rates on October 1, October 31, and December 20 are 1 Chilean peso = $.002821, $.00283, and $.002826, respectively.

Required:
Record all the necessary entries related to this sale.

EXERCISE 5-7

Weston Lamps, a small manufacturer of wood-base lamps, purchases much of its lumber from a Canadian sawmill. Lumber was delivered on September 15. A bill for 15,000 Canadian dollars arrived at the same time. Payment for the lumber is required by November 15. Weston enters into a forward contract to protect itself against exchange rate fluctuations. Weston prepares financial statements on June 30 and December 31. The spot and forward exchange rates on September 15 are 1 Canadian dollar = $.88 and $.8684, respectively. The spot rate on November 15 is 1 Canadian dollar = $.886.

Required:
Record the purchase, forward contract hedge, and subsequent cash flows.

EXERCISE 5-8

Fiber Optics, Inc. manufactures and sells fiber-optic cable for use in high-speed data transmission lines. A large sale is made to the national telephone company of Australia. The cable is delivered on November 1 and receipt of 350,000 Australian dollars is expected by December 15. Fiber Optics immediately purchases put options totaling 350,000 Australian dollars and pays a $750 premium. The strike price for the December option is $.54. The spot rates on November 1 and December 15 are 1 Australian dollar = $.52 and $.51, respectively. Fiber Optics prepares financial statements on December 31.

Required:
Prepare the journal entries for the sale, put option acquisition, and subsequent cash flows.

EXERCISE 5-9

Midwest Agricultural Co-op sells wheat to the Saudi government for 6,500,000 riyals on November 1 with payment due by February 1. The wheat is to be transported FOB shipping point. Midwest Agricultural has a policy of hedging all foreign currency transactions and therefore enters into a forward exchange contract on November 1 to sell riyals for delivery on February 1. Midwest Agricultural prepares financial statements on December 31. The spot rates on November 1, December 31, and February 1 are 1 riyal = $.26663, $.2662, and $.2657, respectively. The forward exchange rate on November 1 for February 1 delivery is 1 riyal = $ .267. The forward contract's fair values on December 31 and February 1 are $2,600 and $8,450, respectively.

Required:
Prepare all necessary journal entries on the books of Midwest Agricultural Co-op with regard to this set of transactions.

EXERCISE 5-10

Cascade Agriculture buys and sells animal feed. Cascade recently started purchasing cattle feed from suppliers in Brazil. A shipment costing 500,000 Brazilian reals is delivered on May 10. Payment is due by July 10. Cascade purchases a July call option with a strike price of $.45 on May 10, when the spot rate is $.47. Cascade paid a $13,750 premium for the call option. On June 30, a financial statement date, the spot rate is 1 real = $.458 and the option's fair value is $5,200. The spot rate on July 10 is $.463 and the option's fair value is $6,500.

Required:
Record the purchase, call option purchase, balance sheet date adjustments, and subsequent cash flows.

EXERCISE 5-11   TPC makes rubber gaskets for sale to various manufacturing firms. TPC must place orders for rubber far in advance of the date needed because there is a shortage of rubber. On July 1, 2005, TPC orders rubber valued at 1,000,000,000 rupiahs from its main Indonesian supplier. The rubber is to be delivered by November 1 and payment is due immediately. The rupiah has been a volatile currency, and TPC decides to hedge the commitment to make the acquisition. A forward contract is initiated on July 1 requiring the exchange broker to deliver 1,000,000,000 rupiahs on November 1. The November 1 forward exchange rate on July 1 is 1 rupiah = $.0005162. The spot rates on July 1 and November 1 are 1 rupiah = $.0005056 and $.0005243, respectively. TPC prepares financial statements semiannually on June 30 and December 31.

Required:
Prepare all necessary journal entries for the foreign currency commitment and the purchase.

EXERCISE 5-12   Richmond's Cushions manufactures seat cushions for use in commercial airplanes. One of its largest customers is Airbus, a French airplane manufacturer. Airbus orders seats when it begins manufacturing a new airplane, but the cushions are not to be delivered until they are needed, approximately three months after they are ordered. Richmond's received an order for 2,000 seat cushions on February 1. The order is priced at 80,000 euros. Delivery and payment are to take place on April 30. Richmond's immediately enters into a forward contract to hedge the contracted sale. Richmond's prepares financial statements on June 30 and December 31. The spot rates and fair values of the forward contract from February 1 through April 30 are as follows.

Date	Spot Rate	November 1 Forward Rate	Forward Contract Fair Value
February 1	$.925	$.916	$0
April 30	$.910	$.910	$480

Required:
Prepare the journal entries on Richmond's book to reflect the commitment and subsequent sale.

EXERCISE 5-13   Avery's Chemical Company produces specialized agricultural products. Some ingredients used in the manufacturing process are of limited supply, so Avery's must order them in advance of when needed. An order (250,000 Australian dollars) is placed on July 10. The chemicals are scheduled for delivery on September 18, and payment is due at time of delivery. Avery's has a policy of hedging this type of transaction. A call option with a $.57 strike price is initiated on July 10, and a $2,600 premium is paid. Spot rates and the fair values of the option contract as of July 10 and September 18 follow.

Date	Spot Rate	Option Contract Fair Value
July 10	$.56	$2,600
September 18	$.59	$5,000

Required:
Assuming that Avery's Chemical prepares financial statements on December 31, record all necessary journal entries from July 10 through September 18.

EXERCISE 5-14   Agricultural Commodities, Inc. represents a group of midwest wheat growers. The organization enters into sales agreements on the behalf of its members. A grain sale was negotiated on February 1 with the Kuwait government to sell excess grain held in the organization's storage facilities. Agricultural Commodities is to deliver the grain to the carrier on May 1. Payment of 375,000 dinars will be wired to Agricultural Commodities' bank as soon as the carrier takes possession. The organization has a policy of hedging all such transactions because of the unknown risk due to fluctuation of the value of foreign currencies. Accordingly, Agricultural Commodities pays $2,000 to purchase a put option on February 1 with a maturity date in May and a strike price of $3.500 per dinar. The spot rate for the dinar on February 1 is 1 dinar = $3.496. The spot rate on May 1 is 1 dinar = $3.568. Agricultural Commodities prepares financial statements on June 30 and December 31.

Required:

Prepare all necessary journal entries for the hedge of the foreign currency commitment and the subsequent sale of grain.

EXERCISE 5-15

Expensive Rentals placed an order on July 1 to buy 25 new Japanese cars for 80,000,000 Japanese yen. Delivery of the cars is scheduled for September 1 and payment will occur on November 1. Management enters into a foreign exchange (forward) contract on July 1 to buy 80,000,000 Japanese yen on November 1. Expensive Rentals prepares financial statements on December 31. The spot rates and fair values of the forward contract from July 1 through November 1 are as follows.

Date	Spot Rate	November 1 Forward Rate	Forward Contract Fair Value
July 1	$.0093	$.0090	$0
September 1	$.0089	$.0085	($40,000)
November 1	$.0086	$.0086	($32,000)

Required:

Prepare the journal entries on the books of Expensive Rentals to reflect the commitment and subsequent purchase transaction.

EXERCISE 5-16

Ma Bell Cable manufactures lines used to install cable television to homes. Sales personnel signed a contract to sell 300 miles of cable to a Canadian communications company for 26,000,000 Canadian dollars on March 15. The cable is to be delivered by July 15 and payment is due on September 1. Ma Bell immediately enters into a forward contract to hedge the contracted sale. Ma Bell prepares financial statements on December 31. The spot rates and fair values of the forward contract from March 15 through September 1 are as follows.

Date	Spot Rate	November 1 Forward Rate	Forward Contract Fair Value
March 15	$.642	$.670	$0
July 15	$.655	$.665	$130,000
September 1	$.662	$.662	$208,000

Required:

Prepare the journal entries on Ma Bell's book to reflect the commitment and subsequent sale.

EXERCISE 5-17

Reliable Computer Company sells network computers to businesses. The high demand for memory has resulted in higher prices and a long lead time for delivery. As a result, Reliable must order memory from its Japanese supplier several months before it is needed. An order (43,750,000 Japanese yen) is placed on May 17. The memory is scheduled for delivery on August 31 and payment is due on October 15. Reliable hedges this transaction by immediately initiating a call option with a $.0085 strike price. A premium of $23,000 is paid to the option writer. Spot rates and the fair values of the option contract from May 17 to October 15 follow:

Date	Spot Rate	Option Contract Fair Value
May 17	$.0090	$23,000
August 31	$.0082	$3,000
October 15	$.0089	$17,500

Required:

Assuming that Reliable prepares financial statements on December 31, record all necessary journal entries from May 17 through October 15.

EXERCISE 5-18   Bonnie's Jewelry Manufacturing designs and produces fine jewelry for special occasions. An order was received from the Canadian government on March 1 for pins to be distributed to Olympic athletes. The order is to be filled by August 1 and payment will occur on September 1. Because the total price of the order (600,000 Canadian dollars) is significant to Bonnie's Jewelry, management hedges the sale from March 1 through September 1 by purchasing a put option with a $.6700 strike price and paying a $7,000 premium. Spot rates and the fair values of the option contract from March 1 through September 1 follow.

Date	Spot Rate	Option Contract Fair Value
March 1	$.6620	$7,000
August 1	$.6645	$4,300
September 1	$.6648	$3,120

Required:
Assuming that Bonnie's Jewelry prepares financial statements on December 31, record all necessary journal entries from March 1 through September 1.

EXERCISE 5-19   Richardson Plumbing sells bathroom fixtures to customers performing renovations. A faucet that has been popular for many years is manufactured by a British company. Richardson is required to pay for the faucets in British pounds, while sales to customers are in U.S. dollars. Richardson's sales staff forecasted, on January 1, that purchases of this particular faucet will total approximately 5,000 British pounds in the first quarter of the year. The owners enter into a forward contract to acquire 5,000 British pounds to protect the company from fluctuations in the British pound's value. Faucets from this supplier were received and paid for on March 25. The relevant forward exchange rate on January 1 for the foreign currency forward contract is $1.46. The January 1 and March 25 spot rates are 1 British pound = $1.52 and $1.49, respectively.

Required:
A. Record the necessary journal entries for the foreign currency forward contract and the inventory purchase and payment.
B. Assume the inventory is not sold till April 15. In interim financial statements prepared on March 31, how is *Other Comprehensive Income* disclosed?
C. What happens to the *Other Comprehensive Income* balance when the inventory is sold?

EXERCISE 5-20   Very Thin Wafers makes silicone wafers for use by the computer industry. For the last five years, Very Thin has made large sales to a Japanese manufacturer (1,250,000,000 yen) every six months. Very Thin's management is certain that sales to the Japanese company will continue. On January 1, Very Thin pays $75,000 to purchase a put option with a strike price of $.009 to hedge the forecasted sales for the next six months. On June 20, the Japanese manufacturer purchases the forecasted amount. The Japanese company pays for the wafers at the time of sale. The spot rate for the Japanese yen on June 20 is $.0088. Very Thin prepares financial statements semiannually, with a December 31 year-end.

Required:
Prepare the journal entries for the hedge and the sales transaction.

EXERCISE 5-21   Johnston and Johnston manufactures and sells baby powder. Its primary source of talc, the main ingredient in baby powder, is in Australia. At the January planning meeting, management forecasts that 500,000 Australian dollars of talc will be purchased at the end of February. The company enters into a forward contract on January 10 to purchase 500,000 Australian dollars on March 15. As forecasted, 500,000 Australian dollars of talc is purchased on February 28 and payment is wired to the supplier on March 15. The relevant spot rates and forward contract fair values are presented below.

Date	Spot Rate	March 15 Forward Rate	Forward Contract Fair Value
January 10	$.5480	$.5370	$0
February 28	$.5375	$.5340	($1,500)
March 15	$.5350	$.5350	($1,000)

Required:
Record the necessary journal entries for the forward contract and the purchase and payment.

EXERCISE 5-22

Performance Tires manufactures tires for the automobile industry. The sales representatives have been particularly successful in working with one Japanese automaker. The July forecast for August sales to this automaker is 75,000 tires for 1,000,000,000 yen. Orders are typically received from this customer on the 20th of the month, with delivery in 10 days and payment 15 days subsequent to delivery. On July 10, management purchases a September put option with a $.0093 strike price for $325,000. Consistent with projections, an order valued at 1,000,000,000 yen is received from the customer on August 20. The tires are delivered on August 30, and payment is received on September 15. Performance prepares financial statements semiannually on June 30 and December 31. The following table presents relevant spot rates and option contract fair values.

Date	Spot Rate	Option Contract Fair Value
July 10	$.0090	$325,000
August 30	$.0092	$110,000
September 15	$.0089	$400,000

Required:
Prepare the journal entries for the option hedge and the subsequent sale.

EXERCISE 5-23

Persian Imports, a Persian rug dealer, has observed that the exchange rate for the Turkish lira is near a 10-year low against the dollar. In an effort to increase profits, the managers of Persian Imports have decided that the firm should speculate in the Turkish currency. Persian Imports, on May 1, entered into a forward contract to purchase 250,000,000 Turkish lira for delivery on November 1. Persian Imports prepares financial statements on December 31. The relevant forward exchange rates and the forward contract fair values are provided below.

Date	November 1 Forward Rate	Forward Contract Fair Value
May 1	$.0002026	$0
November 1	$.0002058	$800

Required:
Record all entries related to the speculative contract.

EXERCISE 5-24

Richard Geswein is the owner of a business located near the Mexican border. He has seen the value of the Mexican peso fluctuate for many years, and he believes he understands why its value changes. Richard decides to trade on his knowledge, purchasing a call option for 100,000 Mexican pesos with a strike price of $.0985 on May 31. Richard pays a premium of $125, and the option matures on August 31. Richard's company prepares financial statements on June 30. Below are the spot rates and forward contract fair values for the period from May 31 through August 31.

Date	Spot Rate	Option Contract Fair Value
May 31	$.0995	$125
June 30	$.1015	$325
August 31	$.0993	$80

Required:
Record all entries related to the speculative contract.

PROBLEMS

PROBLEM 5-1

On May 1, Chipper Enterprises, a manufacturer of heavy-duty wood chippers, accepted a special order from a Canadian logging firm for 300 wood chippers. Chipper negotiated a price of 2,500 Canadian dollars for each chipper, with delivery due on August 1 and payment due at time of delivery. The size of the order causes Chipper Enterprises to hedge the commitment by initiating a forward contract on May 1 to sell Canadian dollars for delivery on August 1. Chipper prepares financial statements on June 30 and December 31. The relevant spot rates and forward contract fair values are provided below.

Date	Spot Rate	August 1 Forward Rate	Forward Contract Fair Value
May 1	$.6749	$.6800	$0
June 30	$.6702	$.6780	$1,500
August 1	$.6860	$.6860	($4,500)

Required:
Prepare the journal entries on the books of Chipper Enterprises to reflect the commitment and subsequent sales transaction.

PROBLEM 5-2

International Press, a large publishing company, entered into a contract to purchase new equipment costing 500,000 euros from Heidelberg Press on September 1, 2005. The state-of-the-art equipment is only produced to meet demand. As a result, delivery will not occur until six months after the order is placed. Heidelberg is to deliver the equipment by February 28, 2006, and payment is to be wired to Heidelberg as soon as the equipment is received. Because exchange rates have been fluctuating wildly, International Press decided to hedge this obligation beginning on September 1. A February call option is acquired with a strike price of $.9100. Relevant spot rates and option contract fair values are presented below.

Date	Spot Rate	Option Contract Fair Value
September 1	$.8600	$4,000
December 31	$.9389	$17,000
February 28	$.9125	$1,250

Required:
Prepare all needed journal entries on the books of International Press for the period beginning September 1, 2005, and ending February 28, 2006. International Press prepares financial statements on June 30 and December 31.

PROBLEM 5-3   Precision Manufacturing makes high-quality valves for use in U.S. Navy ships. An important part of the manufacturing process is the application of a special compound that extends the valve's life when used in saltwater systems. The compound is manufactured only by a company in Britain. Because demand for the compound is high relative to the supply, Precision has to place orders far in advance of when the compound is needed. On August 31, Precision orders 50,000 kilograms of the material for 20 British pounds per kilogram. The compound will be delivered on December 1, and payment is due on February 1. On August 31 Precision initiates a forward contract to purchase British pounds on February 1 for $1.60 each. The following table presents the spot and forward rates and the forward contract fair values from August 31 until February 1. Precision prepares quarterly financial statements, with a December 31 balance sheet date.

Date	Spot Rate	February 1 Forward Rate	Forward Contract Fair Value
August 31	$1.670	$1.60	$0
September 30	$1.654	$1.64	$40,000
December 1	$1.700	$1.72	$120,000
December 31	$1.682	$1.69	$90,000
February 1	$1.620	$1.62	$20,000

Required:
Prepare the journal entries necessary on August 31, September 30, December 1, December 31, and February 1.

PROBLEM 5-4   High Flying Airline Manufacturing builds planes for passenger airlines. Contract negotiation with Australian Airlines ended on March 1 with an agreement whereby Australian Airlines will purchase a new aircraft from High Flying for 30,000,000 Australian dollars. Management believes it will take approximately three months to assemble the airplane and deliver it to Australian Airlines. Payment for the aircraft is scheduled to occur two months after delivery. High Flying pays a premium of $1,120,000 to purchase a 30,000,000 Australian dollar put option with a strike price of $.56 to hedge from the date of commitment until the payment date. Financial statements are prepared quarterly, and the fiscal year ends on December 31. The following table presents the spot rates and option contract fair values for the relevant time period.

Date	Spot Rate	Option Contract Fair Value
March 1	$.5240	$1,120,000
March 31	$.5245	$1,080,000
June 1	$.5400	$630,000
June 30	$.5350	$760,000
August 1	$.5570	$90,000

Required:
Record all necessary journal entries for March 1, March 31, May 1, June 30, and August 1.

PROBLEM 5-5   Hewitt Company sells bicycle frames to major bicycle manufacturers. The business is seasonal, with most bicycle frame sales occurring in early spring to allow bicycles to be manufactured and delivered to dealers for summer sales. One of Hewitt's major customers is located in Mexico. Management forecasts that sales to this customer will continue to be approximately 3,000,000 pesos every April. On January 1, Hewitt establishes a foreign currency forward contract to deliver 3,000,000 pesos. Consistent with the forecast, Hewitt ships the frames and collects 3,000,000 pesos on April 30. Hewitt prepares financial statements quarterly, with a December 31 year-end. Relevant spot rates and forward contract fair values are as follows.

Date	Spot Rate	April 30 Forward Rate	Forward Contract Fair Value
January 1	$.0950	$.0990	$0
March 31	$.0975	$.1010	($6,000)
April 30	$.0980	$.0980	$3,000

Required:

Prepare the journal entries for the forward contract and the related sales transaction.

PROBLEM 5-6 Cruising Cars is a U.S. company that manufactures high-performance automobiles. Many of the company's raw materials are purchased in Europe. As a result, the company has a large exposure to foreign exchange fluctuation risk with regard to the euro. At the December planning meeting, management forecasts that purchases of tires from a German supplier will be 312,500 euros in February. On December 15, Cruising Cars' treasurer purchases a February call option with a strike price of $.89. The tires are delivered and payment is made on February 26. Cruising Tires prepares financial statements quarterly, with a December 31 balance sheet date. The following table presents the spot rates and option contract fair values for December 15 through February 26.

Date	Spot Rate	Option Contract Fair Value
December 15	$.9000	$5,000
December 31	$.9080	$6,000
February 26	$.9240	$10,625

Required:

Prepare the journal entries for the hedge and the subsequent purchase.

PROBLEM 5-7 Swell Computers assembles computers for sale to individual customers. While some components are purchased from bids submitted, RAM is always purchased from the same Japanese supplier. On September 26, management forecasts that RAM purchases during the fourth quarter will amount to 112,500,000 yen. Swell's treasurer immediately initiates a forward contract to deliver yen on February 8, the expected payment date. On November 20, Swell purchases the RAM, and payment is made on February 8. Swell prepares financial statements quarterly, with a December 31 balance sheet date. Relevant spot and forward rates and the forward contract fair values are presented below.

Date	Spot Rate	February 8 Forward Rate	Forward Contract Fair Value
September 26	$.0089	$.0087	$0
September 30	$.0088	$.0086	($11,250)
November 20	$.0091	$.0094	$78,750
December 31	$.0093	$.0092	$56,500
February 8	$.0090	$.0090	$33,750

Required:

Prepare the journal entries for the forecasted transaction hedge as well as the purchase and payment.

PROBLEM 5-8 Jacksonville Shipyards builds barges for many different companies. Recently negotiations have been underway to construct a grain barge that will be owned and operated by a British company. In January, management forecasts that the barge will be sold for 18,000,000 British pounds on May 31 and payment will occur by August 31. On January 20, Jacksonville's treasurer purchases an 18,000,000 British pound put option with an August maturity month. The option has a strike price of $1.470, and Jacksonville pays a premium of $65,000. Jacksonville prepares quarterly financial statements, and the balance sheet date is December 31. The following table provides the spot rates and the option contract fair values for the period from January 20 through August 31.

Date	Spot Rate	Option Contract Fair Value
Jan. 20	$1.486	$65,000
Mar. 31	$1.433	$916,000
May 31	$1.400	$1,413,000
June 30	$1.420	$1,000,000
Aug. 31	$1.463	$126,000

Required:
Assume that the dates provided above are the dates when the economic events occur. Prepare the journal entries for the forecasted transaction's hedge and the subsequent sale.

PROBLEM 5-9   Mid-America Manufacturers produces custom computer-operated equipment. Sales representatives travel to many different countries to meet with potential customers. One result of all the international travel is that management has become convinced that they understand how some currency values fluctuate. In an effort to profit on this knowledge, Mid-America pays an option writer a $500 premium on October 5 to acquire a call option for 250,000 Australian dollars at $.53 strike price and a maturity on December 31. Mid-America prepares financial statements on December 31. The spot rates and option contract fair values for the period from October 5 to December 31 follow.

Date	Spot Rate	Option Contract Fair Value
October 5	$.52	$500
December 31	$.51	$0

Required:
Prepare the journal entries from October 5 through December 31.

PROBLEM 5-10   PSC Corporation manufactures and distributes consumer products worldwide. The treasurer's department has noticed that the exchange rate of the Swiss franc is unusually high compared to historical rates. In a move to take advantage of this situation, PCS enters into a forward contract on July 1 to sell 100,000 francs for delivery on December 1. PCS prepares financial statements on February 28 and August 31. The following table presents the forward rates and the forward contract fair values from July 1 to December 1.

Date	November 1 Forward Rate	Forward Contract Fair Value
July 1	$.6019	$0
August 31	$.6101	($820)
December 1	$.5991	$280

Required:
Record all necessary journal entries for this speculative contract.

CHAPTER *6*

FOREIGN CURRENCY FINANCIAL STATEMENTS

LEARNING OBJECTIVES

After reading this chapter, you should be able to:

- Identify currencies relevant to a foreign investee.
- Determine which method to apply when converting a foreign currency trial balance into U.S. dollars.
- Convert a foreign currency trial balance into a U.S. dollar trial balance for a foreign investee.
- Prepare equity method journal entries for a foreign investee.
- Prepare the worksheet eliminations to consolidate a foreign investee and a U.S. parent.
- Prepare a consolidation worksheet for a foreign investee and a U.S. parent.

Multinational operations: operations that result from activities conducted outside of the country where an entity is headquartered

Multinational operations result from activities conducted outside of the country where an entity is headquartered. For example, a U.S. entity may sell all its product in the United States but may purchase some its component parts from manufacturers in Taiwan or Mexico. Another U.S. entity may manufacture all its products in the United States but have sales in Canada and Mexico. A third company may have manufacturing facilities located around the globe and sell products in most countries of the world. The operation of these entities is referred to as multinational operations.

Multinational operations may result from the importing or exporting of goods and services. Goods and services produced in the United States may be exported to foreign markets in a variety of ways, such as through an independent foreign distribution network, a foreign marketing branch of the U.S. entity, or a foreign subsidiary of the U.S. entity. An independent foreign distribution network exists when the product is sold to an independent foreign distributor. As a result of the sale, the U.S. entity relinquishes legal title of the product when it is sold to the distributor. The distributor is responsible for marketing the product and making final sales to foreign consumers. Foreign marketing operations exist when the U.S. entity establishes a branch office or a subsidiary to sell the entity's products to foreign consumers. Regardless whether a branch or a subsidiary is formed, the U.S. entity retains ownership of the products until the products are purchased by a foreign consumer. When a product is sold to a foreign distributor, the U.S. entity recognizes a sale on the consolidated income statement. When a product is distributed to a foreign branch or subsidiary, a sale is not recognized on the consolidated income statement because the product is still owned by the consolidated entity. A sale is recognized only when the foreign branch or subsidiary sells the product to an unrelated party.

Manufacturing a U.S. entity's products in a foreign facility can also occur in a variety of ways, including contracting with an independent foreign manufacturer, establishing a manufacturing plant in a foreign country, or having the product manufactured by a foreign subsidiary. Contracting with an independent foreign manufacturer is conceptually the same as contracting with an independent U.S. manufacturer, although some differences exist. The differences pertain to the risks of conducting business in a foreign country, such as currency fluctuation or management's lack of knowledge about the foreign manufacturer. For example, the U.S. entity's management may be unaware of the foreign manufacturer's record of product liability suits resulting from inferior production operations. Buying products from an independent foreign manufacturer results in the U.S. entity recognizing the purchase of inventory. This transaction may result in the payment of U.S. dollars to the foreign manufacturer or in the payment of a foreign currency, creating a **foreign currency transaction** and currency fluctuation risk.

Foreign currency transaction: a transaction in a currency other than the one in which the financial records are maintained

Establishing a foreign manufacturing facility (branch or subsidiary) provides the U.S. entity with greater control over the manufacturing operations; however, some of the same risks, such as currency fluctuations, still exist when conducting business in a foreign country. Additional risk also exists with regard to items such as political instability. Rapid change in the political leadership of a country may lead to expropriation of private assets when an industry is nationalized by a new government. This occurred in the late 1970s, when Iran nationalized the oil industry after a change in government.

If U.S. government negotiators succeed in reducing or eliminating tariffs and trade barriers, the volume of business activity across borders will continue to increase. Some of this increase will result from entities producing goods and services in their own countries and selling the output in foreign countries. On the other hand, increased investment in productive assets in foreign countries is also likely to occur. The following table indicates the dollar amount (in millions of dollars) of investments made by foreign entities in U.S. entities and by U.S. entities in foreign entities from 1990 to 2000.

Direct investments abroad by U.S. entities

1990	1995	1997	1998	1999	2000
616,655	885,506	1,067,436	1,196,765	1,327,954	1,445,177

Direct investments in the U.S. by foreign entities

1990	1995	1997	1998	1999	2000
505,346	680,066	823,126	912,187	1,094,439	1,369,505

Source: U.S. Census Bureau, *Statistical Abstract of the United States*, July 2002.

The focus of this chapter is U.S. entities that have a significant investment in a foreign entity. This type of investment may result in the U.S. investor reporting the investment using the equity method or it may result in the U.S. entity being the parent company and preparing consolidated financial statements. Regardless of whether the investor has significant influence or control over the investee, information provided by the investee is necessary to prepare the investor's financial statements. For the investor to prepare equity method journal entries and possibly consolidated financial statements, investee information usually has to be modified so that it complies with generally accepted accounting principles (GAAP) of the investor's country (assumed to be the United States in this chapter).

This chapter introduces the procedures necessary to convert a foreign entity's trial balance so it can be used to record journal entries on a U.S. investor's financial records and prepare consolidated financial statements for a U.S. parent company. The first section presents the objectives of current GAAP, including an explanation of important terminology. The next section presents the consolidation of a foreign subsidiary at the date of acquisition. The last two sections present the two methods used to convert foreign currency trial balances into U.S. dollars. These sections also illustrate the equity method journal entries under both methods and the worksheet eliminations necessary to consolidate a foreign subsidiary subsequent to the acquisition date.

OBJECTIVES OF STATEMENT OF FINANCIAL ACCOUNTING STANDARDS NO. 52

U.S. companies are required to consolidate all entities (including foreign entities) over which they have control. The ultimate goal of Statement of Financial Accounting Standards (SFAS) No. 52 is to establish standards for conversion of the U.S. based investor's account balances measured in foreign currencies into U.S. dollar equivalents to enable the investor to prepare journal entries and, if appropriate, consolidated financial statements. To accomplish this goal, the Financial Accounting Standards Board (FASB) stated two objectives:

  a. *Provide information that is generally compatible with the expected economic effects of a rate change on an enterprise's cash flows and equity, and*

  b. *Reflect in consolidated statements the financial results and relationships of the individual consolidated entities as measured in their functional currencies in conformity with U.S. generally accepted accounting principles.*[1]

Functional currency: the currency of the primary economic environment in which the entity operates

The **functional currency** of an entity is defined as "the currency of the primary economic environment in which the entity operates; normally, that is the currency of the environment in which an entity primarily generates and expends cash."[2]

---

[1] **Statement of Financial Accounting Standards (FAS),** No. 52, "Foreign Currency Translation" (Stamford, CT: Financial Accounting Standards Board, 1981), par. 4.

[2] Ibid., par. 5.

Some changes in exchange rates between currencies will have cash flow effects for the investor while other changes will not. For example, if a foreign subsidiary holds an investment in land throughout an accounting period, the investor will not experience a cash flow effect regardless of any exchange rate changes. The Board's position is that compatibility of information with regard to equity is achieved if changes in exchange rates result in comparable changes in equity. Similarly, compatibility with regard to cash flow is achieved if changes in exchange rates that would be reasonably expected to impact the cash flow in either the functional currency or the reporting currency of the U.S. entity (the U.S. dollar) appear on the income statement as gains or losses, while changes in the exchange rate with a remote chance of impacting cash flows are not reflected on the income statement.[3] This difference is the impetus for two different methods of converting the trial balance of foreign investees into U.S. dollars.

The second objective indicates that the Board believes the financial results and relationships that exist among the elements of the financial statements should be retained, to the extent possible, when the foreign entity's financial information is converted into the functional currency. The results and financial relationships referred to by the Board are such performance measures as reported income and cash flows. The functional currency of the foreign entity is the currency of the primary economic environment of the entity, and the financial relationships existing in the functional currency should be retained. Therefore, when the functional currency is the foreign currency, the conversion process should not restate the financial statement elements as if the foreign entity's operations were conducted in the reporting currency. However, in some instances the functional currency is the U.S. investor's reporting currency. In those instances, the conversion process should restate the foreign entity's trial balance as if the operations were conducted in U.S. dollars.

The second objective also states that the foreign financial information must be converted to conform with U.S. GAAP. This conversion process is undertaken to make the foreign entity's financial information conform to financial reporting requirements for inclusion in the reporting entity's financial records and consolidated financial statements. Modifying the financial information to conform to U.S. GAAP is required *before* the foreign financial information can be converted into U.S. dollars. For example, the financial accounting rules in some countries do not require the capitalization of leases; that is, all leases are operating leases. Leases that meet the requirements for capitalization in the United States would have to be capitalized on the foreign entity's trial balance to conform with U.S. GAAP. Then the foreign currency amounts would be converted into U.S. dollars. The examples in this chapter assume that all adjustments to conform with U.S. GAAP have been made on the foreign entity's trial balance.

RELEVANT CURRENCIES

The foreign entity's financial records are typically maintained in a currency different from the U.S. investor's reporting currency (U.S. dollar) and apply accounting principles other than U.S. GAAP. The foreign currency amounts must be converted into U.S. dollars to prepare equity method journal entries and possibly consolidated financial statements. Before converting the foreign entity's trial balance into U.S. dollars, the currencies relevant to the foreign entity must be determined.

[3] Ibid., par. 71.

Determining the Local, Foreign, Reporting, and Functional Currencies

Local currency: the currency of the country where the foreign entity is located

One relevant currency of a foreign entity is its **local currency**, the currency of the country where the foreign entity is located. Most entities headquartered in a given country will use the local currency of that country to maintain the entity's financial records. For example, the local currency of a Brazilian subsidiary is typically the Brazilian real.

Reporting currency: the currency used by the parent company to prepare the consolidated financial statements

The manner in which the financial information of the foreign entity is incorporated into the U.S. investor's financial records and consolidated financial statements, when applicable, depends on the functional currency, the currency of the entity's primary economic environment. The functional currency may be the local currency of the foreign entity, the investor's **reporting currency**, or some other **foreign currency**. The reporting currency is the currency used by the parent company (investor) in a parent–subsidiary relationship to prepare the consolidated financial statements. The reporting currency is generally the local currency of the parent company. For an entity located in any given country, a foreign currency is any currency other than the entity's functional currency. The FASB stated that the local currency of the foreign entity is the functional currency when the

Foreign currency: any currency other than the entity's functional currency

> foreign operations are relatively self-contained and integrated within a particular country or economic environment. The day-to-day operations are not dependent upon the economic environment of the parent's functional currency; the foreign operation primarily generates and expends foreign currency. The foreign currency net cash flows that it generates may be reinvested or converted and distributed to the parent.[4]

On the other hand, the parent's currency (U.S. dollar) is the functional currency when the

> foreign operations are primarily a direct and integral component or extension of the parent company's operations … the day-to-day operations are dependent on the economic environment of the parent's functional currency, and the changes in the foreign entity's individual assets and liabilities impact directly on the cash flows of the parent company in the parent's currency.[5]

While the functional currency may appear to be reasonably well defined, determining which currency is the functional currency may not be as apparent. Management judgment is essential in determining the functional currency as long as management's judgment does not contradict the observed facts. In FAS No. 52, the FASB outlined the economic factors to be considered in the determination of the functional currency.[6] Several of the major indicators and factors are included in Figure 6-1. These items are not meant to be an exhaustive list, but rather a sample list of relevant items.

To illustrate, the foreign currency would be the functional currency when a Brazilian company purchases production inputs in the local (Brazilian) market, sells its products primarily in the local market, and receives and expends cash in the Brazilian currency, reals. On the other hand, the functional currency would be the parent's currency when a Mexican subsidiary receives inventory from its U.S. parent, assembles the parts, and sells the product for U.S. dollars in a U.S. market. The Mexican subsidiary may pay labor costs in Mexican pesos, but labor may only be 20 percent of the product's cost while the rest of the manufacturing costs are paid in dollars. An example of another foreign currency being selected as the functional currency is a Uruguayan subsidiary located near the border of

---

[4] Ibid., par. 80.

[5] Ibid., par. 81.

[6] Ibid., par. 42.

	Factors Suggesting the Functional Currency is the:	
Sample Economic Indicators	**Local or Other Foreign Currency**	**Parent's Reporting Currency**
Cash Flow	Cash flows are primarily in the foreign currency and do not directly impact the parent's cash flows.	Cash flows directly impact the parent's cash flows and are available for remittance to the parent company.
Sales Price	Sales prices are primarily determined by local competition or government regulation and do not respond to short-term exchange rate changes.	Sales prices are primarily determined by international competition and prices and respond to short-term exchange rate changes.
Sales Market	An active local sales market exists.	The primary sales market is in the parent's country, or sales are made in the parent's currency.
Expense	Goods and services are primarily purchased in the local market and paid in the local currency.	Goods and services are primarily purchased in the parent's market and paid in the parent's currency.
Financing	Financing is obtained locally, and local operations generate sufficient cash flow to service the debt.	Financing is obtained in the parent currency or from the parent, and local operations do not generate sufficient cash flow to service the debt.
Intercompany Transactions and Arrangements	Intercompany transactions are rare, and there is not an extensive interrelationship between the foreign entity and the parent.	Intercompany transactions are common, and there is an extensive relationship between the foreign entity and the parent.

FIGURE 6-1 Economic Determinants of the Functional Currency

Brazil that primarily hires Brazilian labor and provides services to Brazilian clients. This subsidiary maintains its financial records in the Uruguayan new peso, but the functional currency of the subsidiary is the Brazilian real because most of the cash flows of the subsidiary are in the real.

The Functional Currency in a Highly Inflationary Economy

A basic assumption of financial reporting is that a stable monetary unit exists.[7] The FASB has determined that if a foreign entity is located in a country with high inflation, the foreign currency is too unstable a measuring unit to be the functional currency. A high inflation rate is defined to be a cumulative inflation rate of approximately 100 percent or more over three years.[8] The 100-percent cumulative inflation rate is a general rule of thumb, not an absolute cutoff. The trend in the rate of inflation is also important in determining whether the foreign entity resides in a country with high inflation. For example, if the rates of inflation over the past three years have been 40 percent, 25 percent, and 15 percent, the three-year cumulative inflation rate is approximately 101 percent, from $1 to $2.0125

[7] **Statement of Financial Accounting Concepts,** No. 5, "Recognition and Measurement in Financial Statements of Business Enterprises" (Stamford, CT: Financial Accounting Standards Board, 1984).

[8] Op. cit., **Statement of Financial Accounting Standards (FAS),** No. 52., par. 11.

[$1(1.4)(1.25)(1.15)]. This country may not be viewed as highly inflationary because the rate of inflation has substantially decreased. On the other hand, if the rates of inflation over the past three years have been 12 percent, 20 percent, and 44 percent, the three-year cumulative inflation rate is 94 percent. This country may be viewed as having a **highly inflationary economy** because the rate of inflation is escalating. The basic concern with the rate of inflation is that the converted values of the foreign entity's assets and liabilities may be distorted by rapidly changing exchange rates as a result of the high rate of inflation. If the country where the subsidiary is located is deemed highly inflationary, the parent's reporting currency (U.S. dollar) is the functional currency.

Highly inflationary economy: economy where the three-year cumulative rate of inflation is approximately 100 percent

Steps in Converting Foreign Financial Statements

The FASB stated that one objective of foreign currency translation is "to reflect in consolidated financial statements the financial results and relationships of the individual consolidated entities as measured in their functional currencies."[9] The Board also stated that "…if an entity's books of record are not maintained in its functional currency, remeasurement (conversion) into the functional currency is required."[10] As a result, the functional currency is the focal point for converting financial records maintained in a foreign currency into the reporting currency of a U.S. investor.

The ultimate objective of converting financial records of a foreign entity into U.S. dollars is to enable the U.S. investor to merge the financial records by preparing equity method journal entries and/or consolidated financial statements. Converting the foreign entity's trial balance into U.S. dollars may require as many as three steps.

The first step is to modify the foreign financial accounting methods so they conform to U.S. GAAP. This process may require numerous modifications to the foreign financial information. For example, the accounting procedures applied in some countries do not require the capitalization of any leases; that is, all leases are classified as operating leases. Other countries do not capitalize goodwill. It is written off to equity in the year the investment is made. Still other countries permit more liberal capitalization of software development costs. All these items must be revised so the accounting procedures conform to U.S. GAAP before the U.S. entity can record equity method journal entries and prepare consolidated financial statements.

Temporal method: the method used to convert foreign trial balance information into the functional currency; purpose is to revalue financial records to appear as they would if maintained in the functional currency

The second step, if necessary, is the remeasurement of the foreign entity's trial balance into the functional currency. The methodology for remeasurement is called the **temporal method**. The temporal method converts nonmonetary foreign entity asset and liability accounts using historical exchange rates. Monetary accounts are converted using the balance sheet date exchange rate. This method will be discussed in detail later in the chapter. *This step is needed only when the currency used to maintain the foreign entity's financial records is not the functional currency.* The purpose of this step is to revalue the financial records so they appear as they would if maintained in the functional currency. For example, assume a U.S. parent company has a British subsidiary that has the U.S. dollar as the functional currency. The historical cost of the British subsidiary's plant assets must be maintained in the U.S. dollar.

Current rate method: the method used to convert functional currency trial balance information into the parent reporting currency; purpose is to change the unit of measure with as little change as possible in relationships that exist among values in the functional currency

The third step, if necessary, is the translation of the foreign subsidiary's trial balance from the functional currency into the investor's reporting currency. The methodology for translation is the **current rate method**, which converts all asset and liability accounts of a

[9] Ibid., par. 70.

[10] Ibid., par. 9.

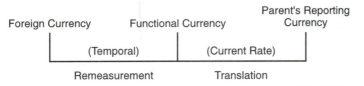

FIGURE 6-2 Methods for Converting Foreign Currency Trial Balances

foreign entity using the balance sheet date exchange rate. This will also be discussed in detail later in the chapter. *This step is needed when the functional currency is not the investor's reporting currency.* The purpose of this step is to change the unit of measure from the functional currency to the U.S. dollar. The objective is to convert the trial balance into the investor's reporting currency with as little change as possible in the relationships that exist among the values in the functional currency trial balance. Figure 6-2 presents a diagram of the different methods that may be used to revalue foreign currency financial statements.

The ultimate objective is to convert the foreign entity's financial information (both trial balance and purchase differentials) from the foreign currency into the parent's (investor's) reporting currency. As Figure 6-2 shows, the temporal method (remeasurement) is applied to convert the foreign currency trial balance from a foreign currency into the functional currency. This method is used when the foreign currency is not the functional currency. It is also used when the subsidiary is located in a country with a highly inflationary economy. If the functional currency is also the parent's reporting currency, the current rate method (translation) would not be applied after the temporal method. If the functional currency is not the parent's reporting currency, the current rate method is applied to convert the functional currency trial balance into the parent's reporting currency. Thus, the conversion process may apply either the temporal method or the current rate method individually, or it may apply the temporal method followed by the current rate method.

After the financial information has been converted into U.S. dollars, the parent company records the equity method journal entries and prepares the worksheet eliminations needed to consolidate the U.S. parent and the foreign subsidiary. The equity method journal entries and worksheet eliminations are required whether the remeasurement approach, translation approach, or both are applied to convert the foreign currency financial information into U.S. dollars.

CONSOLIDATING FOREIGN SUBSIDIARIES AT THE DATE OF ACQUISITION

The acquisition of a foreign subsidiary may involve an exchange of stock or a transfer of assets to the stockholders of the foreign entity. This transaction may be stated in U.S. dollars or in units of foreign currency; however, the economic substance of the transaction can always be converted into U.S. dollars by considering the exchange rate that exists between the U.S. dollar and the foreign currency at the date of acquisition. For example, assume Palmer Corporation acquires 80 percent of Fabryka Manufacturing (a Polish company) on January 1, 2005, for 26,350,000 Polish zloty. The exchange rate at the date of acquisition is 1 Polish zloty (Zl) = $.24. As a result, the value of the investment recorded on Palmer's books is $6,324,000. Assuming that Palmer pays $3,324,000 in cash and issues 150,000 shares of common stock with a market and par value of $20 and $1, respectively, the following journal entry would be recorded by Palmer at the acquisition date:

Journal Entry—Palmer Corporation Books

Jan. 1, 2005	Investment in Fabryka	6,324,000	
	(26,350,000 Zl × $.24 = $6,324,000)		
	Cash		3,324,000
	Common Stock		150,000
	Additional Paid-In Capital		2,850,000
	To record the acquisition of Fabryka stock.		

Palmer's management may desire a pro forma consolidated balance sheet as of the acquisition date to assess the impact of the acquisition on the consolidated entity's liquidity and coverage ratios. The trial balances (in Polish zloty and U.S. dollars) at January 1, 2005, are presented in Illustration 6-1. The book value columns present Fabryka's book values in both Polish zloty and U.S. dollars at the date of acquisition, while the market value columns present the estimated market value of Fabryka's assets and liabilities in Polish zloty and in U.S. dollars.

Notice that the exchange rate existing at the date of acquisition is used to convert all the trial balance accounts (balance sheet and/or income statement) from Polish zloty into U.S. dollars at that date. This exchange rate is used because it represents the U.S. dollar equivalent of Fabryka's assets and liabilities at the acquisition date. The procedure of using only one exchange rate applies only on the acquisition date, including acquisition dates during the year.

If Palmer prepares consolidated financial statements at the date of acquisition, a worksheet elimination is needed. Illustration 6-2 presents the allocation of the purchase differentials to individual accounts. The resulting worksheet to consolidate Palmer and Fabryka at the date of acquisition is presented in Illustration 6-3. Worksheet Elimination 6-3

ILLUSTRATION 6-1
Fabryka's Assets and Liabilities
Book Values and Market Values
January 1, 2005

(Credit) Accounts	Book Values			Market Values		
	Debit (Credit) Polish Zloty	Exchange Rate	Debit (Credit) U.S. Dollars	Debit (Credit) Polish Zloty	Exchange Rate	Deb U.S. Dollars
Cash	1,650,000	.24	396,000	1,650,000	.24	396,000
Accounts Receivable (net)	2,050,000	.24	492,000	2,050,000	.24	492,000
Inventory (FIFO)	3,590,000	.24	861,600	4,025,000	.24	966,000
Plant Assets	24,750,000	.24	5,940,000	22,412,500	.24	5,379,000
Accumulated Depreciation	(6,600,000)	.24	(1,584,000)			
Patents	7,850,000	.24	1,884,000	10,600,000	.24	2,544,000
Totals	33,290,000		7,989,600			
Current Liabilities	(4,300,000)	.24	(1,032,000)	(4,300,000)	.24	(1,032,000)
Bonds Payable	(10,000,000)	.24	(2,400,000)	(9,750,000)	.24	(2,340,000)
Discount on Bonds Payable	250,000	.24	60,000			
Common Stock	(4,000,000)	.24	(960,000)			
Additional Paid-In Capital	(10,625,000)	.24	(2,550,000)			
Retained Earnings	(4,615,000)	.24	(1,107,600)			

ILLUSTRATION 6-2
Purchase Differential Analysis in U.S. Dollars
80 Percent–Owned Subsidiary
January 1, 2005

Value	Analysis of Marke
Fabryka's **imputed** total market value ($) [(26,350,000 ZI × $.24)/.80]	$7,905,000
Book value ($) [(4,000,000 + 10,625,000 + 4,615,000) ($.24)]	4,617,600
Purchase differential ($)	$3,287,400

Purchase differential allocated to identifiable net assets:

Accounts	Debit (Credit) Market Value	Debit (Credit) Book Value	Difference
Inventory (FIFO)	966,000	861,600	$104,400
Plant and Equipment	5,379,000	5,940,000	(561,000)
Accumulated Depreciation		(1,584,000)	1,584,000
Patents	2,544,000	1,884,000	660,000
Total imputed goodwill			1,500,000

presents the journal entry form of the worksheet elimination needed to consolidate Palmer and Fabryka at the date of acquisition.

Notice that the date of acquisition information makes no mention of the approach (remeasurement or translation) used to convert the trial balance from Polish zloty into U.S. dollars. At the date of acquisition, all accounts are converted using the exchange rate that exists at that date. Differences do exist between the remeasurement and the translation approaches, but they arise in periods subsequent to the date of acquisition. Furthermore, the worksheet elimination at the date of acquisition is the same for a foreign subsidiary and a domestic subsidiary. In either case, both the subsidiary's equity accounts and the parent's investment account are eliminated. In addition, purchase differentials and noncontrolling

	Worksheet Elimination 6-3—Journal Entry Form		
(1)	Common Stock	960,000	
	Additional Paid-In Capital	2,550,000	
	Retained Earnings (January 1, 2005)	1,107,600	
	Inventory	104,400	
	Accumulated Depreciation	1,584,000	
	Patent	660,000	
	Goodwill	1,500,000	
	Plant Assets		561,000
	Investment in Fabryka Manufacturing		6,324,000
	Noncontrolling Interest in Fabryka [($6,324,000/.80).20]		1,581,000

To eliminate the subsidiary's beginning of period stockholders' equity as well as the parent's beginning of period Investment in Fabryka account, to establish the beginning of period purchase differentials, and to create the beginning of period Noncontrolling Interest in Fabryka account. (See Illustration 6-2 for details).

ILLUSTRATION 6-3
Worksheet for Consolidation of Palmer Corporation and Subsidiary, Fabryka Manufacturing
80 Percent–Owned Foreign Subsidiary
Consolidation at Acquisition Date (Beginning of Year)
Price More Than Book Value
January 1, 2005

	Separate Financial Statements		Adjustments and Eliminations		Consolidated Financial Statements
	Palmer	Fabryka	Debit	Credit	
Balance Sheet					
Cash	4,300,000	396,000			4,696,000
Accounts Receivable (net)	2,000,000	492,000			2,492,000
Inventory (FIFO)	5,000,000	861,600	(1) 104,400		5,966,000
Other Current Assets	1,700,000				1,700,000
Total Current Assets	13,000,000	1,749,600			14,854,000
Plant Assets	20,000,000	5,940,000		(1) 561,000	25,379,000
Less: Accumulated Depreciation	(5,900,000)	(1,584,000)	(1) 1,584,000		(5,900,000)
Patent		1,884,000	(1) 660,000		2,544,000
Investment in Fabryka	6,324,000			(1) 6,324,000	0
Other Noncurrent Assets	1,600,000				1,600,000
Goodwill			(1) 1,500,000		1,500,000
Total Long-Term Assets	22,024,000	6,240,000			25,123,000
Total Assets	35,024,000	7,989,600			39,977,000
Current Liabilities	8,750,000	1,032,000			9,782,000
7% Bonds Payable (due 6/30/2010)	4,000,000				4,000,000
Less: Discount on Bonds Payable	(150,000)				(150,000)
9¾% Bonds Payable (due 12/31/2007)		2,400,000			2,400,000
Less: Discount on Bonds Payable		(60,000)			(60,000)
Total Liabilities	12,600,000	3,372,000			15,972,000
Common Stock ($1 par):					
Palmer, 10,000,000 shares authorized, 6,150,000 shares issued and outstanding	6,150,000				6,150,000
Fabryka, 1,000,000 shares authorized, issued and outstanding		960,000	(1) 960,000		0
Additional Paid-In Capital	9,350,000	2,550,000	(1) 2,550,000		9,350,000
Retained Earnings (1/1/2005)	6,924,000	1,107,600	(1) 1,107,600		6,924,000
Noncontrolling Interest in Fabryka				(1) 1,581,000	1,581,000
Total Stockholders' Equity	22,424,000	4,617,600			24,005,000
Total Liabilities and Stockholders' Equity	35,024,000	7,989,600			39,977,000
			8,466,000	8,466,000	

(1) To eliminate the subsidiary's beginning of period stockholders' equity as well as the parent's beginning of period Investment in Fabryka account, to establish the beginning of period purchase differentials, and to create the beginning of period Noncontrolling Interest in Fabryka account.

interest at the acquisition date are recognized. The only procedure unique to a foreign subsidiary is that the foreign subsidiary's trial balance must be converted from a foreign currency to the U.S. dollar using the exchange rate that exists at the acquisition date prior to the preparation of the worksheet elimination.

ACCOUNTING FOR FOREIGN ENTITIES SUBSEQUENT TO ACQUISITION

Subsequent to an investment in a foreign entity, equity method journal entries may be required on the investor's books and the U.S. investor may be required to consolidate the foreign entity. The process once again begins with the conversion of the subsidiary's foreign currency trial balance into U.S. GAAP followed by remeasurement, translation, or both, as appropriate. With regard to the subsidiary's trial balance, assume that on December 31, 2005, Fabryka's controller revises the financial records to conform to U.S. GAAP and provides Palmer with the Polish zloty trial balance presented in Illustration 6-4.

ILLUSTRATION 6-4
Fabryka's Trial Balance
December 31, 2005

Accounts	Debit (Credit) Polish Zloty
Cash	2,650,000
Accounts Receivable (net)	2,810,000
Inventory (FIFO)	5,220,000
Plant Assets	26,250,000
Accumulated Depreciation	(8,325,000)
Patents	7,065,000
Cost of Goods Sold	9,500,000
Depreciation Expense	1,725,000
Amortization Expense	785,000
Interest Expense	925,000
Dividends Declared	1,250,000
Total	49,855,000
Current Liabilities	(5,200,000)
Bonds Payable	(10,000,000)
Discount on Bonds Payable	200,000
Common Stock	(4,000,000)
Additional Paid-In Capital	(10,625,000)
Retained Earnings	(4,615,000)
Sales	(15,615,000)
Total	(49,855,000)

Assume that inventory was purchased evenly throughout the year and that inventory records are maintained on a first-in, first-out basis. All the ending inventory was acquired during the last three months of the year. Assume also that plant assets include a purchase on March 31, 2005, for 1,500,000 Polish zloty. The newly acquired plant assets are assigned an estimated life of 15 years, and straight-line depreciation is taken on all plant assets. Dividends are declared and paid on September 1. The following table provides the relevant 2005 exchange rates for Fabryka.

Date	Exchange Rate—Dollars/Zloty
January 1	.24
March 31	.25
September 1	.18
December 31	.23
Average for March 31–December 31	.20
Average for fourth quarter	.22
Average for year	.21

Once the financial records have been revised to conform to U.S. GAAP, the next step is to determine the functional currency for the foreign entity. The determination of the functional currency is the key issue in converting the Polish zloty trial balance into U.S. dollars. If the foreign entity is basically an extension of the U.S. investor, the U.S. dollar is the foreign entity's functional currency. If the foreign entity is relatively self-contained in the foreign country, the foreign currency (Polish zloty in this example) is the foreign entity's functional currency.

Determining the functional currency is important when accounting for an investment in a company located in a foreign country because U.S. GAAP must be applied in the foreign entity's functional currency. For example, if the Polish zloty is Fabryka's functional currency, the historical cost of plant assets will be maintained in zloty. However, if the functional currency is the U.S. dollar, the historical cost will be maintained in U.S. dollars. In addition, purchase differentials are also amortized in the subsidiary's functional currency.

APPLICATION OF THE TEMPORAL (REMEASUREMENT) METHOD

When the subsidiary is basically an extension of the parent company or the subsidiary is in a highly inflationary economy, the functional currency is the parent's reporting currency and the temporal method (remeasurement) is used to convert the subsidiary's trial balance into the parent's reporting currency. The FASB states that "the remeasurement process is intended to produce the same results as if the entity's books of record had been maintained in the functional currency."[11]

Remeasuring the Foreign Currency Trial Balance into U.S. Dollars

The trial balance presented in Illustration 6-5 includes the remeasurement necessary to convert the Polish zloty trial balance into a U.S. dollar trial balance, assuming the functional currency for Fabryka is the U.S. dollar. A discussion is provided to examine the various exchange rates applied and the supporting schedules developed.

Denominated: the expressed currency in which a transaction is to be completed

Monetary account: account fixed in units of currency

Monetary and Nonmonetary Accounts   As was mentioned above, U.S. GAAP must be applied in the functional currency, so the temporal method results in the subsidiary's trial balance being converted into U.S. dollars in a manner that maintains GAAP in U.S. dollars. FAS No. 52 specifies that when a balance sheet is **denominated** in a foreign currency, each **monetary account** must be revalued using the exchange rate on the balance sheet date so the account reflects the U.S. dollar equivalent value of the foreign currency at that date. This can be seen in the Exchange Rate column of Illustration 6-5 for *Cash, Accounts Receivable, Current Liabilities, Bonds Payable,* and *Discount on Bonds Payable.* Each of these accounts is revalued at 1 Polish zloty = $.23, the exchange rate that exists at the balance sheet date.[12] These amounts represent the dollars that would be received or paid if the asset or liability were settled on the balance sheet date.

---

[11] Ibid., par. 10.

[12] The exchange rate between two currencies on any given date is referred to as the spot rate. The term *spot rate* is explained in detail in Chapter 5.

ILLUSTRATION 6-5
Remeasurement of Fabryka's Trial Balance
Functional Currency—U.S. Dollar
December 31, 2005

Accounts	Debit (Credit) Polish Zloty	Exchange Rate	Debit (Credit) U.S. Dollars
Cash	2,650,000	.23 C	609,500
Accounts Receivable (net)	2,810,000	.23 C	646,300
Inventory (FIFO)	5,220,000	Schedule A	1,148,400
Plant Assets	26,250,000	Schedule B	6,315,000
Accumulated Depreciation	(8,325,000)	Schedule B	(1,998,750)
Patents	7,065,000	.24 H	1,695,600
Cost of Goods Sold	9,500,000	Schedule A	2,050,500
Depreciation Expense	1,725,000	Schedule B	414,750
Amortization Expense	785,000	.24 H	188,400
Interest Expense	925,000	.21 A	194,250
Dividends Declared	1,250,000	.18 H	225,000
Totals	49,855,000		11,488,950
Current Liabilities	(5,200,000)	.23 C	(1,196,000)
Bonds Payable (net)	(10,000,000)	.23 C	(2,300,000)
Discount on Bonds Payable	200,000	.23 C	46,000
Common Stock	(4,000,000)	.24 H	(960,000)
Additional Paid-In Capital	(10,625,000)	.24 H	(2,550,000)
Retained Earnings (January 1, 2005)	(4,615,000)	.24 H	(1,107,600)
Sales	(15,615,000)	.21 A	(3,279,150)
Remeasurement (Gain) Loss			(142,200)
Totals	(49,855,000)		(11,488,950)

A = average; C = current; H = historical.

Schedule A
Remeasurement of Inventory and Cost of Goods Sold

	Polish Zloty	Exchange Rate	U.S. Dollars
Beginning Inventory (Illustration 6-1)	3,590,000	.24	861,600
Purchases	11,130,000	.21	2,337,300
Goods Available for Sale	14,720,000		3,198,900
Ending Inventory	5,220,000	.22	1,148,400
Cost of Goods Sold	9,500,000		2,050,500

Schedule B
Remeasurement of Plant Assets

Date	Polish Zloty	Exchange Rate	U.S. Dollars
Beginning Balance	24,750,000	.24	5,940,000
Purchase March 31, 2005	1,500,000	.25	375,000
Ending Balance	26,250,000		6,315,000

(Continued)

ILLUSTRATION 6-5 *Continued*

Schedule B
Remeasurement of Depreciation Expense

Date	Polish Zloty	Exchange Rate	U.S. Dollars
On plant assets owned at date of acquisition	1,650,000	.24	396,000
On purchase March 31, 2005 [(1,500,000/15)(9/12)]	75,000	.25	18,750
Totals	1,725,000		414,750

Remeasurement of Accumulated Depreciation

Date	Polish Zloty	Exchange Rate	U.S. Dollars
On plant assets owned at date of acquisition (6,600,000 + 1,650,000)	8,250,000	.24	1,980,000
On purchase March 31, 2005	75,000	.25	18,750
Totals	8,325,000		1,998,750

Nonmonetary account: account not fixed in units of currency

Each **nonmonetary** asset and liability account has the historical cost principal applied in the U.S. dollar because, in this example, the dollar is the functional currency. Illustration 6-6 presents example accounts that would be remeasured using historical exchange rates when the temporal (remeasurement) approach is applied. Note that while most nonmonetary accounts are assets, there can also be nonmonetary liabilities. For example, a publisher that receives payment for a magazine in advance of delivery has incurred a liability, *Unearned Revenue*. This liability is not a claim by the subscriber to cash but a claim for a fixed number of issues of the magazine. As a result, the *Unearned Revenue* account is a nonmonetary liability. The remainder of this discussion pertains to

ILLUSTRATION 6-6
Example Accounts to be Remeasured Using Historical Exchange Rates

Marketable securities carried at cost
Inventories carried at cost
Prepaid expenses
Plant assets
Accumulated depreciation on plant assets
Patents, trademarks, licenses, and formulas
Goodwill
Other intangible assets
Deferred charges and credits
Deferred income
Common stock
Preferred stock carried at issuance price
Cost of goods sold
Depreciation on plant assets
Amortization of intangible items
Amortization of deferred charges or credits

assets for simplification of presentation, but the same rationale applies to nonmonetary liabilities.

For historical cost to be preserved in U.S. dollars, the exchange rates between the Polish zloty and the U.S. dollar must not change from period to period. To accomplish this objective, the exchange rate used to remeasure a nonmonetary asset is the exchange rate that existed when the asset was acquired unless the asset was owned when the parent acquired the subsidiary. The exchange rate that existed at the date of the parent's investment is applied to all nonmonetary assets owned at that date because the exchange rate that existed at the date of acquisition established the parent's historical cost for the investment. This exchange rate is applied until the asset is sold or abandoned. In this manner, the remeasured U.S. dollar values will not change over time for nonmonetary assets, and the historical cost in U.S. dollars will be maintained.

Remeasuring Inventory and Cost of Goods Sold

To apply the historical cost principle, schedules are often used to determine the remeasured values of nonmonetary asset accounts because the individual assets in the account may have been purchased at different points in time. Thus, the exchange rates applicable to various items within a nonmonetary account may be different. This can be seen in Schedule A of Illustration 6-5, where the remeasured values for the *Inventory* and *Cost of Goods Sold* accounts are determined. The beginning inventory is remeasured using the exchange rate that exists at the date Palmer acquired Fabryka. This rate is used because the inventory was owned by Fabryka at the date of Palmer's investment. The inventory purchased during the period uses the average exchange rate for the period to accomplish the remeasurement. The FASB permits the average exchange rate to be used when the purchases are assumed to have occurred evenly throughout the year. Under this purchasing scenario, the average rate will provide approximately the same results as the application of specific historical rates for each purchase. In fact, the use of the average exchange rate as a surrogate for the historical rates is permissible in converting any account that has an even flow of activity during the year.

If much of the inventory had been purchased during a particular month, the purchases would be remeasured using more than one exchange rate to reflect the amounts of purchases made at different times. The ending inventory is remeasured at the average exchange rate for the last three months of the year, the period of time when the ending inventory is acquired. The example presented in this schedule is based on the first-in, first-out cost flow assumption. The same concept applies regardless of the inventory method applied. For example, if the last-in, first-out cost flow assumption is used, two layers of inventory might be created. The beginning inventory layer retains its $.24 exchange rate and a second inventory layer, if one is created during the period, applies the exchange rate when purchased. The rate would be $.22 in this example.

Remeasuring Plant Assets, Depreciation Expense, and Accumulated Depreciation

The scheduling rationale applied to inventory also applies to other nonmonetary accounts, such as *Plant Assets*. The account *Plant Assets* requires more detailed scheduling because the historical cost, *Depreciation Expense,* and *Accumulated Depreciation* must all be remeasured using the historical exchange rates. Notice that the exchange rate for a particular group of plant assets is consistent across all related accounts remeasured in Schedule B of Illustration 6-5. For example, the March 31 *Plant Assets* purchased is remeasured using an exchange rate of $.25 per Polish zloty. The *Depreciation Expense* and *Accumulated Depreciation* related to the March 31 purchase are also remeasured using an exchange rate of $.25. If the same exchange rate is not used, the sum of the

Depreciation Expense for several years would not equal the balance in the *Accumulated Depreciation* account. In addition, when any asset is fully depreciated, the balance in the *Accumulated Depreciation* account would not equal the balance in the *Plant Assets* account.

Note that the income statement accounts associated with nonmonetary assets and liabilities also use the historical exchange rates for those assets and liabilities. For example, the remeasured historical cost of inventory in the functional currency must be allocated to the income statement when the inventory is sold. Given that the functional currency is the U.S. dollar, this allocation is accomplished by applying the historical exchange rate to the units of inventory sold. The same rationale applies to *Depreciation Expense* and *Amortization Expense.*

Remeasuring Owners' Equity

The final accounts to be discussed are equity accounts, both permanent equity accounts and temporary equity accounts (i.e., income statement accounts). The remaining income statement accounts (i.e., those not directly related to nonmonetary assets or liabilities) are remeasured using the average exchange rate for the period. For example, the *Sales* and *Interest Expense* accounts in Illustration 6-5 are remeasured in this manner. This approach implicitly assumes that these account balances are the result of transactions occurring evenly throughout the period. The FASB initially proposed that the exchange rate that exists when a transaction occurs be used to revalue these types of income statement accounts; however, the Board determined that using specific exchange rates may impose a cost on the entity greater than the marginal benefit when compared to applying an average exchange rate.[13] Thus, the average exchange rate was permitted and serves as an approximation of the actual historical rates that existed at each transaction date.

The exchange rate applied to contributed capital accounts (e.g., *Common Stock, Preferred Stock, Additional Paid-In Capital*) is the exchange rate that existed when Palmer acquired Fabryka unless a transaction affecting contributed capital occurred after the acquisition date. One way to see the importance of using the acquisition date exchange rate for the contributed capital accounts is to consider the worksheet eliminations that must be made to prepare the consolidated financial statements. The worksheet elimination amounts to remove Fabryka's contributed capital accounts are the same each period, assuming there are no transactions in Fabryka's stock subsequent to Palmer's investment. This dollar amount can remain the same only if the exchange rate applied to the contributed capital accounts is the same every period.

The *Dividends Declared* account is remeasured using the exchange rate that exists at the transaction date because relatively few dividend transactions occur and gathering exchange rate data is not viewed as an undue burden. On the other hand, determining the trial balance amount in U.S. dollars for the earned capital account *(Retained Earnings)* can be an involved process. The U.S. dollar balance at the acquisition date is determined by applying the exchange rate in existence at the acquisition date. In subsequent periods, the *Retained Earnings* amount on the trial balance is always the beginning of period balance. The beginning *Retained Earnings* is a function of the subsidiary's net income and dividends declared during the previous period. Both the subsidiary's net income and dividends declared amounts are determined using a variety of exchange rates. As a result, it is not possible to directly determine the beginning *Retained Earnings* balance in periods subsequent to the first year of ownership. To determine the U.S. dollar amount for beginning *Retained Earnings*, the ending balance from the prior period is carried forward to the

[13] Ibid., par. 29.

current period. For example, the December 31, 2005, *Retained Earnings* is the beginning balance ($1,107,600) plus the net income for 2005 ($573,450, from Illustration 6-7) less the dividends declared during 2005 ($225,000). This amount will be placed on the 2006 trial balance as the beginning *Retained Earnings* in U.S. dollars. A discussion of subsequent-period procedures can be found in the appendix to this chapter.

Balancing the Trial Balance and the Remeasured Income Statement

After the trial balance has been converted from Polish zloty into U.S. dollars, an adjustment is made to equate debit and credit balances in U.S. dollars. The converted trial balance would normally be out of balance in U.S. dollars because of the different exchange rates used to revalue various accounts. The amount needed to bring the U.S. dollar trial balance into balance, when applying the temporal method, is titled *Remeasurement Gain or Loss*. This amount is included in income because the temporal method is applied when the U.S. dollar is the functional currency, and changes in the subsidiary's assets and liabilities are likely to be realized in the form of cash flows to the parent. As a result, changes in the values assigned to assets and liabilities resulting from changes in exchange rates have a direct effect on the parent's cash flows and should be included in the determination of consolidated net income. The amount of the *Remeasurement Gain or Loss* will be recorded on the parent's income statement via equity method journal entries. Fabryka's remeasured 2005 income statement, which includes the *Remeasurement Gain*, is presented in Illustration 6-7.

> **Remeasurement Gain or Loss:** the amount needed to bring the U.S dollar trial balance into balance when applying the temporal method.

Recording Equity Method Journal Entries

The temporal method results in the same three equity method journal entries that would be made for a domestic subsidiary: recognition of the parent's ownership interest in the subsidiary's net income, recognition of the parent's ownership interest in dividends declared by the subsidiary, and amortization of the parent's ownership interest in the purchase differentials. The first journal entry below presents Palmer's recognition of its ownership interest in Fabryka's net income.

Journal Entry—Palmer Corporation Books

Dec. 31,2005	Investment in Fabryka ($573,450 × .8)	458,760	
	Investment Income		458,760
	To record Palmer's ownership interest in Fabryka net income.		

ILLUSTRATION 6-7
Fabryka Manufacturing
Remeasured Income Statement
December 31, 2005

	U.S. Dollars
Sales	$3,279,150
Cost of Goods Sold	(2,050,500)
Gross Profit	1,228,650
Depreciation Expense	(414,750)
Amortization Expense	(188,400)
Interest Expense	(194,250)
Remeasurement Gain	142,200
Net Income (Loss)	$573,450

Notice that the remeasurement gain from the trial balance is included in the determination of Fabryka's net income as stated in dollars. Recall that the temporal method is applied when the functional currency is deemed to be a currency other than the one in which the subsidiary maintains its financial records. In the current example, the U.S. dollar is the functional currency. Based on this premise, business transactions of Fabryka in the Polish zloty expose the consolidated entity to the risk of fluctuation between the zloty's value and the functional currency's (U.S. dollar's) value. Changes in the value of Fabryka's assets and liabilities have a direct impact on Palmer's cash flows. As a result, these fluctuations are reflected through gains and losses in the functional currency *(Remeasurement Gain or Loss)*. Only 80 percent of the *Remeasurement Gain or Loss* is recognized on Palmer's financial records because the $142,200 represents the change in values of all the assets and liabilities and Palmer has only an 80 percent ownership interest in Fabryka. The remainder of the gain or loss is allocated to the noncontrolling interest in the consolidation process.

The second journal entry presents Palmer's recognition of its ownership interest in the dividends declared by Fabryka. As with a domestic subsidiary, the declaration of the dividend reduces Palmer's investment account balance.

Journal Entry—Palmer Corporation Books

Sept. 1, 2005	Cash ($225,000 × .8)	180,000	
	Investment in Fabryka		180,000
	To record the distribution of Fabryka's dividend.		

The third journal entry recognizes the amortization of Palmer's ownership in the purchase differentials created at the date of acquisition (see Illustration 6-2 for purchase differential amounts). Assume that the purchase differential assigned to *Inventory* at the date of acquisition is amortized over three months. The *Plant Assets* and the *Patents* purchase differentials are amortized over 11 years and 10 years, respectively. No goodwill impairment recognition is needed in the current year.

Journal Entry—Palmer Corporation Books

Dec. 31,2005	Investment Income [$104,400 + ($1,584,000 − $561,000)/11 + ($660,000/10)](.8)	210,720	
	Investment in Fabryka		210,720
	To record Palmer's ownership percentage in the amortization of the purchase differentials relevant for the investment in Fabryka stock. (See Illustration 6-2 for total purchase differential amounts.)		

Generally, the journal entries presented for Palmer are the same as the journal entries that would be recognized had Fabryka been a domestic subsidiary. The only difference is that an additional item, *Remeasurement Gain or Loss*, is included in the calculation of Fabryka's net income.

Preparing Consolidated Financial Statements

Once the subsidiary's accounts are remeasured, the process of preparing the consolidated financial statements for a foreign subsidiary when the remeasurement approach is applied is the same as preparing the consolidated financial statements for a domestic subsidiary. Four basic worksheet eliminations are prepared. Illustration 6-8 presents the worksheet to consolidate Palmer and Fabryka at December 31, 2005. Worksheet eliminations in journal entry form are presented in Worksheet Elimination 6-8.

ILLUSTRATION 6-8
Worksheet for Consolidation of Palmer Corporation and Subsidiary, Fabryka Manufacturing
80 Percent–Owned Foreign Subsidiary Consolidation Subsequent to Acquisition Date
Temporal Method (U.S. Dollar Functional Currency)
December 31, 2005

	Separate Financial Statements		Adjustments and Eliminations		Consolidated Financial Statements
	Palmer	Fabryka	Debit	Credit	
Income Statement					
Sales	10,000,000	3,279,150			13,279,150
Investment Income, Fabryka	248,040		(2) 248,040		0
Remeasurement Gain		142,200			142,200
Cost of Goods Sold	5,600,000	2,050,500	(3) 104,400		7,754,900
Selling Expenses	1,400,000				1,400,000
General and Administrative Expenses	2,330,000	797,400	(3) 159,000		3,286,400
Consolidated Net Income					980,050
Noncontrolling Interest in Net Income of Fabryka			(4) 62,010		62,010
Net Income (to Statement of Retained Earnings)	918,040	573,450	573,450	0	918,040
Retained Earnings Statement					
Retained Earnings (1/1/2005)	6,924,000	1,107,600	(1) 1,107,600		6,924,000
Add: Net Income (from Income Statement)	918,040	573,450	(X) 573,450	(X) 0	918,040
Subtotal	7,842,040	1,681,050			7,842,040
Less: Dividends	(380,000)	(225,000)		(2) 180,000	(380,000)
				(4) 45,000	
Retained Earnings (12/31/2005 to Balance Sheet)	7,462,040	1,456,050	1,681,050	225,000	7,462,040
Balance Sheet					
Cash	4,780,000	609,500			5,389,500
Accounts Receivable (net)	1,800,000	646,300			2,446,300
Inventory (FIFO)	5,500,000	1,148,400	(1) 104,400	(3) 104,400	6,648,400
Other Current Assets	1,600,000				1,600,000
Total Current Assets	13,680,000	2,404,200			16,084,200
Plant Assets	20,800,000	6,315,000		(1) 561,000	26,554,000
Accumulated Depreciation	(6,510,000)	(1,998,750)	(1) 1,584,000	(3) 93,000	(7,017,750)
Patent		1,695,600	(1) 660,000	(3) 66,000	2,289,600
Investment in Fabryka	6,392,040			(1) 6,324,000	0
				(2) 68,040	
Other Noncurrent Assets	1,400,000				1,400,000
Goodwill			(1) 1,500,000		1,500,000
Total Long-Term Assets	22,082,040	6,011,850			24,725,850
Total Assets	35,762,040	8,416,050			40,810,050
Current Liabilities	8,930,000	1,196,000			10,126,000
7% Bonds Payable (due 6/30/2010)	4,000,000				4,000,000
Less: Discount on Bonds Payable	(130,000)				(130,000)
9¾% Bonds Payable (due 12/31/2007)		2,300,000			2,300,000
Less: Discount on Bonds Payable		(46,000)			(46,000)
Total Liabilities	12,800,000	3,450,000			16,250,000

(Continued)

ILLUSTRATION 6-8 *Continued*

Common Stock ($1 par):						
Palmer, 10,000,000 shares authorized, 6,150,000 shares issued and outstanding	6,150,000					6,150,000
Fabryka, 1,000,000 shares authorized, issued and outstanding		960,000	(1) 960,000			0
Additional Paid-In Capital	9,350,000	2,550,000	(1) 2,550,000			9,350,000
Retained Earnings (12/31/2005 from Statement of Retained Earnings)	7,462,040	1,456,050	(X) 1,681,050	(X) 225,000		7,462,040
Noncontrolling Interest in Fabryka				(1) 1,581,000		1,598,010
				(4) 17,010		
Total Stockholders' Equity	22,962,040	4,966,050				24,560,050
Total Liabilities and Stockholders' Equity	35,762,040	8,416,050				40,810,050
			9,039,450	9,039,450		

(1) To eliminate the subsidiary's beginning of period stockholders' equity as well as the parent's beginning of period Investment in Fabryka account, to establish the beginning of period purchase differentials, and to create the beginning of period Noncontrolling Interest in Fabryka account.
(2) To eliminate the change in the Investment in Fabryka account and the parent's Investment Income account.
(3) To amortize purchase differentials for the current period.
(4) To recognize the change in the Noncontrolling Interest in Fabryka account during the period.

Worksheet Eliminations 6-8—Journal Entry Form

(1)	Common Stock	960,000	
	Additional Paid-In Capital	2,550,000	
	Retained Earnings (January 1, 2005)	1,107,600	
	Inventory	104,400	
	Accumulated Depreciation	1,584,000	
	Patents	660,000	
	Goodwill	1,500,000	
	Plant Assets		561,000
	Investment in Fabryka		6,324,000
	Noncontrolling Interest in Fabryka		1,581,000

To eliminate the subsidiary's beginning of period stockholders' equity as well as the parent's beginning of period Investment in Fabryka account, to establish the beginning of period purchase differentials, and to create the beginning of period Noncontrolling Interest in Fabryka account.

(2)	Investment Income ($458,760 – $210,720)	248,040	
	Investment in Fabryka		68,040
	Dividends Declared ($225,000 × .8)		180,000

To eliminate the change in the Investment in Fabryka account and the parent's Investment Income account.

(3)	Cost of Goods Sold	104,400	
	Depreciation Expense (G&A)[($1,584,000 – $561,000)/11]	93,000	
	Patent Amortization Expense (G&A) ($660,000/10)	66,000	
	Inventory		104,400
	Accumulated Depreciation		93,000
	Patents		66,000

To amortize purchase differentials for the current period.

(4)	Noncontrolling Interest in Net Income of Subsidiary [($573,450 – $104,400 – $93,000 – $66,000)(.2)]	62,010	
	Noncontrolling Interest in Fabryka		17,010
	Dividends Declared ($225,000 × .2)		45,000

To recognize the change in the Noncontrolling Interest in Fabryka account during the period.

Notice that it is not possible to look at the Palmer Corporation equity method journal entries or the worksheet eliminations and determine whether the subsidiary resides in the United States or in a foreign country. Only the worksheet itself reveals the *Remeasurement Gain (Loss)* on the subsidiary's Income Statement.

APPLICATION OF THE CURRENT RATE (TRANSLATION) METHOD

When a foreign entity is relatively self-contained in the foreign country, the local currency of that country is generally the functional currency. As in all cases, the trial balance of the foreign entity is first revised so as to conform to U.S. GAAP. The foreign currency trial balance is then converted into U.S. dollars in a manner that minimizes any changes in relationships that exist among the trial balance accounts.

Translating The Foreign Currency Trial Balance into U.S. Dollars

The trial balance presented in Illustration 6-9 includes the translation necessary to convert the Polish zloty trial balance into U.S. dollars when applying the current rate method.

Translation of Assets and Liabilities Illustration 6-9 indicates that all of Fabryka's assets and liabilities are translated using the exchange rate at the balance sheet date (the current exchange rate). This simplifies the translation process because it is not necessary to track the purchase date on individual assets as was required under the temporal method. One exchange rate is used for translation of the assets and liabilities because the objective of this process is to change the unit of measure while retaining the relationships that exist among the accounts. For example, the current ratio calculated in Polish zloty is the same as the current ratio calculated in U.S. dollars.

Translation of Income Statement Accounts and the Translated Income Statement Income statement accounts are generally translated using the average exchange rate for the period. As was discussed in the section Application of the Temporal (Remeasurement) Method, the FASB initially proposed that the exchange rate that exists when a transaction occurs should be used to revalue income statement accounts; however, the Board determined that using specific exchange rates may impose a cost greater than benefit. As a result, an average exchange rate may be used to translate income statement accounts. This does not always mean that the same exchange rate will be applied for all income statement accounts. The current example has *Depreciation Expense* translated into dollars using two exchange rates. Depreciation expense on assets owned by Fabryka for the entire year are translated using the average exchange rate for the year. Depreciation expense on the significant asset purchase during the year is translated into dollars using the average exchange rate for the period the assets are owned by Fabryka (March 31–December 31). Another possible reason for the use of multiple average exchange rates to translate income statement accounts is because the income statement amount is not recognized evenly throughout the year (e.g., 40 percent of sales occur in the fourth quarter of the year). Fabryka's translated 2005 income statement is presented in Illustration 6-10.

Translation of Equity Accounts on the Subsidiary Trial Balance The equity accounts are revalued in approximately the same manner as in the temporal method. Contributed capital accounts (e.g., *Common Stock, Preferred Stock, Additional Paid-In*

ILLUSTRATION 6-9
Translation of Fabryka's Trial Balance
Functional Currency—Polish Zloty
December 31, 2005

Accounts	Debit (Credit) Polish Zloty	Exchange Rate	Debit (Credit) U.S. Dollars
Cash	2,650,000	.23 C	609,500
Accounts Receivable (net)	2,810,000	.23 C	646,300
Inventory (FIFO)	5,220,000	.23 C	1,200,600
Plant Assets	26,250,000	.23 C	6,037,500
Accumulated Depreciation	(8,325,000)	.23 C	(1,914,750)
Patents	7,065,000	.23C	1,624,950
Cost of Goods Sold	9,500,000	.21 A	1,995,000
Depreciation Expense	1,725,000	Schedule A	361,500
Amortization Expense	785,000	.21 A	164,850
Interest Expense	925,000	.21 A	194,250
Dividends Declared	1,250,000	.18 H	225,000
Totals	49,855,000		11,144,700
Current Liabilities	(5,200,000)	.23 C	(1,196,000)
Bonds Payable (net)	(10,000,000)	.23 C	(2,300,000)
Discount on Bonds Payable	200,000	.23 C	46,000
Common Stock	(4,000,000)	.24 H	(960,000)
Additional Paid-In Capital	(10,625,000)	.24 H	(2,550,000)
Retained Earnings	(4,615,000)	.24 H	(1,107,600)
Sales	(15,615,000)	.21 A	(3,279,150)
Cumulative Translation Adjustment			202,050
Totals	(49,855,000)		(11,144,700)

A = average; C = current; H = historical.

Schedule A
Translation of Depreciation Expense

Date	Polish Zloty	Exchange Rate	U.S. Dollars
On plant assets owned at date of acquisition	1,650,000	.21	346,500
On purchase March 31, 2005	75,000	.20	15,000
Totals	1,725,000		361,500

ILLUSTRATION 6-10
Fabryka Manufacturing
Translated Income Statement
December 31, 2005

	U.S. Dollars
Sales	$3,279,150
Cost of Goods Sold	(1,995,000)
Gross Profit	1,284,150
Depreciation Expense	(361,500)
Amortization Expense	(164,850)
Interest Expense	(194,250)
Net Income (Loss)	$563,550

Capital) are translated using the exchange rate that exists when the subsidiary is acquired, assuming that no additional stock transactions have occurred. For practical purposes, the rationale for this can be based on the worksheet elimination that must be prepared to consolidate a foreign subsidiary. The worksheet elimination to contributed capital accounts does not change from period to period unless there have been additional equity transactions. Thus, the translated values of the equity accounts should remain the same. The use of a historical exchange rate accomplishes this objective.

Dividends are translated using the exchange rate that exists when the dividends are declared. Few dividend transactions occur during the period, and capturing the exchange rates that exist on these dates is not an undue burden. *Retained Earnings* is carried forward from the prior period, as in the temporal method. For example, the December 31, 2005, *Retained Earnings* is the translated beginning balance of ($1,107,600), plus the net income for 2005 ($563,550), less the dividends declared during 2005 ($225,000). The translated U.S. dollar amount of ending *Retained Earnings* will not be the same as the remeasured dollar amount beyond the date of acquisition because different exchange rates are used to convert the income statement accounts, and the current rate method does not generate a *Remeasurement Gain (Loss)* in the income statement.

Balancing the Trial Balance   Similar to the temporal method, an adjustment is generally necessary to equate debit and credit balances in U.S. dollars once the trial balance is converted from the Polish zloty to the U.S. dollar. Debits and credits of a translated trial balance are not normally equal in U.S. dollars because of the different exchange rates used to translate various accounts. Whereas the *Remeasurement Gain (Loss)* is the account used to balance the temporal method remeasured trial balance, when applying the current rate method, the amount needed to bring the U.S. dollar trial balance into balance is titled **Cumulative Translation Adjustment**. This amount is *not* included in the determination of consolidated net income because the subsidiary operates independently of the parent, so changes in the value of the assets and liabilities are not likely to have a direct cash flow effect for the parent. Instead, the *Cumulative Translation Adjustment* is reported as a component of other comprehensive income. Therefore, a separate parent company journal entry is recorded to recognize the parent's share of the *Cumulative Translation Adjustment*.

Cumulative Translation Adjustment: the amount needed to bring the U.S. dollar trial balance into balance when applying the current rate method

Recording Equity Method Journal Entries

The current rate method requires as many as five equity method journal entries on the parent's financial records. The first journal entry represents Palmer's recognition of its ownership interest in Fabryka's net income.

Journal Entry—Palmer Corporation Books

Dec. 31, 2005	Investment in Fabryka ($563,550 × .8)	450,840	
	Investment Income		450,840
	To record Palmer's ownership interest in Fabryka net income.		

Note that this entry is the same as an equity method journal entry that would be required for a domestic subsidiary. Palmer recognizes its 80 percent–ownership interest in Fabryka's reported net income on its separate financial records. The remaining 20 percent ownership interest in Fabryka's net income is recognized as part of the worksheet elimination for noncontrolling interest.

The second journal entry presents Palmer's recognition of its 80-percent share in the dividends distributed by Fabryka. As with a domestic subsidiary, the dividend distribution reduces Palmer's investment account balance.

Journal Entry—Palmer Corporation Books

Dec. 31, 2005	Cash ($225,000 × .8)	180,000	
	Investment in Fabryka		180,000
	To record the distribution of Fabryka's dividend.		

The third journal entry addresses the change in the *Cumulative Translation Adjustment*.

Journal Entry—Palmer Corporation Books

Dec. 31, 2005	Cumulative Translation Adjustment ($202,050 × .8)	161,640	
	Investment in Fabryka		161,640
	To record Palmer's pro rata share of the cumulative translation adjustment on Fabryka's trial balance.		

As with the income of Fabryka, Palmer recognizes 80 percent of the *change* in the *Cumulative Translation Adjustment* because the trial balance amount represents the change in the translated value of 100 percent of Fabryka's net assets and Palmer owns only 80 percent of Fabryka's net assets. The journal entry is based on the full $202,050 in the current example because it is the first year Palmer has owned Fabryka, so the beginning balance in the *Cumulative Translation Adjustment* account is $0. In 2006, the amount of the journal entry will be based on the change in the *Cumulative Translation Adjustment* from its current balance.

Similar to the temporal method, the purchase differential amortization is accomplished in the functional currency. However, in the current example, the functional currency is the Polish zloty, not the U.S. dollar. As a result, the purchase differential allocation and the purchase differential amortization schedule must be prepared in the Polish zloty and translated into the U.S. dollar. Recall that the purchase differential assigned to *Inventory* at the date of acquisition is amortized over three months. The *Plant Assets* and the *Patents* purchase differentials are amortized over 11 years and 10 years, respectively. No *Goodwill*

ILLUSTRATION 6-11
Purchase Differential Analysis in Polish Zloty
80 Percent–Owned Subsidiary
January 1, 2005

	Analysis of Marke
Value	
Fabryka's **imputed** total market value (26,350,000 Zl/.80)	32,937,500
Less: Book value (Zl) (4,000,000 + 10,625,000 + 4,615,000)	19,240,000
Purchase differential (Zl)	13,697,500

Purchase differential allocated to identifiable net assets:

Accounts	Debit (Credit) Market Value	Debit (Credit) Book Value	Difference
Inventory (FIFO)	4,025,000	3,590,000	435,000
Plant and Equipment	22,412,500	24,750,000	(2,337,500)
Accumulated Depreciation		(6,600,000)	6,600,000
Patents	10,600,000	7,850,000	2,750,000
Total imputed goodwill			6,250,000
Allocated purchase differential (Zl)			13,697,500

ILLUSTRATION 6-12
Amortization of Purchase Differentials When Applying the Current Rate Method

Account	Beginning Balance			Amortization			Ending Balance		
	Zloty	Exchange Rate	Dollars	Zloty	Exchange Rate	Dollars	Zloty	Exchange Rate	Dollars
Inventory	435,000	.24	104,400	435,000	.21	91,350	0	.23	0
Plant Assets	(2,337,500)	.24	(561,000)	0	.21	0	(2,337,500)	.23	(537,625)
Accumulated Depreciation	6,600,000	.24	1,584,000	387,500*	.21	81,375	6,212,500	.23	1,428,875
Patents	2,750,000	.24	660,000	275,000	.21	57,750	2,475,000	.23	569,250
Goodwill	6,250,000	.24	1,500,000	0	.21	0	6,250,000	.23	1,437,500
Totals	13,697,500		3,287,400	1,097,500		230,475	12,600,000		2,898,000

	Translation Adjustment			
	Beginning	Amortization	Ending	Translation Adjustment
Inventory	104,400	91,350	0	13,050
Plant Assets	(561,000)	0	(537,625)	(23,375)
Accumulated Depreciation	1,584,000	81,375	1,428,875	73,750
Patents	660,000	57,750	569,250	33,000
Goodwill	1,500,000	0	1,437,500	62,500
Totals				158,925

* (6,600,000 – 2,337,500)/11

impairment recognition is needed in the current year. Illustration 6-11 presents the purchase differential allocation in Fabryka's functional currency (zloty). The purchase differential amortization and translation adjustment schedules that are the basis for the fourth and fifth equity method journal entries are presented in Illustration 6-12.

Note that the purchase differential amortization schedule is divided into three parts (Beginning Balance, Amortization, and Ending Balance). The beginning of period balance for each purchase differential is based on the exchange rate that exists as of the beginning of the current period. Information from this part of the illustration also supports the beginning purchase differential that will appear in worksheet elimination (1) when consolidated financial statements are prepared.

The purchase differential amortizations for the current period are computed in the functional currency (Polish zloty in this example) and translated into U.S. dollars using the average exchange rate that exists for the period. This is generally consistent with the exchange rates used for the income statement accounts on the trial balance. Information from this part of the illustration also supports the amortization of the purchase differentials on Palmer's financial records. Additionally, this information is used in worksheet elimination (3) that will amortize purchase differentials in the consolidated income statement. The fourth journal entry recognizes the amortization of Palmer's purchase differentials created at the acquisition date.

Journal Entry—Palmer Corporation Books

Dec. 31, 2005	Investment Income	184,380	
	Investment in Fabryka ($230,475 × .8)		184,380

To record the amortization of the purchase differentials relevant for the investment in Fabryka stock. (See schedule in Illustration 6-12 for supporting calculations.)

The unamortized purchase differentials as of the end of the period are based on beginning of period Polish zloty balances less amortization in the current period (in Polish zloty). The Polish zloty amounts are then translated using the exchange rate that exists at the balance sheet date. This is consistent with the exchange rate used to translate assets and liabilities on the trial balance. Information from this part of the illustration supports the net change in value that should be included in the consolidated balance sheet.

The three parts of the purchase differential amortization schedule (Illustration 6-12) reconcile in the functional currency (the Polish zloty in this example). The beginning purchase differential balance (Zl 13,697,500) less the amount amortized (Zl 1,097,500) equals the ending balance (Zl 12,600,000). However, the schedule does not reconcile in U.S. dollars. The beginning balance of $3,287,400 (translated at an exchange rate of $.24) less the amortization of $230,475 (translated at an exchange rate of $.21) numerically equals $3,056,925. However, the ending purchase differential must be presented using the balance sheet date exchange rate of $.23. Therefore, the ending balance to be reported is $2,898,000 (Zl 12,600,000 × $.23). The amount by which the schedule fails to reconcile in U.S. dollars ($3,056,925 − $2,898,000) results from the change in the exchange rates during the current year and is classified as an additional translation adjustment, a loss of $158,925. It is a loss in this example because the required end-of-period unamortized purchase differential balance to the asset accounts ($2,898,000) is less than the ending purchase differential balance numerically expected ($3,056,925).

The fifth journal entry recognizes Palmer's percentage of the translation adjustment for the purchase differentials. It is based on the amount the purchase differential schedule fails to reconcile each year as a result of the changes in exchange rates that have occurred during the year. Palmer records a $127,140 journal entry ($158,925 × .8) to recognize its portion of the amount by which the purchase differential amortization schedule does not reconcile in U.S. dollars.

Journal Entry—Palmer Corporation Books

Dec. 31, 2005	Cumulative Translation Adjustment	127,140	
	Investment in Fabryka		127,140

To record Palmer's ownership interest in the cumulative translation adjustment on Fabryka's purchase differentials. (See schedule in Illustration 6-12 for supporting calculations.)

In each subsequent year, the beginning purchase differential balance will be the ending purchase differential balance from the previous year. Therefore, the beginning purchase differential balance has already been adjusted for the net translation adjustment for all prior years. For example, assume that further exchange rate changes during 2006 result in an additional $300,000 translation adjustment. The journal entry to the *Cumulative Translation Adjustment* account will be $240,000, Palmer's 80 percent of the change in the *Cumulative Translation Adjustment*.

Preparing Consolidated Financial Statements

Illustration 6-13 presents the worksheet needed to prepare the consolidated financial statements for Palmer and Fabryka at December 31, 2005, when the current rate method is applied. Worksheet Eliminations 6-13 presents the worksheet eliminations in journal entry form.

As many as six worksheet eliminations may be required when the current rate method is used to convert the foreign subsidiary's trial balance into U.S. dollars. Four of the worksheet eliminations are the basic worksheet eliminations prepared in previous

ILLUSTRATION 6-13
Worksheet for Consolidation of Palmer Corporation and Subsidiary, Fabryka Manufacturing
80 Percent–Owned Foreign Subsidiary Consolidation Subsequent to Acquisition Date
Current Rate Method (Polish Zloty Functional Currency)
December 31, 2005

	Separate Financial Statements		Adjustments and Eliminations		Consolidated Financial Statements
	Palmer	Fabryka	Debit	Credit	
Income Statement					
Sales	10,000,000	3,279,150			13,279,150
Investment Income, Fabryka	266,460		(2) 266,460		0
Cost of Goods Sold	5,600,000	1,995,000	(3) 91,350		7,686,350
Selling Expenses	1,400,000				1,400,000
General and Administrative Expenses	2,330,000	720,600	(3) 139,125		3,189,725
Consolidated Net Income					1,003,075
Noncontrolling Interest in Net Income of Fabryka			(4) 66,615		66,615
Net Income (to Statement of Retained Earnings)	936,460	563,550	563,550	0	936,460
Retained Earnings Statement					
Retained Earnings (1/1/2005)	6,924,000	1,107,600	(1) 1,107,600		6,924,000
Add: Net Income (from Income Statement)	936,460	563,550	(X) 563,550	(X) 0	936,460
Subtotal	7,860,460	1,671,150			7,860,460
Less: Dividends	(380,000)	(225,000)		(2) 180,000	(380,000)
				(4) 45,000	
Retained Earnings (12/31/2005 to Balance Sheet)	7,480,460	1,446,150	1,671,150	225,000	7,480,460
Balance Sheet					
Cash	4,780,000	609,500			5,389,500
Accounts Receivable (net)	1,800,000	646,300			2,446,300
Inventory (FIFO)	5,500,000	1,200,600	(1) 104,400	(3) 91,350	6,700,600
				(6) 13,050	
Other Current Assets	1,600,000				1,600,000
Total Current Assets	13,680,000	2,456,400			16,136,400
Plant Assets	20,800,000	6,037,500	(6) 23,375	(1) 561,000	26,299,875
Accumulated Depreciation	(6,510,000)	(1,914,750)	(1) 1,584,000	(3) 81,375	(6,995,875)
				(6) 73,750	
Patent		1,624,950	(1) 660,000	(3) 57,750	2,194,200
				(6) 33,000	
Investment in Fabryka	6,121,680		(5) 161,640	(1) 6,324,000	0
			(6) 127,140	(2) 86,460	
Other Noncurrent Assets	1,400,000				1,400,000
Goodwill			(1) 1,500,000	(6) 62,500	1,437,500
Total Long-Term Assets	21,811,680	5,747,700			24,335,700
Total Assets	35,491,680	8,204,100			40,472,100
Current Liabilities	8,930,000	1,196,000			10,126,000
7% Bonds Payable (due 6/30/2010)	4,000,000				4,000,000
Less: Discount on Bonds Payable	(130,000)				(130,000)
9¾% Bonds Payable (due 12/31/2006)		2,300,000			2,300,000

(Continued)

ILLUSTRATION 6-13 *Continued*

	Separate Financial Statements		Adjustments and Eliminations		Consolidated Financial Statements
	Palmer	**Fabryka**	**Debit**	**Credit**	
Less: Discount on Bonds Payable		(46,000)			(46,000)
Total Liabilities	12,800,000	3,450,000			16,250,000
Common Stock ($1 par):					
Palmer, 10,000,000 shares authorized, 6,150,000 shares issued and outstanding	6,150,000				6,150,000
Fabryka, 1,000,000 shares authorized, issued and outstanding		960,000	(1) 960,000		0
Additional Paid-In Capital	9,350,000	2,550,000	(1) 2,550,00		9,350,000
Retained Earnings (12/31/2005 from Statement of Retained Earnings)	7,480,460	1,446,150	(X) 1,671,150	(X) 225,000	7,480,460
Noncontrolling Interest in Fabryka			(5) 40,410	(1) 1,581,000	1,530,420
			(6) 31,785	(4) 21,615	
Cumulative Translation Adjustment	(288,780)	(202,050)		(5) 202,050	(288,780)
Total Stockholders' Equity	22,691,680	4,754,100			24,222,100
Total Liabilities and Stockholders' Equity	35,491,680	8,204,100			40,472,100
			9,413,900	9,413,900	

(1) To eliminate the subsidiary's beginning of period stockholders' equity as well as the parent's beginning of period Investment in Fabryka account, to establish the beginning of period purchase differentials, and to create the beginning of period Noncontrolling Interest in Fabryka account.

(2) To eliminate the change in the Investment in Fabryka account resulting from the parent's recording of dividends and Investment Income.

(3) To amortize purchase differentials for the current period.

(4) To recognize the change in the Noncontrolling Interest in Fabryka account resulting from the subsidiary's recognition of income, purchase differential amortizations, and declaration of dividends.

(5) To allocate trial balance cumulative translation adjustment to Investment in Fabryka and Noncontrolling Interest in Fabryka accounts.

(6) To allocate current period purchase differential translation adjustments to individual accounts.

Worksheet Eliminations 6-13—Journal Entry Form

(1) Common Stock 960,000
Additional Paid-In Capital 2,550,000
Retained Earnings (January 1, 2005) 1,107,600
Inventory 104,400
Accumulated Depreciation 1,584,000
Patents 660,000
Goodwill 1,500,000
    Plant Assets 561,000
    Investment in Fabryka 6,324,000
    Noncontrolling Interest in Fabryka 1,581,000

To eliminate the subsidiary's beginning of period stockholders' equity as well as the parent's beginning of period Investment in Fabryka account, to establish the beginning of period purchase differentials, and to create the beginning of period Noncontrolling Interest in Fabryka account.

(2) Investment Income ($450,840 – $184,380) 266,460
    Investment in Fabryka 86,460
    Dividends Declared 180,000

To eliminate the change in the Investment in Fabryka account resulting from the parent's recording of dividends and Investment Income.

(3)	Cost of Goods Sold	91,350	
	Depreciation Expense (G&A)	81,375	
	Patent Amortization Expense (G&A)	57,750	
	Inventory		91,350
	Accumulated Depreciation		81,375
	Patents		57,750

To amortize purchase differentials for the current period.

(4)	Noncontrolling Interest in Net Income of Subsidiary	66,615	
	[($563,500 – $230,475)(.2)]		
	Noncontrolling Interest in Fabryka		21,615
	Dividends Declared ($225,000 × .2)		45,000

To recognize the change in the Noncontrolling Interest in Fabryka account resulting from the subsidiary's recognition of income, purchase differential amortizations, and declaration of dividends.

(5)	Investment in Fabryka ($202,050 × .8)	161,640	
	Noncontrolling Interest in Fabryka ($202,050 × .2)	40,410	
	Cumulative Translation Adjustment		202,050

To allocate the change in the trial balance cumulative translation adjustment to Investment in Fabryka and Noncontrolling Interest in Fabryka accounts.

(6)	Investment in Fabryka ($158,925 × .8)	127,140	
	Noncontrolling Interest ($158,925 × .2)	31,785	
	Plant Assets	23,375	
	Inventory		13,050
	Accumulated Depreciation		73,750
	Patents		33,000
	Goodwill		62,500

To allocate current period purchase differential translation adjustments to individual accounts.

examples. The two additional worksheet eliminations that may be necessary are a result of the *Cumulative Translation Adjustment.*

Note that there is a *Cumulative Translation Adjustment* in both the parent and the subsidiary columns on the trial balance presented in Illustration 6-13. Recall that 80 percent of Fabryka's trial balance translation adjustment ($202,050) is recognized on Palmer's financial records through a journal entry. The *Cumulative Translation Adjustment* on Palmer's trial balance is made up of $161,640 from Fabryka's trial balance plus $127,140 from the purchase differential amortization schedule. This total ($288,780) is the balance to be reported in the consolidated balance sheet. The $202,050 on Fabryka's trial balance must be eliminated and allocated on a pro rata basis to the parent and the noncontrolling interest. Worksheet elimination (5) removes the *Cumulative Translation Adjustment* from Fabryka's trial balance and adjusts Palmer's *Investment in Fabryka* account for the parent's share of the translation adjustment because $161,640 is included in the investment account. The remainder ($40,410) amends the *Noncontrolling Interest in Fabryka* balance because the *Cumulative Translation Adjustment* represents a decrease in the value of Fabryka's net assets and the noncontrolling interest is a part owner in the net assets.

An additional worksheet elimination (6) is prepared to allocate the translation adjustment relating to purchase differentials to the individual purchase differential accounts. The parent's 80 percent share of the translation adjustment ($127,140) as well as the noncontrolling interest's 20 percent share ($31,785) are assigned to the individual purchase differential accounts according to the individual values calculated in Illustration 6-12. These adjustments are necessary because the beginning purchase differentials established in worksheet elimination (1) were measured using the beginning of period exchange rate and the amortization of the purchase differentials was measured using the average exchange rate in worksheet elimination (3). Yet the consolidated balance sheet must present the unamortized purchase differential balances using the current exchange rate. The individual account translation adjustments calculated in Illustration 6-12 provide the appropriate dollar amounts for adjusting the individual purchase differentials in worksheet elimination (6).

SUMMARY

This chapter presented the basic issues relevant to converting a foreign entity's trial balance from a foreign currency into U.S. dollars. Conversion of the trial balance is needed any time the investor has significant influence or control over the investee. The preparation of consolidated financial statements is not required for the conversion process to be relevant. Equity method journal entries also require the conversion of the investee's trial balance.

The two methods used under current GAAP to convert the investee's trial balance were presented. The temporal and current rate methods were introduced as the appropriate conversion methods under alternative circumstances. The top two sections of Figure 6-3 summarize the application of each method. The bottom section of Figure 6-3 illustrates an additional case that occasionally arises. Assume that Foreign Entity A is an Egyptian sales office of Foreign Entity B, which is

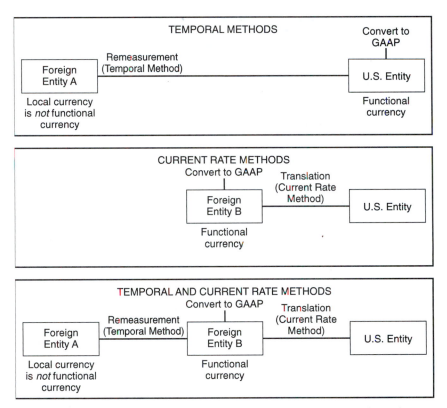

FIGURE 6-3   Summary of Foreign Financial Statement Conversion Procedures

located in Germany. Foreign Entity B is a relatively independent subsidiary of a U.S. entity, so its currency, the euro, is the functional currency. The Foreign Entity A trial balance, measured in Egyptian pounds (EGPs), must first be remeasured (temporal method) into euros so that the financial information of Foreign Entity A and Foreign Entity B can be combined. Once they are combined, the resulting trial balance, in the functional currency, is converted into GAAP and then translated (current rate method) into U.S. dollars.

APPENDIX 6-1
SUBSEQUENT YEAR OWNERSHIP AND CONSOLIDATION

Illustration 6A-1 presents Fabryka's trial balance as prepared by the controller at December 31, 2006. The amounts in the trial balance are stated in Polish zloty and the financial records have been modified to conform to U.S. GAAP.

Assume that inventory is purchased evenly throughout the year and that Fabryka continues to maintain inventory records on a first-in, first-out basis. All of the ending inventory has been acquired during the last three months of the year. Assume also that additional plant assets were purchased on May 31, 2006, for 2,250,000 Polish zloty. These plant assets were assigned an estimated life of 15 years and straight-line depreciation is taken on all plant assets. Dividends were declared and paid on September 1. The following table provides the relevant 2006 exchange rates for Fabryka.

ILLUSTRATION 6A-1
Fabryka's Trial Balance
December 31, 2006

Accounts	Debit (Credit) Polish Zloty
Cash	3,100,000
Accounts Receivable (net)	3,250,000
Inventory (FIFO)	5,750,000
Plant Assets	28,500,000
Accumulated Depreciation	(10,162,500)
Patents	6,280,000
Cost of Goods Sold	11,400,000
Depreciation Expense	1,837,500
Amortization Expense	785,000
Interest Expense	1,250,000
Dividends Declared	1,600,000
Total Debits	53,590,000
Current Liabilities	(5,220,000)
Bonds Payable	(10,000,000)
Discount on Bonds Payable	150,000
Common Stock	(4,000,000)
Additional Paid-In Capital	(10,625,000)
Retained Earnings	(6,045,000)
Sales	(17,850,000)
Total Credits	(53,590,000)

Date	Exchange Rate—Dollars / Zloty
May 31	.16
September 1	.13
December 31	.19
Average for May 31–December 31	.14
Average for fourth quarter	.17
Average for year	.15

The first section that follows demonstrates the continued application of the temporal method. The second section demonstrates the continued application of the current rate method. Each section includes the restatement of the foreign currency trial balance into U.S. dollars, the recording of the equity method journal entries, and the preparation of the worksheet eliminations in journal entry form. The consolidation worksheet is not presented in either section because the posting procedures are the same as presented in the body of the chapter.

APPLICATION OF THE TEMPORAL (REMEASUREMENT) METHOD

When the subsidiary is basically an extension of the parent company, the functional currency is the parent's reporting currency and the temporal method (remeasurement) is used to convert the subsidiary's trial balance into the parent's reporting currency.

Remeasuring the Foreign Currency Trial Balance into U.S. Dollars

The trial balance presented in Illustration 6A-2 includes the remeasurement necessary to convert the Polish zloty trial balance into a U.S. dollar trial balance at December 31, 2006.

The temporal method requires monetary accounts to be revalued using the current exchange rate on the balance sheet date (1 Polish zloty = $.19) so the accounts reflect the U.S. dollar equivalent value of the foreign currency at that date. This can be seen in the Exchange Rate column for *Cash, Accounts Receivable, Current Liabilities, Bonds Payable,* and *Discount on Bonds Payable.* These amounts represent the dollars that would be received or paid if the asset or liability were settled on the balance sheet date.

Each nonmonetary asset and liability account has the historical exchange rate applied to convert the foreign currency amount into U.S. dollars. The historical exchange rate is the exchange rate that existed when the asset was acquired unless the asset was owned when the parent acquired the subsidiary. For example, the *Plant Assets* account presented in Schedule B has three rows in the body of the table. In the previous year there were two rows (see Illustration 6-5, the temporal method example in the body of the chapter). The first two rows of Schedule B in Illustration 6A-2 are the same as in Illustration 6-5. The additional row is for the 2006 purchase of plant assets for 2,250,000 Polish zloty. Notice that the exchange rate for a particular group of plant assets is consistent across all related accounts remeasured in Schedule B. For example, if the $.16 exchange rate is not used for all three accounts remeasured in Schedule B, the sum of the *Depreciation Expense* over time will not equal the balance in the *Accumulated Depreciation* account. In addition, if the same exchange rate is not used, the balance in the *Accumulated Depreciation* account will not equal the balance in the *Plant Assets* account when an asset is fully depreciated.

Other income statement accounts (i.e., those not directly related to nonmonetary assets or liabilities) are remeasured using the average exchange rate for the period ($.15).

ILLUSTRATION 6A-2
Remeasurement of Fabryka's Trial Balance
Functional Currency—U.S. Dollar
December 31, 2006

(Credit) Accounts	Debit (Credit) Polish Zloty	Exchange Rate	Deb U.S. Dollars
Cash	3,100,000	.19 C	589,000
Accounts Receivable (net)	3,250,000	.19 C	617,500
Inventory (FIFO)	5,750,000	Schedule A	977,500
Plant Assets	28,500,000	Schedule B	6,675,000
Accumulated Depreciation	(10,162,500)	Schedule B	(2,433,750)
Patents	6,280,000	.24 H	1,507,200
Cost of Goods Sold	11,400,000	Schedule A	1,960,400
Depreciation Expense	1,837,500	Schedule B	435,000
Amortization Expense	785,000	.24 H	188,400
Interest Expense	1,250,000	.15 A	187,500
Dividends Declared	1,600,000	.13 H	208,000
Totals	53,590,000		10,911,750
Current Liabilities	(5,220,000)	.19 C	(991,800)
Bonds Payable (net)	(10,000,000)	.19 C	(1,900,000)
Discount on Bonds Payable	150,000	.19 C	28,500
Common Stock	(4,000,000)	.24 H	(960,000)
Additional Paid-In Capital	(10,625,000)	.24 H	(2,550,000)
Retained Earnings	(6,045,000)	Schedule C	(1,456,050)
Sales	(17,850,000)	.15 A	(2,677,500)
Remeasurement (Gain) Loss			(404,900)
Totals	(53,590,000)		(10,911,750)

A = average; C = current; H = historical.

Schedule A
Remeasurement of Inventory and Cost of Goods Sold

	Polish Zloty	Exchange Rate	U.S. Dollars
Beginning Inventory (Illustration 6A-1)	5,220,000	.22	1,148,400
Purchases	11,930,000	.15	1,789,500
Goods Available for Sale	17,150,000		2,937,900
Ending Inventory	5,750,000	.17	977,500
Cost of Goods Sold	11,400,000		1,960,400

Schedule B
Remeasurement of Plant Assets

Date	Polish Zloty	Exchange Rate	U.S. Dollars
Date of Acquisition	24,750,000	.24	5,940,000
Purchase March 31, 2005	1,500,000	.25	375,000
Purchase May 31, 2006	2,250,000	.16	360,000
Ending Balance	28,500,000		6,675,000

ILLUSTRATION 6A-2 *Continued*

Remeasurement of Depreciation Expense

Date	Polish Zloty	Exchange Rate	U.S. Dollars
On plant assets owned at date of acquisition	1,650,000	.24	396,000
On purchase March 31, 2005	100,000	.25	25,000
On purchase May 31, 2006			
[(2,250,000/15)(7/12)]	87,500	.16	14,000
Totals	1,837,500		435,000

Remeasurement of Accumulated Depreciation

Date	Polish Zloty	Exchange Rate	U.S. Dollars
On plant assets owned at date of acquisition	9,900,000	.24	2,376,000
On purchase March 31, 2005	175,000	.25	43,750
On purchase May 31, 2006	87,500	.16	14,000
Totals	10,162,500		2,433,750

Schedule C
Remeasurement of Retained Earnings

	U.S. Dollars
Balance from January 1, 2005	$1,107,600
2005 Net Income	573,450
2005 Dividends	(225,000)
Balance January 1, 2006	$1,456,050

For example, the accounts *Sales* and *Interest Expense* are remeasured in this manner. This approach implicitly assumes that these account balances are the result of transactions occurring evenly throughout the period.

As with the temporal method example in the body of the chapter, contributed capital accounts (e.g., *Common Stock, Preferred Stock, Additional Paid-In Capital*) are remeasured using the exchange rate that existed when Fabryka was acquired by Palmer. Recall that the worksheet elimination (1) amounts to remove the contributed capital accounts are the same each period assuming there are no transactions in Fabryka's stock after Palmer's investment. The dollar amount of the elimination to these accounts can remain the same only if the exchange rate applied to them is the same every period.

The *Dividends Declared* account is remeasured using the exchange rate that exists at the transaction date ($.13) because relatively few dividend transactions occur and gathering exchange rate data is not viewed as an undue burden. On the other hand, determining the trial balance amount in U.S. dollars for *Retained Earnings* in years subsequent to the acquisition year is more involved. The U.S. dollar balance at the acquisition date was determined by applying the exchange rate in existence at the acquisition date. However, over time, Fabryka's *Retained Earnings* is altered by its net income and by dividends declared. These amounts are determined using a variety of exchange rates. As a result, it is not possible to directly determine Fabryka's beginning *Retained Earnings* balance in

ILLUSTRATION 6A-3
Fabryka Manufacturing
Remeasured Income Statement
December 31, 2006

	U.S. Dollars
Sales	$2,677,500
Cost of Goods Sold	(1,960,400)
Gross Profit	717,100
Depreciation Expense	(435,000)
Amortization Expense	(188,400)
Interest Expense	(187,500)
Remeasurement Gain	404,900
Net Income (Loss)	$311,100

periods subsequent to the first year of ownership. Schedule C presents the calculation of the U.S. dollar amount of *Retained Earnings* for the 2006 trial balance. The January 1, 2006, *Retained Earnings* presented in the December 31, 2006, trial balance ($1,456,050) is the sum of the January 1, 2005, balance ($1,107,600) plus the 2005 net income ($573,450, from Illustration 6-7), less the 2005 dividends declared ($225,000).

After the trial balance has been converted from Polish zloty into U.S. dollars, an adjustment is made to equate debit and credit balances in U.S. dollars. The *Remeasurement Gain or Loss* is included in income because the temporal method is applied when the U.S. dollar is the functional currency, and changes in the value of Fabryka's assets and liabilities directly impact Palmer's cash flows. Fabryka's remeasured 2006 income statement is presented in Illustration 6A-3.

Recording Equity Method Journal Entries

The temporal method results in the same three equity method journal entires that would be made for a domestic subsidiary: recognition of the parent's ownership interest in the subsidiary's net income, recognition of the parent's share of dividends declared by the subsidiary, and amortization of the parent's ownership interest in the purchase differentials. The first journal entry presents Palmer's recognition of its ownership interest in Fabryka's net income.

Journal Entry—Palmer Corporation Books

Dec. 31, 2006	Investment in Fabryka ($311,100 × .8)	248,880	
	Investment Income		248,880

To record Palmer's ownership interest in Fabryka net income.

The second journal entry presents Palmer's recognition of its ownership interest in the dividends declared by Fabryka. As with a domestic subsidiary, the declaration of the dividend reduces Palmer's investment account balance.

Journal Entry—Palmer Corporation Books

Sept. 1, 2006	Cash ($208,000 × .8)	166,400	
	Investment in Fabryka		166,400

To record the distribution of Fabryka's dividend.

The third journal entry recognizes the amortization of Palmer's ownership in the purchase differentials created at the date of acquisition in the body of the chapter (see Illustration 6-2). The purchase differential assigned to *Inventory* at the date of acquisition was fully amortized during the first year. The purchase differentials for *Plant Assets* ($1,584,000 – $561,000) and for *Patents* ($660,000) are being amortized over 11 years and 10 years, respectively.

Journal Entry—Palmer Corporation Books

Dec. 31, 2006	Investment Income	127,200	
	[($1,023,000/11) + ($660,000/10)](.8)		
	Investment in Fabryka		127,200

To record the amortization of the purchase differentials relevant for the investment in Fabryka stock.

The journal entries presented for Palmer are the same as the journal entries that would be recognized had Fabryka been a domestic subsidiary. The only difference is that an additional item, *Remeasurement Gain or Loss*, in included in the calculation of Fabryka's net income.

Preparing Consolidated Financial Statements

Once the subsidiary's accounts are remeasured, the process of preparing the consolidated financial statements for a foreign subsidiary when the remeasurement approach is applied is the same as preparing the consolidated financial statements for a domestic subsidiary. As in 2005, four basic worksheet eliminations are prepared. These four eliminations in journal entry from are presented in Worksheet Eliminations (Temporal Method).

Worksheet Eliminations (Temporal Method)—Journal Entry Form

(1)	Common Stock	960,000	
	Additional Paid-In Capital	2,550,000	
	Retained Earnings (January 1, 2006)	1,456,050	
	Accumulated Depreciation ($1,584,000 – $93,000)	1,491,000	
	Patents ($660,000 – $66,000)	594,000	
	Goodwill	1,500,000	
	Plant Assets		561,000
	Investment in Fabryka ($6,324,000 + $68,040)		6,392,040
	Noncontrolling Interest in Fabryka ($1,581,000 + $17,010)		1,598,010

To eliminate the subsidiary's beginning of period stockholders' equity as well as the parent's beginning of period Investment in Fabryka account, to establish the beginning of period purchase differentials, and to create the beginning of period Noncontrolling Interest in Fabryka account.

(2)	Investment Income ($248,880 – $127,200)	121,680	
	Investment in Fabryka	44,720	
	Dividends Declared		166,400

To eliminate the change in the Investment in Fabryka account and the parent's Investment Income account.

(3) Depreciation Expense (G&A) [($1,584,000 − $561,000)/11]	93,000	
Patents Amortization Expense (G&A) ($660,000/10)	66,000	
Plant Assets		93,000
Patents		66,000
To amortize purchase differentials for the current period.		
(4) Noncontrolling Interest in Net Income of Subsidiary	30,420	
[($311,200 − $93,000 − $66,000)(.2)]		
Noncontrolling Interest in Fabryka	11,180	
Dividends Declared ($208,000 × .2)		41,600
To recognize the change in the Noncontrolling Interest in Fabryka account during the period.		

The worksheet eliminations to *Common Stock* and *Additional Paid-In Capital* are the same as in 2005. The beginning 2006 *Retained Earnings* worksheet elimination amount was calculated in the trial balance. Recall that this amount was the net of the beginning 2005 *Retained Earnings* balance ($1,107,600), plus the 2005 net income ($573,450), less the 2005 dividends ($225,000). The 2006 unamortized purchase differentials recognized in worksheet elimination (1) can be determined from the worksheet elimination (1) unamortized balance in 2005 less the 2005 worksheet elimination (3) amortization (see Illustration 6-8 in the body of the chapter). For example, the *Patents* 2005 beginning unamortized balance ($660,000) less the 2005 worksheet elimination adjustment ($66,000) is the 2006 unamortized balance ($594,000). The 2006 worksheet elimination (1) *Investment in Fabryka* amount is the actual January 1, 2006, account balance. This can also be calculated by adjusting the 2005 worksheet elimination (1) amount for the 2005 changes in the account. The *Noncontrolling Interest in Fabryka* amount can also be calculated from the 2005 worksheet eliminations that create the December 31, 2005, *Noncontrolling Interest in Fabryka* balance.

As with a domestic subsidiary, worksheet eliminations (2), (3), and (4) adjust the amounts in worksheet elimination (1). Worksheet elimination (2) eliminates the change in the *Investment in Fabryka* account and Palmer's *Investment Income* account. Worksheet elimination (3) amortizes the purchase differentials. Worksheet elimination (4) adjusts the recognized amount of noncontrolling interest.

APPLICATION OF THE CURRENT RATE (TRANSLATION) METHOD

When a foreign entity is relatively self-contained in the foreign country, the local currency of that country is generally the functional currency and the current rate method (translation) is used to convert the subsidiary's trial balance into the parent's reporting currency. The following example assumes that the Polish zloty is Fabryka's functional currency.

Translating the Foreign Currency Trial Balance into U.S. Dollars

The trial balance presented in Illustration 6A-4 includes the translation necessary to convert the Polish zloty trial balance into U.S. dollars when it is appropriate to apply the current rate method.

Illustration 6A-4 indicates that all Fabryka's assets and liabilities are translated using the exchange rate at the balance sheet date. One exchange rate is used for the translation of the assets and liabilities because the objective of this process is to change the unit of measure while retaining the relationship that exists among the accounts. Income statement

ILLUSTRATION 6A-4
Translation of Fabryka's Trial Balance
Functional Currency—Polish Zloty
December 31, 2006

Accounts	Debit (Credit) Polish Zloty	Exchange Rate	Debit (Credit) U.S. Dollars
Cash	3,100,000	.19 C	589,000
Accounts Receivable (net)	3,250,000	.19 C	617,500
Inventory (FIFO)	5,750,000	.19 C	1,092,500
Plant Assets	28,500,000	.19 C	5,415,000
Accumulated Depreciation	(10,162,500)	.19 C	(1,930,875)
Patents	6,280,000	.19 C	1,193,200
Cost of Goods Sold	11,400,000	.15 A	1,710,000
Depreciation Expense	1,837,500	Schedule A	274,750
Amortization Expense	785,000	.15 A	117,750
Interest Expense	1,250,000	.15 A	187,500
Dividends Declared	1,600,000	.13 H	208,000
Totals	53,590,000		9,474,325
Current Liabilities	(5,220,000)	.19 C	(991,800)
Bonds Payable (net)	(10,000,000)	.19 C	(1,900,000)
Discount on Bonds Payable	150,000	.19 C	28,500
Common Stock	(4,000,000)	.24 H	(960,000)
Additional Paid-In Capital	(10,625,000)	.24 H	(2,550,000)
Retained Earnings	(6,045,000)	Schedule B	(1,446,150)
Sales	(17,850,000)	.15 A	(2,677,500)
Cumulative Translation Adjustment			1,022,625
Totals	(53,590,000)		(9,474,325)

A = average; C = current; H = historical.

Schedule A
Translation of Depreciation Expense

Date	Polish Zloty	Exchange Rate	U.S. Dollars
On plant assets owned at beginning of year	1,750,000	.15	262,500
On purchase May 31, 2006 [(2,250,000/15)(7/12)]	87,500	.14	12,250
Totals	1,837,500		274,750

Schedule B
Translation of Retained Earnings

	U.S. Dollars
Balance from January 1, 2005	$1,107,600
2005 Net Income	563,550
2005 Dividends	(225,000)
Balance January 1, 2006	$1,446,150

ILLUSTRATION 6A-5
Fabryka Manufacturing
Translated Income Statement
December 31, 2006

	U.S. Dollars
Sales	$2,677,500
Cost of Goods Sold	(1,710,000)
Gross Profit	967,500
Depreciation Expense	(274,750)
Amortization Expense	(117,750)
Interest Expense	(187,500)
Net Income (Loss)	$387,500

accounts are generally translated using the average exchange rate for the period (the exception is depreciation expense where two average exchange rates are used because of the mid-year acquisition of plant assets). Fabryka's translated 2006 income statement is presented in Illustration 6A-5.

The equity accounts are revalued in approximately the same manner as in the temporal method. Contributed capital accounts (e.g., *Common Stock, Preferred Stock, Additional Paid-In Capital*) are translated using the exchange rate that exists when Fabryka was acquired, assuming that no additional stock transactions have occurred. Dividends are translated using the exchange rate that exists when the dividends are declared. The beginning *Retained Earnings* balance is carried forward from the prior period, as in the temporal method. For example, the January 1, 2006, *Retained Earnings* presented in the December 31, 2006, trial balance is the translated beginning 2005 balance ($1,107,600), plus the 2005 net income ($563,550), less the 2005 dividends declared ($225,000). The translated U.S. dollar amount of ending *Retained Earnings* will not be the same as the remeasured dollar amount beyond the date of acquisition because different exchange rates are used to convert the income statement accounts and the current rate method does not generate a *Remeasurement (Gain) Loss* in the income statement.

The adjustment necessary to equate debit and credit balances in U.S. dollars once the trial balance is converted from the Polish zloty to the U.S. dollar is titled *Cumulative Translation Adjustment*. Just as in 2005, this amount is *not* included in the determination of consolidated net income because the subsidiary operates independently of the parent, so changes in the value of the assets and liabilities are not likely to have a direct cash flow effect for the parent. Instead, the *Cumulative Translation Adjustment* is reported as a balance sheet adjustment to stockholders' equity. The *Cumulative Translation Adjustment* balance at the end of 2005 was a $202,050 debit, and the 2006 *Cumulative Translation Adjustment* is a $1,022,625 debit. Thus, there is an $820,575 debit change in the *Cumulative Translation Adjustment* balance ($1,022,625 – $202,050).

Recording Equity Method Journal Entries

Consistent with 2005, the current rate method requires as many as five equity method journal entries on the parent's financial records. The first journal entry presents Palmer's recognition of its ownership interest in Fabryka's net income.

Journal Entry—Palmer Corporation Books

Dec. 31, 2006	Investment in Fabryka ($387,500 × .8)	310,000	
	Investment Income		310,000
	To record Palmer's ownership interest in Fabryka net income.		

Note that the first journal entry is the same as an equity method journal entry that would be required for a domestic subsidiary. Palmer recognizes its 80 percent–ownership interest in Fabryka's reported net income on its separate financial records. The remaining 20 percent–ownership interest in Fabryka's net income is recognized as part of the worksheet eliminations for noncontrolling interest.

The second journal entry presents Palmer's recognition of its 80-percent share in the dividends distributed by Fabryka. As with a domestic subsidiary, the distribution of the dividend reduces Palmer's investment account balance.

Journal Entry—Palmer Corporation Books

Sept. 1, 2006	Cash ($208,000 × .8)	166,400	
	Investment in Fabryka		166,400
	To record the distribution of Fabryka's dividend.		

The third journal entry addresses the change in the *Cumulative Translation Adjustment*.

Journal Entry—Palmer Corporation Books

Dec. 31, 2006	Cumulative Translation Adjustment	656,460	
	Investment in Fabryka [($1,022,625 − $205,050)(.80)]		656,460
	To record Palmer's pro rata share of the cumulative translation adjustment on Fabryka's trial balance.		

As with the income of Fabryka, Palmer recognizes 80 percent of the change in the *Cumulative Translation Adjustment* because the difference between the 2005 and 2006 trial balance amounts represents the change in the translated value of 100 percent of Fabryka's net assets, and Palmer owns only 80 percent of Fabryka's net assets. The journal entry is based on the change in the trial balance amount from 2005 to 2006 ($1,022,625 − $202,050) because the *Cumulative Translation Adjustment* is a balance sheet account. As a result, the 2005 balance is carried forward to 2006.

As with the temporal method, the purchase differential amortization is accomplished in the functional currency. However, the functional currency is the Polish zloty when applying the current rate method, not the U.S. dollar. As a result, an amortization schedule must be prepared in the Polish zloty and translated into the U.S. dollar to prepare the journal entry. Illustration 6A-6 presents the purchase differential amortization and translation adjustment schedules that lead to the fourth and fifth equity method journal entries.

The beginning 2006 purchase differential in dollars for each account is the unamortized purchase differential in Polish zloty translated at the January 1 exchange rate ($.23). Note that the beginning 2006 purchase differential is the same as the ending 2005 purchase differential presented in the chapter section entitled Application of the Current Rate (Translation) Method (see Illustration 6-12).

The purchase differential amortizations for the current period are calculated in the functional currency (Polish zloty in this example) and translated into U.S. dollars. The translated amounts are based on the average exchange rate that exists for the period. This is consistent with the exchange rates used for most income statement accounts on the trial

ILLUSTRATION 6A-6
Amortization of Purchase Differentials When Applying the Current Rate Method

Account	Beginning Balance			Amortization			Ending Balance		
	Zloty	Exchange Rate	Dollars	Zloty	Exchange Rate	Dollars	Zloty	Exchange Rate	Dollars
Plant Assets	(2,337,500)	.23	(537,625)	0	.15	0	(2,337,500)	.19	(444,125)
Accumulated Depreciation	6,212,500	.23	1,428,875	387,500*	.15	58,125	5,825,000	.19	1,106,750
Patents	2,475,000	.23	569,250	275,000	.15	41,250	2,200,000	.19	418,000
Goodwill	6,250,000	.23	1,437,500	0	.15	0	6,250,000	.19	1,187,500
Totals	12,600,000		2,898,000	662,500		99,375	11,937,500		2,268,125

	Translation Adjustment			
	Beginning	Amortization	Ending	Translation Adjustment
Plant Assets	(537,625)	0	(444,125)	(93,500)
Accumulated Depreciation	1,428,875	58,125	1,106,750	264,000
Patents	569,250	41,250	418,000	110,000
Goodwill	1,437,500	0	1,187,500	250,000
Totals				530,500

* (6,212,500 − 2,337,500)/10

balance. The income statement accounts are the relevant points of reference because purchase differential amortizations are adjustments to the consolidated income statement. Information from this part of the illustration supports the amortization of the purchase differentials on Palmer's financial records and the worksheet elimination that amortizes purchase differentials in the consolidated income statement. The fourth journal entry recognizes the amortization of Palmer's purchase differentials created at the acquisition date.

Journal Entry—Palmer Corporation Books

Dec. 31, 2006   Investment Income   79,500
                    Investment in Fabryka ($99,375 × .8)   79,500
To record the amortization of the purchase differentials relevant for the investment in Fabryka stock. (See Illustration 6A-6 for supporting calculations.)

The unamortized purchase differentials as of the end of the period are based on beginning of period Polish zloty balances less amortization in the current period (in Polish zloty). The ending unamortized Polish zloty amounts are translated using the exchange rate that exists at the balance sheet date. This is consistent with the exchange rate used to translate assets and liabilities on the trial balance. Values from this part of the illustration are the unamortized purchase differentials included in the consolidated balance sheet.

The fifth journal entry recognizes the Palmer's portion of the translation adjustment for the purchase differentials. The purchase differential translation adjustment is determined by the amount that the unamortized beginning purchase differential ($2,898,000) less the amortization ($99,375) fails to equal the ending unamortized purchase differential ($2,268,125). This journal entry is for $424,400 ($530,500 × .8), the amount by which the Palmer's ownership percentage of the purchase differential amortization schedule does not reconcile in U.S. dollars.

Journal Entry—Palmer Corporation Books

Dec. 31, 2006	Cumulative Translation Adjustment	424,400	
	Investment in Fabryka		424,400

To record Palmer's ownership interest in the cumulative translation adjustment on Fabryka's purchase differentials. (See Illustration 6A-6 for supporting calculations.)

Preparing Consolidated Financial Statements

Worksheet Eliminations (Current Rate Method) presents the worksheet eliminations in journal entry form. Worksheet elimination (1) in 2006 is constructed in the same manner as worksheet elimination (1) in 2005 except that the 2006 worksheet elimination includes an additional equity account (*Cumulative Translation Adjustment*). Fabryka's beginning of period *Cumulative Translation Adjustment* amount is the $202,050 recognized in the 2005 worksheet elimination (5) (see Illustration 6-13 in the body of the chapter). The beginning *Cumulative Translation Adjustment* is eliminated in worksheet elimination (1) because it was included in the *Investment in Fabryka* account when Palmer made its 2005 journal entries. The elimination of the *Cumulative Translation Adjustment* also changes Fabryka's total equity, and its elimination adjusts the *Noncontrolling Interest in Fabryka* account.

Worksheet eliminations (2), (3), and (4) are prepared as they have been in previous consolidation examples. Worksheet elimination (2) eliminates Palmer's *Investment Income* and the change in the *Investment in Fabryka* account due to Fabryka's reported income, dividends declared, and purchase differential amortizations. Worksheet elimination (3) allocates the purchase differential amortizations to the appropriate income statement accounts. Worksheet elimination (4) recognizes *Noncontrolling Interest in Net Income of Subsidiary* on the consolidated income statement and adjusts the *Noncontrolling Interest* on the consolidated balance sheet due to the noncontrolling interest's portion of Fabryka's recognized income, amortization of the purchase differentials, and dividends declared.

Worksheet elimination (5) allocates the change in the trial balance *Cumulative Translation Adjustment* to Palmer and the noncontrolling interest. Palmer recorded its share of the change (with a debit to *Cumulative Translation Adjustment* of $656,460) in the third equity method journal entry presented previously. Worksheet elimination (5) removes the change in the *Cumulative Translation Adjustment* from Fabryka's trial balance with a credit elimination, reverses the entry made to the *Investment in Fabryka* account in the journal entry, and assigns the remainder to the *Noncontrolling Interest*. The *Noncontrolling Interest* is debited in this instance because the change in Fabryka's *Cumulative Translation Adjustment* on the trial balance (from a debit of $202,050 in 2005 to a debit of $1,022,625 in 2006) is a debit adjustment. As a result, the *Cumulative Translation Adjustment* is credited in worksheet elimination (5) to remove it from the consolidated balance sheet. The *Noncontrolling Interest* is reduced (debit worksheet elimination) to show that its portion of Fabryka's book value has decreased due to the change in the exchange rate.

The worksheet elimination (6) translation adjustment allocation to the purchase differential accounts includes only the translation adjustment for 2006. The purchase differential translation adjustment from 2005 is included in the beginning purchase differential amounts presented in worksheet elimination (1). A specific recognition of the beginning translation adjustment on the purchase differentials is not required because the ending unamortized purchase differentials in the previous period are translated at the balance sheet date exchange rate. As a result, these balances include the 2005 translation adjustments.

As in 2005, worksheet elimination (6) is prepared to eliminate the purchase differential translation adjustment from the *Investment in Fabryka* account ($424,400) and reduce the *Noncontrolling Interest in Fabryka* account for its share of the purchase differential translation adjustment ($106,100) while assigning the translation adjustment to the individual purchase differential accounts according to the amounts calculated in Illustration 6A-6. The purchase differential translation adjustments are necessary to create the balance sheet purchase differential amounts. The consolidated balance sheet must present the unamortized purchase differential balances using the current exchange rate. The beginning purchase differential created in worksheet elimination (1) using the beginning of period exchange rate less the purchase differential amortization in worksheet elimination (3) measured using the average exchange rate does not create the necessary ending pruchase differential amount for the consolidated balance sheet. The individual account translation adjustments calculated in Illustration 6A-6 provide the appropriate dollar amount of adjustment for the individual purchase differential accounts. For example, the $569,250 beginning *Patent* purchase differential less the $41,250 amortization less the $110,000 translation adjustment amount creates the required $418,000 balance sheet purchase differential amount. These amounts can be seen in Illustration 6A-6 and Worksheet Eliminations (Current Rate Method).

Worksheet Eliminations (Current Rate Method)—Journal Entry Form

(1) Common Stock	960,000	
Additional Paid-In Capital	2,550,000	
Retained Earnings (January 1, 2006)	1,446,150	
Accumulated Depreciation	1,428,875	
Patents	569,250	
Goodwill	1,437,500	
Cumulative Translation Adjustment		202,050
Plant Assets		537,625
Investment in Fabryka ($6,324,000 + $86,460 − $161,640 − $127,140)		6,121,680
Noncontrolling Interest in Fabryka ($1,581,000 + $21,615 − $40,410 − $31,785)		1,530,420

To eliminate the subsidiary's beginning of period stockholders' equity (including the beginning Cumulative Translation Adjustment balance) as well as the parent's beginning of period Investment in Fabryka account, to establish the beginning of period purchase differentials, and to create the beginning of period Noncontrolling Interest in Fabryka account.

(2) Investment Income ($310,000 − $79,500)	230,500	
Investment in Fabryka		64,100
Dividends Declared		166,400

To eliminate the change in the Investment in Fabryka account resulting from the parent's recording of dividends and Investment Income.

(3) Depreciation Expense (G&A)	58,125	
Patent Amortization Expense (G&A)	41,250	
Accumulated Depreciation		58,125
Patents		41,250

To amortize purchase differentials for the current period.

(4)	Noncontrolling Interest in Net Income of Subsidiary [($387,500 − $99,375)(.20)]	57,625	
	Noncontrolling Interest in Fabryka		16,025
	Dividends Declared ($208,000 × .20)		41,600

To recognize the change in the Noncontrolling Interest in Fabryka account resulting from the subsidiary's recognition of income, purchase differential amortization, and declaration of dividends.

(5)	Investment in Fabryka ($820,575 × .8)	656,460	
	Noncontrolling Interest in Fabryka ($820,575 × .2)	164,115	
	Cumulative Translation Adjustment ($1,022,625 − $202,050)		820,575

To allocate the change in the trial balance cumulative translation adjustment to Investment in Fabryka and Noncontrolling Interest in Fabryka accounts.

(6)	Investment in Fabryka	424,400	
	Noncontrolling Interests	106,100	
	Plant Assets	93,500	
	Accumulated Depreciation		264,000
	Patents		10,000
	Goodwill		250,000

To allocate current period purchase differential translation adjustments to individual accounts.

QUESTIONS

6-1. Technology Edge is a small regional computer manufacturer. Management is considering expanding the company's business because current operations, in the United States only, are limiting the company's profitability. The problem is that management does not have experience in multinational operations. Prepare a memo to management explaining some ways in which they can expand the company's sales into foreign markets.

6-2. Management of Maxwell Industries is considering some changes in its inventory policies to increase the importing of inventory from South Korea, which has only recently began producing this inventory item. The division manager responsible for product quality has little experience in international operations. As a result, she is concerned about potential quality problems when purchasing inventory from this source. Prepare a memo to the division manager explaining some ways in which Maxwell Industries can acquire more inventory from South Korea.

6-3. You open an e-mail from a colleague and read the following: "I realize that there is more than one way to convert foreign financial currency financial information into U.S. dollars. Is the method used something that is chosen by management or are there guidelines?" Prepare a response to this request to explain the underlying reason for the existence of two methods for converting foreign currency financial information into U.S. dollars. Provide the reference from accounting standards so your colleague can get some additional information if needed. (*Hint*: Search FAS No. 52.)

6-4. Compare and contrast the local, foreign, functional, and parent reporting currencies.

6-5. Sam Kippel is a new staff member in a large multinational corporation's international operations group. Sam just returned from two days of training and has indicated that there is a lot of information to understand in international operations. He has asked for some clarification on the difference between the local currency of a foreign subsidiary and a foreign currency. How do you respond?

6-6. Is the functional currency of a foreign subsidiary easy to determine? Why or why not?

6-7. You are the controller in a company with a new CFO. She tells you that senior management is not pleased with the performance of one of the foreign subsidiaries. Her suggestion is to change the functional currency of the subsidiary to the *subsidiary's local currency*. You recall that there is something in the standards to provide guidance when determining the functional currency. Prepare a brief memo, including the appropriate reference to the standard outlining the factors that would indicate that the local currency is the foreign subsidiary's functional currency. (*Hint*: Search FAS No. 52.)

6-8. You are the controller in a company with a new CFO. She tells you that senior management is not pleased with the performance of one of the foreign subsidiaries. Her suggestion is to change the functional currency of the subsidiary to the *parent's reporting currency*. You recall that there is something in the standards to provide guidance when determining the functional currency. Prepare a brief memo, including the appropriate reference to the standard outlining the factors that would indicate that the parent's reporting currency is the foreign subsidiary's functional currency. (*Hint*: Search FAS No. 52.)

6-9. Bill Baker and Jennifer Harris are having a disagreement. Bill believes that the functional currency of an Italian subsidiary must be either the Italian lira, the local currency, or the U.S. dollar, the parent's reporting currency. Jennifer says that it can also be some other currency. Bill and Jennifer ask for some information on this issue. Prepare a memo explaining what currencies can be the functional currency.

6-10. Why do high inflation rates make it inappropriate to use the foreign subsidiary's local currency as the functional currency?

6-11. Discuss the three steps that may be required to convert foreign financial information into U.S. dollars and include the information in the consolidated financial statements.

6-12. Compare the worksheet eliminations needed to consolidate a U.S. parent and a foreign subsidiary under the temporal method versus a U.S. parent and a domestic subsidiary.

6-13. Compare the worksheet eliminations needed to consolidate a U.S. parent and a foreign subsidiary under the current rate method versus a U.S. parent and a domestic subsidiary.

6-14. Explain the reason for the exchange rate(s) used to convert a foreign subsidiary's trial balance into U.S. dollars at the date of acquisition.

6-15. Ben Sanders is a new member of Webster, Incorporated's board of directors. Webster is a multinational corporation with several foreign subsidiaries. A recent presentation to the board included a brief statement that mentioned two methods used to convert the trial balance of foreign subsidiaries into U.S. dollars. Ben asked why management did not choose the same method for all subsidiaries. Prepare a memo to Ben outlining the need for two methods. (*Hint*: Search FAS No. 52 for authoritative support.)

6-16. Dwayne Lewis was recently promoted to senior management. He was previously head of domestic operations. As a result, he has little knowledge of the entity's three foreign subsidiaries. Dwayne is reviewing some information on the foreign subsidiaries when he notices that the trial balance of one subsidiary is converted into U.S. dollars differently from the other two subsidiaries. The corporate controller comments that he applies the temporal method for this subsidiary. Dwayne asks why there are so many different exchange rates used for this method. The corporate controller has given you the opportunity to respond to Dwayne's inquiry. How do you respond?

6-17. What is the basis for deciding whether to use the spot rate or some other exchange rate when converting a foreign subsidiary's trial balance accounts into U.S. dollars under the temporal method?

6-18. Compare and contrast monetary and nonmonetary accounts.

6-19. Prepare a short discussion, including authoritative support, indicating why historical exchange rates are used to convert a foreign subsidiary's nonmonetary account balances into U.S. dollars under the temporal method. (*Hint*: Search FAS No. 52).

6-20. Sheila Thompson is the division manager of a foreign subsidiary. She recently received the U.S. dollar trial balance for the subsidiary and she wants to know why the income statement accounts are not all converted into U.S. dollars at the same exchange rate. Prepare a memo responding to Sheila's inquiry.

6-21. Brian Jacobi is reviewing the U.S. dollar financial statements for a German subsidiary when he notices that there is an item on the income statement with which he is unfamiliar (Remeasurement Gain). Prepare a note to Brian explaining the purpose of the remeasurement gain and the reason it is on the income statement.

6-22. Compare the equity method journal entries recorded for a domestic subsidiary with the equity method journal entries recorded for a foreign subsidiary when the temporal method is applied.

6-23. Marge Hemingway is a new member of senior management. She has been part of the management team for some time, but this is her first occasion to review the corporation's foreign operations. She notices that some foreign subsidiaries have an additional equity account that is not on the converted trial balance of other subsidiaries (Cumulative Translation Adjustment). Prepare a memo to Marge explaining the reason for this account.

6-24. Is the journal entry required to recognize the Cumulative Translation Adjustment for a foreign subsidiary's trial balance always equal to the parent's percentage ownership times the figure on the trial balance? Why or why not?

6-25. Is the dollar amount of the foreign subsidiary's purchase differentials established at the date of acquisition the same regardless of whether the temporal or current rate method is applied? Why or why not?

6-26. Is the purchase differential amortization for a foreign subsidiary the same regardless of whether the temporal or current rate method is applied? Why or why not?

6-27. Jim Skiles is the new vice president for international operations. Jim has worked in international operations for some time, but he is not an accountant. He recently asked the corporate controller why some procedures applied are not the same for all foreign subsidiaries. The controller asked Jim to be more specific, and Jim commented about the way purchase differentials are amortized. The corporate controller said they are basically handled the same. Jim is confused because the calculations are different. Prepare a memo to Jim clarifying what the corporate controller meant.

6-28. The purchase differential schedule for a foreign subsidiary, when the current rate method is applied, is broken into three parts. Explain how the information in the beginning balance portion of the purchase differential schedule is used by the parent when preparing journal entries and/or consolidated financial statements.

6-29. The purchase differential schedule for a foreign subsidiary, when the current rate method is applied, is broken into three parts. Explain how the information in the amortization portion of the purchase differential schedule is used by the parent when preparing journal entries and/or consolidated financial statements.

6-30. The purchase differential schedule for a foreign subsidiary, when the current rate method is applied, is broken into three parts. Explain how the information in the ending balance portion of the purchase differential schedule is used by the parent when preparing journal entries and/or consolidated financial statements.

6-31. Why is it possible that there will be more journal entries on the parent's financial records when the current rate method is applied to convert a foreign subsidiary's financial information into U.S. dollars as compared to when the temporal method is applied?

MULTIPLE CHOICE

6-1. Stewart Enterprises (a U.S. company) purchased 80 percent of Sanchez Corporation (a Mexican company) for 6,500,000 pesos on March 1, 2005. At that date Sanchez had land on its financial records for 250,000 pesos. The land was appraised at 400,000 pesos at the acquisition date. The exchange rate on March 1 and December 31, 2005, was 1 peso = $.16 and $.19, respectively. What is the dollar amount of the purchase differential assigned to land in the 2005 worksheet elimination (1)?

 a. $24,000
 b. $28,500
 c. $19,200
 d. $22,800

6-2. RX Corporation owns 70 percent of Matsuzuka Corporation of Japan. Beginning inventory for the year was purchased for 280,000,000 yen when the exchange rate was 1 yen = $.0008. Purchases of 970,000,000 yen occurred during the year, and the average exchange rate was 1 yen = $.00076. The ending inventory (310,000,000 yen) was acquired when the exchange rate was 1 yen = $.00082. What is Cost of Goods Sold on Matsuzuka's trial balance if the U.S. dollar is the functional currency?

 a. $707,000
 b. $752,000
 c. $714,400
 d. $770,800

6-3. When a foreign subsidiary's trial balance is remeasured into the functional currency, debits and credits often are not equal in the functional currency. Where is the balancing amount placed on the financial statements?

 a. Statement of cash flows
 b. Income statement
 c. Balance sheet
 d. In the footnotes to the balance sheet

6-4. Francis Company (a French entity) is a 60 percent–owned subsidiary of Sunberg Enterprises. What is the dollar amount of the equity method journal entry to recognize Investment income if the remeasured trial balance includes the following accounts (in U.S. dollars).

Current Assets	$ 50,000
Plant Assets	320,000
Cost of Goods Sold	480,000
Depreciation Expense	18,000
Dividends	7,000
Liabilities	140,000
Stockholders' Equity	100,000
Sales	620,000
Remeasurement Gain	15,000

 a. $122,000
 b. $137,000
 c. $64,200
 d. $82,200

6-5. Aussie Corporation is an Australian subsidiary (90 percent) of Mellencamp Enterprises. Aussie's plant assets (A$600,000) were owned all year. Depreciation expense in Australian dollars was A$60,000. The exchange rates at the beginning, ending, and the average for the year were 1A$ = $.52, $.57, and $54, respectively. Assuming that the Australian dollar is the functional currency, what amount of depreciation expense (in U.S. dollars) will be included in Aussie's trial balance?

a. $32,400

b. $31,200

c. $24,200

d. $32,600

6-6. Fraction Company (British) is a 60 percent–owned subsidiary of Review Corporation (U.S.). Fraction's controller prepares a trial balance in conformity with U.S. GAAP and sends it via e-mail to Review's controller. When the trial balance in translated into U.S. dollars, a credit Cumulative Translation Adjustment of $63,000 exists. What is the dollar amount of the journal entry to the Cumulative Translation Adjustment account on Review's financial records if the previous year's trial balance Cumulative Translation Adjustment was a debit of $10,000?

a. $37,800 credit

b. $37,800 debit

c. $43,800 credit

d. $43,800 debit

6-7. Rite Company is a foreign subsidiary of Perfect, Incorporated. At the date of acquisition (when the exchange rate is $.30), the plant assets' purchase differential (10-year life) applicable to Perfect's ownership percentage is 50,000 foreign currency units. What is the amount of purchase differential amortization if the average and ending exchange rates for the period are $.32 and $.37, respectively, and the current rate method is applied?

a. $1,850

b. $1,600

c. $1,500

d. $15,000

6-8. Rite Company is a foreign subsidiary of Perfect, Incorporated. At the date of acquisition (when the exchange rate is $.30), the plant assets' purchase differential (10-year life) applicable to Perfect's ownership percentage is 50,000 foreign currency units. What is the entry to the Cumulative Translation Adjustment account if the average and ending exchange rates for the period are $.32 and $.37, respectively?

a. $3,150 credit

b. $3,150 debit

c. $3,250 credit

d. $3,250 debit

6-9. U.S. Corporation acquired 80 percent of Canada Company on March 15, 2005, for 2,000,000 Canadian dollars when the exchange rate is C$1 = $.64. One purchase differential existed at the acquisition date (C$100,000). Canada's income for 2005 is C$250,000 and the average exchange rate for the year is $.62. Dividends paid during the year are C$40,000 when the exchange rate is $.63. U.S. recorded a Cumulative Translation Adjustment debit entry of $6,400 in 2005. What is the balance in the Noncontrolling Interest account at December 31, 2005?

a. $344,360

b. $280,360

c. $345,704

d. $347,560

6-10. Wilkensen Company purchased 70 percent of the Gillette Corporation (French) on January 1, 2005. At December 31, Gillette's trial balance includes a credit Cumulative Translation Adjustment of $60,000. Wilkensen recorded two Cumulative Translation Adjustment journal entries during 2005. The entry to recognize the trial balance translation adjustment was a credit of $42,000, and the purchase differential translation adjustment was a credit of $10,000. What amount of Cumulative Translation Adjustment is included in the December 31, 2005, consolidated balance sheet?

a. $112,000 credit

b. $32,000 credit

c. $70,000 credit

d. $52,000 credit

EXERCISES

EXERCISE 6-1	Date of acquisition trial balance and worksheet elimination, 100-percent acquisition, positive goodwill
EXERCISE 6-2	Date of acquisition trial balance and worksheet elimination, 100-percent acquisition, negative goodwill
EXERCISE 6-3	Date of acquisition trial balance and worksheet elimination, less than 100-percent acquisition, positive goodwill
EXERCISE 6-4	Date of acquisition trial balance and worksheet elimination, less than 100-percent acquisition, negative goodwill
EXERCISE 6-5	Purchase differential amortizations for temporal and current rate methods, 100-percent ownership

EXERCISE 6-6 Purchase differential amortizations for temporal and current rate methods, less than 100-percent ownership

EXERCISE 6-7 Inventory balance and cost of goods sold for current rate and temporal methods under FIFO and LIFO

EXERCISE 6-8 Plant assets, accumulated depreciation, and depreciation expense for the current rate and temporal methods

EXERCISE 6-9 Trial balance and journal entries for current rate and temporal methods, 100-percent ownership

EXERCISE 6-10 Trial balance and journal entries for current and rate temporal methods, less than 100-percent ownership

EXERCISE 6-1 Hines Corporation purchased 100 percent of the outstanding stock of Lima, Incorporated (a Peruvian company) on January 1, 2005, for 8,000,000 Peruvian new sol. The following abbreviated trial balance, in new sol, was prepared for Lima at the date of acquisition.

	Book Value	Market Value
Cash and Receivables	1,140,000	1,140,000
Inventory	3,509,000	3,600,000
Plant and Equipment (net)	14,600,000	15,900,000
Current Liabilities	(2,300,000)	(2,300,000)
Long-Term Debt	(12,000,000)	(11,400,000)
Common Stock	(1,000,000)	
Retained Earnings	(3,949,000)	

The exchange rate at the date of acquisition is 1 Peruvian new sol = $.22

Required:
A. Prepare a trial balance in U.S. dollars at the date of acquisition.
B. Prepare the journal entry to recognize the acquisition of Lima by Hines.
C. Prepare the worksheet elimination, in journal entry form, at the date of acquisition.

EXERCISE 6-2 Management of Boston Corporation (a U.S. company) is trying to expand operations into Asia. A proposal has been made to acquire a Japanese manufacturing company (Sonyo Enterprises) to meet this objective. The management of Boston has requested information on the dollar values that would appear on the consolidated financial statements if Boston acquires 100 percent of Sonyo for 1,111,500,000 Japanese yen. The exchange rate that exists when this request is made is 1 Japanese yen = $.008. The following is the most recent trial balance, in Japanese yen, for Sonyo Enterprises.

	Book Value	Market Value
Cash and Receivables	125,000,000	125,000,000
Inventory	200,000,000	250,000,000
Plant and Equipment (net)	640,000,000	900,000,000
Patents	375,000,000	450,000,000
Current Liabilities	(187,500,000)	(187,500,000)
Long-Term Debt	(300,000,000)	(300,000,000)
Common Stock	(62,500,000)	
Retained Earnings	(790,000,000)	

Required:
A. Prepare a trial balance in U.S. dollars at the date of acquisition.
B. Prepare the journal entry to recognize the acquisition of Sonyo by Boston.
C. Prepare the worksheet elimination, in journal entry form, at the date of acquisition.

EXERCISE 6-3 Micro Electronics purchased 70 percent of the outstanding stock of LRB, Incorporated (a Canadian company) on January 1, 2005, for 21,000,000 Canadian dollars. The following abbreviated trial balance, in Canadian dollars, was prepared for LRB at the date of acquisition. The exchange rate at the date of acquisition is 1 Canadian dollar = $.65.

	Book Value	Market Value
Cash and Receivables	4,600,000	4,600,000
Inventory	11,000,000	14,000,000

Plant and Equipment (net)	29,000,000	33,000,000
Current Liabilities	(7,000,000)	(7,000,000)
Long-Term Debt	(15,000,000)	(16,200,000)
Common Stock	(2,600,000)	
Retained Earnings	(20,000,000)	

Required:

A. Prepare a trial balance in U.S. dollars at the date of acquisition.

B. Prepare the journal entry to recognize the acquisition of LRB by Micro Electronics.

C. Prepare the worksheet elimination, in journal entry form, at the date of acquisition.

EXERCISE 6-4   Premier Watch Corporation is a U.S. company. To control manufacturing costs, management has decided to acquire 60 percent of a Swiss maker of watch movements. Management has located a closely held Swiss company (Run Right Movements) that has recently had some financial problems because the owner has had a serious illness. When Premier acquired Run Right for 8,430,000 Swiss Francs, the exchange rate was 1 Swiss franc = $.61. The following is the most recent trial balance, in Swiss francs, for Run Right Movements.

	Book Value	Market Value
Cash and Receivables	1,000,000	1,000,000
Inventory	3,600,000	4,000,000
Plant and Equipment (net)	9,200,000	12,600,000
Patents		4,200,000
Current Liabilities	(2,000,000)	(2,000,000)
Long-Term Debt	(5,000,000)	(5,000,000)
Common Stock	(1,900,000)	
Retained Earnings	(4,900,000)	

Required:

A. Prepare a trial balance in U.S. dollars at the date of acquisition.

B. Prepare the journal entry to recognize the acquisition of Run Right Movements by Premier Watch.

C. Prepare the worksheet elimination, in journal entry form, at the date of acquisition.

EXERCISE 6-5   Patterson, Inc. purchased 100 percent of Wilson Corporation, a British company, on January 1, 2006. At that date, the exchange rate was 1 pound = $1.50. The following table presents the purchase differentials that existed at the date of acquisition.

Account	Purchase Differential (Pounds)	Remaining Life
Inventory	640,000	4 months
Plant and Equipment (net)	3,200,000	10 years

The average and ending exchange rates for the current period, 2006, are the following: 1 pound = $1.43, and 1 pound = $1.40, respectively.

Required:

A. Record the journal entry on the parent's financial records to amortize the purchase differential assuming the temporal method is applied to remeasure the subsidiary's financial information into U.S. dollars.

B. Record the journal entry on the parent's financial records to amortize the purchase differential, assuming the current rate method is applied to translate the subsidiary's financial information into U.S. dollars.

EXERCISE 6-6   Kioko Corporation of Japan was purchased (75 percent) by Victorian Enterprise on January 1, 2005. The exchange rate at the date of acquisition was 1 yen = $.0097. The following table presents 100 percent of the purchase differentials that existed at the date of acquisition.

Account	Purchase Differential (Yen)	Remaining Life
Inventory	690,000,000	5 months
Plant and Equipment (net)	1,600,000,000	16 years
Patents	310,000,000	10 years

The beginning, average, and ending exchange rates for 2006, the second year of ownership, are the following: 1 yen = $.0092, 1 yen = $.0090, and 1 yen = $.0086, respectively.

Required:
A. Record the 2006 journal entry on the parent's financial records to amortize the purchase differential, assuming the temporal method is applied to remeasure the financial information of the subsidiary into U.S. dollars.
B. Record the 2006 journal entry on the parent's financial records to amortize the purchase differential, assuming the current rate method is applied to translate the financial information of the subsidiary into U.S. dollars.

EXERCISE 6-7 Jerry's Furniture Company purchased 100 percent of Miller's Hardwood Corporation of Canada on January 1, 2005. The following table presents the inventory levels for Miller's Hardwood in Canadian dollars.

	Exchange Rate	Inventory (Canadian Dollars)
January 1, 2005	.680	600,000
First-quarter average 2005	.725	
2005 average	.710	
Fourth-quarter 2005 average	.690	
December 31, 2005	.682	700,000
First-quarter average 2006	.700	
2006 average	.720	
Fourth-quarter average 2006	.727	
December 31, 2006	.730	850,000

Inventory purchases were made uniformly throughout the year. The purchases, in Canadian dollars, are C$2,500,000 and C$3,300,000 for 2005 and 2006, respectively.

Required:
A. Determine the 2005 and 2006 inventory and cost of goods sold amounts, in U.S. dollars, for Miller's Hardwood, assuming that Miller's Hardwood sells 70 percent of its production to Jerry's Furniture so that the functional currency is the U.S. dollar. Assume also that Miller's maintains first-in, first-out inventory records and that ending inventory results from purchases made in the fourth quarter of the year.
B. Determine the 2005 and 2006 inventory and cost of goods sold amounts, in U.S. dollars, for Miller's Hardwood, assuming that Miller's Hardwood sells 20 percent of its production to Jerry's Furniture so that the functional currency is the Canadian dollar. Assume also that Miller's maintains first-in, first-out inventory records and that ending inventory results from purchases made in the fourth quarter of the year.
C. Determine the 2005 and 2006 inventory and cost of goods sold amounts, in U.S. dollars, for Miller's Hardwood, assuming that Miller's Hardwood sells 70 percent of its production to Jerry's Furniture so that the functional currency is the U.S. dollar. Assume also that Miller's maintains last-in, first-out inventory records and that changes in inventory levels result from purchases made in the fourth quarter of the year.
D. Determine the 2005 and 2006 inventory and cost of goods sold amounts, in U.S. dollars, for Miller's Hardwood, assuming that Miller's Hardwood sells 20 percent of its production to Jerry's Furniture so that the functional currency is the Canadian dollar. Assume also that Miller's maintains last-in, first-out inventory records and that changes in inventory levels result from purchases made in the fourth quarter of the year.

EXERCISE 6-8   TDJ, Incorporated (a Japanese company) is a 70 percent–owned subsidiary of Clarke Enterprises (a U.S. company). TDJ was acquired by Clarke on January 1, 2005. The following table presents information relevant to plant and equipment transactions during a two-year period.

	Exchange Rate	Historical Cost (Yen)
January 1, 2005	.0080	3,750,000,000
October 1, 2005, purchase	.0073	360,000,000
October 1–December 31, 2005, average	.0076	
2005 Average	.0074	
December 31, 2005	.0077	
August 1, 2006, purchase	.0071	288,000,000
December 31, 2006	.0068	
August 1–December 31, 2006, average	.0072	
2006 average	.0070	

Accumulated depreciation at the date of acquisition was 1,600,000,000 yen. All assets are depreciated on a 10-year life with no estimated salvage value.

Required:

A. Determine the amounts that would be disclosed on the 2005 and 2006 balance sheets and income statements with regard to TDJ's plant and equipment, assuming TDJ is closely controlled by Clarke and the functional currency is determined to be the U.S. dollar.

B. Determine the amounts that would be disclosed on the 2005 and 2006 balance sheets and income statements with regard to TDJ's plant and equipment, assuming TDJ operates independent from Clarke and the functional currency is determined to be the Japanese yen.

EXERCISE 6-9   Fredericks, a German corporation, was acquired (100 percent) by Jefferson Enterprises, a U.S. corporation, on January 1, 2005, for 12,700,000 euros when the exchange rate was 1 euro = $.85. Total stockholders' equity of Fredericks at that date was 10,000,000 euros. The purchase differential is assigned as follows: 20 percent to inventory, 30 percent to plant assets, 10 percent to patents, and 40 percent to goodwill. The purchase differentials are amortized over four months for inventory, nine years for plant assets, and five years for patents. The following trial balance, in euros, was received by Jefferson on December 31, 2005.

	Book Value
Cash	800,000
Accounts Receivable	1,900,000
Inventory	3,590,000
Plant Assets	16,200,000
Accumulated Depreciation	(3,400,000)
Patents	1,250,000
Cost of Goods Sold	5,000,000
Depreciation Expense	1,580,000
Patent Amortization Expense	250,000
Other Expenses	500,000
Dividends Declared	1,080,000
Total	28,750,000
Current Liabilities	(3,000,000)
Long-Term Debt	(7,000,000)
Common Stock	(900,000)
Additional Paid-In Capital	(2,600,000)
Retained Earnings	(6,500,000)
Sales	(8,750,000)
Total	(28,750,000)

Fredericks made inventory purchases evenly throughout the year. The ending inventory was purchased during the fourth quarter and first-in, first-out inventory records are maintained. The inventory level at the date of acquisition was 2,800,000 euros. Fredericks owned 13,800,000 euros of plant assets at the date of acquisition. The remainder was acquired on March 1, 2005. All plant assets are depreciated on a 10-year life with no salvage value. There are no patent transactions other than periodic amortization during 2005. Dividends were declared and paid on August 31. No goodwill impairment is necessary for 2005. The following exchange rates (dollars per euro) exist during 2005.

March 1	$.83
August 31	.86
Fourth-quarter average	.88
March 1–December 31 average	.87
2005 average	.89
December 31	.90

Required:

A. Prepare a trial balance in U.S. dollars and record the journal entries on Jefferson's financial records if the temporal method is applied.

B. Prepare a trial balance in U.S. dollars and record the journal entries on Jefferson's financial records if the current rate method is applied.

EXERCISE 6-10   Rossi Corporation, an Italian entity, was acquired (70 percent) by Spectrum, Incorporated, a U.S. corporation, on January 1, 2005, for 8,400,000 euros when the exchange rate was 1 euro = $.860. Total stockholders' equity of Rossi at that date was 9,000,000 euros. The purchase differential is assigned as follows: 15 percent to inventory, 25 percent to plant assets, 20 percent to patents, and 40 percent to goodwill. The purchase differentials are amortized over 5 months for inventory, 5 years for plant assets, and 10 years for patents. The following trial balance, in euros, was received by Spectrum on December 31, 2005.

	Book Value
Cash	260,000
Accounts Receivable	390,000
Inventory	800,000
Plant Assets	14,000,000
Accumulated Depreciation	(4,000,000)
Patents	2,500,000
Cost of Goods Sold	1,400,000
Depreciation Expense	1,300,000
Patent Amortization Expense	200,000
Other Expenses	550,000
Dividends Declared	300,000
Total	17,700,000
Current Liabilities	(700,000)
Long-Term Debt	(2,800,000)
Common Stock	(450,000)
Additional Paid-In Capital	(1,350,000)
Retained Earnings	(7,200,000)
Sales	(5,200,000)
Total	(17,700,000)

Rossi made inventory purchases evenly throughout the year. The inventory at the date of acquisition was composed of two layers: 400,000 euros and 300,000 euros. The relevant exchange rates that existed when these inventory layers were created in 2004 were 1 euro = $.93 and 1 euro = $.95, respectively. Inventory records are maintained on a last-in, first-out basis, and the additional inventory purchased in 2005 was acquired during the fourth quarter. Rossi owned 10,100,000 euros of plant assets at the date of acquisition. An additional 3,000,000 was acquired on February 1, 2005, and 900,000 was acquired on November 1, 2005. All plant assets are depreciated on a 10-year life with no salvage value. Dividends were declared and paid on June 30. The following exchange rates (dollars per euro) exist during 2005.

February 1	$.880
June 30	.874
November 1	.846
February 1–December 31 average	.852
November 1–December 31 average	.846
Fourth-quarter average	.842
2005 average	.870
December 31	.850

Required:

A. Prepare a trial balance in U.S. dollars and record the journal entries on Spectrum's financial records if the temporal method is applied.

B. Prepare a trial balance in U.S. dollars and record the journal entries on Spectrum's financial records if the current rate method is applied.

PROBLEMS

Number	Percent owned	Year	Conversion Method	Other Problem Features
6-1	100	First	Temporal	Mid-year acquisition, goodwill, trial balance, journal entries, worksheet eliminations
6-2	100	First	Current Rate	Mid-year acquisition, goodwill, trial balance, journal entries, worksheet eliminations
6-3	100	Second	Temporal	Continuation of Problem 6-1, year 2 journal entries, worksheet eliminations, consolidation worksheet, and worksheet elimination (1) year 3
6-4	100	Second	Current Rate	Continuation of Problem 6-2, year 2 journal entries, worksheet elimination, consolidation worksheet, and worksheet elimination (1) year 3
6-5	100	First	Temporal	Beginning of year acquisition, trial balance, negative goodwill, journal entries, worksheet eliminations, consolidation worksheet
6-6	100	First	Current Rate	Beginning of year acquisition, trial balance, negative goodwill, journal entries, worksheet eliminations, consolidation worksheet
6-7	100	Second	Temporal	Continuation of Problem 6-5, year 2 journal entries, worksheet eliminations, and worksheet elimination (1) year 3
6-8	100	Second	Current Rate	Continuation of Problem 6-6, year 2 journal entries, worksheet eliminations, and worksheet elimination (1) year 3
6-9	80	First	Temporal	Beginning of year acquisition, goodwill, trial balance, journal entries, worksheet eliminations
6-10	80	First	Current Rate	Beginning of year acquisition, goodwill, trial balance, journal entries, worksheet eliminations
6-11	80	Second	Temporal	Continuation of Problem 6-9, year 2 journal entries, worksheet eliminations, consolidation worksheet, and worksheet elimination (1) year 3
6-12	80	Second	Current Rate	Continuation of Problem 6-10, year 2 journal entries, worksheet eliminations, consolidation worksheet, and worksheet elimination (1) year 3
6-13	60	First	Temporal	Beginning of year acquisition, trial balance, journal entries, worksheet eliminations, consolidation worksheet
6-14	60	First	Current Rate	Beginning of year acquisition, trial balance, journal entries, worksheet eliminations, consolidation worksheet
6-15	60	Second	Temporal	Continuation of Problem 6-13, year 2 journal entries, worksheet eliminations, and worksheet elimination (1) year 3
6-16	60	Second	Current Rate	Continuation of Problem 6-14, year 2 journal entries, worksheet eliminations, and worksheet elimination (1) year 3

PROBLEM 6-1   Henderson Corporation, a U.S. company, acquired 100 percent of Westminster, Incorporated of Great Britain on March 1, 2005, for 5,568,800 British pounds when the exchange rate was 1 pound = $1.425. At the date of acquisition, the following remaining lives were assigned to items with purchase differentials: inventory, 6 months; plant assets, 8 years; patents, 5 years; and long-term debt, 12 years. The following book and market values (in British pounds) exist at the date of acquisition and book values at December 31, 2005.

| | Date of Acquisition | | December 31, 2005 |
	Book Value	Market Value	Book Value
Cash	245,900	245,900	325,000
Accounts Receivable	478,000	478,000	576,000
Inventory	750,000	990,000	840,000
Plant Assets	6,308,000	5,203,200	7,208,000
Accumulated Depreciation	(1,508,000)		(2,023,000)
Patents	960,000	840,000	880,000
Cost of Goods Sold	430,000		2,900,000
Depreciation Expense	100,000		615,000
Patent Amortization	16,000		96,000
Other Expenses	112,000		611,600
Dividends Declared	131,200		274,400
Totals	8,023,100		12,303,000
Current Liabilities	(670,700)	670,700	(780,000)
Long-Term Debt	(2,036,000)	2,266,400	(2,033,000)
Common Stock	(250,000)		(250,000)
Additional Paid-In Capital	(850,000)		(850,000)
Retained Earnings	(3,390,000)		(3,390,000)
Sales	(826,400)		(5,000,000)
Totals	(8,023,100)		(12,303,000)

Inventory records are maintained on a last-in, first-out basis, and the increase in inventory was acquired during March and April. Purchases were made uniformly during the year. Additional property, plant, and equipment were acquired on October 31, 2005. Depreciation expense on the new plant assets is computed on a 10-year life with no salvage value. Dividends are declared and paid on January 31 and July 31.

The following exchange rates exist during 2005.

January 31	1.495
April 30	1.572
July 31	1.485
October 31	1.511
December 31	1.475
March 1–April 30, 2005, average	1.500
March 1–December 31, 2005, average	1.515
October 31–December 31, 2005, average	1.506

Required:
Prepare the following based on the assumption that the U.S. dollar is the functional currency.

A. The trial balance for Westminster in U.S. dollars on December 31, 2005.

B. The journal entries that would be recognized on Henderson's financial records in 2005.

C. The worksheet eliminations needed to prepare the consolidated financial statements at December 31, 2005.

PROBLEM 6-2   (Refer to the information in Problem 6-1.)

Required:
Prepare the following based on the assumption that the British pound is the functional currency.

A. The trial balance for Westminster in U.S. dollars on December 31, 2005.

B. The journal entries that would be recognized on Henderson's financial records in 2005.

C. The worksheet eliminations needed to prepare the consolidated financial statements at December 31, 2005.

PROBLEM 6-3   (Refer to Problem 6-1 for date of acquisition and 2005 information.) Westminster continues to operate as a 100 percent–owned subsidiary during 2006. Westminster purchases additional plant assets on May 1 (1,500,000 pounds). Straight-line depreciation is recorded based on a 10-year estimated life with no salvage value. During the year, Westminster increased inventory levels by 70,000 pounds. The increase in the inventory level is attributed to purchases made in January, February, and March. Inventory purchases were generally made evenly throughout the year, and the last-in, first-out inventory method continued in use. Dividends of 200,000 and 328,000 pounds were declared and paid on January 31 and July 31, respectively. The controllers of Henderson and Westminster prepare the following trial balances at December 31, 2006.

	Henderson	(Pounds) Westminster
Cash	1,470,000	370,000
Accounts Receivable	2,053,000	640,000
Inventory	4,690,000	910,000
Plant Assets	13,746,000	8,708,000
Accumulated Depreciation	(8,329,000)	(2,813,000)
Patents		784,000
Investment in Westminster	9,105,705	
Cost of Goods Sold	14,609,000	3,400,000
Depreciation Expense	2,050,000	790,000
Patent Amortization		96,000
Other Expenses	5,760,000	740,000
Dividends Declared	4,200,000	528,000
Totals	49,354,705	14,153,000
Current Liabilities	(4,100,000)	(930,000)
Long-Term Debt	(6,240,000)	(2,030,000)
Common Stock	(700,000)	(250,000)
Additional Paid-In Capital	(1,480,000)	(850,000)
Retained Earnings	(9,409,731)	(3,893,000)
Sales	(25,766,540)	(6,200,000)
Investment Income	(1,658,434)	
Totals	(49,354,705)	(14,153,000)

The following exchange rates are applicable to 2006.

January 31	1.487
May 1	1.504
July 31	1.498
December 31	1.550
January 1–March 31, 2006, average	1.492
May 1–December 31, 2006, average	1.530
January 1–December 31, 2006, average	1.525

Required:
Prepare the following based on the assumption that the U.S. dollar is the functional currency.

A. The trial balance for Westminster in U.S. dollars on December 31, 2006.

B. The journal entries that would be recognized on Henderson's financial records in 2006.

C. The worksheet eliminations needed to prepare the consolidated financial statements at December 31, 2006.

D. The consolidation worksheet for Henderson and Westminster at December 31, 2006.

E. The worksheet elimination to remove Westminster's beginning of period stockholders' equity, remove Henderson's beginning of period investment account, and create the beginning of period purchase differentials for the 2007 consolidation worksheet.

PROBLEM 6-4   (Refer to the information in Problem 6-3 for current year activities; ignore the trial balances.) The controllers of Henderson and Westminster prepare the following trial balances at December 31, 2006.

	Henderson	(Pounds) Westminster
Cash	1,470,000	370,000
Accounts Receivable	2,053,000	640,000
Inventory	4,690,000	910,000
Plant Assets	13,746,000	8,708,000
Accumulated Depreciation	(8,329,000)	(2,813,000)
Patents		784,000
Investment in Westminster	9,962,470	
Cost of Goods Sold	14,609,000	3,400,000
Depreciation Expense	2,050,000	790,000
Patent Amortization		96,000
Other Expenses	5,760,000	740,000
Dividends Declared	4,200,000	528,000
Totals	50,211,470	14,153,000
Current Liabilities	(4,100,000)	(930,000)
Long-Term Debt	(6,240,000)	(2,030,000)
Common Stock	(700,000)	(250,000)
Additional Paid-In Capital	(1,480,000)	(850,000)
Retained Earnings	(9,446,684)	(3,893,000)
Sales	(25,766,540)	(6,200,000)
Investment Income	(1,778,870)	
Cumulative Translation Adjustment	(699,376)	
Totals	(50,211,470)	(14,153,000)

Required:

Prepare the following based on the assumption that the British pound is the functional currency.

A. The trial balance for Westminster in U.S. dollars on December 31, 2006.

B. The journal entries that would be recognized on Henderson's financial records in 2006.

C. The worksheet eliminations needed to prepare the consolidated financial statements at December 31, 2006.

D. The consolidation worksheet for Henderson and Westminster at December 31, 2006.

E. The worksheet elimination to remove Westminster's beginning of period stockholders' equity, remove Henderson's beginning of period investment account, and create the beginning of period purchase differentials for the 2007 consolidation worksheet.

PROBLEM 6-5   Western Corporation is a Canadian manufacturer of precision equipment. Western's management is supporting a proposed acquisition of Western by Clemens, Incorporated, a U.S. company. The agreement is for Clemens to pay Western's stockholders 447,785,000 Canadian dollars for all of the outstanding common shares. Clemens hired an appraiser to estimate the market value of Western's assets and liabilities. At the date of acquisition, the following remaining lives are assigned to items with estimated market values different from book values: accounts receivable, 3 months; inventory, 5 months; plant assets, 10 years; and patents, 12 years. Clemens' controller has worked with the appraiser to estimate the following book and market values (in Canadian dollars) that will exist at the date of the proposed acquisition (January 1, 2005) and book values expected to exist at the end of the year of acquisition (December 31, 2005).

	Date of Acquisition		December 31, 2005
	Book Value	Market Value	Book Value
Cash	79,785,000	79,785,000	63,160,000
Accounts Receivable	109,975,000	100,000,000	140,000,000
Inventory	201,400,000	250,000,000	255,000,000
Plant Assets	351,000,000	371,200,000	396,000,000
Accumulated Depreciation	(115,200,000)		(140,530,000)
Patents		92,800,000	

Cost of Goods Sold			360,000,000
Depreciation Expense			25,330,000
Patent Amortization			
Other Expenses			30,000,000
Dividends Declared			64,000,000
Totals	626,960,000		1,192,960,000
Current Liabilities	(170,000,000)	(170,000,000)	(258,000,000)
Long-Term Debt	(226,000,000)	(226,000,000)	(224,000,000)
Common Stock	(14,750,000)		(14,750,000)
Additional Paid-In Capital	(76,130,000)		(76,130,000)
Retained Earnings	(140,080,000)		(140,080,000)
Sales			(480,000,000)
Totals	(626,960,000)		(1,192,960,000)

Inventory records are maintained on a first-in, first-out basis, and the ending inventory is assumed to be acquired during November and December. Purchases are assumed to be made uniformly during the year. Western is expected to purchase additional plant assets on June 1, 2005. Depreciation expense on the new plant assets is computed on a 15-year life with no salvage value. Dividends of 25,000,000 and 39,000,000 Canadian dollars are declared and paid on June 30 and December 31, respectively.

The following estimated exchange rates for 2005 are based on historical rates for the past five years.

January 1	.575
June 1	.630
June 30	.607
December 31	.644
June 1–December 31, 2005, average	.650
November 1–December 31, 2005, average	.665
January 1–December 31, 2005, average	.616

The board of directors is interested in how the acquisition of Western will impact the consolidated financial statements based on the assumptions made above. As a result, the controller has prepared the following pro forma trial balance for Clemens based on the Western assumptions presented previously.

	Clemens
Cash	1,163,923,625
Accounts Receivable	800,000,000
Inventory	600,000,000
Plant Assets	4,825,000,000
Accumulated Depreciation	(854,109,000)
Patents	300,000,000
Investment in Western	256,576,040
Cost of Goods Sold	780,000,000
Depreciation Expense	275,000,000
Patent Amortization	40,000,000
Other Expenses	165,000,000
Dividends Declared	108,000,000
Total	8,459,390,665
Current Liabilities	(850,000,000)
Long-Term Debt	(900,000,000)
Common Stock	(50,000,000)
Additional Paid-In Capital	(530,000,000)
Retained Earnings	(4,690,000,000)
Sales	(1,400,000,000)
Investment Income	(12,480,665)
Extraordinary Gain from Acquisition of Western	(26,910,000)
Total	8,459,390,665

Required:
Prepare the following based on the assumption that the U.S. dollar is the functional currency.

A. The trial balance for Western in U.S. dollars on December 31, 2005.

B. The journal entries that would be recognized on Clemens' financial records in 2005.

C. The worksheet eliminations needed to prepare the consolidated financial statements at December 31, 2005.

D. The consolidation worksheet for Clemens and Western at December 31, 2005.

PROBLEM 6-6   (Refer to the information in Problem 6-5.) The controller has prepared the following pro forma trial balance for Clemens based on the Western assumptions.

	Clemens
Cash	1,163,923,625
Accounts Receivable	800,000,000
Inventory	600,000,000
Plant Assets	4,825,000,000
Accumulated Depreciation	(854,109,000)
Patents	300,000,000
Investment in Western	280,545,720
Cost of Goods Sold	780,000,000
Depreciation Expense	275,000,000
Patent Amortization	40,000,000
Other Expenses	165,000,000
Dividends Declared	108,000,000
Total	8,483,360,345
Current Liabilities	(850,000,000)
Long-Term Debt	(900,000,000)
Common Stock	(50,000,000)
Additional Paid-In Capital	(530,000,000)
Retained Earnings	(4,690,000,000)
Sales	(1,400,000,000)
Investment Income	(3,048,220)
Extraordinary Gain from Acquisition of Western	(26,910,000)
Cumulative Translation Adjustment	(33,402,125)
Total	8,483,360,345

Required:

Prepare the following based on the assumption that the Canadian dollar is the functional currency.

A. The trial balance for Western in U.S. dollars on December 31, 2005.

B. The journal entries that would be recognized on Clemens' financial records in 2005.

C. The worksheet eliminations needed to prepare the consolidated financial statements at December 31, 2005.

D. The consolidation worksheet for Clemens and Western at December 31, 2005.

PROBLEM 6-7   (Refer to Problem 6-5 for date of acquisition and 2005 data.) The board of directors is intrigued with the first year pro forma information. They ask for a second year of information before the acquisition talks continue. The controller of Western reveals that the following events are anticipated. Western expects to sell plant assets with a historical cost of 77,300,000 Canadian dollars and accumulated depreciation of 37,700,000 Canadian dollars (after accruing depreciation expense on these assets of 3,300,000 Canadian dollars) on September 30 for 42,000,000 Canadian dollars. These plant assets were owned at the date Western was acquired by Clemens, and the sale is viewed as a significant transaction. Western's controller provided the following table outlining the expected changes in the plant asset accounts and the depreciation expense expected to be recognized in 2006.

	Plant Assets	Depreciation Expense	Accumulated Depreciation
Jan. 1, 2005	351,000,000		115,200,000
June 1, 2005, purchase	45,000,000		
2005 depreciation expense		25,330,000	25,330,000
December 31, 2005	396,000,000		140,530,000

September 30, 2006, sale	(77,300,000)	(37,700,000)
2006 depreciation expense*	25,480,000	25,480,000
December 31, 2006	318,700,000	128,310,000

* Date of acquisition assets held January 1–December 31, 2006: [(351,000,000 − 77,300,000) − (115,200,000 + 23,580,000 − 37,700,000)]/9	19,180,000
Assets purchased June 1, 2005, and held January 1–December 31, 2006: 45,000,000/15	3,000,000
Date of acquisition assets held January 1–September 30, 2006: [(77,300,000 − 37,700,000)/9](9/12)	3,300,000
Depreciation Expense 2006	25,480,000

Inventory purchases will be made uniformly throughout the year and ending inventory will be purchased during November and December. Dividends of 40,000,000 and 45,000,000 Canadian dollars will be declared and paid on June 30 and December 31, respectively. The following exchange rates are estimated for 2006.

January 1	.644
June 30	.627
September 30	.626
November 1	.624
December 31	.620
January 1–September 30, 2006, average	.635
November 1–December 31, 2006, average	.621
January 1–December 31, 2006, average	.634

The following pro forma trial balance, in Canadian dollars, is prepared for December 31, 2006, based on conversations with Western's controller.

	December 31, 2006 Book Value
Cash	124,080,000
Accounts Receivable	190,000,000
Inventory	230,000,000
Plant Assets	318,700,000
Accumulated Depreciation	(128,310,000)
Cost of Goods Sold	370,000,000
Depreciation Expense	25,480,000
Other Expenses	35,000,000
Dividends Declared	85,000,000
Total Debits	1,249,950,000
Current Liabilities	(218,120,000)
Long-Term Debt	(205,000,000)
Common Stock	(14,750,000)
Additional Paid-In Capital	(76,130,000)
Retained Earnings	(140,750,000)
Sales	(592,800,000)
Gain on Sale of Plant Assets	(2,400,000)
Total Credits	(1,249,950,000)

Required:

Prepare the following based on the assumption that the U.S. dollar is the functional currency.

A. The trial balance for Western in U.S. dollars on December 31, 2006.

B. The journal entries that would be recognized on Clemens' financial records in 2006.

C. The worksheet eliminations needed to prepare the consolidated financial statements at December 31, 2006.

D. Prepare the worksheet elimination to remove Western's beginning of period stockholders' equity, Clemens' beginning of period investment account, and create the beginning of period purchase differentials for the 2007 consolidation worksheet.

PROBLEM 6-8   (Refer to the information in Problem 6-7 for current year activities.)

Required:

Prepare the following based on the assumption that the Canadian dollar is the functional currency.

A. The trial balance for Western in U.S. dollars on December 31, 2006.

B. The journal entries that would be recognized on Clemens' financial records in 2006.

C. The worksheet eliminations needed to prepare the consolidated financial statements at December 31, 2006.

D. Prepare the worksheet elimination to remove Western's beginning of period stockholders' equity, remove Clemens' beginning of period investment account, and create the beginning of period purchase differentials for the 2007 consolidation worksheet.

PROBLEM 6-9   Richmond, Incorporated is a manufacturing company located in Brownsville, Texas. Richmond's management is interested in making selected component parts used in some of its products in Mexico. Management has decided that Sanchez Machine Corporation should be acquired to meet this need. Richmond's management initiates a dialogue with Sanchez's management, and an agreement to an 80-percent acquisition is attained. Sanchez has 500,000 shares of stock outstanding at the date of acquisition—January 1, 2005. Each share of stock has a par value of 14,000 pesos. Richmond is to pay 122,920 pesos for each share of stock acquired. Accounts receivables are expected to be collected during the first two months of 2005. Inventory is determined to have an estimated life of six months as of the date of acquisition. Plant assets are being depreciated with an average remaining life of 12 years. The following book and market values (in Mexican pesos) exist at the date of acquisition and book values at December 31, 2005.

	Date of Acquisition		December 31, 2005
	Book Value	*Market Value*	*Book Value*
Cash	10,280,000,000	10,280,000,000	12,000,000,000
Accounts Receivable	13,500,000,000	12,500,000,000	15,760,000,000
Inventory	37,500,000,000	45,000,000,000	49,000,000,000
Plant Assets	59,720,000,000	49,680,000,000	59,720,000,000
Accumulated Depreciation	(5,000,000,000)		(9,560,000,000)
Cost of Goods Sold			112,500,000,000
Depreciation Expense			4,560,000,000
Other Expenses			7,000,000,000
Dividends Declared			8,000,000,000
Totals	116,000,000,000		258,980,000,000
Current Liabilities	(25,000,000,000)	(25,000,000,000)	(34,960,000,000)
Long-Term Debt	(40,000,000,000)	(40,000,000,000)	(40,000,000,000)
Common Stock	(5,500,000,000)		(5,500,000,000)
Additional Paid-In Capital	(19,500,000,000)		(19,500,000,000)
Retained Earnings	(26,000,000,000)		(26,000,000,000)
Sales			(133,020,000,000)
Totals	(116,000,000,000)		(258,980,000,000)

Inventory records are maintained on a first-in, first-out basis, and the ending inventory was acquired during November and December. Purchases were made uniformly during the year. Dividends of 4,000,000,000 pesos are declared and paid on March 31 and September 30.

The following exchange rates exist during 2005.

January 1	.0003390
February 1	.0003396
March 31	.0003370
September 30	.0003282
December 31	.0003235
November 1–December 31, 2005, average	.0003340
January 1–December 31, 2005, average	.0003245

Required:

Prepare the following based on the assumption that the U.S. dollar is the functional currency.

A. The trial balance for Sanchez in U.S. dollars on December 31, 2005.

B. The journal entries that would be recognized on Richmond's financial records in 2005.

C. The worksheet eliminations needed to prepare the consolidated financial statements at December 31, 2005.

PROBLEM 6-10   (Refer to the information in Problem 6-9.)

Required:

Prepare the following based on the assumption that the Mexican peso is the functional currency.

A. The trial balance for Sanchez in U.S. dollars on December 31, 2005.

B. The journal entries that would be recognized on Richmond's financial records in 2005.

C. The worksheet eliminations needed to prepare the consolidated financial statements at December 31, 2005.

PROBLEM 6-11   (Refer to Problem 6-9 for date of acquisition and 2005 information.) Sanchez continues to operate as an 80 percent–owned subsidiary during 2006. Sanchez purchases additional plant assets on March 1 (2,700,000,000 pesos). Straight-line depreciation is recorded on these assets based on a 15-year estimated life with no salvage value. During the year, Sanchez decreased inventory levels by 17,000,000,000 pesos. Inventory purchases were generally made evenly throughout the year, and the first-in, first-out inventory method continued in use. Ending inventory was acquired in November and December. Dividends of 4,280,000,000 and 5,000,000,000 pesos were declared and paid on March 31 and September 30, respectively. The following trial balances are prepared at December 31, 2006.

	Richmond	(Pesos) Sanchez
Cash	10,400,000	14,310,000,000
Accounts Receivable	8,000,000	18,000,000,000
Inventory	27,000,000	32,000,000,000
Plant Assets	165,000,000	62,420,000,000
Accumulated Depreciation	(47,000,000)	(14,270,000,000)
Patents	10,750,000	
Investment in Sanchez	16,710,728	
Cost of Goods Sold	95,000,000	125,000,000,000
Depreciation Expense	13,250,000	4,710,000,000
Patent Amortization	1,075,000	
Other Expenses	4,600,000	8,100,000,000
Dividends Declared	7,200,000	9,280,000,000
Totals	311,985,728	259,550,000,000
Current Liabilities	(20,000,000)	(22,000,000,000)
Long-Term Debt	(50,000,000)	(34,000,000,000)
Common Stock	(3,000,000)	(5,500,000,000)
Additional Paid-In Capital	(43,000,000)	(19,500,000,000)
Retained Earnings	(32,525,352)	(26,960,000,000)
Sales	(160,000,000)	(151,590,000,000)
Investment Income	(3,460,376)	
Totals	(311,985,728)	(259,550,000,000)

The following exchange rates are applicable to 2006.

January 1	.0003235
March 1	.0003260
March 31	.0003265
April 30	.0003261
September 30	.0003251
December 31	.0003210
March 1–December 31, 2006, average	.0003240
November 1–December 31, 2006, average	.0003305
January 1–December 31, 2006, average	.0003250

Required:
Prepare the following based on the assumption that the U.S. dollar is the functional currency.

A. The trial balance for Sanchez in U.S. dollars on December 31, 2006.
B. The journal entries that would be recognized on Richmond's financial records in 2006.
C. The worksheet eliminations needed to prepare the consolidated financial statements at December 31, 2006.
D. The consolidation worksheet for Richmond and Sanchez at December 31, 2006.
E. The worksheet elimination to remove Sanchez's beginning of period stockholders' equity, remove Richmond's beginning of period investment account, and create the beginning of period purchase differentials for the 2007 consolidation worksheet.

PROBLEM 6-12   (Refer to the information in Problem 6-11 for current year activities.)

	Richmond	(Pesos) Sanchez
Cash	10,400,000	14,310,000,000
Accounts Receivable	8,000,000	18,000,000,000
Inventory	27,000,000	32,000,000,000
Plant Assets	165,000,000	62,420,000,000
Accumulated Depreciation	(47,000,000)	(14,270,000,000)
Patents	10,750,000	
Investment in Sanchez	15,731,568	
Cost of Goods Sold	95,000,000	125,000,000,000
Depreciation Expense	13,250,000	4,710,000,000
Patent Amortization	1,075,000	
Other Expenses	4,600,000	8,100,000,000
Dividends Declared	7,200,000	9,280,000,000
Totals Debits	311,006,568	259,550,000,000
Current Liabilities	(20,000,000)	(22,000,000,000)
Long-Term Debt	(50,000,000)	(34,000,000,000)
Common Stock	(3,000,000)	(5,000,000,000)
Additional Paid-In Capital	(43,000,000)	(20,000,000,000)
Retained Earnings	(32,143,624)	(26,960,000,000)
Sales	(160,000,000)	(151,590,000,000)
Investment Income	(3,641,048)	
Cumulative Translation Adjustment	778,104	
Total Credits	(311,006,568)	(259,550,000,000)

Prepare the following based on the assumption that the Mexican peso is the functional currency.

A. The trial balance for Sanchez in U.S. dollars on December 31, 2006.
B. The journal entries that would be recognized on Richmond's financial records in 2006.
C. The worksheet eliminations needed to prepare the consolidated financial statements at December 31, 2006.
D. The consolidation worksheet for Richmond and Sanchez at December 31, 2006.
E. The worksheet elimination to remove Sanchez's beginning of period stockholders' equity, remove Richmond's beginning of period investment account, and create the beginning of period purchase differentials for the 2007 consolidation worksheet.

PROBLEM 6-13   Smith Enterprises is a U.S. company involved in assembling electronic components for the automobile industry. Management recently signed a long-term contract with one of the major automobile manufacturers to deliver computer analysis assemblies for new cars. The problem is that some of the electronic components needed to complete the computer assemblies are in short supply. Management of Smith has determined that a good long-term strategy would be to acquire control of Inca Enterprises, a Peruvian manufacturer. Smith's board of directors has asked for information on the impact of paying 300,000,000 Peruvian new soles for 60 percent of Inca's 35,000,000 outstanding common shares. At the acquisition date, the following remaining lives would be assigned to items with estimated market values different from book values: accounts receivable, 3 months; inventory,

8 months; plant assets, 10 years; patents, 5 years; and long-term debt, 20 years. Below are the book values and the estimated market values that would exist at the date of the proposed acquisition (January 1, 2005) and book values expected to exist at the end of the year of acquisition (December 31, 2005).

| | Date of Acquisition | | December 31, 2005 |
	Book Value	Market Value	Book Value
Cash	25,000,000	25,000,000	32,000,000
Accounts Receivable	45,000,000	40,000,000	51,000,000
Inventory	65,000,000	80,000,000	76,000,000
Land	20,000,000	60,000,000	20,000,000
Plant Assets	703,200,000	420,000,000	823,200,000
Accumulated Depreciation	(270,000,000)		(314,820,000)
Patents	96,000,000	120,000,000	76,800,000
Cost of Goods Sold			380,000,000
Depreciation Expense			44,820,000
Patent Amortization			19,200,000
Other Expenses			26,000,000
Dividends Declared			15,000,000
Totals	684,200,000		1,249,200,000
Current Liabilities	(50,000,000)	(50,000,000)	(83,000,000)
Long-Term Debt	(200,000,000)	(212,000,000)	(200,000,000)
Common Stock	(35,000,000)		(35,000,000)
Additional Paid-In Capital	(150,000,000)		(150,000,000)
Retained Earnings	(249,200,000)		(249,200,000)
Sales			(532,000,000)
Totals	(684,200,000)		(1,249,200,000)

Inventory records are maintained on a last-in, first-out basis, and the increase in ending inventory is assumed to be acquired during January and February. Inventory purchases are assumed to occur uniformly during the year. Inca is expected to purchase additional plant assets for 120,0000,000 new soles on October 1, 2005. Depreciation expense on the new plant assets is computed using the straight-line method based on a 20-year life with no salvage value. Dividends of 6,000,000 and 9,000,000 new soles are declared and paid on May 31 and November 30, respectively.

The following exchange rates are projected for 2005.

January 1	.200
May 31	.183
October 1	.209
November 30	.194
December 31	.182
January 1–February 28, 2005, average	.186
October 1–December 31, 2005, average	.190
January 1–December 31, 2005, average	.188

The following pro forma trial balance for Smith is based on assumptions presented previously.

Cash	3,960,000
Accounts Receivable	6,500,000
Inventory	25,000,000
Plant Assets	320,000,000
Accumulated Depreciation	(125,000,000)
Patents	20,000,000
Investment in Inca	66,799,500
Cost of Goods Sold	130,000,000
Depreciation Expense	32,000,000
Patent Amortization	5,000,000
Other Expenses	47,000,000

Dividends Declared	18,000,000
Total Debits	549,259,500
Current Liabilities	(23,000,000)
Long-Term Debt	(100,000,000)
Common Stock	(1,000,000)
Additional Paid-In Capital	(36,000,000)
Retained Earnings	(60,393,600)
Sales	(320,360,000)
Investment Income	(8,505,900)
Total Credits	(549,259,500)

Required:

Prepare the following based on the assumption that the U.S. dollar is the functional currency.

A. The trial balance for Inca in U.S. dollars on December 31, 2005.

B. The journal entries that would be recognized on Smith's financial records in 2005.

C. The worksheet eliminations needed to prepare the consolidated financial statements at December 31, 2005.

D. The consolidation worksheet for Smith and Inca at December 31, 2005.

PROBLEM 6-14   (Refer to the information in Problem 6-13.)

The following pro forma trial balance for Smith is based on assumptions presented previously.

Cash	3,960,000
Accounts Receivable	6,500,000
Inventory	25,000,000
Plant Assets	320,000,000
Accumulated Depreciation	(125,000,000)
Patents	20,000,000
Investment in Inca	58,323,720
Cost of Goods Sold	130,000,000
Depreciation Expense	32,000,000
Patent Amortization	5,000,000
Other Expenses	47,000,000
Dividends Declared	18,000,000
Total Debits	540,787,320
Current Liabilities	(23,000,000)
Long-Term Debt	(100,000,000)
Common Stock	(1,000,000)
Additional Paid-In Capital	(36,000,000)
Retained Earnings	(60,395,400)
Sales	(320,360,000)
Investment Income	(5,536,680)
Cumulative Translation Adjustment	5,506,560
Total Credits	(540,787,320)

Required:

Prepare the following based on the assumption that the Peruvian new sol is the functional currency.

A. The trial balance for Inca in U.S. dollars on December 31, 2005.

B. The journal entries that would be recognized on Smith's financial records in 2005.

C. The worksheet eliminations needed to prepare the consolidated financial statements at December 31, 2005.

D. The consolidation worksheet for Smith and Inca at December 31, 2005.

PROBLEM 6-15   (Refer to Problem 6-13 for date of acquisition and 2005 data.) The board of directors is intrigued with the first-year pro forma information. They ask for a second year of information. The controller of Inca reveals that the following events are anticipated. Inventory purchases will be made uniformly throughout the year, and the increase in inventory will be purchased during January and February. Additional plant assets will be purchased for 180,000,000 new soles on May 1. These assets will be assigned an estimated useful life of 15 years. Dividends of 7,000,000 and 10,000,000 new soles will be declared and paid on May 31 and November 30, respectively. The following exchange rates are estimated for 2006.

January 1	.182
May 1	.184
May 31	.185
November 30	.169
December 31	.170
January 1–February 28, 2006, average	.181
May 1–December 31, 2006, average	.189
January 1–December 31, 2006, average	.180

The following pro forma trial balance, in new soles, is prepared for December 31, 2006, based on conversations with Inca's controller.

	December 31, 2006 Book Value
Cash	45,000,000
Accounts Receivable	70,000,000
Inventory	85,000,000
Land	20,000,000
Plant Assets	1,003,200,000
Accumulated Depreciation	(372,140,000)
Patents	57,600,000
Cost of Goods Sold	442,000,000
Depreciation Expense	57,320,000
Patent Amortization	19,200,000
Other Expenses	31,000,000
Dividends Declared	17,000,000
Totals	1,475,180,000
Current Liabilities	(124,000,000)
Long-Term Debt	(200,000,000)
Common Stock	(35,000,000)
Additional Paid-In Capital	(150,000,000)
Retained Earnings	(296,180,000)
Sales	(670,000,000)
Totals	(1,475,180,000)

Required:

Prepare the following based on the assumption that the U.S. dollar is the functional currency.

A. The trial balance for Inca in U.S. dollars on December 31, 2006.

B. The journal entries that would be recognized on Smith's financial records in 2006.

C. The worksheet eliminations needed to prepare the consolidated financial statements at December 31, 2006.

D. The worksheet elimination to remove Inca's beginning of period stockholders' equity, remove Smith's beginning of period investment account, and create the beginning of period purchase differentials for the 2007 consolidation worksheet.

PROBLEM 6-16   (Refer to the information in Problem 6-15 for current year activities.)

Required:

Prepare the following based on the assumption that the Peruvian new sol is the functional currency.

A. The trial balance for Inca in U.S. dollars on December 31, 2006.

B. The journal entries that would be recognized on Smith's financial records in 2006.

C. The worksheet eliminations needed to prepare the consolidated financial statements at December 31, 2006.

D. The worksheet elimination to remove Inca's beginning of period stockholders' equity, remove Smith's beginning of period investment account, and create the beginning of period purchase differentials for the 2007 consolidation worksheet.

CHAPTER 7

PARTNERSHIP FORMATION, OPERATION, AND CHANGE IN OWNERSHIP

LEARNING OBJECTIVES

After reading this chapter, you should be able to:

■ Discuss the features of a partnership entity.

■ Be familiar with the common features of partnership agreements.

■ Determine partnership profit and loss allocation based on the partnership agreement.

■ Determine the financial reporting required when a new partner is admitted or an existing partner withdraws.

Entity structure is a significant element in the understanding of accounting for owners' equity. The form of an entity can have a significant impact on the accounting process: **tax implications, asset valuation, income determination,** and **accountable interests** are all impacted by the organizational form of an economic entity. Economic entities are usually classified as **private-sector** entities and **public-sector** entities. Private-sector entities can be classified into **for-profit** or **business-type** entities and **not-for-profit** entities. **Public-sector** entities include **government** and **not-for-profit** entities.

This chapter emphasizes accounting for **general partnerships,** one of the basic types of business entities in the private sector. Other types of business entities include **proprietorships** and **corporations.** Although seemingly simple, a plethora of entity structures have evolved out of the basic business types. Some of these include **S corporations, joint ventures, limited partnerships, limited liability partnerships,** and **limited liability corporations.** Over the last several decades, numerous hybrid forms of business entities have been created to meet the particular needs of business owners and investors. Risk management, diversified financial interests, and tax considerations are primary reasons that investors and proprietors seek alternate forms of business entities.

Partnerships have been of particular interest to accounting professionals for several reasons. Traditionally, the partnership has been the predominant form of business entity for certified public accounting firms. Until recently, most states required CPAs to organize their practices as **sole proprietorships** or **partnerships**, where the personal assets of the partner or proprietor would not be protected from attachment by creditors and litigants in the event of business failure or malpractice. Presumably, with all assets of the partner or proprietor exposed to risk of loss in the event of a breach of professional competence, CPAs would have an incentive to ensure the quality of service from their professional practice. In recent years, devastating losses from legal actions have prompted many state legislatures to permit the creation of the limited liability partnerships and professional corporations.

Many other professional firms (e.g., lawyers, doctors, dentists, architects, real estate investors) also conduct their business in the partnership format. A special form of partnership, the **joint venture**, is a useful entity type for real estate development, natural resource investment, research and development endeavors, special heavy construction projects, and international ventures. Despite the emergence of hybrid entity types for partnerships, the partnership remains an important entity form, and accounting students should be cognizant of the special features of partnerships. This chapter provides comprehensive coverage of the characteristics, formation, and accounting for the activities of general partnerships.

The objective of this chapter is to introduce some of the issues common to most partnership entities. This first part of the chapter presents an overview of partnership entities. In particular, some basic features of partnership entities are compared and contrasted with those of proprietorships and corporations, and the equity theories applicable to partnerships are discussed. The second part of the chapter includes a discussion and illustration of some of the issues unique to partnership entities. These issues include the formation of a partnership, the special issues relating to the continuing operation of the partnership, and changes in ownership of partnership entities.

COMPARING PARTNERSHIPS, PROPRIETORSHIPS, AND CORPORATIONS

Partnerships and Proprietorships

As defined in the Uniform Partnership Act (see Appendix 7-1), a partnership is an association of two or more persons to carry on as co-owners a business for profit,[1] where a person can be an individual, a partnership, or a corporation. Partnerships may be formed for many different reasons, including combining economic resources, managerial talent, and time to undertake specific business objectives. Partnerships and proprietorships are similar from a legal, an accounting, and a tax perspective (see Table 7-1).

Legal Perspective Similarity From a legal perspective, both types of entities are easily formed. There is no requirement to attain state approval to form a business entity as a

---

[1] Uniform Partnership Act, §6 (1).

TABLE 7-1   Comparison of Proprietorship, Partnership, and Corporation

Perspective	Proprietorship	Partnership	Corporation
Legal perspective			
Formation	Easily formed	Easily formed Written agreement common	File articles of incorporation with state for approval
Liability	Unlimited liability for owners	Unlimited liability for owners	Liability of owners generally limited to investment
Change in ownership	Not applicable	Adding additional owners requires approval of current partners	Easy to change owners
Management	Managed by owner	Each partner shares in management	Stockholders vote for board of directors, who hire management
Accounting perspective	May use a comprehensive basis of accounting other than GAAP	May use a comprehensive basis of accounting other than GAAP	GAAP required
Tax perspective	Proprietorship an extension of the owner Proprietorship not a taxable entity	Partnership an extension of the owners Partnerships not a taxable entity Information return required	Corporation a taxable entity Dividends paid to stockholders taxable to the stockholders

partnership or a proprietorship. In fact, there is no requirement to have anything in writing to form either type of entity, although it is risky to form a partnership without a written agreement because there are many issues that can become sources of disagreement among the partners. Another legal consideration where partnerships and proprietorships are similar is the owners' liability. The owners in both partnerships and proprietorships have unlimited liability. All the general partners in a partnership are liable for all the debts of the partnership (joint and several liability). This liability does not pertain only to assets invested in the business. It can also extend to the owners' personal assets (some exceptions exist in the case of limited liability partnerships).

Accounting Perspective Similarity   From an accounting perspective, neither partnerships nor proprietorships are required to comply with generally accepted accounting principles (GAAP) unless the entity has publicly traded debt securities (unlikely in all but a small number of instances) or the entity is required to comply with GAAP by a creditor. For example, a bank may require financial statements prepared in conformity with GAAP as a condition for evaluating a loan request. The bank may also require an audit as a condition of evaluating a loan request; however, an audit does not necessarily mean that the partnership or proprietorship would have to conform to GAAP to attain an unqualified audit opinion. The Auditing Standards Board has recognized other comprehensive bases of accounting such as the cash basis, the modified accrual basis, and the tax basis. These bases may be applied without impairing the fairness of the entity's financial statements. As a result, it is common for partnerships and proprietorships to use a comprehensive basis of accounting other than GAAP. For smaller partnerships, the tax basis is popular. This eliminates the need for dual sets of books and, therefore, minimizes cost. Furthermore, lenders usually will accept financial information prepared on the tax basis. On the other hand, there is nothing to prevent the owners of a partnership or proprietorship from complying with GAAP. Unless specifically noted, this chapter assumes that GAAP is applied.

Tax Perspective Similarity Tax authorities (e.g., federal and state tax agencies) basically view both partnerships and proprietorships as an extension of the owners. Neither entity is separately taxed on income; however, the owners of these types of entities are required to pay other types of taxes, including payroll, sales, and franchise taxes. The taxable income or loss (not net income or loss)[2] is allocated to the owners according to the partners' profit and loss sharing agreement. Once a partner's taxable partnership income is determined, the income is included on the partner's individual tax return. The partnership is required to file an informational tax return (Form 1065) to disclose how the taxable income has been allocated to the partners. A proprietorship is not required to file an informational return form because all of the taxable income is assigned to the one owner. Instead, the individual files his/her personal return with a Schedule C for business income. The requirement to determine taxable income or loss is the primary reason why many partnerships and proprietorships keep accounting records on a tax basis. This essentially keeps the owners, or the owners' accountants, from maintaining two sets of accounting records or from keeping track of the adjustments necessary to convert financial accounting information into income tax information.

Differences The only inherent differences between partnerships and proprietorships result from the number of owners. Proprietorships have only one owner, so there is no allocation of profit or loss among several individuals and there is no concern about how to admit new owners to the entity or address the withdrawal of existing owners from the entity. Admitting a new owner would convert the proprietorship into a partnership, and the withdrawal of the only owner would result in the liquidation of the business. Profit allocation and ownership changes are important to a partnership. Profits and losses must be allocated to the partners in some agreed-upon manner. In addition, the partnership should have provisions for the admission of new owners to the partnership and for withdrawal of existing owners from the partnership. Each of these issues is discussed later in the chapter.

Partnerships and Corporations

Similarity While proprietorships and partnerships have many similarities and few differences, partnerships and corporations have many differences and few similarities. Partnerships and corporations may be similar from an accounting perspective, but they are different from both a legal and a tax perspective.

Accounting Perspective Differences If the accounting records of a partnership are maintained in conformity with GAAP, the only accounting difference that exists between partnerships and corporations is with regard to the reporting of ownership equity.

---

[2] Net income or loss is determined in accordance with generally accepted accounting principles, while taxable income is determined by applying income tax regulations.

The partnership maintains one "Capital Account" for each partner and posts changes to that account according to a partnership agreement. Thus, new investment of capital by any partner increases that partner's capital account. Similarly, both income (or losses) and withdrawals are allocated into each partner's capital account according to the distribution agreement of the partners. On the other hand, a corporation maintains a *Capital Stock* account, *Additional Paid-In Capital* accounts, and a *Retained Earnings* account. Net income or loss becomes part of retained earnings, and dividends are always paid equally to all shareholders of a particular class of stock. The corporation can also reacquire some of its own equity interest in the form of treasury stock.

Legal Perspective Differences From a legal perspective, partnerships and corporations differ substantially. The differences begin with the way in which the entity is initially created. A partnership is created by an agreement between two or more parties. This agreement is typically in writing (articles of partnership), but a written agreement is not required. A corporation is created by filing articles of incorporation to obtain a charter with the state in which the entity is to be incorporated. The articles of incorporation include a variety of provisions, such as the name of the corporation, the purpose of the entity, and the number of shares of stock to be authorized. Both the partnership and the corporation are governed by the applicable laws of the state in which the entity resides. Across states, partnership laws typically conform to the Uniform Partnership Act (UPA).[3] Each type of entity may carry out the activities outlined in the agreement that creates the entity, either the articles of partnership or the articles of incorporation.

Another major difference is the liability exposure of the entity's owners.[4] This is particularly important in that a partner may bind the partnership by contract when conducting business in the name of the partnership. This results in each partner being liable for the partnership business dealings of the other partners. Stockholders of a corporation do not share such legal liability. The corporation is a legal entity separate from the owners, and management can commit the corporation to legal contracts in the name of the corporation but not the stockholders. Thus, management of the corporation can sue in the name of the corporation and the corporation can be sued. As a result, the stockholders are generally not liable for the debts of the corporation beyond the amount invested. In addition, a stockholder cannot bind the corporation by contract unless the stockholder is also authorized to do so as an agent of the corporation.

The legal liability issues directly relate to two additional differences between partnerships and corporations—transferability of ownership interest and the life of the business entity. Change in the ownership of a partnership occurs when a new partner is admitted, an existing partner withdraws from the entity, or a partner dies. Existing partners basically cannot stop a partner who wants to withdraw from the partnership if the exiting partner sells his/her ownership interest to existing partners or to the partnership itself (a **dissolution**); however, existing partners can stop new partners from entering the partnership because the existing partners would become liable for the business dealings of the new partners. It is common for the articles of partnership to require consent of *all* existing

Dissolution: the legal ending of a partnership agreement through the cessation of operations, the admission of a new partner, or the withdrawal of an existing partner

---

[3] Most states have adopted the UPA or a variation to serve as a means of governing the business operations of partnerships. While most of the provisions of the UPA can be circumvented by the creation of a specific agreement or articles of copartnership, the UPA is reasonably comprehensive in addressing the general business relationships that should be considered by parties forming a partnership.

[4] Partners have unlimited liability for the debts of the partnership unless limited by contract, and this limitation is subject to legal limitations.

partners for a new partner to enter the partnership. An exception to this is some large partnerships, such as CPA firms. In these instances the partners agree to permit a committee of partners to determine who should be admitted as new partners. In essence, the partners not on the committee have given a proxy to the committee to vote for new partner admission on their behalf. In a large partnership it is basically impossible for a partner to know all the other partners. Each partner, therefore, would not be capable of making an informed decision regarding the desirability of admitting all new partners.

Legally, an existing partnership ceases to exist and a new partnership is formed when a new partner is added to the partnership, an existing partner withdraws from the partnership, or a partner dies. A partnership may also cease to exist if the articles of partnership contain a termination date (unlikely in most instances). In many cases, the partnership as an entity continues to operate as a going concern even though a change in ownership occurs. The partnership often continues in operation when partners join or withdraw by defining "a continuation of the partnership agreement" in the articles of partnership. On the other hand, transferability of ownership in a corporation is not restricted unless there is a contractual agreement prohibiting sale of shares (common only in closely held corporations). Transferability of ownership includes the sale of stock among existing owners or the sale of stock to investors who are not currently stockholders. As a result, a corporation has an unlimited life unless specified in the corporate charter (unlikely in most instances); that is, changes in ownership (stockholders) do not result in the formation of a new business entity.

The final major legal difference between partnerships and corporations is how the entity is managed. Partnerships are often established in such a manner that each partner has a voice in the partnership's management unless the articles of partnership contractually change this arrangement. A corporation is governed by the board of directors. The corporation's officers are hired by the board of directors. The owners of the corporation (stockholders) typically do not have a direct voice in the management of the corporation. The owners' voice in corporate management exists in the form of voting for the members of the board of directors. An exception to this would be an owner of a large block of stock. This investor could have sufficient voting power to elect him/herself to the board of directors and take an active role in management. Even if not on the board of directors, a major stockholder may have an influence on the operation of the corporation. For example, Chrysler Corporation's single largest shareholder (9 percent) indicated that he would increase his investment in the corporation unless the board of directors took steps to increase the value of Chrysler's stock.[5] The steps proposed by the investor included an increase in the dividend, implementation of a stock buyback, declaration of a stock split, and elimination of the "poison pill" restriction that prevented any individual from owning more than 10 percent of the corporation's stock.

Tax Perspective Differences Partnerships and corporations are also different from a tax perspective. As discussed previously, partnerships are viewed as conduits of income by tax authorities. Taxable income of the partnership is determined and allocated to the partners. Each partner's pro rata share of the entire reported partnership income is included on the individual partner's tax return. When actual distributions of assets are made to the partners, they are not taxed again. The corporation, on the other hand, is a taxable entity. The corporation pays tax on its taxable income. Distribution of earnings to

---

[5] Lavin, D., and P. Yoshihashi, "Kerkorian Plans to Raise Stake in Chrysler Corp," *The Wall Street Journal,* November 15, 1994, pp. A3, A8.

stockholders, in the form of dividends, results in additional taxation of corporate earnings on the investor's tax return (in effect a form of double taxation).[6]

EQUITY THEORIES APPLICABLE TO PARTNERSHIPS

Proprietary theory: views the business entity as an aggregation of the business owners

Entity theory: views the business entity as separate and distinct from the business owners

The two equity theories applicable to partnerships are the proprietary theory and the entity theory. The manner in which an entity is viewed from a legal, accounting, and taxation perspective depends on the equity theory applied to the entity. The **proprietary theory** is based on the notion that the business entity is an aggregation of the individual owners; that is, the entity is an extension of the owners. The **entity theory** is based on the notion that the business entity is distinct and separate from the owners; that is, the entity has its own existence. Proprietorships conform to the proprietary theory and corporations conform to the entity theory, but partnerships contain elements of both the proprietary and entity theories. Some supporting arguments for the proprietary theory include the following:

* Individual partners are liable for all debts of the partnership.[7]
* Salaries of partners are viewed as distributions of income, not components of net income.
* The admission of a new partner or withdrawal of an existing partner results in the dissolution of the partnership.
* Assets contributed to the partnership retain the existing tax basis to the partner contributing.
* A partner's income tax includes the partner's share of partnership net income, and the partnership does not pay income taxes.

Supporting arguments for the entity theory include the following:

* Assets contributed to the partnership become property of the partnership.[8]
* A partnership can enter into contracts.
* Partners do not have claims to specific assets.
* Partnership creditors have priority claim to partnership assets, and the creditors of partners have priority claim to a partner's assets in the event of liquidation.[9]
* The partnership continues to exist when admission or withdrawal of partners occurs.[10]

The existence of both proprietary theory and entity theory characteristics in partnership equity issues gives rise to unique accounting treatments. For example, the proprietary theory leads to some partnerships revaluing partnership assets when a new partner is admitted or an existing partner withdraws, while the entity theory leads to some partnerships retaining historical cost values. As a result, it is not possible to predict whether assets will or will not be revalued when there is a change in the number of partners. The revaluation of assets is determined by the articles of partnership signed when the partnership is created or it is determined by state laws if not addressed in the articles of partnership.

---

[6] An exception occurs if the investor is another U.S. corporation where a dividend exclusion rule permits the exclusion of some portion of dividends received from other U.S. corporations from the corporate tax return.

[7] Uniform Partnership Act, §15.

[8] Ibid., §8.

[9] Ibid., §40.

[10] Ibid., §23 and §27.

PARTNERSHIP FORMATION

Prior to forming a partnership, the prospective partners should agree on the provisions that will guide the partnership's operations. Some areas that should be considered include initial formation of the partnership, routine operations, changes in ownership interest, and dissolution of the partnership. Time invested in reaching agreement on these issues can help avoid future problems for the partnership.

Articles of Partnership

Uniform Partnership Act: uniform statutes that outline formation, operation, and dissolution partnerships; most states have adopted the Uniform Partnership Act as state law governing partnership operation

Partnerships can be formed with or without a formal written agreement. If a partnership is formed without articles of partnership, the partnership laws (often the **Uniform Partnership Act**) of the state in which the partnership is created will establish the basic legal doctrine for the partners. Some provisions of the Uniform Partnership Act impose obligations on the partnership that cannot be avoided, such as joint liability for partnership debts; however, most provisions in state law apply only if there is no agreement among the partners with regard to that specific issue. A written partnership agreement is preferred because it enables the partners to detail the agreed-upon working relationship among the partners. An attorney experienced in partnership law should draft the articles of partnership to ensure the partners are made aware of the mandatory provisions of the Uniform Partnership Act, to avoid conflicts with the Uniform Partnership Act, and to be advised of common provisions included in articles of partnership. The following is a list of some of the provisions often found in articles of partnership:

1. Partnership name and address
2. Partners' names and addresses
3. Date on which partnership was formed
4. Nature of the business
5. Term of the partnership
6. Initial capital contribution by partners and agreed-upon valuation of noncash assets
7. Capital interest received by each partner
8. Duties of partners
9. Powers of partners
10. Provision for allocating profits and losses
11. Provisions for salaries and withdrawals, including limitations on withdrawals
12. Payment or receipt of interest on loans
13. Enumeration of matters requiring consent of all partners
14. Procedures for admitting new partners
15. Procedures for withdrawal or death of a partner
16. Procedures for the arbitration of disputes
17. Situations that may result in dissolution of the partnership and provision for the termination or continuation of business
18. Fiscal period
19. Basis for accounting

20. Accounting practices
21. Requirement of an audit
22. Expulsion of a partner for cause

Initial Capital Contributions

The previous section indicated that the relationship between partners is often a contractual relationship set forth in the articles of partnership. A common feature of the articles of partnership is the **initial capital contribution** of each partner and agreement on how non-cash assets are to be valued. The **initial capital balance** to be assigned to each partner is a separate but often related item. It is also important for the partners to distinguish between capital contributions and loans to the partnership by individual partners. Loans should be evidenced by the appropriate legal documents, such as a promissory note, and the loan should include a market interest rate and a maturity date.

Determining the initial capital contribution to be made by each partner is essential when planning the formation of the partnership. One way to determine the total initial capital contribution needed is to prepare a budget for the partnership. The amount of capital contribution needed may be based on the projected needs of the business. Assume three prospective partners (Peterson, Richards, and Smith) prepared a budget and determined that total initial capital contributed should be approximately $150,000. The $150,000 total capital needed does not imply that each partner would be expected to contribute $50,000. It is possible that one or more partners may not be financially capable of making a $50,000 capital contribution. One partner may be willing to invest a larger share of the initial capital contribution in return for additional consideration. For example, this partner may expect a greater share of profits from the business or a greater voice in the operations of the business.

After determining the total initial capital needs of the partnership and the amount each partner is going to contribute, the partners must agree on the value to assign to any noncash assets contributed to the partnership. The three most likely valuations that could be assigned to noncash assets are the (1) contributor's carrying value, (2) contributor's tax basis, or (3) market or appraised value of the asset. The amount to be assigned to the noncash assets can be determined by agreement among the partners or by appraisal (if market values are used). Each valuation may be used, but it is important to understand the consequences of each valuation alternative. The following table presents information about a delivery truck contributed to the partnership by Peterson.

	Peterson's Books	*Tax Basis*
Cost	$48,000	$48,000
Accumulated Depreciation	22,000	28,000
Carrying Value	$26,000	$20,000
Market Value	$32,000	

EXAMPLE 7-1   **Carrying value assigned to contributed noncash assets**   Assigning the truck its carrying value ($26,000) at the date the partnership is formed may result in an understatement of Peterson's initial capital. Assume the truck is sold soon after the partnership begins operations because business has been better than expected and the truck is not capable of accommodating the volume of deliveries to be made. At the date of sale, the partnership will record a gain of $6,000 ($32,000 − $26,000). The gain will be shared by the partners

in some manner as specified in the articles of partnership. It is possible that Peterson will receive the entire $6,000 gain if the articles of partnership address the assigned value of the truck and the allocation of any depreciation expense or gain related to the truck. However, if the truck is not addressed in the articles of partnership, Peterson's capital will be understated by the amount of the gain allocated to Richards and Smith at the date the truck is sold. This potential result would likely cause Peterson to not agree to assigning the truck its carrying value.

EXAMPLE 7-2

Tax basis assigned to contributed noncash assets Assigning the tax basis to the delivery truck ($20,000) is a viable alternative because the partnership must prepare an information return (Form 1065) indicating how partnership income is allocated to each partner regardless of whether the partner withdraws his/her share of income from the partnership. The asset's tax basis must be used to determine this income allocation; that is, the income allocation presented to the IRS would likely not be the same as the accounting income allocation. Any difference between the asset's tax basis and its carrying value on the partnership's books would normally be allocated to the contributing partner. The assignment of the $20,000 tax basis to the asset would alleviate the partnership from keeping two sets of records for the delivery truck, one for accounting and one for the IRS.

EXAMPLE 7-3

Market value assigned to contributed noncash assets The assignment of the asset's market value to the truck ($32,000) would avoid the problem that exists when the contributor's carrying value is used. If the truck is sold soon after the partnership begins operations, there will be no gain or loss and Peterson's capital will reflect the full market value of the contribution. However, Peterson's tax return would reflect the difference between the sales price and the tax basis when the truck was contributed to the partnership. While all three of these options may be used, generally the market value is assigned to noncash assets to ensure equity for partners' capital balances. Market values will be used in the remaining examples in the chapter, unless specifically noted.

Liabilities Assumed by the Partnership

The examples presented above did not include any liability related to the truck contributed to the partnership. Any liability assumed by the partnership must also be considered when determining the basis of the contributing partner. The assumption of a liability by the partnership results in a decrease in the value of the contribution to the partnership. Assume, for example, that the truck contributed had an outstanding loan. The loan assumed by the partnership is now jointly owed by Peterson, Richards, and Smith. As a result, it is no longer an obligation of Peterson; it is an obligation of the partnership. Therefore, Peterson's capital balance is reduced by the amount of the obligation assumed by the partnership. The impact of an assumed liability on each partner's book basis is not the same as the impact on each partner's tax basis. The tax basis of a contributing partner is reduced only by the part of the loan assumed by the partnership because the IRS interprets this event as all three partners sharing the obligation; therefore, Peterson would still be obligated for part of the liability.

EXAMPLE 7-4

Comprehensive illustration In addition to determining the values to be assigned to noncash assets contributed to the partnership, the partners must also agree on the initial capital balance of each partner. Assume that Peterson, Richards, and Smith form a partnership by contributing the net assets listed below with the following market values:

	Peterson	Richards	Smith	Total
Cash	$13,000		$50,000	63,000
Inventory	3,000	$5,000		8,000
Truck	32,000			32,000
Building		65,000		65,000
Mortgage Payable		(30,000)		(30,000)
Total Market Value	$48,000	$40,000	$50,000	$138,000

One alternative is to assign to each partner's capital an amount equal to the market value of the net assets contributed by that partner. This allocation will establish the partnership's accounting records with the following journal entry.

Cash	63,000	
Inventory	8,000	
Truck	32,000	
Building	65,000	
Mortgage Payable		30,000
Peterson, Capital		48,000
Richards, Capital		40,000
Smith, Capital		50,000

To record the initial contributions by partners to form a partnership.

Note that each of the capital accounts used to represent ownership equity in a partnership is the same as the capital account used to represent ownership equity in a proprietorship. Note also that the truck and the building were recognized on the partnership's books at market value at the time of contribution. In addition, there is no accumulated depreciation account. The financial records of the partnership appear just as they would have had all the partners contributed cash and had the partnership acquired the noncash assets.

Accounting for Unidentifiable Intangible Assets

Assume the partners agreed that, while the initial capital contribution is not the $150,000 desired, the initial capital contributions are adequate for the partnership to start business operations. The journal entry presented above does not give consideration to unidentifiable intangible assets that may have been contributed to the partnership. It is possible that Richards has an existing business where significant management experience was gained. In addition, Richards may also have many loyal customers who will provide a solid base of business for the new partnership. As a result of the existing business, Richards is contributing more than the monetary value of the tangible assets. One way to consider this additional contribution by Richards is to modify the initial recognition of the contributions made to form the partnership. Two alternatives are common in practice, the bonus method and the goodwill method.

Bonus method: method of accounting for premium or discount in the creation of a partnership or a change in ownership; this method reallocates equity among partners in lieu of recognizing unidentifiable assets

Bonus Method The **bonus method** adjusts for the contribution or existence of unidentifiable intangible assets by reallocating the partners' capital accounts. One or more partners agree to give up some assigned capital to one or more other partners.

EXAMPLE 7-5

Accounting for a bonus Assume that Peterson, Richards, and Smith agree that the beginning capital balance of each partner should be $46,000 [($48,000 + $40,000 + $50,000)/3]. Note that the partners could have agreed on any beginning capital balances; that is, they do not have to be equal. Note also that this does not imply that the partners are going to share everything equally. Profits and losses may be shared in any manner prescribed in the articles of partnership. The agreement in this example states only that the initial capital balances will be the same for all partners. As a result of this agreement, Peterson's initial capital account balance is reduced by $2,000 and Smith's initial capital account balance is reduced by $4,000. Richards' initial capital account balance is increased by $6,000, and the following journal entry would be used to recognize the formation of the partnership:

Cash	63,000	
Inventory	8,000	
Truck	32,000	
Building	65,000	
Mortgage Payable		30,000
Peterson, Capital		46,000
Richards, Capital		46,000
Smith, Capital		46,000

To record initial contribution by partners to form a partnership applying the bonus method.

Goodwill method: method of accounting for premium or discount in the creation of a partnership or a change in ownership; this method recognizes unidentifiable intangible assets (goodwill) and assigns the value to the equity of the appropriate partner(s)

This may be interpreted as recognition of the value being contributed by Richards in excess of the tangible assets. Notice that this approach does not directly recognize the unidentifiable intangible asset being contributed by Richards. Thus, no goodwill is recorded at the date it is contributed.

Goodwill Method It is possible that some partners may object to being assigned an initial capital account balance less than the *value of the net assets contributed*. Another way to recognize the contribution of intangible assets while maintaining the initial capital account balance of the other partners is the **goodwill method**. This approach requires the partners to agree on a value to assign the intangible asset being contributed by Richards.

EXAMPLE 7-6

Accounting for goodwill Assume that the partners do not require the initial capital account balances to be equal and they agree that the value of Richards's experience and customer base should be recognized and goodwill should be assigned a $10,000 value. Therefore, the revised assets being contributed are as follows.

	Peterson	Richards	Smith	Total
Cash	$13,000		$50,000	63,000
Inventory	3,000	$5,000		8,000
Truck	32,000			32,000
Building		65,000		65,000
Goodwill		10,000		10,000
Mortgage Payable		(30,000)		(30,000)
Total Market Value	$48,000	$50,000	$50,000	$148,000

This agreement results in the following recognition at the formation of the partnership.

Cash	63,000	
Inventory	8,000	
Truck	32,000	
Building	65,000	
Goodwill	10,000	
Mortgage Payable		30,000
Peterson, Capital		48,000
Richards, Capital		50,000
Smith, Capital		50,000

To record initial contribution by partners to form a partnership applying the goodwill method.

Articles of partnership: written agreement that outlines the terms by which a partnership is formed, operated, and terminated

The only difference between the amounts recognized in this journal entry and the one presented in Example 7-4 is that goodwill is placed on the balance sheet, and Richards' capital account is $10,000 greater. The primary issue to understand in recognizing the initial capital contribution is that the partners may allocate the initial capital in any manner they choose. The only requirement is that the allocation presented in the partnership's financial records has to conform to the **articles of partnership**.

PARTNERSHIP OPERATION

Generally, the accounting procedures used for a partnership do not differ from those used for a corporation (assuming the partnership applies GAAP) except for ownership equity transactions. Partnerships and corporations will record most transactions in the same way. For example, the recognition of sales transactions, inventory purchases, plant and equipment acquisitions, and depreciation expense is identical for partnerships and corporations. One area that is different when comparing a partnership and a corporation is distributions to owners. Corporate distributions are recorded in a *Dividend* account that is ultimately closed to *Retained Earnings*, while partnership distributions are recorded to a *Drawing* account that is closed to the partner's capital account. Another difference between a partnership and a corporation is the allocation of net income. In a corporation, net income becomes part of *Retained Earnings*, while in a partnership net income is allocated to the partners' capital accounts. This allocation, for accounting purposes, is generally controlled by the articles of partnership. In the event that the partnership agreement does not address the allocation of profits and losses, the Uniform Partnership Act allocates profits and losses equally among the partners.[11]

Drawing Accounts

It is common for partners to withdraw resources periodically from the partnership. The ability of partners to remove resources from the partnership—that is, make withdrawals—is often stipulated in the articles of partnership. This agreement may determine when withdrawals may be made and limit the size of the withdrawals. Withdrawals include such items as direct removals of assets (e.g., cash or inventory) from the partnership as well as payments made by the partnership on behalf of the partner. An example of such a payment would be partnership payment of country club dues for individual partners. When noncash assets are withdrawn from the partnership, it is common to recognize such withdrawals at the market value of the asset. The difference between market value and book value becomes part of partnership income.

Drawing account: a contra partnership equity account where withdrawals from the partnership are recorded; the drawing account is closed and transferred into the partnership capital account at the end of the accounting period

Withdrawals are recognized in some partnerships as a reduction of the partner's capital account, while other partnerships may recognize a withdrawal by using a **drawing account** (a contra equity account) that is closed to the capital account at the end of the accounting period. These approaches are the same as a corporation recognizing dividends as a direct reduction to *Retained Earnings* or to a *Dividends Declared* account that is subsequently closed to *Retained Earnings*. Regardless of whether a partnership recognizes withdrawals directly to the capital account or to a drawing account, only the capital account appears on the partnership's balance sheet. The use of the drawing account does provide a

---

[11] Ibid., §18.

concise record of withdrawals by partners, but the recognition of withdrawals directly into the capital account is theoretically identical to recognition in a separate drawing account. Thus, whether to use a drawing account or not is at the discretion of the partners. As discussed later in the chapter, it is possible that the drawing account may make it slightly easier to perform profit and loss allocations depending on the wording of the articles of partnership.

Sharing Profits and Losses

The articles of partnership can include any provisions for allocating profits and losses that are legally enforceable in the state where the partnership is located. For example, it is possible for the partners to agree to cut cards, with the winner taking all the profits, if the partnership is located in Nevada, where that form of gambling is legal. In this instance, the accountant may want to ensure that the rules are fully understood,[12] be present to verify the winner of the game, and make the profit or loss allocation to the appropriate recipient partner. The accountant should also ensure that the partners are fully aware of the riskiness of this method of profit and loss allocation; however, the accountant cannot tell the partners they cannot allocate profits and losses in this manner if it is legal in the state where the partnership is located. In many states such a provision would not be enforceable because that type of gambling is illegal.

The allocation of profits and losses to the partners may be based on the partners' capital account balances. For example, Peterson, Richards, and Smith may choose to share profits and losses in proportion to their relative capital balances. If the partners agree to share profits and losses in this manner and if the withdrawals made by the partners are proportionate to the capital account balances, this relationship can be maintained. However, if the partners agree initially to share profits and losses in this manner but have different levels of withdrawals, then the relative size of the capital accounts will change. As a result, it is common for the allocation of profits and losses to be independent of the initial capital account balances.

Accountants should be very cautious in recommending or endorsing specific profit and loss sharing methods. It is reasonable for the accountant to prepare an analysis of alternative methods and to evaluate and compare specific methods. This would often include illustrations of the resulting allocation outcomes using a range of hypothetical profit (and loss) levels. However, the selection of the particular profit and loss allocation provisions should be left to the partners themselves. Generally, the following components are far more likely to be included in the articles of partnership with regard to profit and loss allocation:

- Interest on capital balance
- Salary
- Bonus
- Residual percentages

These components provide a reward structure that ties the allocation of profits to the type of input provided by each owner. The interest component rewards for capital contributions. Salary and bonuses are designed to reward labor and expertise contributions.

---

[12] For example, if there is a loss, does the partner who draws the high card or the low card receive the loss allocation?

Theoretically, the first three profit and loss allocation components listed above can be determined in any order; however, the articles of partnership may require them to be determined in a specific order. The reason for this will be discussed later in this section. The only component that has a predetermined place is the residual percentages. **Residual percentages** are used to allocate all profits and losses not allocated with other allocation components. Residual percentages are also the component stipulated by the Uniform Partnership Act if the articles of partnership do not specify the method for allocating profits and losses.

The inclusion of a profit and loss allocation method in the articles of partnership may not be important if the partners contribute equally in the partnership's operation. All partners may contribute the same financial resources and perform the same amount of work on behalf of the partnership, so the partners may agree to share profits and losses equally. An equal sharing of profits and losses can be included in the articles of partnership, but it is not necessary because profits and losses are shared equally if the articles of partnership are silent regarding this issue. The profit and loss allocation must be specified in the articles of partnership only when they are not to be shared equally. An unequal sharing of profits and losses usually occurs when the partners do not contribute equally to the partnership. For example, one partner may contribute greater financial resources to start the partnership while another partner may be more active in the day-to-day operations and decision making. Each of these individuals would want to be compensated according to the nature of the contribution made.

Interest on Capital Balances   Interest on each partner's capital balance is often included to compensate partners who contribute economic resources to the partnership. This component of the profit or loss allocation is often stated as a percentage return on the capital balance. The capital balance used for determining this component of the profit and loss allocation may be the beginning capital balance, the ending capital balance, a simple average of the beginning and ending capital balances, or a weighted-average capital balance. The first three approaches are simpler than the weighted-average capital balance, but they are easy for partners to manipulate.

EXAMPLE 7-7

Interest on capital balances   Suppose two partners (Briscoe and Mitchell) begin business operations with Briscoe contributing $100,000 and Mitchell contributing $25,000. It is also agreed that the interest paid on invested capital is 10 percent and that the capital balance to be used for this allocation is the end-of-year capital account balance. If Mitchell becomes unhappy with his profit allocation, he may decide to borrow $200,000 at the end of the year and invest it in the partnership. His capital account balance at the end of the year will be $225,000, resulting in a marginal increase in profit allocation of $20,000 ($200,000 × .1). The $200,000 could then be withdrawn during the first month of the subsequent year.

The same manipulation can occur if the capital account balance used for the interest component allocation is based on the beginning capital account or a simple average of the beginning and ending capital account balances. This type of manipulation is much less likely if a weighted-average capital account balance is used for the interest component allocation.[13] The time frame used to compute the weighted-average capital account balance

---

[13] The procedural technique applied to determine the weighted-average capital balance for the partner's capital accounts is the same technique used to determine the weighted-average number of shares outstanding when determining earnings per share for a corporation.

can be any time frame agreed to by the partners, such as monthly or daily. The example below uses a monthly calculation for illustrative purposes. In addition to Briscoe's initial $100,000 contribution to the partnership, he also invests $60,000 on May 1 and withdraws $24,000 on November 30. Subsequent to his initial $25,000 contribution, Mitchell invests an additional $30,000 on August 1 and makes withdrawals of $10,000 and $5,000 on September 30 and December 31, respectively. Recall that withdrawals may be separately recognized in the *Drawing* account or may be included in the partner's capital account. The interest component of the profit and loss allocation would be determined as follows:

Briscoe's Average Capital Balance

Date	Invest/Withdraw		Capital Balance	Time Invested	Average Capital
January 1	Invest	$100,000	$100,000	4 months	400,000
May 1	Invest	$60,000	160,000	7 months	1,120,000
November 30	Withdraw	$24,000	136,000	1 month	136,000
					1,656,000
	Average capital ($1,656,000/12)				138,000

Mitchell's Average Capital Balance

Date	Invest/Withdraw		Capital Balance	Time Invested	Average Capital
January 1	Invest	$25,000	$25,000	7 months	175,000
August 1	Invest	$30,000	55,000	2 months	110,000
September 30	Withdraw	$10,000	45,000	3 months	135,000
December 31	Withdraw	$5,000	40,000	0 month	-0-
					420,000
	Average capital ($420,000/12)				35,000

As a result of the weighted-average capital calculations presented above, Briscoe would receive a profit allocation of $13,800 ($138,000 × .1) while Mitchell would receive $3,500 ($35,000 × .1). Keep in mind that the interest allocated to the partners as a result of this computation is not interest expense and is not included on the partnership's income statement. The interest component is part of an allocation process to determine how much of the partnership's profit and loss is to be allocated to each partner.

Salary Another common element of the profit and loss allocation procedure is a salary to the partners actively involved in the operation of the business. This element can be used to compensate partners for the time and effort expended actively working in the business in an attempt to make the business successful. This item could be expected to be renegotiated in the articles of partnership periodically as the duties of the partners change.

EXAMPLE 7-8

Salary allocation Assume that Briscoe and Mitchell agree that the salary for the two partners will be $10,000 and $25,000, respectively. As with the interest component of the profit and loss allocation, the salary component is generally considered to be part of an allocation process to determine how much of the partnership's profit or loss is to be allocated to each partner; it is not a component of the partnership's net income.

Bonus A third component that may be included in the profit and loss allocation is bonuses. Bonuses may be paid to any individuals the partners agree to include in the articles of partnership; however, the most likely recipient of a bonus is the partner serving as the manager of the business. The bonus computation may be as straightforward as taking net income in excess of some predetermined amount and multiplying this excess by an agreed-upon percentage.

EXAMPLE 7-9

Bonus to partner   Assume Briscoe and Mitchell agree that Mitchell will receive a bonus equal to 5 percent of the amount of net income in excess of $150,000. For this example, the formula to determine the bonus to allocate to Mitchell is:

$$\text{Bonus} = (\text{Net income} - \$150,000) \times .05$$

If the partnership's net income is $200,000, Mitchell's bonus is $2,500 [($200,000 − $150,000) × .05]. On the other hand, if partnership net income is $149,999, Mitchell's bonus is $0. The computation of the bonus can also be more involved. For example, the bonus may be based on net income after deducting the bonus. In this case the formula may look like the following:

$$\text{Bonus} = (\text{Net income} - \text{Bonus} - \$150,000) \times .05$$
$$1.0 \ \text{Bonus} = .05 \times \text{Net income} - .05 \times \text{Bonus} - .05 \times \$150,000$$
$$1.05 \ \text{Bonus} = .05 \times \text{Net income} - \$7,500$$
$$\text{Bonus} = (.05 \times \text{Net income} - \$7,500)/1.05$$

If net income is $200,000, Mitchell's bonus is now $2,380.95:

$$\text{Bonus} = (.05 \times \$200,000 - \$7,500)/1.05$$
$$\text{Bonus} = \$2,500/1.05$$
$$\text{Bonus} = \$2,380.95$$

The main issue regarding bonuses is that the accountant must understand the bonus arrangement and calculate the bonus based on the articles of partnership. Bonuses are sometimes based on attaining particular levels of profit (net income, operating income), revenue, or market share. Other bonus arrangements are based on improvements in items such as profits, revenue, or market share. An aspect that all good bonus arrangements should include is that the bonus should be based on a criteria under the control of the person to receive the bonus. For production managers, bonuses are sometimes based on the achievement of cost controls or maintaining average cost per unit levels below an established target. There is no set way to make the bonus calculation; it depends on the agreement reached by the partners and included in the articles of partnership.

Residual Interest   The final common component of the profit and loss allocation is the residual interest allocation to the various partners. This amount is often fixed percentages among the partners, although it is not required to be fixed. The residual amount to be allocated to each partner may depend on many factors. The only requirement is that the allocation of residual profits and losses must be included in the articles of partnership if it is going to be an allocation different from sharing the residual equally among all partners.

EXAMPLE 7-10

Residual percentages for profit and loss allocation (Part A)   Assume that Briscoe and Mitchell agree that both residual profits and losses will be allocated 60 percent to Briscoe and 40 percent to Mitchell. The allocation of the residual profits and losses can also be determined by other factors such as relative capital balances or number of billable hours. The amount of partnership income or loss remaining after the allocation in the other allocation steps is shared using the residual percentages.

The allocation of profits does not have to be the same as the allocation of losses, although they are often the same. If the allocations of profits and losses differ, the articles of partnership must explicitly address the allocations. Below is an example of the allocation of the Briscoe/Mitchell partnership assuming the relationships discussed above and a partnership net income of $80,000.

	Briscoe	*Mitchell*	*Totals*
Interest on capital account	$13,800	$3,500	17,300
Salary	10,000	25,000	35,000
Bonus ($80,000 – $150,000) × .05		0	0
Subtotal	23,800	28,500	52,300
Residual			
($80,000 – $52,300) × .6	16,620		16,620
($80,000 – $52,300) × .4		11,080	11,080
Totals	40,420	39,580	80,000

Notice that Mitchell does not receive a bonus in this example. The net income of the partnership was not large enough to result in the inclusion of a bonus.

EXAMPLE 7-11

Residual percentages for profit and loss allocation (Part B) This example is based on the same facts, but the net income is now assumed to be $250,000.

	Briscoe	*Mitchell*	*Totals*
Interest on capital account	$13,800	$3,500	17,300
Salary	10,000	25,000	35,000
Bonus ($250,000 – $150,000) × .05		5,000	5,000
Subtotal	23,800	33,500	57,300
Residual			
($250,000 – $57,300) × .6	115,620		115,620
($250,000 – $57,300) × .4		77,080	77,080
Totals	139,420	110,580	250,000

The difference between the partnership income allocated to Briscoe and Mitchell is greater here than in Example 7-10. Briscoe has benefited from the 60 percent allocation of the residual amount of partnership net income. The amount of bonus assigned to Mitchell does not make up for the greater residual granted to Briscoe because of the low bonus percentage relative to the residual percentage and the high income level required before the bonus becomes a significant factor in the profit or loss allocation.

It is also possible that the net income of the partnership will not be great enough to fully allocate the interest on the capital accounts and the salaries. This occurrence can be addressed in either of two ways when performing the profit and loss allocation. One approach is to perform the allocation until all of the partnership's net income is allocated and then stop the allocation process.

EXAMPLE 7-12

Insufficient income to perform all allocations (Part A) Assume that the Briscoe and Mitchell partnership net income is $30,000 and that the order of allocation for profits and losses is (1) interest on invested capital, (2) salaries, (3) bonus, and (4) residual. The following allocation will be made. There are insufficient profits for each partner to receive his/her entire salary allocation. Given that the profit allocation in the current example stops when the profits are exhausted, each partner is allocated a share of his/her respective salary. As a result, each partner is allocated a salary amount in proportion to his/her share of the total salaries of all partners.

	Briscoe	Mitchell	Totals
Interest on capital account	$13,800	$3,500	17,300
Salary			
($30,000 – $17,300) × ($10,000/$35,000)	3,629		3,629
($30,000 – $17,300) × ($25,000/$35,000)		9,071	9,071
Bonus ($30,000 – $150,000) × .05		0	0
Subtotal	17,429	12,571	30,000
Residual	0	0	0
Totals	17,429	12,571	30,000

EXAMPLE 7-13

Insufficient income to perform all allocations (Part B)   Assume now that the order of allocation is changed to the following: (1) salaries, (2) interest on invested capital, (3) bonus, and (4) residual. The following allocation would occur:

	Briscoe	Mitchell	Totals
Salary			
$30,000 × ($10,000/$35,000)	8,571		8,571
$30,000 × ($25,000/$35,000)		21,429	21,429
Interest on capital account	0	0	0
Bonus ($30,000 – $150,000) × .05		0	0
Subtotal	8,571	21,429	30,000
Residual	0	0	0
Totals	8,571	21,429	30,000

Note that the order of the first three allocation items in the examples above does not matter as long as the amount of profit to be allocated is greater than the amounts to be allocated to the first three items (in this case $17,300 + $35,000 + $5,000 = $57,300). If the partnership's net income is less than the sum of these items, the order of the allocation may make a difference in the total partnership profit and loss allocated to each partner.

The other approach that can be used to allocate profits and losses when there are insufficient profits to perform all the allocation is to continue the allocation process as if there is sufficient profit and allocate the resulting negative residual to the partners using the residual profit and loss ratios.

EXAMPLE 7-14

Insufficient income resulting in negative residuals   Assume this process is used with the $30,000 partnership net income from Example 7-12. It will again be assumed that interest on invested capital is the first allocation, although the order of the first three allocations does not make a difference when this procedure is applied because the full allocation will be made regardless of the order.

	Briscoe	Mitchell	Totals
Interest on capital account	$13,800	$3,500	17,300
Salary	10,000	25,000	35,000
Bonus ($30,000 – $150,000) × .05		0	0
Subtotal	23,800	28,500	52,300
Residual			
($30,000 – $52,300) × .6	(13,380)		(13,380)
($30,000 – $52,300) × .4		(8,920)	(8,920)
Totals	10,420	19,580	30,000

The above examples illustrated the allocation process when there is a small partnership profit. It is also possible that the partnership will have an absolute loss. The partnership agreement should contain provisions for allocating the net loss to the partners. If the partnership agreement calls for the allocation of profit until it is fully allocated (as presented above) and the articles of partnership do not mention how to allocate a net loss, then the loss is allocated equally to all partners. The residual interest percentages (60 percent and 40 percent) in the previous examples are applicable because Briscoe and Mitchell applied the residual ratios to the allocation of profits and losses.

Accounting for Unrealized Holding Gains and Losses

As stated above, the allocation method used to assign each partner's share of the partnership's income or loss to that partner's capital account is typically included in the articles of partnership. The agreed-upon profit and loss allocation method may continue unaltered for some time or it may be periodically amended. The amendment may occur for a variety of reasons, but the most likely reason is that a partner wants to change his/her active involvement in the operations of the partnership and is willing to accept a larger (smaller) allocation of profits and losses.

The issue that should be considered when renegotiating the profit and loss allocation agreement is that some assets and liabilities may have a market value different from book value due to holding gains and losses that have not been recognized in net income. Any unrealized gains and losses in existence at the date of change in the profit and loss allocation method should be assigned to the partners using the previous profit and loss agreement because it was over time that holding gains and losses occurred. This assignment can occur in three ways. First, the partners can prepare an itemized list of items that have market values different from book values. The articles of partnership could then be amended to indicate the amount of unrealized gain or loss that should be allocated using the previous profit and loss allocation method.

EXAMPLE 7-15   **Holding gains and losses allocated with an itemized list**   Assume the Briscoe and Mitchell partnership has always allocated profits and losses 60 percent to Briscoe and 40 percent to Mitchell (interest in invested capital, salaries, and bonuses are excluded from this example for simplification). Briscoe is nearing retirement and wants to curtail active involvement in the partnership. As a result, the partners agree that the new profit and loss allocation will be 30 percent to Briscoe and 70 percent to Mitchell.

Assume also that the partnership owns land with a book value of $100,000 and a market value, at the date the profit and loss allocation method is changed, of $300,000. The partners could include, in the amended articles of partnership, that the $200,000 increase in the land's value should be allocated 60 percent to Briscoe and 40 percent to Mitchell when the land is sold or the partnership dissolves.

Notice that this agreement did not state that the first $200,000 of gain should be allocated 60 percent to Briscoe and 40 percent to Mitchell. This is important because it is possible for the land's value to fall below $300,000 before it is sold. If this occurs, Briscoe and Mitchell should still receive 60 percent and 40 percent of $200,000, respectively. Any additional gain (market value greater than $300,000) or loss (market value less than $300,000) should be allocated 30 percent to Briscoe and 70 percent to Mitchell to reflect the change in value since the profit and loss allocation method was changed. For example, the land may be sold for $350,000 some time after the profit and loss allocation method is changed, resulting in the following journal entry.

Cash	350,000	
Land		100,000
Gain on Sale of Land		250,000

To record sale of land.

The *Gain on Sale of Land* is ultimately closed to the partner's capital accounts, resulting in the following journal entry.

Gain on Sale of Land	250,000	
Briscoe, Capital ($200,000 × .6) + ($50,000 × .3)		135,000
Mitchell, Capital ($200,000 × .4) + ($50,000 × .7)		115,000

To allocate $200,000 of the gain on sale of land to the partners based on prior profit and loss allocation method and $50,000 of the gain based on current profit and loss allocation method.

The approach demonstrated above requires special recordkeeping for this arrangement and makes the allocation of profits and losses more detailed when the specified assets are sold or liabilities settled.

A second alternative is to revalue the assets and liabilities at the date of the change in the profit and loss allocation method. Revaluation of the assets and liabilities would result in the immediate assignment of the gain or loss to the partners based on the old profit and loss allocation method. This would eliminate the need to keep a record of the items requiring special consideration when the asset is sold or the liability settled. The problem with this approach is that such recognition of unrealized gains and losses is not in conformity with GAAP, and some partners may not want to deviate from GAAP to this extent. It could be argued, however, that the change in the profit and loss allocation method in essence dissolves the previous partnership and forms a new partnership, so revaluation of the partnership's assets and liabilities is appropriate.

EXAMPLE 7-16   **Revaluing assets before sale**   Continuing with the previous example, Briscoe and Mitchell would recognize the $200,000 increase in the value of the land when the profit and loss allocation method was changed with the following journal entry.

Land	200,000	
Briscoe, Capital ($200,000 × .6)		120,000
Mitchell, Capital ($200,000 × .4)		80,000

To record the increase in the value of land on the date of change in profit and loss allocation method.

The subsequent sale of the land would base the gain or loss recognized on the $300,000 land valuation, the adjusted cost basis. Any subsequent gain or loss from the sale of the land would be shared 30 percent to Briscoe and 70 percent to Mitchell. Sale of the land for $350,000 would result in the following journal entry.

Cash	350,000	
Land		300,000
Gain on Sale of Land		50,000

To record sale of land.

The *Gain on Sale of Land* is ultimately closed to the partner's capital accounts resulting in the following.

Gain on Sale of Land	50,000	
Briscoe, Capital ($50,000 × .3)		15,000
Mitchell, Capital ($50,000 × .7)		35,000

To allocate the gain on sale of land to the partners based on current profit.

The third approach to considering the change in the profit and loss allocation method is to adjust the capital accounts of the partners without altering the value of the asset or liability. This process will result in the same partners' capital account balances, after the asset is sold or the liability is settled, that existed in the previous examples. The only difference is that the change in the allocation of the unrealized gain or loss is assigned directly to the partners' capital accounts. The allocation of the total gain or loss is the same as it would have been had the cost basis of the asset or liability been changed and the unrealized gain or loss allocated (as it was in the previous example).

EXAMPLE 7-17

Adjust partners' capital accounts   Keeping the same assumption that the land has increased in value from $100,000 to $300,000, the following journal entry would be made.

Mitchell, Capital [$200,000 × (.70 − .40)]	60,000	
Briscoe, Capital [$200,000 × (.30 − .60)]		60,000

To restate the capital accounts to reflect the unrealized increase in value of the land and the impact of the change in the profit and loss allocation method.

Subsequent sale of the land for $350,000 would result in the following journal entry.

Cash	350,000	
Land		100,000
Gain on Sale of Land		250,000

To record sale of land.

The *Gain on Sale of Land* is ultimately closed to the partners' capital accounts, resulting in the following journal entry.

Gain on Sale of Land	250,000	
Briscoe, Capital ($250,000 × .3)		75,000
Mitchell, Capital ($250,000 × .7)		175,000

To allocate the gain on sale of land to the partners based on current profit and loss allocation method.

Regardless of the method used to recognize the change in the market value of the land, the total gain or loss allocated to the partners is the same. The form of the allocation has changed but the substance is the same. The following table shows the change in the capital accounts of the two partners (Briscoe and Mitchell) for each of the three methods.

Note that the unrealized gain on the land was allocated using residual profit and loss percentages; that is, it was assumed that interest on invested capital, salaries, and bonuses were not an issue. This would be accurate if the partnership's net income before the unrealized gain was greater than the sum of the interest on invested capital, salaries, and bonuses. If the partnership's net income before the unrealized gain was not greater than the sum of these three items, the allocation would have to consider the impact of the additional income on those items. This would increase the level of detail necessary to compute the

	Change in Briscoe's Capital Account		
	Gain Recognized at Date of Change in Profit Allocation	*Gain Recognized at Date of Sale*	*Total*
Change in allocation is accomplished with itemized list	-0-	135,000	135,000
Change in allocation is accomplished by revaluing assets	120,000	15,000	135,000
Change in allocation is accomplished by reallocating capital among partners	60,000	75,000	135,000

	Change in Mitchell's Capital Account		
	Gain Recognized at Date of Change in Profit Allocation	*Gain Recognized at Date of Sale*	*Total*
Change in allocation is accomplished with itemized list	-0-	115,000	115,000
Change in allocation is accomplished by revaluing assets	80,000	35,000	115,000
Change in allocation is accomplished by reallocating capital among partners	(60,000)	175,000	115,000

allocation of the unrealized gain on the land but it would not change the underlying theoretical reason for the allocation.

Another item that could lead to an adjustment to the partners' capital accounts is the correction of an error. A material error should always be corrected when discovered. In many instances, any change in the partnership's net income can be included in the current period net income and allocated to the partners using the current period profit and loss sharing agreement. The exception to this allocation is if the profit and loss sharing agreement has changed. If the profit and loss sharing agreement changed, the change in net income resulting from correcting an error should be determined using the profit and loss agreement in effect when the error occurred (if possible). It is possible that the year in which the error occurred may not be determinable; that is, it may be the result of assumptions made in several periods (for example, a change in the allowance for bad debts as a percentage of credit sales). It is also possible that the impact of the error on the partners' capital accounts due to a change in the profit and loss allocation method may be immaterial. In these cases it may be impossible or impractical to allocate the impact of the error on partnership income using a prior period profit and loss agreement and the partners may choose to use the current profit and loss agreement as a matter of convenience.

CHANGE IN OWNERSHIP

Change in the ownership structure in the corporate form of business is a frequent occurrence. Shareholders sell stock to current investors and new investors. Corporations update the list of stockholders for the purpose of paying dividends, buying and selling treasury stock, and issuing new stock. In addition, some corporations will update the list of stockholders to monitor the list of owners for potential takeovers. Changes in the ownership of corporations has no impact on the financial records of the corporation except for the acquisition or reissuance of the corporation's own capital stock (treasury stock). These transactions are recognized in the corporation's financial records, but they rarely affect the corporation's business operations.

In contrast to changes in the owners of a corporation, changes in the owners of a partnership may result in changes in the operation of the partnership. The admission of a new partner or the withdrawal of an existing partner results in the dissolution of the partnership. *Dissolution* of the partnership is defined in the Uniform Partnership Act as "the change in the relation of the partners caused by any partner ceasing to be associated in the carrying on as distinguished from the winding up of the business."[14] A change in the relationship among partners is important because of the unlimited liability that exists in a partnership. Every partner is liable for the actions of all the other partners taken in the name of the partnership. However, new partners assume the rights and responsibilities of existing partners as of the date of admission, so the new partner has unlimited liability for the actions of the partners beginning with the date of admission. Liability for actions of partners prior to the date of the new partner's admission is limited to the amount invested in the partnership; that is, partnership creditors cannot attach the personal assets of a new partner for action taken prior to the new partner being admitted to the partnership. This limitation of the new partner's liability makes it important for the partnership to itemize the liabilities in existence at the new partner's admission date.

The dissolution of the partnership does not mean that the partnership ceases operation. The articles of partnership usually include a clause that provides for the continued operation of the partnership in the event of a change in the relationship among the partners. It is likely that a new profit and loss allocation method will be created as a result of the change in the relationship among partners.

A concept distinct from the admission of a new partner or the withdrawal of an existing partner is the assignment of the interest of a current partner to a third party. An assignment of all or part of the capital and/or profits of an existing partner to a third party does not result in the dissolution of the partnership if the third party does not become a partner. For example, the judgment in a civil suit against one of the partners may result in the court attaching 75 percent of that partner's share of the partnership's profits and losses to pay damages to the third party; however, the third party has no vote in the operations of the partnership and may request intervention by the court only if fraud is suspected. The only change that occurs is that 75 percent of that partner's share of the partnership's profits and losses are allocated to the third party as stipulated by the court. There is no change in the relationship among the partners with regard to the management of the partnership's operations. The only journal entry that may be required is when there is an assignment of a partner's capital to a third party. The partnership records should disclose the transfer of the capital balance from the existing partner to the assignee.

Admission of a New Partner

A change in the ownership structure of a partnership (e.g., admission of a new partner) results in either (1) no change in the net assets of the partnership or (2) a change in the net assets of the partnership.

No Change in Net Assets A change in the ownership structure resulting in no change in the partnership's net assets occurs when a new partner purchases an ownership interest directly from an existing partner. In this instance, the new partner is transferring assets to the existing partner's personal assets. Because there is no change in the partnership's total assets, the only recognition required is the transfer of capital from one party to another,

---

[14] Ibid., §29.

if applicable. For example, Briscoe may desire to reduce the amount of time spent working in the partnership's business. Because of the partner's unlimited liability, Mitchell must agree to the new partner who will enter the partnership. Assume that Mitchell agrees that Johnson would be an acceptable person to become an additional partner in the partnership. Briscoe and Johnson agree to a transaction external to the partnership; for example, Johnson agrees to pay Briscoe some unknown amount (based on an appraisal or a negotiation between Briscoe and Johnson) in return for a 25 percent–ownership interest in the partnership's total capital. Prior to admitting Johnson as a partner, Briscoe and Mitchell may want to revalue the partnership's assets because the current partners would likely believe that any increase in the value of the partnership's net assets that has already occurred should accrue to the current partners and not the new partner. This allocation of unrealized profits can also occur through a separate profit and loss agreement with regard to those net assets, but such an agreement requires an itemized list. After admission, Johnson will be allocated a share of profits and losses based on a new profit and loss agreement.

Keep in mind that the transfer of 25 percent of the partnership's capital does not always mean that Johnson is going to receive 25 percent of the total profits of the partnership. The profit and loss allocation method is not dependent on the partners' capital balances unless the partners define that relationship in the articles of partnership. Additionally, because the profit and loss allocation method may include a number of criteria—including interest on invested capital, salary, bonus, and residual—the amount of profit and loss allocation received by Johnson may not be a simple set percentage.

EXAMPLE 7-18

New partner purchases capital of an existing partner Assume that Johnson receives a 10 percent interest on invested capital (the same as Briscoe and Mitchell in earlier examples), 70 percent of the salary previously received by Briscoe (if Johnson is going to spend a substantial amount of time working in the business), but only 30 percent of Briscoe's residual allocation. In addition, the amount Johnson agrees to pay Briscoe is not disclosed because Johnson's investment is not a necessary piece of information for the recognition in the partnership's financial records. The journal entry that would be required (assuming Briscoe's capital account is $200,000 and the partnership's total capital is $300,000) is as follows.

Briscoe, Capital ($300,000 × .25)	75,000	
Johnson, Capital		75,000

To recognize the transfer of Briscoe's capital to Johnson.

It is also possible that Johnson may receive no initial capital balance. In that instance, Johnson's capital account will not be recorded initially; it will be created the first time profits and losses are allocated. Johnson may agree to this type of arrangement in return for a larger allocation of the profits and losses.

The relationships presented above illustrate a new partner entering the partnership and the partial withdrawal of an existing partner. The relationships would have been exactly the same had Briscoe sold his entire ownership interest to Johnson. The only difference is that Briscoe's entire capital account would have been transferred to Johnson.

Change in Net Assets—Investment at Book Value A change in the relationship among the partners may also result in a change in the partnership's net assets. A new partner may contribute assets directly to the partnership to gain admission or the partnership may purchase the ownership interest of a withdrawing partner. In addition, a change in the ownership interest may occur at book value or at some other amount. While the occurrence of a book value admission to a partnership or withdrawal from a partnership is rare, it is illustrated below to provide a foundation for subsequent non–book value examples.

EXAMPLE 7-19

New partner investment at book value Assume that the Briscoe and Mitchell partnership has total capital of $300,000 and that Johnson is joining the partnership with a 20-percent ownership by investing $75,000.

Book value of capital before the investment	$300,000
Johnson's investment	75,000
Total book value of capital after the investment	$375,000
Johnson's percentage ownership	0.20
Book value of Johnson's ownership percentage capital	$75,000

As a result of this investment, the following journal entry would be made.

Cash	75,000	
Johnson, Capital		75,000

To admit a new partner (Johnson) to the partnership.

If Johnson was the member of the partnership who was withdrawing and the amount of the payment to Johnson was the book value of his capital, the journal entry would be the following.

Johnson, Capital	75,000	
Cash		75,000

To retire an existing partner (Johnson) from the partnership.

Change in Net Assets—Revaluation of Existing Assets

It is more common for the change in the relationship among partners to occur at some amount other than book value. Three approaches are commonly used to recognize such a change in the relationship among partners at an amount other than the book value: (1) revaluation of existing partnership assets, (2) bonus method, and (3) goodwill method. The revaluation of assets and goodwill methods are problematic for some because these methods results in partnership financial records that deviate from historical cost. This deviation concerns some who contend that the partnership is still in operation and that there should be no change in the values assigned to assets and liabilities while the partnership is in operation. Proponents of these approaches contend that there has been a change in ownership resulting in the legal dissolution of the old partnership and the establishment of a new partnership. Even though partnership operations may have continued through the change in the relationship among the partners, there is a new legal entity. Such a change, proponents contend, warrants the changes that result. Keep in mind that the partners do not have to choose one of the three approaches; a combination of approaches may be utilized.

EXAMPLE 7-20

Revaluation of assets, new partner investment at revised book value Assume that the book value of the Briscoe and Mitchell partnership is $480,000 and that Johnson has agreed to pay $125,000 for a 20-percent interest in the partnership's capital. Briscoe and Mitchell may desire to revalue the partnership's assets to market value because Johnson is to receive a share of partnership's profits and losses after admission to the partnership. For this example, assume that the partnership's fixed assets are undervalued by $20,000. Assume also that Briscoe and Mitchell agree to divide the increase in the value of the fixed assets in proportion to their residual interests in the partnership (60 percent and 40 percent for Briscoe and Mitchell, respectively), resulting in the following journal entry.

Fixed assets	20,000	
Briscoe, Capital		12,000
Mitchell, Capital		8,000

To recognize the increase in the value of the fixed assets prior to admitting Johnson.

The admission of Johnson into the partnership is prepared in a manner similar to the previous example.

Book value of capital before the investment	$500,000
Johnson's investment	125,000
Total book value of capital after the investment	$625,000
Johnson's percentage ownership	0.20
Book value of Johnson's ownership percentage capital	$125,000

As a result of this investment, the following journal entry would be made.

Cash	125,000	
Johnson, Capital		125,000

To admit a new partner (Johnson) to the partnership.

The revaluation of the net assets, in this example, resulted in Johnson being admitted to the partnership at an investment level proportionate to the percentage of resulting book value (.20 of $625,000 in this case). In this example, the value of the partnership and the capital to be assigned to the new partner can be determined by considering the sum of the values of the tangible assets.

In practice it is likely that the revaluation of the net assets will not result in a book value admission of a new partner (unless the partners make it occur in such a manner). One possibility is that the existing partnership may have some intrinsic value (goodwill) not recognized in the financial records of the partnership. This intrinsic value may result from the perceived quality of the product delivered by the partnership as evidenced by a strong base of loyal customers. Another possibility is that the prospective new partner may bring needed expertise to the partnership resulting in some intrinsic value (goodwill) in the new partner. These examples are not meant to be an exhaustive list of the ways that intangible assets may become part of the partnership entity; they are only representative examples.

The partners must determine whether goodwill is going to be recorded on the financial records of the partnership. Some argue that because intangible assets can be recorded only when they are acquired from another entity, goodwill should not be recognized when a new partner is admitted to, or when an existing partner withdraws from the partnership. Others contend that because the ownership structure of the partnership has changed, the partnership is justified in recognizing all assets invested in the new partnership. The two accounting options illustrated below are the bonus method (goodwill is not directly recognized) and the goodwill method (goodwill is directly recognized). The similarity between the two methods is that the net assets (other than goodwill) contributed by a new partner must be recognized at their market values on the date the new partner is admitted. Keep in mind that it is also possible that the net assets of the partnership may be revalued before the new partner is admitted to the partnership or an existing partner withdraws from the partnership. In the examples below, it is assumed that the revaluation of the existing net assets has already occurred, so a revaluation step is not included. This permits the examples to focus exclusively on the bonus or goodwill methods.

Change in Net Assets—Bonus Method When the bonus method is applied, the capital account of the new partner is assigned that partner's percentage interest in the total book value of capital after the investment. The difference between the investment and the capital assigned often represents the unrecognized intangible asset. If the partners choose not to directly recognize the intangible asset, a bonus either to or from the existing partners will result.

EXAMPLE 7-21

New partner investment, bonus to existing partners Assume that Johnson is contributing $150,000 to become a new partner in the Briscoe and Mitchell partnership. The partnership has total capital of $500,000 after revaluing the assets and before Johnson is admitted. Johnson is to receive a 20 percent capital interest in the new partnership. Assume also that the articles of partnership indicate that the *bonus method* is to be used to admit new partners into the partnership. Regardless of the approach used to recognize the admission or withdrawal of a partner, the cash being exchanged is $150,000 in the current example and an entry in that amount must be made to *Cash*. The bonus method is used when the partners do not want to recognize goodwill on the partnership's balance sheet. After the investment by Johnson, the total partnership capital is $650,000, and Johnson's share of the new book value is $130,000, as presented below.

Book value of capital before the investment	$500,000
Johnson's investment	150,000
Total book value of capital after the investment	$650,000
Johnson's percentage ownership	0.20
Book value of Johnson's ownership percentage capital	$130,000

In this instance Johnson is paying more than the capital assigned, resulting in a bonus to the existing partners. This could indicate that the partnership has goodwill attached to it. It could also indicate that Johnson agreed to accept a lower initial capital balance in return for a greater allocation of profits and losses.

The difference between the value of the new partner's contribution and the capital assigned to the new partner is allocated to the existing partners in this example because Johnson's investment is greater than the proportionate book value of capital. This bonus is allocated to the existing partners in a predetermined ratio (often the residual profit and loss sharing ratio). The profit and loss ratio for the Briscoe and Mitchell partnership prior to admitting Johnson is 60 percent to Briscoe and 40 percent to Mitchell. The following journal entry recognizes the admission of Johnson into the partnership.

Cash	150,000	
Briscoe, Capital [($150,000 – $130,000) × .6]		12,000
Johnson, Capital		130,000
Mitchell, Capital [($150,000 – $130,000) × .4]		8,000

To recognize the admission of Johnson into the Briscoe and Mitchell partnership using the bonus method.

The recognition of a bonus allocated to the existing partners does not necessarily indicate that Johnson does not bring goodwill to the partnership. It may indicate that the existing partnership has more goodwill than does the new partner. The adjustment is in essence a net adjustment, not an adjustment for the goodwill associated with all the partners. The unrecognized goodwill is assigned to the existing partners' capital accounts using the profit and loss ratios because it came into existence over time and is essentially a form of undervalued assets in existence at the date the new partner is admitted.

Example 7-21 was based on the assumption that the bonus was allocated to the existing partners. This circumstance could change if Johnson was contributing significant intangible assets to the partnership.

EXAMPLE 7-22

New partner investment, bonus to new partner   Assume that Johnson had significant experience operating a business similar to the Briscoe and Mitchell partnership and Johnson also had many loyal customers who would become customers of the partnership Johnson joins. As a result, Briscoe and Mitchell may find Johnson's membership in the partnership to be highly desirable, and they may offer a higher initial capital balance to entice Johnson to join their partnership. Assume all the facts of the previous example remain the same except that the initial capital investment required by Johnson is only $90,000 for a 20 percent interest. After the $90,000 investment by Johnson, the total partnership capital is $590,000, but Johnson's share of that book value is now $118,000, as presented below.

Book value of capital before the investment	$500,000
Johnson's investment	90,000
Total book value of capital after the investment	$590,000
Johnson's percentage ownership	0.20
Book value of Johnson's ownership percentage capital	$118,000

The following journal entry recognizes the admission of Johnson into the partnership:

Cash	90,000	
Briscoe, Capital [($118,000 – $90,000) × .6]	16,800	
Mitchell, Capital [($118,000 – $90,000) × .4]	11,200	
Johnson, Capital		118,000

To recognize the admission of Johnson into the Briscoe and Mitchell partnership using the bonus method.

In this example Johnson is granted a capital account ($118,000) in excess of the amount of the investment ($90,000). This results in a transfer of capital from Briscoe and Mitchell to Johnson. Briscoe and Mitchell are willing to make such a transfer because the perceived benefits of having Johnson in the partnership outweigh the economic sacrifice of transferring ownership interest to Johnson. The reduction of the existing partners' capital accounts is a transfer of economic value to Johnson because, if the partnership were to liquidate on the date Johnson is admitted at book value, Johnson would receive $28,000 more than his investment while, in total, Briscoe and Mitchell would receive $28,000 less.

Change in Net Assets—Goodwill Method   Rather than applying the bonus method to admit Johnson, Briscoe and Mitchell could have elected to apply the _goodwill method_. This method results in the recognition of goodwill on the partnership's balance sheet. The net result is that the partnership's total assets are greater when applying the goodwill method than when applying the bonus method because of the goodwill recognition.

The new partner may contribute both identifiable (tangible and intangible) assets and goodwill to the partnership. The sum of these two amounts makes up the total contribution by the new partner. On the other hand, the goodwill may be contributed by the existing partners, so the "new partner goodwill" will be assigned the value of $0. As with the bonus method, this does not mean that the new partner is not contributing goodwill; it means that the partnership's goodwill is viewed as being more substantial than the new partner's goodwill and the adjustment is a net adjustment.

The "new partner percentage ownership" is the agreed-upon percentage of total capital to be assigned to the new partner. In a general expression, the new partner makes an investment and is granted a percentage of ownership as follows.

$$\text{Investment by new partner} = \text{New partner \% ownership} \times \text{Total value of partnership}$$

The investment by the new partner can include both identifiable assets and goodwill contributed. In addition, the total value of the partnership, after admission of the new partner, becomes the identifiable net assets prior to admission plus identifiable net assets contributed by the new partner and the goodwill recognized. The equation may now be expanded to the following.

$$\begin{array}{l}\text{Identifiable assets} \\ \text{contributed by} \\ \text{new partner}\end{array} + \begin{array}{l}\text{Goodwill} \\ \text{contributed by} \\ \text{new partner}\end{array} = \begin{array}{l}\text{New partner \%} \\ \text{ownership}\end{array} \times \left(\begin{array}{l}\text{Identifiable} \\ \text{net assets}\end{array} + \begin{array}{l}\text{Goodwill} \\ \text{recognized}\end{array} \right)$$

By applying the above equation, one can solve for the amount of goodwill to be recognized. The goodwill contributed by the new partner and the resulting goodwill recognized by the partnership are equal when the new partner brings goodwill into the partnership. When the goodwill contributed by the new partner is $0, the resulting goodwill recognized is from the existing partners. Both cases are illustrated in the examples below.

EXAMPLE 7-23   **New partner investment, goodwill to existing partners**   Assume the same facts as in Example 7-21, where Johnson was admitted to the Briscoe and Mitchell partnership with a 20 percent beginning capital balance for an investment of $150,000. The same initial computation is used to determine whether the goodwill is being contributed by the existing partners or the new partner. The computation from Example 7-21 is reproduced as follows.

Book value of capital before the investment	$500,000
Johnson's investment	150,000
Total book value of capital after the investment	$650,000
Johnson's percentage ownership	.20
Book value of Johnson's ownership percentage capital	$130,000

Johnson invested $20,000 more than the book value of the capital that would be assigned to him ($150,000 − $130,000) if no goodwill were to be recognized. This indicates that the existing partners are contributing the goodwill because the new partner is paying more than book value for the right to join the partnership. However, the computation does not indicate the value being assigned to goodwill.

Substituting the information from the current example into the formula leads to the calculation of goodwill as follows.

$150,000 = (.20)($650,000 + Goodwill)
$150,000 = $130,000 + (.2) (Goodwill)
$20,000   = (.2) (Goodwill)
Goodwill = $100,000

This computation indicates that the partnership should recognize goodwill of $100,000. Previous computations indicated that the goodwill should be assigned to the existing partners, so the following journal entry should be made to admit Johnson to the partnership.

Cash	150,000	
Goodwill	100,000	
Briscoe, Capital ($100,000 × .6)		60,000
Johnson, Capital [($650,000 + $100,000) × .2]		150,000
Mitchell, Capital ($100,000 × .4)		40,000

To admit new partner (Johnson) to the partnership for $150,000 investment.

Note that Johnson's capital account is not established at the book value of Johnson's ownership percentage presented ($130,000) in the computation, where it was determined that the goodwill was to be allocated to the existing partners. The reason for this difference is that the $130,000 amount does not include the recognition of goodwill. Johnson is to receive a capital balance equal to 20 percent of the total partnership capital after the new partnership is formed. The book value of the partnership's net assets is increased from $650,000 to $750,000, with the recognition of the goodwill associated with the existing partnership. A revised schedule illustrates this result.

Book value of capital before the investment	$500,000
Johnson's investment	150,000
Goodwill recognized	100,000
Total book value of capital after the investment	$750,000
Johnson's percentage ownership	.20
Book value of Johnson's ownership percentage capital	$150,000

The book value of Johnson's ownership interest in the partnership is recorded at $150,000, resulting in Johnson's ownership interest being equal to the 20-percent ownership in the revalued partnership.

EXAMPLE 7-24

New partner investment, goodwill to new partner   Assume the same facts as in Example 7-22 when Johnson was to receive an initial capital account balance equal to 20-percent of the new partnership's total capital with only a $90,000 investment of identifiable assets. The computation of the book value of Johnson's ownership interest is reproduced as follows.

Book value of capital before the investment	$500,000
Johnson's investment	90,000
Total book value of capital after the investment	$590,000
Johnson's percentage ownership	.20
Book value of Johnson's ownership percentage capital	$118,000

In this example, Johnson invests $28,000 ($118,000 − $90,000) less than the book value of the capital that would be assigned if no goodwill were to be recognized, indicating that the goodwill is being contributed by Johnson. Once again, the computation does not indicate the value being assigned to the goodwill. This amount can be determined by evaluating the capital of the new partner using the same formula presented previously.

The goodwill is being assigned to Johnson, so the "new partner goodwill" is equal to "total partnership goodwill." As in the previous example, the "new partner percentage ownership" is the agreed-upon percentage of total capital to be assigned to the new partner. The "total capital after new partner investment" is the total capital including the identifiable assets invested by the new partner; it does not include any goodwill that may be contributed by the new partner. The final component, "total partnership goodwill," is the goodwill that would appear if a partnership balance sheet is prepared immediately after the new partnership is formed. In this example, goodwill is determined as follows.

$$\$90,000 + \text{Goodwill} = (.20) (\$590,000 + \text{Goodwill})$$
$$\$90,000 + \text{Goodwill} = \$118,000 + (.20) (\text{Goodwill})$$
$$(.80) (\text{Goodwill}) = \$28,000$$
$$\text{Goodwill} = \$35,000$$

The above computation indicates that the partnership should recognize $35,000 of goodwill. Previous computations indicated that the goodwill should be assigned to Johnson, so the following journal entry should be made to admit Johnson to the partnership.

Cash	90,000	
Goodwill	35,000	
Johnson, Capital		125,000

    To admit new partner (Johnson) to the partnership for an investment of $90,000.

Note that Johnson's capital account is once again not established at the book value of Johnson's ownership percentage presented ($118,000) in the computation determining who is contributing goodwill. The reason for this difference is that the $118,000 amount does not include the recognition of goodwill. Johnson is to receive a capital balance equal to 20 percent of the total partnership capital after the new partnership is formed. The book value of the partnership's net assets is increased from $590,000 to $625,000 with the recognition of the goodwill associated with the existing partnership. As a result, the book value of Johnson's ownership interest in the partnership is $125,000 as illustrated below.

Book value of capital before the investment	$500,000
Johnson's investment	90,000
Goodwill recognized	35,000
Total book value of capital after the investment	$625,000
Johnson's percentage ownership	.20
Book value of Johnson's ownership percentage capital	$125,000

Practical Considerations In practice, when negotiations to bring in a new partner occur, the dollar amount of goodwill either that a new partner is bringing into the partnership or that exists in the partnership is sometimes agreed to first. Then the desired ownership percentage to be granted to the incoming partner is agreed to by the parties. Using those agreed-upon factors, the dollar amount of required cash (or tangible) asset investment is calculated. The equations used above can still be applied to calculate the required investment.

    For example, assume the parties agree that $500,000 of tangible assets and $100,000 of unrecorded goodwill are in the existing partnership. If Johnson wants to invest new capital for a 20 percent interest, the cash investment required would be as follows:

$$\begin{pmatrix} \text{Identifiable assets} \\ \text{contributed by} \\ \text{new partner} \end{pmatrix} + \begin{pmatrix} \text{Goodwill} \\ \text{contributed by} \\ \text{new partner} \end{pmatrix} = \begin{pmatrix} \text{New partner \%} \\ \text{ownership} \end{pmatrix} \times \begin{pmatrix} \text{Identifiable} \\ \text{net assets} + \begin{array}{c}\text{Goodwill} \\ \text{recognized}\end{array} \end{pmatrix}$$

or

$$\text{Contribution Required} + \$0 = (.20) (\$500,000 + \text{Contribution Required} + \$100,000)$$
$$(.80) (\text{Contribution Required}) = \$100,000 + \$20,000$$
$$\text{Contribution Required} = \$150,000$$

    Similarly, a required $90,000 cash contribution required can be calculated when Johnson is bringing in an agreed-upon amount of goodwill totaling $35,000 and is to receive a 20-percent interest in the business as follows:

$$
\begin{array}{c}
\text{Identifiable assets} \\
\text{contributed by} \\
\text{new partner}
\end{array}
+
\begin{array}{c}
\text{Goodwill} \\
\text{contributed by} \\
\text{new partner}
\end{array}
=
\begin{array}{c}
\text{New partner \%} \\
\text{ownership}
\end{array}
\times
\left(
\begin{array}{c}
\text{Identifiable} \\
\text{net assets}
\end{array}
+
\begin{array}{c}
\text{Goodwill} \\
\text{recognized}
\end{array}
\right)
$$

Contribution required + $35,000 = .20 ($500,000 + Contribution required + $35,000)

Contribution required + $35,000 = $100,000 + (.2) (Contribution required) + $7,000

(.8) (Contribution Required)   = $107,000 – $35,000

Contribution Required   = $90,000

Overall, three types of negotiable factors affect the agreement: (1) the existing or invested goodwill, (2) the percentage interest to be granted to the incoming partner, and (3) the dollar value of identifiable assets that are to be invested. Once the parties agree to any two, the third can be derived.

Withdrawal of an Existing Partner

The withdrawal of a partner from a partnership results in the dissolution of the partnership in the same manner as the admission of a new partner results in a dissolution. The articles of partnership may include a clause that will result in the continued operation of the partnership without interruption. The articles of partnership should also include procedures for the withdrawal of a partner, such as the length of advanced warning that a partner wishing to withdraw must give to the other partners and the method used to determine the value of the withdrawing partner's capital if the partner's interest is to be acquired by the partnership. In addition, the Uniform Partnership Act states that "unless otherwise agreed, he or his legal representative … may have the value of his interest at the date of dissolution ascertained, and shall receive as an ordinary creditor an amount equal to the value of his interest in the dissolved partnership with interest."[15] Withdrawal in violation of the articles of partnership may result in the withdrawing partner being liable for damages sustained by the remaining parties.

The three approaches discussed for the admission of a new partner into a partnership (revaluation of assets, bonus, and goodwill) may also be applied when an existing partner withdraws from a partnership. Partners may have the assets and liabilities of the partnership revalued to market value. This recognition of gains and losses may result in allocations to all the partners' capital accounts or the partners may choose to revalue only the portion relevant to the partner withdrawing with accompanying revaluing of that partner's capital account.

EXAMPLE 7-25   **Revaluation of assets, recognizing withdrawing partner's interest only**   Assume that Briscoe, Johnson, and Mitchell have operated their partnership for a number of years. Mitchell decides that other pursuits are more important and informs Briscoe and Johnson that he is going to withdraw from the partnership. Keep in mind that Briscoe and Johnson cannot stop Mitchell from withdrawing from the partnership. Mitchell can always elect to assign his share of profits and losses to someone else and cease taking part in the management of the partnership. Briscoe and Johnson can refuse to admit another partner for a variety of reasons, but one of the more important reasons is the exposure to unlimited liability. Briscoe and Johnson must decide whether to admit another partner in Mitchell's place, purchase Mitchell's ownership interest themselves, or purchase Mitchell's interest using partnership assets. Regardless of the method chosen to transfer Mitchell's ownership interest, all the partners may want to revalue the partnership's net assets to determine the dollar value of Mitchell's proportionate value of the partnership. Assume the book values of the

[15] Ibid., §42

capital accounts and the profit and loss residual percentages (the agreed-upon method of allocating changes in the value of net assets for this partnership) are presented in the following table.

	Briscoe	Johnson	Mitchell
Capital Account Balance	$600,000	$175,000	$445,000
Residual profit and loss allocation percentage	45	30	25

If the market value of the fixed assets is $400,000 greater than the book value and the partners want to recognize only Mitchell's percentage of the change in value, the following journal entry would result.

Fixed Assets	100,000	
Mitchell, Capital ($400,000 × .25)		100,000

To recognize Mitchell's proportion of the increase in the value of fixed assets at the date of Mitchell's withdrawal.

Mitchell's ownership interest could then be acquired by the partnership or the remaining partners. The journal entry that would result if the partnership acquired Mitchell's ownership interest is the following.

Mitchell, Capital	545,000	
Cash		545,000

To recognize the withdrawal of Mitchell from the partnership.

If Mitchell's ownership interest was purchased by Briscoe and Johnson, the credit to *Cash* would be credits to *Briscoe, Capital* and *Johnson, Capital* in proportion to the capital acquired from Mitchell. In either case, Briscoe and Mitchell must determine how to allocate profits and losses after Mitchell's withdrawal.

EXAMPLE 7-26 **Revaluation of assets allocated to all partners** The partners may also wish to revalue all of the partnership's assets, not just Mitchell's proportion. This is particularly true if another partner is going to take Mitchell's place because the new partner will receive an allocation of profits and losses. Therefore, Briscoe and Johnson may wish to include the increase in the value of the fixed assets in their capital accounts to indicate that they are to receive the full change in value. Full recognition of the increase in the value of the fixed assets would require the following journal entry.

Fixed Assets	400,000	
Briscoe, Capital ($400,000 × .45)		180,000
Johnson, Capital ($400,000 × .3)		120,000
Mitchell, Capital ($400,000 × .25)		100,000

To recognize the increase in the value of the fixed assets at the date of Mitchell's withdrawal.

A new partner, the existing partners, the partnership, or some combination of the three could then acquire Mitchell's ownership interest.

The assumption made in Examples 7-25 and 7-26 is that the change in the value of the net assets accurately explains the difference between the book value of the partnership and the market value. It is possible that the recognized value of all identifiable assets may not equal the value of the going concern; that is, there may be goodwill. The remaining partners, Briscoe and Johnson, may choose to apply the bonus method or goodwill method to recognize any goodwill that may exist. The underlying rationale and the computations and allocations are identical to those presented earlier for the admission of a new partner into the partnership.

EXAMPLE 7-27

Withdrawal using bonus method   Assume that Briscoe and Johnson are anxious for Mitchell to withdraw from the partnership, so they offer to distribute to Mitchell $635,000 of partnership assets for his immediate withdrawal (Mitchell's capital account is $545,000 after revaluation of the fixed assets). Mitchell accepts this offer and leaves the partnership.

Assume also that Briscoe and Johnson agree to continue sharing residual profits and losses proportionate to their prior relationship (i.e., .45 for Briscoe and .30 for Johnson). Thus, the new residual profit and loss ratio is .6 for Briscoe (.45/.75) and .4 for Johnson (.30/.75), as calculated below.

	Old Ratio Percentages		New Ratio Percentages	
	Before Withdrawal	After Withdrawal		
Briscoe	.45	.45	.45/.75	.60
Johnson	.30	.30	.30/.75	.40
Mitchell	.25			
Total	1.00	0.75		1.00

If Briscoe and Johnson object to recording goodwill in this situation, the bonus method may be used, resulting the in the following journal entry.

Briscoe, Capital ($90,000 × .6)	54,000	
Johnson, Capital ($90,000 × .4)	36,000	
Mitchell, Capital	545,000	
Cash		635,000

To recognize Mitchell's withdrawal from the Briscoe, Johnson, and Mitchell partnership.

The remaining partners may view the bonus paid to a withdrawing partner as being similar to early retirement options occasionally offered to employees of corporations to entice some individuals to retire.

Briscoe and Johnson could also have elected to recognize goodwill at the date of Mitchell's withdrawal. The recognition of goodwill at the date of a partner's withdrawal is subject to the same dispute that exists when goodwill is recognized at the date of admission for a new partner. Opponents contend that because the entity is still in existence, there would be no recognition. Proponents contend that because one partnership has ceased to exist while another has been created, the recognition of goodwill is appropriate because of the formation of a new partnership. The recognition of goodwill, as with the recognition of the change in the value of identifiable assets, may be a partial recognition or a full recognition.

EXAMPLE 7-28

Withdrawal using partial goodwill method   Partial recognition would assign to goodwill the amount the partnership paid Mitchell in excess of the capital account balance, resulting in the following journal entries at the date of withdrawal.

Goodwill	90,000	
Mitchell, Capital		90,000

To recognize goodwill applicable to Mitchell at the date of withdrawal.

Mitchell, Capital	635,000	
Cash		635,000

To recognize the withdrawal of Mitchell from the partnership.

EXAMPLE 7-29   **Withdrawal recognizing all goodwill**   Briscoe and Mitchell could also have decided to recognize goodwill for the entire partnership, not just Mitchell's proportion. If full goodwill is recognized, the portion being paid to Mitchell would be used as an indication of the full value of goodwill resulting, based on the following calculation.

$$\frac{\text{Excess payment to}}{\text{withdrawing partner}} = \frac{\text{Percent of profit and loss}}{\text{to withdrawing partner}} \times \frac{\text{Total goodwill to be}}{\text{recognized}}$$

$$\$90,000 = (.3)\,(\text{Goodwill})$$
$$\$90,000/(.3) = \text{Goodwill}$$
$$\text{Goodwill} = \$300,000$$

The following journal entry recognizes the complete goodwill at the date of Mitchell's withdrawal.

Goodwill ($90,000/.3)	300,000	
Briscoe, Capital ($300,000 × .45)		135,000
Johnson, Capital ($300,000 × .25)		75,000
Mitchell, Capital ($300,000 × .30)		90,000

To recognize the full amount of goodwill associated with the Briscoe, Johnson, and Mitchell partnership at the date of Mitchell's withdrawal.

Following the recognition of the goodwill, the withdrawal of Mitchell would be recorded with the following journal entry.

Mitchell, Capital	635,000	
Cash		635,000

To recognize the withdrawal of Mitchell from the partnership.

Death of a Partner

As with a withdrawal, the death of a partner results in the dissolution of the partnership. The partnership can continue uninterrupted operations by having a clause in the articles of partnership addressing the death of a partner. The same procedures applied for the withdrawal of a partner may be applied when one of the partners dies. The partners should have procedures for determining the value assigned to the deceased partner's ownership equity to help avoid litigation with the estate. Many partnerships have life insurance policies on each partner's life to enable the partnership to continue in business if one partner dies. The proceeds from the life insurance policy would be used to purchase the deceased partner's ownership interest in the partnership. The articles of partnership should stipulate that each partner agrees that the partnership interest will be sold by the estate to the existing partners.

SUMMARY

This chapter introduced the form of business entity known as the partnership. First, some of the major legal and theoretical considerations that make the partnership a unique form of business entity were discussed. Then, the chapter explored the accounting issues associated with the formation of a partnership, the allocation of income during the operation of a partnership, and the recording of changes in owners' equity interests when new owners buy into the organization or individual owners leave the organization.

Partnership formation was examined focusing on the valuation problems that occur when a partnership is initiated. As with all contributions of assets to any entity, the investment of assets by a partner into a partnership results in valuation choices. The alternative valuation choices—existing carrying value, existing tax basis, and current market value—were presented as the alternatives that are most often agreed to by the partners. The assumption of liabilities of a contributing partner by the partnership was also discussed. Because unidentifiable intangibles having significant value to the partnership are often brought into a new partnership by individual partners, the bonus and goodwill methods of accounting for this type of asset were introduced.

The operation of a partnership was examined. The routine recording of daily business transactions presents no particular accounting problems. However, the allocation of profits and losses to partners' capital accounts can be involved. This section discussed the allocation procedures that are usually followed to provide returns to partners for factors such as interest on capital balances, salaries for time spent working in the partnership, bonuses, and sharing of residuals. Most partnership agreement will have a unique profit allocation agreement that must be followed. Any or all of the factors above may exist in a particular partnership agreement, so many examples were provided to cover the various outcomes, including the possibility of negative residuals and net losses. Finally, this section also discussed the problem of unrealized holding gains and losses that must be considered when the partnership profit and loss sharing agreement is amended.

The final section explored the accounting for changes in ownership that may occur. The various possibilities that were covered are presented below here on outline form:

1. Admission of a new partner
    A. No change in assets
    B. Change in net assets—investment at book value
    C. Change in net assets—revaluation of existing assets
    D. Change in net assets—bonus method
    E. Change in net assets—goodwill method
2. Withdrawal of an existing partner
    A. Revaluation of assets
        (1) Withdrawing partner's interest only
        (2) Revaluation of assets allocated to all partners
    B. Revaluation of assets—recognition of unidentifiable intangibles
        (1) Bonus method
        (2) Goodwill method

A detailed discussion of all of the above situations was provided, including examples for each circumstance.

APPENDIX 7-1
UNIFORM PARTNERSHIP ACT

PART I

PRELIMINARY PROVISIONS

§ 1. Name of Act

This act may be cited as Uniform Partnership Act.

§ 2. Definition of Terms

In this act, "Court" includes every court and judge having jurisdiction in the case. "Business" includes every trade, occupation, or profession.

"Person" includes individuals, partnerships, corporations, and other associations.

"Bankrupt" includes bankrupt under the Federal Bankruptcy Act or insolvent under any state insolvent act.

"Conveyance" includes every assignment, lease, mortgage, or encumbrance.

"Real Property" includes land and any interest or estate in land.

§ 3. Interpretation of Knowledge and Notice

(1) A person has "knowledge" of a fact within the meaning of this act not only when he has actual knowledge thereof, but also when he has knowledge of such other facts as in the circumstances shows bad faith.

(2) A person has "notice" of a fact within the meaning of this act when the person who claims the benefit of the notice:

(a) States the fact to such person, or

(b) Delivers through the mail, or by other means of communication, a written statement of the fact to such person or to a proper person at his place of business or residence.

§ 4. Rules of Construction

(1) The rule that statutes in derogation of the common law are to be strictly construed shall have no application under this act.

(2) The law of estoppel shall apply under this act.

(3) The law of agency shall apply under this act.

(4) This act shall be so interpreted and construed as to effect its general purpose to make uniform the law of those states which enact it.

(5) This act shall not be construed so as to impair the obligation of any contract existing when the act goes into effect, not to affect any action or proceedings begun or right accrued before this act takes effect.

§ 5. Rules for Cases Not Provided for in This Act

In any case not provided for in this act the rules of law and equity, including the law merchant, shall govern.

PART II

NATURE OF A PARTNERSHIP

§ 6. Partnership Defined

(1) A partnership is an association of two or more persons to carry on as co-owners of a business for profit.

(2) But any association formed under any other statute of this state, or any statute adopted by authority, other than the authority of this state, is not a partnership under this act, unless such association would have been a partnership in this state prior to the adoption of this act; but this shall apply to limited partnerships except in so far as the statutes relating to such partnerships are inconsistent herewith.

§ 7. Rules for Determining the Existence of a Partnership

In determining whether a partnership exists, these rules shall apply:

(1) Except as provided by section 16 persons who are not partners as to each other are not partners as to third persons.

(2) Joint tenancy, tenancy in common, tenancy by the entireties, joint property, common property or part ownership does not of itself establish a partnership, whether such co-owners do or do not share any profits made by the use of the property.

(3) The sharing of gross returns does not of itself establish a partnership, whether or not the persons sharing them have a joint or common right or interest in any property from which the returns are derived.

(4) The receipt by a person of a share of the profits of a business is prima facie evidence that he is a partner in the business, but no such inference shall be drawn if such profits were received in payment:

(a) As a debt by installments or otherwise,

(b) As wages of an employee or rent to a landlord,

(c) As an annuity to a widow or representative of a deceased partner,

(d) As interest on a loan, though the amount of payment vary with the profits of the business,

(e) As the consideration for the sale of a good-will of a business or other property by installments or otherwise.

§ 8. Partnership Property

(1) All property originally brought into the partnership stock or subsequently acquired by purchase or otherwise, on account of the partnership, is partnership property.

(2) Unless the contrary intention appears, property acquired with partnership funds is partnership property.

(3) Any estate in real property may be acquired in the partnership name. Title so acquired can be conveyed only in the partnership name.

(4) A conveyance to a partnership in the partnership name, though without words of inheritance, passes the entire estate of the grantor unless a contrary intent appears.

PART III

RELATIONS OF PARTNERS TO PERSONS DEALING WITH THE PARTNERSHIP

§ 9. Partner Agent of Partnership as to Partnership Business

(1) Every partner is an agent of the partnership for the purpose of its business, and the act of every partner, including the execution in the partnership name of any instrument, for apparently carrying on in the usual way the business of the partnership of which he is a member binds the partnership, unless the partner so acting has in fact no authority to act for the partnership in the particular matter, and the person with whom he is dealing has knowledge of the fact that he has no such authority.

(2) An act of a partner which is not apparently for the carrying on of the business of the partnership in the usual way does not bind the partnership unless authorized by the partners.

(3) Unless authorized by the other partners or unless they have abandoned the business, one or more but less than all the partners have no authority to:

(a) Assign the partnership property in trust for creditors or on the assignee's promise to pay the debts of the partnership,

(b) Dispose of the good-will of the business,

(c) Do any other act which would make it impossible to carry on the ordinary business of a partnership,

(d) Confess a judgment,

(e) Submit a partnership claim or liability to arbitration or reference.

(4) No act of a partner in contravention of a restriction on authority shall bind the partnership to persons having knowledge of the restriction.

§ 10. Conveyance of Real Property of the Partnership

(1) Where title to real property is in the partnership name, any partner may convey title to such property by a conveyance executed in the partnership name; but the partnership may recover such property unless the partner's act binds the partnership under the provisions of paragraph (1) of section 9, or unless such property has been conveyed by the grantee or a person claiming through such grantee to a holder for value without knowledge that the partner, in making the conveyance, has exceeded his authority.

(2) Where title to real property is in the name of the partnership, a conveyance executed by a partner, in his own name, passes the equitable interest of the partnership, provided the act is one within the authority of the partner under the provisions of paragraph (1) of section 9.

(3) Where title to real property is in the name of one or more but not all of the partners, and the record does not disclose the right of the partnership, the partners in whose name the title stands may convey title to such property, but the partnership may recover such property if the partner's act does not bind the partnership under the provisions of paragraph (1) of section 9, unless the purchaser or his assignee, is a holder for value, without knowledge.

(4) Where the title to real property is in the name of one or more or all the partners, or in a third person in trust for the partnership, a conveyance executed by a partner in the partnership name, or in his own name, passes the equitable interest of the partnership, provided the act is one within the authority of the partner under the provisions of paragraph (1) of section 9.

(5) Where the title to real property is in the names of all the partners a conveyance executed by all the partners passes all their rights in such property.

§ 11. Partnership Bound by Admission of Partner

An admission or representation made by any partner concerning partnership affairs within the scope of his authority as conferred by this act is evidence against the partnership.

§ 12. Partnership Charged with Knowledge of or Notice to Partner

Notice to any partner of any matter relating to partnership affairs, and the knowledge of the partner acting in the particular matter, acquired while a partner or then present to his mind, and the knowledge of any other partner who reasonably could and should have communicated it to the acting partner, operate as notice to or knowledge of the partnership, except in the case of a fraud on the partnership committed by or with the consent of that partner.

§ 13. Partnership Bound by Partner's Wrongful Act

Where, by any wrongful act or omission of any partner acting in the ordinary course of the business of the partnership or with the authority of his co-partners, loss or injury is caused to any person, not being a partner in the partnership, or any penalty is incurred, the partnership is liable therefor to the same extent as the partner so acting or omitting to act.

§ 14. Partnership Bound by Partner's Breach of Trust

The partnership is bound to make good the loss:

(a) Where one partner acting within the scope of his apparent authority receives money or property of a third person and misapplies it; and

(b) Where the partnership in the course of its business receives money or property of a third person and the money or property so received is misapplied by any partner while it is in the custody of the partnership.

§ 15. Nature of Partner's Liability

All partners are liable

(a) Jointly and severally for everything chargeable to the partnership under sections 13 and 14.

(b) Jointly for all other debts and obligations of the partnership; but any partner may enter into a separate obligation to perform a partnership contract.

§ 16. Partner by Estoppel

(1) When a person, by words spoken or written or by conduct, represents himself, or consents to another representing him to any one, as a partner in an existing partnership or with one or more persons not actual partners, he is liable to any such person to whom such representation has been made, who has, on the faith of such representation, given credit to the actual or apparent partnership, and if he has made such representation or consented to its being made in a public manner he is liable to such person, whether the representation has or has not been made or communicated to such person so giving credit by or with the knowledge of the apparent partner making the representation or consenting to its being made.

(a) When a partnership liability results, he is liable as though he were an actual member of the partnership.

(b) When no partnership liability results, he is liable jointly with the other persons, if any, so consenting to the contract or representation as to incur liability, otherwise separately.

(2) When a person has been thus represented to be a partner in an existing partnership, or with one or more persons not actual partners, he is an agent of the persons consenting to such representation to bind them to the same extent and in the same manner as though he were a partner in fact, with respect to persons who rely upon the representation. Where all the members of the existing partnership consent to the representation, a partnership act or obligation results; but in all other cases it is the joint act or obligation of the person acting and the persons consenting to the representation.

§ 17. Liability of Incoming Partners

A person admitted as a partner into an existing partnership is liable for all the obligations of the partnership arising before his admission as though he had been a partner when such obligations were incurred, except that his liability shall be satisfied only out of partnership property.

PART IV

RELATIONS OF PARTNERS TO ONE ANOTHER

§ 18. Rules Determining Rights and Duties of Partners

The rights and duties of the partners in relation to the partnership shall be determined, subject to any agreement between them, by the following rules:

(a) Each partner shall be repaid his contributions, whether by way of capital or advances to the partnership property and share equally in the profits and surplus remaining after all liabilities, including those to partners, are satisfied; and must contribute towards the losses, whether of capital or otherwise, sustained by the partnership according to his share in the profits.

(b) The partnership must indemnify every partner in respect of payments made and personal liabilities reasonably incurred by him in the ordinary and proper conduct of its business, or for the preservation of its business or property.

(c) A partner, who in aid of the partnership makes any payment or advance beyond the amount of capital which he agreed to contribute, shall be paid interest from the date of the payment or advance.

(d) A partner shall receive interest on the capital contributed by him only from the date when repayments should be made.

(e) All partners have equal rights in the management and conduct of the partnership business.

(f) No partner is entitled to remuneration for acting in the partnership business, except that a surviving partner is entitled to reasonable compensation for his services in winding up the partnership affairs.

(g) No person can become a member of a partnership without the consent of all the partners.

(h) Any difference arising as to ordinary matters connected with the partnership business may be decided by a majority of the partners; but no act in contravention of any agreement between the partners may be done rightfully without the consent of all the partners.

§ 19. Partnership Books

The partnership books shall be kept, subject to any agreement between the partners, at the principal place of business of the partnership, and every partner shall at all times have access to and may inspect and copy any of them.

§ 20. Duty of Partners to Render Information

Partners shall render on demand true and full information of all things affecting the partnership to any partner or the legal representative of any deceased partner or partner under legal disability.

§ 21. *Partner Accountable as a Fiduciary*

(1) Every partner must account to the partnership for any benefit, and hold as trustee for it any profits derived by him without consent of the other partners from any transaction connected with the formation, conduct, or liquidation of the partnership or from any use by him of its property.

(2) This section applies also to the representatives of a deceased partner engaged in the liquidation of the affairs of the partnership as the personal representatives of the last surviving partner.

§ 22. *Right to an Account*

Any partner shall have the right to a formal account as to partnership affairs:

(a) If he is wrongfully excluded from the partnership business or possession of its property by his co-partners,

(b) If the right exists under the terms of any agreement,

(c) As provided by section 21,

(d) Whenever other circumstances render it just and reasonable.

§ 23. *Continuation of Partnership Beyond Fixed Term*

(1) When a partnership for a fixed term or particular undertaking is continued after the termination of such term or particular undertaking without any express agreement, the rights and duties of the partners remain the same as they were at such termination, so far as is consistent with a partnership at will.

(2) A continuation of the business by the partners or such of them as habitually acted therein during the term, without any settlement or liquidation of the partnership affairs, is prima facie evidence of a continuation of the partnership.

PART V

PROPERTY RIGHTS OF A PARTNER

§ 24. *Extent of Property Rights of a Partner*

The property rights of a partner are (1) his rights in specific partnership property, (2) his interest in the partnership, and (3) his right to participate in management.

§ 25. *Nature of a Partner's Right in Specific Partnership Property*

(1) A partner is co-owner with his partners of specific partnership property holding as a tenant in partnership.

(2) The incidents of this tenancy are such that:

(a) A partner, subject to the provisions of this act and to any agreement between the partners, has an equal right with his partners to possess specific partnership property for partnership purposes; but he has no right to possess such property for any other purpose without the consent of his partners.

(b) A partner's right in specific partnership property is not assignable except in connection with the assignment of rights of all the partners in the same property.

(c) A partner's right in specific partnership property is not subject to attachment or execution, except on a claim against the partnership. When partnership property is attached for a partnership debt the partners, or any of them, or the representatives of a deceased partner, cannot claim any right under the homestead or exemption laws.

(d) On the death of a partner his right in specific partnership property vests in the surviving partner or partners, except where the deceased was the last surviving partner, when his right in such property vests in his legal representative. Such surviving partner or partners, or the legal representative of the last surviving partners, has no right to possess the partnership property for any but a partnership purpose.

(e) A partner's right in specific partnership property is not subject to dower, curtesy, or allowances to widows, heirs, or next of kin.

§ 26. Nature of Partner's Interest in the Partnership

A partner's interest in the partnership is his share of the profits and surplus, and the same is personal property.

§ 27. Assignment of Partner's Interest

(1) A conveyance by a partner of his interest in the partnership does not of itself dissolve the partnership, nor, as against the other partners in the absence of agreement, entitle the assignee, during the continuance of the partnership, to interfere in the management or administration of the partnership business or affairs, or to require any information or account of partnership transactions, or to inspect the partnership books; but it merely entitles the assignee to receive in accordance with the contract the profits to which the assigning partner would otherwise be entitled.

(2) In case of a dissolution of the partnership, the assignee is entitled to receive his assignor's interest and may require an account from the date only of the last account agreed to by all the partners.

§ 28. Partner's Interest Subject to Charging Order

(1) On due application to a competent court by any judgment creditor of a partner, the court which entered the judgment, order, or decree, or any other court, may charge the interest of the debtor partner with payment of the unsatisfied amount of such judgment debt with interest thereon; and may then or later appoint a receiver of his share of the profits, and of any other money due or to fall due to him in respect of the partnership, and make all other orders, directions, accounts and inquiries which the debtor partner might have made, or which the circumstances of the case may require.

(2) The interest charged may be redeemed at any time before foreclosure, or in case of a sale being directed by the court may be purchased without thereby causing a dissolution:

(a) With separate property, by any one or more of the partners, or

(b) With partnership property, by any one or more of the partners with the consent of all the partners whose interests are not so charged or sold.

(3) Nothing in this act shall be held to deprive a partner of his rights, if any, under the exemption laws, as regards his interest in the partnership.

PART VI

DISSOLUTION AND WINDING UP

§ 29. Dissolution Defined

The dissolution of a partnership is the change in the relation of the partners caused by any partner ceasing to be associated in the carrying on as distinguished from the winding up of the business.

§ 30. Partnership Not Terminated by Dissolution

On dissolution the partnership is not terminated, but continues under the winding up of partnership affairs is completed.

§ 31. Cause of Dissolution

Dissolution is caused:

(1) Without violation of the agreement between the partners,

    (a) By the termination of the definite terms or particular undertaking specified in the agreement,

    (b) By the express will of any partner when no definite term or particular undertaking is specified,

    (c) By the express will of all the partners who have not assigned their interests or suffered them to be charged for their separate debts, either before or after the termination of any specified term or particular undertaking,

    (d) By the expulsion of any partner from the business bona fide in accordance with such a power conferred by the agreement between the partners;

(2) In contravention of the agreement between the partners, where the circumstances do not permit a dissolution under any other provision of this section by the express will of any partner at the time;

(3) By any event which makes it unlawful for the business of the partnership to be carried on or for the members to carry it on in partnership.

(4) By the death of any partner;

(5) By the bankruptcy of any partner or the partnership;

(6) By decree of court under section 32.

§ 32. Dissolution by Decree of Court

(1) On application by or for a partner the court shall decree a dissolution whenever:

    (a) A partner has been declared a lunatic in any judicial proceeding or is shown to be of unsound mind,

    (b) A partner becomes in any other way incapable of performing his part of the partnership contract,

    (c) A partner has been guilty of such conduct as tends to affect prejudicially the carrying on of the business,

    (d) A partner wilfully or persistently commits a breach of the partnership agreement, or otherwise so conducts himself in matters relating to the partnership business that it is not reasonably practicable to carry on the business in partnership with him,

    (e) The business of the partnership can only be carried on at a loss,

    (f) Other circumstances render a dissolution equitable.

(2) On the application of the purchaser of a partner's interest under sections 27 or 28;

    (a) After the termination of the specified term of particular undertaking,

    (b) At any time if the partnership was a partnership at will when the interest was assigned or when the charging order was issued.

§ 33. General Effect of Dissolution on Authority of Partner

Except so far as may be necessary to wind up partnership affairs or to complete transactions begun but not then finished, dissolution terminates all authority of any partner to act for the partnership,

(1) With respect to the partners,

    (a) When the dissolution is not by the act, bankruptcy or death or a partner; or

    (b) When the dissolution is by such act, bankruptcy or death of a partner, in cases where section 34 so requires.

(2) With respect to persons not partners, as declared in section 35.

§ 34. Rights of Partner to Contribution from Co-partners after Dissolution

Where the dissolution is caused by the act, death or bankruptcy of a partner, each partner is liable to his co-partners for his share of any liability created by any partner acting for the partnership as if the partnership had not been dissolved unless

    (a) The dissolution being by act of any partner, the partner acting for the partnership had knowledge of the dissolution, or

    (b) The dissolution being by the death or bankruptcy of a partner, the partner acting for the partnership had knowledge or notice of the death or bankruptcy.

§ 35. Power of Partner to Bind Partnership to Third Persons after Dissolution

(1) After dissolution a partner can bind the partnership except as provided in Paragraph (3).

    (a) By any act appropriate for winding up partnership affairs or completing transactions unfinished at dissolution;

    (b) By any transaction which would bind a partnership if dissolution had not taken place, provided the other party to the transaction.

        I. Had extended credit to the partnership prior to dissolution and had no knowledge or notice of the dissolution; or

        II. Though he had not so extended credit, had nevertheless known of the partnership prior to dissolution, and, having no knowledge or notice of dissolution, the fact of dissolution had not been advertised in a newspaper of general circulation in the place (or in each place if more than one) at which the partnership business was regularly carried on.

(2) The liability of a partner under Paragraph (1b) shall be satisfied out of partnership assets alone when such partner had been prior to dissolution

    (a) Unknown as a partner to the persons with whom the contract is made; and

    (b) So far unknown and inactive in partnership affairs that the business reputation of the partnership could not be said to have been in any degree due to his connection with it.

(3) The partnership is in no case bound by any act of a partner after dissolution

    (a) Where the partnership is dissolved because it is unlawful to carry on the business, unless the act is appropriate for winding up partnership affairs; or

    (b) Where the partner has become bankrupt; or

    (c) Where the partner has no authority to wind up partnership affairs; except by a transaction with one who

        I. Had extended credit to the partnership prior to dissolution and had no knowledge or notice of his want of authority; or

        II. Had not extended credit to the partnership prior to dissolution and, having no knowledge or notice of his want of authority, the fact of his want of authority had not been advertised in the manner provided for advertising the fact of dissolution in Paragraph (1b II).

(4) Nothing in this section shall affect the liability under Section 16 of any person who after dissolution represents himself or consents to another representing him as a partner in a partnership engaged in carrying on business.

§ 36. Effect of Dissolution on Partner's Existing Liability

(1) The dissolution of the partnership does not of itself discharge the existing liability of any partner.

(2) A partner is discharged from any existing liability upon dissolution of the partnership by an agreement to that effect between himself, the partnership creditor and the person or partnership continuing the business; and such agreement may be inferred from the course of dealing between the creditor having knowledge of the dissolution and the person or partnership continuing the business.

(3) Where a person agrees to assume the existing obligations of a dissolved partnership, the partners whose obligations have been assumed shall be discharged from any liability to any creditor of the partnership who, knowing of the agreement, consents to a material alteration in the nature or time of payment of such obligations.

(4) The individual property of a deceased partner shall be liable for all obligations of the partnership incurred while he was a partner but subject to the prior payment of his separate debts.

§ 37. Right to Wind Up

Unless otherwise agreed the partners who have not wrongfully dissolved the partnership or the legal representative of the last surviving partner, not bankrupt, has the right to wind up the partnership affairs; provided, however, that any partner, his legal representative or his assignee, upon cause shown, may obtain winding up by the court.

§ 38. Rights of Partners to Application of Partnership Property

(1) When dissolution is caused in any way, except in contravention of the partnership agreement, each partner, as against his co-partners and all persons claiming through them in respect of their interests in the partnership, unless otherwise agreed, may have the partnership property applied to discharge its liabilities, and the surplus applied to pay in cash the net amount owing to the respective partners. But if dissolution is caused by expulsion of a partner, bona fide under the partnership agreement and if the expelled partner is discharged from all partnership liabilities, either by payment or agreement under section 36(2), he shall receive in cash only the net amount due him from the partnership.

(2) When dissolution is caused in contravention of the partnership agreement the rights of the partners shall be as follows

  (a) Each partner who has not caused dissolution wrongfully shall have,

    I. All the rights specified in paragraph (1) of this section, and

    II. The right, as against each partner who has caused the dissolution wrongfully, to damages for breach of the agreement.

  (b) The partners who have not caused the dissolution wrongfully, if they all desire to continue the business in the same name, either by themselves or jointly with other, may do so, during the agreed term for the partnership and for that purpose may possess the partnership property, provided they secure the payment by bond approved by the court, or pay to any partner who has caused the dissolution wrongfully, the value of his interest in the partnership at the dissolution, less any damages recoverable under clause (2a II) of this section, and in like manner indemnify him against all present or future partnership liabilities.

  (c) A partner who has caused the dissolution wrongfully shall have:

    I. If the business is not continued under the provisions of paragraph (2b) all the rights of a partner under paragraph (1), subject to clause (2a II), of this section.

    II. If the business is continued under paragraph (2b) of this section the right as against his co-partners and all claiming through them in respect of their interests in the partnership, to have the value of his interest in the partnership, less any damages caused to his co-partners by the dissolution, ascertained and paid to him in cash, or the payment secured by bond approved by the court, and to be released from all existing liabilities of the partnership; but in ascertaining the value of the partner's interest the value of the good-will of the business shall not be considered.

§ 39. Rights Where Partnership Is Dissolved for Fraud or Misrepresentation

Where a partnership contract is rescinded on the grounds of the fraud or misrepresentation of one of the parties thereto, the party entitled to rescind is, without prejudice to any other right, entitled.

  (a) To a lien on, or a right of retention of, the surplus of the partnership property after satisfying the partnership liabilities to third persons for any sum of money paid by him for the purchase of an interest in the partnership and for any capital or advances contributed by him, and

(b) To stand, after all liabilities to third persons have been satisfied, in the place of the creditors of the partnership for any payments made by him in respect to the partnership liabilities; and

(c) To be indemnified by the person guilty of the fraud or making the representation against all debts and liabilities of the partnership.

§ 40. *Rules for Distribution*

In settling accounts between the partners after dissolution, the following rules shall be observed, subject to any agreement to the contrary:

(a) The assets of the partnership are:

I. The partnership property,

II. The contributions of the partners necessary for the payment of all the liabilities specified in clause (b) of this paragraph.

(b) The liabilities of the partnership shall rank in order of payment as follows:

I. Those owing creditors other than partners,

II. Those owing to partners other than for capital and profits,

III. Those owing to partners in respect of capital,

IV. Those owing to partners in respect of profits.

(c) The assets shall be applied in the order of their declaration in clause (a) of this paragraph to the satisfaction of the liabilities.

(d) The partners shall contribute, as provided by section 18(a) the amount necessary to satisfy the liabilities; but if any, but not all, of the partners are insolvent, or, not being subject to process, refuse to contribute, the other partners shall contribute their share of the liabilities, and, in the relative proportions in which they share the profits, the additional amount necessary to pay the liabilities.

(e) An assignee for the benefit of creditors or any person appointed by the court shall have the right to enforce the contributions specified in clause (d) of this paragraph.

(f) Any partner or his legal representative shall have the right to enforce the contributions specified in clause (d) of this paragraph, to the extent of the amount which he has paid in excess of his share of the liability.

(g) The individual property of a deceased partner shall be liable for the contributions specified in clause (d) of this paragraph.

(h) When partnership property and the individual properties of the partners are in possession of a court distribution, partnership creditors shall have priority on partnership property and separate creditors on individual property, saving the rights of lien or secured creditors as heretofore.

(i) Where a partner has become bankrupt or his estate is insolvent the claims against his separate property shall rank in the following order:

I. Those owing to separate creditors,

II. Those owing to partnership creditors,

III. Those owing to partners by way of contribution.

§ 41. *Liability of Persons Continuing the Business in Certain Cases*

(1) When any new partner is admitted into an existing partnership, or when any partner retires and assigns (or the representative of the deceased partner assigns) his rights in partnership property to two or more of the partners, or to one or more of the partners and one or more third persons, if the business is continued without liquidation of the partnership affairs, creditors of the first or dissolved partnership are also creditors of the partnership so continuing the business.

(2) When all but one partner retire and assign (or the representative of a deceased partner assigns) their rights in partnership property to the remaining partner, who continued the business without liquidation of partnership affairs, either alone or with others, creditors of the dissolved partnership are also creditors of the person or partnership so continuing the business.

(3) When any partner retires or dies and the business of the dissolved partnership is continued as set forth in paragraph (1) and (2) of this section, with the consent of the retired partners or the representative of the deceased partner, but without any assignment of his right in partnership property, rights of creditors of the dissolved partnership and of the creditors of the person or partnership continuing the business shall be as if such assignment had been made.

(4) When all the partners of their representatives assign their rights in partnership property to one or more third persons who promise to pay the debts and who continue the business of the dissolved partnership, creditors of the dissolved partnership are also creditors of the person or partnership continuing the business.

(5) When any partner wrongfully causes a dissolution and the remaining partners continue the business under the provisions of section 38(2b), either alone or with others, and without liquidation of the partnership affairs, creditors of the dissolved partnership are also creditors of the persons or partnership continuing the business.

(6) When a partner is expelled and the remaining partners continue the business either alone or with others, without liquidation of the partnership affairs, creditors of the dissolved partnership are also creditors of the person or partnership continuing the business.

(7) The liability of a third person becoming a partner in the partnership continuing the business, under this section, to the creditors of the dissolved partnership shall be satisfied out of partnership property only.

(8) When the business of a partnership after dissolution is continued under any conditions set forth in this section the creditors of the dissolved partnership, as against the separate creditors of the retiring or deceased partner or the representative of the deceased partner, have a prior right to any claim of the retired partner or the representative of the deceased partner against the person or partnership continuing the business, on account of the retired or deceased partner's interest in the dissolved partnership or on account of any consideration promised for such interest or for his right in partnership property.

(9) Nothing in this section shall be held to modify any right or creditors to set aside any assignment on the ground of fraud.

(10) The use by the person or partnership continuing the business of the partnership name, or the name of a deceased partner as part thereof, shall not of itself make the individual property of the deceased partner liable for any debts contracted by such person or partnership.

§ 42. *Rights of Retiring or Estate of Deceased Partner When the Business Is Continued*

When any partner retires or dies, and the business is continued under any of the conditions set forth in section 41(1, 2, 3, 5, 6), or section 38(2b) without any settlement of accounts as between him or his estate and the person or partnership continuing the business, unless otherwise agreed, he or his legal representative as against such persons or partnership may have the value of his interest at the date of dissolution ascertained, and shall receive as an ordinary creditor an amount equal to the value of his interest in the dissolved partnership with interest, or, at his option or at the option of his legal representative, in lieu of interest, the profits attributable to the use of his right in the property of the dissolved partnership; provided that the creditors of the dissolved partnership as against the separate creditors, or the representative of the retired or deceased partner, shall have priority on any claim arising under this section, as provided by section 41 (8) of this act.

§ 43. *Accrual of Actions*

The right to an account of his interest shall accrue to any partner, or his legal representative, as against the winding up partners or the surviving partners or the persons or partnership continuing the business, at the date of dissolution, in the absence of any agreement to the contrary.

PART VII

MISCELLANEOUS PROVISIONS

§ 44. *When Act Takes Effect*

This act shall take effect on the _____ day of _____ two thousand and _____.

§ 45. *Legislation Repealed*

All acts or parts of acts inconsistent with this act are hereby repealed.

QUESTIONS

7-1. What are the three basic forms of business entities?

7-2. Sam and Susan are discussing different business forms. Susan says that proprietorships, partnerships, and corporations are each very different from one another. Sam states that he believes that two are similar and the other one is generally different from these two. You just joined the conversation. Sam and Susan have asked for your opinion. How do you respond?

7-3. A friend is considering starting a new business. She has not previously operated a business and has requested your advise. One of the first questions you ask is which business form she is going to apply. She is puzzled by this question and asks why it makes a difference. How do you respond?

7-4. The headlines read "The IRS Taxes Everyone." Is this true with regard to business entities?

7-5. Compare and contrast proprietorships, partnerships, and corporations with regard to taxation of owners on the income of the entity.

7-6. What is the proprietary theory of equity and how is it applicable to partnerships?

7-7. What is the entity theory of equity and how is it applicable to partnerships?

7-8. Two friends, Ted Richards and Jim Francis, are planning to start a partnership. These individuals know you and have asked for any insights you could provide. One question you ask pertains to a written partnership agreement. Ted and Jim state that they have been friends for many years and they know who is going to do what and how the profits are to be shared. How do you respond to these prospective partners?

7-9. Why is it important to outline the nature of the business to be conducted in the articles of partnership?

7-10. How should partnerships determine the capital needed to start business?

7-11. Larry Sprague and Jennifer Bennett are forming a partnership. A number of noncash assets are being contributed to the partnership by the two prospective partners. Larry and Jennifer have asked your assistance because they do not know what value to assign to these assets. Prepare a brief note outlining the possible bases that can be used to assign a value to noncash assets. Be sure to discuss the advantages and disadvantages of using each basis.

7-12. Dana Wilson and Joe Spalding have just started a business as a partnership. They are reviewing the accounting records that established the partnership operation and have come to you to clarify something they do not understand. Noncash assets were contributed by both Dana and Joe. The noncash assets were recognized in the partnership's records using the assets' tax basis. Dana and Joe want to know why the accumulated depreciation for the noncash assets was not recognized on the partnership's financial records. Prepare a brief note explaining this issue.

7-13. Fred and Susan are entering the final stages of preparing a partnership agreement. Susan has suggested that the capital accounts created at the date the partnership is formed should be equal even though Fred is contributing more tangible assets. Fred does not object to this in theory but he is concerned with the impact of altering the initial capital balances on the profit and loss distribution. Prepare a memo to Fred and Susan clarifying the relationship between the initial capital balances and the allocation of profits and losses among the partners.

7-14. Two partners, David Franz and Greg Ingersoll, are discussing the allocation of profits and losses in their company. There are a number of partners in this partnership. David and Greg believe the order of profit and loss allocation should be changed from its current format (salaries, bonuses, interest, and residual) to interest, salaries, bonuses, and residuals. The other partners say that the allocation order makes no difference and they are not interested in changing the articles of partnership. David and Greg have asked for your opinion on the importance of the order of income or loss allocation. How do you respond?

7-15. Alex Carpenter and Elliott Keene are business associates in a nearby town. They have been discussing some provisions that exist in partnerships to which they separately belong. Alex has been telling Elliott about one partnership where a bonus was paid to a partner even though the partnership had a loss for the period. Elliott says this is not possible because bonuses can only be paid out of profit, not out of losses. You happened to walk into the middle of this conversation and have been asked to comment on this issue. What do you say?

7-16. Contrast the dissolution of a partnership and the liquidation of a partnership.

7-17. Discuss the basic difference between the two ways in which a new partner may be admitted into an existing partnership.

7-18. Max Strange and Norman Williams are considering adding another partner to their company. The combined capital for the two partners is approximately $60,000. Max states that a new partner who invests $15,000 into the partnership will have to be given a 20 percent–ownership interest in the capital of the company. Norman does not like the idea of giving someone else such a large percentage of the company's equity. Is there a way that a partner can be admitted to the partnership without giving up such a large percentage of the company's capital?

7-19. Peggy Simpson and Vincent Chadwick are the current partners in a local retailing company. A new partner is desired because the company needs additional capital to expand. Peggy and Vincent have located several potential partners. One potential partner has asked for a 40 percent interest in the partnership's equity. Vincent is concerned because he does not want to give up that much of the company's profits. Peggy and Vincent have asked for your insights into this issue. How do you respond?

7-20. You have an opportunity to join the partnership of Richards and Schroeder. An examination of the company's books indicated that total owners' equity is $100,000. In addition, you estimate that the company's assets are undervalued by approximately $20,000. You have informed Richards and Schroeder that you will invest $25,000 for a 25-percent interest in the partnership's equity. The partners believe you are asking for too large a percentage of the partnership's equity. How do you justify the ownership interest requested?

7-21. Jim Sylvester is in the process of joining a partnership. The partners have agreed to give him a 20-percent interest in the partnership's owners' equity for a $40,000 investment. Total owners' equity after the investment will be $150,000. Jim questions the fact that his capital account will be less than the amount of his investment. Prepare a memo outlining the reasons why the existing partners may make such an offer to Jim.

MULTIPLE CHOICE

7-1. Which of the following is not true with regard to a partnership form of organization?

   a. State approval is required to form the business.

   b. It may use a comprehensive basis of accounting other than GAAP.

   c. Admission of additional owners requires approval of current owners.

   d. Unlimited owner liability exists.

7-2. Which of the following supports the entity theory as it applies to partnership?

   a. Salaries of partners are viewed as distributions of income, not components of net income.

   b. The admission of a new partner or withdrawal of an existing partner results in the dissolution of the partnership.

   c. Assets contributed to the partnership retain the existing tax basis to the partner contributing.

   d. A partnership can enter into contracts.

7-3. Pritchard, Gumbel, and Glass are forming a partnership. The following table shows the assets being contributed by each partner and the liabilities assumed by the partnership.

	Pritchard		Gumbel		Glass	
	Book	Market	Book	Market	Book	Market
Cash	$9,000	$9,000	$5,000	$5,000	$2,000	$2,000
Inventory			$15,000	$20,000	$18,000	$25,000
Equipment	$65,000	$82,000				
Liabilities	$10,000	$10,000				

What are the capital account balances at the date the partnership is formed if the partners agree that market values are to be used?

   a. Pritchard: $84,000; Gumbel: $20,000; Glass: $20,000

   b. Pritchard: $64,000; Gumbel: $20,000; Glass: $20,000

   c. Pritchard: $81,000; Gumbel: $25,000; Glass: $27,000

   d. Pritchard: $101,000; Gumbel: $25,000; Glass: $27,000

7-4. Alex, Bob, and Caroline are forming a partnership. The market values of the assets being contributed by Alex, Bob, and Caroline are $63,000, $58,000, and $92,000, respectively. The partners agree that Alex's experience warrants a higher initial capital account value than would result from recognizing only the market value of the assets contributed. Bob and Caroline agree that Alex should receive a bonus of $30,000 and that Bob and Caroline should contribute the bonus in a 1/3 and 2/3 ratio. What is the dollar amount of each partner's capital account at the date the partnership is formed?

   a. Alex: $93,000; Bob: $48,000; Caroline: $72,000

   b. Alex: $93,000; Bob: $43,000; Caroline: $77,000

   c. Alex: $63,000; Bob: $58,000; Caroline: $92,000

   d. Alex: $93,000; Bob: $58,000; Caroline: $92,000

7-5. Alex, Bob, and Caroline are forming a partnership. The market values of the assets being contributed by Alex, Bob, and Caroline are $63,000, $58,000, and $92,000, respectively. The partners agree that Alex's experience warrants a higher initial capital account value than would result from recognizing only the market value of the assets contributed. The partners all agree goodwill in the amount of $30,000 should be recognized and allocated to Alex. What is the dollar amount of each partner's capital account at the date the partnership is formed?

   a. Alex: $93,000; Bob: $48,000; Caroline: $72,000

   b. Alex: $93,000; Bob: $43,000; Caroline: $77,000

   c. Alex: $63,000; Bob: $58,000; Caroline: $92,000

   d. Alex: $93,000; Bob: $58,000; Caroline: $92,000

7-6. Kim, Cheryl, and Nicole have been partners for several years. During the current year the partnership had net income of $270,000. The profit and loss sharing agreement allocates salaries of $20,000, $40,000 and $60,000 to Kim, Cheryl, and Nicole, respectively. How much of the partnership income is allocated to Nicole?

   a. $135,000

   b. $110,000

   c. $90,000

   d. $60,000

7-7. Jim, Carol, and Sarah are partners. The profit and loss sharing agreement allocates 7 percent interest on capital account balances. For the current year, the capital accounts are $50,000, $70,000, and $85,000 for Jim, Carol, and Sarah, respectively. The agreement also grants Sarah a bonus equal to 5 percent of profits above $200,000. Remaining income is allocated 30 percent, 30 percent, and 40 percent for Jim, Carol, and Sarah, respectively. Profits for the year are $370,000. How much income is allocated to Sarah?

   a. $133,930

   b. $148,000

   c. $153,310

   d. $158,350

7-8. Bonnie and Gwen are partners with capital account balances of $250,000 and $150,0000, respectively. Gwen desires to reduce her participation in the company, and the partners agree to admit Sarah to the partnership. Sarah pays $90,000 to Gwen for one-half of her equity in the partnership. What is Sarah's capital account balance immediately after she joins the partnership?

a. $0

b. $75,000

c. $90,000

d. $200,000

7-9. Scott and Philip are partners whose capital accounts are $300,000 and $500,000, respectively. Additional capital is needed for expansion, so Scott and Philip agree to allow Jason to join the partnership. Jason will invest $225,000 for a 20-percent equity interest in the partnership. What is Jason's capital account balance immediately after he joins the partnership if the bonus method is applied?

a. $200,000

b. $160,000

c. $45,000

d. $205,000

7-10. Gail, Charlie, and Tim are partners whose capital account balances are $600,000, $480,000, and $320,000, respectively. Gail is interested in retiring and has approached the other partners about the partnership acquiring her interest. The partnership has limited liquidity, and Charlie and Tim offer to have the partnership pay Gail $550,000 for her partnership interest. If Gail accepts the offer and the bonus method is applied, what will be Charlie's capital balance immediately after Gail retires?

a. $510,000

b. $480,000

c. $425,000

d. $505,000

EXERCISES

EXERCISE 7-1	Different bases for noncash assets
EXERCISE 7-2	Initial capital accounts contributing assets and transferring liabilities
EXERCISE 7-3	New partnership formation, bonus method applied
EXERCISE 7-4	New partnership formation, goodwill method applied
EXERCISE 7-5	Interest component of profit and loss allocation using different bases
EXERCISE 7-6	Bonus calculation under two alternatives
EXERCISE 7-7	Impact of changing profit and loss ratios on profit allocation
EXERCISE 7-8	Admission of new partner by purchasing existing partner's interest
EXERCISE 7-9	Admission of new partner by purchasing existing partner's interest
EXERCISE 7-10	Partial purchase of one partner's capital by another partner
EXERCISE 7-11	Admission of new partner, bonus to new partner
EXERCISE 7-12	Admission of new partner, bonus to existing partners
EXERCISE 7-13	Admission of new partner, goodwill to existing partners
EXERCISE 7-14	Admission of new partner, goodwill to new partner
EXERCISE 7-15	Withdrawal of partner, partial recognition of change in asset value
EXERCISE 7-16	Withdrawal of partner, full recognition of change in asset value
EXERCISE 7-17	Withdrawal of partner, bonus to withdrawing partner
EXERCISE 7-18	Withdrawal of partner, goodwill to withdrawing partner recognized
EXERCISE 7-19	Withdrawal of partner, full partnership goodwill recognized

EXERCISE 7-1 Allen Bates, Fred Gregory, and Sam Smith are forming a partnership. The three partners contribute the following assets to establish the business.

	Allen	*Fred*	*Sam*
Cash	$5,000	$12,000	$21,000
Plant Assets—historical cost	$30,000	$20,000	$27,000
Plant Assets—book value	$17,000	$10,000	$23,000
Plant Assets—tax basis	$7,000	$9,000	$6,000
Plant Assets—market value	$27,000	$17,000	$10,000

Required:

A. Determine the dollar amounts that would be assigned to the capital accounts of Allen, Fred, and Sam if the (1) book value, (2) tax basis, and (3) market value of noncash assets are recognized.

B. Which of the bases for recognizing noncash assets seems to have been used to determine the amount of cash each would contribute to the partnership?

EXERCISE 7-2   Bill Jones and Fred Phillips contribute the following assets to begin partnership operations.

	Bill	Fred
Cash	$25,000	$40,000
Inventory		$73,000
Plant Assets	$158,000	
Accounts Payable		$15,600
Notes Payable	$82,700	

Required:
Record the journal entry to establish the assets and owners' equity of the partnership.

EXERCISE 7-3   Jim Snyder, Ken Tucker, and Gail Enriquez are forming a partnership. Each partner is contributing tangible assets to the partnership as indicated in the following table.

	Jim	Ken	Gail
Cash	$30,000	$9,000	$20,000
Inventory	$5,000	$7,000	$26,000
Plant Assets	$17,000	$15,000	$6,000

Ken is also contributing his experience in managing a business similar to the one he, Jim, and Gail are starting. During the discussion of the partnership agreement, all the partners agree that Ken should be compensated for his expertise. As a result, the partners agree that Ken's capital account should equal the capital accounts of Jim and Gail.

Required:
Record the journal entry to establish the partnership, assuming the partners agree to apply the bonus method to recognize Ken's expertise. Prepare a schedule for the partners to ensure they understand the method applied to prepare the journal entry.

EXERCISE 7-4   Philip, Jeff, and Carol are forming a partnership. Carol has significant experience in the marketing of products similar to the one that will be sold by the new partnership's company. As a result of her experience, Philip and Jeff agree that goodwill of $25,000 should be recognized with regard to her experience. Tangible assets contributed to the partnership by each of the partners is listed in the following table.

	Philip	Jeff	Carol
Cash	$50,000	$65,000	$40,000
Plant Assets	$93,000	$106,000	$20,000
Liabilities	$30,000	$27,000	$8,000

Required:
Record the journal entry to establish the partnership.

EXERCISE 7-5   Chris and Darrell are partners. Part of the profit and loss sharing agreement is based on the capital contributed to the partnership. The interest allocation is 8 percent of the invested capital. Chris had a beginning capital account balance of $75,000. He withdrew $20,000 on April 1 and invested $36,000 on October 31. Darrell had a beginning capital account balance of $50,000. He invested $40,000 on April 30, withdrew $25,000 on September 1, and invested $32,000 on December 1.

Required:
Determine the interest portion of the profit or loss allocation when the:

A. Beginning of the period capital balance is the basis for the interest allocation.

B. End of the period capital balance is the basis for the interest allocation.

C. Weighted-average capital balance is the basis for the interest allocation.

EXERCISE 7-6

Mike Harris and Tom Skinner are partners in a local partnership. Part of the profit and loss agreement in the articles of partnership is a bonus to be paid to Tom. Partnership income before considering the bonus is $250,800 in the most recent year. The bonus agreement had been 15 percent of net income in excess of $180,000. The partners are now renegotiating the bonus. One proposal is that the bonus will be 12 percent of net income in excess of $150,000 after deducting the bonus.

Required:
Determine the bonus to be paid to Tom under the current bonus system and the proposed alternative.

EXERCISE 7-7

Bart Harris and Judy Elmers changed the profit and loss allocation in their partnership last year. Prior to the change, profits and losses had been allocated 75 percent to Bart and 25 percent to Judy. After the reallocation, profits and losses are allocated 60 percent to Bart and 40 percent to Judy. A building owned at the time of the reallocation had a book value of $300,000 and a market value of $500,000.

Required:
A. Allocate the gain on the sale of the building two years after the profit and loss agreement was changed, assuming the book value is $230,000 at the time of the sale and the market value is as follows.
   (1) $520,000.
   (2) $470,000.
   (3) $350,000.
   (4) $280,000.
B. Record the journal entry necessary if the partners choose to revalue only their capital accounts for the change in the profit and loss allocation.

EXERCISE 7-8

Mark Baker and Amy King are partners with capital balances of $45,000 and $75,000, respectively. Amy wants to reduce her professional activity so she would like to bring another partner into the business. Mark and Amy have located a potential partner they both believe would be valuable to the company, Ted Williams. Ted has agreed to purchase an ownership interest from Amy.

Required:
A. Record the journal entry to admit Ted into the partnership, assuming:
   (1) Ted pays Amy $30,000 for 40 percent of her ownership equity.
   (2) Ted pays Amy $40,000 for 40 percent of her ownership equity.
B. Is it possible for Ted to pay Amy $25,000 and receive none of Amy's ownership equity? If it is possible, why would Ted make such an investment?
C. Is it possible for Ted to pay Amy $50,000 and receive all of Amy's ownership equity? If it is possible, why would Amy agree to such a transaction?

EXERCISE 7-9

David Barrett and Christian Thomas are partners with capital accounts of $68,500 and $80,750, respectively. Both partners agree to admit Claire Roberts as a new partner. Claire will purchase 30 percent of David's capital balance for $30,825.

Required:
Record the admission of Claire to the partnership.

EXERCISE 7-10

Joe Black and Richard Hill have been partners for many years. During the term of their partnership, Joe has accumulated $189,430 of capital while Richard has accumulated $234,300 of capital. Joe is nearing retirement and wants to slowly withdraw from the partnership. As part of this process, Richard has agreed to purchase 40 percent of Joe's capital balance for $86,000.

Required:
Record the purchase of Joe's capital by Richard.

EXERCISE 7-11

Martin Hooks and Sally Slater are partners in a moderately successful business. Martin and Sally become aware that Albert Brown (a successful businessperson) is interested in becoming involved in another business venture. This is of interest to Martin and Sally because they would like to expand their business. They have several conversations with Albert and reach an agreement whereby Albert would join Martin and Sally's partnership. At the date Albert joins the partnership, he invests $125,000. Martin's and Sally's capital accounts at that time are $300,000 and $450,000, respectively. For his investment, Martin and Sally agree to give Albert a 20 percent interest in the capital of the partnership. Martin's and Sally's residual ratios are 40 percent and 60 percent, respectively, before Albert joins.

Required:
Record Albert's admission to the partnership, assuming the bonus method is applied.

EXERCISE 7-12   Manuel Rodriguez and Michelle Dexter are partners in a very successful business. They have been considering adding an additional partner to help share in the workload. After having conversations with numerous potential partners, they have agreed that Richard Keefer is the person they would prefer to include in the company. Richard is excited about the opportunity because Rodriguez and Dexter are well known and respected in the business community. Keefer is offered a 10 percent partnership equity interest in return for an investment of $50,000. Rodriguez's and Dexter's capital accounts at the time of Keefer's admission are $150,000 and $250,000, respectively.

Required:
Record Keefer's admission to the partnership, assuming the bonus method is applied.

EXERCISE 7-13   Ken Smith and Victor Williams are partners in a local company. They have capital accounts in the amounts of $220,000 and $300,000, respectively, when they agree to admit a new partner, Sam King, to the company. Sam has agreed to contribute $180,000 for a 25 percent interest in the owners' equity of the partnership. Prior to Sam's admission to the partnership, Smith and Williams shared profits and losses 80 percent and 20 percent, respectively.

Required:
Record the admission of Sam to the partnership, assuming goodwill is to be recognized.

EXERCISE 7-14   Wilbur Ashmont and Art Most are partners in a struggling company. They have had difficulty because they lack the liquidity needed to advertise and compete in the local market. An investor, Jesse Fitzpatrick, has offered to join the partnership and provide the needed increase in liquid assets. Wilbur and Art have capital account balances of $80,000 and $125,200, respectively, at the date Jesse is admitted to the partnership, and their respective profit and loss ratios are 40 percent and 60 percent. Jesse agrees to invest $50,000 for a 28 percent interest in the partnership capital.

Required:
Record the admission of Jesse to the partnership, assuming goodwill is to be recognized.

EXERCISE 7-15   Sally Baker, Jesse Caldwell, and Jane Clark are partners with capital accounts of $75,000, $82,000, and $101,000, respectively. Jesse informs his two partners that he is leaving the company. The partnership agreement stipulates that changes in the value of assets and liabilities applicable to the withdrawing partner are to be recognized at the date of withdrawal. Inventory is the only asset that has a market value ($220,000) significantly different from book value ($150,000). The residual profit and loss percentages for Baker, Caldwell, and Clark are 30 percent, 25 percent, and 45 percent, respectively.

Required:
Record the revaluation of the assets and the withdrawal of Jesse, assuming partnership assets are used to acquire Jesse's ownership interest.

EXERCISE 7-16   Jim Richards, Tony Adams, and Cory Stewart are partners who share profits and losses 15 percent, 45 percent, and 40 percent, respectively. Jim has decided to leave the partnership. The fixed assets of the partnership are undervalued by $120,000. The capital accounts of Jim, Tony, and Cory prior to Jim's withdrawal are $42,000, $110,000, and $136,000, respectively. The articles of partnership state that the full market value of all assets and liabilities should be recognized when a partner leaves the partnership.

Required:
Record the revaluation of the assets and the withdrawal of Jim, assuming a new partner, Chet Dexter, purchases Jim's ownership interest.

EXERCISE 7-17   Bill Callahan, Emily Alexander, and Scott Gregory are partners with capital accounts of $200,000, $185,000, and $160,000, respectively. Emily must withdraw from the partnership for medical reasons. The partners have agreed that the partnership will purchase Emily's ownership interest for $215,000. The profit and loss residual ratios before Emily's retirement are 35 percent, 25 percent, and 40 percent for Bill, Emily, and Scott, respectively.

Required:
Record Emily's withdrawal from the partnership, assuming the bonus method is applied.

EXERCISE 7-18   Albert Alexander, Bart Bonds, and Clyde Cunningham are partners in a local CPA firm. Since Bart is nearing retirement age, the partners are planning his withdrawal. The articles of partnership indicate that the retiring partner's goodwill is to be recognized at the date of retirement. Albert, Bart, and Clyde share profits in a 30 percent, 25 percent, and 45 percent ratio, respectively, and their respective capital accounts just prior to the withdrawal are $175,000, $160,000, and $125,000, respectively. Estimated goodwill attributable to Bart's ownership percentage is $38,000.

Required:
Record the journal entry(ies) related to these facts, assuming partnership assets are used to acquire Bart's equity.

EXERCISE 7-19   Alvin Miller, Jessica Smith, and Judy Lawson are partners who have residual profit and loss ratios of 55 percent, 30 percent, and 15 percent, respectively. The capital balances of Miller, Smith, and Lawson just before Lawson's withdrawal are $300,000, $270,000, and $145,000, respectively. The partners' best estimate of Lawson's share of the goodwill attributed to the entire company is $13,200. The partnership agreement states that all goodwill should be recognized when a partner withdraws.

Required:
Record the journal entry(ies) related to these facts, assuming partnership assets are used to acquire Lawson's equity.

PROBLEMS

PROBLEM 7-1   Value assigned to noncash assets contributed by partners
PROBLEM 7-2   Value assigned to noncash assets contributed by partners
PROBLEM 7-3   Profit and loss allocation
PROBLEM 7-4   Evaluating changes in profit and loss allocation
PROBLEM 7-5   Profit allocation, admission of partner by purchasing existing partner's interest, profit allocation
PROBLEM 7-6   Change in profit and loss ratios, revaluation of assets
PROBLEM 7-7   Change in profit and loss ratios, adjustment to capital accounts
PROBLEM 7-8   Profit allocation, admission of new partner by investing, goodwill recognized, compute weighted-average capital, profit allocation
PROBLEM 7-9   Partner withdrawal, partial asset revaluation, bonus method
PROBLEM 7-10   Partner withdrawal, full asset revaluation, withdrawing partner goodwill recognized

PROBLEM 7-1   Jan Levy, Steve Dugan, and Mike Suzuki are contributing cash and noncash assets to begin a new business formed as a partnership. Assume the initial capital account balances will be determined based on the value of the assets contributed. Assume also that the partners have agreed that the relative size of the initial capital accounts will determine the residual percentage allocation of profits and losses when profit and loss distributions occur. Information regarding the initial contributions is provided below.

	Jan	*Steve*	*Mike*
Cash	$50,000	$75,000	$32,000
Plant Assets—historical cost	$180,000	$250,000	$340,000
Plant Assets—book value	$120,000	$107,000	$300,000
Plant Assets—tax basis	$100,000	$90,000	$259,000
Plant Assets—market value	$145,000	$126,000	$310,000

Required:

A. Record the journal entry to establish the initial partners' capital accounts and the assets assuming the (1) book value, (2) tax basis, and (3) market value are used to determine the value assigned to noncash assets contributed. Assume also that each partner's capital account is assigned a value equal to the cash and noncash assets contributed by that partner.

B. Record the journal entry to establish the initial partners' capital accounts and the assets assuming the (1) book value, (2) tax basis, and (3) market value are used to determine the value assigned to noncash assets contributed. Assume also that all the partners' capital accounts are equal when the journal entry is completed.

C. Contrast the entries in parts A and B. Why might the partners agree to equal capital accounts as presented in part B?

D. What basis would each partner prefer for the recognized value of noncash assets contributed to the partnership?

PROBLEM 7-2   Paul Rodriguez, Bill Hayes, and Richard Smith are creating a partnership. The partners contribute the following assets to the partnership.

	Paul	Bill	Richard
Cash		$40,000	$20,000
Inventory	$82,000		
Computer			$-0-
Delivery truck		$17,000	
Liabilities	$30,000	$8,000	$15,000

The value shown for each noncash assets is the tax basis. The tax basis of the computer equipment contributed by Richard is $0 because Richard opted to apply IRS Code Section 179, which permits the taxpayer to take a current period deduction for a limited amount of business property rather than capitalizing the property and recognizing depreciation for tax purposes. The liabilities assumed by the partnership on behalf of Richard pertain to the computer equipment.

Required:

A. Record the journal entry to recognize the assets contributed using the tax basis and the capital balances at the date the partnership is formed.

B. Record the journal entry to recognize the assets contributed and the capital balances at the date the partnership is formed assuming the following market values are recognized: inventory, $86,000; delivery truck, $23,000; computer, $18,000.

C. Is there any necessary relationship between the amounts recognized in the journal entry to record the initial contributions by the partners, tax basis or market value, and the continuing operations of the partnership? Why or why not?

PROBLEM 7-3   Neil Lynch, Jan Groff, and Mark Pentel are partners. Profits are shared in the following manner.

	Neil	Jan	Mark
Weighted-average capital balance	$250,000	$190,000	$400,000
Salary	$10,000	$75,000	$30,000
Bonus		(.1) (Net income – $200,000)	
Residual	40%	35%	25%

The interest portion of the profit and loss allocation is 8 percent of the weighted-average capital balance. Profit allocation is determined in the order presented above. Assume the allocation is completed regardless of the level of profit. Partnership losses, on the other hand, are allocated by the residual ratios only.

Required:

A. Determine the profit allocation if the partnership net income is $300,000.

B. Determine the profit allocation if the partnership net income is $190,000.

C. Determine the loss allocation if the partnership net loss is ($60,000).

D. Determine the loss allocation if the partnership net loss is ($60,000) and all steps of the profit and loss allocation are used, even for net losses.

PROBLEM 7-4 Jane Caldwell, Julia Mitchell, and Robert Smith have been partners for some time. The following outlines the profit and loss distribution provision of the articles of partnership.

	Jane	Julia	Robert
Return on weighted-average capital balance	9%	9%	9%
Salary	$40,000	$30,000	$50,000
Bonus			(.15) (Net income – $250,000 – Bonus)
Residual	25%	55%	20%

Weighted-average capital balances for the current year are $250,000, $400,000, and $350,000 for Jane, Julia, and Robert, respectively. The current partnership agreement stipulates that the allocation be completed, in the order presented, regardless of the profit level. The partners are considering alternative allocations. Assume the company's net income is $162,000.

Required:

A. Prepare the profit allocation based on the current articles of partnership.

B. Prepare the profit allocation, assuming the allocation stops when all the profits have been allocated.

C. Prepare the profit allocation based on a change in the order of allocation where salary is allocated first and interest second. The allocation is completed through all the components.

D. Prepare the profit allocation based on a change in the order of allocation where salary is allocated first and interest second. The allocation stops when all of the profits have been allocated.

E. Which partner(s) would prefer which method of allocating profits and losses?

PROBLEM 7-5 Betty Powers and Gary Cummings have been partners for just over five years. During 2003, profits and losses were allocated using the following information.

	Betty	Gary
Weighted-average capital balance for 2003	$150,000	$195,000
Salary	$17,000	$20,000
Residual	60%	40%

Interest on the weighted-average capital balance is 10 percent. Income in 2003 was $90,000. After posting the 2003 profit allocation, the capital accounts for Betty and Gary are $220,000 and $275,000, respectively. At the beginning of 2004, Betty and Gary admit a new partner, Philip Lawrence. Philip purchases 20 percent of Betty's capital balance for $50,000. Betty and Gary agree that Philip should be allocated a $10,000 salary and that the residual ratios should be changed to 55 percent, 35 percent, and 10 percent for Betty, Gary, and Philip, respectively. Weighted-average capital balances for 2004 are $185,000, $300,000, and $55,000 for Betty, Gary, and Philip, respectively. Net income for 2004 is $140,000.

Required:

A. Determine the profit allocation for 2003.

B. Record the admission of Philip into the partnership.

C. Determine the profit allocation for 2004.

PROBLEM 7-6 Jeremy and Scott are partners who are changing their profit and loss ratios from 25/75 to 45/55. At the date of the change, the partners chooses to revalue assets with market value different from book value. One asset revalued is land with a book value of $160,000 and a market value of $300,000. Two years after the profit and loss ratio is changed, the land is sold for $420,000.

Required:

A. Record the revaluation of the land.

B. Record the sale of the land.

C. Record the distribution of the gain on sale of land to the partners.

PROBLEM 7-7   Alex and Doug are partners. Their current profit and loss ratios (30/70) are being changed to (45/55). The partners decide to adjust their capital accounts at the date of the change in the profit and loss ratios to reflect the differrence between market value and book value of assets and liabilities. At the date of the change, a building has a market value of $520,000 and a book value of $430,000.

Required:

A. Record the adjustment to the capital accounts at the date of the change in the profit and loss ratios.

PROBLEM 7-8   Fred O'Reilly and Shawn Mitchell have operated their business as a partnership for the past three years. During the three years the partnership has been in operation, the following profit and loss agreement has been in effect.

	Fred	Shawn
Interest on weighted-average capital balance 2003	10%	10%
Salary	$26,000	$20,000
Profit/loss residual	40%	60%

The 2003 weighted-average capital balances for Fred and Shawn were $110,000 and $135,000, respectively. The partnership's net income for 2003 is $86,000.

The business has been growing and it is time for them to consider adding another partner to help share the workload. Fred and Shawn have worked with Jeff Mills for some time and would be interested in having Jeff join the partnership, if appropriate arrangements can be made. Jeff has several meetings with Fred and Shawn and agrees to invest $74,400 into the partnership to become a partner. Jeff becomes a partner on July 31, 2004. As part of Jeff's admission, the articles of partnership were changed to reflect the following profit and loss allocation.

	Fred	Shawn	Jeff
Interest on weighted-average capital balance	10%	10%	10%
Salary	$30,000	$23,000	$15,000
Profit/loss residual	30%	45%	25%

All salaries are stated on an annual basis. Investments and withdrawals recorded in the capital accounts of the three partners during 2004 are as follows (this table does not include Jeff's initial investment or any adjustments that may occur to Fred's or Shawn's capital accounts as a result of Jeff joining the partnership).

Date	Fred		Shawn		Jeff	
1/1	Balance	$140,000	Balance	$150,000		
4/30	Withdraw	$18,100				
9/30	Invest	$20,000	Withdraw	$20,000		
12/1	Invest	$10,400	Invest	$15,300	Withdraw	$36,000

Net income for 2004 is $118,095.

Required:

A. Determine the profit allocation for 2003.

B. Record the admission of Jeff into the partnership, assuming Jeff receives a 15-percent interest in the partnership's equity and goodwill is recognized. Any direct investments or withdrawals by

Fred and Shawn must be considered in the calculation of goodwill, but current period income is not to be considered in the calculation of goodwill.

C. Determine the profit allocation for 2004 after considering the entry recorded in part B.

D. Record the admission of Jeff into the partnership, assuming Jeff receives a 37.5-percent interest in the partnership's equity and goodwill is recognized.

E. Determine the profit allocation for 2004 after considering the entry recorded in part D.

PROBLEM 7-9

Rick Brown, Craig Johnson, and Phyllis Newberry have been partners for many years. Craig has indicated that he plans to withdraw from the partnership. To prepare for his departure, the following information is gathered.

	Book Value	Market Value
Current Assets	$160,000	$160,000
Fixed Assets	590,000	740,000
Total Assets	$750,000	
Current Liabilities	$90,000	90,000
Long-Term Debt	200,000	190,000
Brown, Capital (30%)	110,000	
Johnson, Capital (25%)	230,000	
Newberry, Capital (45%)	120,000	
Total Liabilities and Partnership Equity	$750,000	

The partnership agreement specifies that the withdrawing partner's portion of the change in value of any assets and liabilities is to be recognized at the date of withdrawal. The partners agree that $300,000 of partnership assets will be used to purchase Craig's ownership equity. The assets are to be financed by borrowing the money on a long-term notes payable.

Required:
Record the journal entry(ies) related to these facts, assuming the bonus method is applied.

PROBLEM 7-10

Walter McCullough, Bryan Springer, and Jeremy Holt are partners in a small service company. Walter has developed his golf game and has indicated to his partners that he is going to withdraw from the partnership to become a professional golfer. The following information was prepared to help the partners plan Walter's withdrawal.

	Book Value	Market Value
Current Assets	$450,000	$450,000
Fixed Assets	190,000	320,000
Total Assets	$640,000	
Current Liabilities	$200,000	200,000
Holt, Capital (35%)	110,000	
McCullough, Capital (20%)	100,000	
Springer, Capital (45%)	230,000	
Total Liabilities and Partnership Equity	$640,000	

The partnership agreement indicates that the increase in the value of identifiable assets and liabilities is to be fully recognized when a partner withdraws from the partnership but only the withdrawing partner's portion of any goodwill should be recognized. The partners estimate that the total market value of the company as a going concern is $600,000. Current assets of the partnership (Cash) are going to be used to acquire Walter's capital.

Required:
Record the journal entry(ies) related to these facts.

CHAPTER 8

PARTNERSHIP LIQUIDATION

LEARNING OBJECTIVES

After reading this chapter, you should be able to:

- Understand the payment priority of partnership creditors and personal creditors.
- Understand the payment priority of partnership creditors during a partnership liquidation.
- Differentiate between a lump-sum and an installment liquidation.
- Prepare a Statement of Realization and Liquidation.
- Prepare a Cash Distribution Plan.
- Prepare a Schedule of Safe Payments.

Dissolution: the legal ending of a partnership that occurs when there is a change in the relationship among partners, typically due to adding a new partner or the withdrawal of a partner

Termination: when a partnership ceases to conduct normal business operations

Liquidation: when a partnership ceases normal operations, sells its remaining assets, pays creditors, and distributes any remaining cash to partners

A change in the business structure of a partnership may result in a dissolution, a termination, and/or a liquidation. A **dissolution** occurs when there is a change in the legal relationship among the partners. This typically occurs as a result of admitting a new partner to a partnership or the retirement of an existing partner from a partnership. A **termination** occurs when the partnership ceases to conduct normal business operations. A **liquidation** occurs when the partnership sells its assets, pays its liabilities, and distributes any remaining assets to the partners. Partnerships may be liquidated for many reasons, such as that the business purpose of the partnership has been fulfilled, the partners do not wish to continue the business, or the partnership is in financial difficulty. While each of these reasons for partnership liquidation is possible, financial difficulty is the most likely reason. Successful partnerships are usually sold to other investors, not liquidated. Partners may decide that the partnership should be liquidated before the financial difficulties become too severe (**voluntary liquidation**) or the partnership may be forced into liquidation by creditors (**involuntary liquidation**).

This chapter analyzes the primary issues relevant to the liquidation of partnerships. The first part of the chapter presents the basic issues that should be considered when planning a partnership's liquidation. The second part considers liquidations where a single distribution is made to the partners. The final part examines planning and performing liquidations in which multiple distributions are made to the partners.

PARTNERSHIP LIQUIDATION GUIDELINES

Voluntary liquidation: when a partnership liquidates before it encounters severe financial difficulties

The accountant has important responsibilities in the liquidation of partnerships. The primary responsibility is to manage the liquidation process in a manner that will ensure the payment of obligations to creditors other than partners. Failure to meet this fiduciary responsibility may result in a liability for the accountant. A secondary responsibility is to ensure that the partnership liquidation is managed in a manner that will result in appropriate distributions to the partners. This does not mean that all partners receive the same amount of cash. In fact, it may mean that some of the partners receive no distribution as a result of the liquidation.

Involuntary liquidation: when a partnership is forced to liquidate by its creditors

The primary duty of the accountant in a partnership liquidation is to ensure that the partnership's assets are distributed in an equitable manner. To accomplish this task, the accountant must understand the rights of the partnership's creditors, the partners' personal creditors, and the partners themselves. The accountant must also understand the difference between the partnership's creditors and the partners' individual creditors and the difference between a partner's claim to partnership assets and a partner's individual assets. Keeping the partnership assets and liabilities separated from the personal assets and liabilities of the individual partners is referred to as the **marshaling of assets**. The partnership's creditors and the individual partners' creditors can have claims against both the partnership's assets and the partners' individual assets; however, the priority of the claims by the partnership's creditors and the individual partners' creditors differs depending on the source of payment. Claims by the partnership's creditors and the partners' personal creditors against the partnership's assets and the partners' personal assets can be summarized as follows:

Marshaling of assets: keeping the partnership assets and liabilities separate from partner personal assets and liabilities

Claims against partnership assets:

1. Partnership creditors.
2. Personal creditors if the creditor's claim is not fully paid from the partner's individual assets. This claim is limited to the credit balance in the partner's capital account.

Claims against a partner's individual assets:

1. Personal creditors.
2. Partnership creditors if the creditor's claim is not fully paid from the partnership's assets. This claim is not limited to the balance in the partner's capital account because of the partner's unlimited liability.
3. Other partners if the partner in question has a deficit capital account. This claim is limited to the deficit in the partner's capital account.

Uniform Partnership Act: the provisions that provide guidance/laws for partnership formation, operation, and liquidation

With regard to claims against a partnership's assets in the case of liquidation, the **Uniform Partnership Act** (UPA) states:

[T]he liabilities of the partnership shall rank in the order of payment as follows:
1. *Those owing creditors other than partners,*
2. *Those owing to partners other than for capital and profits,*
3. *Those owing to partners in respect of capital,*
4. *Those owing to partners in respect of profits."* [1]

---

[1] Uniform Partnership Act, §40.

As the UPA priority list indicates, the partnership's creditors have the first claim to the partnership's assets. This does not mean that the accountant would be required to pay all of the partnership's liabilities before any distributions could be made to the partners. The creditor's first claim does mean that the accountant has a fiduciary responsibility to the partnership's creditors if assets are distributed to the partners and subsequently insufficient assets are available to pay all the creditor claims. This concept is important because some liquidations take many months to complete and partners often desire partial distribution in the interim. The listing of the partnership's creditors as a single item also does not mean that all the partnership's creditors have equal priority in the distribution of the partnership's assets. Several features determine which partnership creditors have priority claims and what assets are to be used as the basis for the payment to creditors, such as claims secured by a mortgage against property. Claims are listed as one category in this chapter to focus on the partnership aspects of the liquidation.

Claims by the partners against the partnership's assets are divided into three groups (i.e., loans from partners, partners' capital contributions, partners' undistributed partnership income). These items are often combined into a single category in practice. The partners' capital contributions and the undistributed profits (items 3 and 4 in the UPA list) are often combined because the partnership's accounting records typically do not contain the information necessary to separate capital from income. Loans from partners are generally combined with the capital accounts under the **right of offset** doctrine. Under this doctrine, loans from partners are combined with the existing partners' capital accounts to determine a net equity position in the partnership. This net position makes it unlikely for the accountant to pay a *Notes Payable* to a partner from partnership assets if there is reason to believe that the partner may have a deficit capital account before the liquidation is completed. A deficit in a partner's capital account is of concern to the accountant because the partner would be expected to make additional contributions to the partnership to eliminate the deficit. This is important because it is conceivable that a partner might be personally insolvent and, therefore, unable to make the needed contribution. Failure of the partner to make such a contribution would require other partners to forgo distributions in the amount of the deficit.

> **Right of offset:** the combining of a partner's capital account with any loans to/from the partnership to determine the partner's net equity position in the partnership

The procedures applied in current practice are not without risk. Combining the loans from partners with the respective capital accounts (capital and undistributed profits) does not conform with the UPA. The total distribution to each partner will be the same so long as the partners are personally solvent. If a partner's capital account has a deficit and the partner is personally insolvent, the total cash distributed to each partner may differ depending on whether the UPA is applied or whether current practice is applied. This dilemma can be avoided by having the partners approve a cash distribution plan before the liquidation begins.[2] The UPA states that the distribution priorities must be followed unless there is an agreement among the parties to the contrary. The one aspect of the distribution that will not be altered is the priority claim of the creditors because they would not be expected to agree to give up their payment preference.

THE LIQUIDATION PROCESS

The liquidation process often begins with closing the accounting records of the partnership and allocating any income or loss for the period to the partners' capital accounts. Following the closing of the partnership's financial records, assets that cannot be used to pay liabilities

---

[2] Whitis, Robert E., and Jeffrey R. Pittman, "Inconsistencies Between Accounting Practices and Statutory Law in Partnership Liquidations," *The Accounting Educators' Journal*, Fall, 1996, pp. 91–105.

in their current form (typically noncash assets) are converted into cash. Gains and losses on the realization of these assets are allocated directly to the partners' capital accounts. The residual profit and loss ratios are generally applied in such allocations because the gain or loss may result from several causes, such as the accounting methods applied in previous periods. As a result, it is often not possible to know when the change in value occurred. The inclusion of other profit and loss allocation components, such as interest on capital balances and salaries, is not applicable because these items are generally relevant to the operation of the partnership and the current issue is the liquidation of the entity.

Assuming that the aggregate market value of the partnership's assets exceeds the partnership's liabilities, the third step in the liquidation process is the distribution of assets to the partners. This distribution may occur after all of the liabilities have been paid or the accountant may determine that it is prudent to distribute assets to the partners before all of the liabilities have been paid. If the accountant distributes assets to the partners before all the creditors have been paid, caution must be used. If too many assets are distributed to the partners and there are not sufficient assets to pay all the creditors, the accountant may be liable to the creditors for a breach of fiduciary duties.

LUMP-SUM LIQUIDATION

Some partnerships may be liquidated in a relatively short period of time. When this occurs, it is often possible to sell all the partnership's assets and pay its liabilities before a distribution is made to the partners. When the assets are sold and all liabilities paid before there is a distribution to the partners, the process is referred to as a **lump-sum liquidation**. The accountant's risk is greatly reduced because there is only a slight probability of not fulfilling the fiduciary responsibility with regard to the creditors; that is, it is unlikely that the partners will receive assets that should be distributed to the creditors. In this case, the only way an improper distribution could be made to partners is if there are undiscovered liabilities that should have been found by the accountant. However, it is also possible for an improper distribution to be made if there are not sufficient assets to pay all the liabilities. As discussed previously, state law establishes priorities among the creditors of the partnership depending on the nature and security of the claim. The accountant should refer to the state's laws regarding priority distributions among creditors.

Lump-sum liquidation: a liquidation that occurs over a relatively short time period during which all assets are sold and all liabilities are paid before the partners receive one (lump-sum)

The examples that follow present several circumstances that could exist when a lump-sum distribution occurs. The examples differ with regard to whether a partner has a deficit created in the capital account and the ability of the partner to make additional contributions if a deficit capital balance does occur. The residual profit and loss ratios for the partners in all of the examples for Briscoe, Johnson, and Mitchell are .45, .35, and .20, respectively.

EXAMPLE 8-1

Lump-sum liquidation, all positive capital accounts Assume that the Briscoe, Johnson, and Mitchell partnership is going to be liquidated. The partners have prepared the following trial balance (book values and market values) on March 1, 2004, immediately prior to starting the liquidation. The aggregate market value of the partnership's net assets exceeds the outstanding liabilities and all the partners have positive capital balances.

	Debit (Credit)	
	Book Value	Estimated Market Value
Cash	50,000	50,000
Receivables	80,000	70,000
Inventory	160,000	250,000

	Debit (Credit)	
	Book Value	Estimated Market Value
Plant Assets	260,000	50,000
Liabilities	(125,000)	(125,000)
Briscoe, Capital	(100,000)	
Johnson, Capital	(250,000)	
Mitchell, Capital	(75,000)	

Assume the following events occur during the liquidation period:

1.	March 13	Receivables are sold to a bank for their estimated market value, $70,000.
2.	March 16	Inventory is sold for $230,000.
3.	March 22	Plant assets are sold for $60,000.
4.	March 25	An unknown liability of $15,000 is discovered.
5.	March 27	All the partnership's creditors are paid in full.
6.	March 31	The remaining assets are distributed to the partners and the partnership liquidation is completed.

Statement of Realization and Liquidation

The events presented above can be evaluated and recognized in a variety of ways. The partnership will prepare journal entries in a manner similar to those for recognizing transactions for an ongoing entity. As the entity wraps up its business activities, the partnership may prepare a schedule that summarizes and documents the realization of the partnership's assets and the liquidation of the liabilities and capital accounts. Such a schedule is often titled **Statement of Realization and Liquidation**. This schedule contains the same information as journal entries but is organized in a tabular format, as presented in Illustration 8-1.

Notice that the trial balance that exists immediately prior to the liquidation is presented in the first row of Illustration 8-1. The first transaction that occurs, the sale of the accounts receivable, is presented in the second row. Note that the cash column increases, while the accounts receivable column decreases. The amount by which the carrying value of the receivables exceeds the cash collected from their sale is charged directly to the capital accounts. This direct allocation is used because there are no income statement accounts. An income statement is only relevant for a going concern, and the partnership is in the process of liquidating. The allocation of gains and losses to each partner's capital account can use any agreed-upon allocation basis, but the allocation is often prepared using the partners' residual profit and loss ratios (which is assumed here).

Subsequent rows present the sale of the *Inventory* and the *Plant Assets* at amounts different from their respective carrying values. The (gain) loss on the sale of each is (credited) debited directly to the capital accounts.

The fourth transaction presents an increase in the liabilities due to the discovery of a previously unrecognized debt. The increase in the liability results in a corresponding decrease in the partners' capital accounts. In a going concern, an accrual of a liability is charged to an expense account, thereby reducing net income and, through routine closing entries, reducing the partners' capital accounts. In a liquidation, the reduction to the capital accounts is direct and immediate because, as mentioned, income statements are no longer being prepared.

The fifth transaction presents the payment of the partnership's liabilities and the corresponding decrease in cash. The capital accounts are not altered in the payment of the liabilities because the net equity of the partnership does not change as a result of paying liabilities at face value. Had some of the liabilities been discharged for less than face value, the capital accounts would have increased.

ILLUSTRATION 8-1
Statement of Realization and Liquidation for the Lump-Sum Liquidation of the Briscoe, Johnson, and Mitchell Partnership

	Cash	Receivables	Inventory	Plant Assets	Liabilities	Briscoe, Capital (.45)	Johnson, Capital (.35)	Mitchell, Capital (.20)
Preliquidation balances	50,000	80,000	160,000	260,000	(125,000)	(100,000)	(250,000)	(75,000)
1. Sale of receivables and distribution of $10,000 loss	70,000	(80,000)				4,500	3,500	2,000
	120,000	0	160,000	260,000	(125,000)	(95,500)	(246,500)	(73,000)
2. Sale of inventory and distribution of $70,000 gain	230,000		(160,000)			(31,500)	(24,500)	(14,000)
	350,000	0	0	260,000	(125,000)	(127,000)	(271,000)	(87,000)
3. Sale of plant assets and distribution of $200,000 loss	60,000			(260,000)		90,000	70,000	40,000
	410,000	0	0	0	(125,000)	(37,000)	(201,000)	(47,000)
4. Accrual of a $15,000 liability previously unrecorded					(15,000)	6,750	5,250	3,000
	410,000	0	0	0	(140,000)	(30,250)	(195,750)	(44,000)
5. Payment to outside creditors	(140,000)				140,000			
	270,000	0	0	0	0	(30,250)	(195,750)	(44,000)
6. Lump-sum payment to partners	(270,000)					30,250	195,750	44,000
Postliquidation balances	0	0	0	0	0	0	0	0

The final transaction presents the distribution of the partnership's remaining cash to the partners. Notice that the amount of cash remaining after all the other events have been recognized exactly equals the amount of the capital accounts. The equality of the cash remaining in the partnership and the capital accounts will always occur when the liquidation process is completed because each successive trial balance (after each transaction) is still in balance.

EXAMPLE 8-2

Lump-sum liquidation, capital account deficit with personally solvent partner
Assume that the Briscoe, Johnson, and Mitchell partnership is going to be liquidated. The partners have prepared the following trial balance (book values and market values) on March 1, 2004, immediately prior to starting the liquidation. The market value of the partnership's net assets exceeds the outstanding liabilities and all the partners have positive capital balances. The following events are displayed in Illustration 8-2.

	Debit (Credit)	
	Book Value	*Estimated Market Value*
Cash	50,000	50,000
Receivables	80,000	70,000
Inventory	160,000	65,000
Plant Assets	260,000	50,000
Liabilities	(125,000)	(125,000)

	Debit (Credit)	
	Book Value	*Estimated Market Value*
Briscoe, Capital	(100,000)	
Johnson, Capital	(250,000)	
Mitchell, Capital	(75,000)	

Assume the following events occurred during the liquidation period:

1.	March 13	Receivables are sold to a bank for their estimated market value, $70,000.
2.	March 16	Inventory is sold for $40,000.
3.	March 22	Plant assets are sold for $60,000.
4.	March 25	An unknown liability of $15,000 is discovered.
5.	March 26	Briscoe contributes $55,250 to eliminate a capital account deficit.
6.	March 27	All the partnership's creditors are paid in full.
7.	March 31	The remaining assets are distributed to the partners, and the partnership liquidation is completed.

The beginning balance presented in Illustration 8-2 is the same trial balance that was presented in Illustration 8-1. The row presenting the sale of the accounts receivable and the allocation of the loss to the capital accounts is the same as in the previous example.

ILLUSTRATION 8-2
Statement of Realization and Liquidation for the Lump-Sum Liquidation of the Briscoe, Johnson, and Mitchell Partnership

	Cash	Receivables	Inventory	Plant Assets	Liabilities	Briscoe, Capital (.45)	Johnson, Capital (.35)	Mitchell, Capital (.20)
Preliquidation balances	50,000	80,000	160,000	260,000	(125,000)	(100,000)	(250,000)	(75,000)
1. Sale of receivables and distribution of $10,000 loss	70,000	(80,000)				4,500	3,500	2,000
	120,000	0	160,000	260,000	(125,000)	(95,500)	(246,500)	(73,000)
2. Sale of inventory and distribution of $120,000 loss	40,000		(160,000)			54,000	42,000	24,000
	160,000	0	0	260,000	(125,000)	(41,500)	(204,500)	(49,000)
3. Sale of plant assets and distribution of $200,000 loss	60,000			(260,000)		90,000	70,000	40,000
	220,000	0	0	0	(125,000)	(48,500)	(134,500)	(9,000)
4. Accrual of a $15,000 liability previously unrecorded					(15,000)	6,750	5,250	3,000
	220,000	0	0	0	(140,000)	(55,250)	(129,250)	(6,000)
5. Additional contribution by Briscoe	55,250					(55,250)		
	275,250	0	0	0	(140,000)	0	(129,250)	(6,000)
6. Payment to outside creditors	(140,000)				140,000			
	135,250	0	0	0	0	0	(129,250)	(6,000)
7. Lump-sum payment to partners	(135,250)						129,250	6,000
Postliquidation balances	0	0	0	0	0	0	0	0

The sale of inventory is the first event where Example 8-2 differs from Example 8-1. The current example results in a $120,000 loss on the sale of the inventory, while the previous example had a $70,000 gain. Events 4 and 5 are the same as in Example 8-1. The allocation of the loss resulting from the sale of inventory, along with the loss from the sale of plant assets and the discovery of the liability, creates a deficit in Briscoe's capital account. This deficit must be eliminated before the liquidation can be completed.

The preference is for the partner with the deficit capital account (Briscoe) to make an additional contribution to the partnership to remove the deficit. Briscoe may perceive that he should not have to make an additional contribution. He may be of the opinion that he has worked diligently trying to make the business successful and has contributed all that should be expected. On the other hand, Briscoe's capital account would not have a deficit balance had one of two events not occurred. First, the partnership may have had losses and Briscoe's percentage ownership resulted in his receiving a large allocation of those losses. In this instance, Briscoe is the partner with the greatest responsibility for covering the losses incurred because he has the greatest ownership interest in the partnership. Remember that, if the partnership had been successful, Briscoe would have also benefited the most (a 45 percent share). But with the greatest potential for high rewards comes the greatest risk of potentially having to absorb losses. Second, Briscoe may have withdrawn a larger portion of the profits available to the partners. In this instance, Briscoe should be expected to replace some of the funds removed as withdrawals. Regardless of the reason for the deficit in the capital account, the accountant will pursue the additional contribution by Briscoe on behalf of the other partners. If necessary, the accountant will obtain legal advice to persuade Briscoe to make the additional contribution. The current example assumes that Briscoe is able and willing to make an additional contribution.

The remainder of Example 8-2 is the same as the previous example. Cash is used to pay the partnership's liabilities, and the remaining cash is distributed to the partners with positive capital balances. In the current example, Johnson and Mitchell receive cash from the distribution.

EXAMPLE 8-3

Lump-sum liquidation, capital account deficit with insolvent partners
Example 8-3 is the same as Example 8-2 except it is assumed that the partners are unable to make an additional investment to eliminate any deficits that may occur in their respective capital accounts as a result of the liquidation. Illustration 8-3 presents the same first four events that were presented in Illustration 8-2.

The inability of Briscoe to make the additional contribution has implications for the other partners. The capital account balances that exist for Johnson and Mitchell do not represent the amount of cash these individuals will receive when the partnership is finally liquidated. The sum of their capital accounts ($129,250 and $6,000) and the outstanding liabilities ($140,000) are greater than the amount of available cash ($220,000). As a result, the deficit in Briscoe's capital account must be allocated to the remaining partners, who have positive capital account balances. This allocation often occurs in the remaining profit and loss sharing ratios but can be made in any agreed-upon manner.

After Briscoe's capital account deficit is allocated to Johnson ($39,159) and Mitchell ($20,091), Mitchell's capital account has a deficit balance of $14,091 ($6,000 – $20,091). Example 8-3 assumes that Mitchell is also unable to make an additional contribution, so the $14,091 deficit in Mitchell's capital account after the first allocation must be allocated to the only remaining partner who has a positive capital balance, Johnson. After this allocation is completed, Johnson's capital account ($80,000) and the outstanding liabilities ($140,000) exactly equals the amount of cash available ($220,000). The liabilities are then paid and the remaining cash is distributed to Johnson to complete the liquidation.

ILLUSTRATION 8-3
Statement of Realization and Liquidation for the Lump-Sum Liquidation of the Briscoe, Johnson, and Mitchell Partnership

	Cash	Receivables	Inventory	Plant Assets	Liabilities	Briscoe, Capital (.45)	Johnson, Capital (.35)	Mitchell, Capital (.20)
Preliquidation balances	50,000	80,000	160,000	260,000	(125,000)	(100,000)	(250,000)	(75,000)
1. Sale of receivables and distribution of $10,000 loss	70,000	(80,000)				4,500	3,500	2,000
	120,000	0	160,000	260,000	(125,000)	(95,500)	(246,500)	(73,000)
2. Sale of inventory and distribution of $120,000 loss	40,000		(160,000)			54,000	42,000	24,000
	160,000	0	0	260,000	(125,000)	(41,500)	(204,500)	(49,000)
3. Sale of plant assets and distribution of $200,000 loss	60,000			(260,000)		90,000	70,000	40,000
	220,000	0	0	0	(125,000)	(48,500)	(134,500)	(9,000)
4. Accrual of a $15,000 liability previously unrecorded					(15,000)	6,750	5,250	3,000
	220,000	0	0	0	(140,000)	(55,250)	(129,250)	(6,000)
5. Distribution of deficit of insolvent partner (Briscoe):						(55,250)		
(35/55 × $55,250)							35,159	
(20/55 × $55,250)								20,091
	220,000	0	0	0	(140,000)	0	(94,091)	14,091
6. Distribution of deficit of insolvent partner (Mitchell)							14,091	(14,091)
	220,000	0	0	0	(140,000)	0	(80,000)	0
7. Payment to outside creditors	(140,000)				140,000			
	80,000	0	0	0	0	0	(80,000)	0
8. Lump-sum payment to partner	(80,000)						80,000	0
Postliquidation balances	0	0	0	0	0	0	0	0

INSTALLMENT LIQUIDATION

Installment liquidation: occurs over an extended time period; partners receive interim (installment) distributions

In many instances the liquidation of a partnership is not accomplished in a short time period. When the sale of assets is expected to occur over several months, the partners may want to receive cash distributions prior to the completion of the liquidation. When distributions are made while liabilities are still outstanding or noncash assets are still owned, the process is called an **installment liquidation**. The accountant has the responsibility of determining the amount of distribution that can be prudently made while protecting the creditor's interests. It is possible that the accountant may determine there is not sufficient protection for the creditors and decline to make any distributions before the noncash assets are all sold and all creditors are paid. In this instance, the lump-sum liquidation discussed in the previous section would apply.

The task of managing a liquidation becomes substantially more involved when the liquidation occurs over a number of months. The ability to estimate the cash flows that will occur during the remaining life of the partnership may be less precise because the business may continue to operate through part of the liquidation. On the other hand, the cash receipts from liquidating assets may be greater when the liquidation takes place over a longer time period because the owners are able to avoid selling quickly. The accountant must take all these factors into consideration when determining whether it is prudent to make cash distributions to the partners before the sale of assets is completed.

The accountant must consider a number of issues when determining the amount of cash to be distributed to the partners when interim payments are to be made. For example, the accountant must ensure that sufficient cash is available to meet the expenses associated with the liquidation process and to pay current and prospective creditors. It may not be prudent to pay all the current creditors immediately, but cash assets are often set aside in a secure location. Payments to creditors can then be made in a timely manner. Having sufficient cash available to meet the current obligations may not be adequate if the liquidation is expected to occur over many months. As a result, the accountant should be conservative when estimating future cash flows. The approach often taken is to assume that the remaining noncash assets are worthless and no additional cash is forthcoming. This conservative approach will prevent the accountant from making a distribution that is not yet justified through the sale of assets. In addition, the accountant should assume that any deficits that occur in the capital accounts of the partners will not result in the partners making additional contributions to the partnership. These conservative assumptions will prevent the accountant from making a cash distribution to a partner and later potentially having to request that the partner contribute some of the distribution back to the partnership to cover a deficit. It is possible that a partner may not be able to make an additional contribution even if the partner received a distribution of partnership assets. Some partners invest all their life savings into a business and may be personally insolvent. A discussion of the risks of distributions to partners was presented earlier in the chapter in the section Partnership Liquidation Guidelines. All the issues described above should be included in a cash distribution plan approved by the partners prior to beginning the liquidation process.

Cash Distribution Plan

Cash distribution plan: document that outlines the order in which partners will receive cash during an installment liquidation

The **cash distribution plan** outlines the order in which partners will receive payments when cash becomes available. The plan does not guarantee the amount of cash that will be distributed to the partners, nor does it specify when such distributions will be made. It specifies only the order in which cash will be allocated if a distribution is made. The cash distribution plan focuses on the capital balances, the loans to and from the partners, and the residual profit and loss ratios that exist among the partners. It predetermines the relative ability of each partner's capital account to absorb losses without having the capital account drop into the deficit range.

EXAMPLE 8-4

Installment liquidation, all positive capital accounts Assume that the Briscoe, Johnson, and Mitchell partnership is going to be liquidated. The partners have prepared the following trial balance (book values and market values) on March 1, 2004, immediately prior to starting the liquidation. The market value of the partnership's net assets exceeds the outstanding liabilities, and all the partners have positive capital balances. The residual profit and loss ratios for the partners in the following examples for Briscoe, Johnson, and Mitchell are .45, .35, and .20, respectively. The partners anticipate that it will take approximately three months to liquidate the partnership's assets and close the business. They have asked that monthly cash distributions be made to the partners.

	Debit (Credit)	
	Book Value	Estimated Market Value
Cash	50,000	50,000
Receivables	80,000	70,000
Note Receivable, Mitchell	30,000	30,000
Inventory	60,000	55,000
Plant Assets	287,000	175,000
Liabilities	(125,510)	(125,510)
Note Payable, Johnson	(45,000)	(45,000)
Briscoe, Capital	(108,000)	
Johnson, Capital	(156,950)	
Mitchell, Capital	(71,540)	

Assume the following events occurred during the liquidation period:

1. March 13   Receivables are sold to a bank for their estimated market value, $70,000.
2. March 16   Inventory is sold for $43,000.
3. March 31   Liquidation expenses for the month are $13,000. Anticipated liquidation expenses for the remainder of the liquidation period are estimated to be $40,000.
4. April 22   Plant assets with a book value of $135,090 are sold for $147,490.
5. April 25   An unknown liability of $15,000 is discovered and recorded.
6. April 30   Liquidation expenses for the month are $25,000. Anticipated liquidation expenses for the remainder of the liquidation period are estimated to be $12,000.
7. May 15   The remainder of the plant assets are sold for $19,510.
8. May 27   All the partnership's creditors are paid in full.
9. May 31   Liquidation expenses for the month are $5,000.

Before a liquidation occurs, the cash distribution plan should be prepared and presented to the partners. Assume that, in the partnership agreement, all the partners have waived their rights to have a superior claim when there is a partnership loan.

    Illustration 8-4 presents the cash distribution plan for the current example. In Illustration 8-4 a new concept, loss absorption power, is introduced. **Loss absorption power** is the measure of the amount of partnership expenses and losses that would have to occur during liquidation to reduce a partner's capital account to zero. Because each partner normally must absorb a pro rata share of liquidation expenses and losses using his/her residual profit and loss percentage, the capital reduction resulting from expenses and losses may be expressed as follows:

Loss absorption power: the amount of partnership expenses and losses that would have to occur to reduce a partner's capital account balance to zero

$$\text{(Partner capital balance reduction)} = \text{(Partner residual profit and loss percentage)} \times \text{(Expense or loss incurred)}$$

Following from this, the total amount of expense or loss that would eliminate a partner's capital account (loss absorption power) is:

$$\text{(Loss absorption power)} = \text{(Total partner capital balance)} \Big/ \text{(Partner residual profit and loss percentage)}$$

For example, Briscoe's capital account balance is $108,000 when the liquidation starts. If the partnership incurs liquidation expenses and losses equal to $240,000, Briscoe's capital

ILLUSTRATION 8-4
Cash Distribution Plan for the Briscoe, Johnson, and Mitchell Partnership

A	B	C	D	E
		Loss Absorption Power: Column A/Column B		
Net Capital and Loan Balance*	Divide by Profit and Loss Ratio	Briscoe (45%)	Johnson (35%)	Mitchell (20%)
$108,000	/.45	240,000		
$201,950	/.35		577,000	
$41,540	/.20			207,700
Distributions:				
Distribution # 1 to Johnson:				
($117,950)	/.35	0	(337,000)	0
		240,000	240,000	207,700
Distribution # 2 to Briscoe and Johnson:				
($14,535)	/.45	(32,300)		
($11,305)	/.35		(32,300)	0
		207,700	207,700	207,700
Any additional allocation is divided .45, .35, and .20				

* Note that the initial capital balances have been adjusted to reflect outstanding loans to (from) partners. The concept of the right of offset has been applied to all partner loans.

account will decrease to a $0 balance because Briscoe's $108,000 capital balance divided by his 45-percent share of expenses and losses equals $240,000.

After distribution #1 and #2 are complete, the balances in the capital accounts of the three partners are in the residual profit and loss sharing ratios, as illustrated in the T-accounts and supporting calculations below.

Briscoe, Capital			**Johnson, Capital**			**Mitchell, Capital**	
	108,000			201,950			41,540
		#1 117,950					
				84,000			
#2 14,535		#2 11,305					
	93,465			72,695			41,540

Each partner's percentage of total capital is now calculated:

	Capital	*Percent of Total Capital*
Briscoe	$93,465	93,465/207,700 = 45%
Johnson	72,695	72,695/207,700 = 35%
Mitchell	41,540	41,540/207,700 = 20%
Total	207,700	

The relative size of the loss absorption power indicates the degree of expenses and losses the partnership would have to incur for that particular partner's capital account to reach a $0 balance. For example, Briscoe's capital account balance is $108,000 when the liquidation starts. If the partnership incurs liquidation expenses and losses equal to $240,000, Briscoe's capital account will decrease to a $0 balance because Briscoe's 45 percent interest in the $240,000 loss is $108,000. The relative size of the loss absorption power indicates the degree of risk the accountant incurs if a cash distribution is made to the partner. Johnson represents the lowest risk to the accountant for a cash distribution because the partnership would have to incur the greatest amount of expenses and losses for the capital account to reach a $0 balance. Briscoe represents the next-lowest risk, and Mitchell represents the highest risk with regard to making a cash distribution. The calculation of the loss absorption power does not indicate that a distribution should be made to the partners. It indicates only the manner in which a distribution should be allocated if it is appropriate to make a distribution.

Following the calculation of the loss absorption power is an allocation schedule for cash distributions. The first allocation is based on the difference between the highest loss absorption power (Johnson) and the next-highest loss absorption power (Briscoe). Keep in mind that the loss absorption power is an indication of the relative risk of making a distribution to a particular partner. When the loss absorption power for two partners becomes equal, a distribution to the partners would be viewed as equally risky by the accountant because the probability of each partner's capital account reaching a $0 balance is the same. Thus, the first cash allocation will be made to Johnson until his loss absorption power becomes equal to Briscoe's loss absorption power. The amount of the cash allocation is not the $337,000 by which the two loss absorption powers differ because the loss absorption power is the net investment in the partnership divided by the partner's residual profit and loss ratio. Thus, for every dollar that Johnson's capital account decreases as a result of a $1 cash distribution, the loss absorption power decreases by $2.86 ($1/.35). The amount of cash that may be initially allocated to Johnson is the change in the loss absorption power ($337,000) times the respective profit and loss ratio (.35), or $117,950. The distribution of the $117,950 does not have to occur at one time. The cash distribution plan indicates only that the first $117,950 of cash distributed will be allocated to Johnson. It does not indicate how many distributions will occur before this allocation is completed.

After the first $117,950 of the cash distributed to the partners has been allocated to Johnson, Johnson's and Briscoe's loss absorption power are equal and both are greater than Mitchell's loss absorption power. The second allocation is based on the $32,300 by which Johnson's and Briscoe's loss absorption power exceeds Mitchell's. The total amount of this allocation is $25,840 ($32,300 × .80), the change in the loss absorption powers times the sum of the residual profit and loss ratios. The .80 factors is used here because it is the sum of the Johnson plus Briscoe (.35 + .45) profit and loss ratios. Both profit and loss ratios must be considered because Johnson and Briscoe each receive a cash allocation. If the amount of cash distributed to Johnson and Briscoe is less than $25,840, the cash is allocated proportionately based on the partners' relative profit and loss ratios, that is, .35/.80 and .45/.80.

Once the loss absorption powers of all partners become equal, they are all viewed as equally risky when making cash distributions. Any future allocations will be made using the residual profit and loss ratios for all three partners.

Statement of Realization and Liquidation

Illustration 8-5 presents the Statement of Realization and Liquidation for the events in the current example. The additional detail in the illustration pertains to the monthly cash payment to the partners as part of the installment liquidation.

The statement of realization and liquidation begins with the trial balance when the liquidation starts, just as it did with a lump-sum liquidation. The first issue addressed is offsetting the note receivable and the note payable against the respective partners' capital accounts. The offsetting of the note receivable against Mitchell's capital account has the same impact as the collection of the note and a distribution of capital to Mitchell. The

ILLUSTRATION 8-5
Statement of Realization and Liquidation for the Installment Liquidation of the Briscoe, Johnson, and Mitchell Partnership

	Cash	Receivables	Note Receivable, Mitchell	Inventory	Plant Assets	Liabilities	Note Payable, Johnson	Briscoe, Capital (.45)	Johnson, Capital (.35)	Mitchell, Capital (.20)
Preliquidation balances, March 1	50,000	80,000	30,000	60,000	287,000	(125,510)	(45,000)	(108,000)	(156,950)	(71,540)
March, 2004:										
1. Offset Mitchell's Note Receivable and Johnson's Note Payable against the capital accounts			(30,000)				45,000		(45,000)	30,000
	50,000	80,000	0	60,000	287,000	(125,510)	0	(108,000)	(201,950)	(41,540)
2. Sale of receivables and distribution of $10,000 loss	70,000	(80,000)						4,500	3,500	2,000
	120,000	0		60,000	287,000	(125,510)		(103,500)	(198,450)	(39,540)
3. Sale of inventory and distribution of $17,000 loss	43,000			(60,000)				7,650	5,950	3,400
	163,000	0	0	0	287,000	(125,510)	0	(95,850)	(192,500)	(36,140)
4. Payment of $13,000 of liquidation expenses	(13,000)							5,850	4,550	2,600
	150,000	0	0	0	287,000	(125,510)	0	(90,000)	(187,950)	(33,540)
April, 2004:										
5. Sale of plant assets (book value $135,090 and distribution of $12,400 gain)	147,490				(135,090)			(5,580)	(4,340)	(2,480)
	297,490				151,910	(125,510)		(95,580)	(192,290)	(36,020)
6. Discovery of a $15,000 liability						(15,000)		6,750	5,250	3,000
	297,490	0	0	0	151,910	(140,510)	0	(88,830)	(187,040)	(33,020)
7. Payment of $25,000 of liquidation expenses	(25,000)							11,250	8,750	5,000
	272,490	0	0	0	151,910	(140,510)	0	(77,580)	(178,290)	(28,020)
8. Distribution of $119,980 to partners	(119,980)							1,142	118,838	
	152,510	0	0	0	151,910	(140,510)	0	(76,438)	(59,452)	(28,020)

(Continued)

ILLUSTRATION 8-5 *Continued*

May, 2004:

	Cash		Plant Assets	Liabilities			
9. Sale of plant assets (book value $151,910 and distribution of $132,400 loss)	19,510	0	(151,910)	0	59,580	46,340	26,480
	172,020	0	0	0	(16,858)	(13,112)	(1,540)
10. Payment to outside creditors	(140,510)	0	0	140,510			
	31,510	0	0	0	(16,858)	(13,112)	(1,540)
11. Payment of $5,000 of liquidation expenses	(5,000)	0	0	0	2,250	1,750	1,000
	26,510	0	0	0	(14,608)	(11,362)	(540)
12. Distribution of $26,510 to partners	(26,510)	0	0	0	(14,608)	(11,362)	(540)
Postliquidation balances, May 31	0	0	0	0	0	0	0

offsetting of the note payable against Johnson's capital account is undertaken because the partners agreed to forgo priority claims for loans to the partnership.

The two transactions that occur in March, the sale of accounts receivable and the sale of inventory, both result in the recognition of losses. The losses are allocated to the partners' capital accounts using the residual profit and loss ratios. The payment of liquidation expenses in March is also allocated directly to the partners' capital accounts because there are no income statement accounts.

March 31 is the first potential date for a cash distribution. The cash balance at this date is $150,000. The accountant should retain sufficient cash to pay the creditor's claims ($125,510) and the estimated remaining liquidation expenses ($40,000). Because the sum of the liabilities and estimated remaining liquidation expenses exceeds the current cash available, there is no cash distribution to the partners in March. Recall that the preparation of a cash distribution plan does not guarantee that cash will be distributed to the partners at any particular point in time. It indicates only how cash will be allocated when it becomes safe to distribute cash to partners.

The plant assets sold during April result in the recognition of a $12,400 gain that is allocated to the partners' capital accounts. In addition, the accountant becomes aware of a liability that was previously unrecognized. This amount is also allocated to the capital accounts, and the partners' equity is reduced. Liquidation expenses of $25,000 are recognized and allocated to the capital accounts.

April 30 is the second potential date for a cash distribution to the partners. The cash balance at this date is $272,490. The total liabilities are $140,510, and the estimated remaining liquidation expenses are $12,000. As a result, it is possible to make a $119,980 cash distribution to the partners and still meet the expected cash disbursements during the remainder of the liquidation process. After the amount of the distribution is determined, the cash distribution plan is used to allocate the distribution among the partners. Illustration 8-6 presents the April 30 cash distribution allocation.

Based on the cash distribution plan prepared previously, Johnson receives the first allocation of the cash to be distributed. This $117,950 allocation reduces the amount of cash available for an additional allocation to $2,030. The cash distribution plan indicates that the next $25,840 is to be divided proportionately between Briscoe and Johnson. The second step results in Briscoe being allocated $1,142 and Johnson being allocated an additional $888. As a result, Briscoe receives a total allocation from the first cash distribution of $1,142 and Johnson receives a total allocation of $118,838. Notice that the entire $1,142 is removed from Briscoe's capital account but only $73,838 is removed from Johnson's capital account. The remaining $45,000 is allocated to pay the note payable to Johnson.

ILLUSTRATION 8-6
Allocation of April Cash Distribution to Briscoe and Johnson

	Totals	Briscoe	Johnson
Total to be distributed	119,980		
First allocation	(117,950)		(117,950)
Remainder	2,030		
Second allocation			
(.45/.8) $2,030	(1,142)	(1,142)	
(.35/.8) $2,030	(888)		(888)
Remainder	0		
Total allocated		(1,142)	(118,838)

ILLUSTRATION 8-7
Allocation of May Cash Distribution to Briscoe, Johnson, and Mitchell

	Totals	Briscoe	Johnson	Mitchell
Total to be distributed	26,510			
Second allocation continued				
(.45/.8) × ($25,840 − $2,030)	(13,393)	(13,393)		
(.35/.8) × ($25,840 − $2,030)	(10,417)		(10,417)	
Remainder	2,700			
Third allocation				
$2,700 × .45	(1,215)	(1,215)		
$2,700 × .35	(945)		(945)	
$2,700 × .20	(540)			(540)
Remainder	0			
Total allocated		(14,608)	(11,362)	(540)

The allocation to the note payable has the same impact on the net capital positions of the partners, but it is common to remove the note payable with the first cash allocation.

The partnership's creditors are paid in May, and $5,000 additional liquidation expense is incurred. As a result, there is an additional $26,510 to be distributed to the partners. This amount exactly equals the sum of the partners' capital balances. Illustration 8-7 is presented to verify the allocation of the cash.

The first allocation is to Briscoe and Johnson. This is the remainder of the second allocation presented in Illustration 8-4. The cash distributed at the end of April results in the first allocation being made to Johnson and part of the second allocation made to Briscoe and Johnson. The allocation presented in Illustration 8-7 starts with the completion of the second allocation. The amount assigned to Briscoe and Johnson is the $23,810 of the second allocation not assigned previously. The remainder of the cash distributed ($2,700) is allocated proportionately to the residual profit and loss ratios among the partners because each of the partners is now equally risky with regard to cash distributions. In this instance, the partnership is fully liquidated; however, it is possible that the allocation to all the partners could occur well before the liquidation is completed.

Schedule of Safe Payments

While the cash distribution plan provides the accountant with an organized approach to making cash payments to partners during a liquidation, there are two instances when complications arise in the preparation of a cash distribution plan. The first instance is when one or more partners have a deficit net position before the liquidation starts. The existence of a deficit in a partner's capital account will result in a reallocation of capital among the partners if the partner with the deficit cannot or will not make an additional contributions to the partnership. As a result, the cash distribution plan cannot be prepared before the partner's deficit is allocated to the partners with positive capital balances. After the allocation of the partner's deficit is completed, the cash distribution plan can be prepared unless the second instance exists. The second instance is when the partners' profit residual ratios are different from the partners' loss residual ratios. The difficulty created is that any gains will increase the partners' capital accounts at one rate, while losses and expenses will decrease the capital accounts at a different rate. Thus, the future loss absorption potential cannot be predicted because every time a gain occurs during the liquidation process, the relative strengths of the partners will change. As a result, it is not possible to estimate the relative risk resulting from making a cash distribution to one partner versus another.

When the cash distribution plan does not provide a usable foundation for allocated periodic cash payments to the partners, a conservative approach should be taken. The most conservative alternative is to consider how the cash would be distributed if all the remaining noncash assets of the partnership were worthless and if any partners who have a deficit capital balance would be unable to make an additional contributions to the partnership. The allocation of the loss and the subsequent allocation of the hypothetical deficit that may be created in the partners' capital accounts would provide an indication of the least risky partner for a cash allocation. The schedule prepared to present this information is often titled a **Schedule of Safe Payments**. The Schedule of Safe Payments is prepared in conjunction with a Statement of Realization and Liquidation for an installment liquidation. It presents the manner in which cash is to be allocated for each cash distribution date. Illustration 8-8 presents the Schedule of Safe Payments at each of the cash distribution dates presented in the installment liquidation example in Illustration 8-5.

The March Schedule of Safe payments would be prepared at the end of March to determine if a cash distribution is possible and, if so, who should receive the distribution. The information presented in Illustration 8-8 indicates that there is not sufficient cash to make a distribution to the partners at the end of March. This conclusion is reached after assuming that the remaining noncash assets will prove to be worthless and the hypothetical loss is allocated to the partners based on their respective residual profit and loss ratios. After the allocation of the losses from plant assets has been made, the sum of the remaining liabilities and estimated liquidation expenses is greater than the available cash in the partnership. Given that a cash distribution cannot be made to the partners, there is no need to allocate deficits in some capital accounts to the partner with a positive capital balance. If sufficient cash is available to make a distribution to the partners, any deficit capital accounts must be allocated to the partner(s) with a positive capital balance to determine which partner is least risky for a distribution.

The Statement of Realization and Liquidation presented in Illustration 8-5 indicates that the Briscoe, Johnson, and Mitchell partnership has $272,490 of cash available at the end of April. The Schedule of Safe Payments presented in Illustration 8-8 indicates that $151,910 of noncash assets remains in the partnership. After this amount and the estimated $12,000 of remaining liquidation expenses are allocated to the partners, Mitchell has a deficit capital balance. Mitchell's deficit is allocated to the remaining partners based on their respective residual profit and loss ratios (45/80 for Briscoe and 35/80 for Johnson). After this allocation is completed, Mitchell has a $0 capital balance, while Briscoe and Johnson both have positive capital balances. It is possible that the allocation could create a deficit capital position for one or more additional partners. The additional deficit would also be allocated to the remaining partner(s) with a positive capital balance. This process continues until all the partners have either a $0 capital balance or a positive capital balance. The conclusion drawn from the April Schedule of Safe Payments is that $1,142 should be distributed to Briscoe and $118,838 should be distributed to Johnson. This is the same conclusion reached when the cash distribution plan was used previously. In the simple case where profit and loss residuals are the same, the Schedule of Safe Payments will always yield the same results as the cash distribution plan.

The final cash distribution date is May 31. Illustration 8-5 indicates that $26,510 of cash remains after all the partnership's creditors and all liquidations expenses have been paid. Each of the partners in the current example has a positive capital balance, and the sum of the capital accounts exactly equals the cash remaining to be distributed. The sum of the capital accounts will always equal the remaining cash balance at the end of the liquidation.

Schedule of Safe Payments: outlines how a cash distribution to partners would be allocated assuming that all remaining noncash assets are worthless and that partners are not capable of making additional capital contributions to eliminate a capital deficit

ILLUSTRATION 8-8
Schedule of Safe Payments for the Installment Liquidation of the Briscoe, Johnson, and Mitchell Partnership*

	Cash	Plant Assets	Liabilities	Briscoe, Capital (.45)	Johnson, Capital (.35)	Mitchell, Capital (.20)
Balances at date of March cash distribution	150,000	287,000	(125,510)	(90,000)	(187,950)	(33,540)
1. Allocation of estimated losses if remaining assets are worthless		(287,000)		129,150	100,450	57,400
	150,000	0	(125,510)	39,150	(87,500)	23,860
2. Estimated remaining liquidation expenses	(40,000)			18,000	14,000	8,000
	110,000	0	(125,510)	57,150	(73,500)	31,860
3. Allocation of cash to pay liabilities	(125,510)		125,510			
Cash remaining for distribution to partners	(15,510)	0	0	57,150	(73,500)	31,860
Balances at date of April cash distribution	272,490	151,910	(140,510)	(77,580)	(178,290)	(28,020)
4. Allocation of estimated losses if remaining assets are worthless		(151,910)		68,359	53,169	30,382
	272,490	0	(140,510)	(9,221)	(125,121)	2,362
5. Estimated remaining liquidation expenses	(12,000)			5,400	4,200	2,400
	260,490	0	(140,510)	(3,821)	(120,921)	4,762
6. Allocation of cash to pay liabilities	(140,510)		140,510			
Cash remaining for distribution to partners	119,980	0	0	(3,821)	(120,921)	4,762
7. Allocation of Mitchell's capital deficit						(4,762)
$4,762 \times (.45/.8)$				2,679		
$4,762 \times (.35/.8)$					2,083	
	119,980	0	0	(1,142)	(118,838)	0
April cash allocation to Briscoe and Johnson	(119,980)			1,142	118,838	
	0	0	0	0	0	0
Balances at date of May cash distribution	26,510	0	0	(14,608)	(11,362)	(540)
8. May cash allocation to Briscoe, Johnson, and Mitchell	(26,510)			14,608	11,362	540
	0	0	0	0	0	0

* Note that the initial capital balances have been adjusted to reflect outstanding loans to (from) partners. The concept of the right of offset has been applied to all partner loans.

SUMMARY

In summary, this chapter covered the procedures that the accountant generally uses to help oversee a partnership's liquidation. Some partnership liquidations are relatively simple and can be completed in a short period of time. In such cases the partners receive no distributions until all assets have been sold and all liabilities paid, and a single, lump-sum distribution is made. These cases are the most simple and were covered first.

Installment liquidations were covered next. These situations arise when the liquidation takes an extended period of time to complete and the partners wish to receive interim cash distributions. The cash distribution plan is prepared prior to the liquidation to ensure that the partners understand the order of the distributions that must be followed. The Statement of Realization and Liquidation is then prepared to recognize the events that occur during the liquidation process (sale of assets, payment of liabilities, incurrence of expenses, distributions to partners).

Finally, the Schedule of Safe Payments is prepared to allocate distributions to partners for special circumstances when it is not possible to use a cash distribution plan. In most instances, the cash distribution plan and the Schedule of Safe Payments yield the same distribution to partners.

The chapter presented several tools that can be used to ensure an orderly liquidation process. One tool, the cash dis- tribution plan, is prepared before the liquidation begins to enable the accountant to educate the partners with regard to the manner in which cash will be allocated when available. The Statement of Realization and Liquidation was presented as a tool used to track the liquidation process. The Schedule of Safe Payments was illustrated as a secondary tool used when determining cash allocation when distributions are made.

QUESTIONS

8-1. Compare and contrast partnership dissolution, termina- tion, and liquidation.

8-2. What is the primary duty of the accountant in a partner- ship liquidation?

8-3. What is the order of priority for claims against a part- nership's assets?

8-4. What is the order of priority for claims against an indi- vidual partner's personal assets?

8-5. Can a partner's personal creditor force a partnership into bankruptcy? Why or why not?

8-6. Richard Stone, Paul Samos, and Julia Smith are part- ners. Richard has had some personal financial problems. Paul and Julia have just been informed that Richard's creditors are going to force payment of his outstanding debts from the partnership's assets. Paul and Julia want to know if the creditors can do this, because the partner- ship's liquidity is limited. Prepare a memo responding to the concerns of these partners.

8-7. How is the right of offset used to manage a partnership liquidation?

8-8. Terri Miller and Jerri Scott have been partners for a num- ber of years. The partnership has recently struggled and is liquidating. Terri has loaned $25,000 to the partnership over the past two years. She was upset when informed that the loan would not be repaid prior to the distribution of capital to the partners. Prepare a memo to Terri explaining why the accountant may have taken such a position.

8-9. Why are residual profit and loss ratios typically used to allocate gains and losses that may result during a part- nership liquidation?

8-10. Mary Dascher is the accountant overseeing a partnership liquidation. The partnership liquidation has been under way for two months and is expected to take several addi- tional months to complete. The partners requested monthly cash distributions, but none have been made. They are upset with Mary and have asked for an expla- nation because there is $40,000 of cash in the partner- ship's bank account. Prepare a memo to the partners outlining some of the reasons Mary may have decided to not distribute cash yet.

8-11. Explain the difference between a lump-sum liquidation and an installment liquidation.

8-12. A liquidation generally ends with cash and capital accounts remaining and the cash equaling the net of the capital account balances. Why does this equality always occur?

8-13. The Baker, Johnson, and Edmunds partnership is going through liquidation. Johnson's capital account had a deficit as a result of losses from the sale of assets. Johnson has been unwilling to make additional contri- butions to the partnership. A meeting was scheduled with all the partners to discuss the issue. Johnson said that he worked harder than all the other partners and he is insulted that he would be asked to make additional contributions to a failing business. In addition, he is the partner with the least financial ability to make such a payment. Explain to Johnson why it is his responsibility to make the additional contribution.

8-14. Why are gains and losses from the sale of assets during a partnership liquidation adjusted directly to the capital accounts?

8-15. Why does the settlement of a partnership debt for less than face value increase the capital accounts?

8-16. Compare and contrast a Statement of Realization and Liquidation with the partnership's regular financial records.

8-17. Why is it essential to allocate a partner's capital account deficit to other partners with positive capital account bal- ances if the partner with the deficit capital account can- not make an additional capital contribution?

8-18. Joan Hubbuch, Jill Fries, and Camellia Anderson are liq- uidating their partnership. Camellia's capital account became negative after large losses resulted from the sale of inventory. Camellia is personally insolvent and is unable to make an additional capital contribution to eliminate the deficit. Joan and Jill became upset when informed that they would have to absorb Camellia's capital account deficit. Jill stated that it is unfair that she will not receive the full amount of her capital just because Camellia has a negative capital account. Explain to Joan and Jill how the capital account deficit may have occurred and why it is essential that they cover the deficit if Camellia cannot make a contribution.

8-19. Jeff Williams and Mike Peters are liquidating their partnership. The partners have heard that there are two types of liquidations—lump-sum and installment. The two methods are unfamiliar to the partners. Prepare a memo outlining the advantages and disadvantages of each type of liquidation to the partners.

8-20. Is it more difficult to estimate the cash flows that may result in an installment liquidation than in a lump-sum liquidation?

8-21. Why might partners ultimately receive more cash in an installment liquidation than in a lump-sum liquidation?

8-22. Discuss the items that the accountant should consider when determining whether a cash distribution should be made during an installment liquidation.

8-23. You are assisting in the liquidation of a partnership. The manager overseeing the liquidation has prepared a cash distribution plan to be approved by the partners. One of the partners has indicated that he sees where the numbers come from but he does not understand the purpose of the cash distribution plan. Prepare a memo to the partner clarifying his misunderstanding.

8-24. Explain the meaning of the loss absorption power.

8-25. Charles Packard, Elaine Mitchell, and Sharon Spencer are liquidating their partnership. The accountant has provided the partners with a cash distribution plan. Elaine has asked a question regarding the loss absorption power item. She is not a businessperson and does not understand what the loss absorption power means. Prepare a memo to Elaine to help her understand the purpose of this item.

8-26. Does the existence of four different allocation levels in the cash distribution plan mean that there will be four cash distributions to the partners? Why or why not?

8-27. Explain the two instances in which it is not possible to prepare a cash distribution plan to guide the allocation of cash to partners during an installment liquidation.

8-28. Explain why a schedule of safe payments can be used when a cash distribution plan is not appropriate.

MULTIPLE CHOICE

8-1. With regard to claims against individual partners' assets, which of the following has the first priority?

   a. Other partners if the partner in question has a deficit capital account

   b. Personal creditors

   c. Partnership creditors if the creditor's claim is not fully paid from the partnership's assets

   d. The claim that is for the largest dollar amount

8-2. Which of the following is not a feature of a partnership installment liquidation?

   a. Cash may be distributed to partners before all liabilities have been paid

   b. The process requires the accountant to periodically estimate remaining liquidation expenses

   c. The process occurs over an extended period of time

   d. The process always results in a single cash payment to partners

8-3. Which of the following is not a feature of a Statement of Realization and Liquidation?

   a. The statement includes all accounts in the accounting records of the partnership

   b. Gains and losses are posted directly to capital accounts

   c. Profit and loss residual ratios are used to allocate gains and losses to partner capital accounts

   d. The statement contains the same basic information as journal entries

8-4. Which of the following statements describes what type of balance can exist in partner capital accounts on a Statement of Realization and Liquidation?

   a. Capital account balances can only be positive

   b. Capital account balances that are negative before the liquidation process begins can be negative, but other capital accounts must remain positive

   c. Capital account balances can be positive or negative

   d. Capital accounts will all be negative when the liquidation process begins

8-5. A partnership liquidation that results in periodic payments to partners is which of the following?

   a. Lump-sum liquidation

   b. Installment liquidation

   c. Statement of Cash Flows

   d. Schedule of Safe Payments

8-6. The accountant must do which of the following during an installment liquidation?

   a. Distribute assets to the partners as quickly as possible

   b. Optimistically estimate the amount of cash that will be received through the sale of long-term assets

   c. Only consider liquidation expenses as incurred

d. Protect the claims of creditors to maximize the likelihood that creditors are paid

8-7. Which of the following is the calculation of the loss absorption power?

a. Cash and accounts receivable account balances / profit and loss residual ratio

b. Capital account balance / profit and loss residual ratio

c. Profit and loss residual ratio / capital account balance

d. Profit and loss residual ratio / long-term asset book value

8-8. What is the purpose of the cash distribution plan?

a. To guarantee the partners of the amount of cash to be distributed

b. To show partners the amount of cash that will be available for distribution

c. To inform the partners of how cash will be distributed if any distributions occur

d. To show the creditors the amount of cash in the company

8-9. Assume that Sabol, Tinker, and Wright are liquidating their partnership. They share profits and losses in a 35 percent,

40-percent, and 25-percent ratio. The accountant has determined that the loss absorption power is $275,000, $400,000, and $315,000 for Sabol, Tinker, and Wright, respectively. If $90,000 is about to be distributed, how much will each partner receive?

	Sabol	Tinker	Wright
a.	$10,500	$62,000	$17,500
b.	$30,000	$30,000	$30,000
c.	$0	$85,000	$5,000
d.	$31,500	$36,000	$22,500

8-10. The Schedule of Safe Payments makes which of the following assumption(s)?

a. It assumes that assets will be liquidated for their book values

b. It assumes that creditors will make concessions to the partnership

c. It assumes that long-term assets are worthless

d. It assumes that future liquidation expenses will be minimal

EXERCISES

EXERCISE 8-1 The Davis and Miller partnership started the liquidation process on April 30, 2004. The partners have closed the books and presented the following trial balance.

Cash	25,600
Receivables	10,250
Inventory	60,700
Plant Assets (net)	168,400
Liabilities	(90,000)
Davis, capital (35%)	(65,000)
Miller, capital (65%)	(109,950)

The partners agreed that each could wait to receive cash until the liquidation is completed. The following events take place during the liquidation.

1. Receivables of $9,550 are collected. The remainder are deemed uncollectible.
2. The inventory is sold for $75,800.
3. Plant assets are sold for $150,000.
4. The liabilities are fully paid.

5. Liquidation expenses of $6,000 are incurred.

6. All remaining assets are distributed to the partners.

Required:

A. Prepare the partnership's Statement of Realization and Liquidation.

B. Sales of assets such as inventory typically result in losses during the liquidation process. Explain why a gain may have been recognized on the sale of inventory in the current circumstance.

EXERCISE 8-2   Denise Flynn, Gail Patterson, and Susan Summer have been partners for many years. Denise is having health problems, so the partnership is liquidating. The liquidation process is planned to take place during September, when inventory levels are typically low. The following trial balance is prepared on August 31, 2004, the financial statement date.

Cash	150,900
Receivables	122,800
Inventory	217,600
Plant Assets (net)	450,400
Current Liabilities	(240,000)
Long-Term Debt	(405,000)
Flynn, capital (20%)	(40,000)
Patterson, capital (35%)	(111,000)
Summer, capital (45%)	(145,700)

The following events take place during the liquidation.

1. The receivables are factored to the bank without recourse. The proceeds of this sale are $107,800.

2. The inventory is sold for $175,000.

3. Plant assets are sold for $270,000.

4. The liabilities are fully paid.

5. Liquidation expenses of $32,000 are incurred.

6. All remaining assets were distributed to the partners.

The following information is available for the personal assets (excluding interest in the partnership) and liabilities of the partners at August 31, 2004.

	Assets	*Liabilities*
Flynn	$250,000	$180,000
Patterson	360,000	225,000
Summer	210,000	240,000

Required:

A. Prepare the partnership's Statement of Realization and Liquidation, assuming that a partner with a deficit capital account balance will make an additional contribution if possible.

B. Prepare the partnership's Statement of Realization and Liquidation, assuming that a partner with a deficit capital account balance will not make an additional contribution.

EXERCISE 8-3   Tom, Ben, and Jeri have been partners for about 10 years. The business originally had modest success, but the owners have had difficulty attracting business recently. As a result, the partners have decided that liquidating the partnership is in everyone's best interest. The trial balance below was prepared the day before the partners met with the accountant who is going to oversee the liquidation.

Cash	68,400
Receivables	90,500
Notes Receivable (Tom)	30,000
Inventory	278,000
Plant Assets (net)	680,000
Current Liabilities	(350,000)
Notes Payable (Ben)	(220,000)

Tom, capital (30%)	(156,000)
Ben, capital (25%)	(177,000)
Jeri, capital (45%)	(243,900)

Required:
Prepare a cash distribution plan outlining the way cash will be allocated during the liquidation.

EXERCISE 8-4   Patty Griffin, Irwin Redding, and Martin Young are liquidating their partnership. The financial records are closed and the income allocated to the capital accounts on March 1, 2004. The following trial balance was prepared at the beginning of the liquidation process.

Cash	45,000
Receivables	60,000
Inventory	124,000
Plant Assets (net)	190,000
Current Liabilities	(110,000)
Griffin, capital (45%)	(144,000)
Redding, capital (30%)	(72,000)
Young, capital (25%)	(93,000)

The accountant prepared the following cash distribution plan based on the above trial balance.

Cash Distribution Plan for the Griffin, Redding, and Young Partnership

	Griffin (45%)	Redding (30%)	Young (25%)
Capital balance	144,000	72,000	93,000
Loss absorption power:			
$144,000/.45	320,000		
$72,000/.30		240,000	
$93,000/.25			372,000
Allocation # 1:			
Young $13,000/.35	0	0	(52,000)
Adjusted loss absorption power	320,000	240,000	320,000
Allocation # 2:			
Griffin $36,000/.45			
Young $20,000/.25	(80,000)	0	(80,000)
Adjusted loss absorption power	240,000	240,000	240,000

Any additional allocation is divided .45, .30, and .25

The partners agreed that the liquidation would probably take three months to complete and that the liquidation expenses are estimated at $5,000 for March, $15,000 for April, and $7,000 for May. The following events occur during the liquidation.

1.	March 8	Receivables are sold to a bank for $50,000.
2.	March 20	Inventory is sold for $75,000.
3.	March 31	Liquidation expenses for the month are $4,500.
4.	April 15	Plant assets with a book value of $90,000 are sold for $70,000.
5.	April 30	Liquidation expenses for the month are $18,000.
6.	May 7	The remainder of the plant assets are sold for $60,000.
7.	May 22	All of the partnership's creditors are paid in full.
8.	May 31	Liquidation expenses for the month are $9,000.

Required:
Prepare a Statement of Realization and Liquidation for the Griffin, Redding, and Young partnership.

EXERCISE 8-5   Peter Mintz, Ruth Oliver, and Steve Smith are starting to have business difficulties and have decided to liquidate their partnership. The financial records are closed and the income allocated to the capital accounts on December 31, 2004. The following trial balance was prepared at the beginning of the liquidation process.

Cash	80,000
Receivables	120,000
Inventory	245,000
Notes Receivable (Mintz)	50,000
Plant Assets (net)	520,000
Current Liabilities	(200,000)
Notes Payable (Oliver)	(30,000)
Mintz, capital (60%)	(550,000)
Oliver, capital (15%)	(40,000)
Smith, capital (25%)	(195,000)

The partners have discussed the liquidation process with the accountant and have estimated that the liquidation would probably take three months to complete and that the liquidation expenses would be approximately $18,000 in January, $30,000 in February, and $12,000 in March. The following events occur during the liquidation.

1.	January 4	Receivables are sold to a bank for $110,000.
2.	January 17	Inventory is sold for $185,000.
3.	January 31	Liquidation expenses for the month are $15,000.
4.	February 5	Plant assets with a book value of $230,000 are sold for $180,000.
5.	February 29	Liquidation expenses for the month are $38,000.
6.	March 10	The remainder of the plant assets are sold for $160,000.
7.	March 27	All the partnership's creditors (excluding partners) are paid in full.
8.	March 31	Liquidation expenses for the month are $10,000.

Required:
Prepare a Statement of Realization and Liquidation and supporting Schedules of Safe Payments for the Mintz, Oliver, and Smith partnership.

EXERCISE 8-6   The partners of the Boatsman, Jensen, and Williams partnership have decided that they should liquidate the business before being forced into bankruptcy. The financial records of the partnership are closed, and the loss for the period is allocated to the capital accounts on May 31, 2004. The following trial balance was prepared at the beginning of the liquidation.

Cash	30,000
Receivables	70,000
Inventory	160,000
Plant Assets (net)	240,000
Current Liabilities	(180,000)
Boatsman, capital (40%)	(80,000)
Jensen, capital (45%)	(100,000)
Williams, capital (15%)	(140,000)

The accountant overseeing the process has a great deal of experience in partnership liquidations. She has estimated that the liquidation would probably take three months to complete and that the liquidation expenses would be approximately $5,000 in June, $12,000 in July, and $8,000 in August. The following events occur during the liquidation.

1.	June 4	Receivables are sold to a bank for $40,000.
2.	June 17	Inventory is sold for $65,000.

3.	June 31	Liquidation expenses for the month are $6,000.
4.	July 5	Plant assets with a book value of $110,000 are sold for $85,000.
5.	July 29	Liquidation expenses for the month are $10,000.
6.	August 10	The remainder of the plant assets are sold for $95,000.
7.	August 27	All the partnership's creditors are paid in full.
8.	August 31	Liquidation expenses for the month are $8,000.

Required:
Prepare a Statement of Realization and Liquidation and supporting Schedules of Safe Payments for the Boatsman, Jensen, and Williams partnership. Assume that no partner is capable of making a contribution if a capital account deficit exists.

EXERCISE 8-7   David Baker, Shannon Rickles, and Jeff Yount have decided to liquidate their partnership. The liquidation begins on September 30, 2004, and will continue for approximately three months. The income statement accounts are closed and the income allocated to the capital accounts when the liquidation begins. The following trial balance was prepared immediately after the income statement accounts are closed.

Cash	38,700
Receivables	55,200
Inventory	190,000
Notes Receivable (Baker)	120,000
Plant Assets (net)	410,000
Current Liabilities	(200,000)
Notes Payable (Rickles)	(250,000)
Baker, capital (40%)	(160,300)
Rickles, capital (32%)	(100,000)
Yount, capital (28%)	(103,600)

The accountant prepared the following cash distribution plan based on the above trial balance.

Cash Distribution Plan for the Baker, Rickles, and Yount Partnership

	Baker (40%)	Rickles (32%)	Yount (28%)
Net capital and loan balance	40,300	350,000	103,600
Loss absorption power:			
$40,300/.40	100,750		
$350,000/.32		1,093,750	
$103,600/.28			370,000
Allocation # 1:			
Rickles $231,600/.32	0	(723,750)	0
Adjusted loss absorption power	100,750	370,000	370,000
Allocation # 2:			
Rickles $86,160/.32			
Yount $75,390/.28	0	(269,250)	(269,250)
Adjusted loss absorption power	100,750	100,750	100,750
Any additional allocation is divided .40, .32, and .28			

Liquidation expenses are estimated to be $9,000 for September, $23,000 for October, and $13,000 for November. The following events occur during the liquidation.

1.	September 8	Receivables are sold to a bank for $35,000.
2.	September 20	Inventory is sold for $105,000.
3.	September 31	Liquidation expenses for the month are $10,000.
4.	October 15	Plant assets with a book value of $200,000 are sold for $170,000.

5. October 30   Liquidation expenses for the month are $22,000.
6. November 7   The remainder of the plant assets are sold for $150,000.
7. November 22 All the partnership's creditors (excluding partners) are paid in full.
8. November 31 Liquidation expenses for the month are $9,000.

Required:

Prepare a Statement of Realization and Liquidation for the Baker, Rickles, and Yount partnership. Assume that no partner is capable of making a contribution if a capital account deficit exists.

PROBLEMS

PROBLEM 8-1 Payment to partnership creditors and personal creditors, deficit capital accounts
PROBLEM 8-2 Statement of Realization and Liquidation assuming different asset sales prices
PROBLEM 8-3 Statement of Realization and Liquidation, income statement accounts, unstated profit and loss ratios
PROBLEM 8-4 Statement of Realization and Liquidation, income statement accounts, loans to and from partners, initial capital account deficit
PROBLEM 8-5 Cash distribution plan, Statement of Realization and Liquidation, deficit capital account, partial contribution
PROBLEM 8-6 Statement of Realization and Liquidation, Schedule of Safe Payments, profit ratios different from loss ratios

PROBLEM 8-1 The partners Caldwell, Maxwell, and Ramirez share profits and losses 33 percent, 25 percent, and 42 percent, respectively. Some of the partners are having personal financial difficulty, so the partnership is going to liquidate. The following table outlines the financial position of the partners.

	Caldwell	Maxwell	Ramirez
Personal assets	$190,000	$70,000	$210,000
Partnership capital	$60,000	$20,000	$145,000
Personal liabilities	$150,000	$100,000	$140,000

In addition, the partnership has assets (book value) of $500,000 and outstanding liabilities of $275,000.

Required:

Prepare a schedule detailing the amount that will be paid to the partnership's creditors and the partners' personal creditors assuming:

A. There are $90,000 of losses and expenses incurred during the liquidation.
B. There are $260,000 of losses and expenses incurred during the liquidation.

PROBLEM 8-2 Several years ago Bryan Ernst, Diane Simpson, and George Young opened an upscale laundromat, Splish Splash. The partners believed that consumers would pay premium prices to have a superior location for doing their laundry. Unfortunately, the partners were incorrect and the partnership is currently liquidating. The following trial balance is supplied by the partners just before the liquidation began on May 1, 2004.

Cash	25,000
Inventory	60,000
Plant Assets (net)	500,000
Current Liabilities	(45,000)
Long-Term Debt	(425,000)
Ernst, capital (28%)	(30,000)
Simpson, capital (40%)	(50,000)
Young, capital (32%)	(35,000)

The following events occur during liquidation:

1. The inventory is sold for $50,000.
2. Plant assets are sold for $420,000.
3. All current and long-term debt is paid.

Required:

A. Prepare a Statement of Realization and Liquidation for the above events.
B. Prepare a Statement of Realization and Liquidation for the above events, assuming that the plant assets are sold for $400,000 and the partners are able to make additional capital contributions.
C. Prepare a Statement of Realization and Liquidation for the above events, assuming that the plant assets are sold for $400,000 and the partners are unable to make additional capital contributions.
D. What would the accountant do if the partners with a deficit capital position are financially capable of making an additional contribution but refuse to do so?

PROBLEM 8-3   John, Paul, and Richard are partners in a failing business. As a result, they have decided to liquidate the business before their personal assets are placed in jeopardy. The following trial balance was prepared just before the liquidation began.

Cash	50,000
Inventory	100,000
Plant Assets (net)	270,000
Cost of Goods Sold	185,000
Depreciation Expense	27,000
Other Expenses	30,000
Current Liabilities	(70,000)
Long-Term Debt	(115,000)
John, capital	(44,000)
Paul, capital	(95,000)
Richard, capital	(75,000)
Sales	(263,000)

The following events occur during liquidation:

1. The inventory is sold for $76,000.
2. The plant assets are sold for $210,000.
3. The liabilities are paid.
4. Liquidation expenses of $63,000 are incurred.

Required:
Prepare a Statement of Realization and Liquidation for the above events.

PROBLEM 8-4   Neal Kiplinger, Amos Stewart, and Jane Turner are liquidating their partnership. They prepared the following trial balance at the date the liquidation began.

Cash	97,000
Inventory	280,000
Note Receivable (Stewart)	75,000
Plant Assets (net)	785,000
Cost of Goods Sold	750,000
Depreciation Expense	78,000
Other Expenses	200,000
Current Liabilities	(190,000)
Note Payable (Turner)	(150,000)
Long-Term Debt	(525,000)
Kiplinger, capital (40%)	(85,000)
Stewart, capital (35%)	(125,000)
Turner, capital (25%)	90,000
Sales	(1,280,000)

The following events occur during liquidation:

1. The inventory is sold for $252,000.
2. The plant assets are sold for $725,000.
3. The liabilities are paid.
4. Liquidation expenses of $135,000 are incurred.

Required:
Prepare a Statement of Realization and Liquidation for the above events.

PROBLEM 8-5   The Danielson brothers—Richard, Scott, and Thomas—are partners in a local family business that is preparing to liquidate. They are planning to liquidate the business over three months to maximize the cash receipts from the sale of assets. The following trial balance is prepared on October 1, 2004, immediately preceding the liquidation.

Cash	87,000
Inventory	240,000
Note Receivable (Thomas)	28,000
Furniture and Fixtures (net)	445,000
Current Liabilities	(145,000)
Long-Term Debt	(225,000)
Richard, capital (25%)	(180,000)
Scott, capital (40%)	(110,000)
Thomas, capital (35%)	(140,000)

Inventory records are maintained on a first-in, first-out basis, so the book values approximate current market values. The brothers have planned three sales, one during each month of the liquidation period. They believe they will sell three-eighths of the inventory at 60 percent of its value in October, one-third of the original inventory at 40 percent of its value in November, and one-fourth of the original inventory at 20 percent of its value in December. The remaining inventory will be donated to a homeless shelter.

The partnership has been recording accelerated depreciation on the furniture and fixtures. The brothers plan to sell the furniture and fixtures at two times, November and December. The first sale will consist of $350,000 of the assets and should net $370,000 in proceeds. The second sale should net $30,000.

Required:
A. Prepare a cash distribution plan so that the brothers understand how cash will be distributed during the liquidation period.
B. Prepare a Statement of Realization and Liquidation for the above events, assuming the brothers' estimates are accurate. The current liabilities are paid in November, and the long-term debt is paid in December. Liquidation expenses are accurately estimated to be $40,000 in October, $60,000 in November, and $15,000 in December. Assume the partners have the following net personal assets: Richard, $500,000; Scott, $7,200; Thomas, $275,000.

PROBLEM 8-6   Anthony Gilbert, George Mason, and Herman Williams are liquidating their partnership. The partners have been sharing profits 35 percent, 40 percent, and 25 percent, respectively, and losses equally. The following trial balance was prepared at the date the liquidation started (February 1, 2004).

Cash	65,000
Inventory	150,000
Plant Assets (net)	270,000
Current Liabilities	(100,000)
Long-Term Debt	(190,000)
Gilbert, capital (35%)	(85,000)
Mason, capital (40%)	(70,000)
Williams, capital (25%)	(40,000)

The liquidation is expected to be completed in three months. The inventory is sold in the first month of the liquidation for $180,000, and liquidation expenses of $24,000 are incurred. Estimated liquidation expenses for the two remaining months of the liquidation are $50,000. Two-thirds of the plant assets are sold for $120,000 in the second month, and the liquidation expenses are $30,000. The estimated liquidation expense for the last month of the liquidation is $15,000. The current liabilities are paid at face value, and the long-term debt is retired for $175,000 in the third month of the liquidation. The remaining plant assets are sold for $48,000. Liquidation expenses for the month are $12,600.

Required:
A. Prior to the liquidation starting, the partners ask about the amount of cash they can expect to receive. Prepare a response to the partners.
B. Prepare a Statement of Realization and Liquidation for the three-month liquidation period.

CHAPTER 9

NONGOVERNMENT NOT-FOR-PROFIT ORGANIZATIONS

LEARNING OBJECTIVES

After reading this chapter, you should be able to:

- Identify a nongovernmental not-for-profit organization.
- Understand the GAAP pertaining to nongovernmental not-for-profit organizations, including the provisions of SFAS Nos. 116, 117, 124, and 136.
- Explain the accounting and reporting criteria for nongovernmental not-for-profit organizations.
- Apply nongovernmental not-for-profit accounting and reporting requirements to record financial transactions.
- Distinguish reporting for health care organizations from other not-for-profit organizations.

Nongovernmental not-for-profit organization (NFP): is an entity that operates without a profit motive and has no defined owners

This chapter presents and illustrates specific accounting and reporting standards for nongovernmental **not-for-profit organizations (NFPs)**. NFPs benefit society by providing services that might otherwise not be offered by the for-profit (business) sector or the government. NFPs consist of people collectively involved in pursuing a benevolent cause, exist outside the competitive market, and are independently organized and self-governing. The mission of the NFP is to accomplish the goals or purposes for which it was established. The purpose of an NFP may be social, religious, educational, charitable, cultural, environmental, or fraternal. Unlike a for-profit business, whose motive is profit for its owners, the mission of the NFP rarely includes a profit motive. Instead, the NFP seeks to realize revenues equal to or greater than expenses. Achieving financial gain from its operation does not make the NFP a for profit business as long as the gain is devoted to accomplishing its mission. Thus, the acid test of the not-for-profit status is the motive of the organization demostrated by its actions and activities.

Society reciprocates by granting various benefits to NFPs in recognition of the services rendered. Advantages flowing to the not-for-profit status include exemption from most federal taxation, exemptions from local real property and other taxes, privileges extended by special kinds of ordinances and statutes, and other preferences such as tax abatements. NFPs represent a rapidly growing source of strength in the economy and social structure of the United States. In 1998, there were almost 1.7 million NFPs, accounting for 6 percent of all organizations in the United States.[1] According to the Statistics of Income (SOI) Division of the IRS, during the 20-year period from 1975 to 1995, the real assets and revenues of nonprofit organizations filing information returns with the IRS more than tripled, to $1.9 trillion and $899 billion respectively. This compares to real growth in gross domestic product (GDP) of 74 percent during the same 20-year period. Organizations exempt under IRS section 501(c) earned an estimated one-eighth (12.4 percent) of the nation's GDP. It is no surprise that accounting standard-setting authorities have begun to focus special interest on this sector.[2]

NFPs exhibit much diversity in origin, size, finances, specific mission, activities, target group, and resource providers. The National Taxonomy of Exempt Entities (NTEE) has divided the largest set of tax-exempt entities into 10 functional categories and 26 major group areas.[3] The categories are arts/culture/humanities, education, environment/animals, health, human services, international/foreign affairs, public/society benefit, religion-related, mutual/membership benefit, and unclassified.

Accounting activities of NFPs seem similar in many ways to those for both governmental not-for-profit organizations and for-profit businesses, but there are fundamental differences. This chapter discusses accounting recognition and reporting requirements that create the differences among a governmental not-for-profit organization, an NFP, and a for-profit organization. Attention is focused on the evolving history of generally accepted accounting principles (GAAP) and the current accounting standards for an NFP. Transactions and resulting end-of-year financial statements for a voluntary health and welfare organization illustrate the accounting principles and reporting requirements for an NFP.

NOT-FOR-PROFIT ORGANIZATIONS' CHARACTERISTICS AND DEFINITIONS

Basic characteristics differentiate not-for-profit organizations (whether governmental or nongovernmental) from for-profit (business) organizations. Distinguishing characteristics of nonbusiness organizations are outlined in Financial Accounting Standards Board (FASB) Concepts Statement No. 4, and they include the following:[4]

---

[1] *New Nonprofit Almanac & Desk Reference* (Washington, DC: Independent Sector and the Urban Institute, 2002). Statistics of Income Bulletin.

[2] Meckstroth, Alicia, and Paul Arnsberger, "*Statistics of Income Division of the IRS, A 20-Year Review of the Nonprofit Sector, 1975–1995.*" (Internal Revenue Service: Washington, D.C. Fall 1999, 149–171).

[3] The NTEE, developed by the IRS, is a nonprofit coalition consisting of corporate, foundation, and voluntary members based in Washington, D.C.

[4] **Statement of Financial Accounting Concepts**, No. 4, "Objectives of Financial Reporting by Nonbusiness Organizations" (Norwalk, CT: Financial Accounting Standards Board, 1980), par. 6.

1. They receive a significant amount of resources from resource providers[5] who do not expect to receive either repayment or economic benefits proportionate to resources provided.

2. Operating purposes are other than to provide goods or services at a profit or profit equivalent.

3. There are no defined ownership interests that can be sold, transferred, or redeemed, or that convey entitlement to a share of a residual distribution of resources in the event of liquidation of the organization.

Both governmental not-for-profit organizations and NFPs may depend largely on contributions for operating capital, provide a service without a profit motive for the benefit of those who are not the resource providers, and have no owners. The 1996 American Institute of Certified Public Accountants (AICPA) Audit and Accounting Guide, *Not-for-Profit Organizations*, defined a not-for-profit organization as an entity that possesses, in varying degrees, the three characteristics that distinguish it from a business enterprise.[6,7]

Organizations that fall outside the definition include all investor-owned enterprises and entities that provide dividends or other economic benefits to their owners, members, or participants. Mutual insurance companies, credit unions, farm and rural electric cooperatives, and employee benefit plans also fall outside the definition.[8] Determining whether a not-for-profit organization is governmental or nongovernmental can be difficult. However, its classification must be established to determine whether to apply FASB or Governmental Accounting Standards Board (GASB) accounting standards. AICPA Audit and Accounting Guides, with the tacit approval of both the FASB and the GASB, provide the following guidance to differentiate between governmental and nongovernmental organizations.[9]

- Nongovernmental organizations are all organizations other than governmental organizations.

- Public corporations[10] and bodies corporate and politic are governmental organizations.

- Other organizations are governmental organizations if they have one or more of the following characteristics:

  - Popular election of officers or appointment (or approval) of a controlling majority of the members of the organization's governing body by officials of one or more state or local governments

---

[5] FASB Concepts Statement No. 4, par. 29(a), defines resource providers to include those who are directly compensated for providing resources—lenders, suppliers, and employees—and those who are not directly and proportionately compensated such as members, contributors, and taxpayers.

[6] **Statement of Financial Accounting Standards**, No. 116, "Accounting for Contributions Received and Contributions Made" (Norwalk, CT: Financial Accounting Standards Board, 1993), App. D.

[7] Audit and Accounting Guide, " Not-for-Profit Organizations," (New York, NY: American Institute of Certified Public Accountants, 1996 par. 1.01).

[8] Op. cit., Statement of Financial Accounting Concepts, No. 4, par. 7.

[9] Op. cit., *Not-for-Profit Organizations*, par. 1.03; Audit and Accounting Guide, *Health Care Organizations* (New York: American Institute of Certified Public Accountants, 1997), par. 1.02c.

[10] *Random House Webster's College Dictionary* defines a public corporation as "a corporation, owned and operated by a government, established for the administration of certain public programs." (New York: Random House, 1991).

- The potential for unilateral dissolution by a government with the net assets reverting to a government
- The power to enact and enforce a tax levy

In addition, organizations are presumed to be governmental if they have the ability to issue directly (rather than through a state or municipal authority) debt that pays interest exempt from federal taxation. However, organizations possessing only that ability (to issue tax-exempt debt) and none of the other governmental characteristics may rebut the presumption that they are governmental if their determination is supported by compelling, relevant evidence.[11]

Although NFPs include many different kinds of organizations involved in a myriad of activities, they must be incorporated under state nonprofit corporation statutes or charitable trust laws to be considered separate legal entities apart from the incorporators.[12] After becoming incorporated in a state, the NFP may then apply to the Internal Revenue Service for tax-exempt status.[13] Even though an NFP may be tax-exempt under state law, it will not be exempt from federal income tax unless the IRS approves the application. The IRS requires NFPs to file an annual information return, Form 990, if their revenue equals $25,000 or more. Churches and religious organizations are exempt from filing the Form 990.

NFPs comprise a wide range of organizations. They include hospitals and health care organizations as well as soup kitchens and small community-based shelters. Universities, elementary and secondary schools, religious organizations, churches, day-care and adult centers, the Special Olympics, libraries, museums, environmental groups, private foundations, drug rehabilitation centers, country clubs, political parties, and human rights organizations are but a few of the assorted types of NFPs.

The various types of NFPs are typically combined into four major categories:

1. Voluntary health and welfare organizations
2. Colleges and universities
3. Hospitals and other health care entities
4. Other not-for-profit organizations

NOT-FOR-PROFIT GENERALLY ACCEPTED ACCOUNTING PRINCIPLES

NFP GAAP has evolved slowly and undergone several changes in accounting and reporting standard-setting bodies. The initial authority was the Committee on Accounting Procedure (CAP), formed by the AICPA in 1938. The CAP published its pronouncements as Accounting Research Bulletins (ARBs), issuing 51 Bulletins before the Accounting Principles Board (APB) replaced it in 1959. The APB issued 31 pronouncements, titled *Opinions of the Accounting Principles Board,* before the Financial Accounting Standards Board (FASB) replaced it in 1973.

---

[11] Op cit., *Health Care Organizations*, par. 1.02c; op. cit., *Not-for-Profit Organizations*, par. 1.03.

[12] State regulation and requirements for NFPs vary greatly among the states.

[13] Application for tax-exempt status is filed on Form 1023 for public charities and Form 1024 for all other organizations.

In 1979, the FASB assumed the authority for setting accounting and reporting standards for all nonbusiness organizations except governments.[14] The Governmental Accounting Standards Board (GASB), created in 1984, was given the authority to establish GAAP for state and local governments. At the conclusion of the GASB's initial five-year sunset review in 1989, the GASB was reaffirmed as the standard-setting body for all state and local governmental entities, including governmental not-for-profit organizations.

The AICPA responded to the challenge of two GAAP authorities by issuing SAS No. 69,[15] which set forth a new GAAP hierarchy. The new GAAP hierarchy, still in effect today, defines GAAP differently for governmental and nongovernmental entities.

The GAAP hierarchy, which consists of four levels of authority and clearly defined guidelines for acceptance as GAAP standards, is displayed in Table 9-1. Level A pronouncements represent the highest authority and must be issued by either the FASB or the GASB. In addition, other standard-setting bodies' work requires FASB and GASB approval before being accepted or incorporated into a category of authority. The GASB has specifi-

TABLE 9-1   GAAP Hierarchy

Hierarchical Level	Nongovernmental	Governmental
A	FASB statements and interpretations, APB opinions, and AICPA ARBs	GASB statements, AICPA and FASB pronouncements made specifically applicable by the GASB
B	FASB technical bulletins and AICPA industry audit and accounting guides and SOPs if cleared by the FASB	GASB technical bulletins and AICPA industry audit and accounting guides and SOPs if made specifically applicable and cleared by the GASB
C	AICPA practice bulletins cleared by the FASB and Emerging Issues Task Force (EITF) consensus positions	AICPA practice bulletins cleared by GASB and Emerging Issues Task Force (EITF) consensus positions, if the GASB creates such a group
	FASB statements and interpretations, APB opinions and AICPA ARBs	GASB statements, AICPA and FASB pronouncements made specifically applicable by the GASB
D	AICPA accounting interpretations, FASB implementation guides, and industry practices that are widely	GASB implementation guides and industry practices that are widely recognized or prevalent

[14] **Statement of Financial Accounting Standards**, No. 32, "Specialized Accounting and Reporting Principles and Practices in AICPA Statements of Position and Guides on Accounting and Auditing Matters" (Stamford, CT: Financial Accounting Standards Board, 1979). The FASB rescinded SFAS No. 32 in **Statement of Financial Accounting Standards**, No. 111, "Rescission of FASB Statement No. 32 and Technical Corrections" (Stamford, CT: Financial Accounting Standards Board, 1992). The FASB considered SFAS No. 32 unnecessary under the new GAAP hierarchy adopted by the AICPA in *Statement on Auditing Standards*, No. 69 (see note 15).

[15] **Statements of Auditing Standards**, No. 69, "The Meaning of *Presented Fairly in Conformity with Generally Accepted Accounting Principles* in the Independent Auditor's Report" (New York: American Institute of Certified Public Accountants, 1992).

cally prohibited NFPs from following the FASB guidelines for nongovernmental NFPs unless the guidance is made specifically applicable.[16]

NFP SPECIFIC ACCOUNTING AND REPORTING GUIDANCE

Following the issuance of SAS No. 69, the FASB began to address the need to increase financial reporting comparability between the diverse NFP groups and to reduce inconsistencies, including accounting for depreciation, recognizing revenue, satisfying restrictions, reporting resources held by others, and accounting for and displaying investments in financial reports. Five FASB pronouncements (Statement Nos. 93, 116, 117, 124 and 136) changed accounting and reporting requirements for NFP general-purpose financial statements.

Depreciation

The FASB directed SFAS No. 93,[17] solely to NFP organizations. The standard requires all not-for-profit organizations to record depreciation expense on capital assets used in operations, including contributed capital assets. Although depreciation expense has long been part of the financial statements of businesses, most NFPs used inconsistent recognition methods or did not record depreciation at all.[18] The declining value of an asset used to provide a service constitutes a reportable expense because the economic benefits (or service potential) used up are no longer available to the organization. By omitting depreciation, the NFP produced financial operating results that did not reflect all costs of the services provided.

Depreciation is not required to be recognized on works of arts or historical treasures, which are considered to have an extraordinarily useful life or indefinite service potential. These items must have verification that demonstrates that the asset has cultural, aesthetic, or historical value that is worth preserving perpetually and that the organization has the ability to protect and preserve the assets.[19]

Contributions

Contribution: unconditional transfer of cash or other asset to an entity or a settlement or cancellation of its liability in a voluntary nonreciprocal transfer by another entity acting other than as an owner

SFAS No. 116[20] established uniform accounting standards for **contributions** received and given by NFPs. The guidance applies to promises to give (pledges), gifts of cash and other assets (such as equipment or artwork), and contributed personal services. SFAS No. 116 does not apply to transactions that purchase goods or services—that is, **exchange transactions**—in which each party receives and sacrifices something of relatively equal value. The standard also does not apply to assets held for others in which the reporting entity acts

---

[16] **Statement of the Governmental Accounting Standards Board**, No. 29, "The Use of Not-for-profit Accounting and Financial Reporting Principles by Governmental Entities" (Norwalk, CT: Governmental Accounting Standards Board, 1996). See Table 9-1.

[17] **Statement of Financial Accounting Standards**, No. 93, "Recognition of Depreciation by Not-for-Profit Organizations" (Norwalk, CT: Financial Accounting Standards Board, 1987).

[18] Ibid.,

[19] Ibid.,

[20] **Statement of Financial Accounting Standards**, No. 116, "Accounting for Contributions Received and Contributions Made" (Norwalk, CT: Financial Accounting Standards Board, 1993).

Exchange transaction: a transaction is one in which items of comparable value are exchanged or traded; also referred to as a quid pro quo

as an agent, trustee, or intermediary—that is, transactions in which the entity holds cash or investment resources in trust for others.

This standard applies to entities that receive or make contributions. Generally, contributions received, including unconditional pledges to give, are recognized as revenue in the period received at their fair value. Contributions made are recognized as expenses in the period made at their fair value. Conditional promises to give, whether received or made, are recognized when the conditions are substantially met.

The guidance requires NFPs to distinguish between contributions received that increase permanently restricted net assets, temporarily restricted net assets, and unrestricted net assets. It also requires the recognition of the expiration of donor stipulations in the period in which the restriction expires.

Details of these recognition and disclosure requirements are discussed and illustrated with journal entries later in the chapter.

Financial Statement Display

Statement of financial position: displays the organization's assets, liabilities, and equity as of a specific date

SFAS No. 117[21] established minimum financial reporting presentation requirements applicable to all nongovernment not-for-profit organizations for general-purpose external financial statements. The statement's objective was to enhance the relevance, understandability, and comparability of financial statements by achieving uniform financial reporting display for the many different types of NFPs. This guidance moved the NFP away from a disaggregated reporting display that reported financial information by types of programs, activities, or divisions in which the organization was engaged. Instead, SFAS No. 117 guidance focuses on the entity as a whole, using aggregated amounts that bring the procedure more in line with for-profit business reporting.

Statement of activity: displays the organization's resource inflows and outflows for a specific period

The statement requires that an NFP provide a **statement of financial position, a statement of activity**, and a statement of cash flows. It also requires that the organization report the total amount of assets, liabilities, and net assets in the statement of financial position; the changes in the organization's net assets in the statement of activity; and the cash and cash equivalents in the statement of cash flows. Comparative statements are encouraged but not required.

Each of the statements required by SFAS No. 117, with the prescribed display format, is discussed and illustrated later in the chapter.

Fair Value Recognition

SFAS No. 124[22] established accounting recognition and disclosure requirements for investments held by NFPs. Key provisions of the guidance include the reporting of investment equity securities with readily determinable fair values and all investments in debt securities at their fair value as well as recognition of losses on restricted investments.

The statement also established guidance for reporting losses on investments held because of a donor's stipulation to invest the gift in perpetuity or for a specified period of term, that is, endowment gifts. These provisions are discussed and illustrated later in the chapter.

[21] **Statement of Financial Accounting Standards,** No. 117, "Financial Statement of Not-for-Profit Organizations" (Norwalk, CT: Financial Accounting Standards Board, 1993).

[22] **Statement of Financial Accounting Standards,** No. 124, "Accounting for Certain Investment Held by Not-for-Profit Organizations" (Norwalk, CT: Financial Accounting Standards Board, 1995).

Resources Held in Trust by Others

Variance power: the ability to redirect or determine the recipient of donated resources

SFAS No. 136[23] provides guidance on how the recipient organization and final beneficiary should record the transaction. When the recipient organization has **variance power**—that is, the ability to redirect the contributed cash or other assets to another beneficiary—or if the recipient organization and the beneficiary are financially interrelated, the recipient organization records the receipt of the assets as a contribution. In this situation, the beneficiary does not recognize anything until resources are received from the recipient organization. The United Way, which raises money and distributes the gifts to others, is an example of a recipient organization that has variance power over contributions received. In the event the recipient organization cannot redirect the assets to some other beneficiary, the recipient organization records the receipt of the assets as a liability (funds held for others). Since the beneficiary has a direct interest in the resources held by the recipient organization, the beneficiary recognizes an asset (funds held by others) and contribution revenue. A foundation that raises money restricted to support of a specific NFP hospital would be an example of a recipient organization without variance power that holds funds in trust for another organization. The hospital would report the funds held by the foundation as an asset and recognize the contribution as contributions revenue in the appropriate net asset class according the donor's stipulations, if any.

Future NFP GAAP Guidance

When the FASB issued SFAS No. 141,[24] the acquisition of a for-profit entity by an NFP and the acquisition of an NFP by another NFP were excluded because the Board decided to undertake a separate project on combinations of NFPs. The Board also delayed the effective date of SFAS No. 142[25] as it applies to NFPs until NFP combinations are addressed.

Combinations between NFPs have situations that distinguish them from business combinations. For example, some combinations do not include the exchange of cash, or other assets, as consideration. Prior guidance has led to diverse practices, although many NFP combinations are accounted for in a manner similar to the pooling method. SFAS No. 141 eliminated the pooling method[26] for acquisitions by business entities. With the prohibition of the use of the pooling method, new guidance is needed to record NFP combinations.

Current deliberations[27] presume that SFAS No. 141 should apply to combinations of NFPs unless a circumstance unique to the combination is identified that would justify a different accounting treatment. Combinations in which the acquiring entity is an NFP cannot be assumed to be an exchange of commensurate value. Acquired NFPs do not have owners who are focused on receiving a return of their investment. Moreover, the parent or governing board of an acquired NFP may place its mission ahead of achieving a maximum price when negotiating a combination agreement. If an entity voluntarily transfers its net

---

[23] **Statement of Financial Accounting Standards**, No. 136, "Transfers of Assets to a Not-for-Profit Organization or Charitable Trust That Raises or Holds Contributions for Others" (Norwalk, CT: Financial Accounting Standards Board, 1999).

[24] **Statement of Financial Accounting Standards**, No. 141, "Business Combinations" (Norwalk, CT: Financial Accounting Standards Board, 2001).

[25] **Statement of Financial Accounting Standards**, No. 142, "Goodwill and Other Intangible Assets" (Norwalk, CT: Financial Accounting Standards Board, 2001).

[26] Op. cit., **FASB Statement** No. 141, par. 15.

[27] Project update, "Combination of Not-for-Profit Organizations," http:www.fasb.org/project/nfp.

assets to an NFP in exchange for assets of substantially lower value or without receiving any consideration, a contribution is recognized.

In contrast, acquisitions by NFPs of another entity in exchange of commensurate value would be recognized in the same manner as a business combination. In those situations where the fair value of the liabilities exceeds the fair value of the assets, the acquiring organization would recognize the excess as an unidentifiable intangible asset (goodwill). The recognition of goodwill and testing for its impairment is presently being considered by members of the FASB working group on NFP combinations.

The FASB established a goal of discussing the remaining project issues—accounting for goodwill, disclosures, effective date, and transition period—and issuing an exposure draft of the guidance in the fourth quarter of 2003. The final standard was not expected until 2004.

NET ASSET CLASSES

NFPs account for and report their financial position and activities using net asset classes rather than equity. Net asset classes are determined by donor stipulations or the lack thereof. The three required classifications of net assets are (1) permanently restricted, (2) temporarily restricted, and (3) unrestricted.

Permanently restricted net assets: those assets with donor-imposed stipulations that whose resources must be held in perpetuity and only income earned from their investment be expended for specified purpose.

Permanently restricted net assets are net assets whose use is limited by donor-imposed stipulations that the net assets must be held in perpetuity and inviolate, for example, an endowment. These resources must be maintained permanently, but the NFP may use up or expend part or all of the income or other economic benefits. The donor-imposed restrictions cannot expire, be fulfilled by the passage of time, or be satisfied by the actions of the NFP. In addition to cash and other economic assets, permanently restricted resources may include land, artwork, or other assets that must be preserved and used for a certain purpose.

For example, assume that Amy Anderson contributed $1 million to the local NFP library to endow future book acquisitions. Because it stipulates that the gift endows future book acquisition, Ms. Anderson's gift cannot be expended. Instead, only the interest earned on the investment of the gift may be used to acquire books for the library. The entry to record the gift is the following. Notice that only the revenue, not the cash, is distinguished by a net asset class designation.

Cash	1,000,000	
Contribution revenue (permanently restricted net assets)		1,000,000

To record the Anderson endowment gift. Income earned on the investment of this gift is restricted by the donor, Amy Anderson, to be used for the acquisition of library books.

Temporarily restricted net assets: net assets with donor-imposed stipulations that can be met either by the passage of time or by actions of the organization

Restriction: a donor-imposed stipulation that can be met either by the passage of time or by actions of the organization

Temporarily restricted net assets are those contributions whose use by the NFP is limited by donor-imposed stipulations that expire either with the passage of time, expenditure of the asset, or fulfillment by the NFP's actions. When donor **restrictions** are fulfilled, the net assets are considered to be "released from restrictions" and are reclassified to unrestricted net assets from temporarily restricted net assets. If two or more temporary restrictions are imposed on a contribution, the effect of the expiration of those restrictions is recognized in the period in which the last remaining restriction expires. In addition, if restrictions on a temporarily restricted gift are fulfilled in the same period the gift is received, then both the revenue and the expenses may be reported in the unrestricted net asset class for that period.

When interest is earned on the investment of the endowment illustrated above, the interest is temporarily restricted until its purpose is satisfied by acquiring library books. Assume that the endowment investments earned $5,000. The following entry would record the income.

Cash	5,000	
Investment income (temporarily restricted net asset)		5,000

To record income earned on the Anderson endowment that is restricted to the acquisition of library books.

As before, the cash has no net asset designation on the revenue that will be reported in the statement of activities. When the income is used to acquire books for the library, the following entries are recorded. The first entry recognizes that the restriction has been met and "reclasses" the net asset from temporarily restricted to unrestricted net assets. The second entry records the purchase of the books for the library. All disbursements and expenses are recorded as unrestricted net asset transactions.

Temporarily restricted net assets	5,000	
Unrestricted net assets		5,000
Books	5,000	
Cash		5,000

To reclassify temporarily restricted net assets to unrestricted net assets and record the acquisition of library books in accordance with the Anderson endowment gift. Note that books have no net asset class designation.

Gifts with stipulations that the asset is to be invested (or held) for a certain length of time and then used for a specific purpose entail both a time and purpose restriction. Gifts of this type are sometimes referred to as term endowments and recorded as contribution revenue in the temporarily restricted net asset class.

Gifts to acquire long-lived assets are recognized as temporarily restricted because the contribution is restricted for a specific purpose. The organization may acknowledge meeting the temporary restriction and its release in one of two ways: (1) Upon placing the long-lived asset into service, the donated funds can be reclassified to unrestricted net assets to match the cost of acquiring or building the long-lived asset. This reclassification recognizes the satisfaction of the donor's restriction when the long-lived asset is acquired or built and placed in service. (2) An amount equal to the current year's depreciation of the acquired long-lived asset is reclassified from the temporarily restricted net assets to the unrestricted net assets. This implies that the restriction is met as the long-lived asset is used or wastes away. Whichever method is chosen, the recognition treatment must be applied consistently to all gifts to acquire or build long-lived assets. If an organization receives a gift of cash that is restricted to acquiring a long-lived asset and the asset is acquired and placed in service in the same reporting period of the donation, the donation may be classified as unrestricted support if that treatment is consistent with the organization's accounting policy.

For example, John J. Smith gave the NFP $30,000 to purchase computer equipment. Because the computer equipment will be purchased immediately, the organization recognized the gift in the unrestricted net asset class and issued a purchase order to acquire the equipment.

Cash	30,000	
Contribution revenue (unrestricted net asset)		30,000

To record a gift from John J. Smith to acquire computer equipment that has been ordered.

When the equipment is delivered, the following entry is recorded.

Computer equipment	30,000	
Cash		30,000

To record acquired computer equipment using the John J. Smith gift. (*Note*: No net asset class is designated because this transaction involves a balance sheet account, that is, capital assets—equipment.)

However if the NFP did not plan to purchase the computer equipment immediately, the gift would have been recognized as revenue in the temporarily restricted net assets.

Cash (no net asset classification)	30,000	
Contribution revenue (temporarily restricted net asset)		30,000

To record a gift from John J. Smith to acquire computer equipment.

When the computer equipment is ordered, the $30,000 in temporarily restricted net assets is reclassed so that the resources will be available in the unrestricted net assets to pay for the equipment when it is delivered.

Reclass (temporarily restricted net assets)	30,000	
Reclass (unrestricted net assets)		30,000

To recognize the satisfaction of the John J. Smith gift restrictions to acquire computer equipment.

When the equipment is delivered, the same entry as illustrated earlier to pay the vendor.

Computer equipment	30,000	
Cash		30,000

To record acquired computer equipment provided by the John J. Smith gift. (*Note*: No net asset class is designated as this transaction involves a balance sheet account, that is, capital assets—equipment.)

Resource amounts held as temporarily restricted net assets are disclosed in notes to the financial statements to distinguish between the different types of temporary donor restrictions. For example, designations such as the following may be reported:

- Support of a particular operating activity (purpose restriction)
- Investment for a specified term (time restriction)
- Use in a specified future period (time restriction)
- Acquisition of long-lived assets (purpose restriction)

Unrestricted net assets: net assets that have no donor-imposed stipulations or restrictions

Unrestricted net assets are neither permanently nor temporarily restricted by donor-imposed stipulations. They include all unrestricted gifts and items such as income from operations, income from producing and delivering goods, revenues from services provided, and unrestricted income from investments. Unrestricted net assets also include temporarily restricted assets "released from restrictions." Resources are presumed to be unrestricted unless there is evidence of donor-imposed restrictions. As noted earlier, all expenses are recorded as unrestricted net asset transactions.[28] For example, suppose the museum uses its cash resources to pay its monthly utility charges. These are ongoing

[28] Op. cit., **FASB Statement of Financial Accounting Standards**, No. 117, par. 20.

operating costs of the museum. No donor stipulation is associated with the operating activities of the organization. Thus the entry to record the utility bill would be the following.

Utility expense (unrestricted net assets)	250	
Cash		250

To record the utility charges payment.

Unrestricted net assets may have institutionally imposed limits, or designations, which are reported in the notes or on the face of financial statements. The designations convey voluntary resolutions imposed by the governing board to set aside or allocate a portion of the organization's unrestricted net assets to serve as a reserve for a future event or to function as an endowment. Capital asset equity (capital asset net value less related capital debt) is included in the unrestricted net assets together with the satisfied donor-imposed restricted gifts to acquire long-lived assets.

TRANSACTION TYPES

Revenues—that is, inflows from ongoing operations—are reported at their fair value and recognized and recorded as either an exchange or nonexchange transaction.

Exchange transactions are defined as "reciprocal transfers in which each party receives and sacrifices approximately equal value."[29] These transactions include providing goods and services for a fee, membership dues, program service fees, and investment income.[30] This income is unrestricted and reported on the statement of activities under the category "changes in unrestricted net assets."

Exchange transaction are arm's-length transactions in which one party (customer) exchanges something of value (cash) with another party (seller) for something of comparable value (services). An example of an exchange transaction is membership fees received by an NFP.

Cash	100	
Membership fees (unrestricted net assets)		100

To record membership fees received from Allen Brown.

Nonexchange transactions: transactions in which the party providing the resources neither expects nor derives a benefit from the transactions; also known as a *gift*

Nonexchange transactions are nonreciprocal transfers of resources, which include gifts, contributions, grants, and donations. These transactions are defined as an unconditional transfer of cash or other assets to an entity, or a settlement or cancellation of its liabilities, in a voluntary nonreciprocal transfer by another entity acting as other than an owner. Nonexchange transactions may be unrestricted or have donor-implied stipulations. Nonexchange transactions are reported in any or all three net asset classes, according to the existence or absence of donor-imposed restrictions. If the donor makes no stipulation regarding the use of the gift, it is recognized as contribution revenue in the unrestricted net assets. If the donor stipulated that the gift is permanently restricted—that is, an endowment—the gift is recognized as contribution revenue in the permanently restricted net

---

[29] FASB **Statement of Financial Accounting Standards**, No. 116, par. 48.

[30] **Concept Statement**, No. 6, "Elements of Financial Statements" (Norwalk, CT: Financial Accounting Standards Board, 1985), par. 78.

assets. If the donor stipulated that the gift be used for a specific purpose or in a specific time period, the contribution revenue is recognized in the temporarily restricted net assets.

Distinguishing exchange transactions from nonexchange transactions is often difficult. Some exchange transactions, such as special event revenue or membership dues, may include a nonexchange (contribution) portion. For example, the ticket to a gala event covers the cost of the meal plus a contribution. In this case, the portion of the ticket price that represents the value of the meal is recognized as an exchange (food revenue) whereas the contribution portion is recognized as a nonexchange contribution. The entry to record this transaction would be the following.

Cash	100	
Food revenue (unrestricted net assets)		20
Contribution revenue (unrestricted net assets)		80

To record the purchase of one ticket to the Gala Ball.

Although the above illustration recognizes the contribution revenue portion of the transaction as an addition to the unrestricted net assets, the contribution portion would have been recognized as an addition to the temporarily restricted net assets if the donor had stipulated the use of the contribution portion of the gala ticket.

Other transactions—such as grants, awards, and sponsorships by foundations, governments, and other resource providers—may have elements of an exchange transaction, a nonexchange transaction, or funds held in trust for others. To determine the type of transaction, it is necessary to assess the extent of discretion the NFP has over the use of the assets received. If the NFP has little or no discretion, the transaction is an agency transaction, that is, funds held in trust for others. If the NFP has discretion over the asset's use, the transaction is a contribution, an exchange, or a combination of the two.

Deferred revenue is an asset received in an exchange transaction from customers, patients, and other service beneficiaries for specific programs or activities that will take place in the future. To the extent that the earnings process has not yet occurred, the fair value of these resources should be reported as a liability. For example, assume that $500 was received by a symphony for concert events scheduled to be performed next fiscal year. Since the revenue is designated for a future period, it must be recognized as deferred revenue.

Cash	500	
Deferred revenue		500

To record the sale of symphony tickets for a future performance.

No net asset class is designated as the transaction only affects balance sheet accounts. When the concert is performed, the following entry is recorded.

Deferred revenue	500	
Performance revenue (unrestricted net assets)		500

To recognize the realization of deferred revenue.

RESTRICTIONS VERSUS CONDITIONS

Although both arise from donor stipulations, restrictions and conditions represent discrete criteria for recognizing contributions. Contributions, in addition to being restricted or unrestricted, may be either conditional or unconditional. Whereas a donor-imposed restriction merely stipulates that donated assets are to be used for a specific purpose or in a certain time period, a condition creates a barrier that must be overcome in order for the recipient of the asset to have an unconditional right to receive it. A **conditional contribution** depends on a specified future and uncertain event to bind the promissor to provide the promised asset. An instance of a conditional gift is one in which the donor agrees to give $1 million if his business income exceeds $5 million in a given year. In other words, the contribution is conditional upon the performance of the donor's business—a circumstance that is beyond the control of the NFP. Conditional promises to give are not recognized until all conditions have been met, but a summary of the outstanding promises is reported in the financial statement disclosures. In this example, the promise would be recognized if and when the business's income exceeds $5 million.

Conditional contribution: a contribution that has a barrier that must be satisfied for the resource recipient to have the right to receive it

In contrast, an **unconditional contribution** is a nonexchange transaction that is recognized upon receipt. It is a transfer of cash or other assets to an entity or a settlement or cancellation of its liabilities in a voluntary nonreciprocal transfer by another entity acting as other than an owner. The key concepts in the definition are the following:

Unconditional contribution: a nonexchange transaction recognized as revenue at its fair value upon receipt

1. *Unconditional.* The contribution has no contingency and depends only on the passage of time or the satisfaction of any donor stipulation.
2. *Non-reciprocal transfer.* The donor transfers an asset or incurs a liability for another without directly receiving any value in exchange.
3. *Acting as other than an owner.* The exchange is not an owner investment in the entity.

Unconditional contributions include cash, "promises to give," marketable securities, fixed assets, use of facilities, goods and services, and other assets. Alternatively, a contribution may be the relief from a liability. Unconditional contributions are recognized as assets and contribution revenues at fair value on the date they are received or promised. Restricted unconditional contributions whose restrictions are met in the same period may be reported as unrestricted revenues or gains provided that an organization maintains that policy for all similar transactions, reports consistently from period to period, and discloses its accounting policy in the financial statement disclosures. Assume, for example, that a donation was received in the current period and restricted by the donor to the purchase of a computer to track membership dues. If the computer was purchased before the end of the year, both the contribution and the purchase of the computer could be classified in the unrestricted net assets as revenue and an acquisition. However, if the computer is not purchased until the following fiscal year, the contribution should be recorded as revenue in the temporarily restricted net assets since the donor's purpose stipulation—that is, purchase of the computer—cannot be met until the following fiscal year. In the following year, the contribution resource is reclassified; that is, temporarily restricted net assets are reduced and unrestricted net assets increased—to recognize the release of the donor's stipulation and to provide resources for the acquisition of the computer.

PROMISES TO GIVE

Promise to give: a written or oral agreement *(pledge)* to contribute resources

Promises to give (also called *pledges*) are written or oral agreements to contribute cash or other assets. Promises to give may be either conditional or unconditional. A promise must be more than an indication of an intent to give, which is not legally binding. To be recognizable, the promise must be substantiated by sufficient evidence in the form of verifiable documentation, such as a letter or signed agreement. Oral promises, such as those received in a telephone fund-raising event, are not precluded because the person who solicited the contribution typically prepares a detailed record of the solicitation conversation. For example, assume that the local public radio station sponsored a telephone fund-raising event. During the evening, $15,000 in unconditional unrestricted contribution pledges was received. Based on past telephone fund-raising experience, the radio station expects 80 percent of the pledges to be paid. The following accounting entry would be recorded to recognize the pledge.

Contribution receivables	15,000	
Allowance for uncollected pledges		3,000
Contribution revenue (unrestricted net assets)		12,000

To record the contribution pledges associated with the telephone fund-raising event.

Subsidiary receivable records would be created based on the details of the name, addresses, and amount data recorded during the solicitation conversation.

Unconditional promise to give: a pledge to give that depends only on the passage of time or the demand of the recipient

An **unconditional promise to give** is a promise that depends only on the passage of time or on demands by the promisee for performances, such as those received in the telephone fund-raising event. A promise is considered unconditional if it is legally enforceable. An unconditional promise to give is reported in a manner consistent with other contributions, at fair value as an asset and contribution revenue when the unconditional promise is received. Unconditional promises are recognized in the appropriate net asset class—unrestricted, temporarily restricted, or permanently restricted—based upon donor specification or lack thereof. A **conditional promise to give** is a promise (pledge) contingent on specified, uncertain future events to bind the promissor to remit the promised amount. A conditional promise to give is not recognized until the conditions upon which it depends are substantially met. However, if the conditional promise to give is a material amount, a footnote disclosure would be included in the financial statements.

Conditional promise to give: a pledge to give that depends on a specified event for the contribution to be recognized

Multiple-year promises to give are by their nature temporarily restricted because future time periods are involved in the gift. Promises of this type are reported as an account receivable in the balance sheet and temporarily restricted contribution revenue when the promise to give is made. If the multiyear promise establishes an endowment, then contribution revenue in the permanently restricted net assets is credited. Both the asset and contribution revenues are recorded at the present value of the future cash collection. If collection is anticipated within one year, the NFP may use net realizable value, but if collection is expected to extend beyond one year, the value used for financial statements is based on the present value of future cash flows. At the end of each period, any difference between the present value originally recorded as temporarily restricted contribution revenue and the current value is recorded as new contribution revenue rather than interest. Several factors must be considered in determining the estimated future cash flows of unconditional multiyear promises to give: length of time before collection, creditworthiness of the donor, past collections experiences, and the NFP's policies regarding enforcing collections. To illustrate, assume that a donor promises to pay $300 in each of the next five years to support the local museum's ongoing operations. The museum uses an interest rate of 4 percent to record pledges to be paid over multiple years. The following entry would be recorded by the museum to recognize the promise.

Contribution receivable	1,336	
Contribution revenue (temporarily restricted net assets)		1,336

To record the multiple-year pledge that is expected to be paid in full. [Calculation: $300 × 4.452 (present value of annuity for five periods at 4 percent) = $1335.60]

At the end of the fiscal year, the museum recognized the payment received and a new contribution rather than interest income as an adjustment in the contribution receivable account to reflect the fair value change in the annuity due.

Cash	300	
Contribution receivable		300

Records the receipt of the first $300 payment when it is received.

Temporarily restricted net assets	300	
Unrestricted net assets		300

Reclasses the portion of the multiple-year pledge that was received

Contribution receivable	53	
Contribution revenue [temporarily restricted net assets]		53

To record the fair value change in the multiyear contribution accounts receivable. [Calculation: $1,336 – $300 = $1,036. 300×3.630 (present value of annuity for four periods at 4 percent) = $1,089. $1,089 – $1,036 = 53.]

NONCASH CONTRIBUTIONS

Gift in kind: contributions of goods or services

Many NFPs, such as the Salvation Army, food banks, and religious organizations, depend heavily on contributed goods and services to support their operations. Donated goods and services may include such items as clothes, food, furniture, and volunteered services. Other noncash contributions include such items as donated office space, donated utilities, and free advertisement. Contributions of this type are called **gifts in kind** and are recorded at their fair value when received. Contributed goods are reported as program expense or costs when the items are consumed. The following entry would be used to record the receipt of $8,000 worth of food products by the area food bank.

Food products inventory	8,000	
Contribution revenue (unrestricted net assets)		8,000

To record the fair value of food received.

Volunteered services are reported as contributed services revenue and as assets or expenses only if the services received fit the criteria established by SFAS No. 116. The criteria include the following:

- The services must enhance nonfinancial assets.
- The services require specialized skills that are possessed by those individuals who provide the services.
- The services would typically be purchased if not provided by donation.

Accountants, lawyers, and teachers in their professional capacity often perform tasks for NFPs. These services would be purchased if they were not donated. Thus, the organization recognizes the fair value on the date of the services as both a revenue and an appropriate program expense. For example, Robert Oliver, a local CPA, donates 20 hours of his time to audit the financial statements of the area food bank mentioned above. Mr. Oliver's time is normally billed at $90 per hour. Since Mr. Oliver's audit constitutes a professional service that the food bank would otherwise have purchased, the food bank records the following entry.

Audit expense	1,800	
Contributed services (unrestricted net assets)		1,800

To record the 20 hours of auditing services contributed by Robert Oliver, CPA.

However, had Mr. Oliver donated his time to inventory food donations rather than perform auditing services, the value of his time would not have been recognized as contributed service because the effort needed to inventory food does not require a professional skill. In addition, the food bank would probably not hire anyone to perform the inventory service but instead would rely on another volunteer.

When an owner contributes utilities or the use of fixed assets to an NFP but retains title to the property, these donations are recognized as contribution revenue at their fair value in the period in which the contribution is received and as an expense during the period in which the benefit is used. If the promise is unconditional for a specific number of future periods, the transaction is recorded as contributions receivable and restricted support that increases temporarily restricted net assets. As the utilities or fixed assets are used, the temporarily restricted net assets are reclassified to unrestricted net assets and the expense recorded.

Contributions of fixed assets are recognized as contributions and an increase in assets at their fair value on the date received. Donor stipulations and organizational policy also affect the status of the contribution. If the donor stipulates a length of time or specific use for the asset, or if the organization's accounting policy implies a time restriction on the use of assets that expires over the life of the asset, the contribution must be classified as temporarily restricted. Fixed asset contributions recorded as temporarily restricted require periodic reclassification from the temporarily restricted net asset class to the unrestricted net asset class in the amount of current depreciation expense or the time restriction, whichever is shorter.

ACCOUNTING FOR COLLECTIONS AND/OR HISTORIC TREASURES

For a contribution to be deemed a work of art or treasure, there must be verifiable evidence that two criteria exist. It must have (1) recognized cultural, aesthetic, or historical value that is worth preserving perpetually, and (2) the NFP must have the technological and financial means to preserve undiminished the service potential and, in fact, be doing so. Collections include artwork, historical assets, and similar treasures. Because it is often impracticable to determine a value for inexhaustible collections or treasures, the NFP may choose whether or not to recognize them as assets. Selective capitalization of collections is prohibited. Financial statement disclosures are required if an NFP does not **capitalize** its collections. To hold the assets as collections and not capitalize them, *all* of the following conditions must be met.[31]

Capitalization: records the value of a capital item or the costs incurred to build or acquire the item as an asset in the financial accounts

1. Collections/treasures are held for public exhibition, education or research in furtherance of public service.
2. They are to be preserved and protected.
3. If sold, the proceeds are to be reinvested in other collection items.

Contributed collection items are recognized as assets and revenues or gains if collections are capitalized. No recognition is required if collections are not capitalized.

---

[31] Op. cit., **FASB Statement of Financial Accounting Standards**, No. 116, par. 11.

Collection items are capitalized at cost if purchased and at fair value if received as a contribution. The recognition of depreciation of capitalized collections is excluded if the character of their economic benefit or service potential is used up so slowly that the amount of depreciation for any accounting period would be insignificant.

INVESTMENTS

All investments in equity securities with readily determinable fair values (except those accounted for under the equity method and investments in consolidated subsidiaries) and all investments in debt securities must be reported at fair value. NFPs are excluded from the provisions of SFAS No. 115[32] that require the display of various categories of investments, including trading, available for sale, and held to maturity.

Investment income (interest and dividends) from investments, along with any realized or unrealized gains and losses on investments, is included in the current period revenues. Income and gains and losses are reported as unrestricted net assets unless donor-imposed restrictions exist or a law legally restricts them.

Gains and investment income limited to specific uses by donor-imposed restrictions may be reported as increases in unrestricted net assets if the restrictions are met in the same reporting period in which the gains and income are recognized, subject to the following conditions:

1. The organization must have a similar policy for reporting contributions received.
2. The organization must report consistently from period to period.
3. The organization must disclose its accounting policy in the notes to the financial statements.

Unless there is a specific donor-imposed restriction, the income and gains from the permanent endowment are reported as unrestricted. A donor may stipulate that any increase in the value of an endowment is restricted until the endowment reaches a stipulated value. In this case the income and gains are permanently restricted until the stipulated value is met, at which time the income and gains are reported as unrestricted. For example, a donor establishes an endowment with an initial contribution or $96,000. The donor intends the endowment to support a specific event of the NFP, but investment income on $96,000 is insufficient. The donor believes that if the endowment were $100,000, sufficient investment income would be earned each year to support the event. Therefore, the donor stipulates that investment income must be added to the endowment corpus until it reaches $100,000. Once the endowment balance is $100,000, the investment income can be used for any operating purpose of the NFP. This year the endowment investments earned $7,500, which is recorded in the following entry.

Cash	7,500	
Investment income (unrestricted net assets)		3,500
Investment income (permanently restricted net assets)		4,000

To record income earned on endowment investments in accordance with donor stipulations. The amount necessary to increase the endowment balance to the designated $100,000 is added to permanently restricted net assets and the balance is unrestricted.

---

[32] **Statement of Financial Accounting Standards**, No. 115, "Accounting for Certain Investments in Debt and Equity Securities." (Norwalk, CT: Financial Accounting Standards Board, 1993).

In the absence of donor stipulations or laws to the contrary, losses on permanently restricted endowments reduce temporarily restricted net assets by an amount equal to the unused temporarily restricted income earned by the endowment. Any remaining loss reduces unrestricted net assets. Therefore, in the event that losses reduce the assets of a donor-restricted endowment below the level required by the donor or by law, organizational resources must be used to restore the endowment to the required level. Any future gains that restore the fair value of the assets of the endowment fund are classified as increases in unrestricted net assets until the amount of the loss is recovered. For example, assume that a local NFP had permanently restricted endowment investments of $100,000. This year the investments lost $15,000, and the organization had expended all temporarily restricted prior year income in accordance with the donor's restrictions. This situation requires that the organization absorb the loss in the unrestricted net assets and restore the investment to its original value so that the endowment investment remains at its original $100,000 value.

Investment loss (unrestricted net assets)	15,000	
Investments		15,000
To recognize the investment loss		
Investments	15,000	
Cash		15,000

To restore the endowment investment account to its original $100,000 balance as stipulated by the donor or law.

Information regarding investments held by the NFP is presented in the financial statement footnotes to display the aggregate carrying amount of the investments by major types together with the basis for determining the carrying amount for investment other than stocks and bonds with readily determinable fair values and all bond securities.

FINANCIAL STATEMENTS

At a minimum, the general purpose financial statements of NFPs include the following statements, along with appropriate notes and disclosures:

- Statement of financial position (may be titled balance sheet) that presents assets, liabilities and net assets (net assets parallel equity in business enterprises) (see Illustration 9-1).
- Statement of activities (operating statement) (see Illustration 9-2).
- Statement of cash flows (see Illustration 9-3).
- Statement of functional expenses—only for voluntary health and welfare organizations are required to present this statement (see Illustration 9-4).

Although in past years NFPs used a disaggregated method for financial reporting by fund or purpose for accountability purposes, they now report their financial activities as a whole entity using an aggregated single column. The aggregated display format brings NFP reporting more in line with the financial reporting model of a for-profit or corporate entity. GAAP, however, does not preclude the NFP from providing disaggregated information by fund group, program, or purpose as long as the required aggregated amounts for each of the three net asset classes are displayed.

ILLUSTRATION 9-1
Urban Community Service Organization
Statement of Financial Position
December 31, 2005

Assets:	
Cash	$ 29,850
Cash restricted for research program	4,275
Accounts Receivable (net of allowance for uncollectibles of $200)	6,100
Contributions receivable (net of allowance for uncollectibles of $535)	3,615
Contributions receivable—temporarily restricted (net of allowance	
for uncollectibles of $750)	3,559
Accrued interest receivable	2,300
Inventory—health care supplies	8,800
Investments—unrestricted	5,920
Assets restricted for investment in plant:	
Cash restricted for plant	8,125
Investments restricted for plant	
Land	10,000
Buildings and equipment (net of accumulated depreciation of $ 16,325)	105,675
Cash permanently restricted for endowment investments	12,100
Long-term investments (restricted for endowment)	122,700
Total assets	$ 323,019
Liabilities and Net Assets:	
Liabilities	
Accounts payable/accrued expenses	$ 10,800
Grants awards payable	850
Refundable advance (prepaid grant)	
Deferred revenue	1,800
Mortgage payable	42,500
Total liabilities	55,950
Net assets:	
Unrestricted—undesignated	98,985
Unrestricted—designated for special education program	4,950
Temporarily restricted—programs	4,850
Temporarily restricted—plant	8,125
Temporarily restricted—time	15,359
Permanently restricted (endowment)	134,800
Total net assets	267,069
Total liabilities and net assets	$ 323,019

NFPs are required to report financial statements using full accrual accounting recognition but have great flexibility in formatting their financial statements as long as certain requirements are met. To make the financial statements more useful, NFPs are encouraged, but not required, to provide nonfinancial information about service efforts and accomplishments (SEA).[33] Comparative statements are encouraged but not required.[34] NFPs are permitted to use other forms of accounting, such as cash basis or

---

[33] Op. cit., **FASB Statement of Financial Accounting Standards**, No. 117, par. 26.

[34] Ibid., par. 70.

ILLUSTRATION 9-2
Urban Community Service Organization
Statement of Activities
for Year Ended December 31, 2005

Changes in Unrestricted Net Assets:

Revenues and gains

Contributions		$ 82,400
Special events	$ 5,500	
Less: Direct costs of special events	675	4,825
Grant awards		21,950
Membership dues		10,700
Health care fees		1,250
Tuition for education classes		875
Interest income		13,000
Unrealized gain on short-term investments		420
Total unrestricted revenues and gains		135,420

Net assets released from restrictions

Satisfaction of program restrictions		725
Satisfaction of equipment acquisition restrictions		45,000
Expiration of time restrictions		3,075
Total net assets released from restrictions		48,800
Total unrestricted revenues, gains and other support		184,220

Expenses and losses

Program services

Health care		53,850
Education		34,830
Research		13,125
Total program services		101,805

Supporting services

Management and general		17,025
Fundraising		11,770
Total supporting services		28,795
Total expenses and losses		130,600
Increase in unrestricted net assets		53,620

Changes in Temporarily Restricted Net Assets:

Contributions		22,009
Gift grants		2,000
Interest Income		1,125
Net assets released from restrictions		(48,800)
Decrease in temporarily restricted net assets		(23,666)

Changes in Permanently Restricted Net Assets:

Contributions		7,000
Realized gains added to principal per donor stipulations		800
Increase in permanently restricted net assets		7,800
Increase in net assets:		37,754
Net assets at December 31, 2004		229,315
Net assets at December 31, 2005		$ 267,069

ILLUSTRATION 9-3
Urban Community Service Organization
Statement of Cash Flows
for Year Ended December 31, 2005

Cash flows from operating activities:	
Cash received from service recipients	$ 3,925
Cash received from contributors	87,200
Cash received from special events	4,825
Cash received from membership dues	6,400
Interest and dividends received	10,975
Cash paid to employees and suppliers	(77,825)
Cash paid to affiliated organizations	(2,100)
Grants awards paid	(5,450)
Interest paid	(3,800)
Net cash provided by operating activities	24,150
Cash flows from investing activities:	
Purchase of property and equipment	(32,000)
Proceeds from sale of investments	37,100
Decrease in cash invested in assets restricted for plant and endowment purposes	(33,225)
Net cash used by investing activities	(28,125)
Cash from financing activities:	
Proceeds from contributions restricted for:	
Investment in endowment	7,000
Investment in plant	20,000
Other financing activities:	
Interest and dividends add to principal per donor stipulations	1,125
Payments on long-term debt	(4,500)
Net cash used by financing activities	23,625
Net Increase (decrease) in cash	19,650
Cash at beginning of year	14,475
Cash at end of year	$ 34,125
Reconciliation of change in net assets to net cash provided by operating activities:	
Change in net assets	$ 37,754
Adjustments to reconcile change in net assets to net cash provided by operating activities:	
Add: depreciation	11,025
decrease in contributions receivable	4,391
decrease in inventories	1,550
increase in accounts payable	9,000
increase in deferred revenue	1,800
Less: increase in accounts receivable	(4,300)
increase in interest receivable	(2,025)
unrealized gain on investments	(420)
decrease in grants payable	(3,750)
decrease in refundable advances	(1,950)
Contributions restricted for long-term investment	(27,000)
Interest and dividends restricted for long-term investment	(1,125)
Net unrealized and realized gains on long-term investments	(800)
Net cash provided by operating activities	$ 24,150

ILLUSTRATION 9-4
Urban Community Service Organization
Statement of Functional Expenses
for Year Ended December 31, 2005

	Program Services				Supporting Services			
	Health Care	Education Class	Research	Total	Management and General	Fund-Raising	Total	Total Expenses
Salaries	$21,367	$ 13,610	$ 5,151	$ 40,128	$ 5,862	$ 2,010	$ 7,872	$ 48,000
Payroll Taxes	2,633	2,640	999	6,272	1,138	390	1,528	7,800
Total salaries and related expenses	24,000	16,250	6,150	46,400	7,000	2,400	9,400	55,800
Interest	926	1,033	812	2,771	937	92	1,029	3,800
Grants and awards		1,700		1,700				1,700
Health care supplies	6,650			6,650				6,650
Supplies	325	1,750	150	2,225	1,350	1,025	2,375	4,600
Postage and shipping	200	300	50	550	845	305	1,150	1,700
Professional services	15,000	4,500	725	20,225	700	2,100	2,800	23,025
Telephone	365	100	370	835	525	540	1,065	1,900
Facility use	2,400	1,200	585	4,185	1,375	640	2,015	6,200
Utility	380	275	420	1,075	225	200	425	1,500
Travel	720		840	1,560	400	240	640	2,200
Meetings & banquets		325	350	675	375	250	625	1,300
Printing	485	4,300	235	5,020	480	3,700	4,180	9,200
Total before depreciation	51,451	31,733	10,687	93,871	14,212	11,492	25,704	119,575
Depreciation of buildings and equipment	2,399	3,097	2,438	7,934	2,813	278	3,091	11,025
Total expenses	$53,850	$34,830	$13,125	$101,805	$ 17,025	$11,770	$28,795	$130,600

fund accounting, for internal purposes as long as the external financial statements conform to GAAP requirements.

The statement of financial position (Illustration 9-1) is focused on the organization as a whole at a specific point in time and reports the amount of total assets, liabilities, and net assets (which is the difference between assets and liabilities). The net asset section is categorized into three classes of net assets—including unrestricted net assets, temporarily restricted net assets, and permanently restricted net assets—based on the existence or absence of donor-imposed restrictions. Disclosure of governing board-designated limitations on the use of unrestricted net assets is permitted on the face of the statement or in the footnotes.

Assets and liabilities are aggregated into reasonably homogeneous groups similar to those of business enterprises. Assets are sequenced according to their liquidity—that is, their nearness to conversion to cash—whereas liabilities are presented according to the nearness of their maturity and use of cash.

Assets (as opposed to net assets) are not required to be disaggregated on the statement of financial position based on the existence or absence of donor-imposed restrictions on their use. For example, unrestricted cash available for current use is not reported separately from cash received with donor-imposed restrictions but also available for current use. However, cash or other assets received with donor-imposed restrictions that limit their use to long-term purposes should not be classified with cash or other assets that are unrestricted and available for current use. For example, cash that has been received with donor-imposed restrictions limiting its use to the acquisition of plant and equipment is reported as a segregated amount, such as restricted or noncurrent cash, in the statement of financial position.

The statement of activities (operating statement) (see Illustration 9-2) also focuses on the organization as a whole and reports in an aggregated manner revenues, expenses, gains, losses, and reclassifications along with the resultant amount of change in permanently restricted net assets, temporarily restricted net assets, unrestricted net assets, and total net assets for the period. The changes in the net assets in the statement of activities articulate (agree) with the net asset balances in the statement of financial position.

Revenues are reported at gross amounts by source and are categorized according to the three classes of changes in net assets: changes in unrestricted net assets, changes in temporarily restricted net assets, and changes in permanently restricted net assets. Expenses are also reported at gross amounts but are always reported as reductions in unrestricted net assets and categorized by the function performed, including major classes of program expenses and support activities. Because the distinction of what is operating and what is nonoperating can be problematic, the NFP is neither precluded from presenting the revenues, expenses, gains, and losses as operating or nonoperating in the statement of activities nor required to do so.

Program services: categories of expenses that describe related expenses that fulfill the mission of the organization

Function categories: a group of related expenses activities that accomplish a major service or regulatory responsibility for which the government is responsible

Support services: administrative and other expenses that enable the organization to perform its mission

Program services are the activities that result in the NFP's fulfilling the purposes or mission for which it exists. **Functional categories** explain the primary activities of the NFP and include both direct expenses and allocations of indirect costs. Examples of functional categories include a health and welfare organization reporting functions for health or family services, research, and education; a university having student programs or functions for instruction, research, and patient care; or a museum having programs or functions for art education, art classes, and lectures on art history.

Support services are all activities of an NFP other than program services. They typically include managerial, general, fund-raising, and membership-development activities. Management and general activities include oversight, business management, general recordkeeping, budgeting, financing, and all management and administration expense unless directly connected with a program service. Fund-raising includes publicizing and conducting fund-raising campaigns, maintaining donor mailing lists, soliciting contributions from donors, and so on. Membership-development activities include soliciting prospective members, collecting dues, and handling member relations.

Realized and unrealized investment income may be reported as a net amount, if properly disclosed. For example, investment revenues may be reported net of related expenses, such as custodial fees and investment advisory fees, provided that the amount of the expenses is disclosed either on the face of the statement of activities or in the financial statement notes. Also reported net are gains and losses from peripheral or incidental transactions that are not part of the NFP's normal operations and that may be largely beyond the control of the organization. For example, an entity that sells land and buildings no longer needed for its ongoing activities commonly reports that transaction as a gain or loss, rather than recording the proceeds of the sale as revenue and the carrying value of the assets sold as an expense. The net amount of those peripheral transactions, in conjunction with information in a statement of cash flows, is usually adequate to help assess how an entity uses its resources and how managers discharge their stewardship duties.

The statement of activity reports reclassifications in a section entitled "Net assets released from restrictions." This section reports reclassifications from temporarily restricted net assets to unrestricted net assets for satisfaction of donor stipulations and is reported in the period during which the stipulations are satisfied. Satisfactions include the fulfillment of program and purpose restrictions as well as and the fulfillment of time restrictions, either actual donor or implied restrictions. Normally satisfaction is achieved by incurring expenses or costs for the restricted purpose or by the passage of time.

Additional classifications are allowed in the statement of activities to report changes in unrestricted net assets from operating activities versus nonoperating activities, expendable versus nonexpendable, earned versus unearned, recurring versus nonrecurring, or to present results by fund groups. These additional classifications allow the NFP to personalize the financials to meet the needs of its users.

The statement of cash flows (Illustration 9-3) classifies cash receipts and cash payments during a period resulting from investing, financing, or operating activities. Separate disclosure of noncash investing and financing activities (for example, receiving contributions of buildings, securities, or recognized collection items) is required. Although NFP organizations are allowed to use the indirect method of reporting cash flows, they are encouraged to use the direct method. If the direct method is used, the NFP must provide a separate schedule on the face of the statement to show the change in total net assets from the statement of activities to net cash used for operating activities as shown in Illustration 9-3.

Although donor-imposed restrictions are not reported separately in the statement of cash flows, some cash flow reporting requirements are unique to the NFP, including the following:

1. Finance activities include cash inflows from contributions and investment income that by donor stipulation are restricted for capital assets, endowment, or other long-term purposes. Also included in this activity are new loans made and loan principal payments.

2. Investing activities include acquiring and disposing of long-term assets. Investment portfolio acquisitions and sales are reported at their gross amounts.

3. Operating activities include any unrestricted gifts. Interest and dividends that are donor restricted for long-term purposes, as above, are not considered operating activities but rather financing activities, as discussed in item 1.

Statement of functional expenses: a matrix that compares the natural class of expenses to the function performed

Voluntary health and welfare organizations (VHWOs) are required to report expenses by functional category as well as natural category—such as salaries, rent, supplies, and utilities—and present a **statement of functional expenses** (see Illustration 9-4) in addition to their other financial statements. NFPs other than VHWOs are encouraged to provide information about expenses by natural category but are not required to do so. Formatted as a matrix, the statement of functional expenses reports expenses by their functional and natural classifications. Note that column headings correspond to the functional categories reported in the statement of activities and row titles represent the natural classifications. This statement is optional for all NFPs other than VHWOs.

HEALTH CARE ORGANIZATIONS

Although health care organizations are covered by the same GAAP as other NFPs, they must adhere to additional requirements found in the AICPA Health Care Audit Guide,[35] which is different from the VHWO financial statements illustrated in this chapter. Private hospitals, home health agencies, nursing homes, and health maintenance organizations

---

[35] Op. cit., *Health Care Organizations* (May 1997).

(HMOs) are examples of health care organizations because they receive substantially all their revenues from providing health care and health related services.

Some of the important reporting requirements are the following:

1. The financial statements of health care organizations include a balance sheet, a statement of operations, a statement of changes in equity (or net assets), a statement of cash flows, and notes to the financial statements. The statement of operations and statement of changes in equity may be combined into a single statement.

2. Health care organizations, excluding the continuing care communities, must present a classified balance sheet with assets and liabilities displayed as current or noncurrent.

3. Patient service revenue is reported net of contractual adjustments based on third-party payer agreements, such as those with insurance companies. Note disclosure describes the methods of revenue recognition as well as the description of the types and amounts of contractual adjustments.

Capitation: a fixed dollar amount of fees per person paid periodically by a third-party payer to a health care organization regardless of the services performed

4. Patient service revenue normally includes (a) net patient service revenue, (b) premium revenue from **capitation agreements** (NFP agreements to provide a service to a group or an individual for a fixed fee), (c) and other revenue from such activities as gift shop and cafeteria sales, parking lot or transcript fees, rentals to nonresidents, investment income and gains, and unrestricted contributions.

5. Patient service revenue does not include charity care, which is recorded neither as a receivable nor as revenue. Note disclosures include management's policy for providing charity care and the level of charity care provided.

6. "Assets limited as to use" is an unrestricted balance sheet category that refers to assets whose use is limited by contracts or agreements with outside parties other than donors or grantors. Examples include proceeds of debt issues or self-insurance funding arrangements. The category can also refer to limitations placed on assets by the governing board plans for future use. Significant contractual limits should be disclosed in the notes to the financial statements.

7. The Statement of Operations contains a performance indicator such as "operating income" to report the result of operations. The performance indicator is computed using figures from unrestricted revenues, gains and other support, expenses, and other income. To determine what goes "above" or "below" the performance indicator, items must first be categorized as operating or non-operating.

Investment income, realized gains and losses, and unrealized gains and losses on trading securities are reported above the performance indicator, whereas the following are reported below the performance indicator:

- Equity transfers involving related entities
- Receipt of restricted contributions
- Contributions of (and assets released from donor restrictions related for) long lived assets
- Unrealized gains and losses on investments not restricted by donors or by law, except for those investments classified as trading securities
- Investment returns restricted by donors or law
- Other items for which GAAP requires a separate report (such as extraordinary items, the effect of discontinued operations, or the cumulative effect of accounting changes)

SUMMARY AND COMPREHENSIVE ILLUSTRATION

Accounting for nongovernment not-for-profit organizations is much the same as accounting for the operations of for-profit organizations because both entities have operating transactions that are recognized in the financial statements. The primary difference between the two is the recognition of, and reporting for, contributions and any donor stipulations relating to the contribution. This chapter presented an overview of GAAP for nongovernment not-for-profit organizations and a discussion of their characteristics together with the recognition and reporting principles for various types of donor stipulations, including restrictions, conditions, and exchange transactions.

The following is a comprehensive illustration of these recognition and reporting principles. The Financial activities of Urban Community Services Organization, a VHWO, are used for the illustration because the organization is required to present a statement of functional expenses in addition to the three basic financial statements—statement of financial position, statement of activities, and statement of cash flows.

Accounting events for Urban Community Services Organization are described and documented in the following journal entries. The account balances displayed in the beginning-of-year trial balance are then adjusted by the journal entries. The new account balances are used to prepare the end-of-period financial statements displayed earlier as Illustrations 9-1 through 9-4.

Recognition and Reporting Comprehensive Illustration for a Nongovernment Not-for-Profit Organization

Urban Community Service Organization
Beginning Trial Balance
as of December 31, 2004

	Debits	Credits
Cash	$ 9,475	
Cash restricted for research program	5,000	
Accounts receivable—membership dues	2,000	
Allowance for uncollectable accounts receivable		$ 200
Contributions receivable—unrestricted	5,350	
Allowance for uncollectable contributions receivable—unrestricted		535
Contributions receivable—temporarily restricted	7,500	
Allowance for uncollectable contributions receivable—temporarily restricted		750
Interest receivable—unrestricted	275	
Inventory—health care supplies	10,350	
Investments—unrestricted	5,500	
Investments restricted for plant	32,000	
Long-term investments—permanently restricted	127,000	
Land	10,000	
Buildings and equipment	77,000	
Accumulated depreciation—buildings and equipment		5,300
Accounts payable		1,800
Grants payable		4,600
Refundable advances		1,950
Mortgage payable		47,000
Unrestricted net assets—undesignated—available for operations		47,015
Unrestricted net assets—designated for education program		3,300
Temporarily restricted net assets—programs		5,000

Temporarily restricted net assets—plant		32,000
Temporarily restricted net assets—time		15,000
Permanently restricted net assets—endowment		127,000
Totals	$ 291,450	$ 291,450

During the fiscal year, the following transactions occurred.

1. Cash contribution and program inflows and revenues were received from the following sources: membership dues of $5,000, which includes a $300 prior year dues accounts receivable payment; health program service fees of $1,250; tuition for education class of $875; unrestricted grants of $20,000 and a gift of $2,000 restricted for acquisition of plant assets.

	Debits	*Credits*
Cash	27,125	
Cash restricted for plant acquisitions	2,000	
Accounts receivable—membership dues		300
Membership dues		4,700
Health care program fees		1,250
Tuition for education classes		875
Grants—unrestricted		20,000
Gift revenue—temporarily restricted—plant		2,000

2. Contribution revenues of $1,875 received in the prior year restricted by donors to be used in the current year are reclassified from the temporarily restricted to the unrestricted net asset class because the time restriction is met.

Temporarily restricted net assets—time	1,875	
Unrestricted net assets—undesignated		1,875

3. $30,000 in cash was collected for unrestricted contributions, including $1,200 in contributions receivable. $6,000 in cash was collected for temporarily (time) restricted contributions stipulated by donors for use in 2006 that includes $4,700 contributions receivable.

Cash	36,000	
Contribution revenue		28,800
Contributions receivable—unrestricted		1,200
Contribution revenue—temporarily restricted—time		1,300
Contributions receivable—temporarily restricted—time		4,700

4. Accounts receivable of $1,400 for membership dues are collected and current membership dues of $6,000 are billed but not collected.

Cash	1,400	
Accounts receivable—membership dues		1,400
Accounts receivable—membership dues	6,000	
Membership dues		6,000

5. Pledges, promises to pay, are received for the following: $700 to be paid next year for unrestricted purposes, $575 restricted by the donor for programs, and an unconditional promise to give $300 each year for the next five years (the annuity of five payments of $300 each discounted at 4 percent = $ 1,336). The first payment of $300 will be paid next year.

Contributions receivable—temporarily restricted	2,611	
Contribution revenue—temporarily restricted—time ($1,336 + $700)		2,036
Contribution revenue—temporarily restricted—programs		575

Promises to give in a future year involve a transfer of assets in a future reporting period and are therefore temporarily restricted by time. They may also be temporarily restricted by purpose. As the annuity matures, the change is considered a new contribution rather than interest revenue.

6. The organization held a special event (art sale) to raise unrestricted funds. Proceeds were $5,500, and related direct costs of $675 were incurred and paid. Supplies expenses of $250 were also incurred and paid. Special events are a major activity for the organization.

Cash	5,500	
Special events contribution		5,500
Special events cost	675	
Fund-raising expenses	250	
Cash		925

7. Interest income of $1,125 for investments restricted for plant and $10,700 of unrestricted investment income from endowments was received in cash. Unrestricted interest receivable of $275 was also received. Unrestricted interest income earned but not yet received was accrued in the amount of $2,300.

Cash restricted for plant	1,125	
Cash ($10,700 + $275)	10,975	
Interest receivable—unrestricted	2,300	
Interest receivable—unrestricted		275
Interest revenue—unrestricted ($10,700 + $2,300)		13,000
Interest revenue—temporarily restricted—plant		1,125

8. All conditions of a prior year's unrestricted prepaid grant of $1,950 were substantially met. The grant proceeds were originally recorded as a refundable advance.

Refundable advance	1,950	
Grant revenue—unrestricted		1,950

9. Health care supplies valued at $600 were donated. The organization uses the periodic inventory method. The use of a facility with annual rent valued at $3,500 was donated. 30 percent of the space was used for fund-raising activities and 70 percent was used by the accounting and budgeting administration.

Health care program expenses	600	
Contribution revenue—unrestricted		600
Fund-raising expenses	1,050	
Management and general expenses	2,450	
Contribution revenue—unrestricted		3,500

Donated supplies must be recorded at their fair value as both an expense and revenue when the periodic inventory method is used. Under the perpetual inventory method, inventory (an asset account) would be debited.

10. Received payment from United Way for annual $30,000 award allocation less 7-percent service fee that is considered fund-raising expenses of Urban Community Service Organization.

Cash	27,900	
Fund-raising expenses	2,100	
Contribution revenue—unrestricted		30,000

11. $900 in cash is received for pledges received last year to support this year's activities. The amount is reclassified from temporarily restricted to unrestricted net assets because the time restriction has been satisfied.

Cash	900	
Contributions receivable—temporarily restricted—time		900
Temporarily restricted net assets—time	900	
Unrestricted net assets		900

12. Last year a donor pledged to pay $300 a year for 10 years and stipulated that the gift could be used for unrestricted operating activities. At that time, using a discount rate of 4 percent, a temporarily restricted contributions receivable of $2,433 was recorded. This year the first payment of $300 is received. This payment is recorded and the amount reclassified from temporarily restricted to unrestricted net assets. A new contribution of $98 is recorded to reflect the fair value change in the annuity due. The difference between the discounted amount of nine payments of $300 at 4 percent, or $2,231, and the receivable amount of $2,133 ($2,433 − $300) in the Contributions receivable—temporarily restricted account ($2,231 − 2,133 = 98) is recognized as new revenue.

Cash	300	
Temporarily restricted net assets—time (reclassified)	300	
Contributions receivable—temporarily restricted—time		300
Unrestricted net assets (reclassified)		300
Contributions receivable—temporarily restricted—time	98	
Contribution revenue—temporarily restricted—time		98

13. Investments restricted for plant acquisitions were sold at par, $32,000, and used to purchase equipment. It is not the policy of Urban Community Service Organization to apply a time restriction on fixed assets acquired with restricted resources.

Cash restricted for plant acquisition	32,000	
Investments restricted for plant purposes		32,000
Buildings and equipment	32,000	
Cash restricted for plant acquisition		32,000
Temporarily restricted net assets—plant (reclassified)	32,000	
Unrestricted net assets (reclassified)		32,000

The only restriction to be fulfilled is the purchase of the fixed asset. Thus, the plant restriction is satisfied and a reclassification to unrestricted net assets is recorded at this time. Had the donor stipulated that the fixed asset was to be used for a number of years, a reclassification would have been recorded each period over the useful life of the asset (depreciation) or the number of years stipulated by the donor, whichever is shorter.

14. Cash donations of $25,000 were received. $18,000 was restricted by the donor for plant costs, and $7,000 was restricted for a permanent endowment.

Cash restricted for plant	18,000	
Cash permanently restricted for endowment	7,000	
Contribution revenue—temporarily restricted—plant		18,000
Contribution revenue—permanently restricted		7,000

15. Salaries and wages during the year totaled $48,000, and payroll taxes totaled $7,800. At end of the year-end $3,300 of the payroll taxes had not been paid.

Salaries and wages expense	48,000	
Payroll taxes expense	7,800	
Cash		52,500
Accounts payable/accrued expenses		3,300

16. Other expenses for programs and support services were health care supplies, $4,500; postage and shipping, $1,700; professional fees, $700; telephone, $1,900; rents, $2,700; utilities, $1,500; travel, $2,200; meetings and banquets, $1,300; printing, $5,500; supplies, $4,000. Of this amount, $5,700 remained unpaid at year's end.

Supplies expense—health care	4,500	
Postage and shipping expense	1,700	
Professional fees expense	700	
Telephone expense	1,900	
Rent expense	2,700	
Utility expense	1,500	
Travel expense	2,200	
Meetings and banquets expense	1,300	
Printing expense	5,500	
Supplies	4,000	
Cash		20,300
Accounts payable/accrued expenses		5,700

17. Classroom tuition is collected in December for classes starting in January of the new year.

Cash	1,800	
Deferred revenue—tuition for education class		1,800

18. Interest of $3,800 and principal of $4,500 were paid on the mortgage during the year.

Interest expense	3,800	
Mortgage payable	4,500	
Cash		8,300

19. A building addition costing $13,000 was acquired with cash restricted for plant.

Temporarily restricted net assets—plant	13,000	
Unrestricted net assets		13,000
Buildings and equipment	13,000	
Cash		13,000

20. Cash restricted for the research program was expended for professional fees as specified by the donor in the amount of $725. $350 in unrestricted resources (designated by the governing board) was used to pay for special education program supply expenses.

Research program expense	725	
Cash restricted for research program		725
Education program expense	350	
Cash		350
Temporarily restricted net assets—programs	725	
Unrestricted net assets designated for special education program	350	
Unrestricted net assets		1,075

When temporarily restricted resources are available to finance a specific program, qualifying expenses are paid from that source first. The reclassification to unrestricted net assets for the expense incurred by the special education program is not required but is used as an internal method of tracking the balance in unrestricted net assets designated for the special education program.

21. The governing board designated an additional $2,000 to be used for the special education program.

Unrestricted net assets	2,000	
Unrestricted net assets—designated for special education program		2,000

Board designation of net assets for a specific purpose does not change the net asset classification from unrestricted to restricted.

22. Donated services and the fair value of work performed include the following.

- A doctor who treated patients at no charge, $15,000
- A teacher who taught classes at no charge, $4,500
- A CPA who participated in the research project by going door to door with survey questionnaires at no charge, $2,500

Health care program expense	15,000	
Education program expense	4,500	
Contribution revenue—unrestricted		19,500

Because the CPA was not performing services in a professional capacity, the value of the service is not recognized.

23. Long-term investments from permanently restricted endowment funds costing $4,300 were sold for $5,100. By donor stipulation, all realized gains on this endowment must be added to the endowment principal until the corpus reaches $10,000.

Cash permanently restricted for endowment	5,100	
Long-term investments—permanently restricted		4,300
Realized gain of investments—permanently restricted		800

According to SFAS No. 124, unless gains or losses are temporarily or permanently restricted by a donor's explicit stipulation or by a law that extends a donor's restriction to them, gains and losses on investments are changes in unrestricted net assets.

24. Educational grants are awarded to local schools for $1,700. The $4,600 balance in the grants payable account and one-half of the current year's grant are paid in cash. The unpaid portion of the current year's award is recorded as grants payable.

Education program expense	1,700	
Grants payable	4,600	
Cash		5,450
Grants payable		850

25. Temporarily restricted contributions for use in the current year to fund the purchase of new plant assets have met the time restrictions imposed by donors. The plant assets are ordered but will not be received until the new year.

No entry is required at this time. Although the time restriction has been met, the purpose restriction has not. When the fixed assets are received, an entry will be made to record the acquisition and to reclassify the resources from temporarily restricted to unrestricted.

26. Late in the year, a fund-raising campaign was launched. Printing costs of $3,700 were paid. The organization did not begin receiving contributions as a result of the campaign solicitations until January of the new year.

Fund-raising expenses	3,700	
Cash		3,700

Year-End Adjusting Entries

27. A count of health care supplies inventory valued at the lower of cost or market reflected a balance of $8,800. The health care program will be charged.

Health care program expenses	1,550	
Inventory—health care supplies ($10,350 – $8,800)		1,550

28. Analysis of the investments account indicated that the fair value of the Investments—unrestricted account was $420 more than the balance being carried on the records.

Investments—unrestricted	420	
Unrealized gains on investments—unrestricted		420

SFAS No. 124 requires that the fair value of investment be reported. Thus the "unrealized" gain must be recorded. If the investments had been sold at a gain resulting in a "realized" gain, the gain would have resulted in the same entry.

29. Depreciation of $11,025 is recorded for the buildings and equipment.

Depreciation expense	11,025	
Accumulated depreciation—buildings and equipment		11,025

No reclassification is necessary because it is the policy of this organization that gifts to acquire long-lived fixed assets that have donor restrictions are released from restriction when the long-lived fixed asset is purchased or placed in service.

Year-End Reclassification Entries

30. The natural classification for salaries and payroll taxes from entry 15 is allocated into services programs and support services according to organizational policy using the following percentages: health care, 43.01 percent; education, 29.12 percent; research, 11.02 percent; management and general, 12.55 percent; and fund raising, 4.30 percent.

Health care program expense	24,000	
Education program expense	16,250	
Research program expense	6,150	
Management and general expense	7,000	
Fund-raising expenses	2,400	
Salaries expense		48,000
Payroll taxes expense		7,800

31. The natural classifications of expenses from entry 16 are allocated to program services and support services according to organizational policy using the following percentages: health care, 36.06 percent; education, 30.38 percent; research, 11.54 percent; management and general, 14.71 percent; and fund-raising, 7.31 percent.

Health care program expense	9,375	
Education program expense	7,900	
Research program expense	3,000	
Management and general expense	3,825	
Fund-raising expenses	1,900	
Supplies expense—heatlh care		4,500
Postage and shipping expense		1,700
Professional fees expense		700
Telephone expense		1,900
Rent expense		2,700
Utility expense		1,500
Travel expense		2,200
Meetings and banquets expense		1,300
Printing expense		5,500
Supplies		4,000

32. Interest expense from entry 18 is allocated to program services and support services according to organizational policy using the following percentages: health care 24.36%, education 27.19%, research 21.37%, management and general 24.65% and fund raising 2.43%.

Health care program expense	926	
Education program expense	1,033	
Research program expense	812	
Management and general expense	937	
Fund raising expenses	92	
Interest expense—mortgage		3,800

33. Depreciation expense from entry 29 is allocated to program services and support services in accordance with organizational policies.

Health care program expense	2,399	
Education program expense	3,097	
Research program expense	2,438	
Management and general expense	2,813	
Fund-raising expenses	278	
Depreciation expense		11,025

The statements presented in Illustrations 9-1 through 9-4 are the results when entries 1 through 33 are recorded.

QUESTIONS

9-1. List and explain the criterion that distinguishes a not-for-profit organization from a for-profit organization. Where is this guidance found?

9-2. List and explain the criterion that distinguishes a nongovenmental not-for-profit organization from a governmental not-for-profit organization. Where is this guidance found?

9-3. How was the GAAP hierarchy for nongovernmental entities established? Explain the GAAP hierarchy as it relates to nongovernmental entities.

9-4. List the important pronouncements that effect nongovernmental not-for-profit organizations as discussed in this chapter.

9-5. Explain the difference between contributions with restrictions and contributions with conditions. What effect does the difference have on revenue recognition?

9-6. List and briefly describe the three classes of net assets required by FASB Statement No. 117.

9-7. Explain the standards for depreciation in FASB Statement No. 93 as they relate to an NFP.

9-8. Describe the different categories of revenue received by an NFP.

9-9. Many different kinds of services are contributed to NFPs. Outline revenue recognition and expense recognition requirements for contributed services.

9-10. Explain the accounting requirements and alternatives for collections.

9-11. Explain the general standards for investments set forth in FASB Statement No. 124.

9-12. List the financial statements required by the AICPA Audit and Accounting Guide *Health Care Organizations*.

9-13. What are the standards that address multiyear unconditional promises to give? When should these contributions be recognized as revenue? What assets classes are affected and how should the revenues be measured?

9-14. What is a voluntary health and welfare organization? What are its distinguishing characteristics? What unique financial statement must it prepare?

9-15. Do health care organizations follow the same GAAP as all other NFPs? Identify the GAAP health care organizations must follow and briefly describe the reporting requirements.

9-16. Using FARS, determine how investments held by not-for-profit organizations should be recorded and reported. (*Hint:* Open FARS, click on File; Open; Nfo; Open; and select FASB-op, click search, enter query.)

9-17. Using FARS, determine how a not-for-profit organization recognizes and accounts for a promise to give. How is the promise to give accounted for relative to cash contributions?

9-18. How should an endowment be displayed in the financial statements of a not-for-profit organization? What FARS citation supports this display?

9-19. Prepare a list of deferred debits and deferred credits that could appear on a not-for-profit organization's statement of financial position. Identify any unique transactions that are recognized as deferred debits and deferred credits and explain what makes the transactions unique.

9-20. Explain the term *variance power*. Just how does variance power determine whether a not-for-profit organization recognizes resources received as revenue or as a liability?

MULTIPLE CHOICE

9-1. What are the three classes of net assets reported by a not-for-profit organization?

  a. Unrestricted, permanently restricted, and exchange

  b. Unrestricted, temporarily restricted, and nonoperating

  c. Unrestricted, temporarily restricted, and permanently restricted

  d. Operating, nonoperating, and restricted

9-2. What are the financial statements required of a voluntary health and welfare organization?

  a. Statement of activities, statement of financial position, and cash flow statement

  b. Statement of financial position, cash flow statement, statement of functional expenses, and statement of activities

  c. Statement of functional expenses, statement of activities, and statement of financial position

  d. Statement of activities, statement of financial position, and statement of net assets

9-3. The financial statements of an NFP are prepared under what basis of accounting?

  a. Cash

  b. Modified accrual

  c. Tax basis

  d. Full accrual

9-4. On December 31, 2005, Good Deeds Community Organization, a nongovernment not-for-profit organization, received $10,000 in pledges to be paid to Good Deeds in 2006. Past pledges show a collection rate of 80 percent. How much revenue would Good Deeds report for 2005 as a result of this transaction?

  a. $10,000

  b. $0

  c. $8,000

  d. None of the above

9-5. United Food Organization received food donations for the year worth $4,000 and distributed 50 percent of the food through its Food for All program by year-end. How would United Food report the receipt and distribution of the food?

  a. $4,000, contribution revenue; $2,000, program expense

  b. $2,000, contribution revenue; $2,000, program expense

  c. $4,000, contribution revenue; $0, program expense

  d. None of the above

9-6. Jane James, a CPA, volunteers her time to the New Home Shelter, a not-for-profit organization, and spent 20 hours serving hot plates to the homeless at the free Christmas dinner. She normally charges $100 an hour for her work. How should New Home Shelter report Ms. James's services?

    a. $2,000, contributions revenue; $2,000, program expense

    b. $0, contribution revenue; $0, program expense

    c. $2,000, contribution revenue; $0, program expense

    d. $0 contribution revenue; $2,000, program expense

9-7. An NFP received $5,000 in 2005 with a donor-imposed restriction that it was to be used to purchase fixed assets in 2006. How is revenue from this transaction reported in the financial statements?

    a. No revenue is reported in 2005; restricted contribution revenue is reported in 2006.

    b. Unrestricted revenue is reported in 2005; no revenue is reported in 2006.

    c. Temporarily restricted revenue is reported only when the fixed asset is purchased.

    d. Temporarily restricted revenue is reported in 2005; no revenue is reported in 2006.

9-8. Goodwill Association, an NFP, received a $3,000 pledge in 2001 with a donor restriction that it was not to be used until 2003. Cash to satisfy the pledge was received in 2002. How would this transaction be reported in the net assets section of the statement of position?

    a. No entry in 2001; temporarily restricted net assets in 2002 and 2003

    b. Temporarily restricted net assets in 2001; unrestricted net assets in 2003

    c. No entry in 2001; temporarily restricted net assets in 2002; unrestricted net assets in 2003

    d. None of the above

9-9. XYZ, an NFP, received a gift of securities. What basis should be used to value this gift in the statement of position?

    a. At donor's cost

    b. A zero basis to XYZ

    c. Fair value at the date of the gift or donor's cost, whichever is lower

    d. Market or fair value at the date of the gift

9-10. Mercy Hospital, an NFP, received a $100,000 unrestricted donation. The governing board of Mercy Hospital decided to place this donation in a permanent endowment. How would this donation be classified in the net assets section of the statement of financial position?

    a. Unrestricted "assets limited as to use"

    b. Permanently restricted net assets

    c. Temporarily restricted

    d. Unrestricted, undesignated

9-11. In order to be recognized as a collection, artwork, historical assets, and similar treasures must satisfy which of the following conditions?

    a. They are held for public exhibition, education, or research in furtherance of public service.

    b. They are to be preserved and protected.

    c. Proceeds are to be reinvested in other collections if sold.

    d. All of the above are true.

Questions 9-12, 9-13, and 9-14 are based on the following information. Community Art Museum incurred the following expenses for the year.

Art program expenses	$1,200
Annual business meeting expenses	300
Soliciting requests for contributions	1,500

9-12. How much of the expenses should be classified as program expenses in the statement of activities for the year?

    a. $1,500

    b. $1,200

    c. $3,000

    d. None of the above

9-13. How much should be classified as fund-raising expenses in the statement of activities for the year?

    a. $1,500

    b. $1,800

    c. $3,000

    d. None of the above

9-14. How much should be classified as support services in the statement of activities for the year?

    a. $1,500

    b. $1,800

    c. $3,000

    d. None of the above

9-15. Expenses of an NFP are always reported in the Statement of Activities as which of the following?

    a. Changes in unrestricted net assets, temporarily restricted net assets, and permanently restricted net assets based on the type of expenditure

    b. Changes in temporarily restricted net assets and permanently restricted net assets, but not unrestricted net assets

    c. Changes in unrestricted net assets but not temporarily restricted net assets or permanently restricted net assets

    d. Changes in unrestricted net assets, temporarily restricted net assets, and permanently restricted net assets according to donor-imposed stipulation on the source of the funds expended

9-16. Contributions may be either temporarily restricted or permanently restricted by donors. Restrictions may be imposed as to which of the following?

a. Time

b. Purpose

c. Both time and purpose

d. None of the above

9-17. Transactions that may result in the recognition of deferred revenues are which of the following?

a. Exchange transactions

b. Nonexchange transactions

c. Either exchange transactions or nonexchange transactions

d. None of the above

9-18. Contributions and promises to give revenue should be reported on the statement of activities as which of the following?

a. Changes in unrestricted net assets but not temporarily restricted net assets or permanently restricted net assets

b. Changes in temporarily restricted net assets and permanently restricted net assets but not unrestricted net assets

c. Changes to permanently restricted net assets, temporarily restricted net assets, or unrestricted net assets, according to donor-imposed restrictions

d. Changes to permanently restricted net assets, temporarily restricted net assets, and unrestricted net assets, according to organizational objectives

9-19. FASB Statement No. 117 amended FASB Statement No. 95 regarding the statement of cash flows by extending its provision to include not-for-profit organizations. According FASB Statement No. 117, cash inflows from contributions and investment income that by donor stipulation are restricted for capital asset–related, endowment, or other long-term purposes shall be reported on the statement of cash flows as which of the following?

a. Financing activities

b. Investing activities

c. Operating activities

d. Financing activities or investing activities

9-20. Depreciation expense is reported on the statement of activities of a not-for-profit organization in the following manner:

a. The reporting of depreciation expense is optional for the not-for-profit organization.

b. Depreciation expense is reported as part of changes in unrestricted net assets as are other expenses.

c. Depreciation expense should be carried as a separate line item and reported in total as part of changes in assets held for fixed assets.

d. Depreciation should be reported as a separate line item as changes to permanently restricted net assets, temporarily restricted net assets, and unrestricted net assets, according to donor imposed restrictions.

9-21. Which of the following is an industry category for NFPs?

a. Voluntary health and welfare organization

b. Colleges or university

c. Hospitals and other health care entities

d. All of the above

9-22. Which of the following are net assets that must be held in perpetuity?

a. Temporarily restricted assets

b. Permanently restricted assets

c. Exchange restricted assets

d. None of the above

9-23. Interest is received on an endowment for community health care. The interest income would be which of the following?

a. Unrestricted

b. Temporarily restricted

c. Permanently restricted

d. Restricted

9-24. Which of the following is not a concept in defining unconditional contributions?

a. Nonreciprocal transfer

b. Acting as other than an owner

c. Arm's-length transaction

d. Contribution depends on the occurrence of an event

9-25. Which of the following condition is required to hold an asset as a collection and not capitalize it as a capital asset?

a. Held for public exhibition

b. Preserved and protected

c. Reinvested in other collections if sold

d. All of the above

9-26. All of the following are examples of program services except which of the following?

a. Heath and welfare training

b. Fund-raising

c. Education and development

d. Museum exhibit

9-27. All of the following are example of support services except which?

a. Museum docent

b. Membership-development activities

c. Administration expenses of general government

d. None of the above

9-28. Voluntary health and welfare organizations are required to report expenses by which of the following?

a. Natural classification

b. Functional and natural category

c. Alpha category

d. Restricted and unrestricted categories

9-29. NFPs consist of participants that can be described by which of the following?

a. Pursuing only a benevolent cause

b. Pursing a profit

c. Independently organized and self-governing

d. All of the above

9-30. The advantages of having a not-for-profit status would include which of the following?

a. Exemptions from local real property taxes

b. Privileges from special ordinances

c. Tax abatements

d. All of the above

EXERCISES

EXERCISE 9-1	Prepare journal entries to record contributions
EXERCISE 9-2	Prepare journal entries to record new research grant
EXERCISE 9-3	Prepare journal entries to record noncash gifts
EXERCISE 9-4	Recognize and record gift notification
EXERCISE 9-5	Prepare journal entries to record contributions and related transactions
EXERCISE 9-6	Identify and record reclassification of net assets
EXERCISE 9-7	Record fixed asset transactions
EXERCISE 9-8	Prepare miscellaneous journal entries
EXERCISE 9-9	Prepare entries to record fund-raising dinner revenues and costs
EXERCISE 9-10	Record transactions to determine revenues reported in each net asset class
EXERCISE 9-11	Restate the accounts receivable data in proper form
EXERCISE 9-12	Prepare statement of cash flow
EXERCISE 9-13	Record entries to recognize contributions
EXERCISE 9-14	Reclassify expenses into natural classifications
EXERCISE 9-15	Record receipts to determine revenue reported in financial statements

EXERCISE 9-1 Neighborhood Hospital received notification of the following contributions during the month. The hospital expects to collect 90 percent of all pledges received.

1. Gene Smith promised to give the hospital $100,000 within the year.
2. Robert Farley promised to give the hospital $100,000 if his business earned a profit greater than $500,000 this year.
3. Randell David sent a $15,000 check to the hospital to be used for current operations.
4. Mary Myers donated a neonatal bassinet warmer valued at $12,000.

Required:
Prepare journal entries (omit explanations) for Neighborhood Hospital to record these transactions.

EXERCISE 9-2 Union Technologies notified New University that it was awarding the university a $100,000 grant to fund research on the knat bug. The grant would be paid over two years in installments of $50,000. The first installment was included with the notification.

Required:
Prepare journal entries to record the grant to New University.

EXERCISE 9-3 The following noncash gifts were received by Knew View, a nonprofit organization.

1. Three acres of land to be used for the new museum building. The donor stipulated that the land, with a fair value of $15,000, could never be sold.

2. Several rolls of canvas valued at $1,200 to be used in the ongoing art classes for underprivileged children.
3. Five hand-carved frames valued at $5,000 to be used in next year's auction to support the organization.
4. Volunteer art instructors rendered 35 hours of service at no cost. Salary rates for comparable instructions are $15 per hour.
5. Two signed painting valued at $5,000 each were donated as an addition to the organization's art collection. The organization uses the collection for educational purposes, maintains the collection is good order, and, when a painting is sold, the proceeds are used to acquire other artwork for the collection.

Required:
Prepare journal entries, if necessary, to record each of the transactions on Knew View's financial records. If no entry is appropriate, explain why not.

EXERCISE 9-4 Community Service received notification that one of its supporters, Dr. R.E. Alexander, had included a $1,000,000 bequest to Community Service in his will. Dr. Alexander requests that his bequest be used to support educational and training programs for at-risk teenagers.

Required:
Prepare journal entries, if appropriate, for Community Service to record this gift. Explain your answer.

EXERCISE 9-5 Wellness Outreach is a voluntary health and welfare not-for-profit organization. Wellness uses a calendar fiscal year. The following transactions were not recorded as of December 31.
1. Promises to give (pledges) of $100,000 were received in 2003, with $25,000 designated by the donor for use in 2003 and $75,000 for use in 2004 operations.
2. All conditions of a prior year's grant for $1,000 were substantially met. When the grant proceeds were originally received, it was recorded as a refundable advance.
3. Cash collections of $5,000 were received for unrestricted pledges including $300 of pledges receivable. Cash collected for pledges temporarily restricted for programs was $3,000 including receivables of $650.
4. A gift of security investments with a fair market value of $12,000 was received to create a permanent endowment. Interest earned on these investments but not collected at year-end was $750. The donor stipulated the interest could be used for unrestricted purposes.
5. Donated services, facilities, and supplies include:
   (a) CPA who audited the agency at no charge, $4,500
   (b) Attorney who served meals to the homeless at no charge, $275
   (c) Office facilities provided at no charge, $3,500
   (d) Supplies with a fair value of $800; supplies valued at $50 remained in inventory at year-end

Required:
Prepare the appropriate journal entries indicating the net asset classification in which each entry is made. Closing entries are not required.

EXERCISE 9-6 Civic Art League, a not-for-profit organization with a calendar fiscal year, entered into the following transactions.
1. A cash contribution of $900 was received in the prior year designated by the donor for use in the current year.
2. The governing board designated $4,000 of unrestricted net assets for use in special exhibit.
3. A. B. Donor named the league as the beneficiary of a paid-up life insurance policy with a cash surrender value of $12,000. Upon his death, the gift must be used to create a permanent endowment. Mr. Donor died in June of this year. Fair market value of the policy is $25,000.
4. $575 was expended for a children's art show from funds restricted for that purpose.
5. Five years ago a donor made cash contribution of $15,000 to create a five-year term endowment that expired this year. Upon the term endowment's expiration, it can be used for current operations and expenses.

Required:

Record the reclassification of net assets to be recorded by Civic. Identify the net asset class associated with each entry.

EXERCISE 9-7

County Humane Society is a not-for-profit organization operating on a calendar fiscal year. The following transactions occurred during the year.

1. A building and lot downtown with a fair market value of $125,000 was donated to the society for resale in order to pay for a new shelter estimated to cost $150,000. The building and lot were sold for $125,000.
2. The building mentioned in item 1 was built using the sale proceeds. An additional $25,000 of cash restricted for investment in plant was used to fund the construction.
3. Depreciation of $6,500 is recognized.
4. Equipment costing $2,000 was acquired with donated resources received in the prior year designated for that purpose.
5. Equipment costing $500 with accumulated depreciation of $300 was sold for $250.

Required:

Prepare any journal entries needed for the above transactions, including the net asset designation if appropriate. Closing entries are not required. County's policy is to record gifts to acquire long-lived plant assets as temporarily restricted until the asset is placed in service. Once the asset is placed in service, the restriction is assumed to be met.

EXERCISE 9-8

Tall Timbers Society, an environmentalist group, has the following transactions to be recorded. Tall Timbers is a not-for-profit organization that uses a calendar fiscal year.

1. Endowment fund interest income of $5,000 cash was received, which was restricted by the donor to increase the permanent endowment until it reaches a stipulated amount of $5,000, after which time any future income will be unrestricted. The endowment currently has a balance of $4,700.
2. Membership dues for the new year totaling $8,500 in cash were collected in December.
3. An analysis of the accounts receivable determined that 10 percent of the contributions (pledge) receivable of $100,000 at year-end would be uncollectable. The allowance for doubtful accounts for contributions receivable currently has a $7,500 balance.
4. Tall Timbers determined that the balance in the unrestricted investments account of $48,000 at year-end had a fair value of $50,000.
5. Tall Timbers held a special tree and plant bazaar to raise unrestricted funds. Cash receipts totaled $1,800, and the cost of trees and plants sold was $200. Advertising expenses of $150 were paid.

Required:

Prepare the necessary journal entries to record the transactions. Closing entries are not required.

EXERCISE 9-9

The Friends of the Arts sponsored a special fund-raising gala dinner at the local hotel. Three hundred tickets were sold at $125 each. The hotel charged the organization $32.50 for each of the 280 dinners served. Direct costs of the event were $675 for secretarial services, $370 for postage, and $425 for stationery and printing.

Required:

Prepare the necessary journal entries to record all transactions associated with the gala fund-raising dinner. What were the total funds raised by the gala dinner?

EXERCISE 9-10

During the current fiscal year, Uptown Art Museum received contributions, support, and program revenues from the following sources;

1. Membership fees of $7,500
2. Program support fees of $6,500
3. Continuing education course fees of $5,200
4. Unrestricted grant of $25,000
5. Unrestricted gift of $8,000
6. New endowment gift of $50,000
7. Contributions restricted by the donors to be used in the following year of $7,500

8. Unrestricted promises to give of $21,500; all promises were expected to be honored
9. $16,250 in cash for the unrestricted promises to give

Required:
A. Prepare the necessary journal entries in the appropriate net asset class to record the contributions, support, and program revenues received by the Uptown Art Museum.
B. Determine the total revenue that will be reported by the Uptown Art Museum in each net asset class in its statement of activities.

EXERCISE 9-11

An examination of the accounting records for Big Sandy College indicates that all receivables are being recorded in a single account entitled Receivables. Analysis of the accounts reveals the following information.

Accounts receivable for tuition and fees	$ 38,900
Accounts receivable for student room and board	24,500
Investment interest receivable	8,100
Travel advances to professors to attend academic meetings	2,500
Student loans receivable, due in five years	93,500
Prepaid supply expenses	6,400
Deposit to guarantee a future campus cultural performance	5,000
Total	$178,900

Required:
A. Prepare a journal entry to separate the preceeding items into their proper accounts.
B. How would each of the preceeding items normally be reflected on Big Sandy College's statement of financial position?

EXERCISE 9-12

The following are several items involving cash flow activities of the not-for-profit Green Acres Animal Shelter for the current year.

1. Net income of $19,000
2. Salary and wages of $12,000
3. Ten-year $28,000 bond payable issued at par value
4. Depreciation expense of $11,000
5. Building acquired at a cost of $43,000
6. Accounts receivable decreased by $2,000
7. Accounts payable decreased by $5,000
8. Equipment acquired at cost of $10,000
9. Animal food and other inventory items increased by $4,000
10. Beginning cash balance of $15,000

Required:
Prepare the current year's statement of cash flows for the Green Acres Animal Shelter.

EXERCISE 9-13

City Symphony Orchestra received the following contributions during the month.
1. John Smith promised to give the orchestra $50,000 within the year.
2. Mary Allen sent a $10,000 check to be used for current operations.
3. Grace Goodson promised to give the orchestra $35,000 if her business earned a profit greater than $300,000 this year.
4. Alan Martin donated a violin valued at $20,000.

Required:
Prepare journal entries for City Symphony Orchestra to record these transactions. Explanations may be omitted.

EXERCISE 9-14

Main Street Day Care had the following expenses during the year: salaries and wages of $50,000; payroll taxes of $7,500, of which $1,500 was not paid at year-end. Main Street Day Care used the following percentages to reclassify expenses using the natural classification method:

Education	28 percent
Research	7 percent
Children care	50 percent
Management and general	13 percent
Fund-raising	2 percent

Required:
Prepare journal entries for the above payroll expenses and reclassify the expenses using natural classification. Explanations may be omitted.

EXERCISE 9-15   The following transactions occurred during 2005 for the Valley Camellia Club. Cash contributions and revenues for program support were received from the following sources: membership dues of $3,000, which includes a $200 prior year dues accounts receivable payment; horticulture program service fees of $1,600; tuition for master gardener classes of $3,000; unrestricted grants of $20,000; and a gift of $5,000 restricted for acquisition of plant assets.

Required:
Prepare journal entries for the Camellia Club transactions. How much revenue will the Camellia Club recognize during 2005 for each net asset class? Explanations may be omitted.

PROBLEMS

PROBLEM 9-1	Prepare a statement of functional expenses for a voluntary health association
PROBLEM 9-2	Prepare a statement of activities for a college
PROBLEM 9-3	Internet research
PROBLEM 9-4	Recast a hospital financial report
PROBLEM 9-5	Prepare a statement of financial position for a private club
PROBLEM 9-6	Prepare a columnar statement of activities
PROBLEM 9-7	Prepare a statement of cash flows for a college
PROBLEM 9-8	Prepare a statement of functional expense
PROBLEM 9-9	Prepare comprehensive financial statements for a dance organization
PROBLEM 9-10	Prepare comprehensive financial statements for a voluntary health and welfare organization

PROBLEM 9-1   The Community Aid for the Elderly, a not-for-profit voluntary health and welfare association, had the following expenses listed by natural (object) classification during the year.

Salaries and benefits	$5,500
Professional fees and contract services	2,000
Supplies	500
Telephone	1,800
Occupancy/facility rent	3,600
Postage and shipping	1,650
Printing	2,300
Interest expense	1,150
Depreciation of buildings and equipment	1,000

The programs sponsored by this association during the year were medical referrals, meals, counseling, and education. Supporting services were management and general, and fund-raising. After discussions with the persons engaged in offering each service and a review of the association's records, auditors have determined that the following distribution would be realistic.

Distribution Percent for Services by Expense Tyler

	Program Services			Supporting Services		
	Medical Referral	*Meals*	*Counseling*	*Education*	*Management and General*	*Fund-Raising*
Salaries and benefits	25	20	20	20	10	5
Professional/services	10	10	50	10	10	10

Supplies	35	25	5	20	10	5
Telephone	20	10	20	20	10	20
Occupancy/facility	20	5	20	30	15	10
Postage/shipping	20	5	25	20	10	20
Printing	15	10	20	35	10	10
Interest	30	10	20	20	10	10
Depreciation	30	10	20	20	10	10

Required:

A. Prepare a statement of functional expenses for the year.

B. If Community Aid were to solicit a contribution from you, and presented the statement of functional expenses as proof of its value to the community, what would be your analysis and response? Why?

PROBLEM 9-2   Central University, a small private college, had the following information for the fiscal year ending June 30.

Student tuition and fees (net of discounts)	$10,000
Government grants for instructional support	2,500
Unrestricted cash donations	6,000
Donated teaching services	5,500
Unrestricted donations (stipulated to finance operations in 2003)	4,000
Permanent endowment gift	5,000
Term endowment gift	3,000
Contributions restricted for plant purposes	20,000
Unrestricted endowments income	1,500
Interest income restricted for plant purposes	2,000
Unrealized gains on unrestricted investments	800
Institutional support expenses	3,500
Instructional expense including fringe benefits	22,500
Instruction costs for which donor-restricted resources are available	1,800
Purchase of fixed assets from donor-restricted resources	1,000
Student services expenses	4,500
Expenses for academic support paid from resources restricted for that purpose	7,500
Expired term endowments	12,000
Unrestricted net assets, July 1 (beginning of the fiscal year)	25,000
Temporarily restricted net assets, July (beginning of the fiscal year)	15,000
Permanently restricted net assets, July (beginning of the fiscal year)	12,000

Central's programs include instruction, student services, institutional support, and academic support.

Required:

Prepare a statement of activities. (*Hint*: For help with the statement format and display, use www.google.com or www.yahoo.com to find a college financial statement posted on the web. Additional information about college and university accounting is available at the website for the National Association of College and University Business Officers at http://www.nacubo.org.)

PROBLEM 9-3   (Internet Research) On the Internet, search for the home pages of two nongovernmental not-for-profit organizations and analyze the information available from the standpoint of a prospective donor. Several websites offer standards and criteria that function as benchmarks for this sector in addition to providing ratings for many of the not-for-profits. For example, the American Institute of Philanthropy (http://www.charitywatch.org), the Charity Reports and Standards section of the Better Business Bureau (http://www.bbb.org), the National Charities Information Bureau (http://give.org), and the Internet Nonprofit Center (http://.nonprofits.org) provide standards, ratings, and links to the home pages of many not-for-profit organizations. Determine appropriate standards for comparisons (Concept Statement No. 4 at http://www.fasb.org.) such as financial relationship between inflows and outflows of resources, service efforts and accomplishments, and internal policies established by the board. Evaluate each organization based on the criteria selected. There are many other websites that provide a wealth of information, including the Learning Center (http://www.guidestar.org), the

Chronicle of Philanthropy (http://www.philanthropy.com), and the National Center of Charitable Statistics (http://nccs.urban.org).

PROBLEM 9-4   The new bookkeeper for Charity General Hospital prepared the following statement.

Charity General Hospital
Balance Sheet
December 31, 2005

	Debit (Credit)
Assets	
Cash	$ 50,000
Accounts receivable	62,000
Allowance for uncollectible accounts	(6,000)
Pledges receivable	40,000
Allowance for uncollectible pledges	(4,000)
Inventory of supplies	40,000
Investments	225,000
Land	20,000
Buildings and equipment	75,000
Accumulated depreciation	(15,000)
Total assets	$ 487,000
Liabilities and fund balance	
Accounts payable	$ 30,000
Mortage payable	50,000
Total liabilities	80,000
Fund balance:	
Investment in plant	113,000
Endowment	105,000
Restricted for specific programs	84,000
Unrestricted	105,000
Total fund balance	407,000
Total liabilities and fund balance	$ 487,000

Additional Information:

1. Investment in plant fund consists of cash $8,000, and investments of $25,000 restricted by donor for investment in plant; also included are land, building, and equipment with a balance of $80,000 net of accumulated depreciation.
2. Endowment fund consists of permanently restricted cash of $5,000 and investments of $100,000.
3. Restricted for specific programs fund consists of cash, $7,500; investments, $22,000; and pledges receivable, $17,000 (net of $1,500 allowance for uncollectible pledges) restricted by donor for specific purposes. This fund also includes cash of $2,500 and investments of $35,000 designated as "assets limited as to use" due to contracts or agreements with outside parties other than donor or grantors.

Required:

Prepare a classified financial statement that conforms to GAAP standards. (*Note:* It is the policy of Charity to record donations of cash and investments restricted for the acquisition of long-lived plant assets as temporarily restricted until the asset is acquired and placed in service. At that time, the restriction is considered to be met and the donation is reclassified to unrestricted net assets.)

PROBLEM 9-5   Hoops for Fun had the following balances as of December 31, 2004.

Supply inventory	$2,000
Pledges (net of allowance of $300)	3,700
Accounts payable	400
Furniture & equipment (net of accumulated depreciation of $500)	6,350
Cash	15,000

Investments—unrestricted	35,000
Cash permanently restricted for endowment	3,000
Pledges temporarily restricted (net of allowance $200)	2,000

Required:
Prepare in a statement of financial position for Hoops for Fun as of December 31, 2004.

PROBLEM 9-6 Brookhill University had the following transactions during the fiscal year ending June 30, 2005.
1. Received student tuition and fees totaling $12,000
2. Received research grants that were unrestricted of $3,000
3. Received cash contributions of $30,000, of which $10,000 was permanently restricted and $10,000 was temporarily restricted
4. Paid salaries to teaching personnel of $25,000
5. Paid institutional support costs of $2,000
6. Released $6,000 of program restricted net assets was from restriction
7. Paid administrative expenses of $6,000
8. Paid academic support costs of $8,000
9. Paid student support costs of $5,000
10. Received interest income of $40,000, of which $10,000 is unrealized and $15,000 is temporarily restricted.
11. Paid other expenses of $3,000

Required:
Prepare the fiscal year 2004–2005 statement of activities in column format for Brookhill University. Brookhill University's net assets on July 1, 2004, were unrestricted net assets of $22,000; temporarily restricted net assets of $10,000; and permanently restricted net assets of $5,000.

PROBLEM 9-7 The following cash flow information was retrieved from the financial records of Elizabeth College for the fiscal year ending June 30, 2006.

Accretion of bond discount	$ 1,875
Amortization of bond issuance costs	19,817
Capitalized interest expense	(65,000)
Cash and cash equivalents at the beginning of the fiscal year	1,322,962
Cash and cash equivalents at the end of the fiscal year	1,322,962
Change in net assets	(3,581,543)
Contribution of investments	(426,103)
Debt issuance costs	(264,709)
Decrease in accounts payable	(335,445)
Decrease in accounts receivable	231,960
Decrease in other liabilities	(12,598)
Decreases in actuarial liability for annuities payable	(95,378)
Decrese in accrued interest receivable	1,118
Depreciation of property and equipment	2,584,601
Federal government advance of funds for student loans	1,494
Increase in deposits and agency accounts	160,821
Increase in amount due from students	(111,095)
Increase in inventory	(3,370)
Increase in postretirement liability	36,817
Increase in prepaid expense	(166,748)
Increase in salary and wages payable	218,061
Loan distributions to students	(217,050)
Net change in pledges receivable	(620,585)
Net loss on investments	1,886,195
Payments of long-term debt	(9,863,508)
Permanently restricted gifts and donations received	(453,147)
Permanently restricted gifts and donations received	453,147
Proceeds from issuance of long-term debt	19,813,066
Proceeds from sales of investments	22,963,183
Provision for uncollectable accounts	538,939

Purchase of investments	(20,778,782)
Purchase of property and equipment	(11,826,652)
Purchase of short-term investments	(309,625)
Repayments of student loans	220,244

Required:

Prepare a statement of cash flows for Elizabeth University for the fiscal year ending June 30, 2006.

PROBLEM 9-8   City Hospital Health Care Affiliate has the following program and support services: medical care, education, management and general, and fund-raising. The following are expenses incurred for the year 2004.

1. Salaries, $4,000
2. Interest, $200
3. Office supplies, $360
4. Medical supplies for medical care, $600
5. Professional fees for management and general, $250
6. Equipment rental for education, $600
7. Occupancy $1200

Required:

Prepare a statement of functional expenses for December 31, 2004, for City Hospital Health Care Affiliate. All expenses are allocated equally unless used specifically for a program or support service.

PROBLEM 9-9   Dance for Joy is a nongovernmental not-for-profit organization that was incorporated on January 1, 2003. On December 31, 2003, Dance for Joy's adjusted trial balance reflected the following balances.

	Debits	*Credits*
Cash	$ 16,500	
Pledges receivable	4,000	
Allowance for uncollectible pledges		$ 400
Pledges receivable—temporarily restricted—plant	2,500	
Allowance for uncollectible pledges—temporarily restricted		250
Inventory of supplies	1,500	
Investments—unrestricted	41,000	
Furniture and equipment	7,500	
Accumulated depreciation		750
Investments—permanently restricted for endowment	4,300	
Accounts payable		300
Unrestricted net assets		—
Temporarily restricted net assets		—
Permanently restricted net assets		—
Contributions—unrestricted		65,000
Contributions—temporarily restricted—plant		13,500
Contributions—permanently restricted		4,300
Investment income—unrestricted		1,875
Bad debt expense	650	
Salaries expense	3,000	
Supplies expense	2,300	
Facility expense	1,700	
Printing expense	400	
Telephone expense	275	
Depreciation expense	750	
Totals	$ 86,375	$ 86,375

Additional Information:

1. All expenses (excluding bad debt expense) are allocated to the programs and supporting services in the following percentages: dance program, 35 percent; dance education, 40 percent; manage-

ment and general, 15 percent; fund-raising, 10 percent. Bad debt expense is recorded as an expense of the management and general support service.

2. All temporarily restricted contributions are donor restricted for plant purposes. Dance for Joy used $7,500 cash from those resources to purchase equipment and furniture.

3. Dance for Joy received the following cash during the year: unrestricted gifts totaling $61,000, a temporarily restricted gift for investment in plant totaling $11,000, $4,300 restricted for a new endowment, and unrestricted interest income of $1,875.

4. Dance for Joy paid cash from unrestricted funds for salaries of $3,000, for purchases of other goods and services of $5,875, and for investments of $41,000.

Required:
Prepare a statement of financial position, statement of activities, and statement of cash flows for Dance for Joy for the year ended December 31, 2003.

PROBLEM 9-10 Mothers Helpers is a nongovernmental not-for-profit voluntary health and welfare organization dedicated to providing prenatal care to at-risk pregnant women in the community. Mothers Helpers conducts two programs: (1) Medical care and (2) educational programs.

Mothers had the following postclosing trial balance at December 31, 2004, the end of its fiscal year.

Cash—unrestricted	$ 450	
Cash—temporarily restricted—time	1,050	
Cash—temporarily restricted—programs	575	
Cash restricted to plant asset acquisitions	1,250	
Short-term investments—unrestricted	2,000	
Contributions receivable—unrestricted	900	
Inventory—medical supplies	400	
Long-term endowment investments	4,500	
Land, buildings, and equipment	5,200	
Accumulated depreciation—buildings and equipment		$ 1,375
Accounts payable/accrued expenses for supplies		750
Refundable advance		500
Grants payable		300
Mortgages payable		3,500
Net assets—unrestricted		2,525
Net assets—termporarily restricted (time)		1,050
Net assets—temporarily restricted (programs)		575
Net assets—temporarily restricted (plant)		1,250
Net assets—permanently restricted		4,500
Totals	$ 16,325	$ 16,325

During the year ended December 31, 2005 the following transactions occurred.

Transactions affecting unrestricted net assets

1. The organization received unrestricted contributions as follows: cash of $4,220, recognizable contributed services of $2,000, medical supplies of $800, and unconditional promises to give to support activites for 2005 of $1,800. (*Note:* The physical count of medical supplies inventory at 12/31/2005 totaled $300.)

2. Cash in excess of daily requirements is invested in short-term investments. Interest earned on those investments totaling $250 was reinvested in short-term investments.

3. All conditions of a prior year prepaid conditional contribution were met. The conditional contribution was originally recorded as a refundable advance of $500.

4. The organization collected $750 of the unpaid contributions receivable.

5. The organization paid the balance of unconditional grants outstanding from the prior year.

6. The organization paid $600 of the accounts payable. It also repaid $800 of the principal and $200 of the interest due on the mortgage.

7. Depreciation of $560 was calculated and recorded. (*Note:* It is the policy of Mothers to record all donations of cash and investments restricted for the acquisition of plant acquisitions as temporarily restricted until the asset is acquired and put into service, at which time it becomes unrestricted.)

8. The organization received temporarily restricted contributions as shown below:

Restricted for	Cash	Promises to Give
Programs	$ 850	$ 140
Time	400	820
Acquisition of plant	650	

9. Cash contribution of $1,000 was received to set up a term endowment that will mature in five years. At the end of the five years, the endowment assets become unrestricted. Income earned on the term endowment is unrestricted.

Transactions affecting permanently restricted net assets

10. A donor contributed cash of $250 to create a permanent endowment. The income from this endowment must be added to the original gift until the endowment value reaches $500. $20 in interest income was earned on this gift during the year.

Transactions affecting more than one class of net assets

11. Expenditures from unrestricted funds consisted of the following:

Office supplies	$ 280
Salaries	940
Rent expense	1,100

$1820 was paid. Of the amount unpaid, $200 represented supply costs and $300 was salary costs. All expenditures are to be allocated equally to the medical care program, educational program, management and general, and fund-raising for financial reporting purposes.

12. Purpose restrictions were met and net assets released from donor restrictions for the following expenses:

Medical care program (equipment rent)	$300
Education program (equipment rent)	250
Equipment acquired and placed in service	750

13. Net assets of $525 were released from donor restrictions because time restrictions were met.

14. $200 interest was earned on the term endowment.

Required:
A. Prepare the journal entries required to record the above transactions.
B. Prepare a statement of financial position, statement of activities, statement of cash flows, and statement of functional expenses for the year ended December 31, 2005.

CHAPTER 10

STATE AND LOCAL GOVERNMENTS: OVERVIEW, COMPREHENSIVE ANNUAL FINANCIAL REPORTS, AND GOVERNMENT-WIDE STATEMENTS

LEARNING OBJECTIVES

After reading this chapter, you should be able to:

- Identify the various aspects of state and local governments, including (1) their characteristics and nature, (2) objectives of their financial reporting, (3) their unique revenue and expense recognition, and (4) applicable financial reporting standards.
- Understand the composition of the financial reporting entity.
- Identify process to maintain accountability and financial controls.
- Be familiar with the required reporting of management discussion and analysis of financial position.
- Know the required components of government-wide financial statements.
- Understand the government-wide financial statement display.

This is the first of two chapters that introduce and illustrate accounting and reporting guidance for state and local governments. Together, they provide an overview of governmental entities as well as a discussion of the financial reporting requirements for state and local governments. This chapter consists of three main sections: a governmental overview, an introduction to the Governmental Accounting Standards Board (GASB) requirement for a comprehensive annual financial report (CAFR), and a discussion of the first of two major classifications of CAFR-required financial statements, which are government-wide financial statements. Chapter 11 follows with an examination of the accounting for individual fund types and preparation of the second major CAFR-required financial statement group, the individual fund statements.

In this chapter, the first section gives an overview of the objectives and characteristics of governments as they relate to the reporting of financial activities. An investigation of the unique features of governments, as entities, is essential to understanding the discussion of financial reporting requirements for such organizations. Following the overview, the second section discusses the general requirements of CAFR and takes a detailed look at the Management Discussion and Analysis section of the report. The third section covers government-wide financial statements, describing and illustrating the required components. The coverage includes the two primary government-wide financial statements, the Statement of Net Assets and the Statement of Activities, as well as the required disclosure notes that communicate information not presented on the face of the statements.

GOVERNMENTAL ENTITIES AND FINANCIAL REPORTING: AN OVERVIEW

Nature of Governments

When thinking about a government, most people tend to think about Washington, D.C., and the federal government. However, in addition to the federal government, there are extensive numbers of state and local government entities. In 2002, the U.S. Census Bureau identified 87,899 state and local government units. These included 50 state governments and 87,849 local government units. The local units comprised 3,043 counties, 35,937 cities and towns, 13,522 school districts, and 35,356 other special government districts that included airports, port authorities, public buildings, and others.[1] All state and local government entities must observe the accounting and financial reporting standards issued by the Governmental Accounting Standards Board (GASB). The Board also establishes accounting standards for government-owned or -controlled not-for-profit organizations such as hospitals, museums, airports, colleges, and universities. Accounting and financial reporting standards for corporations and nongovernmental not-for-profit organizations are established by the Financial Accounting Standards Board (FASB). GASB and FASB operate under the guidance of the Financial Accounting Foundation, which governs the two Boards' activities and appoints their members.

GASB and FASB are considered independent standard-setting bodies that direct the formation and basis of generally accepted accounting principals (GAAP). The GASB was established in 1984 as the successor to the National Council on Government Accounting (NCGA).[2] GASB Statement No. 1[3] raised a majority of the NCGA accounting and reporting guidance to Level A GAAP. In 1987, GASB issued Concept Statement No. 1,[4] stressing **accountability**. Accountability is the obligation to explain the government's actions, to justify what the government does, to justify the rationale for raising resources, and to offer an explanation for the expenditure of those resources. Governments are accountable to their constituencies for several reasons. Elected officials are empowered by citizens to act on their behalf. Elected officials are evaluated by votes on their financial decision-making performance in addition to the operating performance demonstrated by the

Accountability: the obligation to explain the government's actions, to justify what the government does, to justify to the citizenry the rationale for raising resources, and an explanation for the expenditure of those resources.

[1] U.S. Census Bureau, *Statistical Abstract of the United States 2002*, p. 5.

[2] For an overview of the history of governmental accounting standards and the creation of GASB, see Bean, David R., "The Evolution of Governmental Accounting Standard Setting," *Governmental Finance,* December 1984, V13, 7–11. Another perspective of GASB's history is found in Ives, Martin, "The Governmental Accounting Standards Board: Factors Influencing Its Operation and Initial Technical Agenda," *The Government Accounting Journal,* Spring 2002, V49(1), 22–27.

[3] Statement No. 1 *Authoritative Status of NCGA Pronouncements and AICPA Industry Audit Guide* (Norwalk, CT: Government Accounting Standards Board, 1984).

[4] **Concept Statement No. 1**, "Objectives of Financial Reporting" (Norwalk, CT: Governmental Accounting Standards Board, 1987).

government. Thus, accountability is based on the transfer of responsibility for resources or actions from the citizens to some other party, that is, management of a governmental entity. The assessment of accountability is fulfilled when financial reporting enables financial data users to determine the extent to which current period costs are financed by current period revenues. This objective is based on the concept of **interperiod equity**, which argues that those who benefit from an expenditure should pay its cost. The federal Social Security program is one of the best examples of a lack of interperiod equity. The Social Security system was conceptually designed so that participants' own contributions would be the source of their retirement benefits. Yet prior to 1999, current Social Security (FICA) collections paid benefits for past entitlements.[5] That is, currently employed workers paid the benefits received by Social Security retirees. Therefore, governmental officials demonstrate and display to citizens that the resources received are utilized for the intended purpose to meet the operating goals and objectives of the government. Financial statements are a primary means of conveying accountability information.

Interperiod equity: a concept that those who benefit should pay the cost

State and local government entities use the governmental GAAP accounting hierarchy shown in Table 10-1 when preparing their financial reports.

In response to the desire for the government to provide financial statements that satisfy the broad information needs and expectations of governments' financial statement users, GASB issued Statement No. 34, which requires the display of two distinct sets of financial statements.

> **Government-wide financial statements** have a long-term focus because they report *all* revenues of the government and *all* costs of the services provided by the government.[7]

TABLE 10-1   Levels of Government GAAP[6]

GAAP Level	Items
A	GASB statements, AICPA and FASB pronouncements made specifically applicable by GASB
B	GASB technical bulletins and AICPA industry and accounting guides and Statements of Position if made specifically applicable and cleared by GASB
C	AICPA practice bulletins cleared by GASB and Emerging Issues Task Force (EITF) consensus positions, if GASB creates such a group
D	GASB implementation guides and industry practice that are widely recognized and prevalent

[5] In 1999, Congress expected the Social Security surplus to exceed $18 billion. Associated Press, November 1, 1999.

[6] **Statement of Auditing Standards**, No. 69, "The meaning of "Present Fairly in Conformity with Generally Accepted Accounting Principles" in the Independent Auditors Report" (New York: American Institute of Certified Public Accountants, 1992).

[7] **Statement No. 34**, "Basic Financial Statements—and Management's Discussion and Analysis—for State and Local Governments" (Norwalk, CT: Governmental Accounting Standards Board, 1999), p. 2.

Fund-based financial statements report the planned use of governmental resources and measures the near-term revenues and expenditures of the government's activities.[8]

Government-wide financial statements report a government's activity and financial position as a whole. This display allows report users to make long-term evaluations of the government's finances that enable them to achieve the following goals.

- Asses the finances of the government, including the current year's operation
- Determine whether the government's overall financial position is improving or not
- Evaluate whether the government's current year revenues were sufficient to pay for all the current year's services
- Identify the government's cost of providing services to its citizens
- Determine how the government finances its programs, such as by program revenues, user fees, or tax revenues
- Determine the extent to which the government has invested resources in capital assets
- Have the ability to compare financial data between governments[9]

To achieve these financial statement user goals, government-wide financial statements report all economic resources and use full accrual accounting, just as do for-profit corporations and businesses. That is, *all* assets and liabilities are reported and transactions that change the financial statements are recorded in the period in which the event occurs. Revenues are recognized and recorded when earned rather than when the cash is received. Expenses are recognized and recorded when incurred regardless of whether the cash has been disbursed. Revenue and expense transactions that relate to a future financial period are recorded as deferred revenue or prepaid expense.

In contrast, fund-based financial statements focus on specific activities, the financial resources provided to those activities, and their use during the fiscal reporting period. Fund-based financial statements display amounts expended on services such as education, police and fire protection, welfare, and construction projects in addition to a host of other services. The primary measurement focus used in the fund-based statements is the flow of resources using a system of **modified accrual accounting**. Modified accrual accounting recognizes revenue when it is measurable and available, and expenditures when they cause a reduction in current financial resources. In other words, modified accrual accounting is very much like cash-based accounting recognition.

Modified accrual accounting: recognies revenue when it is measurable and available, and expenditures when they result in a reduction of current financial resources

Government Characteristics

Governments typically create various entities to carry out their mission. These entities may be classified as general-purpose governmental units (such as cities and towns created by states) or special-purpose governmental units (such as school districts or public authorities created by cities). Special-purpose units enjoy certain exemptions, such as being excluded from the state's civil service law; however, they are governmental in nature and must observe public-sector GAAP accounting. Other government creations—such as state airports, hospitals, colleges, and universities—are distinctly classified as governmental

[8] Ibid., p. 1.
[9] Ibid., p. 2.

not-for-profit entities and are subject to the same GAAP guidelines as general-purpose and special-purpose government entities. Regardless of the diverse nature of government entities, they have several common characteristics including the following:

- They are organized to serve the citizens in their jurisdiction and typically do not serve those outside the jurisdiction unless the full costs of the services rendered are paid.
- The principal source of revenue is taxes even if the tax is the result of a self-assessment. Taxes paid by an individual taxpayer generally are based on the value of property owned or income earned and are rarely proportional to the value of the services received.
- A profit motive rarely exists.
- Each entity has an accountability and stewardship responsibility for the resources entrusted to it.
- Measuring optimal quality or quantity of services provided is often a challenge. For example, the quality of city-governed services such as primary and secondary education or planning and zoning is difficult, if not impossible, to measure.

Some entities are difficult to categorize as either a governmental entity or a not-for-profit organization. For example, local cities and towns establish economic development commissions or housing authorities that are separate legal entities and tax exempt under Internal Revenue Service Code section 501(c)3. The question is, "Are these separate entities part of the government or not?" To resolve whether such organizations are governmental entities, GASB, FASB, and the American Institute of Certified Public Accountants (AICPA) agreed on the following definition of a governmental organization.

Organizations are governmental entities—that is, public corporations—if they have one or more of the following characteristics.

1. *Officers of the organization are elected by popular election. Or, officials of one or more state or local government appoint (or approves) a controlling majority of the members of the organization's governing body.*
2. *The potential exists for unilateral dissolution of the organization by a government with the net assets reverting to a government.*
3. *The organization has the power to enact and enforce a tax levy.*
4. *The organization has the authority to issue tax-exempt debt directly to other parties.*[10]

However, an entity may achieve nongovernmental status by offering compelling evidence that it is, in fact, nongovernmental. For example, in several states private universities issue tax-exempt debt that, given characteristic 4, would identify the university as a governmental entity. Yet in each case, the university has presented prevailing evidence in the debt prospectus that the university is not a governmental entity.

Public corporation: an entity created for the administration of public affairs

In applying the definition, a **public corporation** is described as an artificial person, such as a municipality or a governmental corporation, created for the administration of public affairs. Unlike a private corporation, a public corporation has no protection against the legislative body passing acts to alter or repeal its charter. Public corporations include instrumentalities created by the state, formed and owned in the public interest, supported by public funds either in whole or in part, and managed by those who derive their authority from the state.

---

[10] *Audits of State and Local Governments* (New York: American Institute of Certified Public Accountants, 2002), (GASB 34 Edition) par. 1.01.

OBJECTIVES OF GOVERNMENTAL FINANCIAL REPORTING

As discussed earlier, the basic foundation of state and local governmental financial accounting and reporting was established by GASB in Concept Statement No. 1,[11] which identified three primary user groups of governmental financial reports that did not include users within the government itself:

1. The citizenry, including taxpayers, voters, and service recipients in addition to the media, advocate groups, and public finance researchers
2. Legislative and oversight officials, including members of state legislatures, county commissions, city councils, boards of trustees, and school boards, as well as executive branch officials
3. Investors and creditors, including individuals and institutional analysts municipal security underwriters, bond-rating agencies, and financial institutions

Although membership in these user groups overlaps with corporate financial statement users, the citizens and legislative users are unique to governments. Governmental financial reports inform the financial statement user about political, social, and economic decisions and display the government's fiscal accountability.

Each user group assesses the government's financial performance and operational results. For example, citizens watch the government's financial condition as an indicator of change in future tax levies to support the services provided by the government. Users look at the government's cash flow to ascertain the source of the government's cash, how the cash is used to support the various governmental activities, and whether there is sufficient cash flow to pay current liabilities. Investors and creditors are interested in whether the government will be capable of paying its current and future obligations.

To achieve its objectives, governments may create boards, commissions, agencies, or other legal entities. The basic assumption is that all functions of government are responsible to the elected officials and that the financial activities of each government function are reported at the lowest level of legal authority.

THE FINANCIAL REPORTING ENTITY

Reporting entity: a combination of the primary government, organizations for which the primary government is financially responsible, and other organizations for which the nature and significance of the relationship with the primary government is such that the exclusion of their data would cause the financial statements of the reporting entity to be misleading or incomplete

The financial **reporting entity** is a combination of the primary government, organizations for which the primary government is financially responsible, and other organizations for which the nature and significance of the relationship with the primary government is such that the exclusion of their data would cause the financial statements of the reporting entity to be misleading or incomplete. The foundation of a financial reporting entity is, however, the primary government task.

A **primary government** is a state or local general-purpose government. It can also be a special-purpose government that has a separately elected governing body. Primary governments are legally separate from or fiscally independent of other state or local governments. They have popularly elected governing bodies, have separate legal standing, and are fiscally independent from other governments. That is, they are sufficiently fiscally independent to establish a legal budget, levy taxes to fund the budget and the government's operations, and issue tax-exempt debt. New York City (NYC) is an example of a primary

---

[11] Op. cit., **GASB Concept Statement No. 1.**

Primary government: a state or local general- or special-purpose government that has an elected governing body and is legally separate from and fiscally independent of other governments

Component unit: a legally separate organization that imposes a financial burden on the primary government or one for which the government is financially accountable

government. NYC is a legally separate independent government that levies taxes to support the services provided. NYC established a legal budget that authorizes its revenue collection and disbursements. NYC also issues tax-exempt bonds as needed to support its development programs.

A **component unit** is a legally separate organization for which the elected officials of the primary government are financially accountable. A component unit can also be another organization whose relationship with the primary government is such that to exclude its financial information would cause the reporting entity's financial statements to be misleading or incomplete. A government reporting entity may include several legally separate entities, such as a utility service, museum, library, golf course, and airport. These separate entities may have their own governing boards and issue audited financial statements. Certain criteria must exist for the primary government to report a component unit; these criteria are discussed later in the chapter.

There are two methods for including the component unit's financial information in the financial statements of the primary government. The first is blending, which involves combining the financial information of the component unit with the financial information of the primary government. This process simply adds each element of the component's financial statement to the same element of the primary government. That is, assets are added to assets, liabilities are added to liabilities, revenues are added to revenues, and so on. The second method is the discrete presentation. A discrete presentation of a component's financial information in the primary government's financial report is accomplished by presenting the information in a separate column in the financial statements of the primary government's financial report without any elimination of between-organization transactions. With the presentation of the component unit's financial information within the financial statements of the primary government, the question becomes one of how fiscal oversight is achieved by the government's control procedures.

Budget and Monitoring

The budget is the government's primary control procedure because it expresses the public policy and financial intent of the government entity in a financial format and provides the primary means of monitoring fiscal activities. The executive branch proposes the budget while the legislative branch reviews, modifies, and enacts it. Once the budget is enacted, the executive branch carries out the provisions. The enacted budget has the force of law, and violations of the budget's spending authority can be considered a violation of the law, in which case the judiciary branch becomes involved.

Budget: a financial plan that documents the legal authority of the governmental entity to collect revenue and disburse resources

A **budget** is a financial plan. Budgets of governments generally must be balanced. That is, revenues must equal or exceed expenses. Most states have adopted legislation that prohibits expenses exceeding budgeted amounts. When the expenditures reach the budgeted amount, disbursements must cease until the budget is amended or modified. As a public policy, excessive revenues might indicate that taxes are too high or that the budgeted expenditures for public purposes were not achieved. Politically, expenditures below budget might not be desirable unless the reduction is intended to achieve efficiencies.

Codification: a compendium of GASB-promulgated accounting principles

GASB **codification**[12] provides the following criteria regarding government budgets.

- Annual budgets should be adopted by every government entity.
- The accounting system should provide the basis for appropriate budgetary control.

[12] *Codification of Government Accounting and Financial Reporting Standards* (Norwalk, CT: Governmental Accounting Standards Board, 1997), sec. 1700.

• A common terminology and classification should be used consistently throughout the budget, accounts, and financial reports.

The budget can be used to evaluate financial performance and accountability. A comparison of budgeted revenues and expenses to actual results, for a fiscal year and over time, determines the government's accomplishments. That is, the budget analysis can identify the resources consumed, the tasks performed, and the outcomes attained, together with the relationship among these items. The analysis also can determine the relationship of resource inflows to outflows—that is, disbursements—in providing services. Illustration 10-1 is the Budget Comparison Schedule for the City of Orange, California. This schedule presents the authorized legal budget only for the city's General Fund rather than for all the city's activities; thus, the amounts do not reconcile with the revenues and expenses displayed in the city's Statement of Activity that is illustrated and discussed later in this chapter. Also note that the original revenue budget (shown in column 1) was modified for revenues from other agencies from $7,113,400 to $7,142,452. The expenditure budget was adjusted for several categories, including the city manager's operations, public safety, parks and library, public works, and capital outlay, as displayed in column 2. Among the variances from the final adjusted budget amount to the actual expenditures, the actual tax revenues were less than the amount budgeted but the actual overall revenue exceeded the budget by a small amount $1,595. The expenditures, however, were significantly less than the budgeted amounts. Also note that the original budget was not a balanced budget because the budget authorized expenditures of $3.2 million more than the budgeted revenue. The $3 million excess expenditures over revenue together with the budgeted $4.9 million transfer to the sinking fund to pay for debt principal and interest resulted in a planned $8.1 million reduction of the equity balance. Since the actual expenditures did not exceed the actual revenues, the equity balance was decreased only $3.2 million.

Governments use two basic types of budgets. The types are the same as those used by corporate entities: annual operating budgets and capital budgets. Government annual **operating budgets** include estimated revenues and authorized expenditures for a specific fiscal year. **Capital budgets** control the expenditures for construction projects, plant, and capital asset acquisitions. Operating or capital budgets are typically recorded in the accounting system as a means of control or compliance. This contrasts with corporate accounting systems, which rarely record budget information to be used as a control mechanism.

Government **business-type activities**—that is, those services that charge a fee for services—use budgets as a managerial planning and control device rather than as a legislative compliance tool. Thus, the budgets for these activities may or may not be recorded in the accounting system.

As a part of the operating or capital budget, government entities often use several different types of sub-budgets, such as object, program, or performance budgets. The object sub-budget emphasizes the object of expenditures—such as salary, benefits, commodities, or contractual services—as a part of the overall budget control. The **program budget** measures the total cost of a specific governmental program regardless of how many different agencies, departments, or divisions are part of the program. Expenditures are of secondary importance in the program budget. The **performance budget** attempts to compare the input of governmental resources to the output of governmental services. For example, the total estimated expenditures for health and sanitation might be compared with the aggregate collection of charges for services budgeted for the fiscal year.

Each budget type includes the estimated revenues for the fiscal year and the authorized expenditures. Many governmental entities are required by law to maintain a balanced budget. A budget deficit occurs when expenditures exceed the authorized expenditures or

---

Operating budgets: identify the estimated revenue and authorized expenditure for a specific fiscal period

Capital budgets: control the expenditures for construction projects, plant, and capital asset acquisitions

Business-type activities: activities operated by a government that are similar to a for-profit activity: they are financed, in whole or in part, by fees charged for the services rendered

Program budget: measures the total cost of a specific governmental program

Performance budget: attempts to compare the input of governmental resources to the output of governmental services provided

ILLUSTRATION 10-1
City of Orange, California
Budgetary Comparison Schedule
General Fund
Year Ended June 30, 2002

	2002				2001
	Budgeted Amounts			Various with Final Budget	
	Original	Final	Actual	Positive (Negative)	Actual
Revenues:					
Taxes	42,888,000	42,888,000	41,341,500	(1,546,500)	42,849,637
Franchise fees	1,948,800	1,949,600	2,096,232	146,632	1,876,179
Licenses and permits	3,229,600	3,229,600	3,267,373	37,773	3,262,770
Revenues from use of money	2,696,900	2,696,900	2,795,178	98,278	3,731,223
Revenues from other	7,113,400	7,142,452	7,992,026	849,574	7,965,648
Charger for services and fees	5,159,500	5,159,500	5,602,039	442,539	5,198,973
Fines and forfeitures	1,422,000	1,422,000	1,406,951	(15,049)	1,423,082
Other revenues	769,100	769,100	757,448	(11,652)	1,115,164
Total revenues	65,228,100	65,257,132	65,258,747	1,595	67,422,676
Expenditures:					
General government					
City council	225,335	225,335	220,268	5,067	188,261
City manager	2,781,732	2,453,429	1,658,138	795,291	1,658,660
City attorney	1,188,207	1,788,207	727,227	460,980	821,342
City clerk	568,212	568,212	531,067	37,145	576,010
Finance	2,482,935	2,480,436	2,192,715	287,721	1,969,734
Personal services	820,629	820,629	820,629		784,051
Public safety:					
Police	25,416,785	25,348,515	24,164,950	1,683,565	22,317,037
Fire	16,270,082	16,540,237	16,414,546	125,691	14,784,528
Parks and library					
Library	3,437,649	3,451,079	3,225,638	225,441	2,867,524
Community services	5,809,803	5,827,453	5,253,041	574,412	4,777,548
Public works	5,083,151	5,272,612	4,309,101	963,511	3,926,551
Community development	2,798,076	2,792,576	2,454,665	337,911	2,311,538
Gas tax exchange	1,400,000	1,400,000	1,399,980	20	1,346,500
Capital outlay	167,247	485,205	243,104	242,101	261,553
Debt services	10,921	10,921	10,921		10,837
Total expenditures	68,460,765	68,864,864	63,625,990	5,238,856	58,601,674
Excess of revenues over (under) expenditures	(3,232,665)	(3,607,694)	1,632,757	5,240,451	8,821,002
Other Financing Sources (USES):					
Transfers out	(4,876,985)	(4,878,475)	(4,878,475)		(13,314,249)
Net change in fund balances	(8,109,650)	(8,486,169)	(3,245,718)	5,240,451	(4,493,247)
Fund balance, beginning of year	31,617,170	31,617,170	31,617,170		36,110,417
Fund balance, end of year	$23,507,520	23,131,001	28,371,452	5,240,451	31,617,170

Source: City of Orange, California, Comprehensive Annual Financial Report, 2002, www.cityoforange.org.

when the authorized expenditures exceed the estimated revenues for the budget period. If a budgetary deficit occurs in a governmental entity with a balanced budget requirement, an additional appropriation of available unrestricted resources or equity (analogous to corporate retained earnings) must be enacted or approved by the legislative process. The federal government is an example of a government entity with a balanced budget requirement. Frequently Congress must enact special budget amendment legislation to enable federal services to continue.

Financial reports provide the data for comparing legally adopted budgets with actual results. Underspending might indicate that the quality of services provided by the government fell below the budgetary stipulations. If, on the other hand, favorable economic events intervened, services might be provided at a significant cost reduction, thus eliminating any expected budget increase. Just as underspending has several possible causes, overspending may indicate poor financial management, inadequate budgetary controls, or unanticipated extraordinary events.

Financial reports are essential for demonstrating compliance with legally mandated activities. For example, the financial reports can document compliance with debt covenants, bond indentures, grants, or debt limits. Financial reports also can demonstrate compliance if the government is required to maintain specific funds for control purposes.

In 1994, GASB issued Concept Statement No. 2,[13] which encouraged states and local governments to provide more information about the government's performance in the financial statements as an addition to the financial information. Indicators of service efforts include the inputs of monetary and nonmonetary resources, while accomplishments include both outputs—that is, production—and outcomes as a result of the outputs. Service efforts, costs, and accomplishment information can be obtained from financial reports to assess or evaluate the government's efficiency and effectiveness. The information can be the basis of voting decisions or political support, although revenue and its recognition are more often used for managerial decisions.

Revenue Recognition

The recognition of revenue historically has been a concern for state and local governments because, unlike for-profit organizations, no earning process exists for most government revenues, such as taxes or fines. Property taxes are not earned because they are assessed, while income and sales taxes, fines, and the like are imposed on the government's citizens. Revenues may result from exchange or nonexchange transactions. Exchange revenue is the result of a transaction that recognizes the revenue earned when a fee is charged for service provided, that is, quid pro quo transactions such as one would expect to find reported by a for-profit organization. That is, the revenue is the result of an exchange of a comparable item for a comparable value, such as an exchange of goods or services for cash. Because governments do not perform a service for many types of revenue they receive, such as taxes, GASB Statement No. 33[14] provides a comprehensive system for recognizing the nonexchange revenues received by state and local governments. GASB Statement No. 33 does not apply to exchange transactions but concentrates on nonexchange transactions that include most tax revenue, as well as fines and grants, because the government does not have to provide an equal benefit for the item or amount received. GASB Statement No. 33 defines a nonexchange transaction as giving value (benefit) to another

[13] **Concept Statement No. 2**, "Service Efforts and Accomplishments Reporting" (Norwalk, CT: Government Accounting Standards Board, 1994).

[14] **Statement No. 33**, "Accounting and Financial Reporting for Nonexchange Transactions" (Norwalk, CT: Governmental Accounting Standards Board, 1998).

party without directly receiving equal value in exchange, or receiving value (benefit) from another party without directly giving equal value in exchange. Statement No. 33 also segregates nonexchange transactions into four classifications, each with its own set of rules for recognition. The nonexchange classifications include derived tax revenue, imposed revenues, government-mandated transactions, and voluntary transactions.

Derived tax revenues: nonexchange transactions imposed by the government as the result of an exchange transaction, such as a sales tax

Derived tax revenues result from assessments imposed by the government when an exchange transaction takes place. Examples include taxes imposed on earned personal income (income tax), corporate income (franchise or income tax), and retail sales of goods and services (sales tax).

Accounting for derived revenue such as income tax or sales tax is relatively straightforward. These revenues are recognized when the underlying transaction has occurred. For example, when a taxpayer earns income, the government recognizes income tax revenue. Likewise, when a sale is made that results in sales tax revenue, the government recognizes the resulting sales tax revenue. Because a government cannot recognize revenue every time that income is earned or a sale made, recognition of these revenues is normally made when the information becomes available.

Assume that the sales in the City of Pleasant View amount to $10 million for the year and a sales tax of 6 percent is assessed. In the year in which the sales are made, the following entry would be recorded. The amounts should be reported net of any estimated refunds or uncollectible balances.

Sales tax receivable	600,000	
Revenue—sales tax		600,000

To recognize the sales tax to be collected for the current period.

Had cash been received prior to the occurrence of the sales upon which the tax was levied, deferred revenue—that is, liability—would be recorded. Later, when the exchange takes place, the liability would be reclassified as revenue.

Another issue is raised with any tax revenue when the government specifies that certain revenues must be used for a specific purpose. For example, if the City of Pleasant View determined that 20 percent of the sales tax revenue must be used for the maintenance of the city's roads and streets, $120,000 of the sales tax revenue must be spent for that purpose. According to GASB Statement No. 33, these restrictions are not recorded as part of the revenue recognition entry but rather disclosed in the financial statements by reclassifying an appropriate amount of the equity to disclose the intended usage. Consequently, in the City of Pleasant View's Statement of Net Assets, $120,000 would be reported as a part of the restricted expendable net assets.

Imposed nonexchange revenues: government assessments such as property tax

Imposed nonexchange revenues result from assessments by governments on nongovernmental entities, including individuals, other than assessments on exchange transactions. These revenues include property taxes, fines, penalties, and property forfeitures, but no transaction exists to support the levy.

Accounting for imposed nonexchange revenues is more complicated than accounting for derived tax revenue because no underlying transaction is available to guide the timing of the revenue recognition. GASB Standard No. 33 asserts that the accounts receivable should be recognized when the government has an enforceable legal claim or when the cash is received (whichever occurs first). Revenue recognition is made when the resources are required to be used or the first period when their use is permitted. Because the government imposes the tax, the period for which the tax proceeds are to be used is usually specified. If a tax is assessed and usage is not allowed for two years, deferred revenue is recognized until the time restriction is met.

The largest source of imposed nonexchange revenue for governments is property tax. Governments, such as the City of Pleasant View, recognize the property tax revenue on the date the taxes are levied. Assume, for example, that in 2005 the City of Pleasant View assessed $5,510,000 in property taxes on the first day of the year and expects to collect $5,400,000. The entry to record the tax levy would be the following.

Property tax receivable—2005	5,510,000	
Allowance for uncollectible property tax		110,000
Revenues—property taxes		5,400,000

To record assessed property taxes for the year 2005.

Mandated nonexchange transactions: those transactions that one government unit requires another government unit to perform, such as state aid to selected individuals mandated by the federal government

Government **mandated nonexchange transactions** result from one government conveying to another government resources to help pay for the costs of a specific program. Examples include federal programs that state or local governments are mandated to perform or programs that state government mandated the local government to perform. For example, the state government grants a local city $200,000 to establish a day-care center for children whose mothers receive welfare. When the city accepts the grant, it has no choice but to use the resources as mandated by the state. That is, the city must establish a day-care center for the children regardless of whether the $200,000 covers the total costs of establishing the center. The following journal entry would record the grant revenue.

Grant receivable	200,000	
Grant revenue		200,000

To record the grant received to support the children's day-care center.

Voluntary nonexchange transactions: contributions and gifts for which the provider expects nothing in exchange

Voluntary nonexchange transactions result from legislation or contractual agreements, other than exchanges, entered into willingly by two or more parties; that is, one party conveys to another party a *gift or donation.*

Government-mandated nonexchange and voluntary nonexchange transactions are identified separately, but the accounting methods for their recognition and reporting are discussed together because the timing of their recognition is the same. Governments recognize government-mandated and voluntary nonexchange transactions when all eligibility requirements have been met. That is, the government is eligible to use the resources because the program is already in place or no time constraint is specified. Using the above information regarding funding for a day-care center, if the grant were specified to support operating costs of the center, the government would not be eligible to use the revenue until the day-care center was established. Thus, the above entry that recorded the grant receivable would have been recorded only if the day-care center were in operation. The entry would not have been recorded if the day-care center were not yet in operation because the eligibility would not be met.

If the grant resources—that is, cash—are received before the day-care center is established, the revenue is recorded as deferred revenue.

Cash	200,000	
Deferred revenue		200,000

To record grant resources received to support the day-care center when it begins operations.

When the day-care center is established, the eligibility is met and the deferred revenue would be reclassed to current revenue.

| Deferred revenue | 200,000 | |
| Grant revenue | | 200,000 |

To recognize grant revenues received to support the day-care operations.

Eligibility requirements that must be met before revenue is recognized are grouped by GASB Statement No. 33 into four categories—required characteristics of the recipient, time requirements, reimbursement, and contingencies.

1. *Required characteristics of the recipient.* The recipient must have the characteristics specified by the provider. For example, the state may provide funding on a per-student basis for Native Americans attending public schools. In order to recognize the revenue, the recipient must be a public school that enrolls Native Americans.

2. *Time requirements.* If time requirements are specified by the resource provider or legislation, they must be met before the recipient is eligible to recognize the revenue. For example, if a state provides resources for a public university for the fiscal year 2005, the university would not recognize the revenue until the beginning of the 2005 fiscal year. If the funds were received by the university in advance of the 2005 fiscal year, the cash and a deferred revenue (liability) would be recognized. If the resource provider does not specify a time requirement, no time requirement condition exists and the revenue and asset are recognized upon receipt. For example, if a donor promised to give $100,000 to the public university at some unspecified future time but did not specify when the funds could be expended, the $100,000 would be recognized by the university as a gift receivable and a revenue at the time of the promise was received.

   | Pledge receivable | 100,000 | |
   | Gift revenue | | 100,000 |

   To record the receipt of pledged gift revenue. An allowance would have been recognized for any estimated uncollectible pledge receivable.

3. *Reimbursement.* Many grants, gifts, and other programs are designed to reimburse a designated government for amounts spent for a specified purpose. That is, accounts receivable and revenue are recognized when the expenditures associated with the grant, gift, or other programs are incurred. Assume, for example, that salaries and wages of $50,000 were paid for a cost-reimbursable grant. The following entries would be recorded.

   | Salary and wages | 50,000 | |
   | Cash | | 50,000 |

   To record the salary and wage payroll.

   | Grant receivable | 50,000 | |
   | Grant revenue | | 50,000 |

   To record the receivable for a cost-reimbursable grant.

4. *Contingencies.* In voluntary nonexchange transactions, *not* government-mandated nonexchange transactions, revenue may be withheld until a specified action occurs. For example, a donor indicates that $50,000 will be donated to the city museum only when the museum has raised an equal amount from some other donors. Until

the museum raises the additional $50,000, a contingency exists and the pledged gift revenue should not be recognized. If the donor provides the cash prior to the funds being raised, the museum must recognize deferred revenue until the additional $50,000 is raised. In the event the funds are not raised, the $50,000 deferred revenue would be refunded to the donor because the condition was not met.

If there is a difference between the provider's fiscal year and the recipient government's fiscal, the government's fiscal year applies for the purpose of determining eligibility requirements.

Expense Recognition

The expenses of a government are similar to those of a for-profit business. Expenses reflect the cost of operating the enterprise and the assets used; they are recognized in the period incurred. Expenses resulting from full accrual accounting recognition are recognized and reported in the government-wide financial statements. Expenditures resulting from the modified accrual funds flow accounting are recognized and reported in the government's fund statements. Business-type activities, also referred to as proprietary funds, use full accrual accounting and report expenses regardless of which statement the activity is displayed on.

Expenditure recognition is unique to governmental accounting because it represents the assets disbursed. It reflects the cost of goods or services acquired during the period whether they are consumed or not, the acquisition of capital assets, and payment of long-term debt principal. Governments also report expenditures in the period when a liability is incurred.

Many operating expenses and expenditures occur simultaneously. For example, payroll costs for salary and wages result in expenses reported in the government-wide statements and in expenditures reported in the fund statements. Other examples of simultaneous expense and expenditures include operating costs such as office supplies, utility consumption, telephone usage, and so on. The acquisition of a police car is an example of an expenditure that does not result in a simultaneous expense. The police car purchase is an expenditure in the fund statements but not an expense because it uses cash in the year the car is acquired. In the government-wide statements, the acquisition of the car is an exchange of asset, that is, cash for a fixed asset. The expense is recognized as depreciation during the expected life of the car to reflect the use of the car rather than the use of cash.

The government often incurs liabilities that do not result in governmental fund liabilities being incurred at the same time. For example, the proceeds of a long-term debt increase the government's equity, that is, fund balance and cash of the governmental fund. The liability is not recorded in the fund statements because is it not an obligation of the current period. In the government-wide statements, both the cash proceeds and the long-term liability are displayed because the government-wide statement looks at the entity as a whole. The following discussion regarding compensated absences, infrastructure, and landfill costs illustrates transactions that are reported in two different ways: to measure current financial resources using modified accrual accounting and to measure the economic resources using full accrual accounting.

Although this sounds very confusing, the discussions and illustrations in both this chapter and Chapter 11 should help clarify the differences between the government reporting expenses and expenditures.

Compensated absences: employee absences such as vacations, holidays and sick time for which it is expected the employee will be paid

Compensated Absences **Compensated absences** are absences for vacations, holidays, sick leave, and other reasons for which employees are paid. These costs are attributable to services already rendered that will be paid in the future. As in for-profit organizations, government employees earn vacation days, sick days, or holidays that can amount to a rather significant amount of liability. At the end of the reporting period, the government clearly has a liability for such compensated absences. However, the recognition of the liability is based on a government GAAP measurement basis and guidance.[15] These costs are an example of both an expense and an expenditure being recognized. For example, assume that Sample City owes it employees $60,000 for compensated absences to be taken in the future for vacation days, holidays, and sick days that have been earned. Of the total costs, $8,000 will be paid within the first 60 days of the new fiscal year. A liability of $60,000 exists for the City, but $8,000 is a claim on the government's current financial resources because the sick and vacation time has been used but the liability has not been recorded.

In the government-wide statements, the following entry would be recorded.

Expenses—compensated absences	60,000	
Liability—compensated absences		60,000

To recognize the accrued amount of compensation owed to employees for vacation, holiday, and sick leave.

In contrast, the governmental funds using the modified accrual accounting method would recognize only the obligation of current financial resources, not a long-term liability, because the long-term liability requires future rather than current resources.

Expenditures—compensated absences	8,000	
Liability—compensated absences		8,000

To recognize the accrued amount of compensation owed to employees for vacation, holiday, and sick leave that will be paid in the new fiscal year that is an obligation of current financial resources.

The unpaid portion of the $60,000 compensated absence is not recorded in the fund statements, although the financial statement reader can determine the total obligation by reviewing the government-wide statements.

Interest Governments recognize interest expense in the government-wide financial statement using full accrual accounting, just as do for-profit organizations. That is, the interest expense is recorded to match the time period in which the interest cost was incurred. However, in the resource flow fund financial statements prepared using the modified accrual accounting recognition, interest expense is not recognized until the date it becomes a "legal" obligation, for example, the date it is due and payable. For example, assume Sample City's fiscal year-end is June 30 and it has $300,000 of long-term bond interest due on July 1. A liability of $300,000 exists for the City, but there is no claim on the government's current financial resources.

The following entry would be recorded in the government-wide statements.

Expenses—long-term bond interest	300,000	
Liability—long-term bond interest		300,000

To recognize the accrued amount of interest expense owed on long-term bond issues.

---

[15] **Statement No. 16**, "Accounting for Compensated Absences" (Norwalk, CT: Governmental Accounting Standards Board, 1992).

In contrast, the governmental funds using the modified accrual accounting method would not recognize any changes in current financial resources. The interest will not use current financial resources until the following fiscal year, when it is paid. Thus no entry would be recorded to recognize the expenditures.

Infrastructure assets: long-lived assets such as roads and bridges that are stationary in nature and can be preserved for a far great number of years than most capital assets

Infrastructure Accounting for **infrastructure assets** is another unique feature of governmental accounting. Infrastructure asses are defined in GASB Statement No. 34[16] as "long-lived capital assets that normally are stationary in nature and can be preserved for a significantly greater number of years than most capital assets." Infrastructure assets include streets and highways, bridges, sidewalks, tunnels, lighting systems, drainage systems, and dams. The cost of these assets must be recorded and depreciation expense recognized on the government-wide statements. In contract, modified accrual accounting recognizes these costs as an expenditure because they represent the consumption of current financial resources.

In addition to recording new infrastructure acquisitions as assets, state and local governments must also capitalize infrastructure assets previously acquired. Prior to GASB Statement No. 34, capitalization of infrastructure was optional. Since the costs of these earlier acquisitions may not be available, estimates must be used.

An argument can be made about the appropriateness of recognizing depreciation of these long-lived assets. For example, the bridge over the Connecticut River near Hartford, Connecticut, was built in the early 1900s. With continuous maintenance, the bridge that was built to handle Model-T traffic continues to provide passage over the river for thousands of cars and trucks each day. With proper maintenance, the bridge could continue the serve modern traffic for another century. The same could be said about highways, such as Route 66 and Route 80, that traverse many states. With appropriate repair and maintenance, the estimated life of these roads could be indefinite.

Modified approach: a specified process to document infrastructure condition established by GASB that allows governments to expense infrastructure maintenance rather than recognize depreciation

GASB responded to this argument by providing an alternate to depreciating eligible infrastructure such as state highways and bridges. The alternate, known as the **modified approach**, eliminates the depreciation for the qualified infrastructure. If the specific modified approach guidelines are met, the government can expense all maintenance costs each year rather than recording depreciation. Additions, improvements, and retirements must still be capitalized, but the costs of maintaining the infrastructure are expensed.

The modified approach requires that the infrastructure assets be part of a network or subsystem of a network and that an asset management system be maintained.[17] The management system must (1) have an up-to-date inventory of the infrastructure assets, (2) perform a condition assessment, and (3) estimate on an annual basis the annual amount needed to maintain and preserve the infrastructure at the condition level established by the government in item 2.

The condition level must be established and documented by government policy or legislative action. A complete condition assessment of eligible infrastructure assets must be preformed in a consistent manner at least every three years. The condition assessment must provide reasonable assurance that the assets are being preserved at the level established by the government.

For example, the City of Corona, California, reported in the notes to its 2001 basic financial statements the following information pertaining to the City's adoption of the modified approach to account for their infrastructure assets.

---

[16] Op. cit., **GASB Statement No. 34**, par. 19.

[17] Ibid., par. 23.

*The City elected to use the Modified Approach as defined by GASB Statement No. 34
for infrastructure reporting of its streets, concrete and asphalt pavements. The City
commissioned a physical assessment of the streets condition in May 2001. This
condition assessment will be performed every 3 years. Each homogeneous segment of
City owned street was assigned a physical condition based on 17 potential defects. A
Pavement Condition Index (PCI) was assigned to each street segment. The index is
expressed in a continuous scale from 0 to 100, where 0 is assigned to the least
acceptable physical condition and 100 is assigned to segments of street that have the
physical characteristics of a new street. The following conditions were defined:
excellent condition is assigned to segments with a scale rating between 86 and 100,
very good condition is assigned to segments with a scale rating between 71 and 85,
good condition is assigned to segments with a rating between 56 and 70, fair
condition is assigned to segments with a scale rating between 41 and 55, poor
condition is assigned to segments with a scale rating between 26 and 40, very poor
segments have a range of 11 to 25 and failed condition is assigned to segments with a
scale rating between 0 and 10. The City's policy relative to maintaining the street
assets is to achieve an average rating of 70 for all street segments. This acceptable
rating allows minor cracking and raveling of the pavement along with minor
roughness that could be noticeable to drivers traveling at the posted speeds.*[18]

Given this policy, the City of Corona would record $4 million of new infrastructure
cost in the government-wide full accrual accounts with the following entry.

Infrastructure capital assets	$4,000,000	
Cash		$4,000,000

To capitalize the acquisition costs of public works infrastructure assets.

The modified accrual accounting recognition in the fund statement would record only the
use of financial recourses.

Expenditures	$4,000,000	
Cash		$4,000,000

To record the disbursement to acquire infrastructure assets.

As long as the modified approach requirements are met and adequate documentation
is maintained, the expenditures incurred to preserve the infrastructure assets should be
expensed in the period incurred. Additions and improvements to the eligible assets should
be capitalized. If the government fails to maintain the assets at or above the established and
disclosed condition level, it must revert to reporting depreciation for its infrastructure
assets and discontinue the use of the modified approach.

Solid Waste Landfills   Cities and local governments collect and dispose of an
incredible amount of garbage and trash in landfills. Some cities and municipalities
charge a user fee to citizens and companies to dispose of their refuse in the government's
landfill. These operations have both cash inflows and outflows during their operating
lives. However, landfills are unique because when they are full, they must be closed. The
government no longer receives any user fees, but the cash outflow continues to cover costs
to ensure that residues produced by the landfill do not damage the groundwater and surrounding environment.

[18] www.ci.corona.ca.us/dept/finance/cafr01, pp. 43–44.

Prior to 1991, landfill operators and owners could be lax about how the landfills were maintained after they were closed. In October 1991, however, the U.S. Environmental Protection Agency (EPA) issued new rules to govern landfill closure and postclosure care. These rules resulted in a variety of accounting practices being established, such as "pay as you go" cash approaches or escrowing (setting aside) cash reserves for future costs. Thus the question became how and when to recognize and record the costs incurred after the closure.

To reduce the diversity of accounting practices, GASB issued Statement No. 18[19] to establish guidance for landfill closure and postclosure cost recognition. The Statement defined the costs to combine both an economic and financial resource perspective.

To illustrate the unique accounting requirements for landfill closure and postclosure maintenance, assume that Sample City opened a landfill this fiscal year and expects it will take 20 years to fill. Closure costs are estimated to be $1 million and postclosure costs to maintain the landfill are estimated at $700,000. This year the City contributed only $135,000 to closure costs. The City also estimates that 10 percent of the landfill space had been filled by the end of the fiscal year.

Regardless of whether the landfill is operated as a governmental activity or as a business-type activity, recognition in the government-wide statements is based on accrual accounting and the economic resources measurement basis. Because the government expects a total closure cost of $1.7 million and the landfill is 10 percent filled, $170,000 in closure costs should be accrued this year.

Expense—landfill closure	170,000	
Landfill closure liability		170,000

To recognize this year's portion of the estimated landfill closure costs.

The $135,000 paid toward these costs would be recognized in the following entry.

Landfill closure liability	135,000	
Cash		135,000

To record the payment of costs required for the landfill closure.

If the closure and postclosure cost estimates change as the landfill is used either increasing or decreasing, the closure expense and liability are adjusted as necessary.

If the landfill is operated as a governmental activity, only the changes in current financial resources are reported in the modified accrual fund statements. Despite the enormous estimated liability to close and maintain the landfill, the change in financial resources is limited to the amount paid. Thus the only entry to the fund-based financial statement is the following one.

Expenditure—landfill closure costs	135,000	
Cash		135,000

To record the payment of costs required for eventual landfill closure costs.

The long-term closure obligation is not reported in the modified accrual statements because it does not fall within the definition of current financial resources. However, financial statement readers can easily determine the future estimated landfill closure costs

---

[19] **Statement No. 18**, "Accounting for Municipal Solid Waste Landfill Closure and Postclosure Care Costs" (Norwalk, CT: Governmental Accounting Standards Board, 1993).

because the long-term liability of the estimated closure cost is reported in the government-wide financial statements.

COMPREHENSIVE ANNUAL FINANCIAL REPORTS

General Discussion of Requirements

General-purpose financial reporting includes not only financial statements but also includes other information that relates directly or indirectly to the information provided by the accounting system. GASB standards state that governmental entities should publish, as a matter of public record, a comprehensive annual financial report (CAFR).[20] A CAFR provides introductory information about the government, government-wide financial statements, individual fund statements, schedules that assist in demonstrating fiscal accountability, and multiple-year comparative statistical data.

In fiscal year 2002, large-sized local and state governments began reporting their financial information using both full accrual and fund-based modified accrual information in accordance with GASB Statement No. 34.[21] Mid-sized governments with annual revenues of more than $10 million but less than $100 million began reporting the two perspectives of financial information in fiscal year 2003. Small governments with annual revenues under $10 million had an additional year before being required to report both full and modified accrual information.

Full accrual information divulges the total cost of providing government services, including details of the direct cost to taxpayers and to specific users of the government's services. Full accrual financial reports are similar to those of profit-seeking corporations and include a narrative description of the past as well as a financial performance forecast much like the management discussion and analysis required by the Securities and Exchange Commission (SEC) of corporations. Modified accrual information is based on the recognition of revenues only in the financial period when the revenue is measurable and available and of expenditures when a liability is incurred.

Although governments are encouraged to prepare a CAFR, governmental GAAP[22] requires that the government financial report include the financial statements and supplementary information illustrated in Figure 10-1.

Management discussion and analysis: a required supplemental component of the financial statements that provides an explanation of the government's financial activities.

The **management discussion and analysis** (MD&A) introduces the basic financial statements and provides an analytical overview of the government's financial activities. Details of the MD&A reporting requirements are discussed later in this chapter.

The basic financial statements contain the most relevant and significant information about the government expressed in quantitative terms and include both the government-wide (full accrual) financial statements and fund (modified accrual) financial statements. The government-wide financial statements display information about the government as a whole, except those resources the government holds for others. Details of this statement are presented and discussed later in this chapter. The fund financial statements are presented following the government-wide statements and display information about the government's governmental, proprietary, and fiduciary funds.

---

[20] Op. cit., *Codification of Government Accounting*, sec. 2200.101.

[21] Op. cit., **GSAB Statement No. 34**.

[22] Op. cit., *Codification of Government Accounting*, sec. 2200.114.

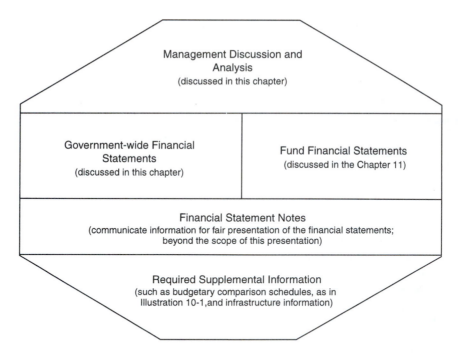

FIGURE 10-1 Governmental Comprehensive Annual Report Financial Statements and Supplemental Information Diagram

Disclosure notes follow the two basic financial statements to communicate information essential for the fair interpretation of data displayed on the face of the financial statements and are an integral part of the basic statements. The financial statement notes are comparable to those presented by for-profit organizations and present information that cannot be easily incorporated into the financial statements.

Required supplemental information is presented immediately following the notes to the financial statements. This includes statistical tables and comparative schedules to provide information on social and economic data, financial trends, and the financial capacity of the government needed by financial statement readers who desire more information about the government entity than a casual reader. Among the schedules in the statistical section is a comparison of the original authorized and final adjusted budget for the reporting period, together with the actual inflows/revenues and outflows/expenditures (see Illustration 10-1).

Figure 10-2 displays the classifications presented in each type of financial statement together with the associated basis of accounting recognition and financial statements.

Details of the individual funds and the fund financial statements that are a part of the government's financial report are discussed and illustrated in Chapter 11.

Management Discussion and Analysis (MD&A)

The MD&A, a component of the financial report that precedes the financial statements, is required supplementary information in the CFAR and is subject to limited auditor review. This section presents an overview of the government's financial activities for the past year

	Government-Wide Reporting	**Fund-Based Reporting**
Governmental activities Includes activities such as administration, public safety, welfare, and education	**Accounting recognition** Use the economic resources measurement focus and accrual accounting for the timing of revenue and expense recognition	**Accounting recognition** Use the current financial resources measurement focus and modified accrual accounting for the timing of revenue and expenditure recognition
	Financial statements Statement of Net Assets and Statement of Activities	**Financial statements** Balance Sheet and Statement of Revenues, Expenditures, and Changes in Fund Balances
Business-type activities Includes those activities that charge a fee for services provided	**Accounting recognition** Use the economic resources measurement focus and accrual accounting for the timing of revenue and expense recognition	**Accounting recognition** Use the economic resources measurement focus and accrual accounting for the timing of revenue and expense recognition
	Financial statements Included as a component of the Statement of Net Assets and Statement of Activities	**Financial statements** Statement of Net Assets; Statement of Revenues, Expenses, and Change in Net Assets; and Statement of Cash Flows
Fiduciary activities Includes pension and other trusts held for nongovernment recipients	Not reported	**Accounting recognition** Use the economic resources measurement focus and accrual accounting for the timing of revenue and expense recognition
		Financial statements Statement of Fiduciary Net Assets and Statement of Change in Fiduciary Net Assets

FIGURE 10-2   Comparison of Government-Wide to Fund-Based Reporting for Government Activities

and is presented prior to the basic financial statements in the financial report. The MD&A provides an objective and easily readable analysis of the government's financial activities based on currently known facts, decisions, or conditions. The discussion compares the government's current year results with the prior year and may include charts, graphs, or tables to illustrate the discussion. Because the discussion is general rather than specific, the most relevant information is provided to avoid a *boilerplate* or repetitious presentation.[23] Projections or assumptions should not be included in the presentation because they are conjecture and are not easily verified or audited.

At a minimum, the MD&A must include the following 8 major information components together with 14 elements that are listed in item 2 below.[24]

1. A brief discussion of the basic financial statements, including the relationship among the financial statements and an explanation of the significant differences in the information provided in the financial statements.

[23] Op. cit., **GASB Statement No. 34**, par. 11.
[24] Ibid., par. 11b.

2. Condensed financial information from the government-wide financial statements comparing the current year to the prior year. The following 14 elements must appear in the discussion.

   a. Total assets, distinguishing between capital and other assets

   b. Total liabilities, distinguishing between long-term and other liabilities

   c. Total net assets, distinguishing between amounts invested in capital assets net of related debt, restricted amounts, and unrestricted amounts

   d. Program revenues identified by major source

   e. General revenues designated by major source

   f. Total revenues

   g. Program expenses displayed by the function performed

   h. Total expenses

   i. Excess revenue over expenses or deficiency

   j. Contributions

   k. Special and extraordinary items

   l. Transfers between government funds

   m. Changes in net assets

   n. Net assets at the end of the year

3. An analysis of the government's overall financial position and the operating results so that the financial statement users can determine whether the financial position has improved or deteriorated as a result of the current year's operation.

4. An analysis of individual fund balances and transactions, including reasons for significant changes.

5. An analysis of significant variations between the original and final budget amounts together with the differences between the final budget amounts and actual expenditures.

6. A description of the capital asset and long-term debt activities, such as additions, deductions, and other changes including expenditure commitments. The discussion should also address credit rating changes and potential effects of debt limitations on financing facilities or services.

7. A discussion of the condition of current infrastructure assets, that is, assets with extraordinary long lives—such as roads, bridges, tunnels, water and sewage systems, dams, and lighting systems—when the modified approach is adopted. The modified approach of reported infrastructure is discussed later in this chapter.

8. A discussion of currently known facts expected to significantly affect the government's financial position or results of operations, such as revenues, expenses, and other changes in net assets.

Although the items and discussion that must be included in the MD&A seem exhaustive, the discussion is comparable to the president's message found in most corporate annual financial reports provided to shareholders. Through the MD&A, government financial managers explain the transactions, events, conditions, and financial data displayed in the financial reports as they relate to government's fiscal policies. As an example, see the CAFR of Orange, California, posted on its website.[25]

---

[25] The CAFR is posted under city documents at www.cityoforange.org.

GOVERNMENT-WIDE FINANCIAL STATEMENTS

Government-wide financial statements are the first of the two types of financial statements required in the CAFR. Government-wide financial statements are presented using full accrual recognition, very much like corporate financial statements. The statements include a statement of net assets, similar to a corporate balance sheet, and a statement of activities, somewhat like an income statement, that displays the current year's revenues, expenses, and changes in net assets (i.e., equity). The presentation distinguishes between the primary government and component units of the government. The primary government information displays the governmental activities and the government's business-type activities with a combined total of the two activities. Component unit information is displayed in a discrete column that is not combined with the primary government financial information.

As defined and described earlier in the chapter, primary governments are general- or special-purpose units of government such as a state, county, or city. They have popularly elected governing bodies, separate legal standing, and fiscal independence from other governments. That is, they are fiscally independent to (1) establish a budget, (2) levy taxes or set other rates or charges, and (3) issue tax-exempt debt. Governmental activities of the primary government include police and fire protection, social welfare services, education, the courts, and other general government activities. Business-type activities are those government activities that charge a fee for the provided services and are not dependent on tax revenues to support their operations, although tax revenues may be used by the primary government to subsidize the business-type operations. Examples of governmental business-type activities are water departments, natural gas services, power companies, solid waste or garbage services, parking garages, governmental hospitals, and governmental colleges and universities.

As discussed earlier in the chapter, although a component unit is not an integral part of the primary government, it may be reported in the government's financial statements. It is reported within the government's financial statements if it is an organization that imposes a financial burden or is financially dependent on the government. This situation results when the primary government is financially accountable for another organization even if the other organization is fiscally independent. In this situation, primary governmental financial accountability exists when both of the following conditions exist:

1. *The primary government either appoints (or has ex officio representation) a voting majority of the other organization's governing body or can unilaterally abolish the other organization AND*
2. *The primary government has the ability to impose its will on the other organization, or can receive either financial benefits or financial burdens from the organization.*[26]

When these conditions exist, the other organization is a component unit of the primary government and is included in the primary government's government-wide financial statements. For example, a component unit could be a separately incorporated museum that relies on the city (primary government) for financial support. According to GASB, an organization cannot be a component unit of two different primary governments. However, GASB guidance does not indicate which primary government should report or not report the component unit. The guidance indicates that the criteria should be applied from the bottom up. For example, if ABC Organization is a component unit of HAL Museum and HAL Museum is a component unit of City XYZ, then ABC Organization is a component unit of City XYZ.

---

[26] **Statement No. 14**, "The Financial Reporting Entity," (Norwalk, CT: Governmental Accounting Standards Board), par. 21–24.

Government-wide statements report all assets; liabilities; capital assets, net of accumulated depreciation; and other net assets—that is, equity, revenues, and expenses. The statements provide information based on the full accrual accounting recognition used in commercial accounting. Two government-wide statements, statement of net assets (Illustration 10-2) and statement of activities (Illustration 10-3), provide a comprehensive demonstration of the government's long-term stewardship responsibility.

Neither illustration displays a discrete column for component unit information. The significant accounting policies note disclosure in the City's financial statements states that the financial statements include the financial activities of the City and its blended component unit, the Orange Redevelopment Agency, for which the City is considered to be financially accountable. Although the Agency is a legally separate entity, it is considered part of the City's operations. Therefore, the data from the Agency were combined with the data of the City.

Statement of Net Assets

The statement of net assets (Illustration 10-2) displays information about the government as a whole, reports for all financial and capital resources, and assists the financial statement user in assessing the medium- and long-term operational accountability of the government. Separate columns on the statement are used to distinguish between the financial data for the governmental activities and business-type activities. A total of the governmental activities and the business-type activities is presented to provide financial statement users with a combined financial position for the total primary government; thus, discrete columns on the statement display the total primary government information and the government's component unit information. The government-wide statement of net assets may include a combined total column for the entity but is not required to do so. Prior year data also may be presented but is not required.

The City of Orange statement of net assets lists assets of $849,426,846 minus liabilities of $106,103,681, yielding total net assets—that is, equity—of $743,323,165. Assets and liabilities are presented in their order of liquidity. That is, assets are presented in the order in which they are expected to produce cash, and liabilities are presented in the order in which they are expected to consume cash. Assets and liabilities may be displayed in a classified format, current and noncurrent, if desired. Illustration 10-2 does not, however, display the classified format.

Net assets are presented in three components. The details of the net asset components may be presented on the face of the statements, as shown in Illustration 10-2, or as total amounts on the face of the statement with the details disclosed in the financial statement note disclosures. The three required net asset components include (1) capital assets net of related accumulated depreciation and debt, (2) restricted net assets, and (3) unrestricted net assets.

Capital assets are reported at their historical cost and depreciated over their estimated useful lives unless they are inexhaustible, such as land. Capital assets are comprised of land, improvements to land, easements, buildings, building improvements, vehicles, machinery, equipment, works of art (if capitalized)[27], infrastructure, and all other tangible and intangible assets. To be classified as a capital asset, the item must both be used in the government's operations and have a useful life extending beyond a single reporting period. Infrastructure assets are long-lived assets that are normally stationary in nature and

---

[27] Works of art need not be capitalized if they are used for educational purposes, maintained in good order, and, if sold, the proceeds are used to acquire other works of art. (**GASB Concept Statement No. 34.**) par. 27.

ILLUSTRATION 10-2
City of Orange, California
Statement of Net Assets
June 30, 2002

	Governmental Activities	Business-Type Activities	Totals 2002	Totals 2001
Assets:				
Cash and investments	$126,266,582	9,055,165	135,321,747	130,148,433
Receivables (net of allowance for estimated uncollectibles):				
Accounts	3,329,781	3,045,566	6,375,347	7,640,697
Taxes	5,040,780		5,040,780	5,162,156
Interest	1,047,638	77,811	1,125,449	1,835,555
Grants	941,814	413,076	1,354,890	1,471,909
Inventories	230,478		230,478	232,378
Prepaid items	143,363		143,363	366,123
Due from other agencies		1,884,855	1,884,855	2,088,266
Loans receivable	11,063,456		11,063,456	10,751,203
Land held for resale	142,200		142,200	1,210,860
Restricted assets:				
Cash and investments	2,376,104		2,376,104	2,000,473
Cash and investments with fiscal agent	28,621,990	41,366	28,663,356	30,416,805
Capital assets, undepreciated (note 1)	386,145,547	4,110,390	390,255,937	337,011,458
Capital assets, net (note 1)	206,315,427	59,133,457	265,448,884	156,955,613
Total assets	771,665,160	77,761,686	849,426,846	687,291,929
Liabilities:				
Accounts payable	3,202,971	2,138,495	5,341,466	5,256,989
Accrued items	3,746,236	169,318	3,915,554	3,872,766
Deposits payable	446,717	46,779	493,496	327,984
Contracts payable	349,700	130,690	480,390	280,393
Due to other agencies	1,598,775		1,598,775	1,286,754
Deferred revenue	695,432	219,591	915,023	2,669,698
Noncurrent liabilities (note 2)				
Due within one year	5,610,560	367,910	5,978,470	5,377,628
Due in more than one year	85,785,357	1,595,150	87,380,507	91,117,478
Total liabilities	101,435,748	4,667,933	106,103,681	110,189,690
Net Assets:				
Invested in capital assets, net of related debt	579,902,224	61,280,787	641,183,011	478,654,114
Restricted for:				
Capital projects	51,880,562		51,880,562	57,766,219
Debt service	8,374,666		8,374,666	12,675,589
Specific projects and programs	44,629,393		44,629,393	42,031,068
Unrestricted	(14,557,433)	11,812,966	(2,744,467)	(14,024,751)
Total net assets	$670,229,412	73,093,753	743,323,165	577,102,239

Source: City of Orange, California, Comprehensive Annual Financial Report, 2002, www.cityoforange.org.

ILLUSTRATION 10-3
City of Orange, California
Statement of Activities
Year ended June 30, 2002

| | | Program Revenues | | | Net (Expense) Revenue and Changes in Net Assets | | | |
	Expenses	Charges for Services	Operating Grants and Contributions	Capital Grants and Contribution	Governmental Activities	Business-Type Activities	Totals 2002	Totals 2001
Governmental activities:								
General government	$5,064,520	383,731			(4,680,789)		(4,680,789)	(4,544,989)
Public safety	41,623,305	4,942,185	1,149,257	616,890	(34,914,973)		(34,914,973)	(31,531,330)
Public works	22,956,131	811,895	4,513,686	6,724,899	(10,905,651)		(10,905,651)	11,204,605
Community development	2,425,190	1,729,472	92,510		(603,208)		(603,208)	(604,446)
Parks and library	9,106,265	800,126			(8,306,139)		(8,306,139)	(8,023,883)
Economic development	3,954,068	4,591	1,919,946		(2,029,531)		(2,029,531)	(691,506)
Health and sanitation	7,684,067	6,889,874	150,662		(643,531)		(643,531)	(746,455)
Interest on long-term debt	5,050,268				(5,050,268)		(5,050,268)	(5,372,394)
Total governmental activities	97,863,814	15,561,874	7,826,061	7,341,789	(67,134,090)		(67,134,090)	(40,310,398)
Business-type activities:								
Water	16,297,130	15,421,443				(875,687)	(875,687)	(412,973)
Total business-type activities	16,297,130	15,421,443				(875,687)	(875,687)	(412,973)
Totals	$114,160,944	30,983,317	7,826,061	7,341,789	(67,134,090)	(875,687)	(68,009,777)	(40,723,371)
General revenues:								
Taxes:								
Property taxes					26,152,013		26,152,013	24,708,683
Less pass-through payments					(2,758,816)		(2,758,816)	(2,527,304)
Sales taxes					25,478,034		25,478,034	27,171,351
Transient occupancy taxes					2,767,866		2,767,866	3,281,626
Franchise taxes					2,117,909		2,117,909	1,856,179
Other taxes					2,659,370		2,659,370	2,667,049
Investment income					4,831,435	594,774	5,426,209	6,866,617
State motor vehicle in lieu					7,409,676		7,409,676	6,829,988
State revenue other					982,272		982,272	1,132,875
Capital contributions					7,504,594	4,269,305	11,773,899	765,884
Other					701,446		701,446	478,576
Transfers					(1,490)	1,490		
Total general revenues and transfers					77,844,309	4,865,569	82,709,878	73,231,524
Change in net assets					10,710,219	3,989,882	14,700,101	32,508,153
Net assets at beginning of year, as restated (note 17)					659,519,193	69,103,871	728,623,064	544,594,086
Net assets at end of year					$670,229,412	73,093,753	743,323,165	577,102,239

Source: City of Orange, California, Comprehensive Annual Financial Report, 2002, www.cityoforange.org.

can be preserved for significantly longer periods of time than most capital assets. As discussed earlier in the chapter, infrastructure assets include, among other long-lived assets, roads; bridges; tunnels; sidewalks; and water, sewer, and lighting systems.

Depreciation of certain infrastructure assets are not recognized and recorded if the government chooses to apply the modified approach for reporting infrastructure assets as provided by GASB Statement No. 34. When the modified approach is used, all expenditures that maintain the eligible infrastructure assets are expensed rather than capitalized. Disbursements that represent additions and improvements to the eligible assets are capitalized and reported together with all other governmental capital assets in the statement of net assets.

The total amount of capital assets net of related accumulated depreciation and debt displayed in the statement of net assets is supported by required schedules in the financial statement note disclosures. Note 1 (Illustration 10-4) discloses information about the capital assets, while Note 2 (Illustration 10-5) discloses information about the primary government's long-term debt.

The required capital asset information note disclosure schedule for the City of Orange (Illustration 10-4) displays capital asset information for both the governmental activities and the business-type activities. It presents the beginning and ending balances together with the increases and decreases for the year for each major class of capital asset and its related accumulated depreciation. The schedule also displays the specific depreciation expense charged to each of the governmental programs or functions. The detail of the governmental $386 million undepreciated and $206 million depreciated capital assets shown on the statement of net assets is comprised of additions by major asset class totaling $16.4 million and reductions totaling $3.1 million for equipment disposals or capitalization of construction in progress adjusted by the associated accumulated depreciation changes. Note that the equipment sold or retired was not fully depreciated. Details of the business-type activities' capital assets are displayed in a similar manner.

The combined total for the primary governments' net capital assets, $655.7 million, is shown on the note disclosure but not displayed on the statement of net assets (see Figure 3).

Financial statement note 2 (Illustration 10-5) discloses detailed information on the City of Orange's long-term debt obligations for both the government and business-type activities presented as a net number on the statement of net assets. The schedule displays the beginning balance of the long-term debt for each major type of long-term liability. New debt issued is displayed as an addition, while debt principal payment or refunding is shown as a reduction. Debt refinancing deferred payments is not shown as part of the reductions but is shown separately. For example, note that the majority of the government activities' long-term debt obligations is for bonds to be paid by tax revenues. The business-type activities' primary debt is the water district's mortgage bond. In addition to the disclosure of the composition of the amount of long-term debt outstanding by major types, the schedule displays the amount due within one year in a discrete column that ties back to the "due within one year" information presented on the statement of net assets.

Note 2 displays not only long-term obligations but also other long-term liabilities such as accumulated unpaid vacation and sick leave earned by employees but not yet

Government activities net capital assets (in thousands)	$592,461
Business-type activities net capital assets (in thousands)	$ 63,243
Combined total (rounded)	$655,704

FIGURE 10-3 City of Orange, California
Summary of Capital Assets Values Reported in the Financial Statement Notes

ILLUSTRATION 10-4
City of Orange, California
Financial Statement Note Disclosure
Note 1, Capital Asset Information
(in thousands)

	Primary Government			
	Beginning Balance	Additions	Retirements	Ending Balance
Government activities:				
Land	$48,088			$48,088
Right of way	331,883	1,307	144	333,046
Construction in progress	4,884	2,144	2,016	5,012
Total nondepreciating assets	384,855	3,451	2,160	386,146
Buildings and improvements	30,946	3,799	22	34,723
Equipment	23,353	1,874	979	24,248
Infrastructure	280,870	7,332		288,202
Total historical costs	720,024	16,456	3,161	733,319
Less accumulated depreciation				
Building and improvements	9,482	2,052	861	10,673
Equipment	11,319	756		12,075
Infrastructure	113,168	4,942		118,110
Total accumulated depreciation	133,969	7,750	861	140,858
Net capital assets	**586,055**	**8,706**	**2,300**	**592,461**
Business-type activities:				
Land	1,805			1,805
Construction in progress	1,490	1,747	932	2,305
Total nondepreciating assets	3,295	1,747	932	4,110
Distribution and collection system	96,300	4,996		101,296
Buildings	566	280		846
Equipment	2,086	125	20	2,191
Total historical costs	102,247	7,148	952	108,443
Less accumulated depreciation				
Distribution and collection system	42,876	1,679		44,555
Buildings	286	17		303
Equipment	296	56	10	342
Total accumulated depreciation	43,458	1,752	10	45,200
Net capital assets	**$58,789**	**$5,396**	**$942**	**$63,243**
Distribution of depreciation expenses:				
General government		$399		
Public safety		721		
Public works		6,350		
Parks and library		247		
Economic development		32		
Community development		1		
Total depreciation expense		**$7,750**		

Source: City of Orange, California, Comprehensive Annual Financial Report, 2002, www.cityoforange.org.

ILLUSTRATION 10-5
City of Orange, California
Financial Statement Note Disclosure
Note 2, Long-Term Liabilities
(in thousands)

	Beginning Balance	New Obligations	Reductions	Ending Balance	Amount Due within one year
Government activities:					
Bonds, notes and leases payable					
Tax allocation bonds	$73,745		$1,295	$72,450	$1,385
Certificate of participation	10,660		570	10,090	600
Notes payable	179		15	164	17
Leases payable	2,342		346	1,996	361
Total bonds and notes payable	86,926	0	2,226	84,700	2,363
Other liabilities					
Compensated absences	3,871	1,886	1,620	4,137	1,821
Judgements and claims	3,387	1,828	2,656	2,559	1,427
Total other liabilities	7,258	3,714	4,276	6,696	3,248
Total payable	**94,184**	**$3,714**	**$6,502**	**$91,396**	**$5,611**
Business-type activities:					
Bonds and leases payable					
Water District mortgage bond	$2,218		$334	$1,884	$353
Lease payable	93		14	79	14
Total payable	**2,311**	**0**	**348**	**1,963**	**367**
Total long-term liabilities	**$96,495**	**$3,714**	**$6,850**	**$93,359**	**$5,978**

Source: City of Orange, California, Comprehensive Annual Financial Report, 2002, www.cityoforange.org.

taken. Observe that the note includes compensated absences and claims or judgments outstanding against the City of Orange. The schedule presents a combined total for all long-term liabilities for each component of the primary government. The total equals the long-term liabilities shown on the statement of net assets. For example, the governmental activities' $5.6 million due within one year shown on the statement of net assets is the same amount detailed on the disclosure schedule for long-term liabilities, as illustrated in Figure 10-4.

	Governmental activities	Business-type activities
Long-term liabilities payable within one year	$ 5,610,560	$ 367,910
Long-term liabilities payable in more than one year	$85,785,357	$1,595,150
Total long-term liabilities	**$91,395,917**	**$1,963,060**

FIGURE 10-4   City of Orange, California
Summary of Long-Term Debt Obligations Reported in the Financial Statement Notes

The second component of net assets displayed on the statement of net assets is restricted net assets. These net assets have constraints imposed on their use by parties outside the government, by laws or regulations of other governments, or by constitutional legislation of the reporting government. Restricted net assets are typically displayed by the major categories of restriction. For example, if net assets of a permanent endowment trust were held by the City, those assets must be held in perpetuity and only its investment income can be used. These net assets would be displayed as unexpendable restricted net assets. Restricted resources that can be used for the benefit of the government or its citizenry are shown as expendable restricted net assets. An example of expendable restricted net assets is the unexpended $51,880,561 that will be used for capital construction projects in the forthcoming fiscal year. Another expendable net asset example is the $8,374,666 held to service future debt obligations and special program support of $44,629,393 held by the City of Orange. When a government manages the pension program for its employees, pensions net assets are reported as restricted expendable net assets because those resources must be disbursed to former employees in accordance with the pension plan benefits.

The third component of net assets displayed in the statement of net assets is unrestricted net assets. These net assets are the resources that may be expended or budgeted for any expenditure in subsequent periods as determined by the government administrative processes. That is, these net assets may be used to fund any government purpose, such as operating costs, program expansion, acquisition of new capital assets, or investment as part of the investment program. Details of the unrestricted net assets *may not* appear on the face of the statement of net assets but may be detailed in a footnote disclosure.

Rather than available unrestricted net assets, the City of Orange has a deficit of $14.5 million due in debt incurred by the City that was used for noncapitalizable redevelopment costs and the acquisition of assets owned by the Redevelopment Agency. Details of the noncapitalized redevelopment costs may be displayed on the face of the statement of net assets because this information must be disclosed to the financial statement reader via a footnote disclosure.

Another example is $3 million of the City's business-type activities' unrestricted net assets designated for future development for the water distribution activities. The $3 million cannot appear in a separate line from the other $11.8 million unrestricted net assets held by business-type activities.

The total governmental and business-type activities net assets articulate to net assets at the end of the year and are displayed on the statement of activities that accounts for the net asset change from the beginning to the end of the year.

Statement of Activities

The governmental entity statement of activities displays the current period's recognized revenues together with the current period's expenses. Although it conveys the same information as the corporate income statement, the statement display is significantly different from the business presentation. An underlying objective of the government display format is the amount of program costs that must be supported by tax and other government revenue. Many financial statement users prefer expense information to be segregated by program so that each activity can be assessed. Thus, the statement of activity reports revenues by type and expenses for functions/programs, unlike corporate income statements, which report expenses by natural classifications such as salary and wages or supplies.

The statement of activities (Illustration 10-3) provides an overview of the government on a program/function basis. Charges for services, grant revenue, or contributions received that are associated with each program/function are deducted from the total expenses to indicate the extent to which each program/function relies on, or contributes to, the general revenue of the government. For example, charges and contributions for the City of Orange, California, health and sanitation program reduced the reliance of that program on the general revenues of the City from $7,684,067 to only $643,531. In contrast, parks and library expenses were reduced by only $.8 million to $8,306,139, which must be funded by taxes and some other general revenues of the City.

The first column in the statement lists the government's program expenses. The next three columns display the various revenues received by each program. The net (expense) revenue column presents the balance of the expenses that must be supported by general revenues. The net expense that must be supported by general revenues is also referred to as the net program cost. In the lower portion of the net (expense) revenue column, the government's general revenues are listed by revenue type. At the bottom of the column, the difference between the total expenses and total revenue is displayed as the change in net assets.

The upper portion of the statement of activities presents the net (expenses) revenues of each function/program together with any unallocated expense, such as interest expense ($5,050,268) or depreciation expense (not shown), which are displayed as a separate line. Net (expenses) revenues are presented separately for governmental and business-type activities, with a combined column representing the total for the primary government. Orange's component unit expenses do not appear as a separate discrete column on the statement because they have been blended into the appropriate program revenues and program net (expenses) revenues.

General revenues comprise all taxes (by type), grants, contributions, interest revenue, and any miscellaneous income received to support the program. Revenues that are not related to any specific program are reported as general revenues. Transfers among primary government activities, contributions for endowments (such as a gift to support the library), or extraordinary items are displayed in the same manner as general revenues but appear as separate line items. For example, Illustration 10-3 for the City of Orange displays on a separate line within the general revenues a reduction of the property taxes ($2,758,816) that represent tax collections that are passed on to some other entity, such as the local art museum. Also displayed separately is the $1,490 transfer to governmental activities from the business-type activities that represents the return of a cash advance.

For example, in Illustration 10-3, the total program costs of Orange's governmental activities are $67.1 million. Because the governmental revenues totaled $77.8 million, $10.7 million was added to the net assets of the governmental activities. Although we know the amount of the change in net assets, we do not know whether net asset additions were restricted or unrestricted. The business-type activities had net program costs of only $.8 million, which were supported by revenues in excess of $4.8 million. So some $3.9 million was added to the business-type activities net assets. The change in net assets is added to the net assets at the beginning of the period to equal the net assets at the end of the period. Thus, the total net assets at the end of the period articulate to the net asset amount displayed on the statement of net assets.

The statement of activity is prepared using the accrual basis of accounting. Thus, the expenses reported for each function or program include all accruals and appropriate depreciation expense. Revenues received from intragovernmental transactions, such as charges by the motor pool for servicing the police cars, are eliminated in a manner similar to the elimination of intercompany sales between parent and subsidiary corporations.

Over time governmental accounting has defined a program to be a function performed by the government entity. Orange, California, reports only seven programs in its governmental activities. Most cities and local government report many more. A function/program is defined as a group of related activities that accomplish a major service or responsibility for which the government is responsible. Figure 10-5 is a set of typical expense programs/functions reported by a state or local government, with those reported by the City of Orange, California, shown in **bold**.

The general ledger of a government is designed to organize expenses in a manner that meets the reporting and informational needs of the government and the financial statement preparer. The government records expenses by using the chart of accounts to collect financial information details such as the following components.

Type of activity being performed—such as governmental, business-type activity or proprietary or fiduciary

Function or program—such as police, fire, or general government

Departments that operate within the function/program—such as police or fire chief's office, or tax collector's office

Projects performed by the department—such as fire safety or auto inspections

Type of expense—such as personal services, operating expenses, capital outlay, and debt service

Objective of expense: a subset of the expense type, such as full-time salary or part-time labor, that provides details of the personal services expense

Objectives of expense are unique expense subsets, such as full-time salary or part-time labor, that provide details of the personal services expense. Given this hierarchy, accounting information can be presented highly summarized or in as much detail as needed by the information user. The statement of activities reports expense only at the function level, although all the above information is available in the government's financial system for the preparation of detailed reports used for financial and management decisions.

The statement of net assets and the statement of activity are full accrual-based financial statements that set forth the government's financial activities as a whole for the fiscal year. These statements display only a portion of the government's annual financial operation because they present a single column of highly aggregated financial information. The financial statement user may want to know what financial sources were received, how those resources were used, or whether any excess resources were available at the end of the fiscal year. In other words, the user may ask: What was the current financial resource flows? To provide this short-term accountability information, fund financial statements sorted by chart of account components are also presented as basic financial statements. Fund financial statements are illustrated and discussed in Chapter 11.

General government	Sanitation
Public safety	Health and welfare
Police and fire	Cultural and recreation
Public works	Education
Street and road or highway maintenance	Judicial system
Community development	Planning and development
Parks and library	**Economic development**

FIGURE 10-5 Typical Functions Used by State and Local Governments

SUMMARY

State and local governments represent a large number of entities in the United States. They follow governmental GAAP accounting and reporting hierarchy when preparing their financial reports in which accountability is identified as the paramount objective. Accountability arises due to the transfer of responsibility for resources or actions from the citizens to the government's administrators. The assessment of accountability is fulfilled when financial reporting enables financial statement users to determine the extent to which current period costs are financed by current period revenues.

State and local government financial reporting entities are the combination of the primary government, organizations for which the primary government is financially responsible, and other organizations for which the nature and significance of their relationship with the primary government is such that to not include them in the financial statements would present misleading information.

Since the timing and recognition of revenue by governments had been a historical concern, GASB issued Statement No. 33, which set forth a comprehensive system for recognizing the wide array of nonexchange revenues received by state and local governments such as taxes, fines, grants, and gifts. The guidance addresses resources from transactions in which

one party either gives value, or benefit, without directly receiving equal value in exchange or receives value, or benefit, from another party without directly giving an equal value in exchange.

State and local governments report their financial information with both full accrual information and fund-based information in accordance with GASB Statement No. 34. The government-wide financial statements discussed in this chapter present a comprehensive overview of the government as a whole, much like corporate financial reports. The government-wide statements display all economic resources, including infrastructure and obligations, with long-term debt accounted for on the accrual basis of accounting. Information reported in the statements includes the full costs of providing government services, with details on how much of the cost is borne by taxpayers and by special users of the government's service. In addition to the required financial statements and note disclosures, specific required supplementary information comprised of a management discussion and analysis, budget data, and statistical information are presented.

The fund-based information that is a part of the government's financial report is discussed and illustrated in the next chapter.

QUESTIONS

10-1. What common qualities exist among state and local governments?

10-2. What are the special characteristics of a governmental organization?

10-3. What is the basic objective of financial reporting for government organizations?

10-4. What is the paramount objective of governmental financial reporting?

10-5. How does governmental financial reporting display interperiod equity?

10-6. Describe and explain four uses of governmental financial reports that center on political, social, and economic decisions in addition to determining the government's accountability.

10-7. What are the characteristics of a primary government?

10-8. Describe the conditions that determine the existence of a component unit.

10-9. Define and describe a government business-type activity.

10-10. Explain the difference between a general-purpose governmental unit and a special-purpose governmental unit.

10-11. What purpose does a budget perform for the governmental entity?

10-12. What types of budgets are used state and local governments?

10-13. What is fund accounting and how is it used by state and local governments?

10-14. Describe the basis of accounting recognition used in state and local governmental financial statements.

10-15. Who are the three primary users of governmental financial reports?

10-16. What does a budget deficit suggest? A budget excess?

10-17. What constitutes minimum state and local government financial statement presentation?

10-18. What is included in the required supplemental information?

10-19. Describe the management discussion and analysis reported by state and local governments. What are the required contents of the discussion and analysis?

10-20. What financial statements are included in government-wide financial reports?

10-21. Discuss the information provided by government-wide financial reports.

10-22. What are the characteristics of the statement of net assets?

10-23. What are infrastructure assets and how do they differ from capital assets?

10-24. Describe the optional reporting method that state and local governments may use for reporting infrastructure assets.

10-25. Describe the information displayed in the statement of activity.

10-26. How are expenses displayed in the statement of activities?

10-27. What information other than program or functional cost is captured in the government chart of accounts?

10-28. Why is revenue recognition a concern for state and local governments?

10-29. What is the difference between an exchange and nonexchange transaction.

10-30. Identify and discuss the four types of nonexchange transactions recognized by state and local governments. Provide an example of each type of nonexchange transactions and outline the assets and revenue recognition criteria for each.

10-31. What are compensated absences? How are they determined and accounted for by governments?

10-32. Identify and discuss the two methods used by state and local governments to account for infrastructure assets.

10-33. Describe how state and local governments recognize costs associated with landfill operations and closure.

MULTIPLE CHOICE

10-1. Which one of the following may not be a target user group of governmental financial reports?

a. Citizens of the governmental entity

b. Members of the Security and Exchange Commission (SEC)

c. Direct representatives of the citizens, such as legislatures and oversight bodies

d. Investors, creditors, and others involved in the lending process

10-2. Which of the following types of budget is not a primary emphasis for a government entity?

a. Capital budget

b. Program budget

c. Performance budget

d. Asset budget

10-3. Which of the following is not one of the major state and local government fund groups?

a. Governmental

b. Proprietary

c. Capital assets

d. Fiduciary

10-4. Which of the following would not be a use of government-wide financial statements?

a. To evaluate whether current year revenues are sufficient to pay current year services

b. To provide data to determine cost of providing services to its citizenry

c. To determine the ability of business-type activities to increase their charge for services provided

d. To provide the ability to make financial comparisons between governments

10-5. A component unit of the city government could be which of the following?

a. Police department

b. Solid waste operation

c. Mayor's office

d. County hospital

10-6. A basic budget used by state and local governments that is also used by corporate entities is which of the following?

a. Fixed budgets

b. Acquisition budgets

c. Capital budgets

d. Control budgets

10-7. Tax revenues levied by state and local governments are authorized by which of the following?

a. Laws

b. Any means necessary

c. Standards set by the head of a department

d. Fund-raisers

10-8. What are the three types of state and local government fund groups?

a. General, enterprising, and agency

b. Governmental, proprietary, and fiduciary

c. General, business-type, and trusts

d. General, revenue, and trusts

10-9. The budget expresses the public policy and financial intent of the government entity. For which of the following is the budget used?

a. It is a financial plan.

b. It is a means of providing financial control.

c. It is used to evaluate performance.

d. It is all of the above.

10-10. Restricted assets are those that have constraints imposed on their use by which of the following?

a. Parties outside the government

b. Laws or regulations of other governments

c. Constitutional legislation of the reporting government

d. All of the above

10-11. Government-wide financial statements use which basis of accounting?

a. Full accrual

b. Modified accrual

c. Cash basis

d. Whatever the government prefers as long as it is consistent

10-12. Which of the following is not required to be included in the management discussion and analysis included in governmental financial statements?

a. Program revenue by major source

b. Budgetary deficit

c. General revenues by major source

d. Contributions

10-13. When assessing or evaluating the government's efficiency or effectiveness, what information should be collected?

a. Service accomplishment

b. Service costs

c. Service efforts

d. All of the above

10-14. Government-wide financial statements do not provide financial statement users which of the following?

a. Data to determine the costs of providing services to its citizenry

b. The ability to understand how the government finances its programs

c. Common terminology and classifications

d. A means to assess the finances of the government in its entirety

10-15. Program revenues are comprised of all of the following except which?

a. Grants

b. Contributions

c. Tax revenues

d. Pension plan benefits

10-16. Which of the following is an example of a component unit?

a. A police department

b. An independent library

c. A motor pool

d. All of the above

10-17. Which of these assets are significantly long lived?

a. Buildings

b. Capital equipment together with its related improvements

c. Infrastructure

d. General long-term assets

10-18. The revenues of a city may be all of the following except which?

a. Property taxes

b. Grants

c. Contributions

d. Individual income taxes

10-19. Government-wide statements do all of the following except what?

a. Report capital assets net of accumulated depreciation

b. Include a balance sheet and a income statement

c. Provide information to user groups

d. Distinguish between the primary government and the business-type activities

10-20. The net assets reported in the government-wide statement of net assets include all of the following except what?

a. Unrestricted net assets

b. Capital assets net of accumulated depreciation and debt

c. Permanently restricted net assets

d. Restricted net assets

10-21. What is (are) the typical number of budgets used by governments?

a. One

b. Two

c. Three

d. Four

10-22. A donation or gift from one party to another would be an example of a what?

a. Voluntary nonexchange transaction

b. Derived tax revenue

c. Imposed nonexchange revenue

d. Government-mandated nonexchange transaction

10-23. When is derived revenue recognized?

a. When the eligibility requirements are met

b. When time requirements are met

c. When the monies are collected

d. When the information becomes available

10-24. Component units typically are included in the financial statements of the primary government using which of the following?

a. Blending or discrete presentation

b. Blending or control presentation

c. Discrete presentation or control presentation

d. None of the above

10-25. Which of the following would not be a typical expense program/function reported by a state or local government?

a. Public safety

b. Health and welfare

c. Judicial system

d. Comptroller's office

10-26. Which of the following is a primary user of Dade County's financial reports?

a. Taxpayers

b. County commissioners

c. Investors

d. All of the above

10-27. An example of a business-type activity would be which of the following?

a. Parking garage

b. Garbage services

c. Water department

d. All of the above

10-28. What is the budget that relates the input of resources to the output of services for each organizational unit?

a. Operating budget

b. Program budget

c. Performance budget

d. Capital budget

10-29. What is a transaction in which items of comparable value are traded or exchanged (also referred to as a quid pro quo)?

a. Exchange transaction

b. Imposed nonexchange transaction

c. Voluntary nonexchange transaction

d. Government-mandated nonexchange transaction

10-30. Financial data for the government as a whole are which of the following?

a. Fund-based statements

b. Statement of activities

c. Government-wide statements

d. None of the above

EXERCISES

EXERCISE 10-1	Determine amount of program costs reported in statement of activities
EXERCISE 10-2	Classify activities reported in statement of activities
EXERCISE 10-3	Prepare the net asset section of a statement of net assets
EXERCISE 10-4	Prepare capital asset note disclosure
EXERCISE 10-5	Determine landfill closure cost
EXERCISE 10-6	Calculate and display compensated absence expense
EXERCISE 10-7	Calculate unrestricted net assets to be reported in statement of net assets
EXERCISE 10-8	Prepare various journal entries
EXERCISE 10-9	Internet research
EXERCISE 10-10	Calculate and display budgetary comparison information

EXERCISE 10-1 During the current fiscal year, the recreation program of Whiteboro City expended $893,468 for salary, wages, and payments for supplies and to vendors. The program received grants totaling $123,450 and fees for service totaling $245,785.

Required:
Determine the amount and format that will be displayed as governmental activities for the recreation program in the City's statement of activities?

EXERCISE 10-2 Identify the classification for each of the following as a governmental activity or a business-type activity.

1. Building permit fees charged by a city
2. A tax levied for highway improvements
3. Bonds issued for a water treatment plant
4. Parking fees for a self-supporting parking garage
5. Court costs in a lawsuit against the city
6. Vacation and sick leave due employees in the state controller's office
7. Payment to a school district
8. Revenue from ticket sales to an athletic arena
9. Equipment purchased for state government offices
10. Revenue from sales tax that is restricted to improve streets

EXERCISE 10-3   The following are selected account balances for the City of Milford at the end of the fiscal year.

Cash and cash equivalents	35,800
Capital assets 13,743,500	
Accumulated depreciation	5,287,000
Compensated absences	412,000
Accounts payable	137,000
Mortgage payable	520,000
Construction bonds payable	4,250,000
Reserve for debt service	375,000
Reserve for construction projects	2,500,000
Unrestricted net assets	3,894,000

Required:
Prepare the net asset (equity) section of the statement of net assets for the City of Milford.

EXERCISE 10-4   At the beginning of the fiscal year, the Town of Athens general ledger has the following balances for the Town's capital assets. During the year the Town sold a building valued at $350,000 that was fully depreciated. Depreciation expenses recognized during the year were building, $828,000; equipment, $2,356,000; and infrastructure, $19,379,000. Capital assets acquired during the year included land, $125,000; buildings, $6,890,000; equipment, $2,690,000; and new streets, $9,975,000.

	Balance	Accumulated Depreciation (in thousands)
Land	$16,254	
Building	52,830	$20,750
Equipment	28,800	5,648
Infrastructure	156,325	51,792
Total	254,209	78,190

Required:
Prepare the Town of Athens required capital asset information footnote disclosure.

EXERCISE 10-5   The City of Doomus is operating a landfill as a government activity. It is estimated that the total closure and postclosure costs will be $15,000,000. The estimated waste to be deposited in the landfill over a 30-year period is 20,000,000 tons. During fiscal year ending June 30, 2005 (its first year of operation), the landfill will accept 750,000 tons of waste.

Required:
Determine the amount that the City of Doomus will recognize as the charge for closure and postclosure care costs for fiscal year 2005. Prepare the journal entry to appropriately record the cost. Show your calculations.

EXERCISE 10-6   During the current year, employees of Gurleyville Village earned vacation and sick leave valued at $89,000. At the beginning of the fiscal year, the Village had reported a compensated absence liability of $165,450. During the current year, the employees of Gurleyville were paid $74,000 for vacation and sick days that were taken.

Required:

Prepare the general journal entry or entries to recognize and report the vacation and sick days earned and taken by Gurleyville Village employees. What amount of compensated absence liability will the Village report in its annual financial report? Where will the financial statement readers find this information in the annual financial report?

EXERCISE 10-7

In its statement of net assets, the City of Summerset reported assets of $125 million, including $75 million in capital assets net of accumulated depreciation, and liabilities of $67 million, including long-term debt of $40 million used to acquire or construct the capital assets. The City also has $1.5 million of cash restricted for debt service payments and $1 million of unexpended bond proceeds.

Required:

What amount will the City of Summerset report as unrestricted net assets in its statement of net assets?

EXERCISE 10-8

Pineville, a small city, entered into the following transactions during the fiscal year.

1. Sold land to a commercial organization for $750,000. The government originally acquired the land for $50,000.
2. Received $25,000 to support a park and recreation program for the following year.
3. Levied taxes in the amount of $9.2 million for the current fiscal year. The city expects to collect only 98 percent of the levy.
4. Received $325,000 in sales tax revenue.
5. Received $52,000 of a grant received last year to support this fiscal year's operation of the library's summer reading series.
6. Recognized estimated landfill closure costs of $125,000.
7. Had a donor promise to give the library $25,000 when the library raises an equal amount from other donors.
8. Withheld $52,000 in federal taxes from employees' salary paid on the last day of the fiscal year. The withheld funds will be forwarded to the federal government on the first day of the new fiscal year.
9. Purchased a new fire truck for $72,000.
10. Built three miles of new street at the cost of $2,500 per linear foot. The project was funded by the proceeds of a bond issued in the prior year.

Required:

Prepare the general journal entries for Pineville to recognize these transactions in its government-wide statements at the end of the fiscal year.

EXERCISE 10-9

Locate the home page for a local government in the area in which your college or university is located. From the home page, locate the government's posted comprehensive annual financial report CAFR). (*Hint*: Use a search engine such as www.google.com or www.yahoo.com to find the local government's posted financial report. Most CAFRs are posted in a pdf format.)

Required:

Using the CAFR that you found, list the programs that reported revenue in the statement of activities. What percent of each program's expenses was funded by program revenues? General revenues and other income support what percent of the total expenses reported by the government in the statement of activity? Did any program not receive any program revenue? Provide a copy of the statement of activity that you used for your analysis.

EXERCISE 10-10

The City of Livingston approved an original budget for the police department totaling $7 million. During the year purchase orders and contracts were issued in the amount of $1,400,000. All the purchase orders were filled and paid except for $156,000. Salaries and wages with fringe benefits totaling $6 million were incurred and paid. During the fiscal year, the police department's budget was increased by $700,000.

Required:

Prepare in good form the budgetary comparison schedule for the police department for the current fiscal year.

PROBLEMS

PROBLEM 10-1 Prepare capital assets disclosure for municipality
PROBLEM 10-2 Prepare municipality statement of net assets
PROBLEM 10-3 Prepare long-term debt obligation disclosure
PROBLEM 10-4 Determine how transactions will be displayed in statement of net assets
PROBLEM 10-5 Internet research
PROBLEM 10-6 Determine the statement of activity effect of various transactions
PROBLEM 10-7 Prepare primary government statement of net assets
PROBLEM 10-8 Prepare primary government statement of activity

PROBLEM 10-1   The City of Easy Street has the following capital assets recorded at historical cost.

Beginning of the fiscal year balances:	
Land (Water and Sewer Department)	$ 25,500
Land (Parking Garage)	15,400
Land (City Hall)	38,248
Building & Improvements (City Hall)	48,627
Accumulated depreciation	10,650
Buildings (Water and Sewer)	82,421
Accumulated depreciation	26,800
Equipment (City Hall)	31,390
Accumulated depreciation	8,765
Equipment (Water and Sewer)	67,358
Accumulated depreciation	15,200
Parking Garage	27,430
Accumulated depreciation on parking garage	4,000
Utility distribution & collection system	42,156
Accumulated depreciation	8,500
Infrastructure	96,765
Accumulated depreciation	25,200

The following were additions and retirements for the period.

1. Retired two computers at City Hall recorded at a cost of $1,500 each with accumulated depreciation of $825 each.
2. Purchased two computers at City Hall for $1,200 each.
3. Purchased additional land for the parking garage for $8,000.
4. Added street lights in a new subdivision for $5,000.
5. Remodeled offices at the Water and Sewer Department for $6,450.
6. Retired a desk at the Water and Sewer Department valued at $350 with accumulated depreciation of $350.
7. The depreciation for the period includes depreciation for new additions and are the following amounts.

Buildings and improvements (City Hall)	$ 803
Equipment (City Hall)	2,985
Infrastructure	1,342
Buildings and improvements (Water and Sewer)	1,437
Equipment (Water and Sewer)	1,350
Parking Garage	932
Distribution and Collection System	2,654

Required:
Prepare the primary government capital asset information required disclosure using the above information.

PROBLEM 10-2   The Evergreen City general ledger trial balance at the end of the fiscal year, June 30, 2004, is the following.

Cash and cash equivalents	$10,456,231
Taxes receivable	17,589,648
Allowance for uncollected taxes	3,325,780
Supply inventory	85,250
Investments	25,687,250
Capital assets net of depreciation	180,689,000
Accounts payable	7,890,250
Deferred revenues	4,500,000
Long-term liabilities due next year	6,350,000
Long-term liabilities due after one year	16,480,000
Capital bonds payable due after one year	75,680,000
Funds reserved to pay debt service	4,950,000
Funds reserved for capital projects	2,300,000

Required:
Prepare the statement of net assets for Evergreen City as of June 30, 2004.

PROBLEM 10-3   At the end of the fiscal year, the following long-term liabilities information was available for Music City.

	Beginning Balance	*Amount Due Within One Year*
General obligation bonds	$ 43,320	$4,943
Revenue bonds	17,432	1,560
Parking garage revenue bonds	27,225	345
Equipment notes (City Hall)	1,501	302
Compensated absences	5,732	2,920
Judgments and claims	7,642	2,875
Economic Development Bonds	25,150	2,198
Special assessment debt		150
Compensated absences (water and sewer)	578	165
Water and Sewer Revenue Bonds	54,874	3684

The following transactions occurred during the fiscal year.

1. Issued $11,390 new parking garage revenue bonds.
2. Paid general obligation bonds principal of $25,432 and issued $32,745 of new general obligation bonds.
3. Purchased additional equipment for Water and Sewer Department for $6,239.
4. Paid water and sewer revenue bonds principal of $3,743.
5. Compensated absences were increased by $3,250 and decreased by $2,954.
6. Special assessment debt was increased by $2,408.
7. Compensated absences for the water and sewer department were increased by $735 and decreased by $632.
8. Judgments and claims were decreased by $3,723 and increased by $908.
9. Equipment notes for city hall equipment were increased by $2,980.
10. Economic Development bonds were decreased by $867 and increased by $3,860.
11. Revenue bonds were increased by $26,460 and decreased by $1,643.

Required:
Prepare an appropriate financial statement disclosure schedule of the long-term obligations for Music City using the provided information.

PROBLEM 10-4   A state government entered into the following transactions during the fiscal year.

1. The state issued $10 million of general obligation bonds to expand the highway system. $9 million of the bond proceeds had been spent by the end of the fiscal year. The balance was restricted to make the next year's debt payment.

2. The state received $4.5 million in grants from the federal government that could not be spent until the next fiscal year.
3. $45 million was invested in equities and securities, while $42.5 million invested in equities and securities matured.
4. $15 million was received in sales tax receipts.
5. Vacation and sick leave of $4 million was earned during the year. Employees are expected to use the amount earned in the new fiscal year.
6. $2.5 million as an allowance for uncollected taxes was recognized at the end of the fiscal year.

Required:
Indicated how each transaction would be reported in the statement of net assets.

PROBLEM 10-5   Locate the home page for a local government that has prepared its comprehensive annual financial report (CAFR) using GASB Statement No. 34.

Required:
Review the CAFR and answer the following questions. Include the government's name, web address, and the date that the home page was accessed.

A. Does the Management Discussion and Analysis (MD&A) include a discussion of the required 14 elements outlined in the chapter?
B. If not, what elements were omitted?
C. Does the MD&A include information other than the required elements? If so, what additional information was included?
D. Locate the budgetary comparison statement. Comment on the extent of the differences between the original and final budget.

PROBLEM 10-6   The City of Lindale entered into the following transactions during the current fiscal year.

1. Lindale paid the mayor's $50,000 salary.
2. A new fire truck was purchased by the Fire Department for $95,000.
3. Principal and 8-percent interest on a $2 million general obligation 90-day note was paid.
4. Equipment at the end of its expected life was sold for $1,200. The equipment had no expected residual value when it was acquired for $15,000.
5. Property tax of $10 million was levied, of which $9.8 million is expected to be received.
6. Engineering supplies costing $98,000 were purchased.
7. 1,000 new tires for the police cars were purchased at $96 for each tire.
8. $25 million was remitted to the independent school district that is considered a component unit.
9. A $2.5 million contract for snow removal for the city's streets and parking lots was executed and paid.
10. $50,000 of "profits" from the city parking garage operation were transferred to the general government.

Required:
Analyze the effects of each transaction and indicate how the transaction would be reported in the statement of activity.

PROBLEM 10-7   Turner City has the following information for the fiscal year ended September 30, 2004. (Amounts are in thousands of dollars.)

Accounts payable	3,574
Assets restricted for capital projects	15,704
Assets restricted for debt service	36,542
Assets restricted for other purposes	6,981
Assets restricted for programs	15,432
Capital assets (net)	562,897
Cash and cash equivalents	23,877
Deferred revenue	3,514

(continues)

Inventories	848
Investments	273,650
Long-term debt obligations related to capital assets	
Due in more than one year	175,984
Due within one year	16,352
Receivables	16,442

Required:

Using the appropriate format and display, prepare a statement of net assets for Turner City for the fiscal year ended September 30, 2004.

PROBLEM 10-8   The following is Day Village primary government's revenue, expense, and net asset information for the fiscal year ended December 31, 2006.

Net assets beginning of the year	$ 26,543
Revenues	
Capital grants	
Development services	560
Police	420
Charges for service	
Development services	5,493
Engineering	645
Fire department	1,672
General government	74
Parks and recreation	3,419
Police	879
Public works	95
Grants and contracts nonprogram	4,265
Investment income	3,828
Miscellaneous	476
Operating grants and contracts	
General government	72
Development services	7
Fire department	6,125
Parks and recreation	892
Police	1,642
Taxes	
Franchise taxes	3,764
Property taxes for debt services	1,685
Property taxes for general purposes	17,265
Utility taxes	7,650
Expenses	
Development services	3,368
Engineering	198
Fire department	8,720
General government	2,906
Long-term debt interest	3,028
Parks and recreation	5,496
Police	16,525
Public works	2,077

Required:

Using good format and display, prepare the primary government portion of Day Village's statement of activity for the fiscal year ended December 31, 2006.

CHAPTER 11

STATE AND LOCAL GOVERNMENTS: ACCOUNTING AND FINANCIAL REPORTING FOR FUND GROUPS

LEARNING OBJECTIVES

After reading this chapter, you should be able to:

- Identify various aspects of state and local government funds, including (1) their characteristics and nature and (2) objectives of their financial reporting.
- Understand the unique accounting recognition processes used by governmental funds.
- Determine the appropriate governmental fund to use to record a transaction.
- Prepare journal entries for governmental fund transactions.
- Understand the fund structure and required financial statement display.
- Convert fund financial statements to government-wide statement presentation.

This chapter is the second chapter that introduces and illustrates accounting and reporting guidance for state and local governments. The previous chapter presented an overview, an introduction to the CAFR, and a discussion of government-wide financial statements. This chapter examines the accounting for the individual fund types and preparation of the second major CAFR-required financial statement group, the individual fund statements.

The chapter contains six main sections. The first provides a discussion of fund accounting and defines the three fund groups used by state and local governments. The second investigates the accounting and control procedures used by one of the fund groups, governmental funds. The next three sections describe and illustrate the required financial statements used to report the financial activity of each of the three fund groups. The final section takes a detailed look at reconciling differences between the equity balances and the change in the equity balances presented in the governmentwide statements and the fund-based statement presentation.

FUND-BASED FINANCIAL STATEMENTS AND ACCOUNTING

Recall from Chapter 10 that the government-wide statement of net assets and the statement of activity are full accrual–based financial statements that present the government's financial activities for the fiscal year. The statements present a single column of highly aggregated financial information that displays only totals without any detail of the government's financial operation for the year. Financial statement users may want to know what financial resources were received, how those resources were used, and whether there were any excess resources available at the end of the fiscal year. In other words, What were the current financial resource flows? To provide this short-term accountability information, fund financial statements are required to be presented as basic financial statements for state and local governments.

Fund Accounting

The diversity of most state and local governments and the need to assure compliance with restrictions and laws preclude the recording and summarizing of all government financial transactions in one single accounting entity. Contrary to for-profit commercial enterprises that account as a single entity, a governmental unit is accounted for through several separate fund group entities that account for designated assets, liabilities, and equity or other balances.[1] Each **fund** is a self-balancing set of accounts used to record financial information. All funds taken together comprise the government's financial reporting system.

Fund: a set of self-balancing accounts that include assets, liabilities, residual balance (equity), revenues, and disbursements

The number of funds established by a government depends upon the extent of services provided. Large governmental organizations will establish a much greater number of funds, since they provide far more services than do small governments. The general rule is that a government establishes the minimum number of separate funds consistent with legal specifications and operations requirements. Too many funds can create complexity and confusion, and it is better to avoid this situation so as to achieve financial administrative efficiency.

Fund accounting reports governmental financial information using the **modified accrual basis**. That is, fund accounting reports revenues when the resources are available. It also reports financial information by fund group. As such, fund accounting statements help assess the government's short-term fiscal accountability. Most funds are established by governing bodies to show restrictions on the planned use of resources or to measure, in the short term, the revenues and expenditures of a particular activity. Note that the term *expenditure* is used rather than *expense* because not all costs are recognized. Costs are recognized when a liability is incurred pursuant to legal authorization. For example, interest cost is not recognized until its due date, since that is when it becomes a legal obligation. The equity component of modified accrual fund financial statements is reported as fund balance rather than net assets, which is used in full accrual–based government-wide statements.

Fund Groups

Three major groups of funds—governmental, proprietary, and fiduciary—are identified in the GASB *Codification*.[2] These fund groups are employed due to the large number of

---

[1] *Codification of Governmental Accounting and Financial Reporting Standards* (Norwalk, CT: Governmental Accounting Standards Board), sec. 1300.101.

[2] Ibid., sec. 1100.103 and 1100.105.

Governmental funds: funds that account for the government's services and include administrative support for those services

Proprietary funds: funds that account for activities that charge a fee for their services; Also referred to as *businesslike* or *income producing governmental activities*

Fiduciary funds: funds that account for resources held in trust for parties outside of the government for which the government acts as an agent or trustee

diverse activities carried out by many governmental entities. The funds are combined into the three broad classifications to facilitate the reporting process because to design an accounting procedure for each fund type would not be feasible or practicable. Descriptions of the three fund groups follow.

Governmental funds account for activities of a governmental entity that provide services to its citizens and are financed primarily by taxes. These are the financial resources used in the day-to-day operations of the government. For example, governmental funds account for public safety activities (police and fire departments), welfare services, and administration of the government, such as the mayor or controller's office.

Proprietary funds are those that account for the government's ongoing activities that are similar to for-profit organizations or commercial entities. These funds can be referred to as government's business-type activities. Governmental business-type activities charge fees for their services. Utility services, a parking garage, and a municipal airport are examples of governmental business-type activities.

Fiduciary funds are funds the government holds in trust for others that cannot be used to support the government's programs. An example of a fiduciary fund is assets of an employee pension fund held and managed by the government.

Because of the diverse activities carried out by state and local governments, subfunds exist within each of the three fund types. Discussion of typical subfunds found in each of the fund groups follows.

Governmental Funds   Governmental funds tend to dominate the government's chart of accounts because the preponderance of activities carried out by the government are those services provided to its citizens. For reporting purposes, individual accounting records are maintained within each fund for the function performed by the fund, such as public police and fire safety, welfare, general administration, education, and so on. In each of the various functions, governmental resources are accumulated and expended to achieve the government's goals and objectives.

Governmental funds are divided into five subfunds or categories to provide information and control as well as provide more precise accounting data. The five subfunds include the general fund, special revenue, debt service, capital projects, and permanent funds. Accounting objectives are typically the same for each subfund, although actual procedures may differ according to the services provided. The subfund classification within the fund type provides accounting information needed by managers while providing an overall structure for financial reporting.

The *general fund* is used to account for all activities of a government that are carried out primarily to provide services to its citizens and that are financed primarily through taxes and intragovernmental revenues. Intragovernmental revenue is received when one fund buys from or sells to another fund within the government. The general fund accounts for all financial resources and their use except those required by law or generally accepted accounting principles (GAAP) to be accounted for in another fund.[3]

The *special revenue fund* accounts for the proceeds of specific revenue sources other than trust or capital projects that are legally restricted for a special purpose. That is, these resources must be expended in a specified way. For example, this subfund would account for a special $\frac{1}{2}$ percent sales tax restricted for city street and road maintenance. Another example would be rental income received for the use of the municipal athletic stadium that can be used only to retire the stadium's long-term debt.

---

[3] Ibid., sec. 1300.104.

The *debt service fund* accounts for the accumulation of resources for the payment of long-term debt principal and interest. This subfund does not account for the government's long-term debt and is comparable to a debt sinking fund used by a for-profit organization. The debt service fund monitors the long-term debt obligations to satisfy the principal and interest payments when they are legally due and payable. That is, interest payments are not recognized until the date the interest is due as determined by the debt instrument. If the interest is not paid on its due date, it is recognized as an accounts payable.

The *capital projects fund* accounts for financial resources used to acquire or construct major capital facilities other than those capital asset acquisitions financed by proprietary funds. Costs associated with the construction of roads, bridges, and buildings of all types are recorded in this subfund. Money to finance the capital project activities is usually provided by new long-term debt, grants, contributions, or transfers from the general fund. For example, if the City of Butterfield sold long-term bonds to build a new fire station, the bond proceeds would be deposited into the capital projects fund, which would then account for the costs as the new fire station is constructed.

The capital projects subfund accounts for the revenue and the expenditures but not the new long-term debt or the capitalized fixed asset—the new fire station. Capitalized state and local government long-lived assets, property, and plant and equipment are maintained in a fixed asset net asset equity account that consists of the assets, accumulated depreciation, and related long-term debt. The fixed asset net asset equity amount is reported only in the government-wide financial statements. It is not in the fund financial statements because the net fixed asset equity is not available—that is, expendable—to support operating activities. The long-term debt activities are also accounted for in a net asset equity account reported only in the government wide statements.

The *permanent fund* accounts for the principal of trusts that must be maintained intact. That is, the corpus of the trust is held in perpetuity, invested with the earnings legally restricted to use for a purpose that benefits the government or its citizenry. For example, an endowment gift received by the city that stipulates that the gift assets be invested and that only the investment income be used to the support of the city's art museum would be accounted for by the permanent fund.

Proprietary Funds   Proprietary funds account for those governmental activities that are similar to activities found in the business world that charges a fee for their services. Two subfunds facilitate the financial reporting of proprietary activities—enterprise and internal service. Accounting rules used by proprietary funds are the same as those used by for-profit businesses because fees are charged for the services rendered. That is, proprietary funds use a full accrual economic focus rather than the modified accrual current resource flow.

The *enterprise activities fund* accounts for business-type activities financed and operated in a manner similar to private business enterprises where the government intends for the costs of providing goods and services to be financed through user charges. The enterprise activities fund receives the revenues, pays the expenses, and measures any profit or loss from the service being provided. For example, the city may operate a municipal airport, mass transit system, swimming pool, golf course, water and utility services, solid waste disposal plant, and so on.

When activities are subsidized by general tax revenues, such as a light-rail or mass transit system, the activities may be accounted for as either general funds or enterprise activities. Because of the recognition differences, activities subsidized by tax revenues are typically reported as an enterprise activity in order to display the full costs of services offered using full accrual accounting recognition rather than only the legal costs recognized under modified accrual accounting employed by governmental funds.

The *internal services fund* accounts for the acquisition and sale of goods and services provided to departments and agencies within the government on a cost-reimbursement basis. Fees are charges for the service, as with enterprise activities, but the only customer is the government. Internal services accounts for such activities as central purchasing, leasing of equipment such as copiers or other small equipment, motor pools for maintenance and repair, central duplicating services, central mail room, communications (telephone and fax), warehouse services, and any other service whose costs can be pooled and then distributed to the governmental user.

Internal service transactions are comparable to sales or services between a home office and a branch operation as both the internal service fund and the subfund that received the goods or service must record the transaction. The dollar amount assigned to the provided goods or service can be referred to as a transfer price because the value of the goods or services provided could be either the original cost to the internal service subfund or some amount in excess of that costs.

Fiduciary Funds Fiduciary funds are also referred to as trust and agency activities. Resources maintained in the fiduciary funds do not belong to the government and cannot be used by the government for its operations. Thus the fund only holds assets to account for the resources held and liabilities to display the amounts due to others. The fund has no equity balance. The resources are held in trust for a person, an organization, or some other government. Since these resources are not available for the government's use, fiduciary funds are reported only in the fund financial statements and are not included in the government-wide financial statements.

Trust funds account for the receipt and disbursement of funds held in trust for others, including employees (pension or postretirement trusts) and other governments. Trust funds are expendable, as both principal and investment revenues may be disbursed. A pension or postretirement benefits trust would be an example of funds held for employees. A pooled investment fund would be an example of funds held for other governments.

Agency funds account for funds held for others for which no trust or legal relationship exists. An example is the tax collected by the government on behalf of another government, such as sales tax collected by the city on behalf of the state. Agency subfunds are often referred to as pass-through funds when their only activities consist of accounting for collected taxes due to some other government, such as sales tax collected on behalf of the state.

Major funds: funds that are displayed in the basic governmental and proprietary statements; funds are considered to be major when they have total assets, liabilities, revenues or expenses/expenditures that (1) constitute 10 percent of the governmental or enterprise activity and (2) 5 percent of the governmental or enterprise category.

Major Fund Accounting and Reporting A specific set of financial statements is required to display information for each of the three groups of funds—governmental, proprietary, and fiduciary. Governmental and proprietary group financial statement presentations display major and nonmajor subfunds determined by criteria established by the Governmental Accounting Standards Board (GASB).[4] The fiduciary fund presentation displays all subfunds regardless of whether they are major or not. The governmental fund group is required by GAAP to display the main operating fund (government's general purpose or general fund) as a major fund. If both of the following conditions (criteria) exist, other subfunds are reported as a **major fund**.

Total assets, liabilities, revenues, or expenditures/expenses are at least 10 percent of the corresponding elements (assets, liabilities, revenues, or expenditures/expenses) for all funds of that category or type displayed—that is, total governmental or total enterprise funds.

[4] **GASB Statement No. 34**, "Basic Financial Statements—and Management's Discussion and Analysis—for State and Local Governments" (Norwalk, CT: Governmental Accounting Standards Board, 1999), par. 75 and 76.

The same element that met the 10-percent criteria is at least 5 percent of the corresponding element (assets, liabilities, revenues, or expenditures/expenses) for the combined total for all governmental and enterprise funds combined.[5]

For example, assume that at the end of the fiscal year the enterprise fund has assets of $100,000,000, total liabilities of 50,000,000, revenues of $100,000,000, and expenses of $95,000,000. If the total parking garage enterprise subfund has assets totaling $71, 000,000, liabilities in excess of $25,000,000, $31,500,000 in revenues, and expenses of $30,000,000, the parking garage would be reported as a major fund in the enterprise fund's financial report because the parking garage activities exceed 10 percent of the criteria totals (assets, liabilities, revenues, and expenses) of the enterprise funds as well as exceeding the 5 percent criteria for subfund amounts within the combined fund groups—that is, the enterprise activities and governmental funds. If any of the parking garage assets, liabilities, revenues, or expenses did not meet the criteria amounts—that is, 10 percent of the total subfunds or 5 percent of the combined funds—the parking garage financial information would be combined with all the other enterprise activity information for financial statement display.

In addition to subfunds that meet the major fund criteria, any other governmental or enterprise fund that the government's management believes to be particularly important to financial statement users may be reported as a major fund. For example, museum activities are of particular interest to a large constituency among the citizenry. Because of the public interest, the government might choose to display the museum activities as a major governmental fund even though it does not meet the asset, liability, revenue, or expenditure test for reporting a major fund.

ACCOUNTING AND REPORTING GOVERNMENTAL FUNDS

As indicated earlier, governmental funds are used to account for financial resources used in the day-to-day operations of the government that typically comprise the bulk of state and local governments' accounting transactions. Governmental funds have five subfunds that account for the transactions and activities of a government entity.

Governmental funds use a modified accrual basis of accounting where revenues are recognized only when they become both measurable and available to finance expenditures for the fiscal period. Expenditures are recognized when the related liabilities are incurred, if measurable, except for unmatured interest on long-term debt, which is recognized when due and payable.

For example, the following entry would be recorded in the debt service subfund of the governmental funds only on the day (May 1) the bond interest is due since the interest is legally payable before May 1.

Interest expenditure	$34,000	
Bond interest payable		$34,000

To record the May 1 interest on the 1998 Series bond issue.

Expenditures and liabilities are recognized when goods are delivered in accordance with the purchase agreement. If the purchase agreement indicates that the goods become

---

[5] Op. cit., GASB Statement No. 30, par. 76.

the property of the government when they are delivered, the expenditure and related payable are recognized when the government receives the goods. If the purchase agreement indicates that the goods become the property of the government when they are shipped, the expenditure and liability are recorded when the government is notified that the goods are in transit. Salary and wage obligations are recognized as expenditures and payables at the end of the payroll period when the amounts are legally due.

Authorization to Collect and Disburse Resources

Governmental funds are created in conformity with legal requirements. A governmental unit may raise revenues only from sources allowed by law. Such revenues are detailed and set forth in a budget (Illustration 10-1 illustrates a legal budget). The budget is prepared for each separate activity, estimating the financial resource inflow and establishing an approved expenditure (outflow) which, in turn, enhances the entity's *accountability*. Through its preparation, the budget expresses public policy, signals the financial intent of the governmental entity for the forthcoming fiscal period, and provides a control mechanism to evaluate financial performance by comparing the planned fiscal events to the actual results. GASB has indicated that many believe the budget to be the most significant document prepared by a governmental organization.[6]

Appropriation: the authorization granted by a legislative body to incur liabilities or disburse resources

The budget is the principal method of directing and controlling the financial process of the governmental entity. Resource revenues set forth in the adopted budget, which becomes a legal document of the government, may be expended only for purposes and in amounts in compliance with the laws of the jurisdiction. This approval of the expenditure process is known as an **appropriation**. The appropriation process is the legal authorization for the government unit to incur liabilities during the budget period for the purposes specified in the appropriations law, statute, or ordinance, not to exceed the amount specified for each purpose. When a liability is incurred as authorized by an appropriation, the appropriation is considered consumed.

Recording the Budget

At the beginning of a budget period, the estimated revenue control account is debited for the total amount of revenues expected from each source specified in the revenue budget. The amounts authorized in the appropriations process are credited for the total amount of expenditures expected to be incurred for each program. The residual amount between the estimated revenues and the appropriations is debited or credited to the **budgetary fund balance** as appropriate (see Figure 11-1).

Budgetary fund balance: a control account that records the net amount of estimated revenues and appropriations that are available for the fiscal period

The estimated revenues account can be considered a pseudo asset control account because it reflects the resources to be received by the governmental funds during the fiscal year. The account is pseudo because it does not meet the accounting definition of an asset as "a probable future economic benefit obtained or controlled by an entity as a result of a past transaction or event".[7] Comparable to the estimated revenue account being a pseudo asset account, the appropriation account can be considered a pseudo liability account. It, too, is not genuine and does not fit the definition of a liability as "a probable future sacrifice of economic benefits arising from present obligations of a particular entity to transfer

---

[6] **Concept Statement No. 1**, "Objectives of Financial Reporting" (Norwalk, CT: Governmental Accounting Standards Board, 1987), par. 9.

[7] **Statement of Financial Accounting Concepts** No. 6, "Elements of Financial Statements" (Norwalk, CT: Financial Accounting Standards Board, 1985), par. 25.

assets or provide services to other entities in the future as a result of past transactions or events".[8] Both the estimated revenue and appropriation accounts can be considered memorandum accounts for control purposes as they will be closed after the preparation of the financial statements at the end of the year.

The budgetary fund balance is an account that balances the debit and credit entries in a budget journal entry. A credit balance indicates that funds are available for additional appropriations during the fiscal period. A deficit balance indicates that the governmental entity does not anticipate receiving sufficient revenues to finance the authorized appropriations. In other words, the government is practicing deficit spending. Although the budgetary fund balance account is similar to the owner's equity account of a commercial enterprise, the account does not imply or show ownership interest in the governmental fund's assets. At the end of the year, the budgetary fund balance account is closed by a journal entry that reverses the original budget entry plus any amendments to the budget.

Recording the budget initiates the accounting cycle and facilitates the preparation of financial statements comparing actual amounts of revenues and expenditures with the budgeted amounts.

The credit entry to the budgetary fund balance indicates that the legal budget anticipates a surplus for the fiscal period. If this were a debit to the budgetary fund balance, a

---

The Legally Adopted General Fund Budget for the City of Pleasant View for the Year Ended December 31, 2005, is Comprised of the Following Information

Estimated Revenues

Taxes	$80,825,000
Licenses, fees, and fines	3,525,000
Intergovernment	7,650,000
Charges for services	13,050,000
Interest	650,000
Miscellaneous	1,450,000
Total estimated revenues	107,150,000
Transfers from other funds	150,000
Less: Appropriations	
General government	11,000,000
Public safety	39,600,000
Public works	5,850,000
Health and sanitation	7,200,000
Cultural and recreation	13,200,000
Education	25,600,000
Other programs	1,925,500
Total appropriations	104,375,500
Transfers to other funds	2,500,000
Excess estimated revenues	**$424,500**

The journal entry to record the adopted budget is as follows.

General Fund

Estimated revenues	$107,150,000	
Estimated other financing source	150,000	
Appropriations		$104,375,500
Estimated other financing use		2,500,000
Budgetary Fund Balance		424,500
To record the annual budget for the City of Pleasant View.		

FIGURE 11-1 General Fund Budget.

---

[8] Ibid., par. 35.

deficit would be predicted. The estimated revenue is the total of all anticipated types of revenues, taxes, fees, charges for service, and so on. Appropriations are the total of all approved expenditures in the functions/programs for which resources may be expended. Although the budget entry is illustrated in Figure 11-1, many governments also record in subsidiary accounts the amount budgeted for the specific revenue types and expenditure function as shown in the legally adopted budget. This subsidiary account enables the government to track the amount of revenue not yet received or appropriations available for expenditure.

The following journal entry records the appropriations in the subsidiary accounts for the amount budgeted for the fiscal year ended December 31, 2005.

General Fund

Appropriations	$104,375,500	
General government		$11,000,000
Public safety		39,600,000
Public works		5,850,000
Health and sanitation		7,200,000
Cultural and recreation		13,200,000
Education		25,600,000
Other programs		1,925,500

To record the adopted budget's authorized appropriations in the subsidiary ledger accounts.

The estimated revenues would be recorded in the subsidiary ledger accounts in a similar journal entry. Figure 11-2 and 11-3 illustrate both a revenue and expenditure account at mid-year that displays revenue not yet received and appropriations available for expenditure.

The balances in the revenue subsidiary ledger accounts provide management information that $1,655,000 in tax revenue has been recognized in excess of the budget's estimated amount. That is, the government has more revenue that expected and can increase the authorized appropriations if appropriate or needed. One possible reason for this excess is that new buildings were added to the tax rolls that increased the amount of taxes billed that were not anticipated or known about during the budget process. The $4,275,000 unexpended appropriations in the general government expenditure ledger is the amount available for the government to spend for general government services between June 30 and December 31, that is, the end of the fiscal year. The amount available is often

FY 2005	Description	Estimated Revenue	Received	Variance Over (Under)
	Budget	80,825,000		(80,825,000)
June 30, 2005	Receipts		82,480,000	1,655,000

FIGURE 11-2   Tax Revenue—Illustrated Subsidiary Ledger Mid-Fiscal Year.

FY 2005	General Government	Appropriation	Expenditures	Available Appropriations
	Budget	11,000,000		11,000,000
June 30, 2005	Expenditures		6,725,000	4,275,000

FIGURE 11-3   General Government—Illustrated Subsidiary Ledger Mid-Fiscal Year.

proportional to the number of months remaining in the fiscal year or the number of program costs not yet committed. Subsidiary ledger data provide management the ability to plan and control fiscal activities during the fiscal year.

Interfund Transfers

Transfer: the shifting of resources from one category to another; in fund reporting, the transfer is between one fund and another; in government-wide reporting, transfer is between one type of activity and another, such as from governmental to business-type activities

The estimated other financing sources ($150,000) and other financing uses ($2,500,000) items shown in the approved budget are accounts created for an anticipated **transfer** among funds included in the authorized budget. These interfund transactions would have resulted in revenues or expenditures had the transaction involved enterprises external to the government. All routine, recurring interfund transfers of resources from one fund to another fund are sometimes referred to as operating transfers. For example, a local law requires that a certain amount of the taxes collected by the general fund must be used to finance expenditures made in another fund, such as repair and maintenance of water towers for the water utility in the enterprise activities within the proprietary funds. Since revenues should be recorded only once, the revenue is "transferred" from the receiving fund (enterprise activity funds) to the expending fund (general funds) to match the expenditure. The following journal entry records the transfer authorized in the City of Pleasant View's budget.

General Fund

Other financing uses (transfer out)	$2,500,000	
Cash		$2,500,000

Enterprise Activities

Cash	$2,500,000	
Other financing sources (transfer in)		$2,500,000

To record the transfer of tax revenues for use in the water tower repair and maintenance according to the authorized budget.

Note that the entry to record the transfer included a debit and a credit for each fund that was a party to the transaction. Because a fund is a set of self-balancing assets, liabilities, and equity accounts, every accounting entry in all funds and fund subfunds must be balanced by including both a debit and a credit for each fund affected.

In contrast to operating transfers that are routine and recurring, a new fund may be created by transferring assets from an existing fund, or residual balances from an inactive fund may be transferred to another fund, as allowed by the law. In this situation, the transfer is a nonreciprocal interfund transaction that is equivalent to a contribution that may or may not have a repayment requirement. These interfund transfers do not create revenue in the receiving fund or an expenditure in the fund that relinquishes the asset. However, the transfers must be reported in the fund financial statements as a change in fund balance. For example, the City of Pleasant View decided to create a new central equipment leasing service to reduce the City's operating costs. The service will need resources to acquire the equipment and repair tools before it can begin to "lease" the equipment to governmental users. The general fund advances the internal service fund $100,000 to establish the service. The advance is not expected to be repaid until the central leasing services is discontinued. The following journal entry would record the nonreciprocal transfer.

General Fund

Other financing uses (transfer out)	$100,000	
Cash		$100,000

Internal Service Fund

Cash	$100,000	
Other financing sources (transfer in)		$100,000

To record the nonreciprocal transfer to establish an equipment leasing service for the City of Pleasant View.

Since the nonreciprocal transfer is neither revenue in the internal service fund nor an expenditure in the general fund, the reduction of the general fund resources is presented in the financial statements in a category following the operating expenditures, much like a for-profit business reports extraordinary expenses. Internal service funds report the receipt of the resources in a comparable special manner.

Typical General Fund Transactions

After the general fund budget is recorded, transactions are recorded using typical accounting processes. The following journal entries illustrate partial general fund revenue activities of the City of Pleasant View during the 2004 fiscal year.

1. Property taxes were billed in the amount of $19,500,000, of which $290,000 was expected to be uncollectible.

2. Property taxes collected in cash totaled $16,000,000. Revenues from building fees were $150,000 in cash, and license fees collected totaled $200,000.

3. Property taxes in the amount of $50,000 were determined to be uncollectible. Before the end of the fiscal year, $10,000 of the taxes written off was paid.

4. At the end of the year, $156,000 in billed property taxes remained unpaid, of which $30,000 was expected to be uncollectible.

1. *To record the taxes billed:*

General Fund

Property Taxes Receivable—Current	19,500,000	
Allowance for Uncollectible Current Taxes		290,000
Tax Revenues		19,210,000

To record the tax levy, of which an estimated 1.487 percent will not be paid.

The modified accrual (funds flow) basis of accounting requires the accrual of property taxes because it is known when the taxes are billed to the property owners. The estimated uncollectible current taxes offset the total taxes billed in order to measure actual revenues received from property taxes for the year. The term *current* is included in the account title so as to differentiate the tax levy from previous years' levy receivables.

2. *To record the taxes collected:*

General Fund

Cash	16,350,000	
Property Taxes Receivable—Current		16,000,000
Fee Revenue		150,000
License Revenue		200,000

To record the receipt of tax receivable payments and other fees payments.

Under the funds flow modified accrual basis of accounting, fees and license revenues collected are recognized on the cash basis. These revenues are not billed but become revenue when collected. Any taxes or other revenues collected in advance of the year to which they apply are credited as Prepaid Revenues and reported as liabilities in the financial statements.

In the event of a cash shortage prior to the collection of property taxes, the government may issue short-term tax anticipation notes to borrow cash, pledging future tax collections as collateral. Tax anticipation notes are repaid from proceeds of the subsequent tax collection.

In the event a tax anticipation note of $5,000,000 was needed to provide cash to the government for operating needs, the following entries would be recorded.

General Fund

Cash	$5,000,000	
Tax anticipation note payable		$5,000,000

To record a note with an annual 6-percent interest rate signed February 1 with the First National Bank to provide operating cash. Current tax receivable accounts totaling $5,500,000 pledged as collateral.

When sufficient cash has been received from tax receivable payments, the note is repaid together with any interest charge.

General Fund

Tax anticipation note payable	$5,000,000	
Interest expenditure	50,000	
Cash		$5,050,000

To repay note held by First National Bank secured by current tax receivable.

3. *To record current taxes being written off that were determined would not be collected:*

General Fund

Allowance for Uncollectible Current Taxes	50,000	
Property Taxes Receivable—Current		50,000

To write off current tax receivables that were deemed to be uncollectible.

Property records would be noted for the uncollectible taxes. Any amounts collected on these delinquent taxes would include revenue for interest and penalties as required by law.

The following journal entry would record the payment of taxes, interest, and penalties for $10,000 of the taxes that were written off. Before the payment can be credited to the taxes receivable, the receivable must be restored.

General Fund

Property Taxes Receivable—Current	10,000	
Allowance for Uncollectible Current Taxes		10,000

To restore the tax receivable that was paid after it had been declared uncollectible.

Cash	11,000	
Taxes receivable—current		10,000
Taxes interest and penalties		1,000

To record the payment of taxes together with interest and penalties.

If unpaid after the passage of an appropriate statutory period, the uncollected taxes become a tax lien that the government can satisfy by selling the property on which the delinquent taxes were levied.

4. *To close the unpaid portion of the current property taxes receivable at the end of the year and establish the receivables as delinquent accounts.* (*Note:* Because the receivable account balance at the end of the year was only $156,000, payments of $19,304,000 had been received, including much of the remaining $250,000 estimated uncollectible receivables. Don't forget that receivables of $40,000 were written off against the uncollectible allowance.)

General Fund

Allowance for Uncollectible Current Taxes	220,000	
Tax Revenues		220,000

To adjust the allowance for uncollectible property taxes billed at the beginning of the year and increase the net revenue recognized. (Math proof: original 290,000 – net write-off 40,000 – this entry 220,000 = 30,000 estimated remaining allowance balance.)

Property Taxes Receivable—Delinquent FY04	156,000	
Allowance for Uncollectible Taxes—Current	30,000	
Property Taxes Receivable—Current		156,000
Allowance for Uncollectible Taxes—Delinquent FY02		30,000

To close the current tax receivable accounts and establish the unpaid accounts as delinquent.

This entry clears the Property Tax Receivable—Current ledger account and the related Allowance account, so they will be available for the accrual of property taxes for the new fiscal year. This process enables the government to track taxes billed, paid, and unpaid to specific years. In accordance with the law, after a prescribed period of time, the government can place a tax lien on the property for unpaid property taxes. Also in accordance with law, the government may have the right to sell the property at some time to satisfy the unpaid taxes receivable.

Encumbrance Accounting

The annual budget is very important and emphasized in accounting for governmental fund expenditure. In fact, many governments have balanced budget laws that prohibit the government from spending more than the budget approved by the citizens. Because the expenditures of governmental entities must not exceed the budgeted and authorized appropriations, an **encumbrance** accounting technique is used to keep track of all purchase orders and outstanding contracts. This process sets aside appropriations at the time the order is placed so that when the goods and services are received and a legal liability is incurred, sufficient resources are available. Encumbrance accounting is appropriate for any type of governmental fund because encumbrances provide an additional means to control spending. When a state or local government uses an encumbrance system, information is available about the amounts expended, the amounts committed, and the amount of budgeted resources that are available at any time during the fiscal year. The encumbrance accounting systems acts as an early warning system and significantly reduces the opportunity for the government to overspend its appropriations. For example, when the purchase order for $5,000 is placed for office supplies from Ables Service, the following entry is recorded in the City of Pleasant View's accounting system to reduce the unexpended balances of the applicable appropriation.

Encumbrance: an estimated amount that represents commitments to be paid from appropriated funds

General Fund

Encumbrances	$5,000	
Fund balance reserved for encumbrances		$5,000

To record Purchase Order #1234 to Ables Service for office supplies.

When the supplies are delivered, the encumbrances are "released" and the expenditure recorded. For example, when the office supplies were delivered, the amount of the order was $4,950 rather than the estimated $5,000 in the purchase order. The encumbrance was released for the full estimated amount and the expenditure recorded for the actual amount, as shown in the following entry.

General Fund

Fund balance reserved for encumbrances	$5,000	
Encumbrances		$5,000
Expenditures	$4,950	
Vouchers payable		$4,950

To record the delivery of office supplies from Ables Supplies ordered on Purchase Order #1234.

To safeguard the cash payments, state and local governments typically use vouchers payable rather than accounts payable processes. By using a voucher system, the government (1) establishes a liability (which may be reported as accounts payable on the financial reports) for each anticipated cash payment, (2) supports each cash payment by a voucher (written authorization) and substantiating documents to prove the validity of the payment, and (3) makes all payments by check.

If the purchase order has not been delivered at the end of the fiscal year, the encumbrance is still outstanding and the current year's appropriations are still reserved for the purchase. However, the encumbrance account must be closed to the fund balance account, just as the revenues and expenditures are. The reserve for encumbrances is reported as a reserved fund balance on the balance sheet in order to display the commitments of resources that have not yet been satisfied. For example, if encumbrances in the amount of $3,500 were outstanding at the end of the fiscal year, the following journal entry would be made.

General Fund

Fund Balance	$3,500	
Encumbrances		$3,500

To close the encumbrance account at the end of the fiscal year.

The fund balance reserved for encumbrances would remain in order to set aside $3,500 to pay the orders when they are received. By continuing to reserve $3,500 of the fund balance, that amount is not available for the future year's appropriations or other uses.

In the new fiscal year, the closed encumbrance journal entry would be reversed to accommodate recording the receipt of the goods (see the earlier journal entry that recorded the releasing of the encumbrance and reserve for encumbrance). The following reversing entry would be made to match the encumbrance to the appropriate fiscal year.

General Fund

Encumbrances—old year	$3,500	
Fund Balance		$3,500

To reverse the end of year closing entry to re-establish the encumbrance for outstanding purchase orders.

Assume that when the goods are received their cost is $3,600. The following entries would be made to record the expenditure of the prior fiscal period for the amount encumbered and recognize the excess as a current year cost.

General Fund

Reserve for Encumbrances	$3,500	
Encumbrances—old year		$3,500
Expenditures—old year	$3,500	
Expenditure—current year	$ 100	
Vouchers Payable		$3,600

To record the receipt of goods ordered in the old fiscal year.

End-of-Year Closing Entries

As mentioned earlier, the budget information remains in the account ledgers for informational purposes throughout the fiscal year. Budget entries are removed at the end of the year as part of the closing entries. For example, the City of Pleasant View would make the following entries to close the revenue and expenditure accounts and to reverse the entry that recorded the annual budget.

Appropriations	104,375,500	
Estimated other financing use	2,500,000	
Budgetary Fund Balance	424,500	
Estimated revenues		107,150,000
Estimated other financing sources		150,000

To remove (or reverse) the original budget entry.

Taxes	81,250,000	
Licenses, fees, and fines	3,498,500	
Intergovernment	7,750,000	
Charges for services	13,275,000	
Interest	700,000	
Miscellaneous	1,500,000	
Transfers from other funds	150,000	
General government		10,985,000
Public safety		39,675,000
Public works		5,805,000
Health and sanitation		7,220,000
Cultural and recreation		13,325,000
Education		26,500,000
Other programs		1,125,500
Transfers to other funds		2,500,000
Fund Balance		988,000

To close the revenue and expenditure accounts at the end of the fiscal year.

The $988,000 credit to fund balance indicates that the City had $563,500 unexpended revenues at the end of the year in addition to the budgeted $424,500. This difference is comprised of the City's receipts of $108,123,500 compared to the budgeted $107,300,000 that yielded $835,000 additional resources. This amount was reduced to $563,500 because the expenditures of $107,135,500 exceeded the budgeted $106,875,000 by $260,500.

Reversing the original budget entry removes any permanent impact on the accounting system of the estimated budget amounts that served as a controlling device during the fiscal year.

GOVERNMENTAL FUND FINANCIAL STATEMENTS

The result of operations, net income, or net loss is not relevant for governmental activities. Instead, how much revenue and other financing sources were received and how they were expended or used is reported on the two required governmental fund financial statements. The statements required for the governmental funds are a balance sheet and a statement of revenues, expenditures, and changes in fund balance. To show the relationship between the fund statement information and the government-wide presentation, the City of Orange, California, funds statements are used as exhibits.

Balance Sheet

The City of Orange's balance sheet (Illustration 11-1) uses the traditional format—assets equal liabilities plus fund balance. Assets and liabilities are presented in liquidity order. The fund balance is reported as either reserved or unreserved. The fund balance items reported as reserved are legally restricted to be expended for the designated purpose. An item among the reserved fund balance not found in corporate financial statements is the amount reserved for encumbrances.

As discussed earlier, encumbrances are those resources set aside to pay outstanding commitments of the current year budget for purchase orders and service contracts. This process ensures that current year resources are used for current year commitments and that the government is not committing future revenues for current year needs. This technique is also known as interperiod equity—the extent to which current year revenues are sufficient to pay for current year services as opposed to the costs of current year services being shifted to future years.

Amounts equal to the value of two asset accounts, inventory ($92,573) and prepaid items ($125,488), are also reported as reserved. These amounts are reserved because the assets are not liquid. That is, the assets cannot be converted to cash and are therefore not legally available. These reserved fund balances are similar to appropriated retained earnings in a commercial entity. The reserved portion of the general fund ($2,612,306, a total of $1,030,000 + 92,573 + 456,169 + 908,076 + 125,488) represents the nonexpendable portion of the general fund's assets that cannot be appropriated or budgeted for expenditures in the new fiscal year. Although $15,842,991 is designated for contingencies, the amount could be used. **Designated resources** are those set aside by management rather than legally restricted by an external party. Since there is no legal prohibition against using the resources, management can rescind the designation so as to use the funds. Special revenue funds and capital project funds are listed as unreserved but are unavailable to pay for governmental goods and service operating needs.

Designated resources: those resources set aside for a specific purpose or use by the government's management rather than an external party, such as a creditor; because no legal restriction to use these resources exist, the designation may be rescinded at any time

Some governmental fund balance sheets use the term *restricted* rather than *reserved* to identify fund balances legally restricted to be expended for a specific purpose by the government. Although the use of the term *restricted* to present reserved fund balances is not the same as that used in Illustration 11-1, it is acceptable under GASB guidance.

Reserved fund balances are those set aside or designated by the government for a specific purpose. Included among the reserved fund balances are the special revenues earmarked by law or regulation to finance specified governmental operations. Fees for state gasoline taxes, taxes on tobacco products and alcoholic beverages, or traffic violations are other examples of governmental revenues that may be reserved for a specific purpose and thus accounted for as special revenue.

As required, the general fund of the government is display on the balance sheet as a major fund because the general fund must be displayed regardless or whether it meets the major fund criteria. Also displayed as major funds are the debt service fund and three capital project subfunds. Because none of the other subfunds within the governmental activities met the major fund criteria, they are combined and reported under "Other Governmental Funds." The aggregate total of all governmental-type subfunds is displayed in a separate column.

Because the total does not equal the total amount of governmental funds displayed in the full accrual Governmentwide Statement of Net Assets presented and discussed in Chapter 10, an explanation (reconciliation) of the differences between the full accrual (economic resource flow) and the modified accrual (current resource flow) statements is required to "articulate" the two presentations.

The required reconciliation to explain the differences between the fund presentation and the government-wide presentation can be part of the balance sheet display. If sufficient room is not available on the face of the balance sheet, the items that comprise the difference may be disclosed as a separate schedule or in the footnotes to the financial statements. The City of Orange, California, presented a separate schedule to detail the components of the required reconciliation. The reconciliation, discussed later in the chapter, describes the adjustments needed to convert the modified accounting fund data to the full accrual governmentwide data for the City of Orange, California.

Comparative totals for the current and prior year are presented as required by GASB guidance to provide an understanding of changes in the City's financial position and operations. However, comparative data by fund type are not presented since their inclusion would have made the statements unduly complex and difficult to read.

Statement of Revenues, Expenditures, and Changes in Fund Balance

The governmental funds statement of revenues, expenditures, and changes in funds balance (Illustration 11-2) reports the revenues, expenditures, and other financial transactions for the same subfunds as presented in the balance sheet (Illustration 11-1). The revenues are displayed by type, including taxation; nonexchange transactions such as fines, licenses, permits, and fees; and exchange transactions such as charges for services, investment income, and operating leases.

Revenues   Revenues from taxation are recognized with a related receivable when the event occurs and the government has demanded the tax by a specific date. Revenues from fines are recognized when the fine becomes enforceable. Accrual for taxes includes delinquent taxes not received when due in addition to tax audit settlements.

Under modified accrual accounting, revenues are recognized when they become measurable and available. For example, if the City of Orange levied $45,975,000 in property taxes for the year 2002 and estimated that $2,495,000 of the amount levied will not be collected, the following journal entry would be made to record the tax levy.

Property Tax Receivable—Current	$45,975,000	
Property Taxes Revenue		$43,480,000
Allowance for uncollectible taxes		2,495,000
To record the property tax levy for 2002.		

Recording the payment of these levies and any subsequent write-off of uncollected accounts is normal accounting processes. Because the $2,495,000 not expected to be collected is unavailable for expenditure in 2002, it is not recognized as part of the tax revenue. Revenue recognition is defined as collectible within the current period or soon enough to

ILLUSTRATION 11-1
City of Orange, California
Balance Sheet
Governmental Funds
June 30, 2002

		Debt Service Fund			Capital Projects Fund	Other Governmental Funds	Totals	
	General	Redevelopment Agency	Capital Improvement	Assessment Districts	Redevelopment Agency		2002	2001
Assets:								
Cash and investments	$ 26,285,441	9,415,126	12,248,699	120,484	15,946,133	38,167,789	102,183,672	99,119,205
Receivables (net of allowance for estimated uncollectibles):								
Accounts	694,122		1,731,440		24,315	879,904	3,329,781	4,887,500
Taxes	4,498,456	190,638				351,686	5,040,780	5,162,156
Interest	440,970	90,218	12,662	22,779	140,301	340,708	1,047,638	1,693,748
Intergovernmental	677,467					264,347	941,814	1,024,143
Inventories	92,573						92,573	102,389
Prepaid items	125,488				475		125,963	124,924
Advances to other funds	297,045						297,045	1,812,072
Loans receivable					1,715,405	9,348,051	11,063,456	10,751,203
Land held for resale						142,200	142,200	1,210,860
Restricted assets:								
Cash and investments					390,000	1,986,104	2,376,104	2,000,473
Cash and investments with fiscal agent		7,003,815		20,998,936		569,239	28,571,990	30,325,750
Total assets	$ 33,111,562	16,669,797	13,992,801	21,142,199	18,216,629	52,050,028	155,213,016	158,214,423
Liabilities and Fund Balance								
Liabilities:								
Accounts payable	$ 923,235		297,483		514,959	947,277	2,686,957	3,105,690
Accrued items	3,422,379		2,892		54,829	242,688	3,722,788	3,347,550
Deposits payable	208,578			61,029	1,000	176,110	446,717	227,359
Contracts payable			59,478	2,536		225,281	287,295	234,152
Due to other agencies	2,430	1,568,383				27,962	1,598,775	1,286,754
Deferred revenue	183,488		1,638,752			495	1,822,735	2,669,698
Advances from other funds						297,045	297,045	1,812,072
Total liabilities	4,740,110	1,568,383	1,998,605	67,568	570,788	1,916,858	10,862,312	12,683,275

(Continued)

ILLUSTRATION 11-1 *Continued*

Fund Balance:

Reserved:

Debt service	1,030,000	15,131,414				247,067		16,408,481	15,146,691
Inventories	92,573							92,573	102,389
Land held for resale						142,200		142,200	1,210,860
Encumbrances	456,169		2,232,126	76,385	373,389	3,114,816		6,252,885	4,800,183
Continuing appropriations	908,076		13,091,148	19,548,481	2,682,611	12,507,465		48,773,781	50,058,184
Advances to other funds— noncurrent									1,527,597
Noncurrent portion of loans receivable					1,640,593	9,258,839		10,899,432	10,771,243
Settlement agreement						900,000		900,000	900,000
Prepaid items	125,488							125,488	124,924

Unreserved:

General Fund:

Designated for contingencies	15,842,991							15,842,991	14,541,114
Undesignated	9,916,155							9,916,155	12,737,183
Special revenue funds			(3,329,078)		22,146,624			22,146,624	18,838,710
Capital project funds				1,413,765	12,949,248	1,816,159		12,850,094	14,772,070
Total fund balance	28,371,452	15,131,414	11,994,196	21,074,631	17,645,841	50,133,170		144,350,704	145,531,148
Total liabilities and fund balance	$ 33,111,562	16,699,797	13,992,801	21,142,199	18,216,629	52,050,028		155,213,016	158,214,423

Source: City of Orange, California, Comprehensive Annual Financial Report, 2002, www.cityoforange.org.

ILLUSTRATION 11-2
City of Orange, California
Statement of Revenues, Expenditures, and Changes in Fund Balances
Governmental Funds
Year Ended June 30, 2002

	General	Debt Service Fund — Redevelopment Agency	Capital Projects Fund — Capital Improvement	Capital Projects Fund — Assessment Districts	Capital Projects Fund — Redevelopment Agency	Other Governmental Funds	Total 2002	Total 2001
Revenues:								
Taxes (note 5)	$41,341,500	10,908,983				5,479,380	57,729,863	58,752,833
Franchise fees	2,096,232					21,677	2,117,909	1,876,179
Licenses and permits	3,267,373		16,700			133,183	3,417,256	3,503,552
Revenues from use of money	2,795,178	542,160	24,189	422,697	858,083	2,116,212	6,758,519	9,291,038
Contributions from property owners								29,024,480
Revenues from other agencies	7,992,026		3,083,185			5,346,939	16,422,150	13,871,392
Charges for services and fees	5,602,039		2,399		2,930	9,084,329	14,691,697	13,747,506
Fines and forfeitures	1,406,951					833	1,407,784	1,424,087
Gas tax exchange						1,399,980	1,399,980	1,346,500
Other revenues	757,448				10	2,197,175	2,954,633	2,551,514
Total revenues	65,258,747	11,451,143	3,126,473	422,697	861,023	25,779,708	106,899,791	135,389,081
Expenditures:								
Current								
General government	6,150,044				177,358	186,690	6,514,092	6,314,105
Public safety	40,579,496					1,672,451	42,251,947	38,311,505
Public works	4,309,101			349		3,316,077	7,625,527	7,738,248
Community development	2,454,665						2,454,665	2,311,538
Parks and library	8,478,679					488,838	8,967,517	8,133,435
Economic development		101,496			3,038,519	829,760	3,969,775	2,999,321
Health and sanitation						7,778,943	7,778,943	7,687,473
Gas tax exchange	1,399,980						1,399,980	1,346,500

(Continued)

ILLUSTRATION 11-2 *Continued*

Capital outlay	243,104		2,864,457	2,026,351	4,133,613	6,489,223	15,756,748	25,482,830
Debt service:								
Principal	8,280	1,295,000			15,340	906,240	2,224,860	2,109,499
Interest	2,641	4,500,508			58,130	587,522	5,148,801	5,399,390
Pass-through payments	2,758,816						2,758,816	2,527,304
Total expenditures	63,625,990	8,665,820	2,864,457	2,026,700	7,422,960	22,255,744	106,851,671	110,361,148
Excess (deficiency) of revenues over (under) expenditures	1,632,757	2,795,323	262,016	(1,604,003)	(6,561,937)	3,523,964	48,120	25,027,933
Other financing sources (uses):								
Transfers in		1,159,102	2,976,985		4,087,202	200,000	8,423,289	16,147,731
Transfers out	(4,878,475)	(4,087,202)				(1,451,312)	(10,416,989)	(20,527,971)
Total other financing sources (uses)	(4,878,475)	(2,928,100)	2,976,985		4,087,202	(1,251,312)	(1,993,700)	(4,380,240)
Net change in fund balances	(3,245,718)	(132,777)	3,239,001	(1,604,003)	(2,474,735)	2,272,652	(1,945,580)	20,647,693
Fund balances, beginning of year, as restated	31,617,170	15,264,191	8,755,195	22,678,634	20,120,576	47,860,518	146,296,284	124,883,455
Fund balances, end of year	$ 28,371,452	15,131,414	11,994,196	21,074,631	17,645,841	50,133,170	144,350,704	145,531,148

Sources: City of Orange, California, comprehensive annual financial report, 2002, www.cityoforange.org.

be used to pay liabilities of the current period.[9] Given the information in the above entry that recorded the tax levy, if any of the $43,480,000 will not be collected until the following fiscal year and therefore not be available to pay the current year's liabilities, that amount should be recognized as deferred revenue.

Property taxes displayed in Illustration 11-2 total $41,341,500. That amount is different from the amount recognized in the above journal entry that recorded the property tax levy for 2002 because the amount in Illustration 11-2 includes prior period delinquent tax collections as well as levy adjustments that were not part of the above journal entry.

License and permit revenues are recognized when the cash is received, assuming that the fees are not refundable. Charges for services and investment income are recognized when earned—that is, when they become both measurable and available to provide resources to finance the current year's expenditures. License, permit, or fine revenues cannot be estimated, and the government's claim to the resources is not met until the revenues are physically received.

Although the City of Orange did not report a separate line item for sales tax revenues, some governments do. For example, when a sale is made in the City of New York, both city and state sales taxes are charged and collected. GASB Statement No. 22[10] requires sales and income taxes to be recognized in the accounting period in which they become susceptible to accrual. This is based on the fact that the government's claim to the sales tax revenue is established when a business makes a taxable sale. Thus, using the current funds flow recognition, the revenue is both measurable and available for governmental expenditures of the fiscal period.

Grants and moneys transferred from some other government for payment to another government or person—that is, pass-through grants—are a common source of revenue to state and local governments. GASB Statement No. 24[11] requires governments to record pass-through grants of cash or food stamps as both revenues and expenditures rather than as cash and a payable on the balance sheet. Pass-through revenues received by state governments from the federal government include food stamps, Aid to Families with Dependent Children, and food supplements to school lunch programs.

There are several items that are highlights among the revenues reported in the City of Orange's governmental fund's revenue. Overall, the total revenues decreased from the previous year by almost $28 million. Apparently the decrease was the result of $29 million in bond proceeds included in the prior period governmental revenue. When the total is adjusted for this anomaly, revenue actually increased about 0.5 percent from fiscal year 2001 to fiscal year 2002.

Another interesting display is the City's tax revenue. The $57.7 million in tax revenue is comprised of three different sources: $26,562,568 of property tax, $27,819,613 of sales and use tax, and other tax revenue of $3,347,682. However, rather than reporting the revenue by each individual tax type, the revenues are combined into the single heading "Taxes" and reported in the fund according to the authorized use of the revenue.

Revenue from use of money is actually investment income. Although the amount the City has had invested over the past two years is about the same according to the balance sheet, the revenue has decreased due to the Federal Reserve fund interest rate reductions.

---

[9] Op. cit., *Codification of Government Accounting*, sec. 1600.106.

[10] **GASB Statement No. 22**, "Accounting for Taxpayer assessed Tax Revenue in Government Funds" (Norwalk, CT: Government Accounting Standards Board, 1993).

[11] **GASB Statement No. 24**, "Accounting and Financial Reporting for certain Grants and Other Financial Assistance" (Norwalk, CT: Government Accounting Standards Board, 1994).

Revenues from other agencies are another unusual revenue item in the governmental funds. The $3,083,185 capital improvement component of the revenue is grants received from Orange County and other agencies for the development of a part within the City of Orange. The $7,992,026 general fund portion is money received from the state motor vehicle department in lieu of automobile leasing and sales. Reimbursements from the state and other agencies were not included in this revenue category but are shown as Other Revenue and described in the financial statement notes. Details of the revenues from other agencies are explained on the face of the statement or in the footnotes because it is typical for cities and governments to receive revenue from other state and local governmental agencies.

Expenditures The statement of revenues, expenditures, and changes in fund balance displays expenditures by program or function similar to the government-wide statement of activities presentation. However, governmental funds account for the expenditure of financial resources using the modified accrual current funds flow recognition rather than full accrual matching expenses against revenues used in the government-wide statements. For example, debt principal payments and capital assets acquisitions are recognized by the modified accrual current funds flow recognition as expenditures rather than balance sheet transactions because there are cash disbursements and use current resources. The full accrual economic flow recognition used in the government-wide statements capitalizes the capital asset acquisition in the balance sheet and recognizes depreciation as an expense to reflect the economic wasting away of the capital asset. Full accrual accounting recognizes the debt principal payment as a reduction of cash and of the debt liability in the balance sheet.

Nonoperating sources and uses of resources are displayed in the other financing sources (uses) component of the statement. These items are typically the operating transfers within the governmental funds that include debt proceeds, debt service, and transfers to and from internal service funds.

The final component on the statement of revenue and expenditures and change in fund balances presents any special items. Although the City of Orange did not report any special items, a special item would have been received if some unusual transaction had occurred. For example, assume that the City sold land that had been acquired to build a new fire station but changed its plans. The proceeds of the land sale would be reported as a special item because governments rarely sell real estate. Another example would be an extraordinary event transaction such as fire damage.

A total column is required for the statement of revenues, expenditures, and changes in fund balance. The net change in fund balance in this total column must be reconciled to the total change in the net assets for governmental activities reported on the government-wide statement of activities. The reconciliation identifies those items and amounts that represent the differences between modified accrual and full accrual accounting recognition. The City of Orange, California, presented a separate schedule to detail the components of the required reconciliation that is discussed later in the chapter.

After the financial statements have been prepared for the City of Orange, the budgetary and actual revenue, expenditure, and encumbrance accounts are closed in order to clear them for the next fiscal year's activities. The budgetary accounts are closed because they are no longer required for control over the revenues, expenditures, and other financing sources and uses.

An analysis of the City's expenditure finds that public safety represents the largest component of the City's expenditures. These cost include both the police and fire departments. Although these costs are collapsed into one amount in this statement, the financial statement reader can determine the expenditures of each department by reviewing the budget comparison schedule that displays the actual expenditures for each department.

Just as the details of the public safety expenditures can be found in the budget comparison schedule, so can the details of the general government as well as the parks and library. For example, the general government expenditures represents only 6 percent of the City's operating cost. What may be of more interest to the financial statement reader are the costs expended for those activities that are a part of the general government, including costs of the city council, the manager, attorney, clerk, and administrative services.

PROPRIETARY FUND ACCOUNTING AND FINANCIAL STATEMENTS

The primary concept for accounting for proprietary funds is income determination rather than current funds flow of financial resources, which is used to report the activities of governmental funds. Costs for proprietary fund business-type activities, also known as enterprise funds and internal service funds, are typically covered through user charges for services rendered rather than taxes or other governmental revenues. Because of the similarity with for-profit commercial businesses, the accounting and financial measurement centers on the determination of operating income or loss, financial position, and change in the financial position. That means that the proprietary funds use full accrual economic flow accounting. Depreciation expense, for example, is recognized to allocate the costs of long-lived fixed assets over their useful lives. Revenues are recognized when the earnings process is substantially complete. Because of this change in reporting recognition from governmental funds, encumbrances are typically not recognized by the proprietary funds, and long-lived asset acquisitions are capitalized rather than being reported as expenditures. Recording fixed assets as long-term assets and long-term debts as long-term liabilities permits the recognition of depreciation and the accrual of interest expense payable. Thus, operating income—that is, net income—of the business-type activity can be determined and reported.

Although budgets are typically adopted for business-type activities, they tend not to be legal documents; thus, budgetary entries may or may not be recorded in the financial accounting system. According to the GASB *Codification*,[12] the demand for goods and services provided largely determines the appropriate level of revenues and expenses. Thus, as in commercial accounting, flexible budgets prepared for several levels of possible activity are better for proprietary fund planning, control, and evaluation purposes than the legal fixed budget used by governmental funds.

State and local governments use proprietary funds to account for operations financed by user charges for the goods and services rendered. However, deciding whether an operation is a proprietary fund or part of the governmental funds can sometimes be difficult, especially when the financing source is a combination of user fees and subsidies from the general fund. Activities are required to be reported as a business-type activity enterprise fund if any one of the following criteria is met based on the activity's principal revenue source.

> 1. *The activity is financed with debt that is secured solely by a pledge of the net revenues from fees and charges of the activity. If the pledge of net revenues from fees and charges is accompanied with the full faith and credit of a related government or component unit, then a sole pledge does not exist.*

[12] Ibid., sec. 1700. 120–122.

2. *Laws or regulations exist that require that the activity's costs of providing services, including capital costs such as depreciation and debt service be recovered with fees for services rather than with taxes or similar revenues.*

3. *The pricing policies of the activity establish fees or charges for services designed to recover its costs including the cost of depreciation and debt service.*[13]

Internal service funds and business-type activities utilize comparable accounting procedures. The functions of these two proprietary funds are the same, so any variation in their accounting and reporting is not appropriate or justified. The difference between the two funds is the internal services fund, which, as the name implies, provides goods and services internally within the government for a fee, whereas the business-type activities provide goods and services to the general public as well as to the government and charge a fee for the services rendered.

Statement of Net Assets

Proprietary fund financial statements report separate columns for each major business-type activity enterprise fund. Other enterprise activities may be reported as a major fund if the government believes that the specific enterprise activity is of significant importance to the financial statement user. Nonmajor enterprise funds are aggregated in a separate column, as is the internal service funds. Illustration 11-3 indicates that the City of Orange has only one major fund—water—in addition to its internal service fund. If the City had reported more than one major enterprise fund, a total of the enterprise activity would have been presented separately from the internal service fund total and a combined total for the proprietary fund financial statements would not be presented.

Because the accounting and reporting processes of business-type activity funds are comparable to those of a for-profit company, a complete overview of the reporting processes is unnecessary. However, a few accounting procedures are unusual. For example, the proprietary funds statement of net assets (see Illustration 11-3) is presented in a classified format, with assets and liabilities listed in the order of their liquidity. The net assets—that is, equity—display capital assets net of accumulated depreciation and debt, funds restricted for debt service, and unrestricted net assets, which is the net equity in the enterprise activities' capital assets.

Another unique reporting concern is the legal restriction of cash and other assets. For example, in Illustration 11-3, the water district reports $41,366 as restricted cash and investments. Local laws may require that certain money be formally segregated in the accounting records. Similar restrictions often result from contractual or debt covenants. For example, bond covenants often stipulate that bond proceeds must be segregated and spent only for the intended purposes. The covenants may also specify that certain amounts, like the $41,366 displayed in Illustration 11-3, be restricted and set aside to ensure the availability of resources to pay debt obligations when they are due. Regardless of the reason for the restriction, the net assets set aside are invested until needed as a cash disbursement.

The proprietary fund statement of net assets displays net assets rather than fund balances in the same manner as does the government-wide statement of net assets. The first item is the amount invested in capital assets—that is, it is the amount of the capital assets less accumulated depreciation less any related debt. Any restricted net assets are presented following the net investment in capital assets. The restricted net assets may be presented as a single number or displayed by type of restriction. If the restricted net assets are presented

---

[13] Op. cit., **GASB Statement No. 34**, par. 67.

ILLUSTRATION 11-3
City of Orange, California
Statement of Net Assets
Proprietary Funds
June 30, 2002

	Business-Type Activities—Enterprise Fund—Water	Governmental Activities— Total Funds	Totals	
			2002	2001
Assets:				
Current assets:				
Cash and investments	$9,055,165	24,082,910	33,138,075	31,029,228
Accounts receivable	3,045,566		3,045,566	2,753,197
Interest receivable	77,811		77,811	141,807
Inventories	413,076	137,905	550,981	577,755
Prepaid items		17,400	17,400	
Due from other agencies	1,884,855		1,884,855	2,329,465
Restricted assets:				
Cash and investments with fiscal agent	41,366	50,000	91,366	91,055
Total current assets	14,517,839	24,288,215	38,806,054	36,922,507
Capital assets:				
Property, plant and equipment, net	63,243,847	8,354,283	71,598,130	55,649,467
Total capital assets	63,243,847	8,354,283	71,598,130	55,649,467
Total assets	77,761,686	32,642,498	110,404,184	92,571,974
Liabilities:				
Current liabilities:				
Accounts payable	2,138,495	1,943,370	4,081,865	3,192,800
Accrued expenses	169,318	442,433	611,751	832,283
Deposits payable	46,779		46,779	100,625
Contracts payable	130,690	62,405	193,095	46,241
Deferred revenue	219,591		219,591	
Lease payable—current	367,910		367,910	347,618
Total current liabilities	3,072,783	2,448,208	5,520,991	4,519,567
Long-term liabilities:				
Claims payable		1,131,802	1,131,802	2,345,234
Lease payable	1,595,150		1,595,150	1,963,061
Total long-term liabilities	1,595,150	1,131,802	2,726,952	4,308,295
Total liabilities	4,667,933	3,580,010	8,247,943	8,827,862
Net Assets:				
Invested in capital assets, net of related debt	61,280,787	8,354,283	69,635,070	53,338,788
Unrestricted	11,812,966	20,708,205	32,521,171	30,405,324
Total net assets	$73,093,753	29,062,488	102,156,241	83,744,112

Source: City of Orange, California, Comprehensive Annual Financial Report, 2002, www.cityoforange.org.

as a single number, the type and amount of each restricted net asset must be reported in the financial statement disclosures. The last item listed among the net assets is the amount of the unrestricted net assets. GASB GAAP prohibits reporting the any of the unrestricted net assets on the face of the statement. If the government has designated portions of the unrestricted net assets to be used for a particular purpose, a description of the designation may be presented in the notes to the financial statement.

Statement of Revenues, Expenses, and Changes in Fund Net Assets

The statement of revenues, expenses, and changes in fund net assets is also presented in a classified format for proprietary funds (Illustration 11-4). Paragraph 102 in GASB Statement 34 directs governments to establish a policy to define what are operating and nonoperating revenues and expenses that are appropriate for the activities being reported. That means that each government must decide what are operating and nonoperating transactions and disclose that policy as part of the significant accounting policies in the footnotes to the financial statements. Because governments differ significantly from one another, enterprise business-type activity, revenue, and expense items reported by one government could be different from those reported by another. The City of Orange chose to report only charges for services and miscellaneous as operating revenues and expenses in its statements of revenues, expenses, and changes in net assets. Although the City reports interest and investment revenue as nonoperating, some governments report a portion of their investment income allocated for ongoing activities as operating revenue.

Proprietary fund expenses are reported by natural classification—that is, personal services or salary, contractual services, utilities, repair, and so on. The display of expense by natural class is required and enables some articulation with the direct method cash flows from operating activities presented in the statement of cash flows.

Business-type activities report income by major types and often receive capital contributions such as grants, development, or endowment gifts. These revenues are reported in the statement of revenues, expenses, and changes in net assets following the nonoperating revenue (expenses) and just prior to the calculation of the change in net assets (see Illustration 11-4).

Any transfer of resources to some other governmental fund is also shown prior to the calculation of the change in net assets. The City of Orange's business-type activities received transfers in of $1,490, and the internal service funds received transfers in of $1,992,210. Both transfers were part of the general fund's transfer out displayed in Illustration 11-2. Note that in the prior year 2001, transfers in of $4,647,248 were received and $267,008 was transferred out to other City fund groups.

Statement of Cash Flows

In addition to a statement of net assets (Illustration 11-3) and a statement of revenues, expenses, and changes in net assets (Illustration 11-4), proprietary funds present a statement of cash flows (Illustration 11-5) based on the provisions of GASB Statement No. 9.[14] The proprietary fund statement of cash flows has four separate sections: cash flow from operating activities, cash flows from noncapital financing activities, cash flows from capital and related financing activities, and cash flows from investing activities. According to

[14] **GASB Statement No. 9**, "Reporting Cash Flows of Proprietary and Nonexpendable Trust Funds" (Norwalk, CT: Government Accounting Standards Board, 1989).

ILLUSTRATION 11-4
City of Orange, California
Statement of Revenues, Expenses, and Changes in Fund Net Assets
Proprietary Funds
Year Ended June 30, 2002

	Business-Type Activities—Enterprise Fund—Water	Governmental Activities—Internal Service Funds	Totals 2002	Totals 2001
Operating Revenues:				
Water sales and services	$14,901,771		14,901,771	14,085,945
Charges for services and fees	354,474	10,039,908	10,394,382	9,210,258
Other revenues	165,198	8,814	174,012	65,400
Total operating revenues	15,421,443	10,048,722	25,470,165	23,361,603
Operating Expenses:				
Salaries and wages	3,019,845	1,232,612	4,252,457	4,259,344
Maintenance and operations	9,827,087	3,141,931	12,969,018	11,180,793
Contractual services		1,473,398	1,473,398	1,342,919
Depreciation	1,751,713	1,180,894	2,932,597	2,359,766
Interfund charge for administration	1,574,650		1,574,650	1,733,366
Insurance claims and charges		1,308,861	1,308,861	2,156,251
Other expenses		734,099	734,099	639,261
Total operating expenses	16,173,295	9,071,785	25,245,080	23,671,700
Operating income (loss)	(751,852)	976,937	225,085	(310,097)
Nonoperating Revenues (Expenses):				
Interest revenue	594,774	1,011	595,785	753,445
Gain on retirement of assets		48,147	48,147	61,698
Interest expense	(123,835)		(123,835)	(139,372)
Total nonoperating revenues (expenses)	470,939	49,158	520,097	675,771
Income (loss) before contributions and transfers	(280,913)	1,026,095	745,182	365,674
Capital contributions	4,269,305		4,269,305	765,884
Transfers in	1,490	1,992,210	1,993,700	4,647,248
Transfers out				(267,008)
Change in net assets	3,989,882	3,018,305	7,008,187	5,511,798
Net assets, beginning of year, as restated	69,103,871	26,044,183	95,148,054	78,232,314
Net assets, end of year	$73,093,753	29,062,488	102,156,241	83,744,112

Source: City of Orange, California, comprehensive annual financial report, 2002, www.cityoforange. org.

GASB Statement No. 34, the proprietary fund cash flows from operating activities must be displayed using the direct method.[15]

As shown in Illustration 11-5, cash flows from the City of Orange's water operating activities inflows include the receipts from the major types of revenue received by the

[15] Ibid., par. 105.

ILLUSTRATION 11-5
City of Orange, California
Statement of Cash Flows
Proprietary Funds
Year Ended June 30, 2002

	Business-Type Activities—Enterprise Fund—Water	Governmental Activities—Internal Service Funds	Totals	
			2002	2001
Cash flows from operating activities				
Cash received from customers	$14,593,526	3,809	14,597,335	15,069,554
Cash received from user departments	354,455	9,352,548	9,707,003	7,561,925
Cash payments to suppliers for goods and services	(9,422,260)	(6,862,936)	(16,285,196)	(17,614,688)
Cash payments to employees for services	(4,753,571)	(1,464,967)	(6,218,538)	(5,926,685)
Cash received for other activities	165,198	723,163	888,361	1,346,169
Net cash provided by (used for) operating activities	937,348	1,751,617	2,688,965	436,275
Net cash flows from noncapital financing activities:				
Transfers in from other funds	1,490	1,992,210	1,993,700	4,647,248
Transfers out to other funds				(267,008)
Net cash provided by noncapital financing activities	1,490	1,992,210	1,993,700	4,380,240
Cash flows from capital and related financing				
Acquisition and construction of capital assets	(1,743,102)	(1,314,680)	(3,057,782)	(3,709,988)
Reimbursement for capital expenditures				135,623
Payment on financing obligation	(347,619)		(347,619)	(328,808)
Interest paid on financing obligation	(123,835)		(123,835)	(119,326)
Proceeds from the sale of capital assets	203,411	92,536	295,947	352,124
Net cash used for capital and related financing activities	(2,011,145)	(1,222,144)	(3,233,289)	(3,670,375)
Cash flows from investing activities:				
Interest and dividends on investments	658,770	1011	659,781	730,677
Net cash provided by (used for) investing activities	658,770	1011	659,781	730,677
Net increase (decrease) in cash and cash equivalents	−413,537	2,522,694	2,109,157	1,876,817
Cash and cash equivalents at beginning of year	9,510,068	21,610,216	31,120,284	29,243,466
Cash and cash equivalents at end of year	9,096,531	24,132,910	33,229,441	31,120,283

(Continued)

ILLUSTRATION 11-5 *Continued*

	Business-Type Activities—Enterprise Fund—Water	Governmental Activities—Internal Service Funds	Totals 2002	Totals 2001
Cash flows from operating activities:				
Operating income (loss)	($751,852)	976,937	225,085	(310,097)
Adjustments to reconcile operating income to net cash provided by (used for) operating activities:				
Depreciation	1,751,713	1,180,883	2,932,596	2,359,766
Gain (loss) on sale of assets	10,547		10,547	36,673
Changes in assets and liabilities				
(Increase) decrease in accounts receivable	(323,165)	29,547	(293,618)	712,835
(Increase) decrease in inventories		215,881	215,881	(13,009)
(Increase) decrease in other assets				(100,354)
Increase (decrease) in accounts payable	307,213	186,859	494,072	(2,444,855)
Increase (decrease) in accrued expenses	(159,076)	(70,699)	(229,775)	73,730
Increase (decrease) in deposits payable	(53,846)		(53,846)	(258,617)
Increase (decrease) in contracts payable	87,068	59,786	146,854	23,331
Increase (decrease) In deferred revenue	68,746		68,746	(36,642)
Increase (decrease) in claims payable		(827,578)	(827,578)	393,514
Total adjustment	1,689,200	774,679	2,463,879	746,372
Net cash provided by (used for) operating activities	$937,348	1,751,616	2,688,964	436,275
Information about noncash capital financing activities:				

Donated assets in the water fund totaled $4,269,305 and $765,884 for fiscal years ended June 30, 2002 and 2001, respectively.

Source: City of Orange, California, Comprehensive Annual Financial Report, 2002, www.cityoforange.org.

entity for the sales of goods and services ($14,593,526), any reimbursement from other funds for operating transactions ($354,455), and all other receipts not included in one of the other three sections ($165,198). Operating activities includes the cash disbursements for the payments to suppliers ($9,422,260) and the payments to employees ($4,753,571). The City of Orange water operations did not report any cash used for the payment for materials used in the production of the goods and services sold, payments for taxes, payments to other governments as grants for operating activities, or other cash payments not included in one of the other three cash flow sections.

Because the direct method is required for reporting cash flows from operating activities, a reconciliation of the operating income (loss) to the direct method cash flows from operating activities is required. The reconciliation is presented as the last category in the cash flow statement. The reconciliation begins with the water operation's operating loss, shown on the statement of revenues, expenditures, and changes in net assets ($751,852). Depreciation, a noncash expense, is added, as is the loss on the sale of assets. Changes in current assets and current liabilities from the beginning of the fiscal year to the end of the fiscal year are added or subtracted to reflect whether cash was received or disbursed. The adjustments totaled $1,689,200, which, when added to the operating loss, resulted in the net cash provided by operating activities to be $937,348, which reconciles to the $937,348 reported in the direct method operation activities section of the cash flow statement.

Cash flows from noncapital financing activities include receipts from bonds or notes not associated with the acquisition, construction or improvement of capital assets, funds held in trust for others, subsidies or grants, and receipts for property taxes and other taxes collected for the governmental entity. Noncapital financing cash outflows include repayment of amounts borrowed, including interest payments, other than those debts related to the acquisition or construction of capital assets. The outflows also include amounts paid for grants and subsidies, funds held in trust for others, and cash transfers paid to other funds. The only noncapital financing activity of the City of Orange's Water operations was the $1,490 transferred from the governmental funds.

Cash flows from financing activities include the cash gifts, grants, or bond proceeds received for the acquisition or construction of fixed assets. Financing activities cash inflows also include fixed asset sale proceeds. Financing activities cash outflows include amounts to acquire, construct, or improve capital assets and to repay amounts borrowed, including interest, to acquire, construct, or improve capital assets.

The City of Orange Water operation used cash to acquire or construct capital assets ($1,743,102) and paid capital asset debt principal ($347,619) and interest ($123,835). The Water operation also received $203,411 in cash for capital assets that were sold.

Cash flows from investing activities include the gross cash inflow from the sale or maturity of investments and the receipt of investment interest and dividends. Investing cash outflows are the payments made to acquire investments and securities with original maturities of more than 90 days. Investments with original maturities of 90 days or less are considered as part of the cash equivalents.

Apparently the City of Orange's Water operation did not buy or sell any investment items, as it reported only investment interest and dividends of $658,770. If investments had matured or new investment been purchased, the gross amount of those transaction would have been reported because GASB GAAP prohibits netting the acquisitions and maturity amounts.[16]

FIDUCIARY FUND FINANCIAL STATEMENTS

Private-purpose trust funds: trust arrangements, other than pensions and investment trust funds, that benefit individuals, private organizations, or other governments

Fiduciary funds are used to account for assets held by the government in trust for others or as an agent for individuals, private organizations, or other governmental units. The fiduciary funds include as many as four types of subfunds, including (1) private-purpose trust funds, (2) investment trust funds, (3) pensions or employee benefit trust funds, and (4) agency funds. A **private-purpose trust fund** results when a donor and a government agree that the trust principal and/or income earned are to be used for the benefit of individuals, organizations, or other governments. Private-purpose trust funds should not be confused with permanent funds held in the governmental funds because the permanent funds' principal cannot be used and only the income can be used for the government's purpose, whereas private-purpose trust funds are used for the benefit of those other than the government. An **investment trust fund** exists when the government holds or sponsors an investment pool that includes other governments' resources and accounts for the resources held for the other governments.

Investment trust funds: investment pools held and managed for other governments

[16] Op. cit., **GASB Statement No. 9**, par. 27 and 28.

Pension or **employee benefit trust funds:** account for pension and other employee benefits held and managed by the government

Agency funds: assets held in trust from individuals, organizations, or other governments

A **pension** or **employee benefit trust fund** exists when the government is the trustee for the employees' defined pension plan, defined contribution pension plan, other postemployment benefits, or other employee benefits. **Agency funds** account for assets held by the government as an agent for individuals, organizations, or some other governmental unit.

Fiduciary funds use the full accrual basis of accounting. Financial reports of the fiduciary funds display the achievement of the government's accountability and fiduciary responsibilities for the resources the government holds in trust. A separate column within the fiduciary financial statements may be used for each activity for which the government acts as an agent or trustee.

The basis of accounting for fiduciary funds follows the nature and measurement of the subfunds' objective. For example, the City of Orange only has an agency fund, shown in Illustration 11-6. Because the agency fund holds assets and liabilities (accounts payable due to others), it has no equity (net assets). That is, the resources held in the agency subfund are not resources of the government. Instead, the resources are held in trust for some other party. Because of this custodial nature, the agency subfund has no statement of changes in net assets.

Agency funds use full accrual accounting to recognize the changes in assets and liabilities but no revenue, expense, or net assets are recognized because the resources held for others are assets (cash or short-term investment) and a liability (accounts payable). For example, when agency funds are received, the following journal entry would be recorded.

Agency Fund

Cash	10,000	
Accounts payable		10,000

To record the receipt of agency funds held for the Friends of the Library.

When the Friends of the Library wish to withdraw a portion of the resources held by the City of Pleasant View, the following entry records the withdrawal.

ILLUSTRATION 11-6
City of Orange, California
Statement of Fiduciary Assets and Liabilities
Agency Funds
June 30, 2002

	2002	2001
Assets:		
Cash and investments (note 3)	6,372,974	3,881,844
Accounts receivable	561	
Interest receivable	95,073	137,999
Restricted assets:		
Cash and investments with fiscal agents (note 3)	4,872,096	5,891,921
Total assets	11,340,704	9,911,764
Liabilities:		
Accounts payable	199,321	6,845
Deposits payable	2,472,614	1,825,193
Due to bondholders	8,668,769	8,079,726
Total liabilities	11,340,704	9,911,764

Source: City of Orange, California, Comprehensive Annual Financial Report, 2002, www.cityoforange.org

Agency Fund

Accounts payable	5,000	
Cash		5,000

To record the withdrawal of agency funds held for the Friends of the Library

Local or state governments act as an agent for the federal government when it withholds income and Social Security taxes from employee payrolls. Local governments act as an agent for the state government when it collects taxes on goods and services sold to the public. Multiple or separate agency subfunds are not established because normal liability accounting procedures are sufficient to demonstrate the government's fiduciary stewardship.

A statement of fiduciary net assets and a statement of change in fiduciary net assets are prepared and reported when a government holds any of the three different types of trust funds identified in the first portion of this section. The statement of fiduciary net assets contains the assets, liabilities, and net assets held for the purpose of the trust. The statement of changes in fiduciary net assets displays the resources received as additions rather than revenue and disbursements as deductions rather than expenditures. Figure 11-4 is statement of changes in fiduciary net assets for the City of Whitehouse, which holds an investment trust fund.

Trust funds, such as an investment pool, retirement plan, or library trust, are accounted for on a full accrual basis. Because both the principal and interest can be expended for the objects of the trust, some governments refer to these trusts as expendable trust funds. The government's fiduciary responsibilities as a trustee are met by accounting for the display of the resources received and the use of those resources. Because trust funds are not the property of the government but rather funds held for others, resources received are additions rather than revenues. Thus, the employee retirement fund records contributions received from both the employer (the government) and employees as additions. The fund also records investment earnings as an addition rather than investment

City of Whitehouse
Investment Trust Fund
Statement of Changes in Fiduciary Net Assets
for the Year Ended December 31, 2004

Additions:	
Contributions	
Local governments	$ 110,000
Local schools	110,000
Total contributions	220,000
Investment earnings	
Interest	62,500
Dividends	87,900
Unrealized change in investments fair value	63,250
Total investment earnings	213,650
Total additions	**433,650**
Deductions:	
Withdrawals by local schools	106,250
Administrative expenses	43,400
Withdrawals by local governments	17,225
Total deductions:	**166,875**
Change in net assets held for others	**266,775**
Net assets held for others—beginning of the year	**18,967,350**
Net assets held for others—end of the year	**$ 19,234,125**

FIGURE 11-4 Investment Trust Fund.

revenue. Uses of the trust resources are displayed as a deduction. Any difference between the addition and deduction is a change in net asset that increases the net assets held for pension benefits.

When governments hold pension trust funds, two additional supplemental schedules are required to report the funding progress and the employer's contributions. A schedule of funding progress displays a comparison of the actuarial values of the assets, the accrued liability, and any unfunded accrued liability. For example, assume that the City of Pleasant View holds the employees' retirement funds in its fiduciary fund group. Figure 11-5 displays the schedule of funding progress for the City of Pleasant View that would be presented in the financial statement. According to the schedule, over the past six years the City of Pleasant View has reduced its unfunded retirement fund liability both as an amount and as a percent of the covered payroll.

The required schedule of the employers' required contribution for the City of Pleasant View is shown in Figure 11-6. This schedule indicates that the City has contributed 100% of the required employer contribution over the past six years. Given the information in the two required retirement fund schedules, the City of Pleasant View is providing all its required annual contribution to the Retirement Fund and is annually reducing the unfunded accrued liability.

City of Pleasant View
Public Employee Retirement Fund
Schedule of Funding Progress (stated in thousands)
for the six years ending December 31, 2003

Actuarial Valuation Date December 31	Actuarial Value of Assets	Actuarial Accrued Liability— Entry Age	Unfunded Accrued Liability	Funded Ratio	Covered Payroll	Unfunded Accrued Liability as a Percent of the Covered Payroll
2003	76,600	112,600	36,000	68%	48,000	75%
2002	71,300	109,700	38,400	65%	44,200	87%
2001	67,200	108,400	41,200	62%	41,600	99%
2000	64,800	109,800	45,000	59%	40,550	111%
1999	61,200	107,400	46,200	47%	37,000	125%
1998	57,600	104,700	47,100	55%	24,400	137%

FIGURE 11-5   Schedule of Funding Progress.

Schedule of Employer Contributions
for the Six Years Ended December 31, 2003

Year Ended	Annual Required Contribution	Percentage Contributed
2003	$ 3,169,002	100
2002	2,963,070	100
2001	2,770,520	100
2000	2,590,480	100
1999	2,422,140	100
1998	2,264,740	100

FIGURE 11-6   Schedule of Employer Contributions.

CONVERTING FUND STATEMENT DATA
TO GOVERNMENT-WIDE DISPLAY

Fund-based financial statements are prepared using the funds flow measurement focus and modified accrual recognition. To comply with GASB reporting requirements, multiple adjustments are needed to convert the fund statement data to the full accrual accounting recognition display in the government-wide financial statements. The adjustments are primarily made to the governmental fund group. No change is needed for the proprietary fund statements because they are already prepared using the full accrual accounting recognition. The fiduciary funds are eliminated from the government-wide financial statements because the funds are held in trust for others and not available for the government's use.

The major adjustments necessary to convert the fund financial data to the government-wide presentation include the following:

1. Remove the expenditures for capital assets, record (i.e., capitalize) the capital assets, and record depreciation expense together with the accumulated depreciation as of the date of the financial statement.

2. Change the proceeds from bonds to debt liabilities. Debt service principal payments are changed to a reduction of the liabilities, and the current period's interest expense is accrued as a payable.

3. Record any earned revenues that have not been received as an accrued receivable.

4. Accrue any expense obligations that have not been paid as payables.

5. Restate proceeds from the sale of fixed assets such as land, buildings, or equipment as a gain, or loss, on the sale of fixed assets as appropriate.

6. Remove the internal service funds from the proprietary funds and eliminate the within-government transactions, much like the between-firm eliminations required by for-profit consolidation.

7. Eliminate any between-fund accounts receivable and related accounts payable.

8. Finally, add the financial statement data for component units as a discrete column in the government-wide financial statement presentation.

Although the adjustments listed above typically convert the fund-based statements to the government-wide presentation, other adjustments may be necessary to convert any unusual items to the full accrual recognition.

For the City of Orange balance sheet assets and liabilities, six items comprise the difference between the two recognition methods (accrual versus modified accrual). Because the value of the capital long-lived assets does not provide resources for current operations, their historical value net of associated depreciation is added as part of the reconciliation. Long-term debt obligations are not a part of current operations, as they will be paid in future periods, so their value must be recognized. Interest expense and revenue accruals are another adjustment. Finally, internal service activities, such as central stores' inventory, that will be used next year are added. The combined total of these adjustments together with the total fund balance equals the total net assets displayed on the government-wide statement of net assets for the City of Orange (Illustration 10-2). A summary of the City's reconciliation of the fund presentation to the government-wide data is displayed in Figure 11-7.

Within the reconciliation items but not a part of the above analysis is an adjustment for government accounts receivables and payables of $297,045, displayed in Illustration 11-1 as advances to other funds. This elimination is similar to the process used for

Government Funds—fund balance per Illustration 11-1	$144,350,704
Add capital assets from Illustration 10-4 plus internal service capital assets from Illustration 11-3	724,964,858
Deduct accumulated depreciation from Illustration 10-4	(140,858,167)
Add internal service funds net assets from Illustration 11-3.	29,062,488
Add accrued revenue previously deferred	1,127,303
Add eliminated accrued payables	418,985
Deduct long-term capital asset liabilities, current portion, from Illustration 10-5 and internal service fund	(4,183,204)
Deduct long-term capital asset liabilities, noncurrent portion, from Illustration 10-5	(84,653,555)
Government-wide Net Assets	$670,229,412

FIGURE 11-7   Reconciliation of the City of Orange's Governmental Funds to the Government-Wide Net Assets.

Total governmental funds net changes in fund balance (Illustration 11-2)	**($1,945,580)**
Governmental funds report capital outlays as expenditures whereas the costs of those assets are allocated over their useful estimated lives as depreciation expense.	
Eliminate capital outlay per Illustration 11-2	15,756,748
Noncapitalized portion of capital outlay	(1,518,513)
Depreciation per Illustration 10-4	(7,750,451)
Eliminate bond principal expenditure per Illustration 11-2	2,224,860
Eliminate interfund internal service transactions	3,018,305
Recognize accrued tax, fees, and other revenue per Figure 11-7	1,127,303
Recognize interest income	39,246
Recognize interest expense	(48,645)
Recognize compensated absence expenses	(193,054)
Total government change in net assets reported in the government-wide statement of activities (Illustration 10-3)	$10,710,219

FIGURE 11-8   Reconciliation of the City of Orange Change in Governmental Fund Balance to the Government-Wide Statement of Activities.

business combinations. The advance to and advance from other funds is comparable to within-company receivables and payables and must be eliminated.

Figure 11-8 displays the details of the conversion of the fund-based revenues, expenditures and other changes in the fund balance to the government-wide statement of activities for the governmental activities. Rather than reporting the reconciliation on the face of the statement, City of Orange included the reconciliation shown in Figure 11-8 as a CAFR financial statement schedule. Notice that the reconciling items identify accrual- versus cash-based recognition differences. For example, the accrual-based (economic flow) depreciation expense was less than the amount expended for capital acquisitions. Other eliminations included the bond principal payment, which was recognized as a use of current resources in the fund statements but will not be recognized in the government-wide presentation because it is a reduction of two balance sheet accounts—cash and long-term liability.

Accruals for revenue earned but not received (interest, taxes, and other) must be recognized, as must compensated absence expenses that were are part of this year's costs but will not be paid until next fiscal year or later.

The interfund internal service transaction elimination from the change in fund balance is comparable to the parent and subsidiary between-organization transaction elimination in consolidated financial statements. The within-organization internal service transactions were eliminated in the government-wide statements but reported as part of the fund-based revenues, expenditures, and changes in fund balances because the internal service fund received and disbursed cash.

The business-type activities are recognized using full accrual accounting recognition; thus, no conversion between the fund-based and government-wide statements is necessary. For a more complete discussion of the composition, components, and accounting recognition for the government-wide financial statements, refer back to Chapter 10.

SUMMARY

Accounting and reporting for state and local government entities uses both full accrual and modified accrual recognition. The required financial reports display the full cost of providing government services, with details on how much of the cost is borne by taxpayers and by specific users of the government's service.

Governments use funds to segregate resources and their uses into identifiable units as a means to control resources, ensure accountability, and demonstrate fiduciary stewardship. The fund groups—governmental, proprietary and fiduciary—were identified and appropriate financial reporting discussed. Government funds report the general fund and other governmental funds to account for the services provided to citizens that are primarily financed by taxes. The governmental fund uses modified accrual accounting recognition, and its financial reports include the balance sheet (Illustration 11-1) and statement of revenues, expenditures, and changes in fund balance (Illustration 11-2). Proprietary funds report the enterprise business-type activities and internal service funds of the government that charge fees to cover the cost of the provided services.

The proprietary fund uses full accrual accounting recognition, and its financial reports include the statement of net assets (Illustration 11-3); statement of revenues, expenses, and changes in net assets (Illustration 11-4); and a statement of cash flows (Illustration 11-5). Fiduciary funds report the various trusts and agency funds held by the government. The fiduciary fund financial reports display the additions and reductions of the resources held in a statement of fiduciary assets (Illustration 11-6) and a statement of changes in fiduciary net assets if appropriate. The fund structure and required financial statements were discussed, together with the appropriate accounting recognition used in the preparation of the statements. Comprehensive guidance to compile each statement was not presented.

As most governments use fund accounting for internal recordkeeping and management processes, adjustments to convert the fund statement data to the government-wide financial statements were identified and detailed within reconciliation schedules, and the articulation between the statements was discussed.

QUESTIONS

11-1. List and discuss the three fund groups used by state and local governments.

11-2. List and discuss the five governmental fund subgroups.

11-3. Two funds facilitate the financial reporting of proprietary funds. List and discuss each of the two funds.

11-4. Fiduciary funds are referred to as trust and agency activities. Explain this statement and provide examples for each trust and agency activity typically performed by state and local governments.

11-5. A specific set of financial statements is required to display information for each of the three groups of funds used by governments. Discuss what must be shown for each group on the financial statements.

11-6. When are revenues and expenses recognized in fund accounting?

11-7. How does fund accounting report financial information?

11-8. What is a fund?

11-9. What is a major fund and how is it determined?

11-10. What purpose(s) do(es) a budget serve?

11-11. What is an appropriation and how is it recorded?

11-12. What is an encumbrance and why do state and local governments use encumbrance accounting?

11-13. Name three items established by the voucher system to safeguard cash payments.

11-14. Net income is relevant information on corporate financial statements. What is relevant information on governmental financial statements?

11-15. What is the format used to display accounts presented on a governmental fund balance sheet?

11-16. What does the governmental statement of revenue, expenditures, and changes in funds balance report and what fund groups are displayed in the statement?

11-17. Explain revenue recognition in regard to GASB Statement No. 22.

11-18. List the four sections of the proprietary fund statement of cash flows.

11-19. List and discuss the four types of fiduciary funds.

11-20. What are the major adjustments necessary to convert the fund financial statement data to the government-wide presentation?

MULTIPLE CHOICE

11-1. Which of the following is not an example of a governmental activity?

a. Parking garage

b. Fire department

c. Education

d. Traffic court

11-2. Which of the following is not an example of a business-type activity?

a. Water department

b. Natural gas utility services

c. Municipal golf course

d. Social welfare services

11-3. State and local governments report fund-based financial information using which of the following?

a. Both full accrual and modified accrual information

b. Full accrual information

c. Modified accrual information

d. None of the above

11-4. Resources held by state and local governments in trust for others that cannot be used to support government services are accounted for by what fund group?

a. Governmental

b. Proprietary

c. Fiduciary

d. Financial

11-5. What is the fund group that provides for the government's day-to-day operations?

a. Governmental

b. Proprietary

c. Fiduciary

d. Financial

11-6. What is the fund group that provides for the government's business-type activities?

a. Governmental

b. Proprietary

c. Fiduciary

d. Financial

11-7. A reconciliation between the government-wide and the fund-based financial statements is required for:

	Governmental Funds	Proprietary Funds	Fiduciary Funds
a.	Yes	Yes	Yes
b.	No	No	Yes
c.	Yes	No	No
d.	No	Yes	No

11-8. Required financial statements for the governmental funds include which of the following?

a. Statement of net assets and statement of activity

b. Balance sheet; statement of revenues, expenditures, and changes in fund balance; and statement of cash flows

c. Balance sheet and statement of change in net assets

d. Balance sheet and statement of revenues, expenditures, and changes in fund balance

11-9. Indicate the appropriate accounting recognition for the following funds groups.

	Government Funds	Proprietary Funds	Fiduciary Funds
a.	Full accrual	Modified accrual	Full accrual
b.	Modified accrual	Full accrual	Full accrual
c.	Full accrual	Full accrual	Modified accrual
d.	Modified accrual	Full accrual	Modified accrual

11-10. Authorized budgets of state and local governments are typically recorded in the accounting records for:

	Government Funds	Proprietary Funds	Fiduciary Funds
a.	Yes	No	No
b.	Yes	No	Yes
c.	No	Yes	No
d.	No	Yes	Yes

11-11. An encumbrance accounting process is used to do which of the following?

a. Record future commitments as required by GAAP

b. Extract reserved resources and future commitments from accounting records

c. Reserve resources for outstanding purchase orders and commitments

d. Audit departmental acquisitions over current and prior fiscal years

11-12. How are approved budgets recorded?

a. As permanent records in the general ledger

b. Only in balance sheet accounts

c. In balance sheet and subsidiary operating accounts

d. Only in operating accounts

11-13. How are governmental general fund expenditures reported in financial statements?

a. Only by natural classes such as salary and wages

b. By natural classes and by function

c. Only by functional designation

d. By departments within major programs

11-14. Budget components are recorded in the accounting records as:

	Estimated Revenues	Appropriations
a.	Credits	Debits
b.	Credits	No entry
c.	Debits	Credits
d.	No entry	Credits

11-15. What is the title of the financial statement that presents the assets and liabilities of governmental funds?

a. Balance sheet

b. Statement of activities

c. Statement of resources

d. Some other title

11-16. How are government fund assets and liabilities are presented in the financial statement?

a. In alphabetical order

b. By classification

c. In liquidity order

d. Some other presentation

11-17. How is the equity of governmental funds reported?

a. Restricted, nonrestricted, and invested in capital assets

b. Reserved, nonexpendable, and unreserved

c. Reserved and unreserved

d. Restricted, reserved, and unreserved

11-18. Major funds reported by governmental funds are determined by which of the following criteria?

a. 10 percent of the total assets, liabilities, revenues or expenses/expenditures of the fund type and 5 percent of the same amounts for all governmental and proprietary funds combined.

b. 5 percent of the fund balance for all governmental funds

c. 5 percent of assets for all fund groups

d. 10 percent of assets for all fund groups

11-19. How are governmental fund capital assets reported?

a. As long-term assets net of accumulated depreciation

b. As part of the fund balance

c. As footnote disclosures

d. As an adjustment to reconcile the fund balance to the net assets of government-wide information

11-20. How do governmental funds report the inflows and outflows that result in a change in equity?

a. As income and expense

b. As revenue and expense

c. As additions and deductions

d. As revenue and expenditures

11-21. How do governmental funds report bond obligation interest costs in financial statements?

a. As an expense/expenditure

b. As capital outlay

c. As debt service

d. As other financing uses

11-22. Governmental fund operating transfers reported in financial statements are which of the following?

a. Routine and recurring transactions between fund groups

b. Advances to some other fund group

c. Noncash transactions

d. Always recorded as a debit amount

11-23. How do governmental funds report resource inflows on financial statements?

a. By type of revenue

b. By natural classification

    c. By object of revenue

    d. By items approved by law

11-24. How do general governmental funds report resource disbursements on financial statement?

    a. By type of disbursement

    b. By natural classification

    c. By object of disbursement

    d. By function or program

11-25. Which of the following is true of equity transfers between fund groups?

    a. They do not create revenue in the receiving fund.

    b. They do not create an expense/expenditure in the fund that relinquishes the asset.

    c. They may be considered an advance.

    d. All of the above are true.

11-26. Which of the following is true of the budget?

    a. It is the principal method of directing and controlling the financial process of a government.

    b. It is a legal document.

    c. It is the authorization to spend governmental resources.

    d. All of the above are true.

11-27. Which of the following is true of the estimated revenues in the budget?

    a. They meet the definition of an asset.

    b. They are considered a pseudo asset control account.

    c. They are considered a contra fund balance equity account.

    d. None of the above are true.

11-28. Proprietary fund capital assets are reported on the financial statements as which of the following?

    a. Long-term assets

    b. Part of the net asset (equity) section net of accumulated depreciation and related debt

    c. Footnote disclosures

    d. An adjustment to reconcile the equity balance to the government-wide financial statement data

11-29. How are proprietary fund financial statement assets and liabilities reported?

    a. In alphabetical order

    b. In a classified format

    c. By program

    d. None of the above

11-30. How is proprietary fund long-term debt reported on financial statements?

    a. As part of the unrestricted equity

    b. As a footnote disclosure only

    c. As current and noncurrent liabilities

    d. As an adjustment to reconcile the equity balance to the government-wide financial statement data

11-31. Proprietary fund financial statements report the activities of which of the following?

    a. Enterprise activities

    b. Business-type activities

    c. Internal service activities

    d. All of the above

11-32. How does the proprietary fund statement of revenues, expenses, and changes in net assets report the resource inflows and outflows?

    a. In a liquidity order

    b. In an operating/nonoperating format

    c. As additions and deductions

    d. None of the above

11-33. How is proprietary fund equity reported on the financial statements?

    a. Retained earnings

    b. Net assets

    c. Fund balance

    d. Some other term

11-34. How are proprietary fund contributed capital assets reported on financial statements?

    a. As revenues

    b. As operating revenues

    c. As nonoperating revenues

    d. As some other inflow

11-35. How does a proprietary fund water department report expenses/expenditures on the financial statement?

    a. In alphabetical order

    b. By natural classification

    c. As function or program types only

    d. None of the above

11-36. Business-type activities are which of the following?

    a. Permanent funds

    b. Governmental subfunds

    c. Fiduciary subfunds

    d. Internal service funds

11-37. Governmental fund revenues for the following items are recognized using:

	Property taxes	*Fines and forfeitures*
a.	Full accrual	Full accrual
b.	Full accrual	Modified accrual
c.	Full accrual	Enforceable claim or cash basis (whichever occurs first)
d.	Cash basis	Modified accrual

11-38. Cash flow statement display guidance for state and local governments is provided by which of the following?

    a. GASB Statement No. 34

    b. FASB Statement No. 95

    c. GASB Statement No. 31

    d. GASB Statement No. 9

11-39. The cash flows from operating activities in the GASB statement of cash flows is presented using which of the following?

    a. The direct method

    b. The indirect method

    c. Either the direct or indirect method

    d. Some other presentation

11-40. Acquisition of capital long-lived assets is displayed in the GASB cash flow statement as cash flow activities of which of the following?

    a. Financing

    b. Investing

    c. Operating

    d. Capital and related financing

11-41. Examples of resources held in the city's fiduciary funds include except which of the following?

    a. Employee retirement funds

    b. County trust funds

    c. Endowment funds to support city library

    d. Agency funds

11-42. Agency funds' equity in the fiduciary fund group is presented as which of the following?

    a. Fund balance

    b. Net assets

    c. Retained earnings

    d. Not presented

11-43. Equity in the fiduciary funds is presented in the financial statements as which of the following?

    a. Restricted

    b. Reserved

    c. Nonexpendable

    d. Held for others

11-44. Funds held in the agency subfunds are displayed in the financial statements as which of the following?

    a. Assets and liabilities

    b. Assets, liabilities, and net assets

    c. Cash, accounts payable, and deferred revenue

    d. Assets, investments, and note obligations

11-45. Funds within the fiduciary fund group are considered which of the following?

    a. Permanent funds

    b. Expendable funds

    c. Nonexpendable funds

    d. Transferred funds

11-46. Changes in the fiduciary equity are presented as which of the following?

    a. Additions and deductions

    b. Revenues and expenses

    c. Revenues and expenditures

    d. Income and disbursements

11-47. Fiduciary financial statements include which of the following?

    a. Balance sheet, statement of activity, and statement of cash flows

    b. Statement of net assets, statement of activities, and statement of cash flows

    c. Statement of fiduciary net assets and statement of changes in fiduciary net assets

    d. Statement of fiduciary net assets and statement of change

EXERCISES

EXERCISE 11-1	Identify the fund and subfund in which selected transactions will be recorded
EXERCISE 11-2	Prepare journal entries and a statement of changes in net assets for the appropriate fund
EXERCISE 11-3	Essay to discuss the importance of the annual budget
EXERCISE 11-4	Prepare journal entries to record the construction of a capital asset
EXERCISE 11-5	Prepare journal entries to recognize transactions associated with a tax levy
EXERCISE 11-6	Record various transactions using an encumbrance system
EXERCISE 11-7	Record journal entries to recognize restricted revenue
EXERCISE 11-8	Discuss details displayed on government balance sheet acquired by web search
EXERCISE 11-9	Prepare journal entries to record adjustments to the annual budget
EXERCISE 11-10	Record appropriate journal entries to recognize permanent fund transactions

EXERCISE 11-1

The following transactions were recognized by the City of Running Springs during the current fiscal year.

1. Toll charges to ride on the mass transit system
2. Property tax levy
3. Bond issued to fund a water utility treatment plant retrofit
4. City garage parking fees
5. Building permit
6. Traffic fine
7. Interest and penalty on delinquent property taxes
8. Sales taxes collected for the state
9. Water utility charges
10. Police salaries
11. Income tax withheld from police salaries
12. City street repair cost
13. Noncapitalized equipment purchased for the mayor's office
14. Principal paid on bond to build City Hall
15. Interest paid on bond issued for the water utility treatment plant retrofit

Required:
Identify the fund group and specific subfund within the fund group where each of the above transactions would be recorded.

EXERCISE 11-2

In March of the current fiscal year, Mr. and Mrs. Gotrocks gave the City of Timball a $20,000 gift to be administered as an expendable trust to buy books for the city library. The gift was immediately invested in a 90-day treasury bill. At the end of the 90 days, the investment earned $400, which was used to buy books. Rather than reinvesting the gift in a treasury bill, the City CFO invested the funds in a Fanguard money market account.

Required:
A. Prepare the general journal entries in good form to record the transactions in the appropriate fund group and subfund. Omit entry explanations.
B. Prepare a statement of changes in net assets.

EXERCISE 11-3

What is the importance of an annual budget for a state and local government?

Required:
Explain why the annual budget is important in accounting for state and local government activities. Be concise.

EXERCISE 11-4

The City of Meomy's fiscal year begins July 1 and ends June 30. The City sold bonds in the amount of $10,000,000 to finance the construction of a new fire station on December 1 of the current year. The newly issued bonds have an interest rate of 5 percent per annum, payable semiannually on June 1 and December 1. The first interest payment is due on June 1.

In addition to issuing bonds, the City of Meomy general fund provided $500,000 by an operating transfer on February 1 to help fund the fire station construction costs.

On January 2 of the current year, a construction contract for $8,900,000 was signed with Reynolds Construction. On the same day, another contract for $1,000,000 was executed with the YXZ General Contractors to serve as general contractors for the fire station project. On May 1, construction costs of $3,000,000 were billed by Reynolds Construction and approved for payment.

Required:

In general journal form, record the above transactions related to the construction of the new fire station in the appropriate fund group and subfund. Journal entry explanations may be omitted.

EXERCISE 11-5   The following are accounting events of Bridgeway Township.

1. Property taxes were billed in the amount of $18,300,000, of which $250,000 is expected to be uncollectible.

2. Property taxes collected in cash totaled $15,000,000. Revenues from building fees were $120,000 in cash, and license fees cash collection totaled $150,000.

3. Property taxes in the amount of $240,000 were determined to be uncollectible.

4. At the end of the year, $425,000 in billed property taxes remained unpaid, of which $27,000 was expected to be uncollectible.

Required:

Prepare journal entries for the transactions in the appropriate fund group and subfund. Explanations may be omitted.

EXERCISE 11-6   The City of Keene uses an encumbrance system as a budget control process. The following transactions occurred during the past fiscal year.

1. Purchase order #390 for $3,000 was issued to Computer Systems for the purchase of computer equipment.

2. The computer equipment was delivered with an invoice of $2,950 and approved for payment.

3. Purchase order #395 for $2,000 was issued to ABC Office Supply for office supplies.

4. Delivery of the office supplies was delayed until after the end of the fiscal year. The supplies were delivered in the new fiscal year at a cost of $2,200.

Required:

Using an encumbrance system, prepare journal entries for the City of Keene transactions to be recorded in the governmental general subfund. Explanations may be omitted.

EXERCISE 11-7   The City of Good Hope is required by law to use 2 percent of the property taxes collected by the general fund for repair and maintenance of the downtown parking garage, which charges parking fees to support the majority of its operating costs. The City's property tax collections totaled $75,650,300.

Required:

Prepare the necessary journal entry or entries to record this transaction in the appropriate fund group and subfund. Journal entry explanation may be omitted.

EXERCISE 11-8   (Internet Research) Major funds whose assets represent 10 percent of the total assets of the governmental fund group must be displayed as a major fund in the entity's comprehensive annual financial report (CAFR) balance sheet. Search the web to find a CAFR posted by at least two state or city governments. Determine whether major funds have been reported in accordance with GAAP in the government's fund financial statement. Write a brief report that details what was found. If possible, attach copies of the balance sheets or part of the balance sheet data used for the report. (*Hint:* Cities that typically post their CAFR on the web include New York City; Akron, Ohio; Nashville, Tennessee; and Orlando, Florida.)

EXERCISE 11-9   The City of Deliverance increased its revenue budget by $680,000. The City also decreased the appropriations budget by $54,000.

Required:

Prepare the journal entries to record the budget revisions. Explanations may be omitted.

EXERCISE 11-10   On September 30, a wealthy individual contributed $250,000 to the City of Atlantis to be maintained as a permanent fund for ongoing replacement of playground equipment in the park. Upon receipt, the contributed resources were invested in 8-percent bonds paying interest semiannually on April 1 and October 1. The City used the calendar year as its fiscal year.

Required:
Prepare the journal entries to record these transactions and any end-of-year entry. Explanations may be omitted.

PROBLEMS

PROBLEM 11-1   Permanent fund transactions and preparation of a statement of revenues, expenditures and change in fund balance

PROBLEM 11-2   Water and sewer utility fund transactions

PROBLEM 11-3   Statement to displays various general fund transactions

PROBLEM 11-4   Recognize delinquent taxes together with interest and penalties

PROBLEM 11-5   Calculate debt service requirements

PROBLEM 11-6   Proprietary fund statement of revenue, expenses and change in net assets

PROBLEM 11-7   Calculate and record a tax levy

PROBLEM 11-8   Transaction to record a construction project using an encumbrance system

PROBLEM 11-9   Acquisition and operating transactions for a sport center

PROBLEM 11-10   Closing entries and balance sheet preparation

PROBLEM 11-1   The City of Mooreville received a cash gift of $500,000 from a resident to create a permanent fund. The interest earned on the fund is restricted to purchasing books for the city library. The following transactions occurred during the fiscal year ended December 31.

1. $500,000 gift was received April 1.
2. Gift money was invested in 6-percent bonds with interest payable on October 1 and April 1.
3. October 1 interest was received.
4. Cash totaling $14,200 was used to purchase books during the year.
5. Year-end accruals were recorded as appropriate.
6. At December 31, the fair value of the bonds was $507,000 exclusive of any interest.
7. Closing entries were recorded.

Required:
A. Prepare the appropriate journal entries to record the transactions.
B. Prepare a statement of revenues, expenditures, and changes in fund balances for the permanent fund for the year ended December 31.
C. What amounts are needed for the reconciliation between the permanent fund statements and the government-wide statements?

PROBLEM 11-2   The following transactions occurred during the current fiscal year concerning the City of Bristow Water and Sewer Utility operations.

1. A prior year closing entry for accrued utility revenues of $31,500 was reversed to water sales.
2. During the year, water sales to nonmunicipal customers totaled $1,067,300. Water sales to the City's general fund totaled $127,500.
3. Materials and supplies valued at $299,300 were received and an accounts payable recorded.
4. Cash of $1,032,000 was received from nonmunicipal customers and credited to the appropriate accounts receivable accounts.
5. Bad debt expense equal to 5 percent of the unpaid accounts receivable balance was recorded.

6. Materials and supplies were issued and charged to the following accounts: supply expense, $28,500; pumping expenses, $45,000; water treatment expenses, $78,300; transmission and distribution expenses, $49,700; and construction in progress, $97,800.
7. The general fund remitted a check for $125,000.
8. Collection efforts were discontinued on accounts receivable totaling $6,370. The customers whose accounts were unpaid had deposits for services totaling $5,890. The deposits were applied to the bills, and the unpaid remainder was charged to the provision for uncollectible accounts.
9. Deposits totaling $4,750 were refunded by check to customers who discontinued service. New customer deposits of $5,270 were received in cash and deposited.
10. Accounts payable totaling $299,000 were paid in cash.

Required:
Prepare journal entries to record the Water and Sewer Utility transactions. Explanations may be omitted.

PROBLEM 11-3   The general fund of the City of Northview had a fund balance at January 1 of $1,598.345. During the year, the following sources and uses of resources were recorded in the general fund accounts.

Miscellaneous revenues	$143,250
Fee and fines received	$987,000
Expended for general government	$17,250,000
Franchise taxes received	$6,250,000
Costs of cultural and recreation activities	$20,295,000
Public safety costs	$32,600,000
Property taxes billed net of estimated uncollectible items	$80,000,000
Funds transferred out	$50,000
Public works	$7,590,000
Transfers received	$297,5000
Health and sanitation	$9,843,000

Required:
Using provided information, prepare in good form a statement that displays these transactions and the change in the fund balance for the City of Northview general fund.

PROBLEM 11-4   The County of Mountain Hill estimated that $55,000 of delinquent taxes and $4,500 of unpaid interest and penalties would not be paid.

Required:
Prepare the journal entries using appropriate account titles to recognize the amounts being written off.

PROBLEM 11-5   The following information is available regarding the long-term debt obligations for Mansfield Village. The Village uses the calendar year as its fiscal year.

Serial bonds payable with a face value of $500,000 were issued on July 1 for $508,000. Six-percent interest is payable semiannually beginning December 31. Ten annual principal payments are to be paid beginning June 30 of the following fiscal year.

Required:
Calculate the amount needed to be transferred to the debt service fund from the general fund to meet the debt service requirement for the current fiscal year.

PROBLEM 11-6   The City of Good Hope's records reflected the following transactions in its proprietary fund during the year ended December 31, 2005.
1. Interest and investment income revenues of $425,000, $150,320, and $125,780 were received for the water and sewer, parking garage, and internal service funds, respectively.
2. Revenues were $14,243,500 for the water and sewer and $2,450,355 for the parking garage.
3. Revenue for internal service funds was $17,450,000 for services provided.

4. Miscellaneous operating revenues for the parking garage and internal service funds were $125,900 and $1,322,345, respectively.

5. Interest expenses were $1,425,150 for water and sewer, $1,270,150 for the parking garage, and $45,325 for internal service funds.

6. Capital contributions were $1,650,425 for water and sewer and $20,850 for the internal service funds.

7. Transfers out were $350,800, $245,300, and 204,820 for water and sewer, parking garage, and internal service funds, respectively.

8. Miscellaneous nonoperating expenses were $52,350 for the parking garage and $203,580 for internal service funds.

9. Miscellaneous nonoperating revenues were $125,900 for the parking garage and $22,345 for the internal service funds.

10. The beginning balances for net assets were water and sewer, $91,050,456; parking garage, $3,625,050; and internal service funds, $4,560,825.

11. The following expenses were incurred.

	Water and Sewer	Parking Garage	Internal Service
Personal services	3,450,250	878,654	4,625,003
Contractual services	402,030	110,950	650,845
Utilities	825,450	118,365	249,832
Repairs and maintenance	870,658	74,862	2,236,450
Other supplies	570,490	19,250	270,125
Insurance claims and expenses			9,265,345
Depreciation	1,460,125	625,412	1,899,736

Required:
Prepare, in good form, the statement of revenues, expenses, and changes in fund net assets for the City of Good Hope proprietary fund.

PROBLEM 11-7   The following information is available concerning Wagner County.

1. The county uses the calendar year as its fiscal year.

2. Estimated expenditures for the current year total $19,000,000.

3. Proposed appropriations for the forthcoming year total $20,000,000.

4. The estimated fund balance at the beginning of the forthcoming year is $1,500,000.

5. The actual fund balance at September of the current year is $3,000,000.

6. Estimated tax revenues to be received before the end of the year total $5,000,000.

7. Miscellaneous (nontax) revenues received during the current year total $1,500,000.

8. The county plans to use any available fund balance at the end of the current year to build a new office building.

9. Three percent of the tax levy is estimated to be uncollectible.

Required:
A. Calculate the amount of tax revenue that will be needed in the forthcoming year.
B. Determine the gross tax levy that must be issued and prepare the general journal entry to record the levy.

PROBLEM 11-8   On January 1, Mountain Hill School District contracted with Racer Construction Company to build a fine arts center for $3,000,000. The construction project is expected to take no more than nine months to complete. On March 31, Racer Construction Company submitted a bill for $1,400,000. The contract stipulated that 2 percent of any amount billed would be retained until 90 days after the construction project was completed. On April 10, the school district paid the first construction bill submitted. On June 30, the contractor submitted a bill for $1,000,000 that was paid on July 15. The remainder of the contracted amount was billed to the school district on October 15 and paid on November 1.

Required:

A. Assuming that the Mountain Hill School District uses an encumbrance system, prepare the journal entries to record the construction of the fine arts center.

B. What is the balance of the accounts payable due to Racer Construction Company on November 1?

PROBLEM 11-9   On January 1 of the current year, the city council of Surprise, Arizona, bought a baseball park to accommodate a minor league baseball team. The City created an enterprise fund called Ballpark Fund as the park is expected to be a self-supporting activity. During the current fiscal year (January 1 through December 31), the following transactions occurred.

1. The general fund contributed $1,000,000 to the enterprise fund to purchase the park.

2. The water utility fund advanced $500,000 to the enterprise fund for operating obligations. This interest-free advance is payable in five equal annual installments beginning December 31 of the current year.

3. Ballpark Fund recorded the purchase of the ballpark and allocated $300,000 of the purchase price to land and $700,000 to buildings and improvements.

4. $1 million in cash was received from 6 percent revenue bonds dated January 1 and maturing in 10 years that were sold at par. Interest is due semiannually. The first payment is due on July 1 in the amount of $30,000, with the next payment due on January 1.

5. $900,000 of various improvements were made to park facilities; maintenance equipment was purchased for $200,000 and $100,000 of general supplies was purchased in preparation for opening day.

6. July 1 interest payment was made and recorded.

7. Park entrance fees generated $1,000,000 in cash receipts during the year.

8. Fifty percent of entrance fees were paid in cash to the baseball team's owner as agreed. An additional $250,000 park management fee was paid in cash to the City.

9. The estimated useful life of the park facility is 20 years. The maintenance equipment is estimated to have five years of useful life. The city uses the straight-line method of depreciation with a half-year convention. Depreciation expense is calculated and recorded.

10. The first advance repayment installment was paid to the Water Utility Fund on December 31.

11. An inventory of the supplies on hand totaled $20,000.

12. Utility expenses of $100,000 and operating expenses of $75,000 were paid to vendors in cash. Another $35,000 of operating expenses was recognized as payable to vendors.

Required:

A. Prepare the journal entries to record the ballpark transactions for the year. Explanations may be omitted.

B. Prepare a trial balance for the ballpark as of December 31.

PROBLEM 11-10   The following is the December 31, 2005 pre-closing trial balance for the City of Euphoria.

City of Euphoria
General Fund
Pre-Closing Trial Balance
as of December 31, 2005

Account	Debit	Credit
Cash	$ 567,040	
Taxes receivable—delinquent	770,752	
Estimated uncollectible delinquent taxes		91,889
Interest and penalties receivable on delinquent taxes	70,262	
Estimated uncollectible interest and penalties		28,114
Due from state government	76,800	
Estimated revenue control	8,000,000	

Account	Debit	Credit
Revenues control		7,784,051
Accounts payable		61,184
Due to federal government		110,400
Due to state government		62,400
Deferred revenues—property taxes		51,200
Appropriations control		6,784,000
Estimated other financing uses control		1,024,000
Expenditures control	6,381,184	
Expenditures—2004	57,600	
Other financing uses—transfers out control	1,024,000	
Encumbrances control	64,000	
Budgetary fund balance		192,000
Fund balance reserve for encumbrances		64,000
Fund balance—reserve for encumbrances—2004		57,600
Fund balance—unreserved		300,800
Special item—sale of proprietary rights		400,000
Total	$ 17,011,638	17,011,638

Required:

A. Prepare the closing entries for the City of Euphoria for the year ended December 31, 2005.

B. Prepare the general fund balance sheet for the City of Euphoria for the year ended December 31, 2005.

CHAPTER 12

GOVERNMENT COLLEGES AND UNIVERSITIES: ACCOUNTING AND REPORTING

LEARNING OBJECTIVES

After reading this chapter, you should be able to:

■ Describe financial reporting for public colleges and universities.

■ Discuss accounting and reporting issues for colleges and universities, such as (1) accounting for assets, liabilities, and net assets, (2) accounting for revenues and expenses, and (3) accounting for cash flows.

■ Understand managerial and reporting issues, such as (1) nonexchange transactions, (2) tuition and fee allowances, and (3) related entities and affiliated organizations.

■ Segment disclosures for revenue pledged to retire debt in addition to other note disclosures.

■ Journalize transactions for governmental colleges and universities following GASB Statement Nos. 34 and 35.

■ Understand governmental college and university statement format and contents.

Of the some 3,461 degree-granting, nonprofit colleges and universities in the United States, almost half (1,729) are public institutions that enroll 11.7 million students. These institutions awarded two-thirds of all degrees and more than half (52 percent) of all bachelor degrees conferred in the 1999–2000 academic year.[1] The governance structures of these institutions vary. Some public institutions are part of a system with many campuses, while others are single-campus institutions; some have elected board members, while others have boards appointed by state or local officials. Thus there is a wide variation in governance and are degrees of autonomy in public colleges and universities. The complexity, size, and number of students enrolled indicate that the financial information of these institutions would be of interest to many within and outside the industry.

After extensive deliberation and due process that spanned almost a decade, the Governmental Accounting Standards Board (GASB) issued Statement No. 35,[2] which

---

[1] *Postsecondary Institutions in the United States* (Washington, DC: U.S. Department of Education, National Center for Education Statistics, 2001).

[2] **Statement No. 35**, "Basic Financial Statements—and Management's Discussion and Analysis—for Public Colleges and Universities" (Norwalk, CT: Governmental Accounting Standards Board, 1999).

amended GASB Statement No. 34[3] to include public colleges and universities. The amendment enables colleges and universities to use GASB Statement No. 34 definitions and reporting guidance. Under Statement No. 34, public colleges and universities can choose to report as a special-purpose government, using the governmental reporting model, or as a business-type activity, using the proprietary fund reporting criteria. Public colleges and universities may continue to utilize fund accounting for internal recordkeeping, management activities, and budget purposes.

The amendment to GASB Statement No. 34 allows public institutions of higher education to use a more commercial accounting approach. Assets, liabilities, and equity accounts are grouped into classes of net assets defined as (1) invested in capital assets, net of related debt; (2) restricted net assets, expendable and nonexpendable; and (3) unrestricted net assets. The terms *equity* and *net assets* are synonymous because they represent the same value. Even though the terms represent the same value, government and not-for-profit organizations use the term *net assets* while for-profit entities use the term *equity.*

Some colleges and universities, such as two-year community colleges, have the authority to levy local property taxes to support their activities. The power to assess taxes meets Statement 34's definition of a primary government, so these institutions may elect to report as a special-purpose government or as an entity engaged in both governmental and business-type activities. Reporting as a special-purpose government, these colleges use the same government-wide and fund-based reporting criteria as a local government with governmental and proprietary activities. That is, the institution prepares statements using both the full accrual– and modified accrual–based accounting required for governmental reporting discussed and illustrated in Chapters 10 and 11. These institutions report resources received by their type and use function types appropriate for governments in reporting expenditures. Institutions that report as a special-purpose government must prepare both government-wide and business-type financial statements. Figure 12-1 displays the required financial statements together with the basis of recognition when an institution chooses to report as an entity engaged in both governmental and business-type activities.

Colleges that have the authority to levy taxes and choose to report as a special-purpose governmental entity prepare as many as nine separate financial statements, identified in Figure 12-1 for governmental, business-type, and fiduciary activities. If, on the other hand, the institution does not have the authority to levy taxes but charges tuition or course fees and operates residential and dining halls that charge a fee for the provided services,[4] the institution may choose to report as an enterprise business-type activity. That is, the institution would prepare the three financial statements required of enterprise business-type activities listed in Figure 12-1. Regardless of which reporting

---

[3] **Statement No. 34**, "Basic Financial Statements—and Management's Discussion and Analysis—for State and Local Governments (Norwalk, CT: Governmental Accounting Standards Board, 1999).

[4] **GASB Statement No. 34**, paragraph 67, provides that the enterprise fund reporting criteria may be used by a business-type when a fee is charged to external users for goods or services.

Activity Type Governmental activities	Government-wide reporting Financial statements	Enterprise reporting Financial statements
Includes activities such as instruction, administration, research activities, student services, academic support, public safety, and endowment activities	Statement of Net Assets and Statement of Activities using full accrual accounting recognition as discussed in Chapter 10	Balance sheet and Statement of Revenues, Expenditures, and Changes in Fund Balances using the modified accrual accounting recognition as discussed in Chapter 11
Business-type activities	**Financial statements**	**Financial statements**
Includes those activities that charge a fee for services, including housing, food services, athletic events, cultural events, testing, and other services	Included as a component of the Statement of Net Assets and Statement of Activities using full accrual accounting recognition as discussed in Chapter 11	Statement of Net Assets; Statement of Revenues, Expenses and Changes in Net Assets; and Statement of Cash Flows using the full accrual accounting recognition as discussed in Chapter 11
Fiduciary activities	**Financial statements**	**Financial statements**
Includes those funds held for students, faculty, and other organizations	Not reported	Statement of Fiduciary Net Assets and Statement of Change in Fiduciary Net Assets using the full accrual accounting recognition as discussed in Chapter 11

FIGURE 12-1 Comparison of Government-wide and Fund-Based Reporting for Public Colleges and Universities.

model the college or university chooses to use, a management discussion and analysis is prepared and presented prior to the financial statements using the same guidance as state and local governments.[5]

Most colleges and universities have chosen to follow the reporting model for public institutions engaged only in business-type activities because they charge tuition and course fees in addition to other fees for services including food and housing for students.[6] Thus, the basic financial statements illustrated and discussed in this chapter are those required for an enterprise (proprietary fund) in a state or local government using college or university terms for assets, liabilities, net assets, revenue, expense, and program types. This chapter's discussion of college and university accounting and reporting includes no guidance pertaining to a higher education institution reporting as a governmental-type activity other than Figure 12-1, which addresses reporting requirements for special-purpose entities. The chapter also addresses the generally accepted accounting principles (GAAP) created by the accounting boards and the American Institute of Certified Public Accountants (AICPA).

[5] Op. cit., **GASB Statement No. 34**, par. 11.

[6] National Association of College and University Business Officers, *Lessons Learned,* GASB 35 Implementation Workshop, Dallas, January 2002.

COLLEGE AND UNIVERSITY VERSUS COMMERCIAL FINANCIAL REPORTING

Many people unfamiliar with the accounting concepts used by public colleges and universities or with the format of their financial statements express concerns when called upon to review such statements. Although there may be little need for such concern, significant differences do exist between the accounting principles followed by public colleges and universities and those followed by commercial enterprises. Even with the GASB financial statement[7] changes that bring the principles closer together, there are still many differences.

The objectives of accounting, whether for a commercial enterprise or for a public college or university, are to provide information that will (1) help managers effectively allocate and use resources and (2) assist others who wish to evaluate the financial operations of the organization. Both commercial enterprises and institutions of higher education are concerned with the proper, effective use of resources and adherence to GAAP and accounting practices.

The differences in accounting practices between these two types of organizations result from their reasons for existence. The objective of a commercial organization is to increase the economic wealth of those who provide resources to finance its operations. In other words, a commercial organization attempts to create a net profit for its owners. In contrast, nonprofit organizations attempt to use available resources to provide goods and services that meet a social need. The objective of a public college or university is to provide a service that meets various educational and social goals. Given this service objective, there is little reason for such institutions to make a profit or for their operations to result in an excess of revenue over expenses. An institution's administration or governing board may desire some excess to provide a reserve to protect the institution against future contingencies. However, the primary objective of the higher education institution and its governing board is to ensure that its institutional resources are used to provide the services for which it was founded.

Commercial enterprises attempt to set prices so that total revenue will exceed all expenses. To accurately measure net income, expenses are matched with the revenue for each period. In higher education, charges for tuition and fees are only one component of revenue; rarely is there a direct relationship between these charges and the actual cost of the services or programs provided. Other important revenue sources for public colleges and universities include state and federal appropriations, grants and contracts, investment income, realized and unrealized gains, and contributions. However, with the full accrual accounting mandated by GASB Statement No. 34, higher education must carefully match expenses against revenues for the accounting period.

Another important difference between financial reporting of a commercial enterprise and that of a college or university is that college and university resource providers often direct how the resources provided are to be used. These resources are referred to as **restricted** resources, and the provider may limit how, when, and for what purpose they may be used. For example, the expenditure of the resources may be restricted to specific uses, such as scholarships for accounting students or support for the accounting program. The provider may also specify that the principal of the gift must be retained intact and that only the income or earnings may be spent. Finally, a provider may stipulate that the resources provided can be used only after a specific period of time.

Restricted: term used to designate resources whose use has been stipulated by a party external to the institution, such as a creditor or vendor

[7] Op. cit., **GASB Statement No. 34**.

All restrictions necessitate adequate disclosure of resource stewardship. Institutions are specifically accountable for restricted resources to comply with the wishes of the resource provider, and they are accountable for the effective use of all resources in meeting institutional objectives.

Colleges and universities use terms and definitions comparable to those used by for-profit organizations to report assets and liabilities. That is, asset categories include accounts receivable net of allowances, short- and long-term investments, capital assets net of depreciation, and prepaid expenses. Liability categories include accounts payable, deferred revenues, short- and long-term debt payable, and other obligations such as compensated absences and postemployment obligations. In addition, the difference between what the institution owns (assets) and what the institutions owes (liabilities) is reported as net assets rather than equity. Net assets represent the institution's unexpended resources, reserves, and capital asset equity, which are displayed in the financial statement as distinct classes.

Proper accounting for revenues and expenses is the foundation of public higher education financial accountability. The accountability is based on accumulating financial information and reporting financial activities based on the existence or absence of restrictions. Accounting systems are used to provide the required information to account for activities carried on at the college or university, such as current operations, student loans and financial aid, endowment investments and similar activities, operation of the plant including capital asset acquisitions, and other activities. While accounting and reporting of financial information for public colleges and universities are similar to methods used by a private enterprise, the display and presentation of the information are vastly different.

ACCOUNTING FOR REVENUES AND EXPENSES

A college and university financial manager's accounting responsibilities are achieved through the effective use of resources to provide the educational and social goals of the organization. To fulfill these obligations, revenues and expenses must be appropriately recognized, recorded, and reported in compliance with managerial and reporting guidelines. Chief among the managed resources and expenses are those associated with the current operating activities of the institutions that must be classified within in the financial statements.

Current Operations

Current operations of a college or university include the economic resources that are received and expended for the primary mission of the institution: instruction, research, and public service. Current operations also include the related supporting services, such as institutional support, which includes financial services expenses, academic support, which includes such activities as the library and admissions costs, and expense of the campus operations and maintenance. The internal service departments—for example, a motor pool, a printing operation, dormitories and dining halls—that support the basic mission are also reported as a part of current operations. Current resources are available for meeting the expenditures necessary for the basic operation of academic and administrative departments. These costs include salaries, wages and benefits, supplies, travel, utilities, facilities, and grounds maintenance. *Current* means that the resources are available for expenditure in the near term, typically within the current fiscal year.

Designations: conditions placed on resources made at the discretion of the governing board or management

Current operating resources include two basic subgroups: unrestricted and restricted. Unrestricted current operating resources include all resources received for which no donor or other external agency has specified how, when, or for what purpose they will be used. Restricted current operating resources are available for financing operations but are limited by donors and other external agencies as to specific purposes, time, programs, departments, or schools. Externally imposed restrictions are not the same as **designations** imposed by institutional administration or governing boards regarding unrestricted resources. Designations do not create restricted resources because the removal of the designation remains at the discretion of the administration or governing board.

When resources flow into an institution, the purpose for which they are made available dictates the account to which they will be added as revenue and recognized as an expense. Resources provided to the institution must be evaluated to determine whether they are operating or nonoperating revenues. Operating revenues generally result from providing services or producing and delivering goods. Operating revenues include all transactions and other events that are not defined as capital assets and their related financing, borrowing for other than capital asset acquisition, or financial investing activities.[8] The reporting criteria for cash flows from operating activities generally help in the determination of transactions and other events that are recognized as operating income.[9]

Although the criteria for reporting cash flows for operating activities on the statement of cash flows can be helpful in determining what is an operating activity, they need not be consistent. GASB Statement No. 34 allows colleges and universities to determine what they consider to be operating activities for financial statement reporting.[10] Given this provision, some institutions report certain items as operating in the statement of revenues, expenses, and changes in net assets but report it as some other activity in the statement of cash flows. For example, many colleges and universities consider endowment investment income that is budgeted to support the current year's activities as operating revenue but report all investment income as investing activities in the cash flow statement. Another example is the interest paid on debt, which is often reported as an operating expense in the statement of revenues, expenses, and changes in net assets but as a noncapital financing activity (i.e., nonoperating) on the statement of cash flows.

State appropriations are not considered operating revenues, even though they may be expended for operating purposes, because they are transfers of revenue from one agency to another within the state. The state agency that provides the resources recognized them as revenue when they were received by that agency. The agency receiving the resources as an appropriation will recognize the expense. That is, within a government, revenues and disbursements are recognized only once. State appropriations are considered subsidies or transfers and nonoperating revenues.

To achieve the objectives of accounting, financial information must be consistently compiled and reported in a manner that corresponds to the users' needs. Colleges and universities accumulate financial information in a series of systematically classified accounts comparable to the internal accounting process used by commercial enterprises. An institution's chart of accounts are typically compatible with its organizational structure that agrees with the financial reports to be presented. For example when a college receives

---

[8] **Statement No. 9**, "Reporting Cash Flows of Proprietary and Nonexpendable Trust Funds and Governmental Entities That Use Proprietary Fund Accounting" (Norwalk, CT: Governmental Accounting Standards Board, 1989), par. 16.

[9] Although operating income is not defined in authoritative governmental accounting literature, the term has become widely used. A nonauthoritive illustration of the calculation of operating income (operating revenue less operating expenses) is provided in GASB Cod. Sec. 2200.906.

[10] Op. cit., **GASB Statement No. 34**, par. 102.

resources restricted for a particular program, the accounting system recognizes the receipt as restricted for the specific program. At the end of the financial period when the financial report is prepared, the accounting system identifies the unexpended revenue that is reported as restricted expendable net assets (equity) on the financial statement.

Other Operating Activities

Financial aid and loan resources for students are typically an integral part of an institution's financial aid program and a subset of the current operating activities. Some colleges and universities use these resources for student financial aid and for emergency loans to students, faculty, and staff. Unrestricted resources available for the financial aid and loans may have been provided by donors, various granting agencies, or the college itself. Most of the loan programs operate on a revolving basis—that is, principal and interest paid by one borrower may be lent subsequently to others. Some loan accounts are created on a temporary basis, and the original resource provider is repaid as loans are repaid by the borrower. In some cases, resource providers forgive repayments if certain conditions are met, such as teaching for a prescribed number of years.

Loans may be either restricted or unrestricted net assets, based on the existence or absence of any donor or provider stipulation. Unless the institution discloses the details of the unrestricted net assets (equity) presented in the financial statements as a disclosure, the financial statement reader has no idea whether any unrestricted financial aid or loan resources exist or their amount.

Operation and maintenance of plant resources are operating resources that can be used for three purposes: acquisition of long-lived assets for institutional purposes, renewal or repair, and replacement of institutional properties. Plant resources can be either restricted or unrestricted. The restricted plan resources are reported as restricted expendable net assets, but the unrestricted portion is part of the operating activities. When plant resources are expended, they may either be capitalized on the statement of net assets or reported as expenses in the statement of revenues, expenses, and changes in net assets. Colleges and universities must establish a capitalization policy that is consistent with the institution's activity for determining those acquisitions that are capitalized and those that are expensed. For example, most research universities establish a policy that capitalizes and recognizes depreciation on any capital asset expense in excess of $5,000 in accordance with the Office of Management and Budget (OMB) Circulars A-21.[11] With a $5,000 capitalization policy, disbursements for capital assets for amounts less than $5,000 are reported as current operating expenses within the program or function acquiring the item.

Funds functioning as an endowment: resources that the governing board chooses to manage as an endowment—investing the resources and expending only the investment income

Funds functioning as an endowment are resources that the institution has received but chosen not to expend. Instead, the resources are managed as an endowment; that is, resources are invested and only the income expended. These resources are also known as quasi-endowments because the governing board, rather than a donor or external agency, determines that the resources are to be retained and invested as though they were an endowment. Since a donor does not require that these resources to be retained and invested, the principal and the earnings may be used at the discretion of the governing board. Since a distribution of the unrestricted net assets reported on the face of the statement of net assets is prohibited, the financial statement reader does not know what portion of the unrestricted net assets are resources functioning as endowment.

[11] U. S. Office of Management and Budget Circular A-21, *Cost Principles for Educational Institutions*, sec. J16, p. 50, revised July 2000.

Funds held in trust for others: those resources held by the institution acting as a custodian; also known as *agency accounts*

Funds held in trust for others are those funds held by the institution acting as a custodian or fiscal agent for individual students, faculty, or staff members. These resources are typically referred to as *agency accounts* and are accounted for in a clearing account. That is, the money is received as cash and held as an accounts payable. There is no institutional equity in these accounts because the resources are held in custody for others. Agency accounts are part of cash or investments in unrestricted net assets of an institution's financial system. The institution must record, in its accounting system, a liability equal to the resources held as fiduciary agent for agency accounts. Both the asset displayed as part of cash and short-term investments and the liability displayed as accounts payable are displayed on the statement of net assets.

Regardless of the type of operating accounts, resources held and used by colleges and universities can be either unrestricted or restricted resources. That is, either the resources can be used to meet any need of the institution (unrestricted) or an external party directs how and when the resources are to be used (restricted).

Restricted Resources

Because an external party directs the utilization of the resources, a specific identity must be maintained for each restricted amount or account. It is possible, to some extent, to group those accounts that have a common purpose. Care must be exercised, however, to ensure proper use of each account. Generally, separate identification in accounting records is maintained for each account with a distinct stipulation or restricted purpose.

Unrestricted resources are considered revenue when they are received, since there are no specific conditions concerning their use. This is not true for restricted resources. Purpose-restricted resources are recognized as revenues but reported as restricted expendable net assets until the designated purpose can be met. Restricted resources may also be limited to the time at which they can be spent. Only when the time restriction is met can the resources be expended. Thus, restricted resources may be both time- and purpose-restricted. For example, when resources are received with the time restriction that they cannot be expended until the next fiscal year, they are recorded as deferred revenue. In the next fiscal year, the deferred revenue is reduced and restricted revenues recognized.

The following journal entries record the receipt of time-restricted resources.

Cash	$50,000	
Deferred restricted revenues		$50,000

To record the receipt of resources for the English Department that cannot be spent until the new fiscal year. [Note that the resources are both time restricted (next fiscal year) and purpose restricted (English Department).]

In the new fiscal year the following entry would be made.

Deferred restricted revenue	$50,000	
Restricted revenue—English Department		$50,000

To recognize restricted net assets available for the English Department.

Exchange Versus Nonexchange Transactions

Based on criteria set forth in GASB Statement No. 33,[12] the recognition of restricted revenue depends on whether the revenues are generated from an exchange or nonexchange

---

[12] **Statement No. 33**, "Accounting and Financial Reporting for Nonexchange Transactions" (Norwalk, CT: Governmental Accounting Standards Board, 1998).

transaction and whether the resources are available for use. As defined and discussed in earlier chapters, exchange transactions are typically those transactions in which resources (effort, cash, goods, services, etc.) are exchanged for resources of comparable value, also referred to as a quid pro quo transaction. Because these are negotiated transactions, the exchange value may be equal to, more than, or less than the value of what was received. It is the normal intent of the college or university to obtain resources that are at least equal to the resources given up. However, sometimes the exchanged resources may not be of like kind, such as when the institution obtains a service for cash or provides cash for some kind of performance. Prepaid exchange transactions are those in which the college receives cash in advance of performing the services, such as prepaid tuition. In this situation, the cash received is recognized and a liability recorded for the deferred revenue.

Exchange Transactions   Revenues from exchange transactions—such as charges for services, investments, grants and contracts, and operating leases—are recognized when earned, regardless of when cash is received, in accordance with accrual accounting concepts. Accrual accounting directs that revenue be recognized when earned and expenses be recognized as soon as liabilities result for the benefits received. *When earned* simply means when the entity has performed what must be done to satisfy its obligation in the transaction.

For example, in an exchange transaction, a federal research grant of $100,000 was received and accompanied by a check for $100,000, but only $70,000 was expended for the grant's intended purpose during the current fiscal year. Because the payment for services was prepaid—that is, a federal grant to fund research—the money is recorded as deferred revenue.

Cash	$100,000	
Deferred revenue—federal research grant		$100,000

To record the advance receipt of $100,000 in support of a federal research grant.

When expenses are incurred for the grant, they are recorded as a normal disbursement. However, a companion entry must recognize the utilization of the prepaid resources.

Expense (by type)	$70,000	
Cash		$70,000

To record expenses associated with the prepaid federal research grant.

Deferred revenue—federal research grant	$70,000	
Federal research grant revenue		$70,000

To record the met restrictions for the federal research grant.

The statement of net assets at the end of the year would report the unexpended $30,000 as deferred revenue in the current liabilities account because the resources are expected to be used within the next fiscal year. In subsequent accounting period, the deferred revenue would be converted to federal grants revenue when it is consumed.

Nonexchange Transactions   In nonexchange transactions, the college or university receives value (benefit) from another party without directly giving equal value in exchange. Typical nonexchange transactions are donations, contributions, grants, promises to give, pledges, or some other gift item. When a nonexchange transaction occurs, it is recognized as revenue in the financial statements, provided that (1) the offer of resources is verifiable, (2) the resources are measurable and likely to be collected, and (3) all applicable eligibility requirements have been met, regardless of the term used. Nonexchange transactions may be either unrestricted or restricted.

Eligibility: term established by GASB that describes the conditions or characteristics that must be met in order to recognize gift revenue

The primary concept in the recognition of a nonexchange transaction is **eligibility**. If the college is not eligible to use the resource, the resource is not recognized as revenue or a pledge receivable. Endowment gifts or pledges to give for future programs are common events that must be reviewed to determine whether the eligibility requirement has been met. The recognition is contingent upon whether the cash has been exchanged or not. The following four journal entries illustrate different eligibility situations and ways of recording the transaction.

1. The college or university receives a gift of $500,000 to be used for construction of a new education building. The building is being designed but construction will not begin until next fiscal year. Since the university cannot utilize the gift until construction begins, the gift revenue is deferred.

Cash	$500,000	
Deferred restricted gift revenue		$500,000

To record the receipt of a gift to be used for the new education building construction.

2. Rather than giving the cash, the donor promised to remit the money when the construction begins for the new education building. The college cannot use the resources because the construction has not yet begun. Thus, the eligibility to utilize the resources has not been met and no recognition of the pledge to give would occur until construction begins.

3. When the construction of the new education building begins, the eligibility criteria are met for the $500,000 gift described in item 2 above. If the donor has not remitted the cash by the time construction begins, a gift receivable is recorded to recognize the satisfaction of the eligibility requirement. That is, the college can now utilize the resources in the construction of the building, which establishes the basis for recognition of the pledge receivable.

Restricted gift receivable	$500,000	
Restricted gift revenue		$500,000

To record the pledge of a gift to be used for the construction of the new education building.

No allowance for uncollectability was recorded as the gift is expected to be received in full within the near term.

4. When the gift is a new endowment, the gift is recognized only if the money is received. Remember that an endowment has the stipulation that the principal must remain intact and only the income used for a restricted or unrestricted purpose. Because the eligibility requirement is met when the money is received and invested, the endowment gift revenue cannot be recognized until the funds are remitted.

Cash (or securities)	$5,000,000	
Endowment gift revenue		$5,000,000

To record the receipt of a new endowment gift. The income is either restricted for a stipulated purpose or unrestricted.

If the new endowment gift had been pledged rather than cash received, no entry would have been recorded because the eligibility requirement had not been met. That is, the institution cannot invest the resources to earn investment income—that is, use the resources.

Except for gifts that have not met an eligibility criteria, colleges and universities recognize assets and revenues from gifts—that is, voluntary nonexchange transactions—when all applicable requirements have been met. Recognition should be the net of any amount that is estimated to be uncollectible. Recognition of assets and revenues should not be delayed pending completion of purely administrative or routine requirements, such as the filing of claims for allowable expenditures under a reimbursement program or the filing of progress reports with the provider.[13]

Restricted nonexchange and exchange receipts that have not been fully used for their stipulated purpose at the end of the fiscal year are reported in the financial statements as restricted expendable net assets. For example, in a nonexchange transaction, a restricted donation of $300,000 was received for the nursing school but only $270,000 of the donation was expended for the restricted purpose. The $300,000 would be included as revenues on the statement of revenues, expenses, and changes in net assets, and the $270,000 would be reported as expended. The $30,000 remaining balance would be reported on the statement of net assets as restricted expendable net assets.

At the end on the fiscal year, the institution's operating and nonoperating activities and accounts are adjusted, as necessary, to full accrual accounting recognition and summarized into financial statement format in accordance with GASB Statement No. 34 display requirements.

COLLEGE AND UNIVERSITY FINANCIAL REPORTING

The objective of financial reporting is full and adequate disclosure of all pertinent financial information. Public colleges and universities prepare and report a management discussion and analysis; statement of net assets; statement of revenues, expenses, and changes in net assets; statement of cash flows; note disclosures; and other required supplementary information as appropriate. The basic requirements for the statements are similar to those used for proprietary fund presentations, addressed in Chapter 11. However, several unique items that pertain solely to colleges and universities must be considered.

Prior to the GASB Statement No. 34, colleges and universities followed the fund accounting format prescribed in the AICPA *Audit Guide for Colleges and Universities*.[14] That guidance established both the funds and functions used by colleges and universities to account for and report their financial activities. Most public colleges and universities continue to use fund groups for management purposes and to satisfy stewardship responsibilities. The fund data are aggregated and between-fund transactions eliminated to prepare the annual financial statements. Figure 12-2 lists the separate self-balancing funds used by colleges and universities that were previously displayed in the financial statements but continue to be used for management and budgetary purposes.

Several unique college and university accounting and reporting concerns must be considered and addressed when the financial statements are prepared. The following discussion addresses three major reporting concerns.

---

[13] Ibid., par. 19.

[14] *Audit Guide for Colleges and Universities* (New York: American Institute of Certified Public Accountants, 1973).

Current funds

Unrestricted	Accounts for the general operations of the institution. An example is instruction costs.
Restricted	Accounts for activities supported by resources that are restricted as to when the resources would be used or the purpose. An example is a research contract.
Auxiliary	Accounts for activities that provided services to students, faculty, and the external public. The bookstore is an example.
Loan funds	Accounts for student loan activities.
Endowment and similar funds	Accounts for endowment gifts and the investment of the resources.
Plant funds	Accounts for all capital assets, including the resources received for their acquisition and construction as well as any long-term capital debt obligation.
Agency funds	Accounts for resources held in trust for students, faculty, and other organizations.

FIGURE 12-2 College and University Fund Groups.

Within-Organization Transactions Internal events of all types are eliminated from the financial statements in the same fashion as business combinations eliminate parent and subsidiary within-organization transactions. For example, due to accounts (payables within the organization) and due from accounts (receivables within organization), such as the business school owning money to the psychology department, are not included in the assets or liabilities of the institution. Balances of due to (or due from) funds held for others are reported as payables and receivables as appropriate because these amounts are either due from or due to an external party. Just as due from receivables and due to payables are eliminated from the assets and liabilities, the other component of the due to/ due from transaction (revenue or expense) is also excluded from the financial statements. For example, a transaction between the English Department and the History Departments would be eliminated because the transaction is neither revenue nor an expense of the institution.

Transactions between institutional departments and cost centers that provide services to the institution, faculty, staff, and students, and that are expected to recover their cost, are not eliminated. Because colleges and universities are nonprofit organizations, they use the term *cost centers* for these activities rather than the term *profit center* used by corporate organizations. For example, in a college or university, the copy center may operate as a cost center. Transactions between this cost center and the faculty, staff, students, and departments within the institution would not be eliminated because the copy center must recover its costs by charging the users for its services. Another exception is the reciprocal activities between auxiliary enterprises (cost centers that provide goods and services to faculty, staff, students, and the external public, such as the bookstore) and other departments. For example, when the dining halls provide catering services to the admissions office, the transactions are reported as sales and service revenue of the auxiliary enterprise activity. If a cost center provides services only to university departments, such as central purchasing or telephone services, the revenue and expense are eliminated because the cost center is considered a clearing activity that pools the charges and distributes the cost to the ultimate user of the service.

Collections Colleges and universities have all sorts of collections, such as artwork, letters, memoirs, music manuscripts, geology specimens, rocks, gems, tissue samples in the biology laboratories, and bugs in the agriculture college. Some of these collections have significant value, while other may only have sentimental value. The individual college or university must decide whether or not to record—that is, capitalize—the collection as a fixed asset.

Public colleges and universities have the option not to capitalize a collection if all the following criteria are met. (1) The collection is held for public exhibition and used for educational purposes. (2) The collection is cared for, maintained, and preserved. (3) If collection items are sold, the proceeds are used to acquire new items to be included in the collection.[15] Because most colleges use their collections for educational purposes and maintain the items, collections are typically not capitalized. Donations of works of art and other collection items are recorded as revenue on the date of the gift. If the items are not capitalized, program expenses are recognized in an amount equal to the revenue.

For example, assume that Sample State University has an institutional policy to not capitalize collections because the collections are used in classroom instruction and the items are maintained. Sample State just received a donation of three paintings to be added to the art collection. The paintings were appraised at a fair value of $48,000. The university would record the following general journal entries to recognize the gift.

Art program expenses	48,000	
Gift revenue		48,000

To record the donation of three paintings added to the art collection used in the art history education program.

Colleges and universities include their collection capitalization policy in the financial statement note disclosures. Although colleges tend not to capitalize their collections, collection items are included in the college's fire and casualty insurance program.

Component Units (Affiliated Organizations)   Legally separate entities that are either a financial benefit or burden to the college or university, such as a university hospital or foundation, are considered **component units** in accordance with the guidance set forth in GASB Statement No. 14.[16] According to definition included in Statement No. 14, a reporting entity is the primary government, an organizations for which the primary government is financially accountable, or any other organization for which the nature and significance of its relationship with the primary government is such that an exclusion from the financial statement could cause the financial statements to be misleading or incomplete. A component unit[17] is a separate legal organization for which the college or university is financially accountable, is subject to the will of the college or university, and can financially benefit or burden the college or university. Component unit financial information may be blended within the primary reporting unit's financial data or presented in a discrete column on the face of the financial statement. Given this guidance, the Clemson University financial statements presented later in this chapter include the Clemson Research Facilities Corporation as discrete information. Although the Research Facilities is a legally separate not-for-profit organization, it is reported by Clemson University as a component unit because the university is financially accountable for the Research Facilities. If the Research Facilities' management were not successful, the university would be responsible

Component units: organizations that provide either a financial benefit or burden to the reporting entity; also called *affiliated organizations*

---

[15] Op. cit., **GASB Statement No. 34**, par. 27.

[16] **Statement No. 14**, "The Financial Reporting Entity" (Norwalk, CT: Governmental Accounting Standards Board, 1991).

[17] This definition is based on **GASB Statement No. 14**, par. 21–41.

for operating the Research Facilities. Another reason for displaying the Research Facilities as a component unit is the construct of its governing board. The university can impose its will on the Research Facilities because university administrators serve as officers on its governing board. Had the Research Facilities been a for-profit organization in which Clemson University owned a majority of stock, the university would have consolidated the Research Facilities' financial data into the its own financial report and eliminated any between-organization transactions.

In a related parties note disclosure that is not a part of this presentation, Clemson University disclosed that several foundations were not reported as component units because the university was not financially accountable for them. These unreported foundations include a research facility, fund-raising organization, real estate center, engineering program, and continuing education organization. With the change in the definition of component units by GASB in its Statement No. 39,[18] financial data for some or all of these organizations will be presented in the university's financial statement beginning in the fiscal year ending June 30, 2004.

The new definition is based on a component unit meeting *all* of following three criteria.

1. The resources received or held by the legally separate organization are entirely or almost entirely for the direct benefit of the primary government, its component units, or its constituents.
2. The government or its component units is entitled to, or has the ability to otherwise access, a majority of the economic resources received by or held by the separate organization.
3. The economic resources received or held by the legally separate organization are significant to the primary government.

Each of the organizations listed in Clemson University's related party note disclosure are separately chartered corporations governed by independent boards. The organizations receive and hold resources that benefit Clemson. Clemson has the ability to access a majority of the resources, and the amount of the resources received or held by the organizations is significant to Clemson University. Thus, in future years, Clemson University will present financial information for these organizations within the university's financial statement as affiliated organizations—that is, component units.

GASB Statement No. 39 requires that component unit financial data must be discretely presented. The challenge becomes how to display the information. Adding several new columns to the face of the financial statement to discretely display the information would be complex and could be confusing. Including one column of aggregate information would add little meaningful information because the economic substance and financial focus of the organizations are probably unique and significantly different. Both these display options are appropriate under Statement No. 39 guidance, and Clemson University must choose which display will be most appropriate for its financial statement users. The component unit's cash flow is not required because the statement of cash flow is not required to be presented in the government-wide statements of the primary government. However, the affiliated organization's cash flow information may be optionally reported. Note that Clemson University did present the optional cash flow information of its component unit in the statement of cash flow.

---

[18] **Statement No. 39**, "Determining Whether Certain Organizations Are Component Units" (Norwalk, CT: Governmental Accounting Standards Board, 2002).

When an institution does not present the affiliated institution's information on the face of its financial statements, a separate statement of the affiliated organization's financial activities must be presented. Illustration 12-1 displays the affiliated organizations' assets, liabilities, net assets, revenues, and expense information for ABC State University. The four separately incorporated nonprofit corporations receive and hold resources to which ABC State University is entitled and has access. The resources received and held by the organizations are significant to ABC State University. Illustration 12-1 will be inserted into ABC University's financial statements just before the statement of cash flows and the note disclosures.

Financial Statements

Public college and university financial statements are prepared using the economic resource measurement focus—that is, full accrual basis of accounting. An economic resources measurement focus and basis of accounting provides that revenues are recorded when earned and expenditures/expenses are recorded as soon as they result in liabilities for benefits received, regardless of when the cash is paid or received.

The purpose of the financial statement is to report the financial position and operating results of the institution in order to assist citizens, legislators, oversight bodies, creditors, and other users of the financial statements in assessing operational accountability. Users of the financial statement information are interested in assessing (1) the financial position and financial condition of the institution, (2) the effect of operations and the ability for the institution to continue current programs or services, (3) the ability of the institution to meet its liabilities as they become due, (4) the cost of the institution's services, (5) how current activities were financed, and (6) the extent to which interperiod equity is being achieved (that is, did current revenues pay for current costs or will current costs be paid by future revenues?).

The annual financial report for a public college or university contains the management discussion and analysis; statement of net assets; statement of revenues, expenses, and changes in net assets; statement of cash flows; notes to the financial statement, which are an integral part of the report; and any supplement information deemed appropriate to report by the institution.

Management Discussion and Analysis (MD&A)

A management discussion and analysis (MD&A) is presented before the various financial statements and is prepared using the same criteria prescribed in paragraph 11 of GASB Statement No. 34. Neither a discussion nor illustration is presented for public colleges and universities because the information for the public college or university presented in its MD&A is the same as that used to prepare the analysis for a primary government, discussed in Chapter 10.

Statement of Net Assets

The statement of net assets (Illustration 12-2) can be viewed as a snapshot of the financial picture of the institution on the reporting date. The general format of the statement is not significantly different from that of commercial enterprises, with two exceptions. First, the statement is required to be presented in a classified format of current and noncurrent assets and liabilities using Accounting Research Bulletin, No. 43,[19] guidance. The required classified

[19] **Accounting Research Bulletin**, No. 43, "Restatement and Revision of Accounting Research Bulletins" (New York: American Institute of Certified Public Accountants, 1953), ch. 3.

ILLUSTRATION 12-1
ABC State University
Affiliated Organizations
Financial Statement Data

	University Research Corporation FY June 30	ABC Foundation FY June 30	University Alumni Association FY June 30	ABC University Health Clinic FY Dec. 31
Assets				
Cash and cash equivalents	$ 680,427	4,997,739	274,492	43,237
Investments	3,082,318	103,544,195	1,101,038	387,428
Accounts receivable		1,690,781		146,046
Capital assets (net)		8,907,571	44,849	332,271
Prepaid expenses	4,581			29,283
Other	91,214	3,450,578		3,909
Total Assets	3,858,540	122,590,864	1,420,379	942,174
Liabilities				
Accounts payable		362,189		222,330
Debt obligations	3,736,368	864,772	127,465	
Deferred revenue		724,942		370,260
Other		1,709,545		
Total Liabilities	3,736,368	3,661,448	127,465	592,590
Net Assets				
Unrestricted	122,172	11,615,700	505,673	318,382
Temporarily restricted		55,871,728	662,241	26,050
Permanently restricted		51,441,988	125,000	5,152
Total Net Assets	$ 122,172	118,929,416	1,292,914	349,584
Statement of Activities Revenue				
Sales and service				$ 606,278
Grants and contracts		3,334,966		413
Interest income	11,977		57,362	16,385
Unrealized investment income		(2,879,949)	23,415	
Gifts		28,595,789	638,548	
Other	298,030	3,270,758		37,950
Total Revenue	310,007	28,986,598	719,325	661,026
Expenses				
Salary and wages		396,548		300,264
Services and supplies	35,407		21,879	214,662
Interest	256,267	308,851	5,480	13,923
Depreciation	10,135		3,210	39,795
Scholarships and research support		17,349,066	568,754	
Other		37,009		66,519
Total Expenses	301,809	17,694,926	599,323	635,163
Change in net assets	8,198	11,291,672	120,002	25,863
Net Assets at beginning of year	113,974	107,637,744	1,172,912	323,721
Net Assets at end of year	$ 122,172	118,929,416	1,292,914	349,584

display contrasts sharply with commercial enterprise display format because the classified presentation is an optional display for commercial entities. Second, items within each classification are required to be arranged in liquidity order, whereas commercial enterprises often present their long-term investments before the inventory or accounts receivable data.

Assets or liability items that have associated contra accounts may be presented net on the face of the statement, with details of the contra disclosed in the footnotes. For example, accounts receivable can be presented in either of the following formats.

Accounts receivable	$8,229,180	
Less allowance for noncollectable	(91,106)	$8,138,074
or		
Account receivable (less allowance $91,106)		$8,138,074
or		
Accounts receivable (see Footnote No. X)		$8,138,074

The difference between the assets and liabilities is reported as net assets rather than equity. Net assets include the following: (1) the amount invested in capital assets net of accumulated depreciation and related debt, (2) restricted net assets distinguished as either expendable or nonexpendable, and (3) unrestricted net assets. Details of the restricted net assets may be displayed on the face of the statement or disclosed in the footnotes to the statements. Details may not be displayed on the face of the statement for the capital assets net of accumulated depreciation and related debt or the unrestricted net assets but may be disclosed in the footnotes.

Capital assets net of accumulated depreciation and related debt compares to the investment in plant currently displayed in the college and university balance sheet. These net assets represent the net equity in the institution's land, buildings, infrastructure, equipment, and all other capitalized fixed assets. Some refer to this amount as brick-and-mortar equity. GASB directed that the amount of net capital assets be displayed as the first item among net assets because this equity is the most nonliquid, nonexpendable net asset. Although the institution has an equity position in its capital assets, this value cannot be used for current operating obligations or programmatic costs unless the capital asset is sold.

Private colleges and universities do not discretely report the equity value of their capital assets net of accumulated depreciation and related debt but rather include the value as part of the institution's unrestricted net assets. This reporting practice allows the nonexpendable equity in capital assets to be commingled with the expendable unrestricted resources reported. Some financial analysts claim that this reporting practice allows private college and university to hide deficits resulting from large postemployment benefit and other fringe benefit obligations that will not be paid until sometime in the distant future.

Note in Illustration 12-2 that the capital assets net of related debt ($252,575,649) is not the value of capital assets ($337,113,861) less the current and long-term liabilities ($84,442,512—current [$6,031,824] plus noncurrent [$78,410,688]). That means that some other payable of $95,700 in addition to the long-term debt liability is related to capital assets. By looking at Illustration 12-3, which displays the details of the long-term liabilities, we find that the long-term debt obligations related to capital assets is $84,538,212. When the capital asset value of $337,113,861 is reduced by the related debt of $84,538,212, the net capital assets net of related debt equals $252,575,649, as shown in Illustration 12-2.

Nonexpendable restricted net assets are resources that have an externally imposed provision that stipulates that the resources must be maintained permanently but permits the institution to use up, or expend, part or all of the earnings (or other economic benefits) derived from the donated assets. Nonexpendable restrictions are created by an externally

ILLUSTRATION 12-2
Clemson University
Statement of Net Assets
for the year ended June 30, 2002

	Clemson University	Clemson Research Facilities Corporation	Total
Assets			
Current Assets			
Cash and cash equivalents	$ 84,641,385	$ 132,627	$ 84,774,012
Restricted assets—current			
Cash and cash equivalents	38,051,946	—	38,051,946
Accounts receivable (Net of provision for Doubtful accounts of $91,106)	8,138,074	—	8,138,074
Grants and contracts receivable	20,105,871	—	20,105,871
Contributions receivable, net	1,724,239	—	1,724,239
Interest and income receivable	1,646,804	—	1,646,804
Student loans receivable	14,159	—	14,159
Inventories	885,437	—	885,437
Prepaid expenses	451,714	4,581	456,295
Investment in direct financing lease	—	246,038	246,038
Other	29,663	10,135	39,798
Total current assets	155,689,292	393,381	156,082,673
Noncurrent Assets			
Restricted assets—Noncurrent			
Cash and cash equivalents	10,113,619	547,800	10,661,419
Student loans receivable	6,874,376	—	6,874,376
Notes receivable	47,740,222	—	47,740,222
Contributions receivable, net	5,213,999	—	5,213,999
Investments	2,997,444	—	2,997,444
Investment in direct financing lease	—	2,836,280	2,836,280
Other	315,272	81,079	396,351
Capital assets, net of accumulated depreciation	337,113,861	—	337,113,861
Total noncurrent assets	393,380,798	2,917,359	396,298,157
Total assets	$ 549,070,090	$ 3,310,740	$ 552,380,830
Liabilities			
Current Liabilities			
Accounts and retainages payable	$ 22,000,193	$—	$ 22,000,193
Accrued payroll and related liabilities	8,304,131	—	8,304,131
Accrued compensated absences and related liabilities	11,564,077	—	11,564,077
Accrued interest payable	679,147	—	679,147
Deferred revenues	18,240,951	—	18,240,951
Bonds payable	5,040,000	—	5,040,000
Certificates of participation payable	—	505,000	505,000
Capital leases payable	942,614	—	942,614
Notes payable	49,210	—	49,210
Deposits	568,174	—	568,174
Funds held for others	1,360,485	—	1,360,485
Arbitrage payable	160,327	—	160,327
Total current liabilities	68,909,309	505,000	69,414,309

(Continued)

ILLUSTRATION 12-2 *Continued*

	Clemson University	Clemson Research Facilities Corporation	Total
Noncurrent Liabilities			
Accounts and retainages payable	187,431	—	187,431
Accrued compensated absences and related liabilities	5,331,923	—	5,331,923
Funds held for others	6,431,035	—	6,431,035
Bonds payable	72,020,000	—	72,020,000
Certificates of participation payable	—	3,231,368	3,231,368
Capital leases payable	6,380,688	—	6,380,688
Notes payable	105,700	—	105,700
Total noncurrent liabilities	90,456,777	3,231,368	93,688,145
Total liabilities	$ 159,366,086	$ 3,736,368	$ 163,102,454
Net Assets			
Invested in capital assets, net of related debt	$ 252,575,649	$ —	$ 252,575,649
Restricted for nonexpendable:			—
Scholarships and fellowships	9,223,406	—	9,223,406
Restricted for expendable:			—
Scholarships and fellowships	66,194,446	—	66,194,446
Research	2,021,885	—	2,021,885
Instructional department use	11,969,602	—	11,969,602
Loans	2,418,206	—	2,418,206
Capital projects	16,177,247	—	16,177,247
Debt service	2,441,574	—	2,441,574
Unrestricted	43,669,984	122,172	43,792,156
Total net assets	$ 406,691,999	$ 122,172	$ 406,814,171

Source: Clemson University comprehensive annual financial report, 2002.
Available at www.comptroller.clemson.edu

imposed stipulation that neither passage of time nor actions of the organization can satisfy. Revenues from the investment of nonexpendable restricted resources are reported as restricted expendable or unrestricted expendable, depending on externally imposed stipulations. Nonexpendable restricted earnings may be recognized as an addition to permanently restricted net assets rather than revenue only if so directed by the donor or stipulated by law. If earnings are designated by the external donor or by law to be unrestricted, the earnings are recognized as unrestricted net assets income and may not be reinvested as nonexpendable net assets.

Most nonexpendable restricted net assets are endowment gifts. When an institution receives endowment gifts, the external donor stipulates, under the terms of the gift, that resources are to be maintained intact in perpetuity and are to be invested for the purpose of producing present and future earnings.

Illustration 12-2 displays a nonexpendable restricted amount of $9,223,406 for scholarships and fellowships. This amount is the corpus of endowment gifts. That simply means that the $9,223,406 cannot be spent, but the income from the investment of the amount can be expended only if used for scholarships and fellowships.

Expendable restricted net assets are those resources provided to institutions for a myriad of purposes. If the provider of resources places a time, purpose, or some other

ILLUSTRATION 12-3
Clemson University
Financial Statement Disclosure
Long-Term Liabilities

	Long-Term Liabilities				
	Beginning Balance	Additions	Reductions	Ending Balance	Current Portion
Long-term liability activity for the year ended June 30, 2002 was as follows:					
Bonds payable, notes payable and Lease obligations:					
General obligation bonds payable	$ 10,900,000	$	$ 985,000	$ 9,915,000	$1,030,000
Plant improvement bonds	6,845,000		570,000	6,275,000	590,000
Revenue bonds payable	43,355,000		2,445,000	40,910,000	2,435,000
Athletic facilities revenue bonds	20,985,000		1,025,000	19,960,000	985,000
Notes payable	201,842		46,932	154,910	49,210
Capital lease obligations	8,204,749		881,447	7,323,302	942,614
Total leases and bonds payable	90,491,591	0	5,953,379	84,538,212	6,031,824
Other liabilities:					
Compensated absences	16,061,000	11,597,016	10,762,016	16,896,000	11,564,077
Funds held for others	6,237,323	315,233	121,521	6,431,035	
Accounts and retainage payable	170,711	187,431	170,711	187,431	
Arbitrage payable	153,021	7,306		160,327	160,327
Total other liabilities	22,622,055	12,106,986	11,054,248	23,674,793	11,724,404
Total long-term liabilities	$ 113,113,646	$ 12,106,986	$ 17,007,627	$ 108,213,005	$ 17,756,228

Note: Amounts shown in "Ending balance" of long-term liabilities include both current and long-term portions.

Source: Clemson University comprehensive annual financial report, 2002.
Available at www.comptroller.clemson.edu

restriction on the use of the resources that requires the institution to classify them as restricted resources, the institution is required to classify them as restricted. Restrictions can be created only by an external party to the organization, such as a creditor, grantor, vendor, or donor.[20]

Some restrictions created by creditors, grantors, vendors, or donors permit the institution to use up or expend the donated assets as specified when external stipulations are satisfied either by the passage of time or by actions of the institution. For these transactions, the institution recognizes revenues when the resources are received, provided that all eligibility requirements have been met. A time requirement is met as soon as the institution begins to honor the provider's stipulation to sell, disburse, or consume the resources, and it continues to be met for as long as the institution honors that stipulation.[21] Earnings from restricted resources are reported as restricted or unrestricted depending upon externally imposed stipulations.

[20] Externally designated restrictions are different from internal designations imposed by a governing board on unrestricted resources. Internal designations, allocations, or commitments do not change the restricted or unrestricted designation of the resource. Internal designations are accounted for by using the institution's chart of accounts.

[21] Op. cit., **GASB Statement No. 33**, par. 22.

Illustration 12-2 displays various different types of expendable restricted net assets. This means that these resources may be expended by Clemson University but must be expended in accordance with the time or purpose restriction designated by the external party. For example, Clemson University has $66,194,446 restricted for scholarships and fellowships. If the institution's financial aid program can disburse these funds for the stipulated purpose, the resources can be used; otherwise the resources must continue to be unused and reported as expendable restricted resources. The same situation exists for the $2,021,885 restricted for research purposes and the $11,969,602 restricted for instructional department uses.

The $2,418,206 displayed as restricted expendable for loans is a bit different because it is not available for disbursement. Instead, the amount represents the total resources restricted for loan purposes. The loan program has assets only in the form of cash or loans receivable and the equity balance. If the loan program is reduced, the equity is refunded to the provider or it becomes unrestricted resources. A primary source of loans is the federal Perkins Loan program, formerly known as the National Direct Student Loan (NDSL) program. In this program, resources provided by the government are matched with institutional resources for loans to students. These institutional resources, which are designated specifically for loans to students, provide a major source of loan funding. Some colleges and universities also hold gift revenues expressly given to the institution to be used for student loans. For example, many institutions have loan programs for nursing, engineering, and other students that were created by gifts to the college.

GAAP[22] requires that any unspent bond proceeds and resources held for the retirement of outstanding long-term debt must be displayed as a restricted expendable net asset. To meet this reporting requirement, Clemson is reporting $16,177,247 of unexpended bond proceeds and other resources and $2,441,574 held in a sinking fund to pay debt principal and interest required by bond covenants as restricted expendable net assets (Illustration 12-2).

Unrestricted net assets represent those resources available to an institution for general operating purposes. Available unrestricted resources associated with operating activities, resources functioning as endowments, financial aid resources, and plant operations and costs are classified as unrestricted net assets. According to GAAP guidance, details of the unrestricted net assets, such as source or designation, may not be displayed on the face of the statement of net assets. However, the details may be disclosed in the notes to the financial statement.[23] The prohibition on displaying the components of the unrestricted net assets is based on the fact that the governing board of the college or university determines the internal designation, allocation, or commitment and can remove or modify the designation at any time. Notice that Clemson University reported $43,669,984 as unrestricted net assets without any explanation. Also note that Illustration 12-2 does not have a reference beside the title "Unrestricted," indicating that no subsequent information is disclosed in the notes to the financial statement. Without the disclosure, the financial statement reader must analyze the display within the statements and the footnote disclosures to understand the major activities that Clemson University is accounting for as unrestricted net assets.

The financial information for component units, such as the Research Facilities, a hospital, or a foundation, are presented in a discrete column on the statement of net assets using the same classified format used for the institution. Unlike a consolidated statement for a commercial enterprise, the between-organizations transactions of the component unit and the institution are not eliminated.

---

[22] **GASB Statement No. 34**, par. 34.

[23] Ibid., par. 37.

Statement of Revenues, Expenses, and Changes in Net Assets

The overall format of the statement of revenues, expenses, and changes in net assets is one that allows the financial statement user to ascertain both operating and nonoperating activities as well as extraordinary items, gains, and losses, as displayed in Figure 12-3.

The statement of revenues, expenses, and changes in net assets (Illustration 12-4) aggregates transactions and events that have similar characteristics into line items of revenues, expenses, gains, losses, extraordinary items, special items, and other support that is presented in a single column for the institution. The statement of revenues, expenses, and changes in net assets reports all changes in the net assets for the institution for the reporting period and must articulate—that is, agree—with the net assets reported in the statement of net assets. That is, the change in net assets reported in the statement of revenues, expenses, and change in net assets ($38,459,392), when added to the beginning-of-the-year net asset balance ($368,232,607), equals the end of the year net asset balance ($406,691,999) displayed in the statement of net assets (Illustration 12-2).

Revenues are reported by source, net of discounts and allowances, with the discount and allowance amount parenthetically disclosed on the face of the statement or in the financial statement footnote disclosures. As an alternative, revenues may be reported gross, with the related discounts and allowances reported directly beneath the revenue account. For example, Clemson University student tuition and fees are reported as $94,061,816 net allowances of $21,907,007, reported parenthetically. Investment income may be reported net of investment expenses provided the amount of expenses netted is disclosed either on the face of the statement or in the footnotes. Clemson University also reports its auxiliary enterprises sales and service income $49,927,309 net allowances of $7,626,291 reported parenthetically.

The tuition and fees allowance as well as the auxiliary enterprise sales and services allowance is the discount allowance for student financial aid. Federal financial aid grants for students are recognized as grant revenue in accordance with GASB Statement

Operating revenues presented by type	$	XXX
Operating expenses detailed by natural class or by function		XXX
Operating income or loss (the net difference between operating revenues and expenses)		XXX
Nonoperating revenues (expenses) listed by type		XXX
Net nonoperating revenues		XXX
Net income (loss) before other revenues, expenses, gains, or losses (combined operating and nonoperating income or loss)		XXX
Other extraordinary and special item revenue, gains, or losses		XXX
Increase (decrease) in net assets		XXX
Net assets—beginning of the year		XXX
Net assets—end of the year	$	XXX

FIGURE 12-3 Typical College and University Format for the Statement of Revenues, Expenses, and Changes in Net Assets.

ILLUSTRATION 12-4
Clemson University
Statement of Revenues, Expenses, and Changes in Net Assets
for the year ended June 30, 2002

	Clemson University	Clemson Research Facilities Corporation	Total
Revenues:			
Operating Revenues			
Student tuition and fees (net of scholarship allowances of $21,907,007)	$ 94,061,816	$—	$ 94,061,816
Federal grants and contracts	51,221,903	—	51,221,903
State grants and contracts	19,884,859	—	19,884,859
Local grants and contracts	1,103,275	—	1,103,275
Nongovernmental grants and contracts	8,656,262	—	8,656,262
Sales and services of educational and other activities	9,481,324	—	9,481,324
Sales and services of auxiliary enterprises—pledged for revenue bonds (net of scholarship allowances of $7,626,281)	49,927,309	—	49,927,309
Sales and services of auxiliary enterprises—not pledged	12,384,121	—	12,384,121
Other operating revenues	11,208,657	298,030	11,506,687
Total operating revenues	257,929,526	298,030	258,227,556
Expenses:			
Operating Expenses			
Compensation and employee benefits	292,247,117	—	292,247,117
Services and supplies	108,321,462	35,407	108,356,869
Utilities	12,006,382	—	12,006,382
Depreciation	19,158,248	10,135	19,168,383
Scholarships and fellowships	9,089,474	—	9,089,474
Total operating expenses	440,822,683	45,542	440,868,225
Operating income/(loss)	(182,893,157)	252,488	(182,640,669)
Nonoperating Revenues (Expenses):			
State appropriations	155,453,023	—	155,453,023
Federal appropriations	9,772,107	—	9,772,107
Gifts	26,892,073	—	26,892,073
Interest income	7,404,845	11,977	7,416,822
Endowment income	(1,788,499)	—	(1,788,499)
Interest on capital asset-related debt	(4,300,280)	(256,267)	(4,556,547)
Other nonoperating revenues	1,423,176	—	1,423,176
Gain/loss on disposal of capital assets	12,621,267	—	12,621,267
Refunds to grantors	(288,718)	—	(288,718)
Net nonoperating revenues	207,188,994	(244,290)	206,944,704
Income before other revenues, expenses, gains or losses	24,295,837	8,198	24,304,035
State capital appropriations	12,482,232	—	12,482,232
Capital grants and gifts	1,864,354	—	1,864,354
Additions to permanent endowments	235,430	—	235,430
Transfers to/from other state funds	(418,461)	—	(418,461)
Increase in net assets	38,459,392	8,198	38,467,590
Net Assets			
Net assets, beginning of year, as restated	368,232,607	113,974	368,346,581
Net assets, end of year	$406,691,999	$122,172	$ 406,814,171

Source: Clemson University comprehensive annual financial report, 2002.
Available at www.comptroller.clemson.edu

No. 24.[24] When the financial aid is used to pay student tuition and fee charges in accordance with student instructions, the payment is considered as a discount because if the transaction were recorded as an expense and revenue, the revenue would recognized twice—once as the grant revenue and once as tuition revenue. This is the basis of Clemson University reporting a scholarship allowance of $21,907,007 in the student tuition and fee display.

The following journal entries illustrate the recognition of the receipt of federal financial aid resources and its application to the students' fee bills in accordance with the students' instruction.

Cash	$4,000,000	
Revenue—federal financial aid (Pell grants)		$4,000,000

To recognize the receipt of the Pell federal financial aid awards.

Student accounts receivable	$6,000,000	
Revenue—tuition and fees		$6,000,000

To record the fall 2002 semester tuition and fee charges.

Tuition discount	$3,500,000	
Expense—scholarship and fellowship	$ 500,000	
Student accounts receivable		$3,500,000
Cash (paid to the student)		$500,000

To record the distribution of the Pell federal financial aid grants. $3,500,000 was used to reduce outstanding student accounts receivable and remaining $500,000 was paid to the students.

The unpaid $2,500,000 student accounts receivable balance must be paid by the students who did not receive financial aid grants and whose bills are still outstanding.

If revenue is received before it is earned—for example, prepaid tuition or dormitory fees—the revenue is reported as deferred revenue within the current liability section of the statement of net assets. For example, $150,000 was received from students in the old fiscal year to reserve their dormitory rooms for the forthcoming year, when the payment will be credited to their dormitory fee bills. The receipt would be recognized as follows.

Cash	$150,000	
Deferred dormitory fees		$150,000

To record prepaid dormitory fees to reserve room selections for the forthcoming term.

At the beginning of the new fiscal year, the deferred fee account would be closed and credited to the students' dormitory fee charges for the current semester.

Deferred dormitory fees	$150,000	
Dormitory fees receivable		$150,000

To credit the prepaid dormitory fees to the appropriate student dormitory fee receivables.

GASB Statement No. 34 requires business-type activities to distinguish their revenue and expenses as either operating or nonoperating. What comprises or determines operating versus nonoperating was not prescribed by GASB.[25] Instead, colleges and universities must establish a policy that defines operating revenues and expenses that are appropriate to the activity being reported, disclose the policy in the significant accounting policies, and use the policy consistently from period to period. Colleges and universities can also use paragraph

---

[24] **Statement No. 24**, "Accounting and Financial Reporting for Certain Grants and Other Financial Assistance" (Norwalk, CT: Governmental Standards Accounting Board, 1994).

[25] Op. cit., **GASB Statement No. 34**, par. 102.

17 in GASB Statement No. 9 "Reporting Cash Flows of Proprietary Funds and Governments that use Proprietary Fund Accounting" to help determine which transactions are operating and which are nonoperating. That is, transactions or other events normally reported as operating transactions in the cash flow statement are displayed as operating activities in the statement of revenues, expenses, and changes in net assets. That is, most nonexchange transactions, transfers from other government agencies, and revenues related to capital asset acquisitions are reported as nonoperating rather than operating income.

Figure 12-4 displays typical (but not all-inclusive) revenue types reported as operating and nonoperating by public colleges and universities. Clemson University chose to report the $9,772,107 in federal appropriations received to support agriculture and mechanical educational programs under the Land Grant Program as nonoperating revenues. Other universities that also received federal appropriations for Land Grant Programs, including the University of Missouri and Oklahoma State University, reported the appropriations they received as operating revenues. This difference highlights the ability of colleges and universities to determine what comprises operating activities under GASB Statement No. 34, paragraph 102, guidance.

Natural classifications: means of describing the expense incurred, such as salary or office supplies

Colleges and universities may report expenses by **natural classifications** or by functional classes, such as major classes of program activities, supporting activities, and auxiliary enterprises. Program activities are the mission-related activities of the institution. Supporting activities generally include student services, institutional support, and academic support, including the operation and maintenance of plant and student aid. Auxiliary enterprises are activities that (1) are conducted to furnish goods and services to faculty, staff, and students; (2) charge a fee directly related to, although not necessarily equal to, full costs; and (3) are managed essentially as self-supporting activities. Auxiliary enterprise–related interest expense on debt incurred to acquire capital assets and depreciation expense are reported as auxiliary enterprise cost. All other capital asset–related interest and depreciation expenses are reported as part of the operation and maintenance of plant. Although GAAP allows the allocation of depreciation costs to the function that utilizes the capital assets, most public colleges and universities report depreciation as a separate function.

Operating Revenues	Nonoperating Revenues
Tuition and fees	State appropriations (government transfers)
Federal appropriations	Endowment gifts
Federal grants and contracts	Annuity contract revenues
State grants and contracts	Investment income
Nongovernment grants and contracts	Capital appropriations not capitalized
Private gifts for operating purposes	Capital gifts
Sales and service of educational activities	Capital gifts not capitalized
Auxiliary enterprises:	Subsidies (listed by source)
Resident hall fees	Intergovernmental transfers
Dining hall fees	
Bookstore revenue	
Other	

FIGURE 12-4   Typical Operating and Nonoperating Revenues Reported by Public Colleges and Universities.

Figure 12-5 provides a list of the activities included within the program activities, together with the type of expenditures that would be reported within the function.

Although public colleges and universities may report expenses by function, Clemson University chose to display its expenses by natural classes (see Illustration 12-4). This format presents the financial statement user with relevant information and precludes the arbitrary allocations that occur in the functional presentation. Some financial statement users believe that the natural class presentation provides some, although not an exact, articulation between the statement of revenues, expenses, and changes in net assets and the direct method statement of cash flows.

In its financial statement note disclosures, Clemson University presented a matrix that displays the natural class of expenses shown in the statement of revenues, expenses, and changes in net assets to the functional expense class. This schedule, operating expenses by function (Illustration 12-5), explains the $440,822,683 total expenses by the

Function	Types of expenditures reported
Program Activities	
Instruction	General academic, vocational and technical, special session, community education, and remedial instruction
Research	Institute and research centers in addition to individual and research grants and contract projects
Public service	Community service, cooperative extension, and radio and television public broadcasting services
Support Activities	
Academic support	Those services that support instruction, such as library, media center, academic computer labs, and curriculum development costs
Student support	Admission, registrar, and student services such as counseling and career guidance, financial aid administration, and student health services
Institutional support	Includes expenditures for the administrative activities, fiscal operations, administrative data processing, space management, human resource management, and logistical activities such as purchasing, central stores, printing, and transportation services
Operation and maintenance of plant	All expenditures for the operation and maintenance of the physical plant, including maintenance costs, custodial services, landscape and grounds maintenance, and building repairs
Scholarship and fellowships	All forms of student financial aid and student fellowships
Depreciation	All recognized depreciation costs
Auxiliary Services	
Auxiliary enterprises	Activities that charge a fee for services to furnish goods to students, faculty, and staff, including the bookstore, dining halls, dormitories, parking garages, concert halls, and intercollegiate athletics
Other Activities	
Hospital activities	Costs associated with patient care operations, including prevention, diagnosis, treatment, and rehabilitation care
Independent activities	Activities unrelated to the college or university, such as a federally funded research laboratory

FIGURE 12-5 Public College and University Functions and Types of Expenditures Reported by Function.

ILLUSTRATION 12-5
Clemson University
Operating Expenses by Function
for Fiscal Year Ended June 30, 2002

	Compensation and Employee Benefits	Services and Supplies	Utilities	Scholarships and Fellowships	Depreciation	Total
Instruction	$ 96,686,142	15,747,271	802,458	109,599		113,345,470
Research	67,446,582	25,151,162	991,913	363,084		93,952,741
Public service	41,111,461	14,207,228	1,189,746			56,508,435
Academic services	23,117,823	5,095,047	598,464			28,811,334
Student services	8,409,766	4,709,523	159,806			13,279,095
Institutional support	14,222,624	2,804,399	259,922			17,286,945
Operation and maintenance of plant	17,052,990	7,235,664	3,877,364			28,166,018
Scholarship and fellowships	34	65,586	4,126,709	8,616,791		12,809,120
Auxiliary services	24,199,695	33,305,582				57,505,277
Depreciation					19,158,248	19,158,248
Total	**$ 292,247,117**	**108,321,462**	**12,006,382**	**9,089,474**	**19,158,248**	**440,822,683**

Source: Clemson University comprehensive annual financial report 2002.
Available at www.comptroller.clemson.edu

function performed. Without this schedule, the financial statement reader would have no idea what portions of the compensation and benefits were used for what function. The one exception is depreciation expense. Depreciation is considered both a natural class of expense and a function for college and university reporting.

The traditional format presented at the beginning of this section is used for revenues, expenses, and changes in net assets, as displayed in Illustration 12-4. This format also provides a measure of operations; since public colleges and universities must report state appropriations as nonoperating revenue, public institutions will typically display an operating loss. This amount is important because it is the beginning amount used in the statement of cash flow reconciliation of net cash flows from operating activities. The line titled *Net income before other revenues, expenses, gains or losses* is considered by most financial statement users to be the net operating measure of public colleges and universities.

Statement of Cash Flows

The primary objective of reporting cash flows is to provide information to financial statement users that is useful in making economic decisions. The information provides data regarding whether the institution has sufficient cash flows to pay outstanding obligations, acquire additional assets, and expand programs, as well as whether the institution is depending on tuition and state appropriations for its continuing operating.

Changes in assets, liabilities, and net assets are explained in the statement of cash flows. The statement provides information about the cash received and disbursements made by an institution during the period of time being reporting in the financial statements. It does not include any transaction or account that is not reflected in the statement of net assets or statement of revenues, expenses, and changes in net assets. The statement of cash flows reports the period's transactions and events in terms of their impact on the cash received or cash disbursed and provides a more complete picture of the institution's operations and financial position.

Colleges and universities prepare a statement of cash flows (Illustration 12-6) in accordance with the provision of GASB Statement No. 9.[26] Public colleges and universities are required to use the direct method to prepare the cash flows from operating activities. That is, the cash flow statement displays the direct operating cash received and the direct operating cash disbursed for operating the organization. In addition, all inflows and outflows are required to be reported gross.

Unlike corporations that report their cash flow using three categories—operating, financing, and investing—public colleges and universities must report their cash inflows and outflows using four categories—operating, noncapital financing, capital and related financing, and investing. Although the categories have similar titles, there are significant differences among what is reported in each category. For example, interest income is reported as a corporate operating activity, while interest income is reported as an investing activity by public colleges and universities. Long-term capital asset debt interest is a corporate operating cash outflow but it is a capital asset financing outflow for colleges and universities. Corporate cash flows report all debt borrowing and repayment as a financing activity, whereas public colleges report debt activity in two categories. Money borrowed to support operating activities and its repayment are reported by public colleges and universities as noncapital-related financing activity. The interest cost and principal payment of any money borrowed for capital asset construction or acquisition are reported as capital-related financing activities.

Operating activities must be presented using the direct method. That is, the cash received is reported for operating transactions—tuition, federal appropriations, research grants and contracts, financial aid grants, resident halls, bookstore, and sale of goods and services. The cash disbursed is reported for operating transactions—salaries, fringe benefits, supplies, and vendor payments. The major types of revenue and expenses displayed in the statement are not prescribed by GAAP. Instead, the college and university must determine which major types of revenue and disbursements more clearly display the character and mission of the institution.

Noncapital financing activities are transactions and events where resources are obtained via transfers such as state appropriations and pass-through grants received from some other state agency. This category also reports new endowment gifts, investment income, direct student lending proceeds and disbursements, and resources held for others receipts and disbursements.

Capital and related financing activities are cash inflows from *all* sources received to acquire capital assets, capital debt proceeds, and fixed asset sale proceeds. This category reports *all* cash disbursements made to acquire capital assets, capital debt principal payments, capital debt interest payments, and capital lease transactions. That is, all cash transactions related to capital assets are reported in this category of the cash flow statement. This differs from corporate cash flow statements, which report debt interest payments as operating activities and capital asset acquisitions as investing activities.

Investing activities are cash transactions and events that involve the purchase and sale of equities, debt securities, and other investments together with the interest earned on the investments. The gross purchase of investment and the gross sale of investments must be displayed in this activity category rather than the net change in investments. Investment transactions include both short- and long-term transactions that do not meet the cash equivalent definition. A cash equivalent is any short-term investment with an original

---

[26] Op. cit., **GASB Statement No. 9**, par. 15–28.

maturity of 90 days or less. Long-term portfolios often hold short-term money market investments with original maturities of less than 90 days. These investments need not be reclassified to cash equivalents if management's intent in investing in these instruments is a portfolio management strategy. Note that public colleges and universities report investment income as part of investing activities, whereas corporate entities report investment income as part of operating activities.

One of the most important items of information reported in statement of cash flows (Illustration 12-6) is the net cash flow provided by (or used by) operating activities. Clemson University paid out more operating cash than it received ($197,999,993) during the fiscal year. Corporate operating activities normally provide operating cash inflow because this amount determines whether or not the enterprise will continue to exist. Because state appropriations are reported as noncapital financing activities rather than operating activities, public colleges and universities will probably report a negative cash flow from operating activities. Cash flows from investing and financing activities are also important, but the cash flow from the major ongoing activities of the college or university is the critical bit of information.

In its statement of cash flows, Clemson University reported receiving $231,433,040 for noncapital financing activities. These activities included the state and federal appropriations, gifts of $66,828,162, and other inflows and outflows of $729,410. This amount was sufficient to fund the negative cash flows from operating activities ($197,999,993) and provide most of the $41,314,902 for capital financing activities not supported by capital gifts ($824,390), appropriations ($10,893,748), and the $14,017684 received from property sales. The interest earned on investments ($7,584,430) provided $3,100,000 that was transferred to the University Foundation. In total, Clemson University used all the cash it received in the fiscal year plus another $3,181,391 of cash on hand at the beginning of the fiscal year, which resulted in total cash and cash equivalents at the end of the fiscal year of $132,806,950. Although the $132 million seems to be a rather large amount of cash and cash equivalent, the financial statement notes indicated that $131.7 million of this balance was deposits held by the state treasurer that were available on demand and were therefore reported as a cash equivalent.

Financial Statement Note Disclosures

An important component of any financial statement, whether it is for a commercial enterprise or for a college or university, is the notes to the financial statement. Primary among the disclosures is the summary of the institution's significant accounting policies. This describes the basis for the financial statement presentation. The disclosures describe in greater detail various data presented in the statements. The notes to the financial statements communicate information that is essential for fair presentation of the financial data and information that is not displayed on the face of the statements. The notes are an integral part of the basic financial statements and the audit opinion.

Figure 12-6 is a list of note disclosures typically reported by public colleges and universities. The list is not intended to be all inclusive because the disclosures are a means of describing the basis of the financial statement presentation to the financial statement user.

The segment note disclosure (Illustration 12-7) is a unique GASB Statements No. 34 disclosure requirement for public colleges and universities that report business-type activity financial statements. A **segment** is defined as any identifiable activity that has a specific revenue stream pledged to retire one or more revenue bonds and has related expenses, gains and losses, assets and liabilities. In other words, an institution that has outstanding revenue bonds is required to disclose segment information if an identifiable

Segments: an identifiable activity that has revenue pledged to retire debt for which the activity's revenue, expenses, assets, and liabilities are required to be separately reported

ILLUSTRATION 12-6
Clemson University
Statement of Cash Flows
for the Year Ended June 30, 2002

	Clemson University	Clemson Research Facilities Corporation	Total
Cash Flows from Operating Activities			
Payments from customers	149,019,554	298,030	149,317,584
Grants and contracts	77,997,431	—	77,997,431
Payments to suppliers	(123,474,616)	(38,446)	(123,513,062)
Payments to employees	(228,645,526)	—	(228,645,526)
Payments for benefits	(54,834,562)	—	(54,834,562)
Payments to students	(19,285,596)	—	(19,285,596)
Loans to students	(18,497)	—	(18,497)
Collection of loans	1,241,819	—	1,241,819
Net cash provided (used) by operating activities	(197,999,993)	259,584	(197,740,409)
Cash Flows from Noncapital Financing Activities			
State appropriations	155,453,023	—	155,453,023
Federal appropriations	8,422,445	—	8,422,445
Gifts	66,828,162	—	66,828,162
Other inflows	1,436,060	—	1,436,060
Other outflows	(706,650)	—	(706,650)
Net cash flow provided (used) by noncapital financing activities	231,433,040	—	231,433,040
Cash Flows from Capital and Related Financing Activities			
State capital appropriations	10,893,748	—	10,893,748
Capital grants and gifts received	824,390	—	824,390
Proceeds from sale of property	14,017,684	—	14,017,684
Purchases of capital assets	(56,517,091)	—	(56,517,091)
Principal paid on capital debt and lease	(5,953,379)	(510,000)	(6,463,379)
Interest and fees	(4,580,254)	—	(4,580,254)
Net cash provided (used) by capital activities	(41,314,902)	(510,000)	(41,824,902)
Cash Flows from Investing Activities			
Interest on investments	7,584,430	11,977	7,596,407
Transfer to Clemson University Foundation	(3,100,000)	—	(3,100,000)
Principal received on direct financing lease	—	226,970	226,970
Proceeds from stock sales	216,034	—	216,034
Net cash provided (used) by investing activities	4,700,464	238,947	4,939,411
Net change in cash	(3,181,391)	(11,469)	(3,192,860)
Cash and cash equivalents, beginning of year	135,988,341	691,896	136,680,237
Cash and cash equivalents end of year	$ 132,806,950	$ 680,427	$ 133,487,377
Reconciliation of net operating revenues (expense) to net cash provided (used) by operating activities:			
Operating income (loss)	$ (182,893,157)	$ 252,488	$ (182,640,669)
Adjustments to reconcile operating income (loss) to net cash provided (used) by operating activities:			
Depreciation expense	19,158,248	10,135	19,168,383

(Continued)

ILLUSTRATION 12-6 *Continued*

	Clemson University	Clemson Research Facilities Corporation	Total
Change in asset and liabilities:			
Receivables net	(41,386,012)	—	(41,386,012)
Grants and contracts receivable	(3,069,558)	—	(3,069,558)
Student loans receivable	(78,638)	—	(78,638)
Prepaid expenses	2,001,239	(3,039)	1,998,200
Inventories	(23,366)	—	(23,366)
Other	8,692	—	8,692
Accounts and retainages payable	(280,965)	—	(280,965)
Accrued payroll and related liabilities	1,550,830	—	1,550,830
Accrued compensated absences and related liabilities	835,000	—	835,000
Deferred revenue	4,886,738	—	4,886,738
Deposits held for others	1,290,956	—	1,290,956
Net cash provided (used) by operating activities	**$ (197,999,993)**	**$ 259,584**	**$ (197,740,409)**
Non-Cash Transactions			
Decrease in fair value of investments	**$ (4,291,740)**	**$ —**	**$ (4,291,740)**

Source: Clemson University comprehensive annual financial report, 2002.
Available at www.comptroller.clemson.edu

stream of revenue, such as a dining hall or dormitory income, is pledged to repay the bonds and the dining hall or dormitory have related expenses, gains, and losses.

Several colleges and universities, such as the University of California system, have extensive numbers of segments because a majority of their dining halls, dormitories, and

Description of the reporting entity
Summary of accounting policies including a description of the measurement focus and basis of accounting, such as operating versus nonoperating activities
Description of cash deposits and investments
Accounts receivable aging and determination of allowances
Capital assets balance by type at the beginning of the year, acquisition, dispositions, current period depreciation, and balance at the end of the year that ties to the statement of net assets
Capitalization policy for capital assets, historical treasures, and collections
Description of restricted assets
Accounts payable description and required reserves, if any
Lease obligations, if any
Long-term liabilities schedule by debt issue and compensated absences—beginning balance, new debt, payments, and end-of-year balance together with the current obligation (Illustration 12-3)
Pension obligations and funding requirements
Postemployment benefits other than pensions
Condensed financial statement for segments whose revenue is pledged to retire debt issues (Illustration 12-7)
Details of any joint venture
Details of related organizations and disclosure of component unit information
Details of construction and any other significant commitments
Description of contingencies and commitments
Description of known financial events subsequent to the fiscal year data being reported

FIGURE 12-6 Public College and University Typical Financial Statement Disclosures.

ILLUSTRATION 12-7
Sample State University
Segment Information Disclosure

The University has issued revenue bonds with the net revenues from the segments shown below pledged to pay the bond interest and principal. The Dorm Bonds of 1984 renovated the five dorms in the Sleepy Hills complex and their net revenue is pledged. Three separate bond issues (1974, 1979, 1985) have the net revenue from parking operations pledged, with the earliest issue having priority. The hospital addition of 1994 is an obligation of the component unit hospital and the net revenues of the hospital are pledged, and the operation of the attached garage pledged. The University has no legal obligation for the component unit debt. The dormitories provide student housing. Parking operations provides student and employee parking for the University. The hospital is a 205 bed regional medical facility. The medical building is rented to local physicians and other health-related providers.

Bonds due serially through	Dorm Bonds of 1982 (Johnson Hall) 2012	Dorm Bonds of 1984 (Renovation of five units) 2004	Parking Operations (Three bond issues) 2015	Hospital Addition of 1994 2024
Condensed Statement of Net Assets				
Assets:				
Current assets	$1,612,409	$3,566,812	$1,625,130	$11,994,777
Capital assets	5,877,970	16,660,004	5,790,691	25,087,969
Total assets	7,490,379	20,226,816	7,415,821	37,082,746
Liabilities:				
Current liabilities	369,115	727,891	281,836	9,155,856
Long-term liabilities	2,645,012	8,300,335	2,557,733	16,728,300
Total liabilities	3,014,127	9,028,226	2,839,569	25,884,156
Net Assets:				
Invested in capital assets, net of related debt	3,164,876	8,550,004	3,077,597	10,266,109
Restricted:				
Expendable:				
Capital projects	385,000	725,889	297,721	153,854
Debt service	197,483	708,755	110,204	136,720
Unrestricted	728,893	1,213,942	1,090,730	641,907
Total net assets	$4,476,252	$11,198,590	$4,576,252	$11,198,590
Condensed Statement of Revenues, Expenses, & Changes in Net Assets				
Operating revenues	$9,250,197	$28,444,165	$9,162,918	$36,872,130
Operating expenses	(8,805,132)	(27,392,221)	(8,892,411)	(36,964,256)
Net operating income (loss)	445,065	1,051,944	270,507	(92,126)
Nonoperating revenues (expenses):	195,978	444,201	108,699	8,872,166
Change in net assets	249,087	1,496,145	379,206	8,780,040
Net assets—beginning of year	4,227,165	9,702,445	4,197,046	2,418,550
Net assets—end of year	$4,476,252	$11,198,590	$4,576,252	$11,198,590
Condensed Statement of Cash Flows				
Net cash flows provided (used) by:				
Operating activities	$559,048	$2,497,118	$471,769	$10,925,083
Noncapital financing activities	(408,459)	(1,276,491)	(131,180)	6,976,474

(Continued)

ILLUSTRATION 12-7 *Continued*

Capital and related financing activities	(218,015)	(1,520,655)	(305,294)	(9,948,620)
Investing activities	157,834	364,891	70,555	(8,063,074)
Net increase (decrease) in cash	90,408	64,863	105,850	(110,137)
Cash—beginning of year	157,834	564,339	70,555	8,992,304
Cash—end of year	$248,242	$629,202	$176,405	$8,882,167

other student service buildings were built with revenue bonds that are being retired with pledged student services net income. Such information was used by GASB to amend its requirements for segment reporting.[27] At its October 2000 meeting, the GASB board decided that if an institution is required to account for segments separately, such as bond covenant requirements, the institution should disclose the condensed financial statement. However, if a college or university is not required to account for the assets, liabilities, revenues, expenses, and gains or losses regarding revenue-backed debt, then the institution does not have to create accounting just for GASB GAAP display. This means that if the institution is not required by some external body to account for assets and liabilities of a revenue-backed bond issue, it does not have a reportable segment for disclosure in the notes to the financial statement.

The required disclosure includes a condensed statement of net assets; condensed statement of revenues, expenses, and changes in net assets; and condensed statement of cash flows. Illustration 12-7 illustrates a typical segment disclosure for a college or university that had pledged revenue to pay debt obligations. Note that the disclosure explains the nature of the pledge revenue stream and all financial information is highly condensed, displaying only the primary classification in all of the statements.

SUMMARY

The GASB has issued many statements directed to the financial reporting of governments that also provide guidance for colleges and universities in preparing their financial reports. Although GASB believes that accountability is the foundation of governmental accounting and financial reporting, the Board has not been too concerned about improving comparability in the financial statements among industries that have both governmental (public) and nongovernmental (private) members. Thus, financial reporting for public colleges and universities has significant differences from that for private colleges and universities.

This chapter summarized the accounting and reporting principles for public colleges and universities and illustrated the applications of many of the accounting and reporting principles. Public colleges and universities report as business-type activities and use accrual accounting for the recognition of revenues and expenses. These recognitions are governed by GAAP criteria for nonexchange and exchange transactions. General restricted versus unrestricted principles were discussed and illustrated with journal entry examples.

The unique aspect of reporting tuition net of scholarship allowances was discussed and illustrated with journal entries. Other transactions particular to public colleges and universities were discussed and illustrated, including restricted versus unrestricted gifts, grants and investment income, collections, within-organization transactions, and affiliated organizations. Financial statements reported by public colleges and universities include a statement of net assets; statement of revenues, expenses, and changes in net assets; and statement of cash flows. Clemson University financial statements were used to illustrate both the format and content of public college and university financial statements. The chapter also included required GAAP information as well as information regarding financial statement disclosures.

---

[27] **Statement No. 37**, "Basic Financial Statements—Management's Discussion and Analysis—for State and Local Governments: Omnibus" (Norwalk: CT: Governmental Standards Accounting Board, 2001), par. 17.

QUESTIONS

12-1. Identify and discuss the changes made by GASB Statement No. 35 for public college and university financial reporting.

12-2. GASB Statement No. 14 sets forth reporting guidance for a component unit. What is a component unit? How does the component unit differ from an affiliated organization? Discuss how and on what financial statements a governmental college or university presents the component unit information. Include examples.

12-3. What are the objectives of accounting for governmental colleges and universities?

12-4. Distinguish between accounting objectives for a commercial organization and for a public college or university.

12-5. Define and discuss current operations for a governmental college or university.

12-6. List the two basic subgroups for current operating resources and discuss each.

12-7. What is a quasi-endowment and how should it be displayed in the financial statements of public colleges and universities?

12-8. Explain the difference between an exchange and nonexchange transaction.

12-9. What are the criteria that a public college or university must meet in order not to capitalize a collection?

12-10. In accordance with GASB Statement No. 34, what note disclosure or disclosures must colleges and universities report if they use the business-type reporting model and pledge revenues to retire long-term debt.

12-11. What financial statements do public colleges and universities prepare and report in their annual financial report?

12-12. Discuss the purpose served by public college and university financial statements. How is the information used?

12-13. Using FARS, find the GAAP guidance that governs the determination of a current asset and current liability. Identify examples of noncurrent cash and investments.

12-14. Explain the difference between expendable restricted net assets and nonexpendable restricted net assets.

12-15. What is an unrestricted net asset? Provide examples of what items would be reported as unrestricted net assets.

12-16. Where would the various unrestricted net assets be reported in the financial statements of a public college or university?

12-17. What are the four categories public colleges and universities use to report their cash inflows and outflows on the statement of cash flows? Provide an example of an inflow and outflow for each category.

12-18. What financial statements should be included in the annual financial report by a special-purpose college or university engaged in both governmental and business-type activities? Be explicit.

12-19. What are funds functioning as endowments? How are they reported in public college and university annual financial reports?

12-20. What type of resources do governmental colleges and universities hold in trust for others. Provide examples.

12-21. Identify the fund groups used by governmental colleges and universities prior to the issuance of GASB Statement Nos. 34 and 35.

12-22. What types of activities are reported in each of the fund groups identified in Question 12-21? Provide examples of activities accounted for and reported in each fund group.

12-23. Using FARS, determine how FASB Statement No. 57 guidance regarding related parties differs from GASB Statement No. 39 guidance regarding the reporting of affiliated organization information.

12-24. Where, other than GASB standards, can you find guidance regarding accounting and reporting issues for governmental colleges and universities?

12-25. Explain why federal financial aid received by students enrolled in governmental colleges and universities often contributes to the recognition of a revenue discount?

MULTIPLE CHOICE

12-1. Financial statements prepared by colleges and universities are which of the following?
   a. Statement of net assets; statement of revenues, expenses, and changes in net assets; and statement of cash flows
   b. Statement of net assets, other changes in fund balance, and statement of cash flows
   c. Statement of revenues, expenses, and changes in net assets; other changes in fund balance; and statement of cash flows
   d. Statement of net assets; other changes in fund balance; and statement of revenues, expenses, and changes in net assets

12-2. What are users of financial statement information interested in assessing?
   a. The effect of operations and the ability of the institution to continue current programs
   b. How current activities were financed
   c. The cost of the services provided by the institution
   d. All of the above

12-3. Which format is appropriate for presenting accounts receivable in the assets section of a college or university financial statement?
   a. Accounts receivable less allowance for noncollectable
   b. Accounts receivable (less allowance)
   c. Accounts receivable (see footnote)
   d. All of the above

12-4. Which of the following is not a typical operating revenue?
   a. Tuition and fees
   b. Endowment gifts
   c. Nongovernment grants and contracts
   d. Private gifts for operating purposes

12-5. Which of the following is not a typical nonoperating revenue?
   a. Investment income
   b. State appropriations
   c. Grants for acquisition of capital assets
   d. Federal appropriations

12-6. College and university net assets may be restricted by which of the following?
   a. Persons or organizations outside the institution
   b. The institution's governing board
   c. Both a and b
   d. None of the above

12-7. A nonexchange transaction has occurred and should be recognized in the college or university financial records provided that which of the following is (are) true?
   a. The offer of resources is verifiable
   b. All applicable eligibility requirements have been met
   c. The resources are measurable and collection probable
   d. b and c only
   e. a, b, and c

12-8. Which of the following statements would not be included in the annual report of a college or university?
   a. Statement of cash flows
   b. Statement of financial activities
   c. Statement of net assets
   d. Statement of revenues, expenses, and changes in net assets

12-9. When federal financial aid revenue is used to pay the student's tuition and fee accounts receivable, it is considered to be which of the following?
   a. A receipt from a third party
   b. The same as if the student had made the payment

c. Tuition discount and recorded in a contra tuition and fee account
   d. A scholarship expense

12-10. During the year, a college received a gift pledge of $50,000 for scholarships to be awarded in the following fiscal year. How would the pledge be recognized?
   a. As a debit to accounts receivable and a credit to restricted scholarship revenue
   b. As a debit to accounts receivable and a credit to deferred revenue
   c. As a debit to accounts receivable and a credit the restricted expendable net assets
   d. None of the above

12-11. A college received $500,000 toward the construction of a new academic building, which will begin in the following fiscal year. How would the funds received be recognized?
   a. As a credit to restricted expendable revenue
   b. As a debit to deferred expense
   c. As a credit to deferred revenue
   d. Both a and b
   e. None of the above

12-12. Which of the following should be used for public college and university accounting recognition?
   a. Fund accounting and full accrual accounting
   b. Fund accounting and modified accrual accounting
   c. Accrual accounting
   d. Neither accrual accounting nor fund accounting

12-13. Which of the following is an example of operating revenues?
   a. Research contracts
   b. Endowment gifts
   c. Investment income
   d. State appropriations

12-14. A large gift was pledged to State University with the stipulation that the gift, when paid, would be used to provide scholarships to students admitted to the engineering college in the following academic year. How would the pledge for the gift be recognized?
   a. As an unrestricted revenue
   b. As a restricted expendable revenue
   c. As a current accounts receivable
   d. It would not be recorded.

12-15. The following receipts were received by State University.

Unrestricted gifts used to support educational activities	$750,000
Federal research contract that was completed this year	$100,000
Scholarship gift restricted for next fiscal year	$ 50,000
Capital appropriations	$250,000

What is the total amount that would be included in the current year's operating revenues?

a. $850,000
b. $1,000,000
c. $800,000
d. $1,150,000

12-16. The following information was available in the Mervale State College financial records for the year ended May 31, 2005.

Restricted gifts for the English Department received	$25,000
Restricted gifts for the English Department expended	$20,000
Unrestricted gifts for the Engineering College received	$75,000
Unrestricted gifts for the Engineering College expended	$60,000

What amount would be recognized as operating revenue for Mervale State College for the year ended May 31, 2005?

a. $80,000
b. $25,000
c. $75,000
d. $100,000

12-17. The following information was available in the Mervale State College financial records for the year ended May 31, 2005.

$25,000 cash gift restricted for the History Department's use was received.

$20,000 of the prior year pledge for the history department was received.

$75,000 education training grant for the Nursing College was received.

$50,000 of the prior year pledge for the Nursing College was received.

What amount would be recognized as operating revenue for Mervale State College for the year ended May 31, 2005?

a. $100,000
b. $70,000
c. $75,000
d. $50,000

12-18. For 2005, North State University billed its students $2,500,000 for tuition and fees. Federal financial aid was used to pay $1,400,000 of the amount billed. The students remitted $900,000, and local service clubs paid $200,000 on behalf of various students. What is the amount of tuition and fee revenue that will be reported by North State University in its statement of revenues, expenses, and changes in net assets?

a. $2,500,000
b. $2,300,000

c. $1,400,000
d. $1,100,000
e. $900,000

12-19. An endowment of $750,000 was received in cash by Southern State College. Which of the following is correct?

a. $750,000 will be reported as nonoperating revenue.
b. $750,000 will be reported as deferred revenue.
c. $750,000 will be reported as other revenue.
d. $750,000 will be reported as a direct addition to the restricted nonexpendable net assets.

12-20. Westfield State University sponsored a fund-raising banquet to celebrate the university's founding in 1937. Each attendee was charged $100 to attend the event. The hotel where the banquet was held catered the event and charged the University $24 for each dinner served. Which of the following statements is true.

a. The university will recognize a restricted gift of $100 for each attendee.
b. The university will recognize unrestricted revenue of $76 for each attendee.
c. The amount charged by the university is considered a nonexchange transaction.
d. The amount charged by the university is considered only as an exchange transaction.

12-21. Which GASB Statement allows colleges and universities to report as a special-purpose government or a business-type activity?

a. GASB No. 35
b. GASB No. 36
c. GASB No. 27
d. GASB No. 14

12-22. The objectives of accounting, whether for a commercial enterprise or for a public college or university, are which of the following?

a. To help managers effectively allocate and use resources
b. To assist others who wish to evaluate the financial operation of the organization
c. Both a and b
d. None of the above

12-23. What are the two basic subgroups of current resources?

a. Exchange and nonexchange
b. Unrestricted and restricted
c. Nonoperating and operating
d. None of the above

12-24. Which of the following determines the use of quasi-endowment resources?

a. Donor
b. Time
c. Governing board
d. Purpose

12-25. Unrestricted resources are considered revenue when which of the following occurs?

a. They are received.
b. They are spent.
c. The time limitation is up.
d. The purpose limitation is met.

12-26. Which of the following is a criterion for recognizing nonexchange transactions?
    a. Offer of resources is verifiable.
    b. Resources are measurable and probable for collection.
    c. All applicable eligibility requirements have been met.
    d. All of the above are true.

12-27. Which of the following is among the criteria for not capitalizing collections?
    a. Collection is held for pubic exhibition.
    b. Collection does not have to maintained.
    c. Proceeds from collections may be used for any purpose.
    d. All of the above are true.

12-28. GASB Statement No. 34 requires business-type activities to distinguish their revenue and expenses as which of the following?

a. Current and noncurrent
b. Restricted and unrestricted
c. Operating and nonoperating
d. None of the above

12-29. A college received an endowment gift of $1,000,000. In what net asset class will the endowment gift be reported?
    a. Unrestricted net assets
    b. Restricted nonexpendable net assets
    c. Restricted expendable net assets
    d. Capital assets net of related debt

12-30. Which of the following is not a category used by public colleges and universities to report cash inflows and outflows?
    a. Operating
    b. Financing
    c. Investing
    d. None of the above

EXERCISES

EXERCISE 12-1   Classification of revenues by public colleges and universities
EXERCISE 12-2   Public college and university recognition of tuition revenue
EXERCISE 12-3   Cash flow classifications used by public colleges and universities
EXERCISE 12-4   Internet problem
EXERCISE 12-5   Public college and university recognition of an unconditional promise
EXERCISE 12-6   Recognition of donated equipment
EXERCISE 12-7   Revenue display used by public colleges and universities
EXERCISE 12-8   Miscellaneous journal entries
EXERCISE 12-9   Recognition of tuition and fee discount
EXERCISE 12-10   Operating versus nonoperating revenues
EXERCISE 12-11   Multiple-year grant revenue recognition
EXERCISE 12-12   Financial statement notes disclosure requirements

EXERCISE 12-1   The following are various types of revenue typically received by a public college or university.
    1. Tuition and fees
    2. Endowment gifts
    3. Annuity contract revenues
    4. Federal appropriations
    5. Capital gifts not capitalized
    6. Auxiliary enterprises
    7. State grants and contracts
    8. Private gifts for operating purposes
    9. Investment income
    10. Sales and service of educational activities

Required:
Classify the types of revenue as either operating or nonoperating. Explain why you classified the revenue as a particular type.

EXERCISE 12-2 Good Hope University received a Pell grant in the amount of $8,000,000, of which $7,000,000 was allocated to reduce student accounts receivable. The university has Student Accounts Receivable in the amount of $10,000,00 for the fall semester.

Required:
Prepare general journal entries to record these transactions.

EXERCISE 12-3 Operating activities, nonfinancing activities, capital and related financing activities, and investing activities are classifications on the cash flow statement reported by governmental colleges and universities.
  A. Tuition and fee revenue
  B. Endowment gifts
  C. Resident halls revenue
  D. Corporate bond purchase
  E. Investment income
  F. Bookstore revenue
  G. Sale of stock
  H. Research grant expense
  I. State appropriations
  J. Proceeds from the sale of capital assets
  K. Salary and wages paid to employees
  L . Purchase of new equity investments
  M. Acquisition of new chemistry laboratory equipment
  N. Research grant revenue
  O. Student financial aid expenses

Required:
Determine the classification for each of the following activities.

EXERCISE 12-4 (Internet Research) On the Internet, find a financial statement for a public college or university. (*Hint*: Try a search question in www.google.com. If that fails, try www.oakton.edu/resource/fin)

Required:
Compare this financial statement to the exhibits in this chapter. Determine and list any display differences. Using information found in the chapter, explain whether the differences are GAAP.

EXERCISE 12-5 Teachum State University received an unconditional promise to give $20,000 with no donor-stipulated restriction. Of this amount, $12,000 was received in the current fiscal year. The university estimated that 2 percent of the pledge would not be collected.

Required:
Prepare the general journal entry, or entries, to record these transactions and indicate the effect that the pledge will have on the net assets of the university.

EXERCISE 12-6 In September 2005, the Goodbill Manufacturing donated research equipment to Wildflower State University. The equipment's original cost was $300,000, and the equipment has a current fair value of half that amount. The equipment has an estimated remaining useful life of six years, with no salvage value. No restrictions were imposed on the gifted equipment.

Required:
Prepare the general journal entry, or entries, to recognize the donated equipment during fiscal year 2005–2006 by Wildflower State University.

EXERCISE 12-7 South Bay Community College billed its students $15,000,000 in tuition and fees for the 2005 spring semester. The college estimates that 2 percent of the tuition and fees will not be paid. During the semester, $3.5 million in institutional scholarship aid was awarded to students. Due to various reasons, refunds to students who withdrew amounted to $85,000.

Required:
Determine the amount of tuition and fee revenue South Bay Community College will report for the 2005 spring semester.

EXERCISE 12-8
The following are various financial transactions at several public colleges and universities.
1. Students attending Statewide University prepaid $350,000 in tuition and fees before the beginning of the fiscal year for the upcoming 2006 fall semester.
2. John Jones promised to give Old State University $4,000,000 to establish an endowed professorship.
3. Pullman State University received $25,000 and is holding the resources in trust for the student History Club.
4. Jefferson State College paid $510,000 in salary together with an additional $112,000 in pension and employer fringe benefits.
5. The English Department at Lakeland Community College acquired $3,500 worth of paper and other office supplies from the Chemistry Department.
6. Bishop State University just received an unrestricted cash gift of $25,000.
7. Jesse James donated copier equipment worth $75,000 to Collins College with the stipulation that the equipment be used in the library. The copier has an estimated three years of remaining life and no salvage value.
8. John Jones delivered a check for $2,000,000 to the president that is part of the gift described in item 2.
9. Seaway College just received $50,000 with a donor stipulation that the gift must be used to support the choir's trip to Europe during the next academic year.
10. Research contract and grant expenses totaling $17,500 were incurred and paid.

Required:
Prepare the general journal entry, or entries, to record the above transactions. Indicate whether the transaction will be reported as an operating transaction, nonoperating transaction, or balance sheet entry.

EXERCISE 12-9
Central College received a Pell grant in the amount of $6,000,000, of which $4,000,000 was allocated to reduce student accounts receivable. Central College has student account receivable in the amount of $8,000,000 for the fall semester.

Required:
Prepare journal entries to record these transactions. Explanations may be omitted.

EXERCISE 12-10
The following information was available in the Central College financial records for the year ended May 31, 2003.

Tuition and fees	$250,000
Endowment gifts	$100,000
Investment income	$350,000
Federal grants	$500,000
Capital gifts not capitalized	$200,000
State appropriations	$400,000
Private gifts for operating purposes	$50,000

Required:
A. What amount would be recorded as operating revenue?
B. What amount would be recorded as nonoperating revenue?

EXERCISE 12-11
During fiscal year 2005, State University was awarded a research project grant of $3,000,000. The grant sponsor agreed to pay the funds in three installments over three years. During the first year, $1,000,000 was spent and the first installment payment was received.

Required:
Prepare a journal entry to record the revenues and expenses recognized by State University during fiscal year 2005.

EXERCISE 12-12   Various financial notes disclosures are presented in the financial statements of public colleges and universities.

Required:
Identify and discuss at least 15 examples of the typical note disclosures reported by public colleges and universities.

PROBLEMS

PROBLEM 12-1   (Internet Research) Retrieve a college or university's financial statement from the Internet, a university financial officer, or the university's library archives.

Required:
Compare the financial information in this financial statement to the financial data displayed in the financial statements in the chapter. In a short report (number of pages determined by your professor), discuss the information provided by the report format and compare it to the financial statements found in the chapter.

PROBLEM 12-2   Good Hope University reported the following information on its financial statements dated June 30, 2005: land, $12,500,000; library materials, $35,200,550; buildings, $105,125,600; furniture, fixtures, and equipment, $45,600,500; land improvements, $3,780,230; capitalized collections, $2,450,000; and infrastructure, $7,040,300. The accumulated depreciation was infrastructure, $1,845,200; library materials, $10,472,104; buildings, $25,780,430; capitalized collections, $1,180,000; furniture, fixtures, and equipment, $15,299,030; and land improvements, $1,240,350. Depreciation for the year was infrastructure, $89,300; library materials, $1,450,300; buildings, $ 2,125,784; capitalized collections, $125,300; furniture, fixtures, and equipment, $2,503,762; and land improvements, $72,890.

Good Hope University also reported the following additions and retirements: infrastructure, additions of $450,340 and retirements of $103,200; land improvements, additions of $356,100; furniture, fixtures, and equipment, additions of $2,345,600; library materials, additions of $1,670,850 and retirements of $450,345; and buildings, additions of $2,650,500.

Required:
Prepare the required disclosure of capital asset information for Good Hope University as of June 30, 2005.

PROBLEM 12-3   Northtown University reported the following information on its financial statements dated June 30,2005: lease obligations, $4,350,780; compensated absences, $3,650,825; revenue bonds payable, $8,659,230; and general obligation bonds payable, $16,675,890. The following were additions and reductions: compensated absences, additions of $467,820 and reductions of $389,465; lease obligations, additions of $525,780 and reductions of $750,802; general obligation bond payable, additions of $2,345,900 and reductions of $1,890,670; and revenue bonds payable, additions of $1,625,900 and reductions of $1,160,500. The current portion of long-term liabilities is as follows:

lease obligations, $560,800; compensated absences, $453,825; general obligation bonds payable, $2,855,325; and revenue bonds payable, $460,358.

Required:

Prepare the required disclosure of information about Northtown University's long-term liabilities for June 30, 2005.

PROBLEM 12-4   Haverton University had the following balances and information as of June 30, 2005.

Net Assets—beginning of year	$165,800,458
Additions to permanent endowments	83,125
Salaries—faculty	33,248,150
Salaries—exempt staff	27,450,600
Salaries—nonexempt staff	4,945,200
Student tuition and fees	35,925,490
Investment income	2,360,250
State and local grants and contracts	3,650,200
Nongovernment grants and contracts	750,835
Sales and services of educational departments	15,803
Residential life (net of scholarship allowances of $435,450)	27,090,282
Bookstore (net of scholarship allowances of $158,300)	9,145,500
Other operating revenue	145,600
State appropriations	38,845,300
Capital appropriations	2,065,750
Federal grants and contracts	9,843,500
Gifts	135,000
Capital grants	743,900
Interest on capital asset–related debt	1,230,125
Benefits	17,485,443
Scholarships and fellowships	2,950,800
Utilities	17,347,200
Depreciation	5,834,290
Supplies and other services	11,780,250
Other nonoperating revenue	254,600

Required:

Prepare a statement of revenues, expenses, and changes in net assets for Haverton University for the fiscal year ended June 30, 2005.

PROBLEM 12-5   During fiscal year 2005, Lewis State University began to conduct a biological research project funded by a $2,500,000 grant. The grant sponsor agreed to pay the funds in four installments over two years. During the first year of the grant, $1,150,000 was spent and the first two installment payments were received.

Required:

Prepare a journal entry to record the revenues and expenses recognized by Lewis State University during fiscal year 2005 for the research grant.

PROBLEM 12-6   The following is a list of transactions that occurred at Buckboard State College during fiscal year 2006.

Required:

Prepare an explanation for each transaction.

1. What accounting recognition should be made regarding an addition to State University's art collection?
2. The governing body of the institution transferred previously unrestricted money into an account to match federal funds provided for the Perkins student loan program in accordance with federal requirements.
3. What recognition should be made for a pledge of $50,000 received by a state college or university?

4. Cash was donated to State University with the stipulation that the money must be used for scholarships. What issues must be addressed in order for State University to record the donation?
5. An unrestricted cash donation of $25,000 was given to the institution by a former student. How is the donation recognized?
6. Groups of stocks and bonds were given to the institution with the stipulation that all income generated from the stocks and bonds would be used to fund scholarships and fellowships in the College of Education. How is the receipt of the stocks and bonds recorded on the institution's accounting records?

PROBLEM 12-7 The cash flow statement has the following classification of activities: (1) operating, (2) noncapital financing, (3) capital and related financing activities, and (4) investing activities. Central State College had the following transactions during the year:

Required:
Determine the classification of each of the following transactions for Central State College. What was the total amount reported on the cash flow statement for each classification?

A. The college collected $500,000 in tuition and fees.
B. The science department received $100,000 for a research grant.
C. Students paid $200,000 in dormitory fees.
D. Corporate bonds in the amount of $80,000 were purchased.
E. The bookstore revenue was $150,000.
F. Stock was sold in the amount of $30,000.
G. $100,000 was received as an endowment gift.
H. The college received $50,000 investment income.
I. The college borrowed $50,000 for operating activities.
J. The college purchased new computer equipment for $10,000.
K. The college purchased new office furniture for the administration for $20,000.

PROBLEM 12-8 Central State College had the following balances and information as of June 30, 2005.

Net Assets—beginning of year	$155,600,000
Salaries—faculty	$25,800,00
Salaries—staff	$20,350,000
Student tuition and fees	$32,690,000
Investment income	$2,700,000
State and local grants and contracts	$2,452,000
Sales and services of educational departments	$600,000

Residential life revenue (net of scholarship allowance of $350,000) is $22,375,000.
All Revenue is pledged as security for revenue bonds Series 1995

Other operating revenue	$160,000
State appropriations	$36,250,000
Capital appropriations	$3,900,000
Gifts	$125,000
Capital grants	$800,000
Interest on capital asset–related debt	$1,350,000
Benefits	$12,500,000
Scholarships and fellowships	$2,400,000
Utilities	$10,600,000
Depreciation	$4,800,000
Supplies and other services	$8,950,000
Other nonoperating revenue	$340,000

Required:
Prepare a statement of revenues, expenses, and changes in net assets for Central State College for the fiscal year ended June 30, 2005.

PROBLEM 12-9 The following is a list of various assets held by Elizabeth State College.

Accrued interest payable	$118,158
Cash and cash equivalents	1,728,123

Construction funds in trust	11,793,706
Current pledge receivable (net)	1,167,950
Current prepaid expenses	602,357
Inventories	249,793
Long-term investments	39,573,677
Other current assets	493,371
Other noncurrent assets	623,927
Pledge receivables and bequest in probate court	3,661,731
Property plant and equipment (net)	48,518,206
Short-term marketable securities	2,362,409
Student educational loans (net)	1,113,286
Student receivables (net)	280,868

Required:

Prepare a schedule of the current assets that Elizabeth State College will list in this year's annual financial report.

PROBLEM 12-10 Jenson State University had the following statement of new assets as of July 1, 2004, the first day of the fiscal year (in thousands of dollars).

Assets	
Current assets	
Cash and equivalents	2,562
Short-term investments	14,266
Accounts receivable (net)	6,027
Inventories	578
Deposit with trustee	3,333
Notes receivable (net)	356
Other assets	426
Total current assets	27,548
Noncurrent assets	
Long-term investments	20,551
Notes receivable	1,946
Investment in real estate	6,341
Capital assets (net)	157,404
Total noncurrent assets	186,242
Total assets	213,790
Liabilities	
Current liabilities	
Accounts payable	4,832
Deferred revenue	2,782
Long-term liabilities	3,999
Total current liabilities	11,613
Noncurrent liabilities	
Deposits	1,109
Deferred revenue	1,727
Long-term liabilities	30,696
Total noncurrent liabilities	33,532
	45,145
Net Assets	
invested in capital assets	122,709
Restricted	
Nonexpendable	
Financial aid	10,799
Research	3,722
Expendable	
Financial aid	3,208
Research	3,117
Department use	100

Student loans	2,324
Capital projects	3,210
Debt service	2,250
Other	239
Unrestricted	16,967
Total Net Assets	168,645

During the fiscal year ended June 30, 2005, the following transactions occurred (in thousands of dollars).

I. Operating revenue and expense transactions during the year

A. Billed tuition and fees	39,913
Students paid in cash	37,000
B. Billed residential life	28,030
Students paid in cash	28,000
C. Bookstore cash sales receipts	10,000
D. New grants revenue received in cash	18,800
E. New grant applied to accounts receivables	3,000
and recognized as tuition discount	
F. Other income received in cash	145
G. Expenses recorded and paid in cash	
Salary, wages, and benefits	88,827
Financial aid paid to students	3,800
Utilities	16,500
Supplies and commodities	12,500
Depreciation	6,800

II. Other revenue received in cash

A. State appropriation	39,800
B. State appropriations for capital	2,075
C. Gifts and contributions	1,820
D. Gifts to acquire capital assets	700
E. New endowment gift	100
F. Nonoperating revenues	310
G. Investment income	2,180

III. Other cash disbursements

Interest paid on capital debt	1,330

IV. Other nonoperating cash transactions during the year.

A. Invested cash in short-term investment	1,100
B. Invested cash in long-term investment	10,000
C. Acquired additional inventory	110
D. Acquired new capital assets	7,000
E. Paid outstanding accounts payable	2,000
F. Paid long-term debt principal	1,000
G. Increased funds on deposit with trustee	500

V. Beginning-of-year restricted net assets expended as part of current year costs recognized

A. Financial aid	300
B. Research supplies	1,500
C. Capital project supplies	2,500
D. Debt service	500
E. Other	200

Required:

A. Prepare the journal entries for each of the transactions. (*Hint*: Record all expenses as unrestricted and reimburse when recording item V entries.

B. Prepare, in good form, a statement of net assets for Jenson State University as of June 30, 2005.

C. Prepare, in good form, a statement of revenues, expenses, and changes in net assets for Jenson State University for the fiscal year ended June 30, 2005.

D. Prepare, in good form, a statement of cash flows for Jenson State University for the fiscal year ended June 30, 2005.

A QUICK GUIDE TO ACCESSING DATABASES FOR THE PROFESSIONAL ACCOUNTANT

LEARNING OBJECTIVES

After reading this chapter, you should be able to:

- Identify research databases commonly used by accounting professionals.
- Perform basic data retrieval from selected databases.
- Be familiar with database search tools and Boolean logic.
- Understand the definitions and concepts of both common and uncommon search terms, words, and commands used in database searches.

The ability to conduct accounting research is as important to an accounting professional as knowledge of accounting, auditing, or tax rules and standards. In fact, an understanding of accounting research may be more important because the rules and standards change, sometimes frequently, while the reason for and basic rules on how to conduct accounting research do not change. As a result, the knowledge of how to conduct accounting research will enable the successful accounting professional to keep up with the rapid change occurring in the profession. In addition to gathering information on new rules and standards, accounting research can also be used to gather important information on clients and legislation relevant to clients and the accountant.

This supplement introduces research tools commonly used in practice by professional accountants. The first section presents basic search information common to most databases. This section also provides helpful tips for conducting searches of these databases. The next section provides an overview of several databases commonly used by accountants. Finally, a glossary of common terms is provided to make conducting keyword searches more readily understandable.

INFORMATION COMMON TO MOST DATABASES

Information in electronic databases is frequently accessed through a keyword search. The person conducting the search provides the search engine with a word or phrase that will result in the computer finding items in the database that match the word or phrase. If the words entered into the search are too general, a large number of matches (hits) will be found. For example, suppose a student is conducting a search in ABI/INFORM (a common database for literature in business) for a paper on goodwill impairment. If the word *goodwill* is entered, more than 700 hits are returned. Some of these articles may address goodwill impairment, but many will not. This may not always be bad when writing a paper for a class. A larger number of articles could provide background information and add to the bibliography. However, when conducting research for clients, a large number of hits could result in additional cost to the client because the search was not conducted efficiently. If the search is narrowed to *goodwill impairment*, the number of hits decrease to fewer than 10.

Searches can be conducted in two ways: from the general to the specific or from the specific to the general. If the search is conducted from the general to the specific, several searches will likely be needed. Each successive search narrows the topic until the desired information is located. It is possible that the searcher may be lucky and the desired result located on the first search. If the search is conducted from the specific to the general, the initial search is defined as narrowly as possible with the intent of locating exactly what is desired. It is possible that the search may be off-target and the desired item may not be included. In that case, an additional inquiry is needed to broaden the search. Care should be taken to broaden the search as little as deemed necessary to locate additional items.

Regardless of the approach taken, conducting a successful keyword search requires conscious effort. Understanding the information included in different databases and how that information is accessed will increase the probability that the initial search will locate the desired information. The search approach supported here is to work from the specific to the general. The following suggestions are provided to reduce the number of searches required, making the search process more efficient.

The first suggestion is to carefully analyze the question when choosing a starting point. Distinctive words or phrases are more likely to result in a limited number of hits when the search is conducted. Think about the word or phrase and how common it might be in the database being searched. It is important to consider the database when choosing words or phrases. Each database used by accounting professionals is specialized, and certain words and phrases will occur more frequently in that database than in other databases. Remember that using only common or general words and phrases may result in too many hits to be useful. When choosing the starting point, it is also important to consider synonyms or equivalent terms that might be in the database. Failure to consider such terms may cause the search to miss the needed item. The purpose of thinking about the topic before starting a search is to determine the search terms and the search tool features that may lead to a successful search. The following list summarizes some approaches that might be helpful in choosing a starting point for a search.

Search Features	Suggestion
Distinctive word or phase	Requires terms to appear in order listed. Enclose in double quotations " ". Test-run word or phrase
No distinctive word	Combine terms to narrow your search using Boolean logic (discussed later)
Narrow aspect of broad or common topic	Keep an open mind about how to focus the search
Synonyms, equivalent term, variants	Use Boolean logic, OR truncation (explained later)
Confused?	Keep you mind open. Luck is always on your side.

The second suggestion is to take the time needed to understand how the database interprets the words provided by the searcher. A keyword search finds all the records with that specific word(s). The example presented previously used the phrase *goodwill impairment* to locate fewer than 10 relevant articles. The ABI/INFORM database interprets *goodwill impairment* as a single search term. Other databases to be discussed later would interpret *goodwill impairment* as a search for *goodwill* and a search for *impairment* unless the search phrase is enclosed in quotes. By surrounding the words in quotes, the search engine finds only those records that contain those exact words in the exact order presented within the " ". Failure to understand how the database search engine interprets search terms can cause the search process to be much longer than necessary.

Another aspect of the search engine's interpretation of the words and phrases pertains to whether the search engine allows the use of Boolean logic. This approach allows the searcher to combine word and phrases in a manner that make the search much more specific. For example, a search can be conducted on *"goodwill impairment"* (placed in quotes) or the search can be for *goodwill and impairment.* Either search will likely result in the search engine looking for information in the database where the words goodwill and impairment are together. The word *and* is part of the Boolean logic, a specific instruction to find one word and the other word together. While it may seem equally as easy to enter either of the above search phrases, an example is provided later where the use of Boolean logic makes the search command much easier to write than attempting to use quotes. The following list provides some of the more common words and symbols that can be used to combine search terms.

Option	Symbols	Example	Result
AND	&	Capital&assets Capital and assets	Finds records that contain both words
OR	|	Capital|assets Capital or assets	Finds records that contain either word
Not	^	Capital^assets Capital not assets	Finds records that contain capital but not assets
Exclusive or (xor)	~	Capital~assets Capital xor assets	Finds records that contain either word but not both
AND and OR		(Fair OR Market) AND "debt instrument"	Finds both *fair* and *market* in combination with *debt* instrument
Wildcards			
Uncertain	?	vest?	Finds words that include *vest*, such as *vested* and *vestee*
Root word search	%	Invest%	Finds words with *invest* as a root, such as *invested, investor, investment*
Letter pattern	+*	Inves*	Finds words with a common beginning, such as *investment* and *invested*
Synonym	$	Invest$	Finds synonyms for *invest*, including *endow, spend, confer, induct, install*

A third suggestion is to remember that keyword searches often require the searcher to learn during the search process. Be careful to notice search approaches that are successful. Future searches will be much more efficient if things learned previously are applied to new situations. Remember that some databases are similarly organized, so approaches that work on one database may work in another.

The fourth suggestion is not to get bogged down in a strategy that does not work. If the search seems to be moving away from the objective, do not hesitate to abandon the approach for something new. Remember that not all databases are organized the same. An approach that works in one database will not necessarily work in another database.

The fifth suggestion is to recall that searches are an iterative process. One step leads to the next. Do not hesitate to return to previous strategies to get back on track. For example, if the search is in the third iteration and the search leads to too many hits, go back to the second iteration results and try to determine another direction that will broaden the search less than the unsuccessful attempt.

OVERVIEW OF COMMONLY USED DATABASES

Most professional accountants have a variety of different databases at their disposal when research is needed. This section focuses on several of the most common databases. A list of additional helpful sites is listed at the end of the section.

Financial Accounting Research System

The Financial Accounting Research System (FARS) is a powerful tool that enables professional accountants to search generally accepted accounting principles (GAAP) and related documents that help the accountant understand how GAAP applies to a particular situation. Understanding how to use FARS enables the professional accountant to better address the challenges that arise. The following information and data are contained in the FARS database:

Original pronouncements. Financial Accounting Standards Board (FASB) and American Institute of Certified Public Accountants (AICPA) pronouncements (including totally superseded pronouncements): FASB Statements, Interpretations, Technical Bulletins, and Concepts Statements; Accounting Research Bulletin (ARB) Nos. 43–51; Accounting Principles Board (APB) Opinions and Statements; and AICPA Accounting Interpretations and Terminology Bulletins.

Current text. Integration of financial accounting and reporting standards arranged by topic. Contains General Standards, Industry Standards, and *Current Text* sections that have been totally superseded but are still applicable due to a delayed effective date.

EITF abstracts. Full text of each abstract for every issue discussed by the FASB's Emerging Issues Task Force since its inception in 1984. Also includes EITF topical index.

Implementation guides. Questions and answers from FASB Special Reports and other published implementation guidance.

Topical index. Combined index of original pronouncements, current text, EITF abstracts, and question-and-answer infobases. This comprehensive index provides information regarding the location of material in the different publications.

Derivative instruments and hedging activities. Presents FASB Statement No. 133 as amended by Statement Nos. 137 and 138.

After installing FARS on the hard drive, an icon will appear on the desktop. Even though an icon exists, the FARS CD is still required to be in the machine to access the database. Clicking on the FARS icon starts the program, and the screen displays a toolbar across the top of the screen, the infobases linked to the FARS menu appear in the middle of the screen, and tabs appear across the bottom of the screen that allow different views of information.

The screen displays drop-down menus at the top of the screen (File, Edit, View, Search, Tools, Window, and Help). These drop-down menu titles are typical of those in many other computer programs. Other than the Help menu, there is likely little reason to use the drop-down menus on the opening page.

The other item at the top of the screen is the toolbar. The toolbar items are unique to FARS. For example, the first toolbar item is the file folder that opens the various infobases. The second item is the export tool that allows the record to be exported to another drive. The third item is the standard printer.

Following the printer are tools that allow the tagging (marking records for future action) or untagging of records. The arrows enable the researcher to move through the windows that have been opened. The next item on the toolbar is the query window, which is followed by binoculars that provide for advanced queries (large binoculars) and queries (small binoculars) and to clear the current query (an X over large binoculars). The balance of the toolbar items are standard symbols used to advance either forward or backward.

The Query Tool, Advanced Query, and Query buttons are active while in the opening screen; however, attempting to conduct a search from the opening screen yields a message of no hits for the current query. Before conducting a search, it is necessary to choose an infobase. For example, click on Original Pronouncements to open a screen where all of the original pronouncement series are listed, such as Accounting Principles Board Opinions, Accounting Terminology Bulletins, and Financial Accounting Standards Board Statements of Financial Accounting Standards. Any of the series can be selected to obtain a detailed listing of original pronouncements in that series.

When the Original Pronouncement screen opens, one change to the toolbar will be visible as the Go Back arrow becomes active. However, an important change occurs to one of the drop-down menus. The Search menu has several additional items added to the bottom of the menu (Search by Issue Date, Search ONLY Current Documents, Search within a single OP document title, and Search within a single OP document type). Selecting other infobases (Current Text, EITF Abstracts, and Implementation Guides) results in fewer additional options on the Search drop-down menu, and selecting the Derivative Instruments and Hedging Activities or the Topical Index does not change the Search drop-down menu.

Click on Statement of Financial Accounting Standards to reveal the list of all FASB Statements. Any Standard can be chosen to reveal the complete text of the document. The same is true for the documents in any of the other lists. When the subcategory (e.g., Statement of Financial Accounting Standards) to the main menu options (e.g., Original Pronouncements) is selected (except the Derivative Instruments and Hedging Activities and the Topical Index), there is an important change to one of the drop-down menus at the top of the screen. Clicking on the View menu reveals an important choice (*All* Records and Records with *hits*). The default when the FARS system was opened is All Records. This default is changed to the Records with Hits when the subcategory is activated. This will result in searches showing only paragraphs that contain hits when searches are conducted. If more information is desired, change this drop-down menu to All Records.

Example: Information is needed on goodwill impairment for a research paper. Preliminary research identifies FAS 142 ("Goodwill and Other Intangible Assets") as the likely place to locate relevant information. Open the FARS database and click on the Original Pronouncements section of the database. Next, click on Statement of Financial Accounting Standards and then on FAS 142. At this point, the top window shows that FAS 142 is the document and the bottom window shows the text of FAS 142.

Now that the correct standard has been located to conduct the search, click on the large binoculars in the toolbar, just to the right of the toolbar area where a search could be typed. A box opens with the heading Advanced Query. Two small screens are at the top of the box (Word and Records with hits—0). Beneath these boxes is a third box titled Query For:. Type *goodwill impairment* in the bottom box. Notice that the top right-hand box now indicates that there are 171 Records with hits. *Goodwill* is found 597 times and *impairment* 587 times, and the two words are found together 171 times. One interpretation might be that this is a lot of hits to find in FAS 142. This would be a misinterpretation. Even though the search was conducted while in the FAS 142 portion of the database, the search was conducted on the entire database. Click on OK in the window and FAS 142 will be replaced by all of the hits. Notice that a small window appears at the top of the screen (Reference Window). This window identifies the paragraph location of each item retrieved from the database. The window in this example shows that the first hit is in FAS No. 38: "Accounting for Preacquisition Contingencies of Purchased Enterprises." Scrolling down through the bottom window while watching the top window will demonstrate that *goodwill impairment* was found in FAS 38, 121, 142, and 144. Clicking on the Hit List tab at the bottom of the screen will also reveal all of the documents where hits were located.

To search only the document desired, the Search drop-down menu must be used. If the document is specifically known, for example FAS 142, click on Search and then click on Search within a single OP document title. A window will appear with the cursor in the top left-hand box. Either type in *FAS 142* in that box or scroll down the top right-hand box until FAS 142 is located and click on it. Type *goodwill impairment* in the Query For box beneath the Document Title box. Notice that there are 144 hits on *goodwill impairment* in the FAS 142 document. While 144 hits is better than 171 hits, it is still a lot, and many may not be relevant. To focus the search further, apply one of the techniques discussed above. One possibility is to place the search term in quotes so the search engine will look for the words *goodwill* and *impairment* together rather than look for *goodwill* and then look for *impairment*. Running this search yields 56 hits in FAS 142. Again, this is an improvement, but it may still be too many hits.

Recall that FARS searches the database for character strings. As a result, there are several important issues that must be considered when constructing the search terms. With regard to one important issue, capitalization, FARS makes no distinction. A search will yield the same number of hits regardless of the case of the letters. With regard to another important issue, spacing, FARS is not so forgiving. FARS recognizes a difference between *FAS 142* and *FAS142*. A third issue of importance is alternative terms. For example, the term *goodwill impairment* may also be phrased *goodwill impairment loss*. As a result, searching for *goodwill impairment* may result in locating too many items. If the search term is expanded to *"goodwill impairment loss,"* the number of hits in FAS 142 decreases to 17. It is now possible to look at each of the hits on the screen or choose the Hits Tab at the bottom of the screen to see a list of hits in an abbreviated manner.

The preceding example is based on the premise that the words desired will occur together. It is also possible that the words will appear near each other but not necessarily one immediately after the other. Searching for two words in proximity of each other is an extension of a search for specific words. The search can either be for (1) words in a particular order separated by not more than a predetermined number of other words or for (2) words separated by not more than a predetermined number of other words. The syntax for an ordered search is:

"search words"/20   This search is for the words in the stated order within 20 words of each other

The syntax for an unordered search is:

"search words"@20   This search is for the words in any order within 20 words of each other

The search examples presented above are based on a situation where the document of interest was known. It is also possible that the specific document is not known but the type of document (Accounting Principles Board Opinion, Accounting Research Bulletins, etc.) is. In that instance, the search should be conducted by applying the within a single OP document type option in the Search drop-down menu. The search can then be conducted on all documents of that type.

When the desired material is located, the relevant section can be tagged so it can be found or the relevant section can be copied into other documents. To tag a document, highlight the record and click on Edit and then Tag Record. To copy the relevant section to another document, highlight the material desired and then right-click the mouse to copy the material. Go to the document, where it will be inserted. Right-click the mouse and paste the copied material into the new document.

CCH Tax Research NetWork

The Tax Research NetWork contains several "libraries" within the database. The available libraries include the following:

Accounting/Auditing

Federal

State

Financial and Estate

Special Entities

Pension and Payroll

International

Perform Plus II

ClientRelate

To get started, click on the library tab that contains material you wish to search. For example, if searching for U.S. IRS tax codes, the Federal library would be selected.

Once in the selected library, type the search term on the button bar and click Search. Browsing through the search results can identify topics to investigate. To browse, click on the underlined title of the item in the results to see the next level of menus or topics for that term. Continue to click on topics until the specific area of interest is found. From this point, a search for information can be executed by clicking in the checkbox next to the item of interest and clicking Search or by continuing to click on topics until the end of the document is reached.

Common Tax Research NetWork's Searching Techniques   To simultaneously search for multiple words with the same root or other common characters without entering each possibility, use wildcards when typing the search term on the button bar.

Use * in a search term to indicate that any one character can appear at a certain position. If two or more * appear together in the middle of a search term, the system will substitute that many characters. However, if two or more * are placed at the end of a term, the system will substitute that many characters or fewer. For example, *a***culture* will retrieve *agri*culture and *aqua*culture, but not a<u>p</u>iculture, while *tax***** will retrieve *tax, taxes,* and *taxable.*

Use ! at the end of a term to indicate that any number of characters may be substituted there. Using the above example, enter *amort!.* This would retrieve *amortize* as well as other variations, such as *amortizing, amortization,* and *amortized.*

To narrow the search, use proximity connectors to specify a relationship between the terms when more than one search term is used. For example, proximity connectors are useful in a search for documents relating to a tax credit allowed for corporate investment in research facilities. Instead of using the search expression "investment tax credit and research", use the expression "investment tax credit w/20 research". The w/# proximity connector tells the system to search for documents in which the search terms appear within 20 words from each other—not just the same document. The documents found should be more relevant to the research question.

Searching using proximity connectors

- At the main menu, select items to search by clicking the checkbox next to them.
- Type your search expression in the word search box (e.g., ***investment tax credit w/20 research***).
- Click the Search Options button.
- Select the Boolean search method.
- Click the Search button on the button bar.

Use document segments to improve the search results   There are many ways to search for documents, but one of the most effective is to search document "segments" or sections. All documents on the CCH Database system are divided into segments. For example, every document has a heading segment and every case has a case name segment.

Thus, to improve the search results use keywords in a particular segment of the document. For example, if searching for a document on the topic of interest rates, search for the phrase *interest rates* in the heading segment to improve the chances of finding documents that pertain to the topic.

Searching document segments

- At the main menu for your research product, click the tab that you wish to search in.
- Click the checkbox next to an item.
- Type your search term in the word search box (e.g., ***interest rates***).
- Select the segment to search.
- Click the Search Options button.
- In the Search Methods section, click the down arrow and select All Terms.
- Locate the field titled "Search in which part of a document." Click once on the down arrow to display the search segments available.
- Type the letter *H* and the list will scroll to the heading segment.
- Click once on heading.
- Click the Search button in the button bar to execute your search.

Note that all the documents on the search results include the phrase *interest rates* in the heading or title of the document.

Searching for particular document segments   If you are interested only in documents from a certain date or range of dates, you can add a date restriction to your search expression and you will retrieve only those documents that fall within that date range. Many documents on CCH research products such as CCH explanations, laws, and regulations have the current year as the default date and cannot be retrieved by a date-restricted search. Date-restricted searches will retrieve only those documents that contain an "issuance" date, such as cases, rulings, and administrative releases.

- At the appropriate tab, select the items you want to search by clicking the checkboxes next to them.
- Type your search terms in the word search box on the button bar.
- Click the Search Options button.
- Click the Search By Date link.
- Under Select Range, click the drop-down arrow and select On.
- In the spaces provided, select the month and type in the day and year for the document you wish to find.
- Click the Search button on the button bar.

The results will include only those documents from the date specified.

Looking for specific or relevant documents   The CCH database includes a feature that enables the researcher to quickly find the most relevant documents on a Search Results List. Select "Display words around hits on results list" in the Search Results section of Search Options. This way, when the results list appears on the monitor screen, all of the search terms are highlighted in the results list so that the results can be scanned to find the relevant documents.

If the search yields a longer list of documents than expected, rather than starting a new search list, search through all the documents on the Search Results List using a more specific expression. The system will then look through each document on the list for the new search expression.

For example, with the Search Results List on the monitor screen, just type the new expression in the word search box and click Search. The new search expression should be more specific about the subject. For example, if the original search expression was *"credit,"* try a more specific search, such as *"investment tax credit"* or *"economic development zone credit"*.

A new search results list will appear on the monitor screen.

Saving search documents   As searches are performed, selected results can be set aside in a separate list called a Keep List. The Keep List allows the researcher to see at one time all selected searches. In addition, multiple lists may be maintained to organize various search findings.

- With the document on your screen or selected on a document list, click Add Document to Keep List.
- The Keep List will open, displaying the name of the document you added (as well as any other documents you have added previously).
- To return to the document, click Return to Document View.

The Keep List can be displayed whenever needed during a research session just by clicking the Keep List button on the button bar.

Continued searching and use of the available libraries in Tax Research NetWork develops skills and competency so as to minimize the time and effort needed to answer tax-related questions. Among the lessons learned will be the appreciation for the vast number of materials included in the database and the ease of retrieval once search tools and techniques are mastered.

RIA Checkpoint

RIA Checkpoint is an Internet database used for tax research. Its features include the ability to search and retrieve tax data by a point and click process rather than knowing the syntax of the cite. RIA Checkpoint uses a table of contents for researchers to begin their searches. For example, using the Table of Contents, the researcher can choose to perform a word search; search for specific information; retrieve a document by citation; browse through the database table of contents of the various federal, state, or other libraries within the database; retrieve previously saved searches; or view recent searches and docs.

After logging on into the Table of Contents from the database main menu, the researcher selects the source library to research, such as primary source materials, legislation, editorial materials, state and local taxes, or archived materials. Once the desired selection is made, the researcher can continue to point and click within the Table of Contents to find the desired information.

For example, suppose the researcher wanted to research the deductibility of business expenses. The following list of pointing and clicking would be used to "drill down" into the library to find the pertinent information.

1. Since the question of the deductibility of a specific business expense concerns a federal tax issue, the researcher would choose the Federal library.

2. Once in the Federal library, the researcher must decide whether to look at tax legislation, federal editorial material, or federal source material. The researcher would click (select) the Federal Source Material, which opens a new page that lists the various federal material, such as codes and regulations, rulings, court decision, pending legislation, and IRS publications. Given that the researcher wants to know about the deductibility of a specific type of business expense, he or she would click on the code and regulations.

3. This takes the researcher to another screen that asks the researcher to choose among Internal Revenue Code, Final Temporary Proposed and Preambles, Code-Arranged Committee Reports, or U.S. Tax Treaties. The researcher would choose Internal Revenue Code, as that would be the area that would address whether the expenses would be deductible.

4. Now the research must decide whether to search Current Code or Code History. Current Code would be more probable, so the researcher selects Current and is presented with an array or different sets of codes, such as income, estate, excise, trust, and so on. Income Tax is selected.

5. That leads to the types of income taxes—normal, self-employed, withholding, and consolidated returns. The researcher is not yet finished. The next level within the Table of Contents asks the researcher to select the appropriate subchapter, which in this search question would be computation of taxable income. At that screen, the researcher is provided a more detailed list of parts within Subchapter B.

6. Given the deductible question being searched, the Part IV Itemized Deductions for Individuals and Corporations would be selected.

7. Within the itemized deductions, the RIA Checkpoint lists the principal types of deduction. Section 162 is appropriate, as that is the section that addresses the allowance of deductions.

8. Once the search reaches the content of the section, the researcher has the full text of the Tax Code Section. After studying the contents, the researcher can print the materials, save the search, or possibly access related documents by clicking on the highlighted buttons provided within the code materials.

Rather than drilling down through the various screens within the library, RIA Checkpoint also allows the researcher to search for keywords. However, this feature, like keyword searches in other databases, may produce far more responses than the researcher desires unless the researcher streamlines the search language. A major characteristic of RIA Checkpoint is it does not accommodate Boolean search techniques. To streamline the search, the researcher can use the following syntax.

To search for documents...	Use this connector	Example
containing all keywords	space, &, AND	funding deficiency
containing any of the keywords	a vertical line, OR	funding OR deficiency
that contain one keyword but exclude another	^, NOT	funding NOT deficiency
containing an exact phrase	" "	"funding deficiency"
containing variations of the keyword	an asterisk*	defic*

A keyword search can produce full text for a code or regulation by typing the code section of regulation citation in the keywords field using quotation marks, such as "381(c)(4)". RIA Checkpoint also allows the researcher to use keyword searches to search for terms and names that appear as acronyms by making use of "equivalencies" to ensure that, for terms with popular acronyms, searches retrieve both the expanded name and its acronym. An example includes generally accepted accounting principles (GAAP), net operating loss (NOL), and Financial Accounting Standards Board (FASB). However, word searches in RIA Checkpoint do not use quotes when creating a citation search because only parentheses are necessary.

To search for a word or phase...	Use this symbol	Example
within *n* words of another (in any order)	/n (where *n* equals number)	"disclosure exception"/7 related party
within *n* words of another (in exact order)	pre/*n* (where *n* equals number)	"disclosure exception" per/7 related party
within the same sentence (or 20 words) as another (in any order)	/s	"disclosure exception"/s related party
within the same sentence (or 20 words) as another (in exact order)	pre/s	"disclosure exception" pre/s related party
within one paragraph (or 50 words) of another (in any order)	/p	"disclosure exception"/p related party
within one paragraph (or 50 words) of another (in exact order)	pre/p	"disclosure exception" pre/p related party

Generally the database searches are confined to a specific topic or practice area. If specific practice areas are the basis of ongoing searches, the researcher can create and save a specific set of sources as a source set that allows the researcher to query that source set on a continuing basis.

When a keyword search returns a larger number of results than the researcher anticipated, sifting through the output can be a time-consuming process. Rather than sifting through everything one entry after another, the researcher can click on Modify Search on the left sidebar of the program. This action return the researcher to the Keyword Search screen where the researcher can change the keywords to choose another library. Alternatively, the researcher can conduct a Search Within Results. That is, the researcher filters the output by adding additional parameters. This procedure searches the documents returned by the original search and retrieves only those that contain the word set forth in the new parameter.

Once the desired data are located, they can be printed or saved. When saved searches use a phrase or term that has been part of a ongoing database upgrade, RIA Checkpoint displays a message under the search name on the My Folder screen, indicating that the search should be re-created to delete any obsolete information in the saved search. Overall, RIA Checkpoint is an easy-to-employ point-and-click Internet database that is tailor made for tax research.

Government Accounting Research System (GARS)

The GASB's Governmental Accounting Research System (GARS), like FARS, provides efficient and effective access to all the necessary governmental accounting literature. The GARS CD-ROM includes the following databases.

Original pronouncements. GASB Statements, Interpretations, Technical Bulletins, Concepts Statements; NCGA Statements; Interpretations; and selected AICPA Statements of Position.

Codification of governmental accounting and financial reporting standards.
Integration of financial accounting and reporting standards arranged by topic.

Implementation guides. Questions and answers pertaining to selected GASB Statements.

Comprehensive topical index. Combined index of concept statements, pronouncements, and implementation guides.

GARS Searches GARS searches are performed using the same procedures and processes used in FARS searches.

The title display lets you know what infobase and document are currently being viewed and exactly where you are within that document. Just as with FARS, the accounting literature within the infobases can be accessed through Table of Contents entries that link to the appropriate document or text in the document. Topical index references link to the corresponding text in the infobases, and predefined query templates facilitate the most common searches. Queries and advanced queries allow customized searches.

After installing GARS on the hard drive, an icon will be placed on the desktop. Clicking on the GARS icon starts the program, and the screen displays a toolbar across the top of the screen, the infobases linked to the GARS menu appear in the middle of the screen, and tabs appear across the bottom of the screen that allow different views of information.

The screen displays drop-down menus at the top of the screen (File, Edit, View, Search, Tools, Window, and Help). These drop-down menu titles are the same as in FARS and are typical of many other computer programs.

The other item at the top of the screen is the toolbar. The toolbar items are the same as in FARS. For example, the first tool item is the file folder that opens the various infrobases. The second item is the export tool that allows the record to be exported to another drive. The third item is the standard printer.

Following the printer are tools that allow the tagging (marking records for future action) or untagging of records. The arrows enable the researcher to move through the windows that have been opened. The next item on the toolbar is the query window, which is followed by binoculars that provide for advanced queries (large binoculars) and query (small binoculars) and to clear the current query (an X over large binoculars). The balance of the toolbar items are standard symbols used to advance either forward or backward.

As with FARS, an infobase must be opened before conducting a search. A search of the GARS infobase follows the same process and procedures as a FARS search. This enables the researcher to employ research techniques learned using FARS, which were described above.

One of the advantages of using either GARS or FARS is the ability to review information regarding FASB and GASB board member's minority opinions in the standard-setting process; resource materials often include highlighted core conceptual issues on which decision makers disagreed even as they moved forward to provide various forms of guidance. This database research provides an opportunity to discover (1) the variety of pronouncements that speak to even basic accounting concepts and issues, just in different contexts, (2) the diversity of business transactions that must be accounted for in business settings, and (3) the nature of changes over time in guidance is (superseded guidance in the FARS and GARS materials is highlighted in gray).

Other Search Vehicles

While the databases discussed previously will address many issues, it is also possible that other searchable databases may need to be accessed to answer questions. This section presents brief information on databases that may be helpful when determining what other databases may be relevant for a particular situation.

The following websites identify a number of professional organizations and government locations where information can be located.

Organization	Address (precede all with http://www.)	Common Use
AICPA	aicpa.org	Information relevant to professional accountancy, publications, and resource information
CPA Net	cpanet.com/home.htm	Community and resource information for the accounting profession
FASB	fasb.org	Information regarding Board activities, summary of standards, current exposure drafts outstanding, meetings, agendas, press, releases position papers, and e-mail addresses to contact Board members and staff
Federal Accounting Standards Advisory Board	financenet. gov/fasab.htm	Information on current accounting standards, Board activities, and pending exposure drafts
Federal Tax Code	fourmilab. ch/uscode/26usc/	Online access to complete text of the IRS code, with hyperlinks to other tax databases and tax code references

(Continued)

GASB	gasb.org	Information regarding Board activities, details of current projects, publications, exposure drafts, meetings, agendas, press releases, position papers, and e-mail addresses to contact Board members and staff
General Accounting Office	gao.gov	Reports, products, available GAO careers, and federal agency issues
Government Finance Officers Association	gfoa.org	Information concerning publications, periodicals national training, and scholarships
Guidestar (990 tax forms)	guidestar.org	National database of U.S. charitable organizations includes 850,000 IRS-recognized nonprofits
International Accounting Standards Board	iasb.org.uk	Information concerning accounting standards around the world that includes standards, latest news, and publications
IRS Digital Daily	irs.ustres.gov	Information regarding careers, tax statistics, news, and publications
Library of Congress	loc.gov	Research arm of the U.S. Congress
Office of Management and Budget	whitehouse. gov/omb	Information on legislative activities and administrative policy, including the single audit requirements
Securities and Exchange Commission	sec.gov/	Information on publicly held companies; many filings in EDGAR
Tax Research Network	tax.cchgroup.com	Accounting and tax publications and tax software information that covers tax research and preparation, accounting and audition, and practice management

In addition to the organizational and government websites listed above, there are many of commercial locations where valuable information can be located. The following list provides information on three commonly used commercial locations.

Organization	Address (precede all with http://www.)	Common Use
Altavista	Altavista.digital.com	Directory of companies and links to their web page
Hoover's Masterlist Plus	hoovers.com/search/srch2.cgi	Directory of companies and links to their websites
LEXIS-NEXIS	lexisnexis.com/	Tax and legal information
Glossary of Financial Terms Ratios	CPACLASS.com/fsa	Common financial ratios

In addition to locating information about accounting standards and tax regulations, it is often important to assess the financial health and prospects of U.S. business for a variety of reasons. To undertake such a task, it is important to know about the business's structure and activities. This part focuses on gathering such background information. The following list provides information on a limited number of sites where company information can be found.

Address (precede all with http://www.)	Type of Information
annualreportservice.com	Annual financial reports
bankersalmanac.com	Global banking details
bloomberg.com	Investment analysis
barrons.com	Financial news and information
compustat.com	Financial statements
disclosure.com	Stock pricing
edgarscan.pwcglobal.com/recruit/other.html	Financial statement including spreadsheets with specific financial information
freeedgar.com	Financial statements
marketguide.com	Financial research reports and market research information
ml.com	Investment analysis
reportgallery.com	Annual financial reports
thonsonib.com	Investment banking and capital market information and analysis
wsj.com	Financial news and information
zpub.com/sf/art	Annual report library with links to other data providers

In addition to accounting and tax rules and company information, it may be important to know about the major firms that make up the accounting profession. Below are the addresses for the websites of four main international accounting firms. Similar websites can be found for many of the regional accounting firms in the United States.

Ernst & Young LLP	http://www.ey.com/
Deloitte & Touche LLP	http://www.deloitte.com/
KPMG International	http://www.kpmg.com/
PricewaterhouseCoopers LLP	http://www.pwcglobal.com/

Finally, it is often necessary to locate information from the websites of specific companies. Almost all major companies have websites where information can be obtained on such things as products, financial reports, and other investment information. Locating these individual company websites can be done in a variety of ways, such as searching on the company name in www.Google.com or similar search engines.

GLOSSARY

Confused by all the different search terms and techniques or web addresses? The following is a short list of common terms together with their definition or explanation.

BOOKMARK/FAVORITES is the process that enables your computer to return to sites that you have previously visited. Netscape includes BOOKMARK on its toolbar that is used to add direct links. Microsoft Internet Explorer used the term FAVORITES that is on its toolbar. Bookmarks can be Imported, Exported, or downloaded to a diskette so as to install on another computer.

BROWSERS are software programs that enable you to view WWW documents. They "translate" HTML-encoded files into the text, images, sounds, and other features you see. Microsoft Internet Explorer (called simply IE), Netscape, Mosaic, Macweb, and Netcruiser are examples of browsers.

CACHE is a storage location that temporarily accumulates web pages you have visited. A copy of documents you retrieve is stored in the cache. If memory allocated to cache in your computer becomes full, some browsers discard older documents. Microsoft Internet Explorer cache is referred to as History and its ability to store visited web pages is determined by the number of days the computer user has selected to retain visited web page addresses.

COOKIE is a message from a WEB SERVER computer, sent to and stored by the browser on the computer. The main use for cookies is to provide customized Web pages according to a profile of your interests.

DOMAIN is a hierarchical scheme for indicating logical and sometimes geographical venue of a web page from the network. In the United States, common domains are .edu (education), .gov (government agency), .net (network related), .com (commercial), .org (nonprofit and research organizations). Outside the United States, domains indicate country such as ca (Canada), uk (United Kingdom), au (Australia), etc.

DOWNLOAD copies a computer file from one source to another such as saving something found on the Web to a floppy diskette or to the computer's hard drive.

EXTENSION or FILE EXTENSION indicate the type of file. For example, *txt* denotes a text file, *.htm* identifies an HTML file, while jpg, jpeg, bmp or gif identifies an image or picture file.

FTP (File Transfer Protocol) allows the transfer of an entire file from one computer to another.

HTML (Hypertext Markup Language) is a standardized language of computer code, imbedded in "source" documents behind all Web documents, containing the textual content, images, links to other documents (and possibly other applications such as sound or motion), and formatting instructions for display on the screen.

HYPERTEXT is a feature built into HTML that allows a text area, image, or other object to become a "LINK" (as if in a chain) that retrieves another computer file (another Web page, image, sound file, or other document) on the Internet.

LINK is a www address imbedded in another document. If the highlighted link is clicked, the imbedded www address is opened.

NESTING is a term used in Boolean Logic searching to indicate the sequence in which operations are to be performed. Enclosing words in parentheses identifies a group or "nest." Groups can be within other groups. The operations will be performed from the innermost nest to the outmost, and then from left to right.

PDF or .pdf or pdf file is an abbreviation for Portable Document Format, a file format developed by Adobe Systems, that is used to capture almost any kind of document with the formatting in the original. Viewing a PDF file requires Acrobat Reader, which can be downloaded free from Adobe.

SITE or WEBSITE is the term typically used to mean "web page" However, a site is a composite of related pages linked to form the site.

STOP WORDS are used in keyword database searches. For example, when *and, or, in, of* are used in keyword searches they are ignored as search terms. When it is appropriate for these words to be a part of the search term, putting them in quotes " "or adding an + immediately before them makes them searchable.

THESAURUS is a search tool procedure that can be used to identify related terms or keywords.

TRUNCATION is a search tool that allows the researcher to enter the first part of a keyword, insert a symbol (usually *), and the search process accepts any variant spellings or word endings, from the occurrence of the symbol forward. For example, the term *tax** would retrieve *taxation, taxability, taxpayer*, and so on.

URL (Uniform Resource Locator) is the unique address of any Web document. The following is the detailed URL for FASB's project regarding fair value measurement.

Anatomy of a URL:

Type of file (could say ftp:// or telnet://)	http://
Domain name (computer file is on and its location on the Internet)	www.fasb.org/
Path or directory on the computer to this file	project/
Name of file, and its file extension (usually ending in a variation of .html or .htm)	fv_measurement.shtml

WORD VARIANTS are different word endings (such as *-ing, -s, es, -ism, -ist*, etc.) to be retrieved when they are a part of the search terms. One technique to do this is by entering the variants either separated by Boolean Logic OR (and grouped in parentheses).

Other Glossary Sources

If a more comprehensive glossary of search, computer or internet terms is desired, the following web addresses provide definitions that are helpful and easy to understand.

http://www.matisse.net/files/glossary.html

http://www.cnet.com/Resources/Info/Glossary/

http://www.lib.berkeley.edu/TeachingLib/Guides/Internet/Glossary.html

http://www.sharpened.net/glossary/index.php

http://www.yahooligans.com/docs/info/glossary1.html

http://www.masterworkdesign.com/lewis/glossary.htm

http://www.walthowe.com/glossary/

http://mindprod.com/jgloss/jgloss.html

http://www.netlingo.com/

SPECIAL-PURPOSE ENTITIES

LEARNING OBJECTIVES

After reading this chapter, you should be able to:
- Understand the definition of, and purposes for, special-purpose entities.
- Trace the historical development of accounting rules relating to special-purpose entities.
- Understand the relationship among the sponsoring company, the special-purpose entity, and third-party equity interests.
- Develop a foundation for the evaluation of the roles and ethics of those involved in the Enron scandal.

A special-purpose entity (SPE) is an entity that has been established for a specific activity, often for a limited time, and most often to benefit a single company known as the sponsor company. The form of the entity may be a corporation, partnership, trust, or joint venture (wherein more than one sponsor company often participates).[1]

SPEs have served the sponsor companies well by providing several types of benefits in various business circumstances. Often the structure permits off–balance sheet financing because the SPE (which holds debt instruments) is not required to be consolidated. Some SPE structures shelter certain sponsor company assets from potential claims by sponsor company creditors. This reduces the risk associated with lending to finance the creation or acquisition of such assets and therefore enables the financing to be obtained at favorable borrowing rates. Since these vehicles (SPEs) first appeared in the late 1970s, they have been used successfully by numerous corporations to achieve various economies and financial reporting goals.

The use of and improper accounting for SPEs by Enron has recently focused a great deal of attention on SPEs. In fact, the FASB's most recent pronouncement relating to the subject refers to these vehicles as variable interest entities (VIEs).[2] The Financial Accounting Standards Board (FASB) believes that the title "VIE" more broadly expresses the varying financial interest that the sponsor company may have in the financial risk of the entity. To some extent this may also be an attempt to offset the negative publicity

---

[1] Hartgraves, A., and G. Benston, "The Evolving Accounting Standards for Special Purpose Entities and Consolidations," *Accounting Horizons* 16 (September) (2002): 246.

[2] **Interpretation No. 46**, "Consolidation of Variable Interest Entities" (Norwalk, CT: Financial Accounting Standards Board, 2003).

resulting from Enron's use of SPEs. In spite of the Enron problems, the vast majority of SPEs have substance and have been accounted for appropriately. For the sake of consistency, the coverage in this supplement refers to all similar entities as SPEs.

The first section will present a summary of the evolution of GAAP relevant to SPEs. Several examples will be presented in the subsequent section, and this supplement will end with a discussion of the Enron abuses of SPEs.

EVOLUTION OF GAAP WITH REGARD TO SPECIAL-PURPOSE ENTITIES

When a sponsor company establishes an SPE, yet maintains control of its resources and continues to assume the risks associated with that entity, the FASB and Securities and Exchange Commission (SEC) have recognized the need to consolidate the SPE. Consolidation of such SPEs by a sponsor company ensures full disclosure of all assets and liabilities that are on the SPE's books because, effectively, such assets and liabilities are controlled by the sponsor company.

Beginning in the 1980s, the FASB's Emerging Issues Task Force (EITF) identified a series of SPE-related issues for which guidance was needed. EITF 84-30 mandated the consolidation of an SPE's assets and liabilities when that SPE was established solely to hold portfolios of loan receivables of financial institutions.[3] Later, in 1989, the SEC established broader guidelines that outlined circumstances when consolidation was not necessary. The conditions that must be present to enable the SPE to remain unconsolidated generally were that majority ownership must be by an independent party that (1) has made a significant capital investment, (2) controls the SPE, and (3) assumes the normal risks and rewards associated with ownership.

In 1990, EITF 90-15 was released.[4] The guidance was specific to leasing transactions housed in an SPE, but the concepts were consistent with the 1989 SEC principles. EITF 90-15 mandates consolidation when the SPE third-party owner has not made a substantive equity investment. This was interpreted by the SEC to be applicable generally at an investment level of 3 percent of total SPE assets.

As the series of pronouncements was released, it became apparent that the key element was the assumption of risk by the third-party equity investor. While the third party was determined to be required to make at least a 3-percent at-risk investment, the risk could be limited by the sponsor. This is because the authoritative guidance did not prohibit the sponsor company from guaranteeing any or all of the SPE's debt. For example, if the SPE balance sheet has the following values:

A	=	L	+	OE
$10,000,000	=	$9,690,000	+	$310,000
(100%)		(96.9%)		(3.1%)

and the Sponsor Company guaranteed all of the debt, then the third-party investor would have been deemed to have made a sufficient investment to qualify the SPE for

---

[3] **EITF 84-30**, "Sales of Loans to Special Purpose Entities" (Norwalk, CT: Financial Accounting Standards Board, 1984).

[4] **EITF 90-15**, "Impact of Nonsubstantive Lessors, Residual Value Guarantees, and Other Provisions in Leasing Transactions" (Norwalk, CT: Financial Accounting Standards Board, 1990).

nonconsolidation. In such cases, the risk to the equity investor was minimized while the potential rewards were intact. In addition, the loan guarantee most likely enabled the SPE to obtain financing at favorable rates.

In 1996 FASB Statement No. 125,[5] introduced the term *qualifying SPE.* The context of FASB No. 125 was very narrow, focusing only on securitization of receivables. The purpose of this standard was to give guidance regarding the conditions that must be met for a transfer of financial assets to qualify as a sale. Consolidation issues were not addressed, and subsequently the EITF (in 96-10) ruled that entities should look to the control of assets as defined in FASB Standard No. 125, not the consolidation requirements previously defined in EITF 90-15, in deciding whether the acquirer of the receivables should be consolidated by the seller.[6] Except for this narrow application, the requirements of EITF 90-15 were to continue to guide the consolidation decision.

In Statement No. 140,[7] the FASB further narrowed and defined the securitization transactions it had attempted to cover in FASB Statement No. 125 and EITF 96-10. The EITF 90-15 policies continued for other SPE activities.

Finally, in January of 2003, in the wake of the Enron scandal, the Board issued FASB Interpretation (FIN) No. 46,[8] an interpretation that effectively increased the required third-party equity participation from 3 percent to 10 percent to enable the sponsor company to avoid consolidation of special-purpose entities. This requirement should serve to greatly reduce the number of special-purpose entities that have no significant substantive economic investment by third parties. A more detailed discussion of FIN No. 46 appears later in this supplement.

EXAMPLES OF SPECIAL-PURPOSE ENTITIES

Consider the following scenario, which gives an example of why one type of SPE structure actually might be established.

SCENE 1: Sponsor corporation, office of the CFO. Meeting of CFO, controller, and assistant controller.

CFO: OK. Our problem today is that we really need to refinance our Production Unit #1. We invested $200 million to build this plant, its current book value is $150 million, and we only have a $100-million note balance outstanding. Yet the plant is appraised currently at $180 million. We are currently saddled with a weak cash flow position and a high debt ratio. Therefore, our interest rate on a refinanced loan will be likely about 3 points above prime. Furthermore, if we default on our note coming due in 6 months, the creditor may attempt to take a lien on Production Unit #1 because of the existing equity it offers. I think we need to find a way to generate cash and protect

[5] **Statement of Financial Accounting Standards, No. 125**, "Accounting for Transfers and Servicing of Financial Assets and Extinguishments of Liabilities" (Norwalk, CT: Financial Accounting Standards Board, 1996).

[6] **EITF 96-10**, "Impact of Certain Transactions on the Held-to-Maturity Classification under FASB Statement No. 115" (Norwalk, CT: Financial Accounting Standards Board, 1996).

[7] **Statement of Financial Accounting Standards, No. 140**, "Accounting for Transfers and Servicing of Financial Assets and Extinguishments of Liabilities—A Replacement of FASB Statement No. 125" (Norwalk, CT: Financial Accounting Standards Board, 2000).

[8] Op. cit., **FASB Interpretation No. 46**.

this asset from creditors. Traditional refinancing is going to be awfully expensive. Your assignment is to research ways to solve this problem.

CONTROLLER: We'll get right on it. *(Controller and assistant controller leave.)*

SCENE 2: Office of the controller (shortly after CFO meeting). Meeting of controller and assistant controller.

CONTROLLER: Wow—what an assignment. I'm expecting great things from you—I want you to drop everything and devote all of your time to this project. Remember, I'm counting on you.

ASST. CONTROLLER: I recently attended a seminar that focused on Enron's abuses of special purpose entities. The speaker emphasized that if used properly, SPEs can offer great benefit to companies in certain circumstances. One of the examples sounded a lot like our situation. I'm going to start by looking at my seminar materials and doing some further research into the possibility of setting up a special-purpose entity.

SCENE 3: Several days later, again in the controller's office. Meeting of controller and assistant controller.

CONTROLLER: I sure hope you have good news for me.

ASST. CONTROLLER: I think I do. It appears that a number of major financial institutions are participating in sale–lease back transactions using a special-purpose entity as the vehicle. As I understand it, we would enter into an agreement with an institution wherein the institution would set up a corporation (SPE) by contributing a small equity investment of cash. The SPE would then buy Production Unit #1 from us at market value, signing a note for the majority of the value. The financed value and payments on the note preferably should be structured so that we can qualify for installment sales treatment for the gain, thus postponing tax on the sale as long as possible. The SPE would lease the asset back to us under a long-term lease agreement with terms that barely qualify the lease as operating. The SPE's primary asset would be Production Unit #1. A note to finance its purchase could be provided at a lower interest rate since the only asset, the plant, would serve as the collateral and no other debt would exist within the SPE.

CONTROLLER: Brilliant. Now what I understand is (1) we get Production Unit #1 off of the books, (2) some initial cash is generated from the sale of the unit, (3) we will have steady net inflow of cash from the collections on the note from the SPE (reduced by operating lease payments), (4) we still get to keep all of the operating profit from Production Unit #1, but the asset is out of reach of our creditors.

ASST. CONTROLLER: Yep.

CONTROLLER: Let's write it up and take it to the CFO. And by the way—good work. I'd better watch out—your work is getting so creative, you'll be looking for your own CFO position soon.

Synthetic Lease SPE

The scenario above is suggesting what is known as a synthetic lease structure. The accounting treatments and effects described by the controller are summarized in Table B-1.

In this SPE, legitimate business purposes underlie the creation of the new entity, including a significant shifting of risks as well as control of the asset. The sponsor company will no longer report the long-term production asset or any debt associated with that asset due to the operating lease structure. This SPE would not have to be consolidated.

TABLE B-1 Synthetic Lease Transactions

Transaction	Third-party equity		Special-purpose entity (SPE)			Sponsor company (SC)		
SPE is created with small (10% of total assets) third-party equity.	Investment in SPE 20		Cash	20				
	Cash	20	Third-party equity		20			
SC sells asset it owns to SPE for 180. SPE obtains new financing or assumes note.			Asset	180		Note Receivable—SPE	80	
			Note Payable		100	Notes Payable—(paid by SC)	100	
			Note Payable—SC		80	Asset (net BV)		150
						Deferred Gain on Sale		30
SPE enters into an *operating* lease with SC. No journal entry as SPE keeps asset and debt on its books.								
Ongoing operating lease transactions to record periodic lease payments over term of lease.			Cash	X		Lease Expense	X	
			Lease Revenue		X	Cash		X
			Depreciation Expense	X		Deferred Gain on Sale	X	
			Accumulated Depreciation		X	Realized Gain on Sale		X
Periodic note payments are made by SPE to SC (inflows of principal to SC will be taxable using installments sales rules).			Note Payable—SC	X		Cash	X	
			Interest Expense	X		Note Receivable—SPE		X
			Cash		X	Interest Revenue		X

Additional Example SPEs

When each SPE is created, the entity acquires financial or other assets and issues debt or ownership certificates (stock, notes, etc.). Under current accounting requirements, the sponsor company (i.e., the corporation wishing to achieve off–balance sheet financing) must participate in less than 90 percent (formally 97 percent) of the equity position. That is, the third-party entity's "substantial" equity investment must now be 10 percent of total SPE assets, whereas it formerly was only 3 percent. The increase to a requirement of a 10 percent investment by outsiders (subsequent to the Enron disclosures) was intended to ensure a more meaningful risk undertaking by the third party. Typically one or more financial institutions make the 10 percent or greater (formally 3 percent or greater) independent investment in the SPE. Several of the most common SPE structures are described below with a discussion of the benefits to the sponsor.

Receivable Transfer SPE Assume the sponsor company is holding $2,900,000 book value of Notes Receivable. The notes will pay 10-percent annually and have a fair market value of $2,700,000. The sponsor company is experiencing cash flow problems and wants to protect its asset (the notes) from its creditors. The sponsor company and a third-party independent investor together agree to form the SPE for the purpose of buying the receivables. The sequence of transactions might occur as illustrated in Table B-2.

This structure is a receivables transfer SPE and is often set up to protect a particular asset from the creditors of the sponsor company. The sale of the notes may be without recourse, but a separate agreement may require that the sponsor company contribute resources to the SPE if the fair market value of the notes fall below some agreed-upon level. Assuming the $2,700,000 fair value of the notes is a true (not inflated) estimate, the likelihood of a future contribution is probably deemed remote, and no contingent liability is even disclosed by the sponsor company. Over the life of the SPE, collections of principal and interest are distributed to the equity holders.

The SPE serves as place to "park" the Notes Receivable and protect them from the sponsor company creditors. Even though a gain or loss must be recorded initially, if the full $2,900,000 initial book value is collected, the cost to the sponsor company is only the third party's 10-percent share of the excess over $2,700,000 collected. If a traditional factoring arrangement was undertaken, the assets would not be protected from creditors. Further, if the arrangement is with recourse, the liability would generally have to be booked.

Financial Instrument SPE A sponsor company needs $90 million to finance the construction of a new production facility but is already heavily indebted. As a result, the available interest rate for traditional long-term financing is relatively high. The sponsor company can use an SPE structure to isolate the debt associated with the construction. This will enable the sponsor company to obtain more favorable financing rates. To achieve this goal, the sponsor company sells forward sales contracts that lock up the sales price of output from the proposed plant and enable the buyer(s) to acquire the output at a set price. Further, the contracts set in place prior to construction reduce the risk of default to the construction and long-term lenders and, therefore, enable the SPE to obtain further interest rate breaks. Accounting for the events is shown in Table B-3.

The result is that the sponsor company keeps the plant asset on the books but does not have to recognize the Long-Term Liability for the permanent financing. The income from the sale of the financial instruments is recognized immediately, while the depreciation on the plant asset will be charged over many years. Often the plant asset serves as

TABLE B-2 Receivable Transfer SPE Transactions

	Third-party equity			Special-purpose entity (SPE)			Sponsor company (SC)		
Investment of cash into SPE by third party	Investment in SPE	300,000		Cash	300,000				
	Cash		300,000	Third-party equity		300,000			
SC sells the Notes Receivable to SPE without recourse				Note Receivable (at Market)	2,700,000		Cash	300,000	
				Cash		300,000	Investment in SPE	2,400,000	
				SC Equity		2,400,000	Loss on Sale of Note	200,000	
							Notes Receivable		2,900,000
Collection of Note Payments	Investment in SPE	X		Cash	X		Investment in SPE	X	
	Equity in SPE		X	Note Receivable		X	Equity in SPE		X
	Earnings			Interest Revenue		X	Earnings		X

TABLE B-3 Financial Instrument SPE Transactions

Transactions	Third-party equity		Special-purpose entity (SPE)			Sponsor company (SC)		
Short-term floating rate construction loan obtained and plant built by SC						Plant Assets Short-Term Note Payable	90	90
During construction, SC sells forward sales contracts for plant output (initially booked at nominal amount).						No entry		
SPE established with contributions of forward contract right to collections from sales by SC and 10% equity contribution by third party.	Investment in SPE Cash	10	10	Forward Sales Contract Liability to SC Cash Third-Party Equity	90 10	90 10	Receivable from SPE Income from Sale of Forward Contracts	90	90
Long-term financing obtained by SPE. Funds transferred to SC and used to pay construction financing note.			Liability to SC Long-Term Note Payable		90 90	Short-Term Note Payable Receivable from SPE	90	90

collateral to the SPE in case the forward sales contracts go into default. As long as the risk of default is minimal, which would normally be the case, there would be no significant contingent liability to the sponsor company. Once the sale of output by the SPE generates enough cash to pay off the long-term note and pay the third-party investors (including a return on their investment), the SPE is no longer needed, and cash generated by the plant benefits the sponsor company from that point forward.

Diamond Structure SPE In this type of SPE, a consortium of companies (three or more) create an SPE to enter into a venture. Such ventures typically include research and development activities or production plant construction for the benefit of the partici-pating sponsors. The asset construction ventures are similar to the previous "Financial Instruments SPE" example, except that the asset (or research and development output) is owned by the SPE. No single sponsor company has enough interest in the SPE to control it. The SPE obtains long-term financing for its project by having output purchase commit-ments signed by the several sponsor companies. These contracts serve as the collateral for the construction loans that the SPE can then obtain to finance the project at a reasonable cost of debt. Sample transactions appear in Table B-4.

The operations of the SPE produce enough revenue to service the debt and provide a rate of return to the sponsor company equity partners. The "Investment in SPE" would not have to be consolidated by any of the equity investors as long as no single party has "control." The sponsor companies each achieve the desired goal without being saddled with either booking the debt, assuming the risks, or exposing the asset to claims of other creditors of the sponsor companies.

THE ENRON SCANDAL

The Scandal Prompts Further Tightening of Standards

Prior to the Enron collapse, the FASB had been attempting for several years to develop a broad standard on consolidation policy. Early in 2001 the Board withdrew its exposure draft of 1999 on Consolidation Policy because there were insufficient votes of the Board members to pass it and make it an official standard. The Board would likely have stayed in total limbo on this matter for a longer period of time except for one major event—the Enron downfall and scandal at the end of 2001. Enron's use of, and accounting for (or misuse of, and misaccounting for), SPEs with the apparent blessing of Andersen, its auditor, created a firestorm of publicity. Congress, the financial press, and stockholder groups, to name just a few, all wanted to know what had gone wrong and what the FASB, American Institute of Certified Public Accountants (AICPA), and SEC were going to do about it.

The FASB responded within months. The result was Financial Accounting Interpretation No. 46 (FIN 46), dated January 2003. It required almost immediate applica-tion. For example, extensive disclosures were required in the as yet unissued financial statements for years ending December 31, 2002. Additionally, all current and future vari-able interest entities (the FASB's new, broadened term for SPEs) had to be evaluated under new criteria that superseded the EITF 90–15 rules. The general premise of the new stan-dard is that identified variable interest entities (VIEs) must be consolidated by the entity that is the primary beneficiary of the VIE's activities if either

> *(1)* *its at-risk equity position (financing by the equity interest) is insufficient to enable the VIE to finance its activities independently, or*

TABLE B-4 Diamond Structure SPE Transactions

Transactions	Special-purpose entity (SPE)			Sponsor company (SC) #1			Sponsor company (SC) #2			Sponsor company (SC) #3		
SPE is created with minimal cash investment by sponsor companies. Contracts to buy output signed.	Cash Equity SC #1 Equity SC #2 Equity SC #3	30	10 10 10	Investment in SPE Cash	10	10	Investment in SPE Cash	10	10	Investment in SPE Cash	10	10
SPE acquires financing to conduct R&D activities (or construct production asset).	Cash Long-Term Notes Payable	200	200									
R&D activities (or start construction).	R&D expense (or plant asset) Cash	200	200									
Output sold under contract to sponsor companies.	Cash Sales	X	X	Patent Rights Cash	X	X	Patent Rights Cash	X	X	Patent Rights Cash	X	X

(2) *its equity investors lack any one of three (new) characteristics that indicate control including*

    (A) **sufficient equity**—*the equity investment is normally presumed to be at least 10 percent of the VIE's total assets, but in all cases the level of investment must be equal to or greater than the projected maximum potential loss that the VIE might suffer,*

    (B) **residual equity**—*the equity investor must be totally at risk to absorb all losses and be totally able to benefit from all of the gains, and*

    (C) **authority to make decisions**—*the equity investors must be the decision makers and that authority must be proportionate to the voting or equivalent rights that they hold.*[9]

Notice the broad applicability of the pronouncement, being applied to all VIEs, with SPEs being a subset. Additionally, notice the major increase in the outside equity participation required relative to the previous standards, 10 percent versus 3 percent. FIN No. 46 promises to force consolidation of many previously unconsolidated SPEs. Conversely, the companies involved may choose to alter the substance of their equity structures to achieve an equity arrangement that meets the new 10-percent rule.

What Did Enron and Andersen Do?

Many have suggested that the authoritative guidance available prior to FIN No. 46 should have been sufficient to keep the Enron abuses from occurring. Enron created hundreds of SPEs, many of which proved to be very profitable. Certain executives at Enron, however, stretched the interpretation of the existing rules to the limit (and apparently beyond) in several areas surrounding their SPEs. Furthermore, the disclosure of the role played by Enron's independent auditor, Andersen, shook the foundations of the entire U.S. financial community.

The auditor of Enron, Andersen, actually worked with Enron financial executives to structure some of the extremely complex ownership arrangements that were then accounted for in ways favorable to the financial reporting objectives of Enron. These objectives included the reporting of the SPEs as unconsolidated subsidiaries, early revenue recognition from the contracts with the SPEs, and, of course, the off balance–sheet debt financing that goes hand in hand with equity method accounting in lieu of consolidation. Andersen's role in the Enron SPEs, some have alleged, probably ensured Andersen's Houston office of about $100,000,000 in combined annual audit and consulting fees. In retrospect, the auditors' independence appears to have been compromised. Outsiders have reviewed the events and the judgments made by Andersen partners. Those reviewing the situation generally concur that Andersen was aware of the Enron objectives to limit disclosure of the true economic substance of the SPEs. Yet Andersen leadership refused to blow the whistle or otherwise challenge the accounting used by Enron. In the chaotic months following Enron's eventual bankruptcy, Andersen paid the ultimate price. The SEC banned Andersen from auditing public companies and effectively forced the dismantling of its entire U.S. operation.

Just what did Enron do to bend the rules? First, through complex ownership arrangements, the (at time) 3 percent of total assets rule was effectively circumvented.

[9] KPMG LLP. "Defining Issues" (January, no. 03-3) (2003), pp. 1–4.

Recall that the purpose of that rule was to ensure that independent third-party investors who controlled the SPE had a substantive (at-risk) investment of their own assets in the business. In many of the Enron SPEs, the investors were largely insulated from risk through complex layering of ownership interests.

Second, much of the SPE debt was guaranteed by Enron. Those guarantees, however, in many cases took the form of pledges of Enron common stock. That was satisfactory as long as the Enron stock has substantial market value. But because the stock itself was a financial instrument, it derived its value from the financial strength of Enron. When some SPEs failed and bad news about Enron in general became public, the stock value fell and the guarantees in turn were weakened. As the stock price fell further, the problem of the guarantees became more and more severe. By using Enron stock instead of "hard" assets as guarantees, the general strength of Enron was the only guarantee being provided.

The "third-party investors" were high-ranking Enron executives in many cases. Because they were related parties, the notion of their true independence was questionable. Furthermore, many of the SPEs were designed to ensure that these individuals could siphon off millions in personal profits while assuming little or no real risk.

Epilogue

In the spirit of full disclosure of the real economic substance of economic transactions, many of the unconsolidated Enron SPEs should have been consolidated. At a minimum, early revenue recognition would have been curtailed, and the full extent of the risk that Enron stockholders were assuming would have been disclosed. Were the actions fraudulent? Such questions are addressed by the courts. The key will be in the answer to the question of whether parties had knowledge of improper actions and intent to deceive.

The newest accounting pronouncement, FIN No. 46, should go a long way toward giving guidance with teeth to the auditors reviewing future transactions of sponsor companies with all types of VIEs. Even if FIN No. 46 does not give auditors the hammer they need, the fear of potentially reliving the fate of Andersen will likely result in auditors, in general, taking a much more conservative and critical view of activities that appear to be designed to limit financial disclosure in publicly held companies.

GLOSSARY

Accountability   the obligation to explain the government's actions, to justify what the government does, to justify to the citizenry the rational for raising resources, and to explain the expenditure of those resources.   (Chapter 10)

Affiliated organizations   organizations that provide either a financial benefit or burden to the reporting entity; also referred to as *component units*.   (Chapter 12)

Agency fund   assets held in trust from individuals, organizations, or other governments.   (Chapter 11)

Appropriation   the authorization granted by a legislative body to incur liabilities or disburse resources. (Chapter 11)

Articles of partnership   written agreement that outlines the terms by which a partnership is formed, operated, and terminated.   (Chapter 7)

Bonus method   method of accounting for premium or discount in the creation of a partnership or a change in ownership. This method reallocates equity among partners in lieu of recognizing unidentifiable assets.   (Chapter 7)

Budget   a financial plan that documents the legal authority of the governmental entity to collect revenue and disburse resources.   (Chapter 10)

Budgetary fund balance   a control account that records the net amount of estimated revenues and appropriations that are available for the fiscal period.   (Chapter 11)

Business combination   when two companies join in an external form of expansion.   (Chapter 1)

Business-type activities   those activities operated by a government that are similar to a for-profit activity. They are financed, in whole or in part, by fees charged for the services rendered.   (Chapter 10)

Capital budget   Controls the expenditures for construction projects, plant, and capital asset acquisitions.   (Chapter 10)

Capitalization   the recording of the value of a capital item or the costs incurred to build or acquire the item as an asset in the financial accounts.   (Chapter 9)

Capitation   a fixed dollar amount of fees per person paid periodically by a third-party payer to a health care organization regardless of the services performed. (Chapter 9)

Cash distribution plan   document that outlines the order in which partners will receive cash during an installment liquidation.   (Chapter 8)

Codification   a compendium of GASB-promulgated accounting principles.   (Chapter 10)

Compensated absences   employee absences such as vacation, holidays, and sick time for which it is expected the employee will be paid.   (Chapter 10)

Component unit   a legally separate organization that imposes a financial burden on the primary government or one for which the government is fiscally accountable. (Chapter 10)

Conditional contribution   a contribution that has a barrier that must be satisfied for the resource recipient to have the right to receive the contribution.   (Chapter 9)

Conditional promise   a pledge to give that depends on a specified event for the contribution to be recognized. (Chapter 9)

Conglomerate combination   when the acquired company is in unrelated or tangentially related businesses.   (Chapter 1)

Consolidated financial statements   the financial statements prepared as a result of combining the financial information of a parent company and its subsidiary(ies).   (Chapter 1)

Contingent consideration   when the resources to be transferred in an acquisition are subject to change based on future events.   (Chapter 1)

Contribution   an unconditional transfer of cash or other asset to an entity or a settlement or cancellation of its liability in a voluntary nonreciprocal transfer by another entity acting other than as an owner.   (Chapter 9)

Control   the power to use or direct the use of the individual assets of an entity to achieve the objectives of the controlling entity.   (Chapter 1)

Cumulative translation adjustment   the amount needed to bring the U.S. dollar trial balance into balance when applying the current rate method.   (Chapter 6)

Current rate method   the method used to convert functional currency trial balance information into the parent reporting currency. Purpose is to change the unit of measure with as little change as possible in relationships that exist among values in the functional currency. (Chapter 6)

Defensive measures   steps taken by a potential acquiree to avoid an undesired acquisition.   (Chapter 1)

Denominated   the expressed currency in which a transaction is to be completed.   (Chapter 5, 6)

Derived tax revenue nonexchange transactions imposed by the government as the result of an exchange transaction such as sales tax. (Chapter 10)

Designated resources set aside for a specific purpose or use by the government's management rather than an external party such as a creditor. No legal restriction to use these resources exist; thus, the designation may be rescinded at any time. (Chapter 11)

Designation conditions placed on resources. They are made at the discretion of the governing board or management. (Chapter 12)

Direct exchange rate number of units of the domestic currency equivalent to one unit of a foreign currency. (Chapter 5)

Direct intercompany debt transaction when one unit of an entity makes a loan directly to another unit of the same entity. (Chapter 4)

Dissolution the legal ending of a partnership agreement through the cessation of operations, the admission of a new partner, or the withdrawal of an existing partner. (Chapter 7, 8)

Downstream transaction an intercompany transaction flowing from the parent to the subsidiary. (Chapter 4)

Drawing account a contra partnership equity account where withdrawals from the partnership are recorded. The drawing account is closed and transferred into the partnership capital account at the end of the accounting period. (Chapter 7)

Eligibility a term established by GASB that describes the conditions or characteristics that must be met in order to recognize gift revenue. (Chapter 12)

Encumbrance an estimated amount that represents commitments to be paid from appropriations. (Chapter 11)

Entity theory views the business entity as separate and distinct from the business owners. (Chapter 7)

Exchange rate the ratio at which one currency can be converted into another currency. (Chapter 5)

Exchange transaction a transaction in which items of comparable value are exchanged or traded; also referred to as a quid pro quo. (Chapter 9)

Executory contract a contract where neither party has yet fulfilled its part of the agreement. (Chapter 5)

External expansion when two or more businesses join together and operate as one entity, or related entities, under the direction and control of one management group. (Chapter 1)

Fiduciary funds funds that account for resources held in trust for parties outside of the government for which the government acts as an agent or trustee. (Chapter 11)

Fixed exchange rate official exchange rate between currencies established and maintained by public officials. (Chapter 5)

Floating exchange rate exchange rate between currencies determined by market conditions. (Chapter 5)

Forecasted transaction a transaction that is expected to occur rather than one that has occurred or is contracted to occur. (Chapter 5)

Foreign currency any currency other than the entity's functional currency. (Chapter 6)

Foreign currency commitment when an entity enters into an agreement to buy or sell goods denominated in a fixed number of foreign currency units at some time in the future. (Chapter 5)

Foreign currency transaction a transaction in a currency other than the one in which the financial records are maintained. (Chapter 5,6)

Forward contract agreement between individual buyer and seller to exchange currency units at a later date and at an agreed-upon exchange rate. (Chapter 5)

Forward rate exchange rate that currently exists for an exchange of currency at a future date. (Chapter 5)

Friendly takeover a tender offer that is publicly supported by acquiree management. (Chapter 1)

Function a group of related expense activities that accomplish a major service or regulatory responsibility for which the government unit is responsible. (Chapter 9)

Functional currency the currency of the primary economic environment in which the entity operates. (Chapter 6)

Fund a set of self-balancing accounts that include assets, liabilities, residual balance [equity], revenues, and disbursements. (Chapter 11)

Funds functioning as an endowment resources that the governing board chooses to manage as an endowment—investing the resources and expending only the investment income. (Chapter 12)

Funds held in trust those resources held by the institution acting as a custodian; also known as *agency funds*. (Chapter 12)

Gift in kind contributions of goods or services. (Chapter 9)

Goodwill method method of accounting for premium or discount in the creation of a partnership or a change in ownership. This method recognizes unidentifiable intangible assets (goodwill) and assigns the value to the equity of the appropriate partner(s). (Chapter 7)

Government funds funds that account for the government's services and include administrative support for those services. (Chapter 11)

Hedging the use of a financial instrument contract to eliminate exchange rate fluctuation risk. (Chapter 5)

Horizontal combination a combination involving two or more entities that are in competition in the same industry. (Chapter 1)

Hostile bid   a tender offer that is opposed by acquiree management.   (Chapter 1)

Imposed nonexchange transaction   government assessments such as property tax.   (Chapter 10)

Imputed market value   the implied total market value of an entity derived by dividing the observed price paid for less than 100 percent of the entity by the actual percentage acquired.   (Chapter 2)

In the money   when the currency spot rate for a call (put) option is less (more) than the option strike price. (Chapter 5)

Indirect exchange rate   number of units of a foreign currency equivalent to one unit of the domestic currency. (Chapter 5)

Indirect intercompany debt transaction   when one unit of an entity acquires, from an unrelated party, debt previously issued by another unit of the same entity.   (Chapter 4)

Infrastructure   long-lived assets such as roads and bridges that are stationary in nature and can be preserved for a far greater number of years than most capital assets. (Chapter 10)

Installment liquidation   occurs over an extended time period; partners receive interim (installment) distributions. (Chapter 8)

Intercompany transaction   a transaction that occurs between two units of the same entity.   (Chapter 4)

Internal expansion   when the business is expanded through new product development or geographic expansion without acquiring another company.   (Chapter 1)

Interperiod equity   a concept that those who benefit should pay for the cost.   (Chapter 10)

Investment trusts   investment pools held and managed for other governments.   (Chapter 11)

Involuntary liquidation   when a partnership is forced to liquidate by its creditors.   (Chapter 8)

Lateral transaction   an intercompany transaction flowing from one subsidiary to another subsidiary.   (Chapter 4)

Liquidation   when a partnership ceases normal operations, sells its remaining assets, pays creditors, and distributes any remaining cash to partners.   (Chapter 8)

Local currency   the currency of the country where the foreign entity is located.   (Chapter 6)

Loss absorption power   the amount of partnership expenses and losses that would have to occur to reduce a partner's capital account balance to zero.   (Chapter 8)

Lump-sum liquidation   a liquidation that occurs over a relatively short time period during which all assets are sold and all liabilities are paid before the partners receive one (lump-sum) distribution.   (Chapter 8)

Major funds   specific funds displayed in the basic governmental and proprietary statements determined by percent criteria. Funds are considered to be major when they have total assets, liabilities, revenues, or expenses/expenditures that (1) constitute 10 percent of the governmental or enterprise activity and (2) 5 percent of the governmental or enterprise category.   (Chapter 11)

Management discussion and analysis   a required supplemental component of the financial statements that provides an explanation of the government's financial activities.   (Chapter 10)

Mandated nonexchange transaction   those transactions that one government unit requires another government unit to perform, such as state aid to selected individuals mandated by the federal government.   (Chapter 10)

Marshaling of assets   keeping the partnership assets and liabilities separate from partner personal assets and liabilities.   (Chapter 8)

Modified accrual accounting   an accounting process that recognizes revenue when it is measurable and available and expenditures when they result in a reduction of current financial resources.   (Chapter 10)

Modified approach   a specified process to document infrastructure condition established by GASB that allows governments to expense infrastructure maintenance rather than recognize depreciation.   (Chapter 10)

Monetary account   account fixed in units of currency. (Chapter 5, 6)

Multinational operations   operations that result from activities conducted outside of the country where an entity is headquartered.   (Chapter 6)

Natural classification   describe the expense incurred, such as salary or office supplies.   (Chapter 12)

Negative goodwill   the amount by which the net appraised value of the subsidiary's identifiable assets and liabilities exceeds the acquisition price.   (Chapter 2)

NFP (Not-for-profit)   an entity that operates without a profit motive and has no defined owners. May be created as a government or nongovernment organization. (Chapter 9)

Noncontrolling interest   the owners of the subsidiary's stock other than the parent company.   (Chapter 2)

Noncontrolling interest in net income (loss) of subsidiary   the prorated share of consolidated net income that increases (decreases) the equity interest of the noncontrolling stockholders.   (Chapter 3)

Nonexchange transaction   a transactions from which the party providing the resources neither expects nor derives any benefit, i.e., a gift.   (Chapter 9)

Nonmonetary account   account not fixed in units of currency.   (Chapter 6)

Object of expense   a subset of the expense type, such as full-time salary or part-time labor, that provides details of the personal services expense.   (Chapter 10)

Operating budget   identifies the estimated revenue and authorized expenditure for a specific fiscal period. (Chapter 10)

Option contract   an agreement wherein the writer will exchange currencies with the holder at a predetermined rate if the holder chooses to exercise the option.   (Chapter 5)

Out of the money   when the currency spot rate for a call (put) option is more (less) than the option strike price. (Chapter 5)

Parent   the acquirer in a stock acquisition form of business combination.   (Chapter 1)

Parent–subsidiary relationship   the ownership relationship that exists in a stock acquisition form of business combination.   (Chapter 1)

Pension trusts   the trusts that account for pension and other employee benefits held and managed by the government. (Chapter 11)

Performance budget   budget that attempts to compare the input of governmental resources to the output of governmental services provided.   (Chapter 10)

Permanently restricted net assets   assets with donor-imposed stipulations that cannot be met and the resources must be held in perpetuity.   (Chapter 9)

Primary government   a state or local general- or special-purpose government that has an elected governing body and is legally separate and fiscally independent of other governments.   (Chapter 10)

Private-purpose trust fund   trust arrangements, other than pensions and investment trust funds, that benefit individuals, private organizations, or other governments. (Chapter 11)

Program budget   a budget that measures the total cost of a specific governmental program.   (Chapter 10)

Program services   categories of expenses that describe related expenses that fulfill the mission of the organization. (Chapter 9)

Promise to give   a written or oral agreement (pledge) to contribute resources.   (Chapter 9)

Proprietary funds   funds that account for activities that charge a fee for their services. Also referred to as *business-like* or *income-producing governmental activities.* (Chapter 11)

Proprietary theory   views the business entity as an aggregation of the business owners.   (Chapter 7)

Public corporation   an entity created for the administration of public affairs.   (Chapter 10)

Purchase differential   the amount by which a subsidiary's book value and market value differ at the acquisition date. (Chapter 2)

Remeasurement gain or loss   the amount needed to bring the U.S. dollar trial balance into balance when applying the temporal method.   (Chapter 6)

Reporting currency   the currency used by the parent company to prepare the consolidated financial statements. (Chapter 6)

Reporting entity   a combination of the primary government, organizations for which the primary government is financially responsible, and other organizations for which the nature and significance of the relationship with the primary government is such that the exclusion of their data would cause the financial statements of the reporting entity to be misleading or incomplete.   (Chapter 10)

Restricted   a term used to designate resources whose use has been stipulated by a party external to the institution, such as a creditor or vendor.   (Chapter 12)

Restriction   a donor-imposed stipulation that can be met by the passage of time or actions of the organizations. (Chapter 9)

Right of offset   the combining of a partner's capital account with any loans to/from the partnership to determine the partner's net equity position in the partnership.   (Chapter 8)

Schedule of safe payments   outlines how a cash distribution to partners would be allocated assuming that all remaining noncash assets are worthless and that partners are not capable of making additional capital contributions to eliminate a capital deficit.   (Chapter 8)

Segment   an identifiable activity that has revenue pledged to retire debt for which the activity's revenue, expenses, assets, and liabilities are required to be separately reported. (Chapter 12)

Settlement date   the date on which the foreign currency transaction is satisfied through the transfer of currency. (Chapter 5)

Speculative foreign currency contract   agreement to buy or sell foreign currency in the future at a known price when there is no underlying transaction, commitment to a future transaction, or forecasted future transaction.   (Chapter 5)

Spot rate   exchange rate that exists for an immediate exchange of currency.   (Chapter 5)

Statement of activity   displays the organization's resource inflows and outflows for as specific period.   (Chapter 9)

Statement of financial position   displays the organization's attest, liabilities, and equity as of a specific date.   (Chapter 9)

Statement of functional expenses   a matrix that compares the natural class of expenses to the function performed. (Chapter 9)

Statement of realization and liquidation   details all business transactions during a partnership liquidation. (Chapter 8)

Statutory consolidation   a business combination that results in two companies being liquidated into a newly created organization.   (Chapter 1)

Statutory merger   a business combination that results in one company continuing to operate and the other company liquidating into the survivor.   (Chapter 1)

Stock acquisition   a business combination where both original companies retain their separate legal existence.   (Chapter 1)

Strike price   the agreed-upon rate at which the option writer will exchange currencies with the option holder.   (Chapter 5)

Subsidiary   the acquiree in a stock acquisition form of business combination.   (Chapter 1)

Support services   administrative and other expenses that enable the organization to perform its mission.   (Chapter 9)

Temporal method   the method used to convert foreign trial balance information into the functional currency. The purpose is to revalue financial records to appear as they would if maintained in the functional currency.   (Chapter 6)

Temporarily restricted net assets   net assets with donor-imposed stipulations that can be met either by the passage of time or by actions of the organizations.   (Chapter 9)

Tender offer   an offer by an acquirer to buy the stock of another company.   (Chapter 1)

Termination   when a partnership ceases to conduct normal business operations.   (Chapter 8)

Transfer   the shifting of resources from one category to another. In fund reporting, the transfer is between one fund and another. In government-wide reporting, it is transfer is between one type of activity and another, such as from governmental to business-type activities.   (Chapter 11)

Unconditional contribution   a nonexchange transaction recognized as revenue at its fair value upon receipt.   (Chapter 9)

Unconditional promise   a pledge to give that depends only on the passage of time or the demand of the recipient.   (Chapter 9)

Uniform Partnership Act   uniform statutes that outline formation, operation, and dissolution of partnerships. Most states have adopted the Uniform Partnership Act as state law governing partnership operation.   (Chapter 7, 8)

Unrestricted net assets   net assets that have no donor-imposed stipulations or restrictions.   (Chapter 9)

Upstream transaction   an intercompany transaction flowing from the subsidiary to the parent.   (Chapter 4)

Variance power   the ability to redirect or determine the recipient of donated resources.   (Chapter 9)

Vertical combination   a combination involving two or more entities which have a potential buyer–seller relationship.   (Chapter 1)

Voluntary liquidation   when a partnership liquidates before it encounters severe financial difficulties.   (Chapter 8)

Voluntary nonexchange transaction   contributions and gifts for which the provider expects nothing in exchange.   (Chapter 10)

INDEX